12/19/13

D0192161

3907504382707

Uruguay

the Bradt Travel Guide

Tim Burford

edition
I

www.bradtguides.com

Bradt Travel Guides Ltd, UK
The Globe Pequot Press Inc, USA

Bradt

**Relax at the Termas de Daymán —
Uruguay's largest hot baths**
page 293

**San Javier is an ideal base for bird-
watching trips along the Río Uruguay**
page 278

**Fray Bentos: discover the history of
the town's former meat-packing plant**
page 270

**Ride with gauchos & spend time on
a traditional *estancia* like La Sirena**
page 269

**Take a tour of the Canelones
Department wineries**
page 135

**Splendid Art Deco architecture along Avenida
18 de Julio & the colourful annual *Carnaval***
page 114 & 102–3

Bella Unión
Quaraí
Artigas
30
30
Santana do
Livramento
Rivera
Tranqueras
31
Salto
Tacuarembó
Minas de
Corrales
26
Valle
Edén
Arsina
Paysandú
Guichón
San Gregorio
de Polanco
San Javier
Young
Paso de
los Toros
Río Negro
Embalse de
Rincón
del Bonete
Nuevo Berlín
Río Uruguay
24
Fray Bentos
Mercedes
14
Durazno
14
Sarandí del Yí
Villa Soriano
21
Dolores
1
Rodó
Trinidad
3
Nueva Palmira
Carmelo
Cardona
5
Florida
San José
11
1
Colonia
Canelones
Atlántida
BUENOS
AIRES
Río de la Plata
MONTEVIDEO
ARGENTINA
Río Uruguay

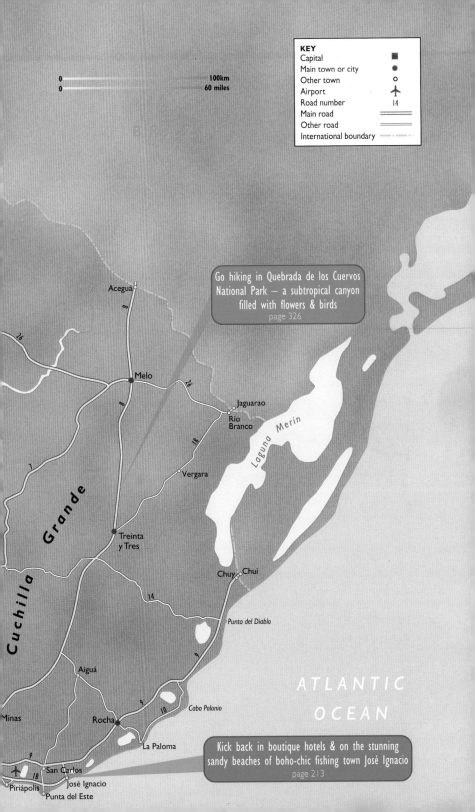

KEY
Capital ■
Main town or city ●
Other town ○
Airport ✈
Road number 14
Main road
Other road
International boundary

0 ____ 100km
0 ____ 60 miles

Aceguá

Go hiking in Quebrada de los Cuervos
National Park — a subtropical canyon
filled with flowers & birds
page 326

Melo

Jaguarao
Río Branco

Laguna Merín

Vergara

Cuchilla Grande

Treinta y Tres

Chuy Chui

Punta del Diablo

Aiguá

Cabo Polonio

ATLANTIC OCEAN

Minas

Rocha

La Paloma

San Carlos

Piriápolis

José Ignacio

Punta del Este

Kick back in boutique hotels & on the stunning
sandy beaches of boho-chic fishing town José Ignacio
page 213

Uruguay
Don't
miss...

Montevideo
Uruguay's capital hosts
the 80-day long *carnaval*
(KD/Dreamstime)
pages 102–3

José Ignacio
This boho-chic fishing village
boasts excellent beaches, boutique
hotels and restaurants
(MF/Alamy) page 213

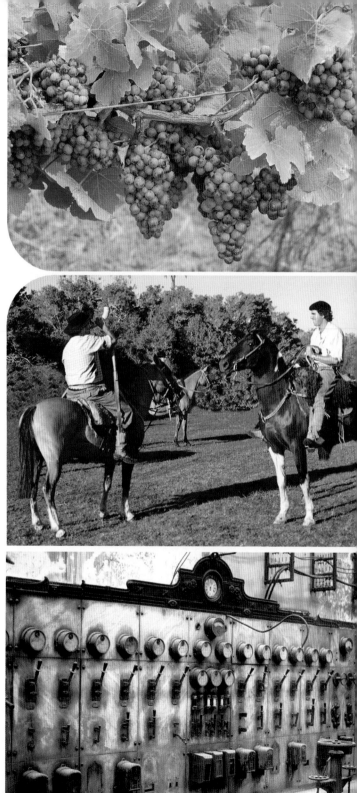

Canelones
Take a tour of the department's wineries
(AG) page 135

Ride with _gauchos_
Stay in a traditional
estancia (JG/DD/Alamy)
page 269

Fray Bentos
The former meat-processing plant is being restored as a wonderful museum of industrial heritage. This is the control room
(JB/Alamy) page 270

above   Sample the excellent eateries housed inside the 19th-century Mercado del Puerto, Montevideo (JH/Corbis) page 110

left   The remarkable Palacio Salvo is built on the site where Uruguay's very first tango was performed in 1917 (NB/Dreamstime) page 115

below   The elegant Plaza Fabini, Montevideo (RR/RHI/Corbis) page 115

The Hotel Escorial is a stunning example of Piriápolis's Art Deco architecture (TB) page 178

AUTHOR

Tim Burford studied languages at Oxford University. In 1991, after a brief career as a publisher, he began writing for Bradt, first covering hiking in eastern-central Europe and then backpacking and ecotourism in Latin America. He has now written nine books for Bradt and also leads hiking trips in Europe's mountains. He lives in Cambridge, loves train travel in Europe and flies only across oceans and as rarely as possible.

AUTHOR'S STORY

I knew before coming to Uruguay that its name meant 'River of Birds', but I had no idea how apt a name this was – except that maybe it should be 'Country of Birds'. I knew that there was a lot of empty pampa in Uruguay, inhabited by plenty of cattle and not many people, but I had no idea what this would mean in terms of wildlife, or that there were extensive wetlands along the Río Uruguay (the country's western border) and that the Atlantic coast is home to an amazing variety of birds.

I also found that the empty countryside, and the small towns hidden in it, had their own very special charm, due to the sense of space in the land and the sense of 'time to spare' in the people – nothing is rushed. Even the capital, Montevideo, is laidback; in fact, many people pop over to rest between wild weekends in Buenos Aires, the Argentine capital.

Compared to the hordes now visiting Argentina, very few tourists reach Uruguay, especially the interior, where there's a real sense of being off the beaten track.

PUBLISHER'S FOREWORD   *Adrian Phillips, Publishing Director*

The bearded Burford has the look of a cowboy – and he's been known to wear the odd checked shirt or two in his time – but these gaucho 'credentials' weren't the only reasons we commissioned him to write this guide. Tim is one of Bradt's longest-standing and most-respected authors, and this guide to Uruguay shows he gets better and better with age. In their rush to visit its bigger neighbour, tourists tend to overlook Uruguay – and, as such, it offers a flavour of traditional, laid-back Latin America that's more difficult to find in Argentina. Here you'll find some of the region's prettiest beaches and most characterful ranches – and, as any self-respecting Uruguayan will tell you, the tastiest beef in the world!

Reprinted April 2013   First published June 2010

Bradt Travel Guides Ltd,
IDC House, The Vale, Chalfont St Peter, Bucks SL9 9RZ, England
www.bradtguides.com
Published in the USA by The Globe Pequot Press Inc, 246 Goose Lane,
PO Box 480, Guilford, Connecticut 06475-0480

Text copyright © 2010 Tim Burford
Maps copyright © 2010 Bradt Travel Guides Ltd
Photographs copyright © 2010 Individual photographers
Editorial Project Manager: Emma Thomson

British Library Cataloguing in Publication Data
A catalogue record for this book is available from the British Library
ISBN-13: 978 1 84162 316 0

Photographs Anne Greenhalgh (AG), Alison Wright/Corbis (AW/Corbis), Andres Stapff/Reuters/Corbis (AS/R/Corbis), Breakers/Dreamstime.com (B/Dreamstime), Carlos Goldin/Corbis (CG/Corbis), Diego Lezama Orezzoli/Corbis (DLO/Corbis), Flip Nicklin/Minden Pictures/FLPA (FN/MP/FLPA), Frans Lanting/FLPA (FL/FLPA), Hiroya Minakuchi/Minden Pictures/FLPA (HM/MP/FLPA), Jack Barker/Alamy (JB/Alamy), Jerry Ginsberg/Danita Delmont/Alamy (JG/DD/Alamy), Jon Hicks/Corbis (JH/Corbis), Jurgen & Christine Sohns/FLPA (J&CS/FLPA), Kobby Dagan/Dreamstime.com (KD/Dreamstime), Konrad Wothe/Minden Pictures/FLPA (KW/MP/FLPA), Kristal Richard/4 Corners (KR/4C), Mark O'Flaherty/Alamy (MF/Alamy), Martin B Withers/FLPA (MBW/FLPA), MedioImages/Corbis (MI/Corbis), Michael & Patricia Fogden/Minden Pictures/FLPA (M&PF/MP/FLPA), Mike Lane/FLPA (ML/FLPA), Neil Bowman/FLPA (NB/FLPA), Nicolás Batista/Dreamstime.com (NB/Dreamstime), Peter Llewellyn/FLPA (PL/FLPA), Rolf Richardson/Robert Harding World Imagery/Corbis (RR/RHI/Corbis), Suzi Eszterhas/Minden Pictures/FLPA (SE/MP/FLPA), Terry Whittaker/FLPA (TW/FLPA), Tim Burford (TB), Tui De Roy/Minden Pictures/FLPA (TDR/MP/FLPA), Vince Alongi/Flickr.com/photos/vincealongi (VA/Flickr), Yacov Dagan/Alamy (YD/Alamy).
Front cover Fiesta della patria gaucha, Tacuarembó (KR/4C)
Back cover Colonial architecture, Montevideo (MI/Corbis), Carnaval, Montevideo (KD/Dreamstime)
Title page Vintage Bedford truck (VA/Flickr), Tango (CG/Corbis), Grapes on the vine (AG)

Illustrations Carole Vincer, Oliver Whalley
Maps David McCutcheon FBCart.S, Malcolm Barnes (colour map)

Typeset from the author's disc by Wakewing, High Wycombe
Production managed by Jellyfish Print Solutions and manufactured in India

Acknowledgements

Thanks to Enrique Facelli and all at the Uruguayan embassy in London, Amy Ucar and all at the Ministry of Tourism in Montevideo, Matias Lasarte, Anne Greenhalgh, Chris Chandler, Adrián Stagi (Eco Tours), Ana Inés Motta (Los Caminos del Vino), Karen Vandergrift (Estancia Tierra Santa), Brian Meissner (El Diablo Tranquilo), Ricardo Hein (Apert-Hotel Bremen), Lucia & Rodney Bruce (Estancia La Sirena), Santiago (La Posada del Faro), Javier & Ximena (La Posta del Vinyet), Sandrine Pont-Nourat (Estancia Finca Piedra), Luis (Planet Montevideo Hostel), Andrea Bresso (Vida Silvestre/Posada al Sur), Melissa Gutiérrez (Retos al Sur/Posada al Sur), Agustín Carriquiry (Aves Uruguay), Juan Andrés Marichal (Bodega Marichal) and Nicolás Villagrán (Museo de la Diáspora Rusa).

DEDICATION

To Katy – you inspire me.

Contents

NOTE ABOUT MAPS

A couple of maps use grid lines to allow easy location of sites. Map grid references are listed in square brackets after listings in the text, with page number followed by grid number, eg: [88–9 C3]. Please note, in order to keep the maps legible, not all sites have been pinpointed on the maps. However, grid references have been nonetheless supplied to highlight their general location.

LIST OF MAPS

FEEDBACK REQUEST

At Bradt Travel Guides we're aware that guidebooks start to go out of date on the day they're published – and that you, our readers, are out there in the field doing research of your own. You'll find out before us when a fine new family-run hotel opens or a favourite restaurant changes hands and goes downhill. So why not write to us and tell us about your experiences? Contact us on 01753 893444 or e info@bradtguides.com. We will forward emails to the author who may post 'one-off updates' on the Bradt website at www.bradtguides.com/guidebook-updates. Alternatively you can add a review of the book to www.bradtguides.com or Amazon.

Introduction

They won the first soccer World Cup; there are places called Fray Bentos and 33; and there are a lot more cattle than people. That's all most people know of Uruguay. Others may have seen a film about the sinking of the *Graf Spee*.

However, it has far more to offer the visitor, from the finest beaches and resorts in the region to traditional estancias (ranches) where you can ride with the gauchos towards the endless horizons, wetlands and lagoons with a fantastic array of birdlife and, in Montevideo, a capital that is fascinating yet laidback, with a totally different vibe to Buenos Aires, just across the water.

Interestingly, Uruguay has a similar relationship to Argentina (and Brazil too) as Canada has to the United States, Ireland to the United Kingdom, or Belgium to France – a permanent sense of being overshadowed by a larger, louder neighbour, while feeling deep inside that they are in fact the smarter, wittier, more creative ones. Indeed, the Uruguayan people are less party-loving than their neighbours in Argentina and Brazil, but more reliable and genuine, with a deep and innate sense of hospitality that delights all who take the time to get to know them. Having said that, come high summer resorts such as Punta del Este are packed with Argentines who ensure non-stop partying for a couple of months at least. And let's not forget the world's longest Carnival season, mainly in Montevideo but in other towns too, when Uruguayans show that they really can let their hair down, bringing the country's Afro-Uruguayan heritage to the fore.

Known in full as the República Oriental del Uruguay (the Oriental Republic of Uruguay), the country takes its name from the river Uruguay, which probably derives from the Guaraní for 'River of Birds'. The term 'Oriental' comes from 'Banda Oriental' (Eastern Shore), the name of the Spanish colonial province that eventually achieved independence from Argentina, its neighbour on the western shore of the Río Uruguay. It is not, as some might think, due to a mistaken notion among early explorers that Uruguay was in the Orient, close to China, Japan or India.

Uruguay continues to be an independent country, culturally distinct from its neighbours, and it is well worth proper exploration rather than a flying visit, or a week spent solely on the – admittedly superb – beaches.

Part One

GENERAL INFORMATION

Location South America – on the northeastern shore of the Río de la Plata (River Plate), between Brazil, Argentina and the Atlantic Ocean. Uruguay shares borders with Brazil to the north (1,068km) and Argentina to the west (580km)

Size 176,215km² (68,037 square miles)

Climate warm-temperate

Time Uruguay is three hours behind UTC (GMT –3), thus four hours behind France and Germany, two hours ahead of Washington and New York and five hours ahead of California. Daylight Saving Time is generally in effect from the first Sunday of October until the second Sunday in March

Electricity 220V, 50Hz. Plugs have either two European-style round plugs (sometimes with an earth plug between them) or three (sometimes two) angled flat prongs

Weights and measures Metric

International telephone code +598

Status Presidential republic

Currency Peso (UYU)

Population 3,494,382 (July 2009 estimate)

Population growth per year 0.466% (2009 estimate)

Life expectancy at birth 76.35 years (male 73.1, female 79.7; 2009 estimate)

Economy Dominated by agriculture, forestry and tourism. GDP US$32.3 billion at the official exchange rate, or US$42.46 billion at purchasing power parity, and US$10,082 per capita (2008)

Capital Montevideo

Main cities Punta del Este, Colonia, Paysandú, Salto

Language Spanish (Español or Castellano)

Religion Roman Catholic 56% (nominally), Protestant 11%, Jewish 0.3%, atheist or agnostic 17%, other 16%

Flag The *pabellón nacional* (national flag) bears five horizontal white stripes alternating with four blue stripes, with a white square in the upper hoist corner with a yellow sun bearing a human face. The flag of Artigas (a white stripe between two blue stripes, with a diagonal red stripe, used mainly by the military) and the flag of the Treinta y Tres Orientales (a white stripe bearing the words *Libertad o Muerte* – Liberty or Death – between a blue stripe and a red stripe) are also official national symbols

Public holidays 1 January (New Year's Day), 6 January (Epiphany; *Día de los Reyes*), February/March (Carnival; the two days before Ash Wednesday), February/March (Five days for Holy Week; dates vary from year to year), 19 April (Day of the Landing of the 33 Orientales), 1 May (Labour Day), 18 May (Battle of Las Piedras), 19 June (Birthday of Artigas; also marking the end of the dictatorship), 18 July (Constitution Day), 25 August (Independence Day), 12 October (Columbus Day; *Dia de la Raza*), 2 November (All Saints), 25 December (Christmas)

Background Information

A small country sandwiched between two large and powerful ones, Uruguay can seem like Luxembourg or Canada, dominated by – and defined in contrast to – its neighbours. Where Argentina and Brazil are large and boisterous, Uruguay is small and quiet; where they have crazy drivers and less than wholly clean politicians, Uruguay has smoothly flowing traffic and boring technocrats. Nevertheless, Uruguay needs its neighbours, who take most of its exports and supply bodies to lie on its fantastic beaches and keep its tourism industry busy.

With near-total literacy and minimal corruption, Uruguay ranks with Chile as one of the two most peaceful countries in Latin America (according to the Global Peace Index), and in December 2008 Montevideo was named by the Economist Intelligence Unit as the most liveable city in Latin America.

GEOGRAPHY

With an area of 176,215km² (68,037 square miles), Uruguay is about 35% larger than England, marginally smaller than Oklahoma and barely half the size of Buenos Aires province. It's the second-smallest country in South America, after Surinam. Its population is much the same as Oklahoma's too. Its coastline (east of Punta del Este) is 220km long, with 450km of estuary shore to the west of Punta del Este; two-thirds of the population and of the economy is along these shores.

The most populated parts of Uruguay are the relatively small level areas along the Atlantic Ocean, the Río de la Plata (River Plate) and the Río Uruguay; the interior of the country is a rolling peneplain (an area almost levelled by erosion) intersected by rivers and by some ranges of hills, mainly in the southeast of the country. The highest and most rugged area of the country is the Cuchilla Grande (literally 'Big Knife'), which contains Uruguay's highest peak, Cerro Catedral (Cathedral Peak, 513.7m), although this does not rise much above the remarkable uniform ridges around it. Indeed, it was only in 1973 that it was found to be higher than the Sierra de las Ánimas (see *Chapter 5*).

Geologically, Uruguay consists of a basement of Precambrian crystalline rocks (more than 542 million years old) that emerges in the centre-south of the country and is elsewhere covered by younger sediments and volcanic rocks. These consist of Early Jurassic basalts (200–176 million years old) in the northwest of the country and Permian sediments (290–251 million years old) in the north-centre, the two separated by the Piriápolis Fraile Muerto fracture zone that runs north–south from Brazil into Argentina. Relatively small areas of Tertiary and Cretaceous sediments (145–1.8 million years old) cover the southern half of the Río Uruguay littoral, together with Cenozoic sands (less than 65 million years old) along the coast.

Until the break-up of the Gondwanan super-continent and the opening of the South Atlantic Ocean (130–110 million years ago), present-day Uruguay abutted what is now Namibia; as Namibia and Brazil are two of the world's major sources

3

of diamonds, there's a possibility that Uruguay also holds large reserves of diamonds, and prospecting is now beginning. The crystalline base may also contain silver, nickel, copper, lead, zinc and other metals; there is already limited gold-mining in Rivera department, and exports of amethysts from Artigas department are worth US$4 million per annum.

The most fertile land is in the west, along the Río Uruguay in the departments of Colonia and Soriano; the rest of the country is largely used for raising livestock (cattle above all), with some rice-growing in the east. The littoral of the Río Uruguay is low-lying, with a considerable risk of flooding. The northern half of the country is stonier and less productive, other than of large birds of prey. In the southeast, the Atlantic coastal plain is sandy, with marshy areas surrounding shallow lagoons.

In socio-geographical terms, the country can be divided into four regions (used as the basis for the chapter divisions of this book's Guide section): Montevideo and its hinterland; the coast to the east of the capital; the littoral (of the Río de la Plata and Río Uruguay) to the west; and the interior, by far the largest in size.

Uruguay has two research bases in Antarctica, one on the Antarctic Peninsula and one nearby on Isla Rey Jorge (King George Island), but has no territorial claim there.

There's no shortage of water, used both for farming and for hydro-electric power generation; to the south and west the country is bordered by the Río de la Plata and the Río Uruguay, while the Río Negro, flowing from east to west, almost cuts the country in half; in the centre of the country it has been dammed to form the Embalse del Río Negro, the largest artificial lake in South America. In addition, the **Guaraní Aquifer** is a huge underground reservoir that lies below Uruguay, Paraguay and parts of Brazil and Argentina, containing fresh water that's around 20,000 years old and is now seen as one of the world's most valuable water resources for the future.

About 90% of the country's area is suitable for growing crops, although only 12% is used in this way. Pasture covers 77% of the country, and forest and woods cover 6%, of which 3.5% is natural and the rest planted, mainly with eucalyptus to feed pulp mills. The area planted with trees is growing fast and may soon cover 1.5 million hectares (9% of the country).

Uruguay is heavily urbanised and rural areas are very lightly populated (although there are over ten million cows). More than 90% of the population lives in towns and cities, 43% of them in Montevideo (almost 1.7 million or 47% in the greater Montevideo area). Similarly, the chief town of each department is usually home to at least half its population. The average population density is 20 persons per km^2 (52 per square mile).

The country is named after the Río Uruguay, rather than the other way round. The name, derived from the Guaraní language, means roughly 'the river where birds dwell' – still a very apt description. The poet Juan Zorrilla de San Martín came up with a more colourful but less accurate translation, 'the river of painted birds'. The full official name of the country is *República Oriental del Uruguay* (Oriental Republic of Uruguay), a consequence of its early identity as the Spanish colony to the east of the Río Uruguay; thus Uruguayans are known as *Orientales*, despite not being in the least Asian. It's worth noting that the Río de la Plata, which people tend to assume flows from west to east, actually flows to the southeast, so much so that Montevideo lies to the south of Buenos Aires, and is in fact the southernmost capital city of South America.

CLIMATE

Uruguay has a warm-temperate (or subtropical) climate – in fact it's the only South American country to be wholly within the temperate zone. The sun shines for most of the year and temperatures hardly ever drop below freezing point.

Nevertheless, the weather can be unstable, owing to the lack of hills to act as barriers, and it can be windy, especially in winter and spring, with storms blowing up on the Plata estuary. In winter, a warm spell is liable to be ended by the pampero, a chilly wind that can howl in from the southwest, while the warmer sudestada brings rain from the southeast when a high-pressure system south of Buenos Aires combines with low pressure over northeastern Argentina. In summer, ocean breezes can bring welcome relief on hot days, while winds from the north only bring heat and humidity.

The seasons are clearly defined, but without great extremes of heat or cold. Spring is usually cool, damp and breezy; summer is hot, autumn is milder, and winter is relatively chilly and wet. The northwest of Uruguay, however, being further from the sea and the River Plate, is hotter in summer and drier and warmer in winter, but it does get more rain than the rest of the country.

Average temperatures range from 12°C in winter (June–September) to 25°C in summer (December–March). Rainfall (1m per annum) is evenly distributed year-round, although the wettest months are July and August, when cold fronts bring grey, drizzly weather; in summer thunderstorms are common (tornados are possible but very rare). Droughts can occur in summer and are likely to become more common with global climate change, even though average rainfall may be increasing – Uruguay is becoming more tropical, with species already extending their range southwards from Brazil. A drought in 2008–09 cost the country US$500–900 million as a result of lost agricultural production and of oil imports needed to replace normally plentiful hydro-electricity. However, natural gas deposits have recently been located offshore.

A 2008 report by Maplecroft (*www.maplecroft.com*) showed that Uruguay was the ninth-best-placed country to adapt to climate change, owing to its combination of geography, low population density, agricultural capacity, education level and infrastructure provision. Increased rainfall will bring more flooding, but Uruguay should cope reasonably well.

NATURAL HISTORY

FLORA While not the flat pampas of popular imagination, most of Uruguay is nevertheless grassland, and remarkably unforested – despite plentiful water resources and seemingly suitable sheltered locations, natural forest covers only 3.5% of the country's area. About 3% more has been planted with trees, most noticeably eucalyptus in the west of the country to feed pulp mills, but also pine, especially around Rivera. In addition large areas along the coasts were planted with pines around a century ago to control the sand dunes and make the area fit for development. The area planted with trees is growing fast and may cover 9,000km² (5% of the country) by 2020, quite a transformation from 310km² in 1987.

The plantations are not quite monocultures but there aren't many other plant species there, and parakeets and pigeons are more or less the only birds that choose to nest in eucalyptus. Eucalyptus also cause neighbouring farmland to dry out. However, the forestry industry has to be environmentally certified, which usually involves setting up nature reserves (where the first step is to exclude cattle). The area planted with soya is also growing fast, which likewise leads to a drop in biodiversity, with no food available for native birds.

In fact conservationists are now realising that *pastizales* (undeveloped grasslands) are the main problem area for bird conservation – cattle ranching has become much more intensive in the last five years, as beef prices were rising fast (until the current global crisis). Over-grazing and use of fertiliser has led to a loss of native grasses (and thus of native birds), while the area planted with introduced grass species grew by 32% in the 1980s alone. In particular there's no winter feed for native bird species so conservation projects are replanting native grasses such as *Bromus auleticus*.

The largest natural area of Uruguay is tall-grass savanna, originally covered with around 400 species of grasses (notably *Andropogon*, *Bromus*, *Paspallum* and *Stipa* spp.), and interrupted by marshy areas (*humedales*) and watercourses lined with gallery forest (*monte ribereño*), the most common form of woodland, dominated by native willow (sauce criollo; *Salix humboldtiana*) and viraró (*Ruprechtia salicifolia*), as well as ceibo (coral tree; *Erythrina crista-galli*), the bright red bloom of which is the national flower.

There are three other main groups of woodland types. First, **bosque parque** (park woodland), *algarrobal* (named after the algarrobo, misnamed the carob tree) and *bosque espinoso del litoral* (spiney coastal woodland), mainly in the west of the country and also in parts of Treinta y Tres and Cerro Largo departments. These range from open land with well-separated trees with plenty of room for grazing cattle, to denser woodland in the transition zones with *espinal* and *chaco* (in Argentina and Brazil). These are mainly composed of deciduous spiney trees such as algarrobo (*Prosopis nigra*), ñandubay (*P affinis*), espinillo (*Acacia caven*), cina-cina (*Parkinsonia aculeata*), quebracho blanco (*Aspidosperma quebracho-blanco*) and chañar (*Geoffroea decorticans*) as well as palms such as palma caranday (*Trithrinax campestris*).

Second, **bosque serrano** (mountain woodland), made up of shorter shrubby trees such as coronilla (*Scutia buxifolia*), aruera (*Lithraea brasiliensis*), tala (*Celtis tala*, *C spinosa*) and arazá (*Psidium cattleyanum*, *P littorale*) is found mainly in the hills of southern and eastern Uruguay. Related to this is *monte de quebrada* (ravine forest), specific to the moist gorges of the north, and dominated by the very spiky *espina de la cruz* (*Colletia paradoxa*), with coronilla, canelon (*Myrsine lactevirens*) and the holly-like congorosa (*Maytenus ilicifolius*) as well. Lastly, the tail-end of the **mata Atlántica** (Atlantic rainforest) of southeastern Brazil (the most biodiverse in the world, with perhaps 25,000 plant species, but now almost wiped out) sneaks across the border in the extreme northeast of Uruguay.

There's also palm savanna, in the southeast and in valleys – grassland dotted with native butia palms, mainly pindo (*Butia capitata*), mostly in Maldonado, and yatay (*B yatay*) in the wetter lowlands of Rocha and the northwest. You'll also see introduced canary palms (*Phoenix canariensis*) and tall Washingtonia palms along roads and in public spaces. The area of palm savanna is shrinking, a result of over-grazing, with young shoots being eaten by cattle.

Uruguay's *monte nativo* (native woodland) is all very low; any tall trees are exotics. The quintessential exotic tree is eucalyptus, first planted in Uruguay by Antonio Lussich (see page 183) in about 1896, to stabilise the sand dunes of Maldonado department (with pines and acacias); it was then planted nationwide for shade and timber, and more recently to feed pulp mills for the paper industry (see page 270). European poplars (alamo; *Populus alba*) are common around farms.

The national tree is the *arbol de Artigas* or ibirá-pitá (*Peltophorum dubium*), a large tree up to 25m in height, that grows in gallery forest in northern Uruguay and has also been widely planted along the streets of Montevideo; however, it should perhaps be the iconic but rare **ombú** (*Phytolacca dioica*), an evergreen up to 18m in height often found growing in a ring around where the parent tree used to be. Its soft wood can be cut with a knife but the sap is poisonous (and the leaves can be used to make a laxative tea), so that cattle and insects leave it alone. Large groups of ombú are found in only two places in Uruguay, by the Laguna de Castillos in Rocha and in the Cerro Arequita in Lavalleja.

FAUNA

Mammals It has to be said that native mammals are not exactly thick on the ground – sometimes it seems as if the European boar (*Sus scrofa*) and hare (*Lepus europaeus*) are the most common animals, together with the introduced axis deer (*Axis axis*) and fallow deer (*Dama dama*).

Deer The **marsh deer** (*Blastocerus dichotomus*), the largest South American deer, is probably extinct in Uruguay, although it survives to the north. Thus the principal surviving large mammals are the *guazuvirá* or **grey brocket deer** (*Mazama gouazoubira*), a small deer found over much of South America, and the *venado de campo* or **pampas deer** (*Ozotoceros bezoarticus*), which survives in two isolated groups, of 100–200 in the Sierra de Ajos (Rocha) and 1,000–1,300 near Arerunguá (Salto), as well as in Argentina; although protected, it is still hunted, as well as being accused of carrying the cattle disease brucellosis. Darwin recorded it as being tame, inquisitive, 'exceedingly abundant' and so indescribably foul-smelling that 'several times whilst skinning the specimen... I was almost overcome by nausea'.

Foxes There are two reasonably common species of fox, the *zorro de campo* or **pampas fox** (*Pseudalopex gymnocercus*) and the *zorro de monte* or **crab-eating fox** (*Cerdocyon thous*), both at the southern end of their range; the crab-eating fox is found more in wooded areas while the pampas fox more in grassland. There's also the *mano pelada* or **crab-eating raccoon** (*Procyon cancrivorus*), which, like the crab-eating fox, is an omnivore that happens to live in humid areas. The *aguaré guazú* or **maned wolf** (*Chrysocyon brachyurus*), a long-legged fox, was thought to be extinct in Uruguay, but in 2007 one specimen was shot near the Brazilian border in Cerro Largo.

Cats With the jaguar and puma no longer found in Uruguay, the largest cat is the **margay** (*Leopardus wiedii*), which weighs just 7kg but is still larger than the *gato montés* or **Geoffrey's cat** (*Oncifelis geoffroyi*) at 5kg or the *gato pajero* or *gato de pajonal* **pampas cat** (*Lynchailurus braccatus*) at 4kg, much the same as a domestic cat. The margay is the most arboreal of all the cats, while the others' habits are largely unknown but largely terrestrial and nocturnal.

Armadillos The *tatú* or **nine-banded armadillo** (*Dasypus novemcinctus*) is the same species found over much of the southeastern United States; it's not rare and is sometimes hunted and eaten. There's also the similar *mulita* or **southern long-nosed armadillo** (*D hybridus*), and the *tatouay* or *tatú de rabo blondo*, the **greater naked-tailed armadillo** (*Cabassous gymnurus*), which is rare, being found only in Cerro Largo, Lavalleja and Treinta y Tres departments. The *peludo* or **yellow/six-banded armadillo** (*Euphractus sexcinctus*) is diurnal and thus the easiest to see of Uruguay's armadillos. The giant anteater is no longer found in Uruguay, but the

Nine-banded armadillo

smaller **tamandua** or *oso hormiguero chico* (*Tamandua tetradactyla*) can be seen in Tacuarembó, Artigas and Cerro Largo departments.

Rodents Rodents are more common, notably the **carpincho** (better known elsewhere as the capybara; *Hydrochoeris hydrochaeris uruguayensis*), the world's largest rodent at up to 70kg in weight – although archaeologists have found a four-million-year-old rodent skull west of Montevideo that they calculate would have weighed around a tonne, or 'more than a car' in newspaper-speak. The world's second-largest rodent is the **paca** (*Agouti paca*), found in the small enclave of *mata Atlántica* that crosses the border in the northeast. Seven of the approximately 50 species of **tuco-tuco** (the exact total is still under debate) are found in Uruguay, including at least two that are found only there and in Entre Ríos province, Argentina, *Ctenomys rionegrensis* and *C pearsoni*. These are gopher-like rodents that spend much of their life underground, largely living alone; its name comes from its throaty call. Fortunately perhaps, the viscacha – a rodent closely related to chinchillas – has never crossed to the east side of the Río Uruguay.

Capybara

Marsupials The *cuica de agua* or **water opossum** (*Chironectes minimus*) is a small aquatic marsupial with a waterproof pouch (otherwise found only in the presumably extinct Tasmanian tiger); it's found only in the patch of *mata Atlántica* that crosses the border in the northeast.

Bats There are 17 species of bats in Uruguay, most excitingly the **vampire bat** (*Desmodus rotundus*), although for some unknown reason this does not generally carry rabies in Uruguay, apart from occasional incursions from Brazil to Rivera department.

Reptiles and amphibians There are over 100 reptiles and amphibians, including around 35 species of snakes, notably the **crossed pit viper** (*crucero, víbora de la cruz* or *yarará; Bothrops alternatus*), up to 1.4m in length, regarded as the most dangerous snake in Uruguay, although its bite rarely kills (and it plays an important role in controlling rodents). A smaller relative is the **yara** (*B pubescens*). The **cascabel** (*vibora de cascabel; Crotalus durissus terrificus*) is almost as long at 1.3m, and is very rare, only being found in northeastern Uruguay. The **coral snake** (*vibora de coral; Micrurus altirostris*) is smaller and has its fangs set at the rear of its jaw, so that it's virtually incapable of poisoning a human. There are other smaller snakes, especially on the islands of the Río Uruguay, where the **yellow anaconda** (*Eunectes notaeus*) may also be found. This is also where the **broad-snouted caiman** (*yacaré; Caiman latirostris*), a small alligator, thrives.

The Argentine **black and white tegu** (*lagarto overa; Tupinambis merianae*) is a large lizard, over 1m long when mature, that you're likely to see scuttling away into the undergrowth; they make good pets and can apparently even be trained to use litter trays. There are also six species of freshwater turtles (*tortuga*) as well as a variety of frogs and toads, notably **Darwin's redbelly toad** (*sapito de Darwin; Melanophryniscus montevidensis*). Sea turtles, which you might just see on boat trips, include **loggerhead** (*tortuga boba* or *tortuga careta; Caretta caretta*), **leatherback** (*tortuga laúd; Dermochelys coriacea*) and **green** (*tortuga verde; Chelonia mydas*) turtles.

Green sea turtles

Fish There are over 400 species of fish in Uruguay – saltwater, freshwater and those in the Río de la Plata which can't quite make up their minds, such as sharks, sea bass (*corvina*) and rays, including the catchily named Plate skate (*Atlantoraja* *platana*), fanskates (*Sympterygia* spp.) and sandskates (*Psammobatis* spp.). There are over 20 species of pejerrey (silverside or silvermelt) of several genuses, including the freshwater silverside (*Odontesthes bonariensis*) and the Río Negro basin silverside (*O humensis*). Sharks in particular, such as the **hammerhead shark** (*tiburón martillo*; *Sphyrna sp*) and the vitamin or **glass-snouted shark** (*tiburón vitamínico/trompa de cristal*; *Galeorhinus galeus*), come to breed in the estuary of the Plate, where the Brazil and Malvinas/Falklands currents meet rivers bearing silt from the interior of the continent, stirring up a very nutritious soup. Other sea fish that you may at least find in restaurants include the *brótola* (*Urophycis brasiliensis*) and **sea bream** (*sargo*; *Diplodus argenteus*).

In the huge rivers that feed into the Plate estuary are fish that grow even bigger than those at sea, most notably the **surubí** (*Pseudoplatystoma coruscans*), a type of catfish that is the biggest freshwater fish of Argentina and Uruguay, the related **manguruyú** (*Microglanis cottoides*) and the **dorado** (*Salminus brasiliensis*), all eagerly sought out by sport fishers in the Río Uruguay. Likewise, the **tigerfish** (*tararira*; *Hoplias malabaricus*) is a large, almost salmon-like beast in the Río Negro and Río Yí. New species of catfish (eg: *Pimelodus* and *Rineloricaria spp.*) are still being identified. The *pacú* (*Piaractus mesopotamicus*) is native to the Uruguay/Paraná system but now widely used for fish-farming elsewhere in the continent. It's known by various names, including: *patí, boga, bagre, sábalo, mojarra*.

Marine mammals
There are large colonies of both sea lions and fur seals on Uruguay's Atlantic coast, and you're very likely to see them, especially the sea lions that breed on the Isla de Lobos and come into the harbour of Punta del Este in search of fish scraps. **Elephant seals** (*Mirounga leonina*) can also turn up on Uruguayan beaches in winter.

Southern sea lions (*lobo común* or *lobo marino de un pelo*; *Otaria flavescens*) are seals with small, clearly visible external ears. They are much more mobile on land than true seals, being able to rotate their rear flippers sideways to propel their bodies forward. Sea lions can move quite fast in this manner: something to remember if you meet an angry bull. A fully grown southern sea lion bull is much larger and more impressive than his northern cousin, the California sea lion. This massive animal measures well over 2m long, and weighs up to half a tonne. His enormous neck is adorned with a shaggy mane, hence the name 'sea lion', which also refers to his roar. The elegant limpid-eyed females that make up his harem weigh only a quarter of his great bulk, but then they expend less energy. From the time he comes ashore in December to when he leaves in March, the bull sea lion neither eats nor sleeps for more than a few minutes at a time. Guarding his harem is a full-time job.

The black, furry pups are born in January. They are not fully weaned for six months, but the females return to the sea for feeding before this time, leaving a nursery or 'pod' of pups to gain safety in numbers. In fact they have few land predators, and the high juvenile mortality rate is largely due to the clumsiness of fighting males.

Only their golden brown fur and upturned noses distinguish **southern fur seals** (*lobo fino austral* or *lobo marino de dos pelos*; *Arctocephalus australis*) from sea lions. This luxurious coat almost led to their extinction through hunting, but now they are fully protected and their numbers are increasing. The fur seal has two layers of fur: a soft, dense undercoat, and an outer layer of coarse hair which traps bubbles of air to increase insulation. In fact, fur seals often seem to get too hot, and you will see them wave their flippers around in an attempt to cool off. Their colonies are most active in January, when you'll hardly be able to tear yourself away.

Fourteen species of whales can be seen in Uruguayan waters, of which the **sperm whale** (*cachalote*; *Physeter macrocephalus*), **pygmy sperm whale** (*cachalote* *pigmeo*; *Kogia breviceps*), **humpbacked whale** (*ballena yubarta*; *Megaptera novoangliae*) and **southern right whale** (*ballena franca austral*; *Eubalaena australis*) pass very close to the coast on their migrations. There are 13 species of porpoise and dolphin (including the orca and the false and pygmy killer whales), of which the easiest to spot are the **Burmeister's porpoise** (*marsopa espinosa*; *Phocoena spinipinnis*), **River Plate dolphin** (*delfín del Plata* or *franciscana*; *Pontoporia blainvillei*), and **bottlenose dolphin** (*tonina* or *delfín nariz de botella*; *Turciops truncatus*).

Birds Uruguay is home to a huge variety of birds relative to its area, with 459 species, a quarter of the total in Brazil (whose area is 48 times larger) and 40% of those in Argentina (16 times larger). The greatest number of species (311) are found in the Bañados del Este, the wetlands along the Atlantic Coast.

In some ways most obvious bird is the **greater rhea** (*ñandú*; *Rhea americana intermedia*), the ostrich-like bird that's easily visible in fields, especially in northern Uruguay; globally it's threatened by intensive farming, but numbers in Uruguay are holding up well enough. Also in pastureland you'll see the **spotted tinamou** (*Nothura maculosa*), popularly known as *perdiz* or partridge; despite hunting it's very common and easily spotted, running away ahead of you. The *hornero* or **ovenbird** (*Furnarius rufus rufus*) is emblematic, because of the rounded mud nests it places on fence-posts and trees (hence its name); it's pretty common, being very happy living close to humans. Endangered birds found in the savanna grasslands include the **yellow cardinal** (*cardenal amarillo*; *Gubernatrix cristata*), **saffron-cowled blackbird** (*dragón*; *Xanthopsar flavus*) and **bearded tachuri** (*Polystictus pectoralis*). The **firewood-gatherer** (*espinero común*; *Anumbius annumbi)* is a relative of the ovenbird, found in grassland (dry or wet), but rather than a mud nest it builds one of twigs, a smaller version of the monk parakeet's (see opposite).

There are nine woodpeckers and flickers, mostly of course in woodland, but the most common in fact feeds on open grassland. This is the **yellowy-green field flicker** (*carpintero de campo*; *Colaptes campestris*) – a flicker being a woodpecker that doesn't peck wood. There are nine species of hummingbirds (in summer).

You'll see large numbers of **turkey vultures** (*buitre cabo roja*; *Cathartes aura*) circling overhead; the **Andean black vulture** (*buitre de cabeza negra*; *Coragyps atratus foetens*) was more common but has been overtaken in recent decades. A third species, the **yellow-headed vulture** (*buitre de cabeza amarilla*; *Cathartes burrovianus*) is rare in Uruguay. There are no fewer than 36 other raptors, including 17 hawks, buzzards and eagles, ten owls, and three caracaras, which are common scavengers of carrion.

The national bird is the *tero* or **southern lapwing** (*Vanellus chilensis*), a crested wader which seems omnipresent, having taken to nesting in fields, parks and gardens. It defends its nest by squawking and then flying at you, although it stops short of actual contact. When not breeding, it lives in wetlands and seasonally flooded grassland, where the attractive **black-and-white monjita** (*viudita blanca grande*; *Heteroxolmis dominicana*) and **red-breasted blackbird** (*pecho colorado grande*; *Sturnella militaris*), actually a meadowlark, are also fairly common. Indeed most Uruguayan birds (perhaps 400 species) are found in wetlands, both on the coast and in the littoral of the Río Uruguay, including 11 species of egret, heron and night-heron, up to 22 ducks, four grebes, three kingfishers, three storks, the **American darter** or snakebird (*Anhinga anhinga*), one spoonbill (*Ajaja ajaja*) and one flamingo (*Phoenicopterus chilensis*). Smaller and less easily seen birds include nine types of rail and crake, three types of moorhen and three types of coot.

The seedeaters (tiny passerines, related to tanagers and Darwin's finches) are a focus of conservation interest at the moment, because of trapping for the cagebird trade, loss of habitat, and problems actually categorising the separate species. The chestnut seedeater (*capuchino corona gris*; *Sporophila cinnamomea*) is found in grassland, while others, such as the **dark-throated seedeater** (*capuchino garganta café*; *S ruficollis*) and **rufous-rumped seedeater** (*capuchino castaño*; *S hypochroma*), are found more in marshes and damper pastures. The white-collared or **Entre Ríos seedeater** (*capuchino de collar*; *Sporophila zelichi*) and **marsh seedeater** (*capuchino pecho blanco*; *S palustris*) are found in marshes and also in gallery forest.

In tidal areas and elsewhere there are seven species of sandpipers, two dotterels, two snipe, the Hudsonian godwit, and other waders – many of these migrate from the northern hemisphere and thus are familiar to North Americans, who are happy to fund conservation initiatives to protect them in Uruguay. Marine birds include five gulls, six albatrosses, 12 terns, 17 petrels, the **snowy sheathbill** (*paloma antártica*; *Chionis albus*), the **frigatebird** (*fregata*; *Fregata magnificens*), and even two penguins, the **rockhopper** (*Eudyptes chrysocome*) and **Magellanic penguin** (*Spheniscus magellanicus*).

Characteristic birds of mountain woodland (*bosque serrano*) include the **diademed tanager** (*cardenal azul*; *Stephanophorus diadematus*), **rufous-browed peppershrike** (*Juan Chiviro*; *Cyclarhis gujanensis*), **long-tailed reed-finch** (*pajonalera cabeza gris*; *Donacospiza albifrons*) and **chopi blackbird** (*mirlo charrúa*; *Gnorimopsar chopi*). In the *monte de quebrada* of the north you may also see the **buff-necked ibis** (*bandurria baya*; *Theristicus caudatus*), **crested-black tyrant** (*viudita copetona*; *Knipolegus lophotes*), **cliff flycatcher** (*viudita colorada*; *Hirundinea bellicosa*), **yellow-rumped marshbird** (*canario de la sierras*; *Pseudoleistes guirahuro*) and (red-legged) **seriema** (*Cariama cristata*), like a secretarybird with its silly crest.

In the *mata Atlántica* you may find some subtropical species such as **brown tinamou** (*perdiz marrón*; *Crypturellus obsoletus*), **red-winged tinamou** (*martineta del monte*; *Rhynchotus rufescens*), **rufous gnat-eater** (*chupadientes castaño*; *Conopophaga lineata*), **scaled woodcreeper** (*trepador escamado*; *Lepidocolaptes squamatus*) and the **blue jay** (*urraca azul*; *Cyanocorax caeruleus*).

There are seven members of the parrot family in Uruguay, of which the most ubiquitous is the **monk parakeet** (*cotorra común*; *Myiopsitta monachus*), which is very talkative (captive birds develop large vocabularies) and makes huge communal nests of twigs. It has taken to nesting in eucalyptus trees, and so its numbers have increased greatly along with the area of eucalyptus plantations; unfortunately it does considerable damage to crops. Otherwise there are various species of attractive Aratinga parakeets in the northwest of the country.

Of the seven introduced bird species, the only common ones are the **European sparrow** (*gorrión*; *Passer domesticus*) and the **rock pigeon** (*paloma doméstica*; *Columba livia*), which you'll see in every town but not outside; however, there are eight species of attractive native doves.

CONSERVATION

In Montevideo at least, people seem always to be carrying bags of rubbish to big wheelie-bins, which are constantly visited by scavenging *hergaderos* with horse carts, mainly taking cardboard. Proper recycling is only getting off the ground slowly, with a few bins for glass, tins and batteries appearing from 2008.

A report in 2008 by the United Nations Environment Programme criticised many aspects of Uruguay's environmental situation, notably problems linked to increasing affluence, such as over-consumption, excessive packaging, poorly organised waste disposal and limited recycling. There's a great lack of monitoring and information and of joined-up government policy, but DINAMA, the National Environment Bureau (*www.dinama.gub.uy*) is now monitoring the emissions of 395 companies.

The UNEP report did note positive new developments such as environmental education initiatives, a new law on returnable bottles and the new Sistema Nacional de Areas Protegidas or National Protected Area System (*SNAP;* *www.snap.gub.uy*); there are now plenty of low-energy bulbs in use.

The SNAP was set up in 2005 (under a law passed in 2000), and will cover 20 state, NGO and private protected areas. The oldest, dating from 1916, is the Parque Roosevelt on the outskirts of Montevideo, which is totally planted with eucalyptus and of no conservation value whatsoever; later additions are more worthwhile, and SNAP's two priority areas are hybrids of various categories of reserve, to be managed holistically. These are Lunarejo, in the north (see page 304) and the Esteros de Farapos y Islas del Río Uruguay, in the west (see page 277). The latter is the country's second Ramsar wetland site, following the Bañados del Este (on the Atlantic coast), which also combines various separate protected areas (including a couple of colonial forts) and became Uruguay's first Coastal-Marine Protected Area in 2007.

HISTORY

It seems that humans first crossed into the Americas from Asia over the Bering land-bridge about 60,000 years ago, and headed south, crossing into South America around 15,000 years ago and reaching Tierra del Fuego approximately 4,000 years later. The oldest human artefacts (arrowheads and spearheads) yet found in Uruguay (in Maldonado department) have been dated to 12,900 years ago; at this time small family bands of nomadic hunter-gatherers were probably moving south from present-day Brazil. Remains dating from around 10,000 years ago have also been found in the northwest of the country.

Around 9,000 years ago larger groups formed, eating a wider range of foods and with more advanced methods of shaping stones for blades, scrapers and bolas (throwing) stones. As the climate warmed, around 8,000 years ago, the megafauna (such as giant sloths and sabre-toothed tigers) died out.

In the centre and west of the country, **rock carvings** (*grabados rupestres*) began to appear *c.*4,000 years ago, to the north of the Río Negro, followed around 2,000 years ago by rock paintings (*pinturas rupestres*, in a range of reds), to the south of the river. In the east of the country, from around 4,000 years ago, large mounds known as **cerritos** (up to 40m in diameter and 7m in height) were constructed; detailed investigation is only now beginning, but it seems that they were not, as assumed, burial mounds, but the sites of villages created as the climate changed and marshlands dried out. Traces of squash, maize and beans (as well as butia palm fruit) indicate that agriculture began far earlier than had been thought in this part of the continent. Strange bird-shaped stones known as *ornitholithos*, carved around 3,300 years ago, have been found mainly in the nearby coastal parts of Rocha and Maldonado departments; ceramics also appeared around 3,000 years ago.

From about 4,000 years ago the people loosely known as the **Charrúa** were driven south into what is now Uruguay by the Guaraní. Although their population only numbered between 5,000 and 10,000, they were the best documented of the peoples encountered by Europeans after their first arrival here in 1516 (at latest), and the last to die out. Other peoples included the Chaná, Guenoa and Yaro.

EUROPEAN COLONISATION Amerigo Vespucci may have reached present-day Uruguay in 1502, but the first certain contact came in 1516 when a Spanish expedition led by **Juan Díaz de Solís** followed the coast south from Brazil, reaching the Río de la Plata (River Plate, which he named the Río Dulce or Sweet River, having found fresh water out at sea) and the confluence of the Río Uruguay and Río Paraná. He and most of his fellows were killed (and allegedly eaten) by the native people, and for the next century the region was left largely undisturbed, due mainly to its presumed lack of gold or silver. Magellan also visited the Plate on his way to the Pacific in 1520.

Sebastián Gaboto was the son of the explorer known to the British as John Cabot, and may have sailed with him to eastern Canada. He entered the service of Spain and in 1526 led a fleet to the Plate and on up the Paraná and Uruguay rivers, establishing the fort of San Salvador at the confluence of the Río Uruguay and the Río San Salvador, west of Dolores – the first European settlement in what is now Uruguay. He also founded the first European settlement in what is now Argentina at Espíritu Santo on the Río Paraná, which was soon wiped out by the indigenous peoples. In 1529 San Salvador was abandoned and the expedition returned to Spain.

In 1580 the city of Buenos Aires was founded (after a failed attempt in 1536) on the Argentine side of the Plate, and in about 1611 cattle were released on the Uruguayan side of the estuary by the legendary Hernandarias (Hernando Arias de Saavedra, 1561–1634, governor of Asunción), with expeditions coming to slaughter some from time to time (for leather more than for meat). The first permanent European settlement in Uruguay came in 1624, when the Jesuits founded the mission of Santo Domingo de Soriano, on Isla Vizcaino (later moved to the mainland; see pages 262–3).

The Portuguese, already established in Brazil, sought to expand their territory to the Plate and the Río Uruguay, establishing a fort at Colonia del Sacramento, across the Plate from Buenos Aires, in 1680. This was resisted by the Spanish, and Colonia was under attack or blockade for much of its early history. The Spanish also established a fort and settlement at Montevideo in 1724.

British involvement was limited in this period to the regular passage of buccaneers and privateers such as Francis Drake (1578), his cousin John Drake (1581), Robert Withrington (1587), John Childley (1589), Thomas Cavendish (1592) and Edward Davis (1683). A little later, in 1768, Captain Cook stopped in Uruguay with the scientists Sir Joseph Banks and Daniel Carl Solander; likewise in 1832 Charles Darwin spent a considerable time in Uruguay, travelling from Maldonado inland to Minas and from Montevideo to Colonia and near Mercedes, and writing perceptively and entertainingly about his experiences.

As the colonisation of the Banda Oriental (the Eastern Shore of the River Plate) became established, further towns were founded, notably Paysandú (in 1749), Maldonado (1755), Salto (1756), San Carlos (1763), San José (1783), Minas (1784), Rocha (1794) and Melo (1795). In addition, forts were built near the Brazilian border, at San Miguel (1734) and Santa Teresa (1762–76).

The War of the Spanish Succession (fought mainly in Europe) ended in 1715 with Colonia confirmed as a Portuguese possession, but from 1737 it was again blockaded by Spain. The Treaty of Tordesillas, in 1494, had set a north–south line 370 leagues (about 1,770km) west of the Cape Verde Islands as the boundary between Portugal and Spain. Portugal's colony in Brazil quickly over-ran this boundary, and it was soon ignored. However, it was only in 1750 that the treaty was officially superseded by the Treaty of Madrid, which settled the southwestern border of Brazil and gave Colonia to Spain, although it was not actually handed over until 1777. Similarly, Spain was required to cede to Portugal the territory of seven Jesuit reductions or missions on the upper Río Uruguay (to the north of present-day Uruguay). This reckoned without their Guaraní inhabitants, who were to be relocated in Spanish territory – when they refused to go, the Spanish and Portuguese armies joined forces to drive them out in the brutal Guaraní War of 1754–56.

This effort was rendered worthless in 1761 when, because of the difficulties of implementing it, the Treaty of Madrid was abrogated by Spain, which now kept the area of the missions; the Treaty of Paris (1763) ending the Seven Years' War, which had set Spain against Portugal in a largely European conflict, returned Colonia to Portugal while Spain held the province of Río Grande do Sul, now the southernmost part of Brazil.

The Portuguese saw the Jesuits as backing the Guaraní in their refusal to be uprooted and, when the Pope died in 1758, moved quickly to dispossess the order of all their possessions in Portuguese territory. Likewise, the Spanish saw the huge and largely autonomous Jesuit estate of Yapeyú, covering the present departments of Paysandú, Salto and Artigas and parts of Río Negro and Tacuarembó, as well as Entre Ríos and Corrientes in Argentina, as a power within the state, and in 1767 the order was expelled from all Spanish domains.

Another Spanish–Portuguese War in 1776–77 was settled by the Treaties of San Ildefonso (1777) and El Pardo (1778), reaffirming the Treaty of Madrid and confirming Portuguese control of Brazil (in particular Río Grande do Sul) and Spanish control of the Banda Oriental (Uruguay), including Colonia.

Also in 1776, the Spanish government created the Viceroyalty of the Río de la Plata, with control of present-day Argentina, Uruguay, Paraguay and southern Bolivia passing from Lima to Buenos Aires, with the aim of better countering the growth of Brazil. The port of Buenos Aires was opened to transatlantic shipping for the first time, leading to a rapid increase in trade, as well as smuggling, in which Montevideo and Colonia played important roles. The original one bull and seven cows released in the Banda Oriental prospered and bred like crazy (as did seven stallions and seven mares); increasingly they were rounded up, branded and kept on huge *estancias* (rural estates), of which there were 102 by 1757, with over 133,000 cattle, 124,000 horses and 71,000 sheep. These were almost all killed or stolen by the Portuguese in the wars of the mid 18th century, and only repopulated after 1819 (with merino sheep introduced from 1832). Nevertheless, the number of cowhides exported increased ten-fold between 1760 and 1780, as the (human) population grew and trade increased. By the end of the 18th century the population of the Banda Oriental was just over 30,000, of whom two-thirds were in the Montevideo area.

THE WARS OF INDEPENDENCE Spain's colonies were never allowed to develop, other than as sources of raw materials, but a *criollo* (native-born) middle-class did grow up and was increasingly able to run its own affairs. Spain allied itself with Napoleon's France, and in June 1806 British forces captured Buenos Aires; the royalist forces proved to be useless, but the British were driven out in August by the naval officer Santiago Liniers, who landed with troops and militia forces from Montevideo. The British, once reinforced, crossed the Plate, capturing Maldonado and then Montevideo after a fierce battle on 3 February 1807. In July they again attacked Buenos Aires, defeated Liniers but failed to occupy the city at once; when they did attack they met fierce resistance in which half the British forces were either killed or wounded. The British surrendered and withdrew to Montevideo, abandoning that as well in September 1807 after a peaceful occupation.

In 1808 Napoleon invaded Spain and forced King Carlos IV to abdicate, putting his brother on the throne instead. The governor of Montevideo, Francisco Javier de Elío, pressured Liniers (now Viceroy of the Plate, but French-born) to declare his loyalty to the Spanish crown, but Liniers issued an ambiguous statement. Accused of complicity with Napoleon by Elío and the *cabildo* (council) of Buenos Aires, he summoned Elío to Buenos Aires, replacing him with Juan Ángel de Michelena. The citizens of Montevideo backed Elío and called for a *cabildo abierto* (open council), held on 21 September 1808; Michelena fled and a royalist Junta (ruling council) was set up, a crucial phase in the Banda Oriental's development of an identity separate to Buenos Aires. Only in May 1810 did the *criollo* people of Buenos Aires set up an autonomous junta, forcing the viceroy to move to Montevideo.

A certain José Gervasio Artigas (see the box on page 16–17), who had fought under Liniers in Buenos Aires and then in the defence of Montevideo where he was wounded and captured, went in the opposite direction, deserting from the army and heading for Buenos Aires in February 1811 to join the movement for independence of the Banda Oriental from Spanish rule, which had begun with the Grito de Asencio (the 'Cry of Asencio') (27 February 1811), and the capture of Mercedes and Santo Domingo de Soriano the next day. He returned in April with around 180 men, defeating Spanish forces at the battle of Las Piedras in May and besieging Montevideo. Threatened by armies from both Buenos Aires and Brazil, he led perhaps 10,000 soldiers and civilians across the Río Uruguay from Salto in the so-called *Exodo del Pueblo Oriental* (Exodus of the Eastern People); having regrouped, he returned in 1812 to beat the Spanish at El Cerrito. In January 1813 a congress in Buenos Aires claimed independence for the whole of the Spanish viceroyalty; in April a meeting of the Orientales (presided over by Artigas) at Tres Cruces accepted this but with conditions (known as the *Instrucciones del Año XIII*) specifying autonomy for the provinces within a federation and the separation of the three branches of government. In 1814 an army from Buenos Aires drove the Spanish from Montevideo, and was in turn driven out in 1815 by Oriental forces under Fructuoso Rivera, securing the autonomy of the Provincia Oriental. Artigas attended the congress in Concepción del Uruguay (in present-day Argentina) at which the provinces of the Banda Oriental, Córdoba, Corrientes, Entre Ríos, Misiones and Santa Fe declared their independence from Spain and formed the Liga Federal (Federal League), in opposition above all to Buenos Aires, which saw itself as capital of the United Provinces of the Plate. With the tacit backing of Buenos Aires, a Portuguese army invaded, capturing Montevideo in January 1817; Artigas held the interior of the country for the next three years, but his federalist allies, the governors of Santa Fe and Entre Ríos, came to an agreement with Buenos Aires and abandoned him. In 1820 he was defeated by the Portuguese at Tacuarembó and went into exile in Paraguay, staying there until his death in 1850.

The Brazilians were welcomed as protection from the domination of Buenos Aires; in 1821 the Congreso Cisplatina in Montevideo voted for the incorporation of the province within the Portuguese Empire (and thus from 1822 the independent Brazil). However, the United Provinces of the River Plate now backed the Orientals (led by Rivera and Juan Antonio Lavalleja) in an independence struggle; the Cruzada Libertadora (Crusade of Liberation) began on 19 April 1825 when 33 Orientals (the famous Treinta y Tres Orientales or 33 Easterners) led by Juan Antonio Lavalleja landed at the Playa de la Agraciada; the next day they joined up with Rivera (although accounts vary as to how willing Rivera was to ally himself with Lavalleja – one version has him being captured and forced to sign on pain of death). In June 1825 a provisional government was formed in Florida, where on 25 August a congress of deputies of the Provincia Oriental voted this time for independence within the United Provinces. Brazil went to war with the United Provinces, blockading the ports of Montevideo and Buenos Aires, but was hampered by internal revolts in raising a decent army. After Lavalleja's victory at Sarandí in October 1825 the Argentines joined the war against Brazil and eventually peace, and **Uruguayan independence**, were mediated by the British diplomat Lord John Ponsonby, Britain being anxious to create a buffer state between Argentina and Brazil to secure its trade interests in the region. The war ended in August 1828 and an *Asamblea Constituyente y Legislativa* (constituent and legislative assembly) met to draw up a constitution, approved in September 1829 and sworn nationwide on 18 July 1830. It created a democratic republic now known as the República Oriental del Uruguay (Oriental Republic of Uruguay).

INDEPENDENCE AND CIVIL WAR Uruguay had finally achieved independence from both Brazil and Argentina, although its borders were still not fixed. Lavalleja became interim head of state, with Rivera elected the country's **first president** in 1830.

The young country got off to an appalling start by massacring its few remaining indigenous people on 11 April 1831 – Rivera's nephew Bernabé Rivera invited the Charrúa (whose numbers had fallen to about 500) to a meeting in the ravine of **Salsipuedes** (aptly named 'Get out if you can') and then ambushed them, killing almost all the men. The women and children were spared and distributed as virtual slaves, but effectively there was now no indigenous culture left in Uruguay (although a few hundred mixed-blood Charrúa remain in Argentina). Four of the surviving Uruguayan Charrúa (ie: pure blood) – Vaimaca-Piru (who had fought with Artigas and Rivera), the medicine-man Senaca and a younger couple, Tacuabe and Guyunusa – were captured at Salsipuedes and in 1833 taken to be exhibited in France (where a baby was born and they all died). A print of *Los Últimós Charrúas* (The Last Charrúas) was produced as publicity (and served as the basis for the

EL PROCER – JOSÉ GERVASIO ARTIGAS

Although the Artigas family settled in Montevideo as early as 1726, and José Gervasio Artigas was born there in 1764, he spent his youth in the country, northeast of the city near Sauce, gaining the outdoor skills that fitted him for military success. Living as a gaucho (and even dabbling in a bit of smuggling), he came to see the indigenous people as equals, an attitude which marked his later career. In 1797 he joined the Blandengues, a cavalry regiment newly created to guard the Banda Oriental's borders, and rose to the rank of captain. Inspired by the movement for independence from Spain, he fled to Buenos Aires and returned with a small amount of men and money to lead an uprising against Spain in the Banda Oriental, laying siege to Montevideo in May 1811, together with troops from Buenos Aires. However he was disgusted by the truce between the Spanish viceroy and the Junta of Buenos Aires and took his troops and many more people across the Río Uruguay to regroup, returning in 1812 once the truce had collapsed to continue the struggle. His delegates to the *Asamblea General Constituyente* in Buenos Aires in 1813 demanded a liberal republican and federalist constitution based on that of the United States of America; this was rejected, and Artigas abandoned the siege of Montevideo. His rivals in Buenos Aires declared him a traitor, but he was able to take control of the rest of the country and then capture Montevideo in 1815, ensuring the independence of the Banda Oriental from Buenos Aires.

Artigas continued to resist the centralising ambition of Buenos Aires, organising the Liga Federal of the Banda Oriental and five provinces on the western side of the Río Uruguay (all now part of Argentina), with free trade between them and land redistributed to his supporters, including native and mixed-race people. Artigas based himself at Purificación, about 100km north of Paysandú, and in June 1815 called a *Congreso de los Pueblos Libres* in Concepción del Uruguay (on what is now the Argentine side of the Río Uruguay) where he was named *Protector de los Pueblos Libres* (Protector of the Free Peoples). The other provines of the former Viceroyalty of the River Plate were invited to join the Liga Federal, provoking Buenos Aires to take control of the other provinces and statue of the same name in Montevideo's Prado park in 1939, by which time attitudes were changing and Uruguayans increasingly deplored the genocide and the loss of part of their heritage). In addition, a group of Guaraní came from the Jesuit missions when these were finally incorporated into Brazil, living from 1833 to 1862 in San Francisco de Borja del Yí (10km from Durazno), until this was forcibly closed down and the remaining Guaraní assimilated into the local population.

In 1834 Manuel Oribe, one of the 33, was elected the country's second president, but the next year Rivera rose in revolt, starting the **Guerra Grande** or Great War, a civil war that polarised the country for the rest of the century. Rivera's party, known as Colorados from their red armbands (torn from the lining of their ponchos), were unitarists, standing for a fully independent Uruguay, while Oribe's Blancos (whose white armbands were torn from a flag) stood for a federal solution – Artigas's dream – and were backed by the landowners and the Argentine dictator Rosas. In October 1838 Oribe fled to Argentina and Rivera became president again, but within days Rosas declared war; Rivera beat his forces at Cagancha in 1839 but fled to Brazil in 1845; Blanco forces (and Argentine ships) blockaded Montevideo from 1843 to 1851, but the war ended as a draw in 1851 (followed by Rosas's overthrow) and Rivera returned in 1853 to rule as part of a triumvirate with Lavalleja and the Colorado Venancio Flores. However, Lavalleja died that year and Rivera in 1854, leaving Flores as interim president until 1855, when he stepped down and went to Argentina.

to connive with Portugal to invade the Banda Oriental and depose Artigas. Montevideo was captured in 1817 but resistance continued until 1820 when Artigas fled into exile in Paraguay.

Not allowed to communicate with anyone abroad, he lived here for another thirty years, with only his trusted companion Joaquín Lenzina, known as 'el negro Ansina', an Afro-Uruguayan who had been enslaved by the Portuguese and whose freedom he had bought at the turn of the nineteenth century. Like San Martín and O'Higgins, the liberators of Argentina and Chile, he was to die in exile. Portraits show him looking increasingly like a Greek philosopher, and he was soon revered as *el procer* or father of the nation (as opposed to the liberator, which title belongs to Juan Antonio Lavalleja); nowadays there's an Avenida Artigas in almost every town. In 1855, five years after his death, his remains were brought back to Montevideo and buried in the Central Cemetery; in 1950 they were moved to the Tres Cruces obelisk, and in 1977 to the mausoleum on Plaza Independencia. In 2009 it was announced that he was to be moved again, to the Casa de Gobierno across the road, due to the mausoleum's association with the military dictatorship.

Artigas's heroic stature is enhanced by the fact that he had fourteen children by eight mothers (including indigenous women); he was married to Isabel Sánchez from 1791 until her death in 1804, then to his cousin Rosalía Rafaela Villagrán. This marriage was annulled due to her mental illness, and in 1815, in his base of Purificación, he took as his third wife Melchora Cuenca, a Paraguayan lancer, no less, and much younger than him; when he went into exile she stayed in Uruguay, putting up with many difficulties due to being his wife.

His first son Juan Manuel, born in 1791, became colonel of a cavalry regiment, and also married in 1815, in his father's camp at Purificación; from 1821 until his death in 1851 he lived in Entre Ríos, now a province of Argentina. José María, born in 1806, also rose to the rank of Lieutenant-Colonel.

When the Blanco government of Bernardo Berro supposedly discriminated against Brazilian-born landowners, Brazil and Argentina invaded Uruguay to put Flores and the Colorados into power in 1865. Later that year Berro's ally, the tinpot dictator of Paraguay, Francisco Solano López, declared war on Uruguay, launching the War of the Triple Alliance in which Uruguay, Brazil and Argentina blockaded Paraguay's access to the sea and still managed to take five years and lose huge numbers of troops before winning. Flores ruled as a virtual dictator until February 1868; four days after stepping down, both he and Berro were assassinated.

The Paraguayan war finally ended in March 1870; in September the Blanco leader Timoteo Aparicio launched the so-called Revolución de las Lanzas (Revolution of the Lances, named after the makeshift weapons of knives tied to sugarcanes), which ended in April 1872 with a power-sharing agreement that was to last until the early 20th century. Although this marked the end of Uruguay's civil war, the political scenery continued to be dominated by the division between conservative, rural Blancos (aka the Partido Nacional) and the liberal, urban Colorados; both were aligned with similar factions in Argentina. The two parties now agreed not to interfere in one another's spheres of influence, but the mindset of *caudillismo* (the dominance of local party bosses who became virtual warlords in their own patch) was difficult to erase, ending only with the death of Aparicio Saravia in 1904 in a failed uprising.

MODERNISATION Industrial development began to take off in the 1860s, with the introduction of railways, barbed wire and Hereford cattle – there was a massive shift from cowhides to huge quantities of beef, processed by the Fray Bentos meat-packing plant and shipped worldwide (in cans until 1905, then also in freezer ships). From the 1870s there was mass immigration, mainly from Spain and Italy, the population growing from 450,000 in 1873 to 1 million in 1900, 1.3 million in 1914 and 1.9 million in 1930. There was also a massive inflow of European investment, with 27 banks and over 100 financial societies founded by 1900 (in addition to the Banco Nacional, created in 1887).

The election of the Colorado **José Batlle y Ordóñez** (1856–1929) as president in 1903 was a major turning-point for Uruguay, the start of a period of economic prosperity, social reform and widening democracy which lasted until the Great Depression. From the defeat of Aparicio Saravia in 1904 until 1907 he concentrated on consolidating democracy after the period of *caudillismo*; church and state were also separated, divorce introduced and education expanded. Re-elected for a second term from 1911 to 1915, Batlle (pronounced 'badge-eh') abolished the death penalty and moved on to the economy, seeking to replace foreign dominance with state control. Unemployment pay was introduced in 1914 and the eight-hour working day in 1915. Similar policies were pursued by Claudio Williman (1863–1934), hand-picked to be president between Batlle's two terms, and by Baltasar Brum (1883–1933), president from 1919 to 1923, who continued reforms of the educational and welfare systems.

This golden age of progress and prosperity came to a sudden end with the arrival of the Great Depression and the collapse of prices for Uruguay's exports, as well as the imposition of tariffs by the developed nations. Gabriel Terra (1873–1942; also a Colorado) became president in 1931 and suspended congress in 1933, introducing a new constitution in 1934 and establishing himself as president with dictatorial powers. Brum was so outraged by the coup and the way that Uruguayans seemed to be accepting it that he killed himself in a dramatic protest; there was a revolt in 1935 but it was swiftly suppressed.

Terra stood down in 1938 and his successors kept Uruguay neutral but aligned with the anti-fascist Allies; in 1949 the British-owned railways and water companies were nationalised (actually in payment for meat supplied to Britain during World War II), as the state tightened its control of the economy. Exports of food for the allied armies fighting in Korea helped boost the economy under president Luis Batlle Berres (nephew of José; 1897–1964). Then in 1952 a new constitution established a ruling college like Switzerland's (as originally proposed by José Batlle y Ordóñez); the Consejo Nacional de Gobierno (National Council of Government) had six members from the majority party and three from the minority party, but because the majority was rarely united and the president had no real power it was ineffective, and in 1967 Uruguay returned to the presidential system. Nevertheless, from 1959 to 1966 the Blancos did have a rare chance to run the country; they tried to implement economic reforms but were blocked by the unions.

MILITARY DICTATORSHIP AND AFTER In 1971 the left-wing Movimiento de Liberación Nacional (National Liberation Movement, known as the Tupamaros) opted for armed struggle; at the same time the legitimate left-wing parties at last formed a united platform, the Frente Amplio (Broad Front). The elections at the end of 1971 were won (with the help of some CIA interference) by Juan María Bordaberry (b1928) who in 1973 'invited' the military to take power. In fact the Tupamaros urban guerrillas had been effectively wiped out by 1972, but a period of brutal repression followed, coupled with neoliberal economic policies that caused real wages to fall to less than half their 1968 levels. Around 10% of the population emigrated for political or economic reasons, and in 1980 the military failed to persuade the electorate to endorse an authoritarian new constitution. In the face of the worst economic crisis since the 1930s, they were increasingly keen to hand back power, and the return of democracy in Argentina after the Falklands/Malvinas war encouraged the opposition, as did the 1983 visit of King Juan Carlos of Spain, seen (ironically) as a symbol of democracy and liberty. Negotiations led to elections in 1984 and the moderate Colorado Julio María Sanguinetti (b1936) became president in February 1985, with an amnesty granted to protect those who committed human rights abuses under the dictatorship. The economy continued to struggle, with inflation reaching 130% by the end of 1990; however, Uruguay played a key role in negotiations leading to the foundation of Mercosur, the South American common market, in 1991. Sanguinetti was succeeded in 1991 by the moderate conservative Luis Alberto Lacalle (b1941), whose free-market policies and budget cuts were unpopular; he lost the 1994 elections to Sanguinetti, who held the presidency again from 1995 to 2000. He worked with the Blancos to reform social security, ending the state monopoly of insurance and pensions; the Frente Amplio, now holding a third of seats in the legislature, won support by backing the welfare state, although it was increasingly unaffordable.

In fact Sanguinetti had won only 24.7% of the vote in the 1994 elections, but was elected as the leading candidate of the party with the most votes in total, although the Frente Amplio's Tabaré Vásquez (named after the half-Charrúa hero of the national poem *Tabaré*) won 30.6% of the vote. In 1996 a referendum approved changes, including a run-off vote for the presidency, but in 1999 Vásquez was again kept from the presidency by an alliance of the Blancos and Colorados, taking 46% of the vote in the run-off against the centrist Colorado Jorge Batlle (b1927, son of Luis). Batlle pushed through controversial reforms, including privatisations and the outsourcing of some public services to the private sector. Although he inherited a strong economy (with GDP growth of around 5% per annum in 1996–98), it was dragged down by the economic problems of Brazil and Argentina, coupled with drought and high oil prices. In 2001 the collapse of the Argentine economy led to bank deposits there being frozen and Argentines making huge withdrawals of US dollars stashed in Uruguayan banks; about a third of the country's deposits were taken out of the financial system and five financial institutions became insolvent, largely the result of a failure of regulation (sound familiar?). In July 2002 the Uruguayan peso plunged, and GDP fell close to 20% in the next four years, while inflation and unemployment soared. Loans from the IMF allowed Uruguay to restructure its external debt, and the country did not default on its debt, unlike Argentina.

As a result of the economic crisis, at the end of 2004 **Tabaré Vásquez** finally managed to get elected, and was remarkably successful and popular, continuing to work part-time at his cancer clinic and taking camping and fishing holidays near Mercedes. One of his first moves was to restore diplomatic ties with Cuba, a declaration of independence from the United States after 170 years of right-wing rule; but in 2007 he signed a trade and investment 'framework agreement' with the US. However, the left wing of the coalition kept him from moving further towards a full free-trade deal. This would also be resisted by Uruguay's partners in the Mercosur trade group; Argentina already tends to be less than neighbourly, doing little to counter the blockades set up at the border bridge to protest against the Botnia pulp mill (see page 270).

Uruguayans seem happy with their mixed economy, with the state controlling most utilities; some are tempted by the more dynamic capitalism of Chile, but they are reluctant to become less egalitarian. With tax breaks and legal safeguards for investors, and an educated workforce, there are hopes that call centres and outsourced back-offices will be established in Uruguay.

MUJICA AND THE FUTURE With the very popular Vásquez unable to run for a second term as president, the ruling Frente Amplio ignored his preferred successor, his former finance minister, Danilo Astori, a technocrat who finds it hard to smile for the cameras, and chose the rather more charismatic José Mujica. A former Tupamaros guerrilla, later agriculture minister and then senator, he had the support of the trade unions; the intelligentsia is wary of him, less because of his guerrilla past than because they see him adopting the same sort of populist policies as the Kirchners in Argentina, as well as Venezuela's Hugo Chávez and Bolivia's Evo Morales. To gain wider acceptability he was forced to select Astori, seen as the architect of Uruguay's steady economic growth over the previous four years, as his running mate.

His main rival was the former president Luis Lacalle of the Partido Nacional (with Jorge Larrañaga as his running mate), followed by Pedro Bordaberry of the Colorados (whose father invited the military to take over in 1973). In the elections of October 2009, Mujica won 47.5% of the vote, followed by Lacalle with 29% and Bordaberry with 17.5%, so that a second round was required in November. In this, Lacalle took 44% of the vote while Mujica won 52%; the Frente Amplio also kept its parliamentary majority. The Colorados received less than 17% of the vote, but that was enough for them to be delighted, given how totally they have been eclipsed by the Partido Nacional. In any case, after the elections all the candidates were very conciliatory, stressing that Mujica was the president of all Uruguayans, not just one party.

GOVERNMENT AND POLITICS

Uruguayans love politics and are always talking about it (and football) – sometimes it seems that campaigning never ends, as parties choose pre-candidates and then one or more candidates proper before the actual election campaign gets under way.

Inaugurated as president of Uruguay at the age of 74 in March 2010, José 'Pepe' Mujica is the most colourful politician the country has seen in half a century. Routinely described in the foreign media as 'a former guerrilla leader', he fought with the Tupamaros in the 1970s, and was jailed from 1972 to 1985 (including two years spent at the bottom of a well). A more ruthless dictatorship would have killed him, but he was eventually released and has stuck to non-violent political action ever since. He founded the Movimiento de Participación Popular (the Movement of Popular Participation), despite the refusal of some former guerrillas to participate in 'bourgeois politics', and was elected to congress in 1994. The MPP is now the largest faction of the Frente Amplio coalition.

Known for his colourful, even profane, way of speaking, and for addressing people as *compañero* (ie: comrade), he's anathema to many on the right and even to those on the more centrist side of the Frente Amplio coalition. He has little interest in economics (or in speaking English), and so it was essential for his defeated rival Danilo Astori to accept the vice-presidential slot and give his campaign a broader appeal. Generally a scruffy-looking believer in the simple vegetarian life, he was tidied up and put into a good suit for meetings with foreign heads of state in the later stages of the campaign, and began speaking from prepared texts. President Vásquez finally embraced him publicly, although he had wanted Mujica as vice-president to Astori. Mujica has stressed that he represents continuity with the highly popular Vásquez government (Uruguay's first elected leftist administration) but in truth the continuity is provided by Astori, rather than Mujica, the agriculture minister who just sat back and benefited from the worldwide boom in commodity prices.

Even so, he has a strong connection with the young, as well as with the widely mocked dinosaurs of the 'Jurassic left'. He admits he doesn't believe in working too hard, and travelled by bus to public meetings throughout his presidential campaign.

Mujica still has a tendency to speak his mind in a way that often gets him into trouble; Uruguay's intelligentsia fears he'll adopt the same sort of populist policies as the Kirchners in Argentina, but in fact he's offended them too by speaking too freely. Nevertheless he had enough of an understanding with them to find a way out of the impasse over the Botnia pulp mill.

He and his wife, Lucía Topolansky, whom he met during the urban guerrilla period and finally married in 2005, live on a simple farm near Montevideo where they grew flowers after the return of democracy. Lucía is a senator too, and in fact received more votes than any other in the 2009 election, so that she became president of the senate and thus next in line to become president herself if both her husband and Astori (neither very young) die or become too ill to stay in office.

Background Information GOVERNMENT AND POLITICS

This means that people generally vote for serious politicians, rather than the charlatans who are usually the only choice in neighbouring Argentina, and thus the standard of governance is generally much higher. This was true even in the 1830s, when Darwin noted:

> There are many [retired generals] always on the watch to create disturbance and to overturn a government which as yet had never rested on any stable foundation. I noticed, however, … a very general interest in the ensuing election for the President; and this appears a good sign for the prosperity of this little country.

Uruguay is a presidential republic with independent legislative, judicial and executive branches. There is a two-chamber legislature comprising the House of

Representatives (Camera de Representantes) and the Senate (Camera de Senadores). National elections, for president and vice-president, 30 senators and 99 deputies, are held in October every five years (next in 2014), with compulsory voting for all those over 18 years of age; the president and vice-president may not serve consecutive terms, but may stand again at later elections. The vice-president chairs the Senate (and occasionally the General Assembly of senators and representatives together); the representatives elect a new speaker every year. Supreme Court judges serve ten-year terms and are nominated by the president and confirmed by the General Assembly.

The country is divided into 19 departments, each governed by an elected *intendant* (mayor). The departments are presently more or less synonymous with their principal city, but local councils are to be set up within the next year or two. Most of these cities (other than Minas, San José and Tacuarembó) are right on the edge of their departments, along the rivers that form the departmental (and national) boundaries, but rural populations are so low that this hardly matters.

ECONOMY

Uruguay's economy is far smaller than those of its neighbours, but it's open and well managed, with very little corruption. With a well-educated labour force and a sizeable middle class, Uruguay's economy is marked by a high level of state involvement, with utilities still publicly owned and government stakes in companies such as PLUNA, the national airline. There's a high level of social spending, funded by a hefty payroll tax, so that it can be hard for small businesses to recruit staff, given the more than comfortable welfare payments.

Whereas Argentina and Brazil, with their large domestic markets, would seem to be better placed to withstand a global recession, in fact Uruguay is likely to suffer less, because of its historical avoidance of populist policies that can lead to economic overheating and subsequent collapse. Although the tourism industry is still largely dependent on Argentine beach-lovers, the economy as a whole is much less tightly coupled to Argentina than it was. In 2007 Brazil replaced Argentina as Uruguay's main trading partner, taking over US$1 billion in exports (17% of Uruguay's total exports – more than to the US and now twice as much as goes to Argentina). Uruguay also now imports more from Brazil than from Argentina. Mercosur, the common market of South America, is dominated by Brazil and Argentina; despite being host to Mercosur's headquarters, Uruguay often finds itself arguing to avert some of their more populist policies, and in particular an Argentine urge to protectionism.

In fact, Uruguay benefits from Argentine misgovernment, as Argentines traditionally move their money abroad, sometimes depositing it in Uruguayan banks or buying farmland in Uruguay. What's more, the government's firm support for the Botnia pulp mill, in the face of Argentine blockades (see page 270), has boosted the confidence of foreign investors. Botnia alone has already boosted Uruguay's GDP by 1%, plus another 1% in indirect gains, since its opening in late 2007.

Uruguay established diplomatic relations with China in 1988, and was one of the few countries not to condemn the Tiananmen Square killings the following year. Bilateral trade between China and Uruguay shot up from US$125 million in 1998 to US$1.6 billion in 2008, and March 2009 saw the first exports of live dairy cattle from Latin America to China. In 2007 Chery, the largest Chinese independent car-maker, opened a factory in Montevideo, producing Tiggo compact SUVs and QQ compact cars, mainly for export to Argentina and Brazil.

Services are now the largest sector of the economy, accounting in 2008 for 57% of GDP and 76% of jobs; this includes banking, retail and **tourism**, which contributes over US$1 billion per year to the economy, with close to two million visitors annually. Half of these come from Argentina, followed by 300,000 from Brazil; the number of visitors from Britain in 2007 and 2008 was around 15,000, double the level of 2002.

In January 2009, despite the global recession, the number of tourists coming to Punta del Este remained much as in the previous year, but it was noticeable that they were staying less long, with an average stay of ten days, compared with three or four weeks a decade or so ago. However, they crammed more shopping into each day, with an average daily expenditure of US$85 per head, so that the total revenue from tourism was actually 40% higher than in 2008. So much for cutting back in hard times!

Cruise tourism is booming, with the number of ships visiting Punta del Este and Montevideo rising from 83 in 2007–08 to over 100, with around 250,000 passengers, in 2008–09; 26% of passengers are Brazilian, 21% from the USA and 13.3% each British and Argentine.

The service sector now also includes outsourced technology services, with engineers in Montevideo working while their colleagues in India sleep.

The industrial sector, including food and wood-pulp processing and leatherworking, accounts for 32.8% of GDP and 15% of jobs; its share of GDP is falling, although the construction sector is growing. Finally, **agriculture** dominates much of the country's area; it's relatively unimportant in terms of revenue and employment, accounting for just 9.8% of GDP and 9% of jobs in 2006, but is very export-oriented. Beef alone accounted for 37% of exports, now worth about US$1.5 billion a year. Traditionally, beef cattle have been raised in the north and east of the country, with dairy farming concentrated on the greener fields of Colonia department, and sheep in the south and west of the country. Uruguayan wool is of relatively poor quality and mostly exported to China; mutton and lamb account for just 6% of meat exports, although this does not include sales of live sheep for halal slaughter in the Middle East. In addition to wineries (see page 135) and forestry (see page 270), there's a well-established citrus-growing industry around Paysandú, in the west of the country, and a newer rice-growing industry around the lagoons of eastern Uruguay; soya is also becoming an important crop, covering 848,000ha.

Economic growth averaged 8% annually from 2004 to 2008; GDP grew at a rate of 13.2% from January to September 2008, but then slowed dramatically to give an average for the year of 8.9%. GDP for 2008 was US$32.3 billion at the official exchange rate, or US$42.46 billion at purchasing power parity (PPP); GDP per capita at PPP was US$10,082.

Uruguay has weathered the global recession remarkably well. GDP fell in the first quarter of 2009 but then recovered to grow by around 2% over the year and

CASINOS

There are 36 casinos in Uruguay (34 run by the state, plus two run by the city of Montevideo – see page 101); they took US$128.1 million in 2007 (paying close to US$44 million to the government), and US$151.6 million in 2008. Over 91% of that revenue comes from *tragamonedas* (slot machines; in most cases an Uruguayan casino is simply a tawdry hall full of these machines), but there are over 15,000 illegal *tragamonedas*, which do not pay tax. In an effort to undermine this illegal gambling, the government announced plans in January 2009 for 13 more casinos, including one in Florida and one in Trinidad, currently the only two departmental capitals without casinos. Most casinos are in tourist resorts and near border crossings, as the main clients are visitors from Brazil, where gambling is banned, although Argentines are also keen on a flutter.

may grow by 4.5% in 2010. Exports were expected to fall by a third in 2009 but actually fell by less than 9%, while imports fell almost 18%, mainly due to reduced demand for oil. Owing to reduced tax revenues and higher energy costs, the budget deficit rose 50% to 2.1% of GDP for 2009.

Inflation was 7.9% at the end of 2008, 5.9% at the end of 2009, and is predicted to be between 4.7% and 6.7% in 2010.

Unemployment rose 1% in 2008 to finish the year at 7.3%, and then dropped slightly to 6.3% by the end of 2009.

Although foreign exchange reserves are healthy, the Uruguayan peso is expected to depreciate slightly in 2009 and 2010, dropping from 24.3 to the US dollar to around 27 by the end of 2010.

PEOPLE

Uruguay's population is close to 3.5 million, almost all on the coast and littoral and overwhelmingly urban, with 43% of the population living in Montevideo. As a largely secular urbanised society, it's no surprise that population growth is low (the lowest in South America, at 0.466%) but that life expectancy is high, at 76.5 years.

The indigenous population has been essentially wiped out (see page 16), although 8% of the population are mestizo (of mixed European and native descent). African slaves were brought in in considerable numbers but have now been largely assimilated – just 4% of Uruguayans are black, but 10% of Uruguayans (over 13% of those under 20) claim to be *afrodescendiente*, although many are broadly indistinguishable from the bulk of the populace. The Afro-Uruguayan cultural influence is, however, far stronger than this would lead you to expect, with *candombé* drumming (see *Music* page 27) and *carnaval* in general a key part of Uruguayan identity throughout the populace. However, 56% of Afro-Uruguayan children live below the poverty line, and the average black wage is 70% of the average white wage; in Montevideo, the Afro-Uruguayan areas of Barrio Sur and Palermo are clearly deprived and run-down, if with pockets of trendiness.

Most Uruguayans are in fact of Spanish and Italian stock – the first mass immigration, from c1824, was of French Basques, followed by their Spanish relatives. In the late 19th and early 20th centuries there was an exodus from southern Italy to Uruguay (as well as to Argentina and the United States) which has left pizza and pasta as omnipresent menu items and Italian words (and gestures) as distinctively Uruguayan aspects of the Spanish language. More Spaniards (especially Basques) arrived after 1936, fleeing Franco's fascists.

You might think there is also a substantial population of Chinese and Koreans in Montevideo, but the groups of men you see hanging around are mainly crew from fishing and cruise ships. Nevertheless there are a few Chinese and Korean restaurants in the city.

Around 45,000 Uruguayans live in the United States, mostly working in professional jobs; many also work in Europe, though mostly in less well-paid jobs. Over 15,000 Uruguayans apply every year for Italian citizenship (granted to all male descendants of Italian immigrants, and some female); some apply for Spanish citizenship, but this is open only to children of Spanish citizens and to grandchildren of victims of Franco's dictatorship.

LANGUAGE

The national language is Spanish (see *Appendix 1* on page 334 for local peculiarities), but a Spanish-Portuguese hybrid called Portunol or Brazilero is also spoken on the Brazilian frontier.

RELIGION

Uruguay is one of the most secular countries in Latin America, although 56% of the population claims to be Roman Catholic and 11% Protestant. Those claiming to be atheist or agnostic total 17% of the populace, with 16% classified as 'other', which presumably includes followers of the animist African Umbanda religion. Just 0.3% are Jewish (and the Simon Wiesenthal Centre says there is virtually no antisemitism in Uruguay), while Muslims, Buddhists and Hindus are too few to be recorded.

Since the economic crisis of 2002 the *Iglesia Universal del Reino de Dios* (Universal Church of the Kingdom of God), a dynamic Brazilian Pentecostalist church, has erupted all over Uruguay, often taking over former cinemas and theatres which can be recognised by banners proclaiming *Pare de Sufrir* (Stop Suffering). Smaller evangelical groups often meet in private homes, and make a surprising amount of noise.

ORIXA Although Umbanda priests and priestesses are available for consultation all year round, they only really emerge in public on 2 February, when the festival of the *orixa* Iemanjá is celebrated in Montevideo and Punta del Este. The seven *orixas* (or *orishas*) are intermediate gods, providing contact between humanity and the supreme creator Olodumare. *Iemanjá*, a river goddess in Yorubá Africa, has here become the *orixa* of the ocean and the patron of fishermen and shipwreck survivors, as well as representing the feminine aspects of creation and motherhood. In Porto Alegre in Brazil, 2 February (the feast of the Virgin of Candelaria) is also celebrated by the Roman Catholic church as the festival of *Nossa Senhora dos Navegantes* (Our Lady of the Seafarers), while a similar celebration is held in Salvador da Bahia on 8 December, as in Río de Janeiro on New Year's Eve. In the voodoo religion of Cuba and the southern USA she is known as Yemaja or Yemalla.

From around sunset devotees clad in white or pale blue gather on the beaches, setting candles in holes in the sand and piling up offerings of fruit and flowers. Some load these on to sand models of boats, while many more bring paper boats that are launched to sea bearing candles, flowers and money. Drums play and men in white and pale blue and women in white 19th-century dresses dance themselves into a trance; others line up for priests to lay on hands and purify them; in addition Iemanjá is said to grant wishes (though not for love, as she keeps the best-looking men for herself).

Meanwhile, on the *rambla* (esplanade) above the beach more and more spectators gather every year, significantly whiter-skinned than the devotees below and not in white, but respectful enough nevertheless. The rites continue to around 03.00 or even dawn, leaving a remarkable quantity of trash on the beaches.

CULTURE

As a small country, Uruguay has one iconic national painter (Joaquín Torres García), one national composer (Eduardo Fabini), one national novelist (Juan Carlos Onetti) and even one national philosopher (Carlos Vaz Ferreira) – but in fact this belies the range and quantity of cultural activity. There's a profusion of artists, writers and musicians, some living and working abroad, and architecture in particular is currently bringing the country worldwide recognition (see page 33).

MUSIC
Leading musical figures Uruguayan classical music became established in colonial times, with the four-part *Misa para día de Difuntos* (Mass for the Day of the Dead) written in 1802 by José Manuel Ubeda. The leading figure in Uruguayan musical

history is **Eduardo Fabini** (1882–1950), born in Lavalleja (see page 167), who studied in Montevideo and at the Brussels Conservatoire (where he won first prize for violin in 1902). He returned to live in Montevideo, but spent much time in Lavalleja, in touch with nature and folk traditions, which were at the heart of his music. His international breakthrough came with the choral symphony *Campo* in 1922, followed by his *Tristes* (1925) for piano and guitar. In 1927 he was appointed artistic attaché at the Uruguayan embassy in the United States. Back in Uruguay, he became the leader of a small group of nationalist composers, including Alfonso Broqua (1876–1946) and Luis Cluzeau-Mortet (1889–1957); in 1946 he became director of the Conservatorio Nacional de Música, which he had co-founded in 1907, and the state paid him a pension for life in exchange for the rights to his music.

The leading contemporary Uruguayan musical figure is **José Serebrier**, best known as a conductor but also a composer, who has been based in the United States for most of his career. One of the most recorded conductors of his generation, his recordings have received 32 Grammy nominations thus far, and eight have won Grammies. He was the first to record Charles Ives's *Fourth Symphony*, previously regarded as almost unplayable and generally performed with three conductors working together. He has not conducted with a baton since stabbing himself in the hand in a moment of over-excitement in an Easter Day concert in 1975. Hailed by the great Leopold Stokowski as 'the greatest master of orchestral balance' when he was just 22, he worked as Stokowski's assistant for five years and as music director of the Cleveland Philharmonic before leaving to work as a guest conductor with any number of orchestras and director of various festivals, leaving time for his composing. Most recently he has gained praise for his recorded cycle of the Glazunov symphonies with the Royal Scottish National Orchestra.

As a composer he has been awarded two Guggenheim Fellowships (the first at 19, the youngest person ever to be granted one), as well as other awards. His *First Symphony* was premiered, by Stokowski, when he was just 17 and was followed two years later by his *Second Symphony*, which he conducted himself with America's National Symphony Orchestra. Perhaps his best work, in his characteristically lively, colourful and tuneful style, is the *Carmen Symphony* of 2004.

Jorge Drexler, born in Montevideo in 1964, gave up a medical career to be a singer-songwriter, also working as a lifeguard and a synagogue singer, and released his first album in 1992. He's best known for his soundtrack to the film of *The Motorcycle Diaries*, the theme song winning him an Academy Award in 2005 – the first Oscar won by an Uruguayan, and the first for a Spanish-language song. Although Drexler wrote both the words and the music, and sang the song himself on the soundtrack, he was snubbed by the organisers of the Oscars, who chose the actor Antonio Banderas to sing it at the ceremony; nevertheless when collecting his award he sang a couple of verses unaccompanied – the scandal and his dignified response largely overshadowing the inauguration on the same day of Uruguay's first leftist government. Based in Spain since 1995, his songs are routinely covered by many Hispanic singers and his live album *Cara B* was nominated for a Grammy as Best Latin Pop Album in 2009.

Tango The tango is almost as important to Uruguayans as it is to Argentines (see page 312 for Carlos Gardel's Uruguayan background). One of the most famous tangos is *La Cumparsita* or The Little Parade (of Endless Miseries), written by Gerardo Matos 'Becho' Rodríguez (1897–1948) and first performed in 1917 where Montevideo's Palacio Salvo now stands. It remains very popular and is commonly played as the last dance of the night at Uruguayan *milongas* (dancehalls); thus there was outrage when the Argentine team at the 2000 Olympics in Sydney marched in to *La Cumparsita*.

The first tango recorded by Gardel, indeed the first tango to be recorded with lyrics, was *Mi Noche Triste* (My Sad Night), written in 1915 by the Argentine Samuel Castriota; lyrics were added without the composer's knowledge by Pascual Contursi (1888–1932) in Montevideo. Gardel recorded it in 1917 and later brought about an agreement between the two writers over the song's copyright.

Tango was born in the port cities of Buenos Aires and Montevideo when the folk music of the poor Italian and Spanish immigrants blended with the rhythms of the African slaves and their descendants (the word *tango* originally meant a social gathering of the slaves, and was then extended to the music they played). In essence it's a simple eight-step dance but with variation and ornamentation (kicks, turns, leaps and lunges); the mournful lyrics are a 20th-century addition. Its most characteristic instrument, the *bandoneón* (button accordion) was introduced by German immigrants after 1870. Originally men danced with men, as if in a duel, and then with prostitutes; gestures and eye contact remain minimal, but charged with meaning. The dancers entangle themselves intimately and yet resist each other, the music straining between tragedy and ecstasy; the eroticism and constrained violence led the upper classes to spurn it as scandalous until it had established itself in Paris and the Old World and made its way back to the New World. Nowadays tango is popular even in the interior where it never existed before, but without the searing (some would say ludicrously over-the-top) intensity of its Argentine form. It's easy enough to find tango in Montevideo (see page 100) but there's little tango tourism, unlike in Buenos Aires. In September 2009 a joint bid by Argentina and Uruguay for tango to be listed as part of the Intangible Cultural Heritage of Humanity was accepted by UNESCO.

Murga *Murga* is a key element of the Uruguayan carnival, a type of musical theatre derived from the *chirigota* of Cádiz in Spain. It's usually performed by a group of up to 17 men in fantastical costumes who sing opening and closing songs (*saludo* and *despedida*) together, along with a series of satirical pieces accompanied by bass drum, snare drum and cymbals. Performed on stages around Montevideo throughout *carnaval* (and in competition at the Teatro del Verano), the musical style also finds its way into Uruguayan popular music.

Candombé *Candombé* (or *candomblé*) is the style of drumming that developed in Montevideo's Afro-Uruguayan barrios and has become an emblematic part of *carnaval* and of Uruguayan culture in general. The thunderous rhythms pounded out by a *cuerda* of scores of drummers marching in a dense block through the city streets can be positively intimidating, leading to the white élite banning *candombé* in 1808; however, it proved impossible to enforce and Afro-Uruguayan culture has made its way to the heart of Uruguayan identity. In 1870 *candombé* was officially incorporated into Montevideo's *carnaval*, and by 1900 the participants were largely white.

The barrel-like drums (*tamboriles*) come in three main sizes, *chico* (small and relatively high-pitched, marking the tempo), *repique* (mid-sized, used for syncopation and improvisation) and *piano* (large and relatively low-pitched, playing a melody). All are carried on shoulder straps and played with one stick and one bare hand – a key rhythmic figure is the *clave*, a 3-2 figure played by striking the side of the drum (*hacer madera* or making wood). Before performing, the leather tops are tuned by holding them over a fire.

The great set-piece of *candombé* is the Las Llamadas procession ('The Calls') at the start of the *carnaval* season in Montevideo, usually in February. Close to 100 *comparsas* (groups of drummers) march through the Barrio Sur and Palermo, the bloc of drummers (in some kind of costume, often with straw hats and blackened faces, to show the music's slave origins) preceded by female dancers (known as *mulatas*), often in scanty samba-style costumes with sequins and feathers, and stock characters such as the *la mama vieja* (the old mother) with fan and parasol, *el gramillero* (the medicine man) with his white cotton-wool beard, top hat, frock coat, glasses and a briefcase of medicinal herbs, and *el escobero* (the stick-holder) juggling a long magical staff – originally a tasselled cane, this now looks exactly like a broomstick. The *comparsas* also compete during *carnaval* in the Teatro del Verano, the open-air theatre near Parque Rodó.

Milonga *Milonga* is a term for a tango dancehall, and also a type of music that derived from Spanish folk forms in the 1870s and was a predecessor of the tango. Originally it was a folk song, partly improvised and set to a lively 2/4 tempo, accompanied by guitar. With time, this came to be accompanied by a syncopated dance, like tango but faster, simpler and with limbs and body held less rigidly. In fact it's like a jerky rhythmic walking, to which can be added *traspiés* or *contrapasos*, a sort of shuffle transferring weight from one foot to the other and back again in double time or three steps in two beats.

The best-known Uruguayan singer of *milongas* and other folk songs was **Alfredo Zittarossa** (1936–89), one of the great voices of Latin America, whose lyrics and poetry were strongly rooted in the Uruguayan countryside and in leftist politics. He lived in exile during the dictatorship, when his music was banned in Uruguay, Argentina and Chile.

Music festivals Uruguay's main popular music festivals are Pilsen Rock in Durazno in October (which attracts 120,000) and jazz festivals in Mercedes and Punte del Este, both held in January.

LITERATURE The earliest noteworthy Uruguayan literature is the gaucho-flavoured poetry of **Bartolomé Hidalgo** (1788–1822). The leading Romantic poet in Uruguay was **Juan Zorrilla de San Martín** (1855–1931; see page 128), whose epic poem *Tabaré* (1886) describes the clash between Spanish colonists and native people that led to the extinction of the aboriginal culture.

José Enrique Rodó (1871–1917) is best known for his essay *Ariel* (1900), based on Shakespeare's *The Tempest*, with Prospero as narrator championing Western classical culture, Caliban standing for utilitarian materialistic North America and Ariel for the rebellious youth of Latin America. Rodó was opposed to democracy, which he saw as entailing mediocrity and vulgarity; nevertheless he remains revered as a theorist of Modernist thought and a champion of Latin America's identity.

Florencio Sánchez (1875–1910) is still Uruguay's best-known playwright; having dropped out of school in Minas, he became an anarchist and a self-taught journalist before turning to plays, which mostly depict life in working-class tenements, including poor immigrant families. Although very successful, he blew it all on bohemian nightlife and died young of tuberculosis.

Julio Herrera y Reissig (1875–1910), nephew of President Julio Herrera y Obes, was a somewhat Proustian figure who was unable to travel much because of a heart defect but hosted a literary salon, and as a poet moved from late Romanticism to avant-garde Modernism, his subtle works finding fame only after his early death. **Juana de Ibarbourou** (1892–1979) remains highly popular (and is still on the thousand-peso banknote), an early feminist whose poetry is largely defined by nature imagery and eroticism.

The philosopher **Carlos Vaz Ferreira** (1872–1958) was particularly influenced by Henri Bergson and William James, and introduced liberal, pluralistic political values and a pragmatic but emotional rationalism to South America. His most important works, such as *Problemas de la Libertad* (Problems of Liberty), *Conocimiento y Acción* (Knowledge and Action), *Moral para Intelectuales* (Morals for Intellectuals), *El Pragmatismo* (Pragmatism) and *Lógica Viva* (Living Logic), were published between 1907 and 1910. There's a locally famous photo of him sitting on a park bench with Einstein, who was visiting a cousin in Uruguay, in 1925. Vaz served as vice-chancellor of the University of the Republic in 1928–31 and 1935–41, taking a break because of ill-health, when he produced other books such as *Sobre el Feminismo* (On Feminism, 1933), one of the earliest discussions of the topic in Latin America.

Horacio Quiroga (1878–1937) was a very popular and influential writer of short stories, many set in the 'jungles' of Argentina's Misiones province and prefiguring Magical Realism. He had a tragic life, his father shooting himself in a hunting accident, then himself shooting a friend while explaining how a gun worked; his first wife killed herself with cyanide as he himself did when diagnosed with cancer; and their two children also later killed themselves.

Felisberto Hernández (1902–64) was a fine short-story writer who had little success, working as a pianist in cinemas and cafés, and remains little known. His deranged first-person narrators produce an off-kilter version of reality that influenced writers such as Gabriel García Márquez, Italo Calvino and Julio Cortázar.

Uruguay's leading 20th-century novelist was **Juan Carlos Onetti** (1909–94), who was born and grew up in Montevideo, dropping out of school to be a journalist, film critic and short-story writer. His first novel, *El Pozo*, was privately published and largely ignored in 1939 but is now seen as the first truly modern Spanish American novel, with its Modernist technique and an alienated protagonist who leads a futile life in a city where he fails to communicate with others. His second novel, *Tierra de Nadie* (No-man's Land, 1941), consisting of brief scenes and conversations, marked the first appearance of the former brothel-keeper Larsen, while the 1950s Santa María trilogy was set in the fictional town of that name on the Plate; perhaps his greatest work, *El Astillero* (The Shipyard, 1961), is also set in Santa Maria, where Larsen takes a job as manager of a bankrupt shipyard, which increasingly comes to resemble his own hopeless interior life.

Having worked as an editor for Reuters in Montevideo and Buenos Aires and as manager of an advertising agency, Onetti became director of Montevideo's municipal libraries in 1957. After being briefly held in a mental hospital in 1974 by the dictatorship, he moved to Madrid and lived there until his death; in *Dejemos Hablar al Viento* (Let the Wind Speak, 1979), his first novel written in Spain, he had Santa María, always a seedy dump, burnt down at the close, reflecting his despair. Nevertheless in 1980 he won the Spanish-speaking world's most prestigious literary prize, the Premio Cervantes, and in 1985 the president of Uruguay flew to Spain to present him with the National Literary Award.

His isolated urban characters, in their existential alienation, are a million miles from the gauchos of earlier Latin American literature, and also have little to do with the fantastical characters and plots of the Magical Realists. In fact there's very little clear narrative, but the portrayal of mood and setting is unparalleled – the use of language owes much to the French novelist Louis-Ferdinand Céline, while the alienation foreshadows Beckett and Camus.

Mario Benedetti (1920–2009) was a prolific poet, novelist and journalist, not well known in the English-speaking world but considered one of the major contemporary writers of Latin America. The most visible member of the political wing of the Tupamaros guerrillas, he also went into exile under the dictatorship and afterwards continued to divide his time between Montevideo and Madrid.

More controversial is **Eduardo Galeano** (b1940), whose writing mixes fiction, journalism, political analysis and history. His best-known work, *Las Venas Abiertas de América Latina* (The Open Veins of Latin America, 1971), is an analysis of Latin American history from European colonisation to the present, arguing against the northern hemisphere's economic and political domination, and especially against globalisation and the IMF. It's still very current – at the April 2009 Summit of the Americas, Venezuela's President Hugo Chávez gave a copy to US President Barack Obama, pushing both the English- and Spanish-language versions high up the bestseller lists. After editing the weekly journal *Marcha* (previously edited by Onetti) and running the University of Uruguay Press, he too went into exile under the dictatorship, ending up in Spain where he wrote the widely praised trilogy, *Memoria del Fuego* (Memory of Fire, 1982–86), a fictionalisation of the history of the Americas, involving the figures actually involved, from pre-Columbian times to the 1980s. In 1985 he returned to Montevideo, and wrote perhaps his most daring work, *El Libro de los Abrazos* (The Book of Embraces, 1989), a collection of stories giving his views on art, emotion and values, as well as another scathing critique of modern capitalism. Then he relaxed a bit, producing *El Fútbol a Sol y Sombra* (Football in Sun and Shadow, 1995), a history of the game that naturally inveighs against its unholy alliance with global capitalism.

Most recently, *Espejos: Una Historia Casi Universal* (Mirrors: Stories of Almost Everyone, 2008) is another broad mosaic of history told through hundreds of kaleidoscopic vignettes, the voices of the unseen, unheard and forgotten, free of the restrictions of chronology.

It's worth mentioning the great Argentine writer **Jorge Luis Borges** (1899–1986), whose mother was Uruguayan; he spent childhood summers near Fray Bentos and in Montevideo and was a perceptive commentator on Uruguayan history and culture; some of his characters are realistically Uruguayan, above all the great Funes the Memorious, who came from Fray Bentos.

Finally, **Isabel Fonseca**, whose father was the Uruguayan sculptor Gonzalo Fonseca, was born in the United States (her mother was the daughter of a grape-juice tycoon) and studied at Columbia and Oxford universities before joining the *Times Literary Supplement*. Writing in English, her first book was *Bury Me Standing* (1995), a very successful non-fiction account of Europe's Roma or gypsies, followed by a memoir about her brother's death from AIDS. The novelist Martin Amis left his wife and family for her in 1993, and from 2003 to 2006 they lived in Uruguay, building a house in José Ignacio (see pages 213–14), where they began work on a fictional account of her family's experiences during the dictatorship. Instead she ended up writing a novel (*Attachment*, 2008) about an American–British couple taking a sabbatical in the tropics, before returning to the original idea.

ART Uruguay's museums are virtually all free and chronically underfunded; however, this matters less in art museums than in others, at least on the surface. The annual *Museos en la Noche* (Museums at Night) event, usually on the first Friday of December, is the peg for a variety of free activities in museums across the country. The website (*www.mnav.gub.uy/artistas.htm*) is the best source of information on Uruguayan artists.

Painters The leading Uruguayan painter of the 19th century was **Juan Manuel Blanes** (1830–1901), after whom the country's main art gallery is named. Born in Montevideo, his education was disrupted by civil war and family break-up, but he was able to train himself as an artist while working as a newspaper typographer. In 1855 he moved to Salto, where he established himself as a portrait painter, and in 1857 to Concepción del Uruguay (in Argentina); in 1861 a government grant took him to Italy, which he revisited several times, the last occasion being in 1899 to search for his son who had gone missing there. He painted in a pretty academic style but, thanks to his Italian Neoclassical training, created some iconic images of Artigas.

Pedro Blanes Viale (1878–1926) was born in Mercedes but in 1893 the family moved back to his father's native Mallorca; nevertheless Blanes Viale returned regularly to Uruguay and indeed died in Montevideo. Although he preferred to paint landscapes (in a Fauvist style in his last years) he is best known for his portraits.

Rafael Barradas (1890–1929) worked as a magazine illustrator and founded his own magazine satirising the Montevideo cultural scene; he moved to Spain in 1914, where he knew Dalí, Bunuel and Lorca, as well as Torres García (see below), and developed his own distinctive style, derived from Cubism and Futurism, which he called Vibracionismo (Vibrationism). After moving to the Catalan countryside he started painting in a more realist style; seriously ill, he returned to Montevideo to die.

Pedro Figari (1861–1938) had a successful legal career while painting as an amateur. In 1915–17 he was interim director of the Escuela Nacional de Artes, reorganising it thoroughly. From 1917 (with his *Piedras*, or troglodyte, paintings) his style changed radically from Realism to a more Expressionist style, and in 1921 he moved to Buenos Aires to dedicate himself to painting fulltime, moving on to Europe for nine years from 1925. In 1927 he was appointed ambassador to Britain, also publishing poems and short stories. His paintings seem not just naïve but amateurish, but he is still highly regarded in Uruguay, partly for his role in portraying Afro-Uruguayan culture and bringing it towards the mainstream.

José Cúneo (1887–1977) studied in Montevideo, Italy and France, absorbing the work of Cézanne, Matisse, Soutine and Van Dongen. He returned to Uruguay in 1917 and the next year held a very successful exhibition in Montevideo which launched the Planismo style, dominant in Uruguay until the 1930s. Derived from Fauvism and Cubism, it was marked by strong colours in flat-seeming planes with no sense of depth or volume (mainly in landscapes, and also some portraits). Although never a school or group as such, it was widely taken up by the generation born between 1875 and 1895 (many marked by their travels to Europe thanks to government scholarships), notably Barradas, Figari, Carlos Federico Sáez (1878–1901), Carlos Roberto Rúfalo (1880–1975), Carmelo de Arzadun (1888–1968), Alfredo de Simone (1898–1950) and Petrona Viera (1895–1960), who had to work especially hard to overcome prejudice against her as the daughter of President Feliciano Viera.

Later, living in rural Florida department, Cúneo developed a freer style, becoming known for his paintings of farms and of the moon. He revisited Europe in 1954, discovering abstraction, and in the 1960s began to be well known abroad as well as at home. He returned to Europe in 1976, and died in Bonn the following year.

The best-known Uruguayan artist remains **Joaquín Torres García** (1874–1949), who moved with his family to Spain in 1891, where he studied at the Academia de Bellas Artes in Barcelona and joined the young artists such as Picasso who met at the El Quatre Gats café. From 1904 he worked with Gaudí on stained glass for the cathedral of Palma de Mallorca and the church of the Sagrada Familia in Barcelona. He painted the Uruguayan pavilion for the 1910 World Fair in Brussels, then after 1915 moved from a Neoclassical style to Modernism, and from 1920 developed a sideline in educational wooden toys (having grown up in the family carpentry shop). From 1926, living in Paris, and influenced by Theo van Doesburg, Piet Mondrian and primitive and African art, he developed his own Constructivismo Universal (Universal Constructivism), a form of abstraction combining a grid-like structure (based on the Golden Section) with symbolic images such as fish, clocks, a ladder, a man and a woman, and even a steam locomotive.

In 1932 he moved to Madrid, developing an interest in pre-Columbian art from the Americas, and in 1934 (feeling that Europe was artistically dead and that there was a need for new approaches) returned to Uruguay where he became an energetic teacher and propagandist. He founded the Taller Torres García (the Torres García Studio), which influenced a generation of Uruguayan painters including José Gurvich, Gonzalo Fonseca, Manuel Pailós, Julio Alpuy and his sons Augusto and Horacio Torres; these are known as the Escuela del Sur (Southern School) after Torres García's saying, 'our north is their south', illustrated with an upside-down map, referring to pre-Colombian culture. Alfredo Testoni (1919–2003) was a painter and also perhaps the best Uruguayan photographer of the 20th century, recording the Taller Torres García and working for *Time* and *Life* magazines.

José Gurvich (1927–74) was born Zusmanas Gurvicius in Lithuania, and came to Uruguay at the age of five. He studied under Cúneo at the Escuela Nacional de Bellas Artes and from 1945 at the Taller Torres García, becoming a teacher there and exhibiting in the studio's collaborative shows. He travelled in Europe and lived on a kibbutz in Israel, returning to Uruguay between 1965 and 1969 and then living from 1970 in New York, where he died of a heart attack at just 47. His paintings, influenced by Bosch, Brueghel and Chagall with their fusion of the fantastic and the everyday, often show scenes of shtetl and kibbutz life as well as Old Testament themes such as Adam and Eve, and included works on leather, plaster casts and ceramics.

Carmelo Arden Quin (b1913) studied with Torres García and moved in 1938 to Buenos Aires, where he was bowled over by abstract art. In 1946 he launched the MADI movement, whose playful, even mad, art sought to liberate painting from the constraints of the frame, with irregularly shaped works, sometimes pierced or articulated, that blurred the distinctions between painting and sculpture. Using brightly coloured circles, spirals, stripes and other shapes, MADI art (and architecture, poetry and dance) is abstract and free of symbolic meaning, focused on form rather than content. The movement's name, with its overtones of Dada, is probably nonsense, although all sorts of theories exist explaining its origin (such as from carMelo ArDen quIn, Movimiento Artístico de Invención or the English 'mad-eye'). By late 1946 he was in Paris, where he's lived ever since, working furiously and leading a chaotic bohemian life.

Two of the leading followers of the MADI movement are the Uruguayans Rhod Rothfuss (1920–69) and Volf Roitmann (b1930), a painter, poet and architect best known for designing the MADI Museum in Dallas, Texas. Roitmann also studied in Buenos Aires but only met Arden Quin after moving to Paris in 1951.

Carlos Páez Vilaró (b1923) is the highest-profile figure in contemporary Uruguayan art, thanks to his successful marketing of himself and his presence in Punta del Este, where his fantastical studio-cum-hotel Casapueblo can be visited (see page 199). He travelled to Europe and visited Picasso in 1957 (recorded in a much-used photo), but the influence of Picasso and Matisse on his art, although obvious, was relatively shallow. Back in Montevideo, he lived in the Mediomundo *conventillo* (tenement) in the Barrio Sur, where he became deeply involved in *candombé* and played a major role in opening up Afro-Uruguayan culture to the middle classes. His brother Jorge (1922–95) was an abstract painter who returned to figurative art in the 1960s, aiming for a universal art rooted in primitive art and folk traditions.

Sculptors As for sculpture, **José Belloni** (1882–1965) spent much of his career in Europe but was also based in Uruguay, where he's remembered for major sculptures in Montevideo such as *La Carreta* and *La Diligencia* in the Prado (see pages 117 and 119) and *El Entrevero* in Plaza Fabini (see page 115). His son Stelio (1920–89) was also a successful sculptor, together with Federico Escalada (1888–1960). **Germán Cabrera** (1903–90), who worked as assistant to José Belloni from 1918 to 1925, then went on a scholarship to France, where he met Despiau and Bourdelle. He spent the years from 1938 to 1951 in Venezuela, then returned to Montevideo, although he made many more trips to Europe as well as to New York City; until World War II he produced mainly stone figures, then moved to a more abstract style, working also in steel.

Like José Belloni, **José Luis Zorrilla de San Martín** (1891–1975) left a significant legacy on the streets of Montevideo, including the statue of the *Gaucho* (see page 116), and the Monument to the Constituents (the *Obelisco*, see page 116).

Octavio Podestá (b1929) studied in Europe and then based himself in Montevideo; he was the first Uruguayan sculptor to make hinged and moving pieces, using pieces of steel and other industrial scrap. **Wifredo Diaz Valdez** (b1932) worked along similar lines, producing articulated wooden sculptures from the 1980s, partly by disassembling violins, guitars and the like. **Pablo Atchugarry** (b1954) works in marble, producing amazingly delicate abstract sculptures; he lives mainly in Italy but has a gallery just east of Punta del Este (see page 212).

ARCHITECTURE After independence, the Baroque style of colonial architecture was soon abandoned for a Neoclassical style that drew on French and Italian – rather than Spanish – roots, while French-style boulevards were superimposed on the Spanish grid of equal-sized streets. Most of Uruguay's churches are Neoclassical in style, with porticos, rounded arches, barrel vaults and domes, while in the late 19th century many public buildings were built in a style known as Belle Epoque or Beaux-Arts eclectic historicism, notably the Teatro Solís (1841–56), Casa de Gobierno (1873), Estación Central (1897) and Palacio Taranco (1908) in Montevideo.

The first individual architect to have a widespread impact in Uruguay was **Giovanni (Juan) Veltroni** (1880–1942), who was born in Florence and came to Montevideo in 1908; he built many public buildings including the port administration building (1910), the Banco de la República (1926–38), the Ministerio de Salud Pública (Ministry of Public Health, 1928) and the *liceos* (high schools) of Canelones and Durazno. Similarly, Mario Palanti (1885–1979) trained in Milan and settled in Buenos Aires in 1909, designing many fine buildings on both shores of the Plate, notably the Palacio Salvo (1928, and still Montevideo's main landmark), with fine Moderne (similar to Art Deco) decoration.

Only a few buildings were constructed in the Art Nouveau style, such as the Edificio Pablo Ferrando (1917) and the Centro Cultural de España (1932) in Montevideo, although it had a greater influence on decorative detailing. In the 1920s and 1930s economic prosperity coupled with an open liberal climate and an educated population led to the construction of many modern buildings, notably schools designed by Juan Antonio Scasso from 1926, the Aduana (Customs House, 1929) and the Palacio Municipal (City Hall, 1930). Art Deco towers and apartment blocks include the Palacio Rinaldi (1929) and Palacio Díaz (1929), and many very successful Art Deco houses, in Montevideo and nationwide. There followed a seamless move into Bauhaus-style Modernism, with buildings such as the Edificio Lapido (1930), Estadio Centenario (1930; see page 117) by Scasso and José Domato, and the Bolsa de Comercio (Stock Exchange, 1936).

Le Corbusier gave a very influential series of lectures in Buenos Aires in 1929, and even drew up a plan for the redevelopment of Montevideo (thanks to the aviation pioneers Jean Mermoz and Antoine de Saint-Exupéry, he was able to fly over Montevideo and other cities), but relatively few buildings were built in

Corbusieresque style, other than a large block near Montevideo's Yacht Club (see page 121) and a few buildings in Punta del Este and Punta Ballena. The leading architect of the 1930s was **Julio Vilamajó** (1894–1948), who taught at the University of the Republic and built its Faculty of Engineering (1937) and many other buildings (including all their fittings in some cases), as well as laying out Villa Serrana in Minas (see page 170).

Eladio Dieste (1917–2000) was an engineer who almost accidentally became one of Uruguay's best-loved architects. Inspired by the Taller Torres García's functional approach to the arts, he devised a structural system to allow double-curved tiled or brick vaults, held by just a thin layer of concrete. After designing a couple of factories and warehouses, in 1957–58 he designed the Iglesia del Cristo Obrero (church of Christ the Worker), 4km north of Atlántida (see page 163), where undulating brick walls magically meet an undulating roof while hidden openings direct light to the altar. To achieve this the construction had to be accurate to within 5mm. He later rebuilt the church of San Pedro in Durazno (see page 316–18), but his main speciality was daringly wide and thin arched roofs for bus stations, gymnasia and the like, as in Salto (see page 291).

Uruguay currently boasts two world-class architects who have done much of their work abroad but have recently returned to design prestigious projects at home. **Rafael Viñoly** (b1944) studied in Buenos Aires and practiced there before moving to New York in 1978; he built many major buildings across the world, such as the Princeton University Stadium, the Kimmel Arts Center in Philadelphia, the University of Chicago's Graduate School of Business, The Curve in Leicester (a theatre, which cost double its budget at £61 million) and the US$1.5 billion Tokyo International Forum. He has built a considerable reputation for his great curving shapes in glass and steel; future projects include a couple in London, the so-called 'Walkie-Talkie' (like a squeezed-in tower block, next to the 'Gherkin') and Battersea Power Station.

His first building in Uruguay, finished in 2008, was the Acqua building in Punta del Este, a luxury apartment block (so called because of its tiers of swimming pools) where the penthouse sold for US$7.3 million. He followed this with the new terminal at Montevideo's Carrasco airport, opened in 2009, where a huge curved roof arches over the approach roads, entry atrium and separate arrival and departure levels, with glazed walls on all four sides allowing plenty of natural light in.

Carlos Ott (b1946), mainly based in Toronto, has designed the new Bastille Opera in Paris, various theatres in China, and the Ushuaia and Calafate airports in Argentina; he returned in 1992 to design Uruguay's 'other' airport, at Punta del Este, as well as the Punta Shopping Centre and the Torre de las Communicaciones (Antel's headquarters), by far the tallest building in Montevideo (see page 117).

CINEMA Uruguay has a tiny film industry, producing around five features a year, but there is considerable interest in cinema, with film festivals in Montevideo, Piriápolis and Punta del Este. Cinema actually has quite a long history here, the first film being shown in 1896, and the second film made anywhere in Latin America, *Una Carrera de Ciclismo en el Velódromo de Arroyo Seco* (A Cycling Race at the Arroyo Seco Velodrome), being made in 1898. However, Uruguayans only saw foreign (mainly Argentine) films until Juan Antonio Borges's *Almas de la Costa* (Souls of the Coast), the first full-length Uruguayan film, was released in 1923 (although the studio only made one more film before closing). Documentaries were made of the 1930 World Cup in Montevideo, but the Depression again killed off the Uruguayan industry. Even after World War II only a few documentaries and comedies had any success, and the first viable full-length dramas, the gaucho story

Guri and *Mataron a Venancio Flores* (The Murder of Venancio Flores), came only in 1980 and 1982, respectively. In the 1980s the return of democracy and the growth of the video industry led to the making of some politically controversial films, and in the 1990s both the city of Montevideo and the national government set up funds to boost the industry, finally allowing it to achieve a degree of stability.

The Memory of Blas Quadra (2000) and *The Southern Star* (2002), both directed by Luis Nieto, did well, as did the slacker comedy *25 Watts* (2002) by Pablo Stoll and Juan Pablo Rebella, whose *Whisky* (2003) won the Un Certain Regard Prize at the Cannes Film Festival. A dark comedy about the owner of a sock factory who sets up a fake relationship with an employee to show his expatriate brother that he has a full life, it's subtle, sad and very smart. Alas, Rebella died in 2006 at just 32.

More recently, *El Baño del Papa* (The Pope's Toilet, 2007), by César Charlone (who lives in Brazil and was nominated for a Best Cinematography Oscar for *City of God*) and Enrique Fernandez, is an excellent comedy about the build-up to a papal visit to the small town of Melo. Charlone is now making a TV film on Artigas. In 2009 both *Gigante* (Giant) by Adrián Biniez and *Mal Día Para Pescar* (Bad Day to Go Fishing; from an Onetti short story) by Álvaro Brechner have been well received.

In fact most people, asked about Uruguayan film, would first think of Costa-Gavras's *State of Siege* (1972), a French classic about the kidnapping and murder of the undercover US agent Dan Mitrione by the Tupamaros guerrillas. It's also worth mentioning the Uruguayan director Israel Adrián Caetano, who works in Argentina, co-directing films such as *Pizza, Beer and Smokes* (1997).

Uruguay's best-known actor is **China Zorrilla** (b1922), daughter of the sculptor Jose Luis Zorrilla de San Martin and granddaughter of the poet Juan Zorrilla de San Martin, who studied at RADA in London, starred on stage and in film in Madrid, Paris and Buenos Aires, won the Best Actress award at the Moscow Film Festival in 2004, and was awarded France's Légion d'honneur in 2008.

SPECTATOR SPORTS Most people know two things about Uruguayan sport – that they won the first World Cup, and that a college rugby team crashed in the Andes on the way to a tour in Chile, with cannibalism ensuing (a story well told by Piers Paul Read in his book *Alive*; see page 338).

Soccer The national sport is, of course, soccer (*fútbol*) and even if Uruguay had not won two World Cups that would still be the case. Uruguay's golden age was the 1920s and 1930s,when they won Olympic gold in 1924 and 1928 and then the inaugural World Cup of 1930. However, they may have had a better team in 1950 when they won their second World Cup, including Juan Alberto 'Pepe' Schiaffino (1925–2002), who moved to Italy after the 1954 World Cup (when Uruguay finished fourth), playing for AC Milano and Roma, and indeed for the Italian national team.

Uruguay's legendary captain Obdulio Varela (1917–96) inspired the team to beat Brazil in the 1950 final in Rio's Maracana stadium, a game still remembered as the *Maracanazo*; it's commonly held that if Varela had not been injured in the 1954 quarter-final against England, Uruguay could have gone on to win the cup again. Instead their first-ever World Cup defeat came in the semi-final against Hungary's legendary 'Golden Team'. Since then they have been less successful, but have qualified for the 2010 World Cup.

To mark the 50th anniversary of the first World Cup, Uruguay hosted the so-called Mundialito (Little World Cup) between the former winners of the cup (with the Netherlands replacing England, who declined their invitation). In the 1980 final (actually in January 1981) Uruguay defeated Brazil 2-1, as they did in the 1950 final; Uruguay's coach, Roque Máspoli, had been Uruguay's goalkeeper in the 1950 game.

It's generally felt that the game is in decline in Uruguay now, with talented youngsters making their names abroad and one agent, Paco Casal, having a stranglehold on all the transfer *pases*. Many players build their careers in Argentina and with luck move on to Europe – the Uruguayan season is the same as Europe's to aid transfers. There are problems with hooligan fans, but nowhere near as bad as in Argentina, where there are half a dozen murders every year. Fans still stand on the terraces, gathering especially behind the goals, but the stadiums are often only a third full – the huge Estadio Centenario is even emptier except for *clásicos* or derbies between the capital's two main teams, Peñarol and Nacional.

When reading the sports pages, *celeste* (sky-blue) refers to the Uruguayan national team and *tricolor* refers to Nacional, who play in red, white and blue; Peñarol play in yellow and black and are known as the *carboneros* or *mirasoles*.

One of the most successful – and popular – players of recent years has been **Gustavo Poyet** (b1967), a powerful midfielder who played in Europe for Zaragoza (captaining the team that won the 1995 Cup Winners' Cup), Chelsea (scoring the winner in the 1998 UEFA Super Cup final) and Spurs, as well as playing for Uruguay. He then became a coach with Swindon Town, Leeds United and Spurs, leaving with manager Juande Ramos when he was sacked in October 2008. In November 2009 he became manager of Brighton and Hove Albion, and is likely to end up coaching the Uruguayan team at some point.

The star of the next generation was **Diego Forlán** (b1979), whose father Pablo played for Uruguay in the 1966 and 1974 World Cups. Diego made his reputation as a striker in Argentina, then transferred to Manchester United in 2002 and failed to score for eight months, becoming nicknamed 'Diego Forlorn' (and when he did score it was from a penalty). Although things did improve for him, he was always inconsistent, and when Wayne Rooney joined the club Forlán moved to Villarreal and then in 2007 to Atlético Madrid. He has found form in Spain, prompting talk of a return to Britain, perhaps with Spurs, Aston Villa or Sunderland.

Álvaro Recoba (b1976) played for Internazionale for ten seasons, and 69 times for the Uruguayan national team, and is now seeing out his career with the Greek team Panionios. The current crop of players include Napoli striker **Marcelo Zalayeta** (b1978), defender **Pablo Lima** (b1981), Mallorca midfielder **Gonzalo Castro** (b1984), Porto's **Cristian Rodriguez** (b1985), defensive midfielder **Alvaro Pereira** (b1985), now with Romania's CFR Cluj, **Juan Ángel Albín** (b1986), an attacking midfielder with Getafe, Barcelona centre-half **Martín Cáceres**, Palermo striker **Edinson Cavani**, striker **Bruno Fornaroli**, currently playing in Argentina on loan from Sampdoria, and Ajax striker **Luis Suárez** (all four born in 1987), and **Tabaré Viudez** (b1989), an attacking midfielder with Milan.

The fast-rising midfielder **Nicolás Lodeiro** (b1989) produced a fine display in the 2009 South American U21 championships and moved from Montevideo's Nacional to Ajax early the next year. His agent is **Daniel Fonseca** (b1969) who also played for Nacional as a forward before moving to Napoli, Roma and Juventus, while also scoring 11 goals in 30 games for Uruguay.

Interestingly, five-a-side football (known as *fútsal* or indoor football) was created for a Montevideo YMCA in 1930 by a local teacher, Juan Carlos Ceriani.

Rugby Rugby was introduced to Uruguay in the 1860s but remains a minority interest, mainly in the wealthier Anglophile suburbs such as Carrasco. Clubs have names like Old Boys, Old Christians and Montevideo Cricket, and all but one are in Montevideo – the exception is Paysandú, half of whose players are

Just as Argentines flock to Uruguay's beaches in summer (because there are no decent beaches near Buenos Aires), so too do their surfers. Although there's no truly demanding surf here, there's plenty of it and you'll usually manage to have fun. The bars and the babes in bikinis are also said to add to the experience.

Surfing is feasible all year, thanks to the reliable Atlantic swell from the southeast. Waves range from 1–1.5m (3–5ft) in January and February (when water temperatures are up to 17°C/68°F) to 2–2.5m (6–8ft) in July and August (when the water is only 13°C/54°F, and a full wetsuit is definitely required, with gloves and booties). Conversely in summer you'll need to protect yourself against the sun. In fact the best surfing is in November, December, March and April when the weather is kind and the beaches are not too busy.

Some airlines classify surfboards as sporting equipment and transport them without charge. Likewise, it's easy to bring boards from Buenos Aires as the ferry and bus companies carry them free. You'll probably want to rent a car (perhaps even a 4x4) if you plan to visit the remoter, emptier beaches; be sure to bring straps to tie the boards to the car.

Punta del Este is the big centre for all beach-related activities: it's often windy, which can spoil surfing proper, but makes this a good site for kite-surfing or windsurfing. Just east of downtown Punta del Este is La Barra, where the young people like to hang out and show off to each other; surfing is good here but it can get very crowded (and with not very skilful surfers at that). There are good breaks on either side of the river mouth, although you need to beware rocks and a strong rip on the right-hand side. Montoya, Bikini and Mantantiales beaches are also very popular, partly because of their trendy bars and nightlife.

Continuing eastwards, surfing is possible more or less everywhere, depending on weather and tides, and the beaches get emptier and emptier as you go. You can also try dune-surfing here with snowboards. José Ignacio, like Punta del Este, has a *Mansa* (sheltered) beach as well as the *Brava* (exposed) one, giving better conditions for novices with fewer cross-currents.

La Paloma is a surfing town, also on a headland with good conditions likely on at least one side; waves of up to four metres have been ridden here. Neighbouring La Pedrera is quieter in terms of nightlife but just as good for surfing. The bohemian enclave of Cabo Polonio, with no road access, apparently has a legendary point break. Punta del Diablo has long empty beaches and good surf; immediately beyond, Santa Teresa occasionally has waves up to four metres high and is popular with Brazilian surfers.

To the west of Punta del Este the surf loses its power as it enters the shallow waters of the River Plate; in Canelones and San José waves are rarely over one metre in height. The water is also an alarming brown colour here, although that's actually nothing to worry about.

It's estimated that there around 12,000 surfers in Uruguay, of whom just a few hundred are members of the Union de Surf del Uruguay, which runs competitive surfing. The only professional surfer is Marco Giorgi, sponsored by a Brazilian surfwear company and generally assumed to be Brazilian himself. Similarly, most of the boards and other equipment you'll see is Brazilian-made, although some accessories are made in Uruguay. There are surf shops and schools in the main resorts, and a well-established bi-monthly magazine, *Mareas*.

Websites with information on surfing in Uruguay include: www.wannasurf.com, www.olasyvientos.com, www.oceanmind.net and www.paipo.com.uy.

Background Information **CULTURE**

|

students in Montevideo and train there. After a slow start the international team (known as Los Teros or southern lapwings) now usually beats other South American nations with the inevitable exception of Argentina. Qualifying for the 1999 and 2003 Rugby World Cups (but not 2007's) boosted the game's popularity, although it's still behind soccer and basketball. At the time of the 2003 World Cup ten players were playing professionally abroad, three in France's top league, which is boosting skill levels. They seem unlikely to qualify for the 2011 World Cup.

Tennis Uruguay's leading tennis player is **Pablo Cuevas** (b1986, across the river in Argentina), who won the men's doubles (with Peru's Luis Horna) at the 2008 French Open, and reached an ATP world singles ranking of No 88 in the same year. In 2009 he won the men's doubles (with Argentina's Brian Dabul) at the Chilean Open, taking him to a world doubles ranking of No 17. Uruguay's No 2 player is **Marcel Felder** (b1984), who was suspended for two months in 2008 for marijuana use.

The only previous Uruguayan to win a Grand Slam event was **Fiorella Bonicelli** (b1951), who won the mixed doubles at the 1975 French Open and the women's doubles at the 1976 French Open.

Boxing It's worth mentioning the female boxer **Chris Namús** (b1987), who is very popular and seen as an excellent role model; with the backing of President Tabaré Vásquez, she trains with the Uruguayan commandos.

OUTDOOR ACTIVITIES The favourite outdoor activity of most Uruguayans is, of course, simply going to the beach, and even towns in the interior have beaches on rivers or lakes which are packed out on sunny weekends. There's not actually much activity involved (exemplified by the fact that most Uruguayans take a folding chair and *matero* (see page 66) to the beach, rather than a towel), but the young bucks will show off by playing *fulbito* (mini-soccer) on the beach. In Punta del Este the beachfront condominiums and hotels stake out a stretch of beach and provide chairs and umbrellas in their own particular colour scheme for their guests – all beaches in Uruguay are public, so it can be contentious if they try to keep non-guests away.

Hiking There's limited scope for hiking, which is best combined with birdwatching in the Bañados del Este or the wetlands of the Río Uruguay *litoral* (see pages 221 and 277). However, there is some attractive hillier terrain in the southeast of the country, including its highest peak, Cerro Catedral (see page 220), as well as the areas of Villa Serrana and the Salto del Penitente, and the Cerro Arequita and Quebrada de los Cuervos protected areas.

Golf There are just 11 golf courses in Uruguay, but four of those have been built since 1994, with more doubtless on the way. Golf brings in US$55 million a year in the Punta del Este area alone, with four clubs all busy with tournaments in January. Two courses, in Montevideo and Fray Bentos, are historical delights, designed in 1928–30 by Dr Alister MacKenzie, a Scottish surgeon who laid out many of the classic American courses, including the Augusta National. Seeing how the Boers used the lay of the land to hide themselves led him to work on camouflage in World War I, and then to become the first great golf course designer who wasn't actually a good golfer himself.

The season lasts for ten months a year; see the Asociación Uruguaya de Golf website (*www.aug.com.uy*) for more information.

Horseriding With 14 million hectares of prairie grassland, it's no surprise that horses are one of the iconic features of the Uruguayan landscape and lifestyle, and riding is a key element of many people's visits to the country. This can range from helping gauchos round up cattle on a working farm to polo courses at luxury *estancias* (ranches). In fact horseriding is increasingly popular in the tourism industry, with rides of a few hours or a day available on and near the beaches (where full-moon rides are the new thing), as well as in grassland and the hills. Equitherapy for the disabled is also developing.

The classic Uruguayan breed of horse (designated by UNESCO as part of the country's Intangible Cultural Heritage) is the *criollo* (native), descended from horses brought from Spain in the 17th century, which are loose-gaited, docile and

THE URUGUAYAN GAUCHO

Uruguayan gauchos have their origins in the *reducciones* (missions) set up by the Jesuits to protect and 'civilise' the native Guaraní people; here they planted *maté*, herded cattle and learnt leatherworking. After the closure of the missions their *mestizo* descendants adopted a semi-nomadic lifestyle, and as the cattle industry developed from simply rounding up wild cattle to more organised ranching, they became the most sought-after workers, thanks to their skills on horseback and their ability to survive happily in the *campo* with almost nothing but a large knife and an unrelieved meat diet.

Darwin observed Uruguayan gauchos in 1832 and wrote in detail about their use of the *lazo* (lasso), made of plaited leather strips, to catch cattle, and the *bolas*, two or three stone balls wrapped in leather and linked by a leather rope, to catch rheas. When he tried to use the *bolas* himself, he got one ball caught on a bush and another around his horse's leg, causing general hilarity but fortunately no injuries to man or beast. He strongly approved of the gauchos' character, finding excuses for their faults:

The gauchos, or countrymen, are very superior to those who reside in the towns. The gaucho is invariably most obliging, polite, and hospitable: I did not meet with even one instance of rudeness or inhospitality. He is modest, both respecting himself and country, but at the same time a spirited, bold fellow. On the other hand, many robberies are committed, and there is much bloodshed: the habit of constantly wearing the knife is the chief cause of the latter. It is lamentable to hear how many lives are lost in trifling quarrels. In fighting, each party tries to mark the face of his adversary by slashing his nose or eyes; as is often attested by deep and horrid-looking scars. Robberies are a natural consequence of universal gambling, much drinking, and extreme indolence.

Even now, *gauchada* refers to an act of kindness or a good deed.

In Montevideo it's well worth visiting the Museo del Gaucho (see page 126) with its displays of silverware and leatherware. Holy Week sees the Semana Criolla in the Prado park, with rodeos and *asados* (barbecues) But to see gaucho culture at its best you should head for Tacuarembó during the second week of March, for the Fiesta de la Patria Gaucha (Gaucho Homeland Festival), with perhaps 3,000 horsemen (and maybe a few women) competing in rodeo events, and many more people in gaucho garb applauding, shopping for crafts and more practical rural bits and pieces. In the evenings there's *asado con cuero* (a cow barbecued with the skin still attached) and performances of dance, song and poetry. If you happen to be here in winter, you'll find horse races held on Sundays in many villages.

willing, and combine speed and stamina. There are also quarter-horses, bred in the United States from the 17th century for quarter-mile sprint races, and introduced to Uruguay from 1980. Polo ponies are mostly crosses of thoroughbreds with *criollo* horses.

A local speciality is endurance riding, with a Pan-American series (held every two years) of 80km and 120km races, in which Uruguay won gold in 2005 and silver in 2007.

Uruguayans ride with both reins held loosely in one hand, using neck-reining to guide the horse (rather than pulling on the bridle). Whereas you may be used to pulling the right rein to turn right, here you lay the left rein against the horse's neck – a subtle difference, but important. Gaucho saddles are flat and wide and have a much bigger pommel than British ones; they are covered with a sheepskin, with two separate girths to hold them in place. They also use longer stirrups than you may be used to, although that's easy to change.

Almost any *estancia* listed in this book will offer riding; see also page 43 for companies offering riding tours, and page 101 for horse-racing in Montevideo.

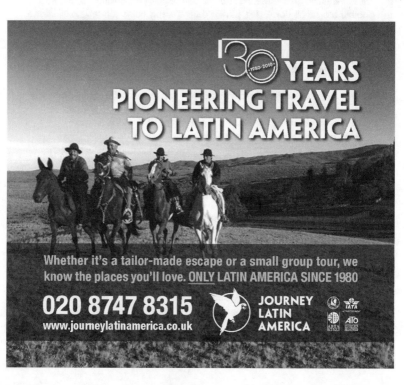

2

Practical Information

WHEN TO VISIT

Uruguay can be visited all year round, but the high season is summer, from late December to February, when it's hot and sunny and perfect for hanging out on the beach. It's never really cold or wet at other times, but it certainly can be chilly in winter. *Carnaval* (carnival) is also a high point, culminating on Shrove Tuesday but starting (in Uruguay) long before then – see page 102.

HIGHLIGHTS

MONTEVIDEO In Montevideo you should enjoy the grand buildings along the main Avenida 18 de Julio, as well as candombé drumming groups rehearsing on Sundays for the Las Llamadas procession. Montevideo's *Carnaval* is also spectacular, and at Easter there are impressive rodeos here. Montevideo is also a good base for visiting the wineries of Canelones department and nearby. See pages 114 and 102–3.

BEACHES Some of the best and most popular beaches in South America lie east of the capital, near the over-developed resort of Punta del Este and also the fashionable little village of José Ignacio, with its boutique hotels and restaurants. See pages 182 and 213.

HIKING AND HORSERIDING Inland there is attractive hill country with opportunities for hiking and horseriding; the country's most dramatic scenery is the Quebrada de los Cuervos, a gorge sheltering subtropical flora and fauna. See page 326.

BIRDWATCHING In the west of the country, there's great birdwatching (and spectacular sunsets) by the Río Uruguay. See page 277.

HOT SPRINGS Further north there are many hot springs resorts, such as the Termas de Daymán, near Salto. See page 293.

TRADITIONAL *ESTANCIAS* Spend time on an *estancia* such as La Sirena, near Mercedes, riding with gauchos, boating, birdwatching, and enjoying the relaxed old-style hospitality. See pages 154 and 269.

FRAY BENTOS The *Anglo* meat-processing plant at Fray Bentos is being restored as a wonderful museum of industrial heritage. See page 270.

SUGGESTED ITINERARIES

Almost all visits to Uruguay quite rightly start in Montevideo, home of half of the country's population, hub of its transport system and a place to enjoy architecture, markets, street life, beaches and a few reasonable museums. From there most people follow the coast, either west to the historic town of Colonia or east to the beach resorts and the lagoons and wetlands. The interior is largely empty, with good roads linking a few towns that make good bases for visiting *estancias* (ranches) for horseriding and country life. To the west larger cities lie along the Río Uruguay, forming the border with Argentina, and make good bases for more riding and birdwatching in the wetlands.

It's possible to continue to Argentina, either by ferry from Montevideo, Colonia or Nuevo Palmira, or by road via Fray Bentos (in theory), Paysandú or Salto; and to Brazil, principally via Rivera, Artigas, Melo or Chuy.

TOUR OPERATORS

Uruguay is ignored by many operators, or features only as a one-day side trip from Buenos Aires to Colonia; overland truck tours pass through pretty quickly between Rio de Janeiro and Buenos Aires (usually via Iguazú Falls). The one exception is horseriding tours, many of which come to Uruguay, especially the coast of Rocha.

TOURS

Adventure Center 1311 63rd St, Suite 200, Emeryville, CA 94608, USA; ✆ 510 654 1879, 1 800 228 8747 (TF); www.adventurecenter.com. Overland trip from Buenos Aires to Rio via Uruguay & Iguazú.

Discover Uruguay 30 Woodland St, Suite 11-JK, Hartford, CT 06105, USA; ✆ 860 246 7777, 1 877 987 8482 (TF); e info@gay-uruguay.com; www.discoveruruguay.com; www.gay-uruguay.com

Dragoman Camp Green, Debenham, Suffolk IP14 6LA, UK; ✆ 01728 861133; www.dragoman.co.uk. Overland trip from Buenos Aires to Rio via Uruguay & Iguazú.

GAP UK: 40 Star St, London W2 1QB, ✆ 0844 410 1030; Canada: 19 Charlotte St, Toronto, Ontario M5V 2H5, ✆ 1 888 800 4100; Australia: 172 Bridge Rd, Richmond, VIC 3121, ✆ 1300 796 618, www.gapadventures.com. Uruguay is a stopover on a variety of South American tours.

Intrepid Travel UK: 40 Station Rd, Westbury BA13 3JN, ✆ 01373 828303, e uk@intrepidtravel.com, www.intrepidtravel.com; Australia: PO Box 2781,

Fitzroy DC, VIC 3065. Uruguay is a stopover on a variety of overland tours (now incorporating Guerba).

Journey Latin America 12 Heathfield Terrace, London W4 4JE, UK; ✆ 020 8747 8315; www.journeylatinamerica.co.uk. The leading Latin America specialists, but their only tours to Uruguay are a 4-day trip from Buenos Aires, & 1 day in a 15-day tour from Buenos Aires to Rio de Janeiro.

Last Frontiers The Mill, Quainton Rd, Waddesdon, Bucks HP18 0LP, UK; ✆ 01296 653000; www.lastfrontiers.com. 3 9-day tours: Montevideo, Punta del Este, Colonia & an *estancia*; horseriding in Maldonadao & Rocha; chic destinations of José Ignacio & Colonia. Also tailormade trips.

Tucan Travel UK: 316 Uxbridge Rd, London W3 9QP, ✆ 020 8896 1600, www.tucantravel.com; Australia: 217 Alison Rd, Randwick, NSW 2031, ✆ 02 9326 6633, 1 300 769 249 (TF). Overland trip from Buenos Aires to Rio via Uruguay & Iguazú.

Tailor-made trips

Austral Tours 20 Upper Tachbrook St, London SW1V 1SH, UK; ✆ 020 7233 5384; www.latinamerica.co.uk/uruguay.htm

Cazenove & Loyd Imperial Studios, 3–11 Imperial Rd, London SW6 2AG, UK; ✆ 020 7384 2332; www.cazenoveandloyd.com. A week in Uruguay from £2,700.

Exsus Travel 118–119 Fenchurch St, London EC3M 5BA, UK; ✆ 020 7337 9000; 10 Rockefeller Plaza, New York, NY 10020, USA; ✆ 212 332 4848; www.exsus.com. Tailormade luxury tours.

Mila Tours 100 S Greenleaf, Gurnee, IL 60031, USA; ✆ 847 249 2111, 1 800 367 7378 (TF);

e milalatin@aol.com; www.milatours.com. Deluxe & tailormade packages, eg: 4-day tour from Buenos Aires.

Steppes Latin America 51 Castle St, Cirencester GL7 1QD, UK; ✆ 01285 880980; www.steppestravel.co.uk. Tailor-made luxury holidays in Montevideo, Colonia & Punta del Este.

Tim Best Travel 1B The Village, 101 Amies St, London SW11 2JW, UK; ✆ 020 7591 0300, 1 866 476 2731 (US: TF); www.timbesttravel.com. 'Luxury Safaris', inc horseriding option at traditional *estancias* & on the beaches.

Specialist operators

Horseriding

Boojum Expeditions 14543 Kelly Canyon Rd, Bozeman, MT 59715, USA; 406 587 0125, 1 800 287 0125 (TF); www.boojum.com

Equitours PO Box 807, 10 Stalnaker St, Dubois, WY 82513, USA; 307 455 3363, 1 800 545 0019 (TF); www.ridingtours.com

Hidden Trails 659A Moberly Rd, Vancouver, BC V5Z 4B3, Canada; 604 323 1141, 1 888 987 2457 (TF); www.hiddentrails.com

In The Saddle Reaside, Neen Savage, Cleobury Mortimer, Shrops DY14 8ES, UK; 01299 272 997, 1 888 732 7505 (Canada/US: TF); www.inthesaddle.com

Ride World Wide Staddon Farm, North Tawton EX20 2BX, UK; 01837 82544; www.rideworldwide.co.uk

South American Experience Welby Hse, 96 Wilton Rd, London SW1V 1DW, UK; 0845 2777 3366; www.southamericanexperience.co.uk. A horseriding tour; or 3 days in Punta del Este at the end of their Argentina Wildlife & Wine tour. **The Ultimate Travel Company** 25–27 Vanston Place, London SW6 1AZ, UK; 020 7386 4646; www.theultimatetravelcompany.co.uk

Wine tours

Arblaster & Clarke Wine Tours Cedar Court, 5 College St, Petersfield, Hants GU31 4AE, UK; 01730 263111; www.winetours.co.uk

Cisplatina Viajes y Turismo Bulevar España 2189, Montevideo; 2 409 9107, m 9963 1547; e senderosdeltannat@cisplatinauruguay.com; www.cisplatinauruguay.com

Lares Tours Wilson Ferreira Aldunate 1341, Montevideo; 2 901 9120, m 9959 2009; e info@lares.com.uy; www.larestours.com

Robertson Wine Tours The Penthouse 1202, Vázquez Ledesma 2865, CP 11200, Villa Biarritz, Montevideo; 707 927 4167 (US); m 9434 5144; Skype: Robertson Wine Tours; www.robertsonwinetours.com

Adventure and nature tourism

Cecilia Regules Viajes Bacacay 1334, Galeria Ciudadela, Local C, Montevideo; 2 916 3011/2; www.ceciliaregulesviajes.com. The longest-established agency for visits to *estancias*.

Eco Tours Avda Rivera 2088, oficina 601, 11200 Montevideo; 2 400 6245; e info@ecotours.com.uy; www.ecotours.com.uy. Founded in 2005, this co-op of experts from NGOs & academia offers tours focusing on birds, mammals, amphibians & reptiles, butterflies, mushrooms, geology & palaeontology, the gaucho experience, plus health tourism w/ends.

Expedición Uruguay 2 696 4006, m 9928 7681; e info@expedicionuruguay.com.uy; www.expedicionuruguay.com.uy. Working with the NGO Vida Silvestre & LMG Turismo (*Cerro Largo 1078 & Río Negro, Montevideo*; 2 902 3395, 2

902 3396), offering 1- & 2-day trips to places of scenic & natural interest, such as the Quebrada de los Cuervos & the Sierra de las Ánimas.

Guyrapytá m 9864 4509, Spain +34 639 333 831; e info@guyrapyta.com; www.birdwatching-guyrapyta.com. Excellent birdwatching tours.

Lares Aldunate 1322, Montevideo; 2 901 9120; www.lares.com.uy. Organises *estancia*, birdwatching, fishing & hunting trips.

Recorriendo Uruguay m 9427 6194; www.recorriendouruguay.com.uy. *Estancia* stays, horseriding & other rural tourism activities.

TransHotel Acevedo Díaz 1671 Montevideo; 2 402 9935, 0800 8161; www.e-transhotel.com. City tours & transfers in Montevideo, Colonia & Punta del Este; birdwatching & other tours.

Cruises All the usual suspects – Costa Cruises (*www.costacruises.co.uk*), Crystal Cruises (*www.crystalcruises.com*), Holland America Line (*www.hollandamerica.com*), Norwegian Cruise Line (*www.ncl.com*), Princess Cruises (*www.princess.com*), Regent Seven Seas Cruises (*www.rssc.com*), Silversea Cruises (*www.silversea.com*) and Swan Hellenic (*www.swanhellenic.com*) – have ships that call in at either Montevideo or Punta del Este on their way to or from Buenos Aires.

RED TAPE

Citizens of most countries (except China, India, Russia and a few smaller countries) require only a passport for visits of up to three months to Uruguay. The same usually applies to Australians (although there was a hiatus in mid-2007 when an agreement lapsed and visas were required for a while).

If you wish to extend your stay for a further three months, contact the Dirección Nacional de Migración (*National Office of Migration, Montevideo*; *www.dnm.minterior.gub.uy – in Spanish only*; see page 109) or in departmental capitals – but it's generally easier to leave the country for a night and return. If you wish to settle in Uruguay, contact the Inspectoría de Migración (e *residencias@ dnm.minterior.gub.uy*), although it's really better to discuss this first with the Uruguayan embassy in your home country.

Arriving by plane, you'll be given two forms, for Immigration and Customs; they are currently in Spanish only but are not difficult to fill in (just remember that your *apellido* is your family name). You'll be given a white form to keep with your passport, but if this gets lost it shouldn't be a problem as long as you have the correct stamp in your passport. Immigration queues are dealt with pretty fast, and there are special desks for disabled and pregnant people and those with babies.

On departure, if you are charged for overstaying, be sure to get a receipt.

E EMBASSIES

OVERSEAS EMBASSIES IN MONTEVIDEO

Argentina Cuareim 1470; ✆ 2 902 8166–9, 2 908 4844; e emargrou@adinet.com.uy, eurug@mrecic.gov.ar; ⏲ 10.00–15.00 Mon–Fri. Consulate: Wilson Ferreira Aldunate 1281; ✆ 2 902 8623–5; e info@consuladoargentino.com.uy; www.consuladoargentino.com.uy; ⏲ 13.00–18.30 Mon–Fri

Australia Honorary Consulate: Cerro Largo 1000; ✆ 2 901 0743; e ausconur@adinet.com.uy

Bolivia Wilson Ferreira Aldunate 1320, 4th Flr; ✆ 2 901 2394

Brazil Bvar Artigas 1328; ✆ 2 707 2036, 2215/19; e montevideu@brasemb.org.uy. Consulate: Convención 1343, 6th Flr; ✆ 2 901 2024/1460

Canada Plaza Independencia 749 office 102; ✆ 2 902 2030; e mvdeo@international.gc.ca; www.montevideo.gc.ca; ⏲ 08.30–12.30, 13.30–17.30 Mon–Thu, 08.30–14.00 Fri

Chile 25 de Mayo 575; ✆ 2 916 4090/4082; e echileuy@netgate.com.uy. Consulate: ✆ 2 916 2346; e cgideouy@netgate.com.uy

France Uruguay 853 & Andes; ✆ 2 902 0077; e ambafranceuruguay@gmail.com; www.amb.montevideo.fr. Consulate: ✆ 1705 0000; ⏲ 09.00–12.00 Mon–Fri

Germany La Cumparsita 1417; ✆ 2 902 5222; e info@montevideo.diplo.de; www.montevideo.diplo.de; ⏲ 07.45–12.30, 13.00–16.45 Mon–Thu, 07.45–13.45 Fri

Israel Bvar Artigas 1585; ✆ 2 400 4164/66; e info@montevideo.mfa.gov.il; http://montevideo.mfa.gov.il; ⏲ 09.15–12.15 Mon–Fri

Italy J Benito Lamas 2857; ✆ 2 708 0542/5316; e amburuit@netgate.com.uy; www.ambitalia.com.uy. Consulate: ✆ 2 710 5980/84

Netherlands Leyenda Patria 2880, 2nd Flr; ✆ 2 711 2956; e mtv@minbuza.nl; www.holanda.org.uy/index.html; ⏲ 09.00–12.30 Mon–Fri

Paraguay Bvar Artigas 1256; ✆ 2 707 2138; ⏲ 10.00–13.00 Mon–Fri. Consulate: ✆ 2 707 9371

Peru Calle Obligado 1384 & Rivera, Carrasco; ✆ 2 707 1420/6862; e emba8@easymail.com.uy; www.embaperu.org.uy

South Africa C Echevarriarza 3335; ✆ 2 623 0161; e safem@netgate.com.uy

Spain Libertad 2738; ✆ 2 708 6010; e emb.montevideo@mae.es; www.mae.es; ⏲ 08.00–13.30 Mon–Fri

Sweden Consulate: Rambla 25 de Agosto de 1825, No 508, 5th Flr; ✆ 2 917 0289, 2 915 4908; e consuladosuecia@smi.com.uy; ⏲ 11.00–13.00 Mon–Fri

UK Marco Bruto 1073 (Buceo), CP 16024, 11300 Montevideo; ✆ 2 622 3630/50; e ukinuruguay@gmail.com; http://ukinuruguay.fco.gov.uk/en; ⏲ 09.00–13.00, 14.00–17.30 Mon–Thu, 09.00–14.30 Fri (Jan–Feb 08.30–14.30 Mon–Fri). Consulate: ⏲ 09.00–14.00 Mon–Fri, visas 09.00–10.00 Mon–Fri

US Lauro Muller 1776, 11100 Montevideo; ✆ 2 418 7777, 2 203 6061; e MontevideoACS@state.gov, webmastermvd@state.gov; http://uruguay.usembassy.gov; ⏲ 08.30–17.30 Mon–Fri

URUGUAYAN EMBASSIES AND CONSULATES ABROAD

Argentina Avda Las Heras 1907, 15th Flr, Buenos Aires 1127; ☎ 4807 3040/60/61; e urubaires@ embajadadeluruguay.com.ar; www.embajadadeluruguay.com.ar; ⏰ 09.00–16.00 Mon–Fri. Main consulate: Avda Las Heras 1907, ground flr; ☎ 4807 3040/44; e conurubaires@ embajadadeluruguay.com.ar; ⏰ 09.30–16.30 Mon–Fri. Other consulates: San Martín 417, 3280 *Colón*; ☎ 3447 421 999; e crou@ciudad.com.ar; ⏰ 08.00–14.00 Mon–Fri; Asunción 131, 3200 *Concordia*; ☎ 345 422 1426, 421 0380; e conurucon@arnet.com.ar; ⏰ 07.00–13.00 Mon–Fri; Edificio St Michel, San Jerónimo 167, 5000 *Córdoba*; ☎ 351 424 1028; e conurucor@ arnet.com.ar; ⏰ 09.00–14.00 Mon–Fri; Rivadavia 510, 2820 *Gualeguaychú*; ☎ 446 426168; e conuruguale@entrerios.net; ⏰ 08.00–14.00 Mon–Fri; Ituzaingó 1422, 5500 *Mendoza*; ☎ 261 425 9877; e conurumen@hotmail.com; ⏰ 09.00–14.00 Mon–Fri; San Luis 441 (between Alem & 1º de Mayo), 2000 *Rosario*; ☎ 341 424 6860, 421 9077; e conururos@ consuladodeluruguay.com.ar; ⏰ 08.00–14.00 Mon–Fri

Australia Suite 2, Level 4, Commerce Hse, 24 Brisbane Av, Barton, ACT 2600; ☎ 02 6273 9100; e urucan@iimetro.com.au; ⏰ 09.00–15.00 Mon–Fri. Consulate: Level 32, Westpac Plaza Bldg, 60 Margaret St, Sydney, NSW 2000; ☎ 612 9251 5544; e curuguay@bigpond.net.au; ⏰ 10.00–17.00 Mon–Fri

Austria Naglergasse 9, 3rd Flr, door 17, Vienna; ☎ 1 535 6657/6636; e uruvien@embuy.at. Consulate: Alpenstrasse 75, Salzburg; ☎ 662 205 1625

Belgium 22 B Franklin Roosevelt Av, 1050 Brussels; ☎ 2 640 1169; e urucon@skynet.be; ⏰ 09.00–17.00 Mon–Fri

Bolivia Calle 21 Calacoto (San Miguel) 8350, Edificio Monroy Velez, 7th Flr, La Paz; ☎ (00 5912) 279 1482/1465. Consulates: Avda Cristobal de Mendoza 214, 12th Flr, office 12C, Edificio Castelo Branco, *Santa Cruz*; ☎ 3 333 5665; e conurucruz@ acelerate.com; Luis Ibanez s/n, *Cochabamba*; ☎ 4 431 8813

Brazil Avda das Naçoes, lote 14, Quadra 803 Sul, CEP 70450-900 Brasilia; ☎ 61 3322 1200/4528/4533; e urubras@emburuguai.org.br; www.emburuguai.org.br; ⏰ 09.30–13.00, 14.00–17.30 Mon–Fri. Consulates: Avda do Contorno 6777, Sala 1301/2, CEP 30110-935 *Belo Horizonte*; ☎ 31 3296 7527/7873; e conurubelo@ terra.com.br; Rua Venezuela 311, CEP 96255-000 *Chuí*; ☎ 53 3265 1151; e conschui@ adinet.com.uy; ⏰ 08.00–14.00 Mon–Fri; Alameda Carlos de Carvalho 417, 31st Flr, office 3101A, Edificio Curitiba Trade Center, CEP 80410-180 *Curitiba*; ☎ 41 3225 5550; e conurucur@ terra.com.br; ⏰ 10.00–16.00 Mon–Fri; Avda Rio Branco 387, 5th Flr, CEP 88015-210 *Florianopolis*; ☎ 48 3222 3718; e conuruflop@yahoo.com.br; ⏰ 14.00–15.00 Mon–Fri; Rua Julio Abreu 383, sala 01, Bairro Varjota, CEP 60160-240 *Fortaleza*; ☎ 85 4006 5880; e conuruceara@gmail.com; ⏰ 10.00–15.00 Mon–Fri; Rua Prudente de Morais 281, CEP 53020-140 *Olinda*; ☎ 81 3439 8849; e conurupe@terra.com.br; ⏰ 10.00–16.00 Mon–Fri; Rua Cornelio Procopio 1101, Apto. 205, Matinhos, CEP 83260-000 *Paranaguá*; ☎ 41 452 2363; ⏰ 09.00–15.00 Mon–Fri; Avda Ferreira Viana 1635, Salas 404 y 405, Barrio Areal, CEP 96085-000 *Pelotas*; ☎ 53 3229 1901/1843; e conurubage@ brturbo.com.br; Avda Cristovão Colombo 2999, Higienópolis, CEP 90560-005 *Porto Alegre*; ☎ 51 3325 6197/94; e cdodistritopoa@terra.com.br; ⏰ 09.00–15.00 Mon–Fri; Rua Bento Gonçalves 180 apt. 23, CEP 97560-000 *Quaraí*; ☎ 55 3423 1802; e conuruquar@mrree.gub.uy; Praia de Botafogo 242, 6th Flr, CEP 22250-040 *Rio de Janeiro*; ☎ 21 2553 6030/15; e conuruguana@consulado-uruguay-rio.org.br; ⏰ 09.00–14.00 Mon–Fri; Rua Gregorio de Matos 20, 1st Flr, Pelourinho, CEP 40025-060 *Salvador*; ☎ 71 322 7093/4; e conurubahia@ terra.com.br; ⏰ 09.30–16.00 Mon–Fri; Rua Estados Unidos 1284, Jardins, CEP 01427-001 *San Pablo* (São Paulo); ☎ 11 2879 6600/04/05, 3085 5941; e conurupa@osite.com.br; ⏰ 11.00–16.00 Mon–Fri; Avda Tamandaré 2080, 5th Flr, CEP 97573-531 *Santa Ana do Livramento*; ☎ 55 3242 1416; e consuliv@terra.com.br; ⏰ 08.00–14.00 Mon–Fri; Rua Venancio Aires 1761, CEP 97010-003 *Santa María*; ☎ 55 3221 1180; ⏰ 13.30–18.00 Mon–Fri; Rua Alexandre Fleming 437 apt. 31, CEP 11040-010 *Santos*; ☎ 13 3238 1886; ⏰ 07.00–13.00 Mon–Fri; Rua 15 de Novembro 554, CEP 96300-000 *Jaguarão*; ☎ 3261 1411; e conuruya@brturbo.com.br; ⏰ 08.00–14.00 Mon–Fri

Canada 130 Albert St, Suite 1905, Ottawa, Ontario KIP 5G4; ☎ 613 234 2727/2937; e embassy@ embassyofuruguay.ca; www.embassyofuruguay.ca; ⏰ 09.30–16.30 Mon–Fri. Consulates: 1411 rue Peel, Bureau 603, *Montréal*, Québec H3A 1S5; ☎ 514 288 0990; e conurumont@gmail.com; ⏰ 09.00–15.00 Mon–Fri; 300 Sheppard Avenue W, Suite 302,

Toronto, Ontario M2N 1N5; ☎ 416 730 1289;
e conrurutor@on.aibn.com; ⏲ 09.00–15.00
Mon–Fri; Three Bentall Centre, Suite 833, 595
Burrard St, PO Box 49058, *Vancouver* BC, V7X 1C4;
☎ 778329 0433; e uruguay@northstar.ca;
⏲ 08.30–17.00 Mon–Fri

Chile Avda Pedro de Valdivia 711, Providencia,
Santiago; ☎ 2 204 7988, 223 8398; e urusgo@
uruguay.cl; consulate: courusgo@netup.cl;
⏲ 10.00–16.00 Mon–Fri, 10.00–12.00 Sat.
Consulates: Copiapó 1071, 5th Flr, office 10,
Antofagasta; ☎ 55 250138; e consuluruguay2@
hotmail.com; 21 de Mayo 345, offices 31–32, *Arica*;
☎ 58 231536; e conurusgo@uruguay.cl; Talca 119,
office 206, *Puerto Montt*; ☎ 65 253155

France 15 rue Le Sueur, 1st Flr, 75116 Paris; ☎ 01
45 00 81 37; e amburuguay.urugalia@
fr.oleane.com; consulate: ☎ 01 45 00 53 32;
⏲ 11.00–15.00 Mon–Fri; & consulates in Marseilles
& Toulouse.

Germany Budapesterstrasse 39, 10787 Berlin; ☎ 030
263 90160; e urubrande@t-online.de;
⏲ 09.00–16.30 Mon–Fri; & consulates in Bremen,
Düsseldorf, Frankfurt, Hamburg, München, Potsdam &
Stuttgart.

Ireland Consulate: Tullycushlin, Bailieborough, Co
Cavan; ☎ 429 665392.

Italy Via Vittorio Veneto 183, 5th Flr, 00187 Roma;
☎ 06 482 1776/77, 482 1001; e uruit@
ambasciatauruguay.it; ⏲ 09.00–14.00 Mon–Fri; &
consulates in Genova, Livorno, Milano & Venezia.

New Zealand Consulate: BNZ Bldg, 137 Armagh St, 4th
Flr, Christchurch; ☎ 3 366 1653; e consulurunz@
gmail.com

Paraguay Avda Guido Boggiani 5832, 3rd Flr,
Asunción; ☎ 021 664244/6; e uruasun@
embajadauruguay.com.py. Consulate: ground flr;
☎ 021 610595; e conrupar@
embajadauruguay.com.py; ⏲ 09.00–15.00 Mon–Fri

Peru José D Anchorena 084, San Isidro, Lima 27;
☎ 01 719 2550/2552/2865; e uruinca@
americatelnet.com.pe; ⏲ 09.30–13.30 Mon–Fri.

Consulate: Calle Quezada 110B, Yanahuara, *Arequipa*;
☎ 54 272512; e consuladoagp-uruguay@
speedy.com.pe

South Africa 1119 Burnett St, MIB House, office 301,
Hatfield 0083, POB 3247, Pretoria 001; ☎ 12 362
6521/2; e urusud@pixie.co.za

Spain Paseo del Pintor Rosales 32, 1st Flr, 28008
Madrid; ☎ 91 758 0475; e urumatri@
urumatri.com. Consulate: 8th Flr; ☎ 91 541 2402,
548 2282; e coruespa@terra.es; summer
09.00–15.00, winter 09.00–18.00 Mon–Fri. Other
consulates: Passeig de Gracia 55, 5th Flr, 08007
Barcelona; ☎ 902 907 315; e couruguay@
consuladouy-bcn.org, conurubar@consuladouy-bcn.org;
⏲ 09.30–15.30 Mon–Fri; & in Bilbao, Las Palmas
(Gran Canaria), Palma (Mallorca), Pamplona,
Salamanca, Santa Cruz (Tenerife), Santiago de
Compostela, Sevilla, Valencia & Vigo.

United Kingdom 125 High St Kensington, 1st Flr,
London W8 5SF; ☎ 020 7937 4170;
e emburuguay@emburuguay.org.uk;
⏲ 10.00–16.00 Mon–Fri

United States 1913 I Street NW, Washington DC
20006; ☎ 202 331 1313–6; e uruwashi@
uruwashi.org; consulate: ☎ 331 8645;
⏲ 09.30–13.00, 14.00–16.00 Mon–Fri. Consulates:
875 North Michigan Av, Suite 1422, *Chicago* IL
60611; ☎ 312 642 3430; e consulado@
uruguaychicago.org; ⏲ 09.30–16.00 Mon–Fri; 1077
Ponce de León Bd, Suite B, Coral Gables, *Miami* FL
33134; ☎ 305 443 9764, 443 7253, 443 7453;
e consulado@uruguaymiami.org; ⏲ 09.00–15.00
Mon–Fri; 420 Madison Av, 6th Flr, *New York* NY;
☎ 212 753 8581/2, 753 8191/92;
e conuruyork@conuruyork.org; ⏲ 09.00–17.00
Mon–Fri; 429 Santa Monica Bd, Suite 400, *Santa
Monica* CA 90401; ☎ 310 394 5777;
e conrula@conurula.org, consulado@conurula.org;
⏲ 09.00–15.00 Mon–Fri; also honorary consulates
in Boston, Honolulu, Houston, Sandy UT, San Francisco
& San Juan PR.

MAPS

The best map of Uruguay is that published by ITMB in Vancouver (Canada), at a
scale of 1:800,000, with detailed insets of Montevideo, Colonia and Punta del Este
(£9.95). ITMB also offers a map of Montevideo at 1:15,000 (£8.95).

Nelles publish a map of Argentina North and Uruguay at 1:2.5m (with an inset
of central Montevideo), as well as one of Argentina South and Uruguay (£7.95 each).

For regional tours, ITMB has a good map of Southern South America at 1:2.8m
(£9.95), Marco Polo and GeoCenter World Map both have maps of Brazil, Bolivia,
Paraguay and Uruguay at 1:4m. Firestone have both a map of Chile, Southern

Brazil, Paraguay and Uruguay at 1:2.75m (£9.95), and a road atlas of Argentina, Bolivia, Chile, Southern Brazil, Paraguay and Uruguay (£27.50).

The Automóvil Cub del Uruguay's road map of Uruguay is available online at www.acu.com.uy/maparutero. There are also rather clunky searchable townplans at http://200.55.6.87/es/a2.asp?vista=MDCA&pais=Uruguay and www.pueblos20.net/uruguay/index.php .

GETTING THERE

✈ **BY AIR** From the northern hemisphere, most people will naturally arrive by air. Montevideo has far fewer long-distance connections than Buenos Aires, in particular, and it may prove cheaper to fly to Buenos Aires and take either the short flight across the River Plate to Montevideo or Punta del Este, or the ferry or bus (see pages 48 and 50). However, this almost always requires transferring from the Ezeiza long-distance airport (EZE) to the Aeroparque (AEP), the airport in the city's northern suburbs that handles flights within Argentina and to neighbouring countries. This is fairly easy and well organised, either by Aerolíneas Argentinas if flying both legs with them or with the Manuel Tienda León shuttle company (*www.tiendaleon.com.ar*). This route is flown by Aerolíneas, Uruguay's flag-carrier PLUNA, and the small Argentine company Sol (*www.sol.com.ar*), which began

---

PLUNA

Founded in 1936, PLUNA (Primera Línea Uruguaya de Navegación Aérea; www.flypluna.com) is Uruguay's national airline. Having been a small, moderately successful local airline for many years, it started long-haul flights to Madrid in 1981 (using a Boeing 707). PLUNA formed an association with Brazil's then flag-carrier Varig in 2002, giving it worldwide connections (via São Paulo) until Varig went bankrupt in 2007. In mid-2007 75% of PLUNA was sold to German-based investment firm Leadgate, which has undertaken a rapid and successful transformation of the airline. They quickly replaced large Boeing jets with smaller Bombardier regional jets, offering more frequent services to business centres such as Buenos Aires, Santiago and São Paulo, and opening up newer destinations such as Asunción, Bariloche, Rosario and Curitiba, benefiting from Open Skies agreements with Paraguay and Chile, and a bilateral agreement with Brazil. Their strategy has been to position Montevideo as a regional hub, and the number of passengers transferring has risen from 10% to 40% and is still rising. It was the first Latin American airline to charge for checking in luggage, but (unlike Europe's predatory low-fares airlines) it waives this for passengers checking in online, which has pushed its online levels up to 33%, a very high rate for Latin America. PLUNA also launched the Smiles frequent-flyer programme in 2006.

In 2008 PLUNA gave up its own flight to Madrid and switched to code-sharing with Spain's Iberia, in the face of strong opposition from the Uruguayan government, which is usually more pragmatic and less interested in pointless national symbols. Nevertheless the airline's core operations are now profitable.

In January 2009 Iberia increased frequency from five to six days a week (not Thursdays). The new BQB airline, being set up by the owner of the Buquebus ferry company, is asking for rights to serve the Montevideo–Madrid route, although it remains to be seen whether this is practical for what is essentially to be a small regional airline.

PLUNA also code-shares with GOL, which took over the bankrupt Varig and is now Brazil's second-largest airline (to Porto Alegre and São Paulo), with TAM, Brazil's largest airline (to São Paulo), and with LAN Airlines (to Santiago).

operating in 2006 and flies to Montevideo Monday to Friday only. In all there are around ten flights each way daily (the last at about 21.00), taking just 40 minutes. Be aware that Aerolíneas in particular is notorious for changing schedules and if you don't check you may turn up to find that your flight has already left.

In addition there's at least one flight a day with PLUNA from Buenos Aires (Aeroparque) to Punta del Este (PDP), with four or five on winter weekends and up to a dozen per day in summer, operated by Aerolíneas Argentinas and Sol as well as PLUNA. The owner of the Buquebus ferry company has established a new airline, BQB (*www.flybqb.com*) operates from Montevideo to Salto and Rivera, and internationally to Porto Alegre, Florianopolis, Iguazú and Asunción, and from Buenos Aires to Punta del Este.

Alternatives are to change planes in São Paulo or Rio de Janeiro, continuing with TAM Linhas Aéreas (TAM) or Gol Transportes Aéreos (GOL), or to fly direct from Madrid to Montevideo. GOL is allied with Air France–KLM, and TAM with Lufthansa and BMI. TAM flies direct from London (Heathrow), Paris, Frankfurt, Milan, Madrid, New York and Miami to São Paulo, with connections to Montevideo. Iberia flies direct every night from Madrid to Montevideo, code-sharing with PLUNA and British Airways and providing connections worldwide with American Airlines and other members of the oneworld alliance.

From North America, American Airlines (code-sharing with PLUNA) flies non-stop from Miami to Montevideo five times a week, between November and March only – at other times you'll have to go via Buenos Aires. Brazil's TAM flies to New York and Miami and code-shares with United Airlines, giving connections across North America.

Within South America, PLUNA flies from Montevideo to Buenos Aires, Santiago, São Paulo, Asunción, Bariloche, Rosario and Curitiba; and TAM serves Rio, São Paulo and Asunción. LanChile (*www.lan.com*) flies to Santiago twice a day; and TACA (*www.taca.com*) has three flights a week to Lima, with onward flights to the United States in conjunction with United Airlines. GOL has around four flights a day from Montevideo to São Paulo, some calling at Porto Alegre, the main transport hub of southern Brazil.

BY FERRY Several companies operate ferries between Argentina and Uruguay. The best known is **Buquebus**, which runs both fast ferries and traditional slower ships from Buenos Aires; these no longer go directly to Punta del Este, but connecting buses go there from both Colonia and Montevideo. Fast ferries reach Colonia in an hour from Buenos Aires, while slower ships are scheduled to take three hours to Colonia or Montevideo. Both types of vessel carry cars. The fast ferries are quick enough but rather cramped, with lots of over-excited children running around, no access to the deck and a disproportionate amount of space set aside for first-class and *primera especial* accommodation – totally unnecessary on a one-hour crossing, but an easy way to part Argentines from their money.

Fares range from US$26 each way tourist class on the slow ship from Buenos Aires to Colonia (US$36 first class, US$41 *especial*, plus US$62 for a car up to 1.2t or US$44 for a motorbike) to US$40 for the fast ferry to Colonia (US$53 first class, US$57 *especial*, US$79 car, US$108 motorbike) and US$72 from Buenos Aires to Montevideo (US$100 first class, US$114 *especial*, US$100 car, US$78 motorbike). Taking the ship to Colonia then a bus to Montevideo costs US$33 each way (US$44 first class, US$49 *especial*); the fast ferry and bus cost US$47 (US$60 first class, US$65 *especial*). Taking the ship to Colonia then a bus to Punta del Este costs US$40 (US$50 first class, US$55 *especial*); the fast ferry and bus cost US$54 (US$67 first class, US$71 *especial*); and the ship to Montevideo plus a bus to Punta del Este cost US$86 (US$109 first class, US$124 *especial*).

It's also possible to book bus connections to Piriápolis, La Paloma, Carmelo and the Termas de Arapey, as well as packages including accommodation. There are discounts for children and senior citizens (formerly only for Argentines and Uruguayans, but now available to all); regular passengers can get every fifth trip free. There's an additional fee for cars leaving Uruguay of US$16 (at Colonia) or US$17.50 (at Montevideo).

Sailings are often fully booked, especially at weekends and peak holiday times, so you should book in advance (particularly with a vehicle), although reservations are only available 90 days ahead. The Buquebus website (*www.buquebus.com*), which used to be notoriously poor, now works well, although it's best to use the Internet Explorer browser. If you can use the Spanish-language site, you'll find it more straightforward than the English version. You'll get an e-ticket, and be told to check in an hour before departure (thus turning a one-hour journey into a two-hour one), giving plenty of time to linger in the departure lounge. Allow plenty of time if buying tickets in person at Buquebus's terminal in Buenos Aires: the counters are unsigned, but you'll book at one counter then queue again to pay at another, in a typically Argentine job-creation scheme. Baggage (and bicycles) can be checked in, but you are free to carry rucksacks on board. There's no ATM at the Buenos Aires terminal, but Uruguay's Banco de la República has an exchange kiosk here. Argentine and Uruguayan immigration procedures are carried out together at the departure port, so you're free to leave rapidly on arrival. At Colonia, a new terminal is under construction, which will offer a café, ATMs and other facilities. There are duty-free shops on board the ships, with cheap alcohol, but the restaurants are overpriced. There's free Wi-Fi between Buenos Aires and Montevideo, which also allows the use of mobile phones at sea.

Two smaller, cheaper competitors are snapping at Buquebus's heels. **Colonia Express** offers web fares as low as US$5 each way from Buenos Aires to Colonia, booking at least 21 days in advance; the fare leaps to US$20 each way if booked 16–20 days ahead, US$27 8–15 days ahead, and US$33 after that. They offer two crossings a day (one on Saturdays) with fast ferries taking an hour from Buenos Aires to Colonia; from here buses connect to Montevideo (from US$10). Passengers for Punta del Este transfer to a COPSA bus at Montevideo's Tres Cruces bus terminal.

SeaCat Colonia operates three fast ferries (one carrying cars), sailing from Buenos Aires to Colonia twice a day (four times on Saturdays), and a ship, sailing daily and also overnight except on Sundays. Fares start at US$26 each way by ship or US$40 by fast ferry, with connecting buses costing US$8 to Montevideo and US$14 to Punta del Este. Cars (up to 1.2 tonnes) cost US$62 each way and motorbikes US$43 by ship, or US$78/53 by fast ferry. First class accommodation is also available on the ferries.

The ship also heads for Montevideo twice daily (once on Saturdays), with fares from US$74 plus US$100 for a car or US$78 for a motorbike; a bus connection to Punta del Este costs US$10.

It's also possible to take the far smaller, simpler boats (which don't carry cars) from the pleasant resort of Tigre through the Paraná Delta, full of birdlife. In Tigre the international boats leave from Lavalle 520, across a bridge from the main Terminal Fluvial (where the tourist office is) at Mitre 319.

Cacciola Viajes in Argentina and **Trans Uruguay** in Uruguay jointly operate a service twice a day from Tigre to Carmelo, with a minibus from downtown Buenos Aires to Tigre, and others from Carmelo to Colonia and Montevideo (a total of eight hours from capital to capital). Fares range from US$17 Tigre–Carmelo to US$27 Buenos Aires–Montevideo.

Similarly, **Líneas Delta Argentinas** sail once daily from Tigre to Nuevo Palmira, north of Carmelo, leaving early in the morning and returning from Uruguay in the afternoon. The fare is US$15 each way, plus US$7 for a connecting bus to Colonia (1¼ hours).

Ferry offices
In Argentina
Buquebus Terminal Fluvial, Avda Antártida Argentina 821, Dársena Norte, Buenos Aires, ☎ 4316 6500, ⊕ 06.30–24.00 Mon–Fri, 06.30–21.00 Sat. Others include: Avda Córdoba 879, Microcentro, Buenos Aires; Posadas 1452, Recoleta, Buenos Aires; Retiro bus terminal, offices 20–22, Buenos Aires All ⊕ 09.00–19.00 Mon–Fri, 09.00–14.00 Sat; sales ☎ 4316 6500 (⊕ 08.00–21.00 Mon–Fri, 09.00–14.00 Sat); www.buquebus.com

Cacciola Viajes Florida 520 casi Lavalle, 1st Flr, Buenos Aires, ☎ 4393 6100, 4394 5520; Terminal Fluvial, Lavalle 520, Tigre; ☎ 4749 2369/0931/0329; www.cacciolaviajes.com

Colonia Express Avda Córdoba 753, Buenos Aires; ⊕ 09.00–20.00 Mon–Fri, 09.00–13.00 Sat; terminal, Avda Pedro de Mendoza 330, Darsena Sur, Buenos Aires; ⊕ 09.00–20.00 Mon–Fri, 09.00–19.00 Sat; sales ☎ 4317 4100, 4313 5100 (⊕ 09.00–20.00 daily); www.coloniaexpress.com

Líneas Delta Argentinas Terminal Fluvial, Tigre, office 6, Buenos Aires; ☎ 4731 1236, 4749 0537; e info@lineasdelta.com.ar; www.lineasdelta.com.ar

SeaCat Colonia Avda Córdoba 772, Buenos Aires; ☎ 4322 9551/3/5/6; e agencias@ ferrylineas.com.ar; ⊕ 07.00–20.00 daily; sales ☎ 4314 5100; www.ferryturismo.com.uy

In Uruguay
Buquebus port, Montevideo; Colonia & Florida, Montevideo Centro; ⊕ 09.30–18.30 Mon–Fri, 09.00–13.00 Sat; Tres Cruces bus terminal, office B29, Montevideo; ⊕ 05.45–01.00 daily, to 23.00 Sat; Shopping Punta Carretas, No 219, Montevideo; ⊕ 10.00–22.00 daily; Hector Miranda 2443 near Ellauri, Punta Carretas, Montevideo; ⊕ 10.00–19.00 Mon–Fri, 09.00–12.00 Sat; bus terminal, Piriápolis; ⊕ 10.00–18.00 daily; bus terminal, office 09, Punta del Este; ⊕ 10.00–18.00 Mon–Fri, 10.00–12.00 Sat; Punta Shopping, No 104, Punta del Este; ⊕ 10.00–22.00 daily; Avda Solari esq Calle de la Virgén, La Paloma; ⊕ 10.00–19.00 Mon–Sat, 09.00–14.00 Sun; telephone sales ☎ 130 (⊕ 08.00–22.00 Mon–Fri, 09.00–19.00 Sat–Sun); www.buquebus.com

Colonia Express Wilson Ferreira Aldunate 1341, Montevideo; sales ☎ 2 901 9597/93, 2 903 2360, 0800 8354; ⊕ 09.00–18.00 Mon–Fri; Tres Cruces bus terminal, Montevideo, offices B17/18; ☎ 2 400 3939; bus terminal, Colonia; ☎ 52 29677/8;

⊕ 10.00–19.00 Mon–Fri, 10.00–16.00 Sat, 10.00–12.00 Sun; Colonia port; ☎ 52 29676 (1hr 45min before departures & for 30min after); & at COPSA bus company offices in Piriápolis, Maldonado, Punta del Este & Solanas (Portezuelo) bus terminals; www.coloniaexpress.com

Líneas Delta Argentinas Colonia; ☎ 5301; Nueva Palmira; ☎ 7589; e ldapalmi@adinet.com.uy; www.lineasdelta.com.ar

SeaCat Colonia Río Negro 1400 & Colonia, Montevideo; ☎ 2 900 6617/2 901 3835; e ventas@ferryturismo.com.uy; ⊕ 09.00–19.00 Mon–Fri, 09.00–12.00 Sat; Tres Cruces bus terminal, offices B28/29, Montevideo; ☎ 2 409 8198/9; ⊕ 07.00–23.00 daily; port, Colonia; ☎ 52 22919; ⊕ 07.30–19.00; bus terminal, office 9, Punta del Este; ☎ 493892; sales ☎ 915 0202; www.ferryturismo.com.uy

Trans Uruguay Tres Cruces bus terminal, Montevideo, office B32; ☎ 2 401 9350/5721; e info@ transuruguay.com; www.transuruguay.com

🚌 **BY BUS** Although it's a long way around, buses do run from Buenos Aires to Montevideo and Punta del Este, offering an overnight journey at a far lower cost than Buquebus. Leaving between 21.30 and 23.30, they take eight hours and charge US$34 each way (US$26 between Buenos Aires and Fray Bentos or Mercedes) or US$38 for a *cama* (a seat that reclines to form a bed). **Bus de la Carrera**, **Cauvi** and **General Belgrano** all run to and from the Tres Cruces terminal in Montevideo (see page 81 for contact details), and General Belgrano also serves Punta del Este. Bus de la Carrera also has a daytime service, leaving at 10.00 in each direction.

Visitors to Uruguay often want to continue to Iguazú Falls, on the border of Argentina and Brazil. There are no direct buses, but the journey can be made relatively simply. From Salto, take the ferry to Concordia (Argentina), then go to the bus terminal at Juan B Justo and Hipólito Yrigoyen and book a ticket to Iguazú with **Expreso Tigre-Iguazú** (*office 7;* ℡ *0345 423 0842/421 4857; www.tigreiguazu.com.ar*). There's a good choice of buses, mostly overnight – you'll be told to return to the terminal about 40 minutes before your scheduled departure to be taken by taxi (no extra charge) to a police checkpoint on the bypass, where the bus will collect you. It's another ten or so hours to Iguazú, with reasonable service and meals, and less good films. From eastern Uruguay you might prefer to go to Florianópolis in Brazil, and take the **Catarinense** bus from there to Foz de Iguaçu, leaving daily at 14.00 and arriving at 07.00 (*www.catarinense.net; US$67*).

There are also regular *leito* (bed) and *executivo* (or *semi-leito*) buses from Montevideo and Punta del Este to southern Brazil, via the Chuy border crossing. **TTL** (Transporte Turismo Limitada) runs an *executivo* bus from Porto Alegre to Montevideo (US$72) nightly except on Fridays (returning nightly except Sundays), via Pelotas, Chuí, San Carlos and Punta del Este; and a *leito* on Friday nights (returning on Sundays; US$90). In addition there's an *executivo* service leaving São Paulo (San Pablo in Spanish) on Monday nights (and Thursdays and Saturdays at busy times), via Curitiba, Florianopolis, Porto Alegre, Pelotas, Chuí and Punta del Este, arriving at Montevideo 30 hours later (US$140; returning on Saturday nights).

Similarly, **EGA** has daily service from Porto Alegre to Montevideo, and on Fridays (and Sundays and Tuesdays at busy times) from São Paulo (US$140), Curitiba and Florianopolis.

You can also cross the border on foot or by taxi and catch an internal bus from the *rodoviaria* (bus station) on the Brazilian side, giving a much greater choice of destinations and departure times. From Chuí there are two buses daily (one overnight) to Porto Alegre (US$32, 6 hours) as well as five to Pelotas, and three a week to Florianopolis, Curitiba and São Paulo; from Jaguarão there are three buses a day to Porto Alegre (US$30, 6 hours), and seven to Pelotas (five on Sundays). From Santana do Livramento three buses daily go to Porto Alegre (*convencional* US$35, *executivo* US$47, *leito* US$62; 7 hours); **NS da Penha** has a daily service to Curitiba (US$77, 19 hours). Uruguaiana is less convenient, with just one bus daily to Curitiba and another to Porto Alegre (US$37, 8 hours), plus one on Saturdays and Sundays only to Santana do Livramento.

There are also services from Brazil to Argentina passing through Uruguay but avoiding Montevideo: in summer **Ouro e Prata** runs (on Sunday night, returning on Fridays) from Porto Alegre to Rivera, Tacuarembó, Salto and Paysandú, for onward connections into Argentina with **FlechaBus** (*www.flechabus.com.ar*). (FlechaBus also provides more convenient services from Brazil to Argentina via Iguazú.) At its hub in Montevideo, EGA's buses from Brazil connect to Asunción (Paraguay) and Foz de Iguaçu (Brazil), to Paraná, Santa Fé, Rosario, Córdoba, San Luis and Mendoza (Argentina) and to Santiago (Chile).

International bus companies
In Argentina
Bus de la Carrera Retiro bus terminal, office 194, Buenos Aires; ℡ 4315 8796, 4313 1700

Cauvi Retiro bus terminal, office 198, Buenos Aires; ℡ 4314 6999

EGA Terminal NETOC, office 27, Córdoba; ☏ 0351 425 4765; Terminal del Sol, office E7, Mendoza; ☏ 0261 431 7758; Terminal M Moreno, Local 32, Rosario; ☏ 0341 438 0038; bus terminal, office 17, Paraná; ☏ 0343 431 5439; bus terminal, office 22, Santa Fé; ☏ 0342 455 7013

Pullman General Belgrano Retiro bus terminal, office 207, Buenos Aires; ☏ 4315 1226/6522; www.gralbelgrano.com.ar

In Brazil

EGA Gonçalves Chávez 659, office 12, Pelotas; ☏ (0532) 223817; Rodoviaria, offices 6 & 18, Porto Alegre; ☏ 051 3225 0324, 3228 2722; e egapoa@zaz.com.br, egapoa@nutecnet.com.br; Rodoviaria Rita María Sector D, Florianópolis; ☏ 048 222 5061/5012; Rodoviaria, Local 29, Curitiba; ☏ 041 323 4221; Rodoviaria Tieté, office 85, São Paulo (San Pablo); ☏ 011 2221 1100; www.egakeguay.com/index.php
Ouro e Prata Rodoviaria, Porto Alegre; ☏ 051 3225 8771; e sac@viacaoouroeprata.com.br; www.viacaoouroeprata.com.br
TTL Rua Dona Teodora 1643, Navegantes, Porto Alegre; ☏ 051 3342 6477; e ttl@ttl.com.br; BR 471, km651, Chuí; ☏ 053 3265 1226; c/o Horizonte

Azul Passagens, Estacao Rodoferroviária, office B 23F, Curitiba; ☏ 041 3233 2192; e josmar.francisco@terra.com.br; Rodoviária, international wing, office 03, Florianópolis; ☏ 048 3224 1416; e ttlflo@ttl.com.br; c/o Unesul de Transporte Ltda, Rodoviaria, Avda Brasil 99, Foz do Iguaçu; ☏ 045 3522 2070; Avda PresidenteJoão Goulart 4605, office 35, Pelotas; ☏ 053 3281 1990 ; e agpel@unesul.com.br; Rodoviária, Rio Grande; ☏ 053 3281 6821; e rdvriog@vetorialnet.com.br; Rodoviária, international wing, Largo Julio Veppo, Porto Alegre; ☏ 051 3224 7557/7690; e ttlrod@ttl.com.br; Rodoviário Tietê, office 385, São Paulo; ☏ 011 2221 3811/3531; e ttlrosao@ttl.com.br; www.ttl.com.br

In Chile

EGA Terminal Sur, office 50, Santiago; ☏ 2 779 3536

In Paraguay

EGA Eligio Axala 693, Asunción; ☏ 021 492 473

In Uruguay

Bus de la Carrera Tres Cruces terminal, office B25/26, Montevideo; ☏ 2 402 1313
Cauvi Tres Cruces terminal, office B31, Montevideo; ☏ 2 401 9196
EGA Tres Cruces terminal, office B30, Montevideo; ☏ 2 402 5164/65, 3225 6767; www.egakeguay.com/index.php

General Belgrano Tres Cruces terminal, office B27, Montevideo; ☏ 2 401 4764
TTL Tres Cruces terminal, office B27, Montevideo; ☏ 2 401 1410

✚ HEALTH with Dr Felicity Nicholson

Uruguay is a clean temperate country with very few nasty diseases or health risks, and a good standard of health care. There is normally no rabies or malaria, and at the moment no dengue fever, although in early 2009 Argentina's health ministry belatedly admitted an outbreak affecting up to 15,000 people in Chaco and other northern states. Cities such as Paysandú are working hard to eliminate the *Aedes aegypti* mosquito, which carries the dengue virus; you should in any case take precautions against mosquito bites in the daytime. Similarly, yellow fever is found in Argentina's Misiones and Corrientes states and in adjacent parts of Brazil, but not as yet in Uruguay. It is recommended to have a yellow fever vaccination at least ten days before visiting the subtropical forests of Argentina and Brazil. The vaccine is not suitable for everyone, so ensure that you seek medical advice before booking your trip if you wish to stray outside of Uruguay. If you are coming from a yellow fever endemic zone into Uruguay then they will ask for a certificate. If you cannot have the vaccine for medical reasons then ensure that you obtain an exemption certificate from your GP or a travel clinic.

Apart from yellow fever, as described opposite, no other vaccinations are required, but make sure you're up to date with tetanus and diphtheria (which now come together with polio as the all-in-one Revaxis) and hepatitis A jabs. Entry requirements can be checked with the **Ministry of Public Health** (✆ *915 4765; 09.00–13.00 Mon–Fri;* e *sanidadfronteras@msp.gub.uy*). Further information is available from NHS Scotland's **Fit for Travel** website (*www.fitfortravel.scot.nhs.uk*), the **National Travel Health Network and Centre** (*www.nathnac.org/ds/ c_pages/country_page_uy.htm*) or the **Centers for Disease Control and Prevention** (*www.cdc.gov/travel/destinations/uruguay.aspx*).

In general, your best health protection is to be fit and well before you set off. Have your teeth checked and carry your prescription if you wear glasses (or leave it as a Hotmail/Yahoo! message).

TRAVEL CLINICS AND HEALTH INFORMATION A full list of current travel clinic websites worldwide is available on www.istm.org. For other journey preparation information, consult www.nathnac.org/ds/map_world.aspx. Information about various medications may be found on www.netdoctor.co.uk/travel.

UK

Berkeley Travel Clinic 32 Berkeley St, London W1J 8EL (near Green Park tube station); ✆ 020 7629 6233; ⏰ 10.00–18.00 Mon–Fri; 10.00–15.00 Sat.

Cambridge Travel Clinic 41 Hills Rd, Cambridge, CB2 1NT; ✆ 01223 367362; f 01223 368021; e enquiries@travelcliniccambridge.co.uk; www.travelcliniccambridge.co.uk; ⏰ 10.00–16.00 Mon, Tue & Sat, 12.00–19.00 Wed & Thu, 11.00–18.00 Fri.

Edinburgh Travel Health Clinic 14 East Preston St, Newington, Edinburgh EH8 9QA; ✆ 0131 667 1030; www.edinburghtravelhealthclinic.co.uk; ⏰ 09.00–19.00 Mon–Wed, 9.00–18.00 Thu & Fri. Travel vaccinations & advice on all aspects of malaria prevention. All current UK prescribed anti-malaria tablets in stock.

Fleet Street Travel Clinic 29 Fleet St, London EC4Y 1AA; ✆ 020 7353 5678; www.fleetstreetclinic.com; ⏰ 08.45–17.30 Mon–Fri. Injections, travel products & latest advice.

Hospital for Tropical Diseases Travel Clinic Mortimer Market Centre, 2nd Flr, Capper St (off Tottenham Ct Rd), London WC1E 6AU; ✆ 020 7388 9600; www.thehtd.org; ⏰ 09.00–16.00. Offers consultations & advice, & is able to provide all necessary drugs & vaccines for travellers. Runs a healthline (✆ 020 7950 7799) for country-specific information & health hazards. Also stocks nets, water purification equipment & personal protection measures. Travellers who have returned from the tropics & are unwell, with fever or bloody diarrhoea, can attend the walk-in emergency clinic at the Hospital without an appointment.

MASTA (Medical Advisory Service for Travellers Abroad), at the London School of Hygiene & Tropical Medicine, Keppel St, London WC1 7HT; ✆ 09068 224100; e enquiries@masta.org; www.masta-travel-health.com. This is a premium-line number, charged at 60p/min. For a fee, they will provide an individually tailored health brief, with up-to-date information on how to stay healthy, inoculations & what to take.

MASTA pre-travel clinics ✆ 01276 685040. Call or check www.masta-travel-health.com/travel-clinic.aspx for the nearest; there are currently 30 in Britain. They also sell malaria prophylaxis, memory cards, treatment kits, bednets, net treatment kits, etc.

NHS travel website www.fitfortravel.nhs.uk. Provides country-by-country advice on immunisation & malaria prevention, plus details of recent developments, & a list of relevant health organisations.

Nomad Travel Stores Flagship store: 3–4 Wellington Terrace, Turnpike Lane, London N8 0PX; ✆ 020 8889 7014; f 020 8889 9528; e turnpike@ nomadtravel.co.uk; www.nomadtravel.co.uk; walk in or appointments ⏰ 09.15–17.00 every day with late night Thu. Six stores in total country wide: 3 in London, Bristol, Southampton, Manchester. As well as dispensing health advice, Nomad stocks mosquito nets & other anti-bug devices, & an excellent range of adventure travel gear.

InterHealth Travel Clinic 111 Westminster Bridge Rd, London, SE1 7HR; ☎ 020 7902 9000; e info@interhealth.org.uk; www.interhealth.org.uk; ⏰ 08.30–17.30 Mon–Fri. Competitively priced, one-stop travel health service by appointment only.
Trailfinders Immunisation Centre 194 Kensington High St, London W8 7RG; ☎ 020 7938 3999 www.trailfinders.com/travelessentials/travelclinic.htm;

⏰ 09.00–17.00 Mon, Tue, Wed & Fri, 09.00–18.00 Thu, 10.00–17.15 Sat. No appointment necessary.
Travelpharm www.travelpharm.com. The Travelpharm website offers up-to-date guidance on travel-related health & has a range of medications available through their online mini-pharmacy.

Irish Republic
Tropical Medical Bureau Grafton St Medical Centre, Grafton Buildings, 34 Grafton St, Dublin 2; ☎ 1 671 9200. Has a useful website specific to tropical destinations: www.tmb.ie.

USA
Centers for Disease Control 1600 Clifton Rd, Atlanta, GA 30333; ☎ (800) 232 4636 or (800) 232 6348; e cdcinfo@cdc.gov; www.cdc.gov/travel. The central source of travel information in the USA. Each summer they publish the invaluable *Health Information for International Travel*.

IAMAT (International Association for Medical Assistance to Travelers): 1623 Military Rd, #279 Niagara Falls, NY 14304-1745; ☎ 716 754 4883; e info@iamat.org; www.iamat.org. A non-profit organisation with free membership that provides lists of English-speaking doctors abroad.

Canada
IAMAT (International Association for Medical Assistance to Travelers) Suite 1, 1287 St Clair Av W, Toronto, Ontario M6E 1B8; ☎ 416 652 0137; www.iamat.org

TMVC Suite 314, 1030 W Georgia St, Vancouver, BC V6E 2Y3; ☎ 905 648 1112; e info@tmvc.com; www.tmvc.com. One-stop medical clinic for all your international travel medicine & vaccination needs.

Australia and New Zealand
TMVC (Travel Doctors Group) ☎ 1300 65 88 44; www.tmvc.com.au. 22 clinics in Australia & New Zealand, including: *Auckland* Canterbury Arcade, 170 Queen St, Auckland; ☎ 9 373 3531; *Brisbane* 75a Astor Terrace, Spring Hill, Brisbane, QLD 4000; (07) 3815 6900; e brisbane@traveldoctor.com.au; *Melbourne* Dr Sonny Lau, 393 Little Bourke St, 2nd

Flr, Melbourne, VIC 3000; ☎ (03) 9935 8100; e melbourne@traveldoctor.com.au; *Sydney* Dr Mandy Hu, Dymocks Building, 7th Flr, 428 George St, Sydney, NSW 2000; ☎ (02) 9221 7133; f (02) 9221 8401
IAMAT PO Box 5049, Christchurch 5, New Zealand; www.iamat.org

South Africa
SAA-Netcare Travel Clinics e travelinfo@ netcare.co.za; www.travelclinic.co.za. Twelve clinics throughout South Africa.

TMVC NHC Health Centre, Cnr Beyers Naude & Waugh Northcliff ☎ 0 11 214 9030; e traveldoctor@wtmconline.com; www.traveldoctor.co.za. Consult the website for details of clinics.

Switzerland
IAMAT 57 Chemin des Voirets, 1212 Grand-Lancy, Geneva; e info@iamat.org; www.iamat.org

HEALTHCARE Uruguay's healthcare system is a mixture of private and socialised provision, with 48 non-profit healthcare bodies providing care to almost half the population through an insurance system. The rest of the population relies on facilities provided by the Ministry of Public Health and the University of the Republic, which also provide free emergency treatment to all. The Ministry of

Public Health also provides an effective system of care for mothers and babies, and for tackling outbreaks of diseases such as dengue fever.

Medical care is good but can be expensive; foreigners will usually be expected to pay cash, and arrange reimbursement from their insurer later. Travel insurance is essential, more so that you can be flown out if necessary. Pharmacies supply most internationally available medications, and the well-trained staff are able to supply most drugs, except for narcotics, without a doctor's prescription.

Expat residents can join a Uruguayan insurance scheme, paying US$55–100 for coverage including a private room; co-payments are just US$5 to see a doctor or for lab tests, from US$15 for an ambulance, or US$70 for a MRI.

FOOD AND WATER HYGIENE Standards of hygiene are generally high throughout Uruguay, but if you are in doubt bottled water is widely available.

RABIES Whilst rabies is not usually present in Uruguay it is in the neighbouring countries of Argentina and Brazil. Any bite, scratch or lick from any warm-blooded mammal should be treated as suspicious. Scrub the wound with soap and water, apply antiseptic and get medical care as soon as possible.

Practical Information **HEALTH**

2

SUN EXPOSURE People say that the ozone layer in Uruguay is thin, leading to increased risk of sunburn, but the problem is (ironically) more the lack of pollution in the air. In any case, you should wear a hat, keep your arms covered in the middle of the day, and use plenty of sunblock.

HIV/AIDS The HIV rate in Uruguay is three times that of the UK, with around 0.6% of the population having HIV or AIDS. If you must indulge in sex, use condoms or femidoms, which help reduce the risk of transmission. If you notice any genital ulcers or discharge, get treatment promptly since these increase the risk of acquiring HIV. If you do have unprotected sex, visit a clinic as soon as possible; this should be within 24 hours, or no later than 72 hours, for post-exposure prophylaxis.

OTHER MEDICAL MATTERS There's a high rate of oesophageal cancer in Uruguay and neighbouring regions, which has been linked to drinking *maté* – research suggests that the problem is not the tea itself but the high temperatures at which some people drink it.

Other problems associated with the beaches are jellyfish, especially Portuguese men-of-war (*fragata portuguesa, Physalia physalis*), increasingly common in 2009 due to the drought which reduced the water flow in the River Plate and allowed other currents to carry them in to the beaches. If stung, wash the contact zone with sea water (not drinking water), remove any remaining parts of the tentacles with gloves or tweezers (not a bare hand!), apply ice in a plastic bag for ten minutes or more, and take painkillers. Do not rub the area with a towel or sand.

SMOKING Not surprisingly with a doctor as president, and a cancer specialist at that, Uruguay has led the way in introducing some of the world's most effective controls on tobacco use. In 2006, smoking was banned in all enclosed public spaces, from shopping malls to restaurants, offices and buses. Coupled with measures to educate and persuade, this has caused the number of smokers to drop from a third of the population to less than a quarter, and President Tabaré Vásquez has been awarded the World Health Organisation's Director-General's award for his achievements. In May 2009 he raised taxes on cigarettes by 29%, so that a pack costs almost US$3 on average.

SAFETY

There's little casual crime in Uruguay, generally seen as an oasis of personal security in South America. Even so, you should take sensible precautions, especially in Montevideo. Avoid looking like a wealthy tourist: leave your jewellery and other such valuables at home. If you carry a bag in addition to your pack, never put it down: keep it under your arm or over your shoulder. Do not keep valuables in it: not only can it be snatched, but it can be picked, slit or slashed open. The same applies to a 'bum bag', although this is a handy way to carry a compact camera.

Divide your money and travellers' cheques between at least two different places, in your baggage and on your body. For your passport and cash reserves, use a money-belt, neck pouch or secret inside pocket. Alternatively, you can sew a hidden pocket into the front of your trousers or shorts. If your passport is too bulky to carry comfortably and safely, take some other form of identification, such as a driving licence or photocopies of the key pages of your passport. Keep the numbers of your travellers' cheques, passport, credit cards and flight itineraries separate from other valuables, so that if they are lost you can replace them more easily; it's also smart to leave them as a Hotmail or Yahoo! message to yourself. You can even scan or take digital photos of passports and flight itineraries and attach them to your email.

If you are robbed and wish to claim on insurance, ask the police for a copy of the official report (*la denuncia*); similarly in the case of a road accident ask for the *constancia*. Even though you presumably won't be around for the official ratification of the complaint in court, explain that you need it for insurance purposes; you may just be given a slip with a reference number and a few lines of explanation, which should be enough for your insurance company.

There were 109,000 reported thefts in 2007, making it the most common crime in Uruguay; but there's little violence and it's not something you're likely to notice at all. Where people in Argentina fear kidnappings, in Uruguay the worst that happens is petnapping.

See the box on page 69 for emergency telephone numbers.

DISABLED TRAVELLERS Facilities for the disabled are very limited, but there are signs of change – in Montevideo bus routes CA1 and 125 are fully accessible to wheelchairs, as is Plaza Independencia, according to signs posted there. Modern Antel phone centres are built to a standard design with ramped access.

There are special immigration desks for disabled travellers at the new Carrasco airport terminal, where there are good facilities for wheelchair users and others. Spa hotels (including those at the hot springs of the northwest) are more likely to have accessible rooms and facilities than other hotels.

GAY AND LESBIAN TRAVELLERS Montevideo doesn't have the kind of gay tourism scene now found in Buenos Aires, but it's a relaxed place, and there are various gay-only and gay-friendly clubs. A Plaza de Diversidad Sexual was created in 2005 (at Sarandí y Mitre, in Montevideo), and in 2008 Uruguay started allowing gay weddings, punished discrimination against gay couples, and allowed transsexuals to change their registered gender. In 2009 gays were allowed to join the military, and gay couples to adopt children.

Some gay men are of course still in the closet, but many, especially the young, are out, as Uruguay is a tolerant, laid-back country where religion has little power. Gay women seem more likely to stay in the closet at work but be out in their private lives.

For more information see www.alianzagayuruguay.com, www.outinuruguay.com (in English) or the blog http://uruguaydiverso.blogspot.com. A map of gay Montevideo is available (*La Lupa Libros, Bacacay 1318, Ciudad Vieja; www.friendlymap.com.uy*). There are at least two gay travel companies, Gay Uruguay, based in the US (*30 Woodland St, Suite 11-JK, Hartford CT 06105;* ℡ *860 246 7777, 1 877 987 8482 (TF);* e *info@gay-uruguay.com; www.gay-uruguay.com*) and Viajes Sunlight in Uruguay (e *info@ viajessunlight.com; www.viajessunlight.com*).

WHAT TO TAKE

Travelling in Uruguay requires pretty much whatever you'd take on a trip in Europe or North America, the only real proviso being to take plenty of sunblock and some long-sleeved clothing.

It's very useful to bring a small daypack, to use as a carry-on for long bus trips, or to leave things in a hotel while you're backpacking; in any case you invariably end up coming home with more luggage than you started with. A lightweight nylon bag with a lockable zip is ideal, or a stuff-sack for your sleeping bag can double up if need be.

Other useful items include pencils or ball-point pens, a notebook and paper, travel alarm clock, penknife (preferably a Swiss Army type), a few Ziploc plastic bags, a universal bath plug (or punctured squash-ball), a sewing kit (with heavy thread and needles for tent repairs), safety pins, clothes-pegs, dental floss (excellent for repairs, as well as teeth), toilet paper and a Latin-American Spanish dictionary or phrasebook.

$ MONEY

The Uruguayan peso (P in this book, though the usual symbol in Uruguay is $) is a stable currency, trading at about P23 to the US dollar, P36 to the pound sterling and P32 to the euro. The cheapest and easiest way to obtain pesos is from the ATMs (*bancomats*) found in virtually every town and airport. The major private banks all belong to the BanRed consortium (*www.banred.com.uy*), whose machines accept virtually all foreign cards; you can also pay with a debit card in shops through the BanRed system. ATMs with a Red Link label, in particular, work with cards bearing the international Plus and Cirrus logos.

The bank with most branches is the state-owned Banco del República Oriental del Uruguay (*BROU; www.bancorepublica.com.uy*). Crédit Uruguay, owned by the Spanish BBVA, is also widespread, along with Spain's Santander and Britain's HSBC and Lloyds TSB, and the American Citibank.

Credit cards (Visa and MasterCard above all) are widely accepted, in better hotels and restaurants and by car-rental companies and the better bus companies.

To change travellers' cheques you'll have to pay a commission of about 3%, or accept a differential rate which comes to the same thing. A few exchange offices (*casas de cambio*), mainly in Montevideo, will oblige, but as a rule you'll need a bank (see page 69 for bank opening hours). If you go to an American Express agent you can change your Amex cheques to US dollars without commission, then exchange the cash at a *cambio* as required. Exchange offices will take US dollars and Argentine pesos, and as a rule euros, sterling and Canadian dollars too. Other currencies may prove more difficult, especially outside Montevideo.

Unlike many of its neighbours, whose money bears the images of generals and presidents, Uruguay's banknotes perpetuate the memory of artistic and cultural luminaries. The lowest-denomination note, P5, bears the image of the painter Joaquín Torres García (1874–1949); the P10 note shows the economist and statesman Eduardo Acevedo Vásquez (1857–1948); the P20 note bears the poet and diplomat Juan Zorrilla de San Martín (1855–1931). On the P50 note is the educational reformer José Pedro Varela (1845–79), on the P100 note the composer Eduardo Fabini (1882–1950), on the P200 note the painter Pedro Figari (1861–1938), on the P500 note Alfredo Vásquez Acevedo (1844–1923), lawyer, academic and politician, and on the P1,000 note the poet Juana de Ibarbourou (1892–1979). There's also the rare P2,000 note, bearing the image of the priest and public figure Dámaso Antonio Larrañaga (1771–1848). At Montevideo's Numismatic Museum (see page 125) you can see all these and many other banknotes.

There are also coins worth P1, P2, P5 and P10; in theory a peso consists of 100 centésimos, although the P0.50 coin is being phased out. There's no lack of change, unlike in Argentina.

Lost American Express travellers' cheques should be reported to Turisport (*San José 930, Montevideo; \ 2 902 0829; Juan B Blanco 837, Local 1, Pocitos, Montevideo; \ 2 712 4797; or Edificio Torre Verona, Gorlero & 21, Punta del Este; \ 42 239226; www.turisport.com.uy*), and lost Thomas Cook travellers' cheques to (\ *000 413 598 2388*). Following are contact details for a lost credit card: Visa (\ *2 902 2200;*

www.visa.com); MasterCard (✆ 2 902 6800; www.mastercard.com); American Express (✆ 2 902 3942; www.americanexpress.com); Diners Club (✆ 2 902 6800; www.dinersclub.com).

BUDGETING

In the last few years Uruguay's currency has strengthened, so the country has become more expensive for foreign visitors. It does remain cheaper than Chile, though pricier than Argentina or Brazil, in general.

The cheapest hostel beds cost around US$12, but you can easily pay over US$100 a night for a good hotel. For food, you can shop in markets and supermarkets and use hostel kitchens, or you can plunge right in and enjoy great steaks every night. Thus it's possible to travel on a budget of just US$20 a day, or you can max out your credit cards. Buses cost about US$10 from Montevideo to Punta del Este or US$14 to Colonia. City buses cost about US$0.60.

A simple restaurant lunch should cost US$4–8, while dinner for two in a posh restaurant could run to US$22–50. A cinema ticket at the weekend costs US$4.50. A small beer is about US$2, and a litre about US$4. A loaf of bread or a litre of milk, or half a litre of petrol, will cost you about US$0.80.

Prices in resorts like Punta del Este fall sharply from April to December. Haggling is not part of the culture, although there may be some leeway in craft markets.

TIPPING In restaurants and hotels a tip (*propina*) of 10% is usual; taxi fares should be rounded up to the nearest peso, and a tip of about P10 is reasonable at filling stations and for tour guides. This is in addition to the IVA or *impuesto de valor agregado* (value-added tax), a levy of 22% on shopping and restaurant meals (10% on some basic goods and medicines). This is usually included in bills where relevant, although it's always sensible to check (*¿IVA incluido?*).

GETTING AROUND

🚗 **BY CAR** Uruguay has excellent infrastructure, with modern main roads (*rutas nacionales*) and bus stations; many minor roads (*caminos*) are unsurfaced but decently maintained. The main roads from Montevideo to Colonia and Punta del Este (Ruta 1 and the Ruta Interbalnearia, abbreviated to IB) are toll roads, and there are tolls on other main roads, often at departmental boundaries; these are fairly inexpensive at about US$2. Payment is accepted in Uruguayan or Argentine pesos, Brazilian reals or US dollars, but change is given only in Uruguayan pesos.

The major highways fan out from Montevideo and are numbered from west to east with single digits. The main route north from Montevideo (dual carriageway as far as Canelones) is Ruta 5; Ruta 6 is pretty minor, Ruta 7 and 8 cross at Melo and are the wrong way around to the north, ie: Ruta 7 runs to the east and Ruta 8 runs to the west. Along the coast, Ruta 10 only exists in isolated sections. The only routes to cross the country are Ruta 14 and Ruta 26, together with Ruta 11 which bypasses Montevideo. Early in 2009 the government announced a US$240 million investment in transport infrastructure, notably access to Montevideo airport and a new bypass just north of the city. Kilometre markers are placed alternately on the left and the right side of most roads. As in much of South America, there's an obsession with speed bumps (*lomadas*), which are often fierce and should be taken very slowly (if you're following a bus, in particular, expect it to almost stop).

Since 2007 it's been obligatory for all drivers and passengers to wear seat belts, and dipped headlights are required on main roads. The national speed limit is

2

Uruguayans once drove on the left-hand side of the road; this changed in 1946, as a near-bankrupt Britain lost its influence. Cars were not built in Uruguay and imports were heavily taxed. Thus drivers rarely replaced their vehicles and an amazing number of classic cars, known as **cachilas**, have survived, generally in pretty poor condition but kept working with ingenuity and persistence. In recent years these have been sought after by foreign collectors and enthusiasts, and many have been exported; this has also had the effect of making Uruguayans appreciate their highway heritage, and many are now being restored and used for Sunday best or displayed in museums. Television advertisements (especially in the US) purportedly set in Cuba are in fact often filmed in Uruguay, especially in Montevideo's Ciudad Vieja, thanks to the availability of these cars.

However, in 2007 *cachilas* ceased to be the only cars exported from Uruguay when Chery, the largest Chinese independent car-maker, opened a factory in Montevideo, producing Tiggo compact SUVs and QQ compact cars, mainly for export to Argentina and Brazil (they also produce bullet-proof cars here and plan to make cars that run on alternative fuels).

110km/h (68mph), although this is only permitted on a few main roads; elsewhere the maximum is 90km/h (56mph). The blood alcohol limit is zero, so don't even think of drinking and driving. Driving is on the right, and there's no right turn at red lights. Traffic gives way to vehicles on the LEFT – thus vehicles on roundabouts have priority. There are lots of scooters and small motorbikes on the roads, which tend to move surprisingly slowly; take care after dark in particular.

Uruguayan drivers are relaxed and patient, and driving standards are far higher than in Argentina – but in summer there are plenty of Argentine drivers, especially along the coast, some performing testosterone-charged stunts (overtaking on the inside, not stopping at crossings) and others just slightly lost.

Petrol (gasoline) is known as *nafta* and diesel as *gasoil*; the fuel alcohol that so many Brazilian cars run on is not available here.

Car crime is minimal, but you should take the usual precautions, at least in Montevideo – lock your car and don't leave valuables or documents visible. Parking is generally free except in the centre of Montevideo (see page 84); even cheap hotels tend to have some kind of secure parking available nearby.

Car rental The major international car rental chains are easily found, especially in Montevideo and Punta del Este, as well as good local companies which may well be cheaper. You'll need only a valid driving licence from your home country. A compact car with manual transmission will probably cost about US$40 a day or US$200 a week outside peak season, with unlimited mileage included, and also child seats if required. Automatics are rarer and much more expensive. Most companies offer a good range of vehicles from compacts to minibuses.

There are no one-way rentals except occasionally between Montevideo, Colonia and Punta del Este. Details of rental companies are given on page 84 for Montevideo (and at Carrasco airport), and in the accounts of other towns. See page 84 for details of taxis.

BY TRAIN There are very limited passenger train services, on just two lines in the Montevideo hinterland. Passenger services have been suspended altogether at various times in the past, and there are currently no Sunday trains. Fares are very low, but the service is too infrequent to be very useful, especially if you want to head out from Montevideo in the morning and back in the evening. However, special trains are put on for passengers from cruise ships visiting the Juanicó winery.

After decades of underinvestment, by 2000 the national freight network was in such poor condition that a maximum speed of 25km/h was imposed, making it even harder to compete for business. In 2003 the state railway company AFE (*www.afe.com.uy*) was restructured into separate infrastructure and operating divisions, to allow private investment and 'open-access' operators. The government was seeking US$56 million of private finance to upgrade the 1,114km core network from Montevideo to Rivera, Río Branco and Minas, as well as branches to Fray Bentos and Salto, to be paid back by payments from freight operators. The rationale was that booming timber production would increase freight traffic from 0.9 million to 1.2 million tonnes within two years, and that it would be cheaper to use the railways than to maintain the roads to cope with that level of traffic. No acceptable bids were received; in 2006 the private sector was invited to bid for a stake in a joint venture with AFE, again without success. Nevertheless the government has continued slowly with upgrading the main line to Brazil via Rivera, using rail supplied by Russia to pay its debts.

In Montevideo there are two railway heritage organisations that struggle to preserve old steam locomotives and carriages. The Círculo de Estudios Ferroviarios del Uruguay (*Railway Studies Circle of Uruguay;* e *cefu@adinet.com.uy; http://cefurailway.com*), at the Peñarol railway works in the northern suburbs, has two British-built Hawthorne-Leslie and Beyer-Peacock locomotives as well as a narrow-gauge German O&K locomotive. The Asociación Uruguaya Amigos del Riel (*Uruguayan Railfans Association; www.trenesavapor.com*) at the Bella Vista yard (nearer the centre, at Lorenzo Carnelli station) has a beautifully preserved Beyer-Peacock 2-6-0, built in Britain in 1910, plus two Dutch coaches from the 1950s, used for excursions for private groups.

BY BUS Being a relatively small country, Uruguay does not generally have separate systems of local and long-distance buses; most interurban buses will stop to pick up passengers who flag them down by the roadside. Standing passengers are allowed, but a point may come at which no more will be picked up. However, at busy times one departure will in fact consist of several buses leaving at the same time, some of which will omit stops at certain towns, as well as roadside pick-ups (check your ticket carefully to see which one you should be on). The bus number and destination are displayed in the front windscreen, often on a dot-matrix screen; middle-distance buses headed for Montevideo may show 'XXX' to represent Montevideo's Tres Cruces terminal, but longer-distance ones simply show 'Montevideo'. There are virtually no buses across the middle of the country – you'll almost always have to pass through Tres Cruces.

Buses are comfortable vehicles with reclining seats (Uruguayans do love to recline their seats at once, and as far back as possible) and good ventilation or air conditioning. There are no *cama* (bed) buses except on international services. They stick to a maximum of 90km/h, but given the country's straight open roads they manage pretty creditable average speeds.

It's often worth booking in advance, especially if you want to go to Punta del Este on a Friday afternoon. If the bus terminal is on the outskirts of town, bus companies will usually have a ticket office downtown. You'll be offered a choice of seats, or perhaps standing space (no cheaper) if the departure is full. Some companies have decent websites, but there's no online booking.

The driver's assistant handles money, tickets and baggage; he (never she) will usually tag your bags – keep the counterfoil to be checked when you get off. At larger terminals a baggage handler may load your bags – if you offer a tip it'll be assumed you're an Argentine tourist. A small departure fee is charged only at shared municipal terminals, as in Montevideo, Punta del Este and Mercedes; elsewhere buses usually leave from the company's own offices. These offices usually have basic toilets (take your own paper) and let you leave baggage for an hour or two; at larger terminals toilets will be better, and usually free, but you will have to pay to leave baggage.

&5% BY BICYCLE There's quite a lot of cycling in Uruguay but (apart from a few clubs of lycra-clad road racers with high-tech gear) it's very much of the popping-around-the-corner variety, almost always without panniers or lights. Most bikes are of the 'beach cruiser' type, with curved double top tubes designed to look a bit like a motorbike – some even have fake fuel tanks, to appeal to boys. There are a few mountain-bike-style machines, but they're really pretty cheap and not much use for serious cycling.

Cycle parking is limited, but given the low crime rate that's probably not a big issue; there are cycle lanes in places, mostly alongside main roads leading out of towns, but these are intermittent, generally unsigned and often with concrete blocks across half the lane at junctions. Touring cyclists looking to maintain a reasonable average speed will probably choose to ride on the main carriageway, which is generally safe given the courteous, laid-back attitude of Uruguayan drivers. The main highways have good shoulders – it's normal to see cyclists even alongside Ruta 5, the busy dual carriageway north from Montevideo to Canelones. Perhaps the most enjoyable touring is in Maldonado department, on Ruta 39 and Ruta 109 north from San Carlos and Rocha towards Aiguá, and the dirt road linking them that passes Cerro Catedral, the country's highest point (see page 220). Just west, in Rocha department, there's also good touring on Ruta 15 from Rocha to Velázquez and Lascano, returning to La Coronilla on the coast by Ruta 14. The coastal Ruta 10 in Maldonado and Rocha can also be pleasant if windy cycling (heading west is advisable), but it's not a continuous route.

Buses will carry bikes, but it's very much dependent on what else needs loading and on the mood of the driver – mention the bike as soon as you ask for your ticket. Trains also carry bikes, although this is only useful as a means of getting out of the greater Montevideo area.

Cycle racing was introduced to Uruguay by the Montevideo Cricket Club in 1888. The country's premium cycle race (the oldest in the continent, founded in 1939) is the Vuelta Ciclista del Uruguay. Held annually during Semana Santa (Easter Week), this covers a circuit of roughly 1,500km from Montevideo, returning there for a grand finish along Avenida 18 de Julio. Over 150 of the leading North and South American cyclists compete, some in national teams and some in sponsored commercial teams.

ACCOMMODATION

There's a good range of places to sleep in Uruguay, although the country does not have the cheap family-owned guesthouses or *residencials* found in neighbouring countries (in fact *residencial* here refers to a home for senior citizens). In Montevideo there's a very wide choice from international-class luxury hotels to real dives, as well as several hostels.

HOTELS Cheap hotels often have a choice of rooms with private (en-suite) bathrooms or with shared bathrooms down the corridor; in the latter case you'll probably have a basin in the bedroom, but the hot tap won't work. The showers, however, always produce very hot water, and are far better than the useless

Brazilian showerhead heaters. Check-out is usually at 10.00, with check-in from noon.

Better hotels usually claim at least one more star than they'd qualify for in the northern hemisphere – thus the many four-star hotels in Montevideo's Centro are really worth three stars at best. However, the luxury hotels around Punta del Este really are world-class.

Moves to stimulate the economy in 2009 included exemption for foreigners from IVA (Value-Added Tax) on hotel bills, as well as a 9% reduction on restaurant bills and car rental if paid by card. Whether these measures will be extended in future years remains to be seen.

MOTELS In a few small towns that are yet to see much tourism, municipal motels in fact consist of a few very simple rooms, perhaps on a campsite, with no additional services.

HOSTELS Some hostels are affiliated to Hostelling International (*national office, Paraguay 1212 & Canelones;* ⟍ *2 900 5749;* e *albergues@hosteluruguay.org; www.hosteluruguay.org*). There are similar backpackers hostels in Colonia, Punta del Este and elsewhere, plus a delightful old-fashioned rural hostel in Villa Serrana. You should bring your own towel if you plan to stay in hostels, plus a padlock for the lockers provided in most of them.

CAMPSITES Many Uruguayans use campsites for day use only (although they bring enough gear for a week's stay), but you should be able to camp overnight – there are 44 major campsites, all along the coast of the Atlantic and the Río Uruguay, that offer pretty decent facilities, although not luxury. These have chalets or *cabañas* for two to eight people, the larger ones with private bathrooms, that provide more comfort than a tent. In the smaller beach resorts there are many *cabañas* and cottages to rent – most Uruguayans just turn up and wing it, looking for *alquila* (for rent) signs, or they just call the number they call every year, but foreigners may need to use an agency.

Practical Information ACCOMMODATION

2

Although Uruguay is famed for its steak and other meat products (even better than Argentina's, at least according to the Uruguayans), there's also a great range of Italian dishes in almost all restaurants, which makes the country surprisingly welcoming to vegetarians (restaurants and bars are also now smoke-free). There's also a strong Spanish influence (especially in seafood, where the Basques excel), as well as Slav and Jewish influences.

The beef is of course grass-fed, with no corn or soya involved, and a year older than in the US – and you can taste the difference. Traditionally it's cooked on an *asado* grill, which is fuelled with wood, rather than charcoal as in Argentina.

In a bid to establish its carnivorous credentials, Uruguay staged the world's biggest barbecue in 2008, when 1,250 *asadors* cooked 12 tonnes (26,400lb – 50% more than the previous record) of meat on 1,500 separate *parrillas* (grills), and fed it to 20,000 hungry people.

A meal should begin with offal – *mollejas* (sweetbreads), intestines, chorizo sausage – although strangely gringos often choose to skip this stage, or to have grilled provolone cheese. Then comes the full **asado** or *parrillada*, a grilled selection of *lomo* (steak), chops, ribs and sausages (including *morcilla*, blood sausages), with some grilled chicken for light relief. Potatoes and bread are frowned upon as unnecessary distractions that just fill you up and distract you from the main mission of eating meat. A few peppers, yams and other vegetables are, however, grilled alongside the meat, and use of the ubiquitous and very tasty *chimichurri* sauce is also encouraged. Supposedly introduced by an Englishman called Jimmy Curry, this is like a spicy version of Italian pesto, made of finely chopped parsley, garlic, red pepper flakes, oil and vinegar, with other ingredients such as paprika (*pimentón dulce*), oregano, cumin and bay leaf (laurel) depending on the region. When you sit down in a restaurant you'll also usually be given a garlic mayonnaise dip with bread.

If this kind of assault course is not what you feel like, a lighter alternative is a **chivito**, which is really Uruguay's national dish, not found in the neighbouring countries. In Argentina a *chivito* is a young goat, as the name implies, but in Uruguay it's a sandwich of skirt steak, with lettuce, tomato, mozzarella, olives and mayonnaise, with possible extras such as fried egg, grilled peppers, beetroot, palm hearts, pickles and ham, served with chips (French fries). It can also be served *al plato*, on a bed of green salad and fries rather than bread, and with Russian salad and other veggies on the side – etiquette requires you to slice through it all and get a bit of everything on your fork. A *chivito canadiense* is served with bacon too. At the La Pasiva chain, in and around Montevideo, Colonia and Punta del Este, you'll get excellent *chivito*, as well

RESTAURANT PRICE CODES

Restaurant listings are laid out in decreasing price order, under the following categories: Luxury, Mid-range and Budget. The following key (also on the inside front cover) gives an indication of prices. Prices are based on the cost of a main meal (including tax) per person.

$$$$$	P400+	£13.30+	US$20+
$$$$	P240–400	£8–13.30	US$12–20
$$$	P150–240	£5–8	US$7.50–12
$$	P40–150	£1.33–5	US$2–7.50
$	<P40	<£1.33	<US$2

as a mystery sauce, in unlabelled plastic squeezy bottles on your table. It's supposedly a mixture of beer and flour, with an unknown secret ingredient.

Less iconic but still very popular is the **pancho** or hot dog, served in a Viennese roll with a choice of sauces; these are bought from *carritos*, the stainless steel trailers semi-permanently parked at street corners all over Montevideo and elsewhere. Alternatively, a chorizo sausage served in a bread roll is called a *choripán*, as in *chorizo y pan* (sausage and bread).

Another Uruguayan speciality is **pamplona de cerdo** or stuffed rolled pork (although chicken and beef can also be used), with meat wrapped around cheese, chopped olives, peppers and whatever else the chef fancies. The cheese is often very bland, but with something more interesting this can be a delight.

Other meat dishes include *milanesa* (steak in breadcrumbs), stews known as *estofado* and *puchero*, and *emapanadas*, like small Cornish pasties or turnovers filled with beef or ham and cheese, or with cheese and onion. An *empanada gallega* or Galician *empanada* is filled with fish, onion and green peppers. *Caprese* refers to any cheese and tomato filling, especially in *empanadas* or sandwiches, while an *Olímpico* is with tomato, egg, ham, cheese and lettuce, often as a double or club sandwich. In fact almost any type of sandwich, with the exception of the *caprese*, comes with compulsory ham. A *pascualina* is a Genoese pie of spinach and hard-boiled egg, which is a reliable vegetarian alternative in cafés and bars; you may also find *tortilla a la española* (with or without chorizo) or *tortilla de papas*, a quiche or omelette with potatoes. Other vegetables include mushrooms, grilled or caramelised sweet potatoes (yams), *zapallo* (pumpkin), which can taste much like sweet potato and is often served as purée or *mermelada*, and a local speciality, the *zapallito*, a small spherical green squash that's often used in pies and quiches.

A local speciality in some of the Atlantic coastal resorts of Rocha is **lechuga de mar** (sea lettuce; *Ulva fasciata, U. lactuca*), a seaweed served in omelettes (and also pies and *buñuelos* or fritters) that is said to contain ten times as much vitamin C as oranges and twice as much vitamin A as cabbage; it needs to be eaten very fresh.

All these meat dishes should not overshadow Uruguay's marvelous **seafood**, with both freshwater and saltwater fish as well as shellfish; all naturally go well with the local white wines.

Virtually every restaurant has a choice of **pasta** dishes, and probably pizza too – usually there'll be vegetarian options, but if not they'll easily knock something up. You'll often have a choice of pastas, often including gnocchi (spelt *ñoqui* here), and then a choice of sauces, such as *tuco* (the tomato sauce known as *sugo* in Italy), *filetto* (also a tomato sauce) or *caruso* (a Uruguayan speciality, made of cream, mushroom, ham and onion). *Sorrentinos* are an Argentine type of pasta, like large round ravioli filled with ham, mozzarella and perhaps ricotta and other cheeses too.

In better restaurants **pizza** is much as you'd expect, with a variety of toppings, but in snack-bars and take-aways it's rather different. It has a thicker, more bready crust, and is square, because of the shape of the *pala* or shovel used to take it in and out of the wood-fired oven – it's even available for sale by the metre in these places. It'll come with nothing but a tomato sauce, with garlic, onion, basil and oregano, that is sweeter than in Italy – if you want cheese, order a *muzarela* or *muza*, which costs twice as much and comes with a light stringy cheese that is less oily than real Italian mozzarella. In cheaper restaurants a 'pizza' is a snack based on a half baguette; if you want real pizza, you'll need to order *pizzeta*.

It's also traditional to order *faina*, a very thin chickpea pancake, topped with white pepper, that's derived from the Genoese *farinata*. *Muza* topped with *faina* is known as *pizza a caballo* (pizza on horseback).

Uruguayan ice cream is superb, but other **dairy products** are not amazing (with a few exceptions – see page 200). The Swiss of Colonia Suiza are particularly

MATÉ

If you're wondering why so many people seem to be carrying an oversized leather binocular case, it's not because they're dedicated birdwatchers but because they are afficionados of *maté*, the infusion of the leaves of the *Ilex paraguianensis* shrub to which many inhabitants of Uruguay and the neighbouring countries seem to be almost addicted. The case is the *matero*, containing a *thermo* or vacuum flask of hot water, a supply of *yerba maté* leaves (pronounced 'zherba mat-ay', at least in Uruguay), a gourd also known as a *maté* (from the Quechua for 'cup'), a silver straw called a *bombilla*, and an *escobilla* with which to clean the *bombilla*. *Maté* can also be drunk from a *pezuña* (cow's hoof) or *guampa* (bull's horn), but this is generally seen as affected. Whoever is in charge of the *thermo* fills the gourd with *maté* and hot water, drinks the first cup himself, adds more water, and passes it to the person on his left. He or she drinks and returns it for recharging, and so it continues to circulate clockwise. It may continue to circulate for hours, as the group relax, chat and watch the world go by. Unlike tea, *maté* does not get bitter when left brewing and can be topped up multiple times. Do not say 'thank you' until you have drunk your fill and don't want another refill; and never wash the gourd with soap. If the gourd is filled to overflowing, or with cold water, or just not filled immediately, this can be taken as a sign that your presence is not welcome.

There's an indefinable difference between Argentina, where you may get the impressions that people would happily drink *maté* for ever rather than risk going to work, and Uruguay, where *maté*-drinking seems more like a justified relaxation before or after getting on with the rest of one's life. The social rites of *maté*-drinking began with the Guaraní people and were then adopted and spread by the Jesuits; now you'll see people happily preparing *maté* on the beach in the hottest of weather, in bus stations, and whenever they're watching TV or hanging out with friends.

The *maté* should not be too hot (there's a possible link between hot *maté* and oesophageal cancer); if it's too bitter (and for some of us, it's always too bitter), wait until the gourd has been around a couple of times. In some places it's normal to take *maté* with sugar (*dulce*) but in Uruguay it's usually without (*amargo*); however, herbs such as mint, or orange or lemon peel, are sometimes added. It can also be found nowadays in teabags and in cans (toasted and sweetened, and drunk cold). In southern Brazil the *yerba* is finer and the gourds are bigger; it can also be made with cold water there (and is called *tereré*).

Yerba maté contains an alkaloid called matteine, very similar to caffeine, which makes one feel more alert and less hungry, but doesn't lead to jitteriness and palpitations; it's also said to ease the digestion and reduce blood pressure. It also contains useful doses of vitamins B1, B6 and C, calcium, phosphate, magnesium, sodium, potassium and iron.

associated with cheese-making, but it doesn't really live up to its reputation. *Dulce de leche*, the caramelised milk spread that's found across South America, is used in a range of typical pastries and desserts, such as *alfajores* (shortbread cookies with a filling of *dulce de leche*), or *chajá*, a dessert from Paysandú that consists of meringue, *dulce de leche* and peach. *Dulce de membrillo* is a quince jelly that's eaten with cheese in a dessert known as *Martín Fierro* after the gaucho hero.

The quintessential restaurant dessert is *flan* or crème caramel (usually *casero* or homemade), which can be served with *dulce de leche* on top. German strudel is popular, most often with an apple filling, while *budín inglés* (English pudding) is a fruit cake that's associated with Christmas and New Year's Eve.

Drinks The best bottled soft drinks are the Paso de los Toros line, produced in the town of the same name (see page 313). Virtually all cafés and restaurants also offer native herbal teas such as *boldo* and *manzanilla*; you may also find other *yuyos medicinales*, infusions of herbs such as *malva* (mallow) and *marcela* (*Achyrocline satureoides, A flaccida*), which is something like camomile, taken as a tea for digestive, gastrointestinal or menstrual disorders and as a sedative. *Marcela* is also said to be rich in antioxidants, so is more popular than ever, also being used in handcreams, for instance.

Uruguay's national drink (even more so than Argentina's) is, of course **maté**, the infusion of the leaves of *Ilex paraguariensis*, a shrub of the holly family (see the box opposite).

Uruguayan **wine** can be excellent (see page 135) and almost any restaurant will serve something decent. While it's red wine you need to go with steak, white wine is very popular, and is also served with orange juice (as *sangría*) and with apples, grapes and perhaps melon or pineapple (as *clericó*). Grappa (brandy) can be quite strong but is made much smoother with the addition of honey, the result being known as *grappamiel*.

Beer is of course widely available – *chopp* means draught, but generally refers to the basic lager-style beer, even if it comes in a bottle. Amber (or red) and dark beers may also be available. The most widely available beer is Pilsen (brewed in Montevideo since 1866), but it's usually possible to find the rather better Patricia (both are now owned by the global giant InBev), which comes in dark (*negra*) or light (*común*) varieties. Zillertal is another premium beer, harder to find and much more expensive than Patricia. The country's only craft beer or real ale is Mastra, which comes in Golden, Scotch Red Ale and Stout varieties, and is only found in a very few bars and upmarket supermarkets such as Tienda Inglesa.

PUBLIC HOLIDAYS AND FESTIVALS

1 January	New Year's Day
6 January	Epiphany (Día de los Reyes)
February/March	Carnival (the two days before Ash Wednesday)
February/March	Five days for Holy Week (dates vary from year to year)
19 April	Day of the Landing of the 33 Orientales
1 May	Labour Day
18 May	Battle of Las Piedras
19 June	Birthday of Artigas (also marking the end of the dictatorship)
18 July	Constitution Day
25 August	Independence Day
12 October	Columbus Day (Dia de la Raza)
2 November	All Saints
25 December	Christmas

A midweek holiday may be transferred to the preceding Monday or following Friday.

Christmas Eve (Nochebuena) and New Year's Eve are a time for partying, with large amounts of fizzy cider and *medio y medio* sprayed around at places like Montevideo's Mercado del Puerto. Fireworks are sold on the street, and let off at midnight; in addition water (to cool people down) and torn-up old calendars may be thrown from upper windows on New Year's Eve.

Christmas starts with fireworks at midnight on the 24th, followed by a family feast, ideally consisting of a whole lamb or piglet. Decorations appear just a week or so beforehand, and buses and shops operate fairly normally until early evening.

2

On Christmas Day nothing is open for most of the day except the main Antel call centres; some long-distance buses run from around 16.00, and by early evening some corner stores and petrol stations will be open.

Children get yet more presents for Epiphany (Día de los Reyes); the previous day shops are open as late as 02.00 for last-minute shopping, but there's only a Saturday bus service.

Easter Week (Semana Santa, or Semana del Turismo) marks the end of the holiday season, with one last rush to the beaches. There are fewer Europeans and North Americans sunning themselves at this season, and more Brazilians.

There are holidays more or less monthly through the autumn and winter. Since the 1970s the evening of 24 August has become known as La Noche de la Nostalgia (Nostalgia Night), when oldie records are played on the radio and in restaurants and bars, and people hold parties to dance to them regardless of age or usual tastes – it's remarkably popular. It's also an excuse to sleep through much of Independence Day (marking independence from Brazil in 1825) on 25 August. Resorts such as Punta del Este are pretty lively for the weekend nearest to Independence Day. The second Sunday of August is Children's Day, when kids get new toys, and events are laid on with music, clowns and bouncy castles.

September is the season of agricultural shows, other than the main one, La Rural, which is held in Montevideo's Prado Park over Easter Week.

The Dia de la Raza (known as Columbus Day in North America), on 12 October, celebrates (somewhat controversially) the union of the Spanish colonisers with the indigenous population, and the continuing links between Spain and Latin America.

SHOPPING

About 35–40% of food sales are in supermarkets, far less than in neighbouring countries where the level is over 70%; however, the rapid development of hypermarkets is likely to push this level upwards. Outside Montevideo in particular, food is largely bought in local private grocery stores.

Ta-Ta is a chain of high-street supermarkets, not to be confused with To To, a chain of shoe shops (or Si Si, selling women's swimwear and underwear, or the scarcely credible Tits, selling women's fashion). Equally misnamed is the Disco Group, which owns Disco supermarkets, Devoto and Géant hypermarkets, and the Fresh Market grocery supermarkets. Other supermarket chains include MultiAhorro and Tienda Inglesa ('English Shop', whose owners are indeed of English descent and have paid close attention to the methods of Tesco and Sainsbury's).

If you want to do something sensible like bringing a backpack to put your shopping in, you won't be allowed to – all bags have to be left in a locker, so you'll more or less have to use their plastic bags.

You'll find various craft markets and specialised shops in Montevideo (see page 106) and elsewhere – look out for leatherware, carved wood and bone, and knitting, in particular the *ruana,* a triangular shawl that opens at the front and is easier to take on and off indoors than a poncho. You might also want a pair of *alpargatas,* the espadrilles or canvas-topped shoes worn by the gauchos, which are also ideal for the beach. Another speciality is semi-precious stones, such as amethyst and agate, from Artigas, Rivera and Tacuarembó departments, which are sold mainly in their unfinished state as geodes or crystal stones, as well as cut and polished gems. They're believed in China to cleanse negative energy from a room, so a kilogram of stones, worth up to US$10 in Uruguay, can fetch as much as US$150 in China.

OPENING HOURS Business hours are from 09.00 to 18.00 Monday to Friday; shops are generally open from 09.00 or 09.30 to 19.00 or 19.30, and on Saturdays from 09.00 to 13.00. Malls and shopping centres are open daily from 10.00 to 22.00, and supermarkets and hypermarkets from between 07.30 and 08.30 (some only at 09.00 on Sundays) to 22.00. Banks are open from 13.00 to 17.00 Monday to Friday (although some now open at 11.00).

Dinner often doesn't start until 21.00 (although there's no problem getting served in restaurants from about 19.00), so it may be wise to take an early evening nap, and not to schedule meetings before 10.00.

Museums are very poor at showing their opening hours, especially when they're closed, and there are no standard hours – some open Monday to Friday, some daily except Mondays, and they may be open quite late into the evening; they're usually free (or almost).

COMMUNICATIONS

POST Uruguayans don't seem to use the postal service much – there are no letter boxes except in Correo offices, and these can be hard to find, many having been relocated from prestigious town-centre properties to anonymous shopfronts. For all locations – including many *farmacías* (with a Correo sign outside) – where you can buy stamps, visit the Correo website (*www.correo.com.uy*) and follow the *locales comerciales* link. Postcards and aerogrammes are also hard to find, although the main post office in Montevideo does have some cards with postage included in the cost.

TELEPHONES The national telephone company, Antel, which still has a monopoly on land lines, provides cardphones on the streets and plazas, and call centres (often several) in most towns. These have very non-standard opening times: for these, go to the Antel website (*www.antel.com.uy*), then click on *telefónia pública* and then on *ubicación* (under *telecentros*). You can buy a *tarjeta telefónica* (a phonecard, worth P25, P50, P100 or P200) at news kiosks or other small shops – make sure you do get an *Antel* card (the assumption is always that you want credit for an *Ancel* mobile phone). The main call centres are open even on Christmas Day, and currently charge from US$0.10 per minute for calls to Uruguayan land lines to US$0.30 per minute to North America and US$0.90 per minute to much of the rest of the world; they also offer internet access, at a slightly higher cost than the private *cibercentros*. These are efficient and easy to find, although there are complaints about the maximum 3 MB/sec speed, which limits the growth of teleworking and

---

USEFUL TELEPHONE NUMBERS

EMERGENCY
Police \ 911
Fire \ 104
Montevideo port emergency \ 106
Ambulance \ 105
Highway police \ 108

OTHER USEFUL NUMBERS
Time \ 16
Long-distance operator \ 120
Directory information \ 122
International operator \ 0007 (Latin America) or 0008 (rest of the world)

outsourcing. There are very few email providers; putting a company name in front of @adinet.com.uy will very often work.

MOBILE PHONES Antel provides mobile phone (cellphone) service through its Ancel brand, but it has been overtaken by Movistar (owned by the Spanish company Telefónica) which now has more customers, and slightly better coverage of the country. You can bring a tri-band GSM phone, or put your own SIM card into a local handset; if you bring in a phone you must register it with Customs (*Aduana*) on arrival, for a fee of US$6, which will then allow you to buy an Uruguayan SIM card and credit.

INTERNET Uruguay is giga-streets ahead of its neighbours in providing wireless internet access – not only do virtually all hostels and many hotels offer free Wi-Fi (*inalámbrica* – but *Wi-Fi* is always understood), but there's also a national policy of providing it on the main plazas of most towns and, in theory, at every school. You'll see children with cute little green-and-white XO laptops, provided under the government's Plan Ceibal (an acronym for 'Basic informatic educative connectivity for online learning' in Spanish), which will soon have distributed 220,000 of these Linux machines. In addition 50% of households now have a personal computer.

MEDIA

There are over 20 television channels (including the state-owned TV Nacional Uruguay), with many more available on cable, and over 100 radio stations (including the state-owned Radiodifusión Nacional SODRE). The main Montevideo daily newspapers are *El País*, *El Observador* and *La Republica*, all of a decent standard. Freedom of speech is well established; although laws against 'insulting the state' are still on the statute book, they are effectively out of use.

TRAVELLING POSITIVELY

As a fairly prosperous and peaceful country with no massive inequality of income, Uruguay is not an obvious target for charities and volunteers. Nevertheless there are things you can do if you want your stay in the country to be a positive exchange.

CRUZ ROJA URUGUAYA (*Uruguayan Red Cross; Avda 8 de Octubre 2990, 11600 Montevideo;* ✎ *2 480 2112;* e *cruzroja@adinet.com.uy; www.uruguay.cruzroja.org*) If you speak good Spanish, the Cruz accepts applications from volunteers 14.00–19.30 Monday to Friday (08.00–13.00 in January and February).

EL ABROJO (↘ *2 903 0144;* e *elabrojo@elabrojo.org.uy*) Works with street children in Las Piedras, a suburb of Montevideo, and volunteers are welcome.

POSADA AL SUR (*Pérez Castillano 1424, Montevideo;* ↘ *2 916 5287;* e *info@ posadaalsur.com.uy; www.posadaalsur.com.uy, www.retosalsur.org*) A self-styled B&B which focuses on sustainable and community tourism, working with local groups both in Montevideo (offering tours of the deprived but very colourful Barrio Sur and Palermo) and in Rocha, Río Negro and Tacuarembó. Taking these tours will support local tourism initiatives and suppliers of food and other services.

KARUMBÉ PROJECT (*D Murillo 6334, 11500 Montevideo;* ↘ *2 401 0101;* e *volkarumbe@adinet.com.uy; www.karumbe.org*) Help to study and protect sea turtles, sea lions and dolphins in Rocha. You'll spend time in boats and the water, and with local villagers, studying fishery practices and helping with workshops and other educational activities. You may also find yourself tending sick turtles or your fellow volunteers, cooking or cleaning as required. Volunteers are needed for periods of two weeks to a month. There's a fee of US$100 for every 15 days, plus US$18 per day for bed and board.

UN TECHO PARA MI PAÍS (*A Roof for My Country; Guayabo 1522, CP 11200 Montevideo;* ↘ *2 400 9545;* e *voluntarios@untechoparamipais.org.uy; www.untechoparamipais.org.uy*) This organisation nearly always requires a steady supply of strapping young labourers to build houses for the poor.

ACADEMIA URUGUAY (*Juan Carlos Gómez 1408, CP 11000 Montevideo;* ↘ *2 915 2496;* e *info@academiauruguay.com; www.academiauruguay.com*) This language school offers the possibility of doing voluntary work while studying Spanish in Montevideo, giving a full immersion in Uruguayan culture. You are asked to pay for a minimum of three weeks of classes (currently US$190 for 20 hours tuition a week), with at least four weeks on your voluntary project, and all payments to the charities or voluntary organisations will be made by the school. Possible tasks include working in a kitchen, bakery or radio station, teaching English, sports or computing skills, or childcare. The programme is also open to couples and families, and accommodation is available with families, groups of fellow volunteers, or in private apartments; there are also combined programmes with the academy's sister school in Buenos Aires.

ASOCIACIÓN NACIONAL DE ONG DE URUGUAY (*National Association of NGOs; Avda del Libertador 1985 esc 202;* ↘ *2 924 0812;* e *anong@anong.org.uy; www.anong.org.uy*) can put you in touch with a relevant group if you have some specific interests or needs.

You could also support two other conservation NGOs, to be found in Montevideo's Catholic Centre (*Canelones 1164*), although they don't have much

---

STUFF YOUR RUCKSACK

This simple idea, the brainchild of British TV presenter Kate Humble, basically consists of a website (*www.stuffyourrucksack.com*) where travellers can look up schools, charities and other organisations which may need items that can easily be stuffed into your rucksack before you go. Those arriving back from a destination where schools need books, orphanages need toys or charities need cash can also register these on the website.

need for foreign volunteers. **Vida Silvestre** (📞 *2 902 5853; http://vidasilvestre.org.uy;* ⏰ *15.00–20.00 Mon & Thu, 13.00–16.00 Wed*) puts on a monthly excursion open to all – a two/three-day hiking and camping trip, as a rule, with a guide and six to ten participants, to explore some wild area and observe nature. **Aves Uruguay** (*Birdlife Uruguay;* 📞 *2 092 8642;* e *gupeca@adinet.com.uy; www.avesuruguay.org.uy;* ⏰ *16.00–20.00 Mon–Fri*) also puts on a monthly trip, focused more on birdwatching, of course.

Part Two

THE GUIDE

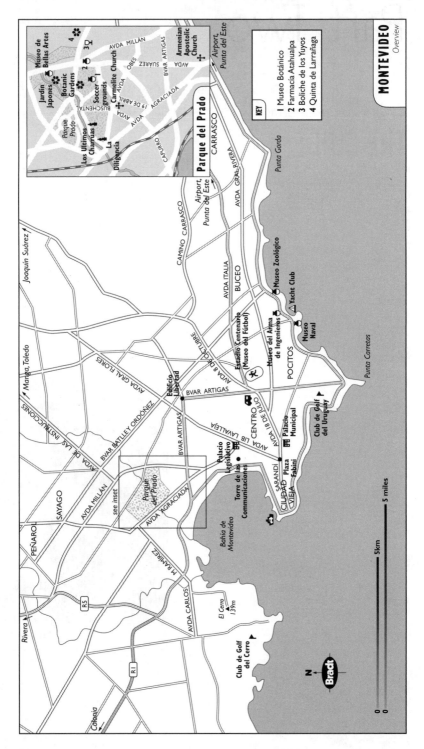

MONTEVIDEO
Overview

KEY
1 Museo Botánico
2 Farmacia Atahualpa
3 Boliche de los Yuyos
4 Quinta de Larrañaga

Parque del Prado

Museo de Bellas Artes
Jardín Japonés
Botanic Gardens
Soccer grounds
Carmelite Church
Armenian Apostolic Church
Los Últimos Charrúas
La Diligencia
Parque Prado
AVDA MILLÁN
AVDA SUÁREZ
OBES
BUSCHENTAL
19 DE ABRIL
AVDA AGRACIADA
AVDA ARTIGAS

Airport, Punta del Este
CARRASCO
Punta Gorda
CAMINO CARRASCO
AVDA ITALIA
AVDA GRAL RIVERA
BUCEO
Museo Zoológico
Yacht Club
Estadio Centenario (Museo del Fútbol)
Museo del Arma de Ingenieros
Museo Naval
POCITOS
Punta Carretas
AVDA 8 DE OCTUBRE
BVAR ARTIGAS
Edificio Libertad
AVDA GRAL FLORES
AVDA BATTLE ORDÓÑEZ
AVDA DE LAS INSTRUCCIONES
Manga, Toledo
Joaquín Suárez
AVDA LAVALLEJA
CENTRO
AVDA 18 DE JULIO
Palacio Municipal
Club de Golf del Uruguay
Palacio Legislativo
Torre de las Communicaciones
CIUDAD VIEJA
SARANDÍ
Plaza Fabini
see inset
Parque del Prado
AVDA MILLÁN
AVDA AGRACIADA
SAYAGO
PEÑAROL
Bahía de Montevideo
M RAMÍREZ
AVDA CARLOS
El Cerro 139m
Club de Golf del Cerro
Rivera
R5
R1
Colonia

N
Bradt

0   5km
0   5 miles

3

Montevideo

Uruguay's capital, indeed its only major city, sits on the estuary of the River Plate, with 13km of beaches linked by a waterfront boulevard known as the *rambla*. In fact one of South America's finest natural harbours is tucked away, half-forgotten, behind the old town. It's a delightfully laid-back, peaceful and friendly town where a normal working day seems like a sleepy Sunday morning in Buenos Aires, but it has all the services you'd expect plus a lively social and cultural scene. In fact in May 2009 the *Economist* magazine ranked Montevideo as the city with the best quality of life (for expats) in Latin America, and third-best in terms of infrastructure. The great Argentine poet Jorge Luis Borges wrote nostalgically of Montevideo:

> You are the Buenos Aires we once had,
> That slipped away quietly over the years.
> False door in time,
> Your streets contemplate a lighter past.

In an area of 525.5km² there's a population of some 1.33 million, or 1.67 million in the wider metropolitan area (in 2004). The city telephone numbers have recently changed from the original seven numbers (prefixed by '02' when called from outside the city) to eight numbers starting with 2 (from anywhere in Uruguay). As many as possible have been updated in this guide. There's useful information at the city council's website (*www.montevideo.gub.uy*).

HISTORY

In 1723 the Portuguese, already established in Colonia, decided to found a settlement at the equally fine natural harbour of Montevideo, but were driven away in January of 1724 by a Spanish force under the governor of Buenos Aires, Bruno Zabala, who began to construct fortifications on the site of the present Plaza Zabala and Palacio Taranco. The city of San Felipe y Santiago de Montevideo was officially founded in November 1726 with the arrival of 96 settlers from the Canary Islands (in fact they were preceded by six families from Buenos Aires), with a second group of Canariots arriving in 1729. In 1726 Pedro Millán distributed land to the settlers (including a certain Juan Antonio Artigas), but large sections of the original site on the tip of the peninsula were as usual reserved for a church and other official buildings on a plaza, plus a strong fortress. In January 1730 Zabala set up the first *cabildo* or council for the fast-growing town, the population of which reached around 7,000 by 1770 and close to 10,000 (perhaps a quarter black and mixed-race) by 1800.

On 3 February 1807 the British attacked the city; after several days of bombardment of the weakest part of the city wall (close to the present Anglican church), soldiers broke through and seized the cathedral, from the tower of which they were able to use their new-fangled rifles to great effect against the *ciudadela* (citadel), which was soon captured. The British occupation of Montevideo was amicable until their departure in September 1807.

In 1808 Napoleon invaded Spain and forced King Carlos IV to abdicate, putting his brother on the throne instead. The governor of Montevideo, Francisco Javier de Elío, pressured the French-born viceroy of the Plate, Santiago Liniers, to declare his loyalty to the Spanish crown, but he only issued an ambiguous statement. Accused of complicity with Napoleon by Elío and the *cabildo* of Buenos Aires, Liniers summoned Elío to Buenos Aires, replacing him with Juan Ángel de Michelena. The citizens of Montevideo backed Elío and called for a *cabildo abierto* or open council, which was held on 21 September 1808; Michelena fled and a royalist junta (ruling council) was set up, a crucial phase in the Banda Oriental's development of an identity separate to Buenos Aires. Only in May 1810 did the *criollo* people of Buenos Aires set up an autonomous junta, forcing the viceroy to move to Montevideo, which remained loyal to the crown. A second siege started in 1813, with the Spanish being driven from Montevideo in 1814 by the forces of

THE *GRAF SPEE*

At the start of World War II, the German navy sent the pocket battleship *Admiral Graf Spee* (one of the most modern ships built, with her electrically welded hull and diesel engines) to raid Allied merchant shipping in the South Atlantic, where she sank nine merchantmen, captured two and left one immobilised, while the Royal Navy scrambled desperately to find her. One of the merchant ships sunk off South Africa managed to get off a radio message first, and Commodore (later Admiral Sir) Henry Harwood correctly guessed the *Graf Spee* would head for the Plate estuary.

On 12 December 1939, 240km off the coast off Brazil, the *Graf Spee's* lookouts saw what they thought was a cruiser and two destroyers escorting a convoy, and she moved in to attack. In fact the destroyers were the light cruisers HMS *Ajax* (with Harwood aboard) and HMNZS *Achilles* (loaned by Britain to New Zealand, although around 40% of the crew were British), with the heavy cruiser HMS *Exeter*, and no convoy.

The next day the so-called battle of the River Plate (in fact well out into the Atlantic, 500km off Punta del Este), the first major naval battle of the World War II, left 36 Germans and 72 British and New Zealanders dead. The *Graf Spee* had six 11-inch (280mm) guns against the *Exeter's* six 8-inch (203mm) guns, which gave her a longer range and allowed her to do a lot of damage – but the *Ajax* and *Achilles*, each with eight 6-inch (152mm) guns, were able to come in on the other side and do enough damage to force the *Graf Spee* to break off and head for the temporary safety of Uruguayan waters. *Exeter* was crippled (having taken three hits, destroying two of her three gun turrets), but the two light cruisers shadowed the *Graf Spee* to Montevideo.

Captain Hans Langsdorff of the *Graf Spee* knew that he'd used up too much fuel and ammunition to be able to fight his way back to Germany for repairs; in addition, the British Minister in Montevideo, Sir Eugen Millington-Drake (also known as a playwright, and as father of Teddy Millington-Drake, artist and lover of Bruce Chatwin), was working hard spreading rumours about the British forces about to arrive. In fact HMS *Cumberland* had been refitting in the Falklands and had to steam flat-out to reach the Plate late on 14 December; and the aircraft-carrier *Ark Royal* was in Rio de Janeiro, 1,600km away. British skullduggery also slowed down the repairs to the *Graf Spee*; by international law she was only allowed to stay for 24 hours in a neutral port, although a presidential decree extended this to 72 hours. The German naval headquarters were pressing for Langsdorff to head out to sea and engage the British ships, but just before the deadline on the independent Buenos Aires, themselves driven out the next year by Rivera. Once Uruguay achieved independence in 1828, Montevideo became the national capital.

The British, who had helped bring about Uruguay's independence from Brazil, promoted Montevideo as an alternative port to Buenos Aires; in 1832 the *Beagle* was anchored there when a government minister was rowed to plead for help against the mutinying black troops. Fitzroy, Darwin and 50 men landed, armed with muskets and cutlasses, but the mutineers melted away. The British group spent the night in the *ciudadela*, cooking steaks, and returned to the ship in the morning with a sense of anticlimax.

The old city walls (with two gates north and south of the present Cabildo, historically open from dawn to sunset, with a wicket open until 20.00) gradually fell into disuse and were demolished. The city was blockaded throughout the Guerra Grande of 1843–51, but there was no actual assault. A rather more effective blockade of Buenos Aires was mounted by Uruguay's French and English allies, with the unexpected result that Montevideo flourished and became the major port of the Río de la Plata, boosted by the British-built railways after 1860. A new town (the present-day Centro) was laid out in 1829–33, but only actually built after

evening of 17 December he scuttled the *Graf Spee* a couple of miles off Punta Yeguas, immediately west of Montevideo.

The crew of over 1,000 men was taken to Buenos Aires, as Argentina was more sympathetic to Germany than was Uruguay (indeed, if Langsdorff had headed for La Plata rather than Montevideo, the outcome might have been rather different); they were interned for the duration of the war, although a few escaped and made it back to Germany. Many of those who remained ended up marrying and staying in Argentina after 1945.

Langsdorff shot himself in the head in his hotel room in Buenos Aires on 19 December; he remains widely respected as an honourable old-school officer who fought bravely but then refused to sacrifice the lives of his crew in a pointless battle – he also ensured that the crews of the merchantmen sunk by the *Graf Spee* were all taken off first, and that not one was killed. At the funeral, in Buenos Aires' Chacarita cemetery, of some of the Germans killed in the battle, when everyone else including the priests gave the Nazi salute, he pointedly gave the old naval salute. Other Germans were buried in Montevideo's Cementerio del Norte. Three sailors from the *Achilles* lie in the British Cemetery, while *Exeter's* dead were buried at sea.

The British merchant seamen held on the *Graf Spee* were released in Montevideo; her supply ship *Altmark*, with 299 others, set sail for Germany, passing through neutral Norwegian waters, where naval officers inspected her but failed to find the prisoners. Nevertheless, on 16 February 1940, the British destroyer HMS *Cossack* followed her in to the Jøssingfjord, where a boarding party seized the ship and rescued the prisoners. This incident may have brought forward the German invasion of Denmark and Norway, which took place on 9 April 1940.

The *Graf Spee* sank in shallow water, with most of her superstructure remaining above water; gradually she sank into the mud and sand until only her masthead was visible. Immediately after the battle British intelligence agents removed her radar equipment, and in 1997 one of the secondary gun mounts was removed and placed outside the naval museum (see page 129). In 2004 it was announced that the wreck was to be raised and moved to become a museum; the huge rangefinder was removed and is now at the entry to the port (see page 112) and in 2006 a bronze eagle was removed from the ship's stern (with its swastika wrapped in tarpaulin). It remains to be seen whether the ship herself can ever be moved.

1861, with wide, tree-lined streets and the new plazas Independencia and Cagancha. By 1867 development had crept beyond the present Palacio Municipal into the Cordón area, and in 1868 the Barrio Atahualpa was laid out near the Prado, until then an area of weekend retreats for the city's affluent citizens. It was only at the start of the 20th century that Avenida 18 de Julio became the city's main thoroughfare.

By 1860 the city's population had grown to almost 58,000; 30 years later it was 215,000 (at least half foreign-born), owing to mass immigration from Europe. This process continued through the 20th century, with large numbers of Italians and Spaniards, then French (and Basques), Poles, Lebanese, Armenians and Jews from all over eastern Europe bringing the great cultural diversity that still marks the city today. The British community was small but affluent and influential, being involved in trade and investment; in 1861 the Montevideo Cricket Club was founded and the same year put on the first rugby[sic] match outside Europe; in 1868 a cricket game against Buenos Aires was the first international cricket match in South America.

An earthquake in 1888 led to many houses being rebuilt around their own central patios (often covered with a glass roof), and the development of *conventillos* or tenements, with rooms occupied by families. Economic prosperity brought large public buildings in the Belle Epoque style, such as the Teatro Solis, Estación Central and Palacio Taranco, as well as grand hotels such as the Parque (by the Parque Rodó) and Carrasco; these were followed in the 1920s by the Palacio Salvo (still Montevideo's main landmark) and many Art Deco towers and apartment blocks include the Palacio Rinaldi and Palacio Díaz, as well as many very successful Art Deco houses, which carried on being built into the 1950s. In the 1930s came Bauhaus-style Modernism, with buildings such as the Edificio Lapido and the Bolsa de Comercio (Stock Exchange).

The first horse-drawn trams appeared in 1917, and motor buses in 1926. Construction of the riverside *ramblas*, one of the city's iconic features, began in 1916 with the Playa Ramírez–Pocitos section, followed from 1926 by the section west from there past the Barrio Sur (considerable areas of estuary being cut off and reclaimed), and the Rambla Gran Bretaña, to the east, in 1935. Avenida Agraciada, to the north, was built in 1927–35, and the Estadio Centenario was built for the first soccer World Cup in 1930, with the surrounding Parque Batlle opened in 1934 and the Palacio Municipal in 1941.

The motor car was taking over at this time (and some of those original cars can still be seen); the first traffic lights appeared on Avenida 18 de Julio (outside the Palacio Municipal) in 1953, and the last electric tram ran in 1956 (the No 9 from Punta Carretas to Estación Goes, as it happens). The Avenida 8 de Octubre tunnel was built in 1961, under the present Tres Cruces bus terminal (itself dating from 1994; until then, bus companies had individual offices on Plaza Cagancha).

There was a construction boom in the late 1970s, when modern buildings (some quite attractive) began to intrude on the main avenues; however, the military dictatorship also led to an exodus, particularly of younger people, giving a sense of stagnation that took a long time to dissipate altogether. Suburban sprawl has now spread across the whole department; the waterfront suburbs to the east of the city centre, as far as Carrasco, developed as weekend resorts for the city's affluent residents, but now, thanks to the development of the road system, are now their permanent homes (with their holiday homes now much further east, in Maldonado and Rocha). Since the 1980s large shopping malls and hypermarkets have appeared as the economy has prospered again, and a progressive council has pushed ahead with improvement projects.

The headquarters of Mercosur, the South American common market, was established here (in the former Hotel Parque) in 1997, and in 1998 the Teatro Solís closed for refurbishment, a process that finally ended ten years later. Also in 2008 the city inaugurated the largest park created in half a century, the Parque Andalucía, north of the centre by the Arroyo Miguelete. Tabaré Vásquez, president of Uruguay to 2010, was mayor of Montevideo from 1990 to 1995, and as a cancer doctor soon began the process of banning smoking on municipal property, which he continued as president.

CLIMATE

Being on the estuary of the River Plate (referred to as *el mar* or the sea), Montevideo has a more maritime version of the Uruguayan climate, ie: slightly warmer in winter and cooler in summer. In summer thunderstorms are common, and you may want a second layer of clothing in the evenings. Sea breezes bring relief from the daytime heat, but are less welcome in winter, when it can really get quite chilly (although there's really no need for the locals to wrap up as if they were in Siberia), and also foggy. There may be a couple of days with temperatures below 10°C (50°F), but they're usually followed by warm sunny days.

Average temperatures are 23°C in summer, 17° in spring, 18° in autumn and 12° in winter (when high humidity makes it feel colder). The average high and low temperatures in January are 28°C and 17°C, with a highest recorded maximum of 43°C; and 14°C and 6°C in July, with a minimum recorded of –4°C. Rainfall averages 950mm annually.

The river is often mud-coloured due to dirt but is fine to swim in, although this is not recommended for 24 hours after rain.

GETTING THERE

Naturally the capital is where most visitors to the country will arrive, chiefly by air or by ferry from Buenos Aires.

BY AIR Passenger traffic at the Carrasco airport [see *Southern Uruguay* map] (*code MVD;* ✆ *2 604 0272/0329; www.aic.com.uy*), 18km east of the centre, grew by 50% from 2003 to 2008, to 1.24 million passengers; fortunately a much larger new terminal (designed by the star architect Rafael Viñoly – see page 34) opened in October 2009. The sweeping curve of its roof seems to float above the departure level, with glazed walls on all four sides; above the departure level a terrace holds a restaurant and other commercial outlets, and arrivals also enter on a mezzanine before descending to the Immigration and baggage halls. It presumably has the free Wi-Fi, ATMs, exchange offices and car rental offices (Avis, Hertz and Europcar) found in the old terminal; the COT bus company has an office (✆ *2 409 4949; www.cot.com.uy*), with buses calling in on the way to Punta del Este and other places along the coast to the east. There's a tourist office (✆ *2 604 0329/86*), run by Canelones department, not the Ministry of Tourism or the city of Montevideo, but helpful and useful enough.

Departing passengers currently have to pay an airport fee of US$31, at the Pago de Tasas (Tax Payment) counter, in dollars or Uruguayan pesos, by cash or credit card; for the Puente Aéreo shuttle to Buenos Aires it's only US$17. The new terminal has cost US$134 million, so we'll be paying for a while. There's duty-free shopping on both arrival and departure; online check-in, not possible at the old terminal, is available in the new one.

Airport transport A taxi costs US$25–35 to the Centro or Ciudad Vieja (US$15 to Pocitos); it's cheaper to book a *remise* (see page 84) for about US$23 to the Centro. Buses currently cost P24 (US$1), with express city buses, notably the

D10 (which boasts Wi-Fi), and regional routes such as Nos 700, 701, 704, 710, 711 and 724 getting you into town pretty efficiently. These take about 30 minutes to the Tres Cruces bus terminal (US$1) and 10–15 minutes more to the Baltasar Brum terminal (*Galicia 911 & Río Branco*) on the north side of the Centro. They all take the busy Avenida Italia to Tres Cruces, except for the DM1 which runs (every 15 minutes) along the coastal *rambla* – a far more attractive introduction to the city, but only going as far as Pocitos, a lovely area but not where most visitors will be staying.

Some long-distance buses, operated by CUT and COPSA, call at the airport, taking you directly to Punta del Este or other places in the east of the country. However, there's little point taking these into the city, as the marginally faster journey is offset by their low frequency, higher fare (US$2–3) and the fact that they only go as far as the Tres Cruces terminal.

Heading out to the airport, regional buses leave from the Baltasar Brum terminal [111 E1], and pick up on Paysandú at its junctions with Río Negro and with Yaguarón, and on Muñoz by the Tres Cruces bus terminal [88–9 F1] (at the junction of Haedo and Acevedo).

Airline offices in Montevideo

✈ **Aerolíneas Argentinas** Plaza Independencia 749 bis; ✆ 2 902 3691, 2902 0828; e mvdrcar@aerolineas.com.uy; www.aerolineas.com.ar; ◷ 09.00–17.30 Mon–Fri; call centre (English spoken) ✆ 0810 222 86527, 4054 86527; ◷ 09.00–21.00 daily

✈ **Air France/KLM** Río Negro 1354; ✆ 2 902 5023/26; www.airfrance.com.uy

✈ **American Airlines** Sarandí 699 bis, Plaza Independencia; ✆ 2 916 3929; www.aa.com; ◷ 09.00–18.00 Mon–Fri, 10.00–13.00 Sat; Benito Blanco 1261, Pocitos; ✆ 2 708 5205; ◷ 11.00–19.00 Mon–Fri

✈ **Copa Airlines** World Trade Center, Luis Alberto de Herrera 1248, Local 028; ✆ 2 707 2672 (24 hours); www.copaair.com; ◷ 08.00–18.00 Mon–Fri, 08.00–12.00 Sat

✈ **Delta** Colonia 981, Oficina 201; ✆ 2 900 7776, 0004 05633; www.delta.com; ◷ 09.00–13.00, 14.00–18.00 Mon–Fri

✈ **Gol** Carrasco airport; ✆ 2 606 0901–3, free ✆ 00040 55127; www.voegol.com.br

✈ **Iberia** Colonia 975 near Herrera y Obes; ✆ 2 908 1032; www.iberia.com.uy; ◷ 09.00–17.30 Mon–Fri

✈ **LAN** Colonia 993, 4th Flr; ✆ 2 902 3881; www.lan.com

✈ **PLUNA** Colonia 1021; ✆ 2 902 1414, 00040 15000; e clientes@flypluna.com, info@pluna.aero; www.flypluna.com; ◷ 09.00–18.00 Mon–Fri; call centre ✆ 2 401 5000, ◷ 09.00–19.00 Mon–Fri, Sat, Sun & hols 09.00–18.00

✈ **Sol** Carrasco airport; ✆ 2 601 2072, 0004 0521 0053; www.sol.com.ar

✈ **TACA** Plaza Independencia 831, Oficina 807; call centre ✆ 00040 51004; www.taca.com

✈ **TAM Mercosur** Plaza Cagancha 1335 near Avda 18 de Julio, Oficina 804; ✆ 2 901 8451, 0004 0190223; e reservas@tam.com.uy; www.tam.com.uy

BY SEA The direct ferry from Buenos Aires operated by **Buquebus** docks at the port on the north side of the Ciudad Vieja (Old Town), where you'll find an attractive terminal [111 A1] with an ATM, Wi-Fi, phones and a café. Unless you get straight on to Buquebus's own connecting bus, you'll walk out between the big Aduana (Customs) building and the Ministry of Tourism, across the road from the Mercado del Puerto, two blocks from city bus stops. Buquebus also offers the cheaper option of going via Colonia, with their own bus direct to the port (see page 48).

Two other companies, **Colonia Express** and **SeaCat Colonia**, operate fast ferries from Buenos Aires to Colonia, with bus connections from the port direct to Montevideo and Punta del Este. **Trans Uruguay** offers a twice-daily Buenos Aires service starting with a three-hour bus journey to Carmelo for the ferry to Tigre and Cacciola Viajes. For all contact details see *By ferry*, under *Getting there* in *Chapter 2*, pages 48–50.

Cruise liners also dock in the port, by the Ciudad Vieja [111 A1], where you'll find the Isla de Información y Servicios (Cruise Service Island), with cafeteria, international phone and internet office, and another office renting mobile telephones and video and digital cameras. Cruise companies usually provide transfers from the dock to Plaza Independencia (between the old and new towns). Tourist police are stationed at the port exit, on the Peatonal Sarandí and in other popular areas (in the Ciudad Vieja and the Centro).

BY BUS Buses arrive in Montevideo at the modern Tres Cruces terminal [88–9 F1] (*Bvar Artigas 1825 at Dr Ferrer Serra, facing the end of Avda Italia;* ☎ *2 401 8998; www.trescruces.com.uy*), about 3km east of the Centro and 4km east of the Ciudad Vieja. It has clean, free toilets; ATMs; *guardería de equipajes* (*luggage storage; 2hrs free; with bus ticket, 24hrs free; without ticket, 4hrs US$1.50 to 12–24hrs US$3.80*); tourist information (*office T-12A;* ☎ *2 409 7399*); currency exchange (*Cambio Indumex;* ⊕ *06.00–24.00 daily*); post office (⊕ *09.00–22.00 Mon–Sat, 10.00–22.00 Sun*) and 24-hour phone and internet centres. It's underneath a shopping mall with a Ta-Ta supermarket and a choice of fast-foody restaurants including a 24-hour McDonald's. The terminal's excellent website gives information on all services, matched by the arrival and departure screens. There are also ticket desks for all the ferry companies to Buenos Aires.

You'll find a boarding fee of P5–16 (US$0.20–0.70) added to the cost of your ticket.

Transport to/from the city From the Tres Cruces terminal there are buses to all parts of the city. From a stop on Bulevar Artigas (by a statue of Rivera), route CA1 goes the length of Avenida 18 de Julio and the Ciudad Vieja (*every 6–10mins 07.30–21.20 Mon–Fri, 08.00–14.00 Sat, not Sun*); the modern, wheelchair-accessible buses cost just P8. From Ferrer Serra, on the south side of the terminal, Nos 21, 64, 180, 187, 188, 330, D9 and D10 run to the Ciudad Vieja via Avenida 18 de Julio and Plaza Independencia. Buses for Pocitos leave from the same stop as the CA1. Buses to and from the airport will also pick you up and set you down here.

A taxi to the Centro costs around P100.

Buses from Montevideo On some routes there are fewer services at weekends, but on others there will actually be more on Sundays, especially heading back to Montevideo in the evening. In summer there may be extra departures, or more commonly multiple buses for each departure, some *directo* and others handling intermediate traffic – be sure to check the number of your *coche*, printed along with your *asiento* (seat number) on your ticket.

The main companies have websites with timetables, but you can't yet book online. The Tres Cruces terminal's website (*www.trescruces.com.uy*) also includes a timetable. 'MDF' means 'not on Sundays or holidays'.

Fares are from mid-2009. Operators will often accept debit cards, but otherwise you'll have to pay cash.

Companies using Tres Cruces terminal include:

🚌 **Agencia Central (including Magic, Chadre, Sabelin)** office B17/18; ☎ 1717; www.agenciacentral.com.uy
🚌 **Bruno Hermanos** office B23B; ☎ 2 402 8212; www.brunohnos.com.uy
🚌 **CITA** office B11/12; ☎ 2 402 5425
🚌 **Copay** office B5; ☎ 2 402 7290
🚌 **COPSA** office B9; ☎ 1975; www.copsa.com.uy

🚌 **Corporacion** office B19; ☎ 2 402 1920
🚌 **COT (Compañia Oriental de Transporte)** office B15/15; ☎ 2 409 4949; e info@cot.com.uy; www.cot.com.uy
🚌 **COTA** office B19; ☎ 2 402 1920
🚌 **COTMI** office B5; ☎ 2 401 7443
🚌 **Cromin** office B10; ☎ 2 403 4657, 402 5451

🚌 **CTTM** office B17/18; ✆ 1717
🚌 **CUT** office B19; ✆ 2 402 1920
🚌 **Cynsa** office B13/14; ✆ 2 402 5363, 2 408 6670
🚌 **El Norteño** office B11/12; ✆ 2 402 1042;
www.bellaunion.com.uy/servicios/elnorteno.htm
🚌 **Emdal** office B23A; ✆ 2 409 0999, 2 408 9738, 2 409 0547
🚌 **Expreso Chago** office B23A; ✆ 2 409 0999/0547, 2 408 9738
🚌 **Expreso Minuano** office B8; ✆ 2 402 5075

🚌 **Intertur** office B23B; ✆ 2 401 7729, 2 409 7098
🚌 **Nossar** office B7; ✆ 1880; www.nossar.com
🚌 **Nuñez** office B13/14; ✆ 2 402 5363, 2 408 6670; www.nunez.com.uy
🚌 **Rutas del Plata** office B24; ✆ 2 402 5129, 2 409 7099
🚌 **Rutas del Sol** office B10; ✆ 2 403 4657, 2 402 5451
🚌 **Turil** office B21/22; ✆ 1990; www.turil.com.uy
🚌 **Turismar** office B23A; ✆ 2 409 0999/0547, 2

Companies using the regional Terminal Baltasar Brum include:
🚌 **CITA** ✆ 2 902 5466

🚌 **Cutcsa** ✆ 2 204 0000; ✉ cac@cutcsa.com.uy; www.cutcsa.com.uy

Major departures from Montevideo, leaving the Tres Cruces terminal:

🚌 **Artigas** (US$24; 7hr–7hr 50min) Corporación/CUT 1–2/day; Turil 2–3/day (1 non-stop)

🚌 **Bella Unión** (US$22; 8hr) Agencia Central (Chadre) 2/day via Colonia — 13hr; El Norteño 1–2/day (Sat–Sun/Mon–Fri)

🚌 **Canelones** (US$3.60; 1hr–1hr 10min) CITA 26–29/day (w/end/Mon–Fri); Turil 5/day (to Rivera)

🚌 **Carmelo** (US$9.50; 3hr–3hr 50min) Agencia Central (Chadre, Sabelin) 3–8/day (Sun/Mon–Fri); Intertur 3–5/day (Sun/Mon–Fri)

🚌 **Castillos** (US$10.70; 3hr 45min) COT 2/4/day (winter/summer); Cynsa 5/day; Rutas del Sol 6/day

🚌 **Chuy** (US$13.50; 4hr 45min–5hr) COT 4/day; Cynsa 4/day; Rutas del Sol 5/day

🚌 **Colonia** (US$7; 2hr 20min–2hr 45min) Chadre 2/day; COT 9–21/day (winter/summer); Turil 7–9/day

🚌 **Dolores** (US$10; 3hr 30min–5hr) Agencia Central (Chadre, Sabelin) 4–5/day (& 2/day via Colonia — 5hr 10min); Intertur 4–5/day

🚌 **Durazno** (US$7.40; 2hr 20min–2hr 50min) Agencia Central (Chadre/CTTM) 3/day; Bruno Hermanos 1–3/day; Nossar 7–10/day; Nuñez 2–3/day; Turil 3/day; Turismar 3–4/day

🚌 **Florida** (US$4; 1hr 30min–1hr 50min) Bruno Hermanos 1–3/day (to Durazno, Sarandí Grande); CITA 14–24/day (Sun/Mon–Fri); CTTM 2/day (to Durazno, San Gregorio de Polanco); Turismar 3/day (to Durazno)

🚌 **Fray Bentos** (US$12.30; 4hr–4hr 40min) Agencia Central (Chadre, Sabelin) 1/day (& 2/day via Colonia — 6hr 45min); CUT 5–8/day

🚌 **José Ignacio** (US$7.65; 3hr 15min) COPSA 2–3/day (winter/summer); COT 3/day via airport

🚌 **La Paloma** (US$9.50; 3hr 20min)/**La Pedrera** (US$10; 3hr 45min) COT 2–3/day (winter/summer); Cynsa 3–4/day (winter/summer); Rutas del Sol 2/day

🚌 **Maldonado** (US$6; 1hr 50min) COPSA 17–26/day (winter/summer); COT 19/day

🚌 **Melo** (US$16; 5hr–6hr 15min, also via Ruta 7, 6–7hr) COTA ; Cynsa/Nuñez 7/day (Ruta 8), 2/day (Ruta 7); Turil 2–4/day; Turismar (Emdal, Expreso Chago, Posada) 2–3/day (Ruta 7), 1/day (Ruta 8)

🚌 **Mercedes** (US$11; 3hr 40min) Agencia Central (Chadre, Sabelin) 6–8/day (& 2/day via Colonia — 6hr); CUT 6–8/day

🚌 **Minas** (US$4.80; 1hr 45min–2hr) Corporación (CUT, Grupo Carminatti) 9–11/day; Cromin 5/day; Cynsa/Nuñez 5–6/day; EGA 1/day (Mon–Fri); Emdal/Expreso Chago 2–3/day; Expreso Minuano 7–11/day; Rutas del Plata 2–4/day; Turil 2–3/day

🚌 **Pan de Azucár** (US$4; 1hr 25min) COT 5/day; Cynsa 6/day; Rutas del Sol 7/day

🚌 **Paso de los Toros** (US$10; 3hr–3hr 45min) CTTM 2/day; Nuñez 2–3/day; Nossar 3–4/day; Turil 3–5/day

🚌 **Paysandú** (US$15; 4hr 30min–5hr) Agencia Central (Chadre, Magic, Sabelin) 3/day via San José/Trinidad/Young, 2/day via Durazno/Trinidad/Young (& 2/day via Colonia 6hr); Copay 4/day; Nuñez 2/3/day

🚌 **Piriápolis** (US$4.30; 1hr 35min) COPSA 12/day; COT 14/day

🚌 **Punta del Diablo** (US$12; 4hr 15min) Cynsa 3–4/day (winter/summer); Rutas del Sol 3–5/day (winter/summer)

🚌 **Punta del Este** (US$6.20; 2hr) COPSA 18–27/day (winter/summer); COT 22/day via airport

🚌 **Río Branco** (US$17; 6hr –6hr 35min) Cynsa/Nuñez 2/day; Rutas del Plata 4/day

🚌 **Rivera** (US$20; 6hr–6hr 45min) Agencia Central (Sabelin) 3–4/day; Nossar 1/day; Nuñez 2–3/day; Turil 6/day (2 non-stop)

🚌 **Rocha** (US$8.35; 3hr) COT 5–6/day; Cynsa 7/day (8 Sun); Rutas del Sol 15/day

Salto (US$20; 5hr 30min–6hr 30min) Agencia Central (Chadre, Sabelin) 8/day (4 direct, 2 via Durazno; & 2 via Colonia – 7hr 20min);El Norteño 1/day; Nuñez 2–4/day (2 non stop, 2 via Trinidad/Young/Paysandú)

San Carlos (US$5.50; 2hr) COT 7/day; Cynsa 6–8/day (winter/summer); Rutas del Sol 8/day

San José (US$4; 1hr 20min–1hr 50min) Agencia Central 8/day (to Trinidad & Paysandú); CITA 17–34/day (Sun/Mon–Fri); Copay 4/day; COTMI 11–16/day (Sun/Mon–Fri)

Tacuarembó (US$15.50; 4hr 30min–5hr) Agencia Central (Chadre) 4/day; Dalfa 1/day; Nuñez 2–3/day; Turil 6–8/day

Treinta y Tres (US$11.50; 4–5hr) Cynsa/Nuñez 9–11/day; EGA 2–3/day; Expreso Minuano 1–2/day; Rutas del Plata 2–4/day; Turil 2–4/day

Trinidad (US$8; 2hr 20min–3hr) Agencia Central (Chadre, ETA, Sabelin) 6/day; Copay 4/day (to Paysandú); El Norteño 1/day (to Salto/Bella Unión); Nossar 2/day; Nuñez 2–3/day (to Salto)

Valizas/Cabo Polonio (US$11; 4hr 40min) COT 1/day (summer only); Cynsa 1/day; Rutas del Sol 5–8/day (winter/summer)

BY RAIL Train travel is almost non-existent in Uruguay, with just a limited commuter service on two lines north of Montevideo. (A line along the coast east from the city would be very useful, but sadly doesn't exist.) Passenger services have been suspended altogether at various times in the past, and there are currently no Sunday trains. Fares are very low, but the service is too infrequent to be very useful, especially if you want to head out from Montevideo in the morning and back in the evening.

Montevideo's Central station was closed in 2004, when it was sold to a state-owned bank (at a low price) for a controversial development project which hasn't yet begun; a modern but much smaller station was provided 500m north. Frequent buses pass the new station, but many passengers declared they would not travel the extra distance to their workplaces, and train loadings may be as much as a third lower than before the closure.

From the fiercely air-conditioned modern station [88–9 C1] (📞 2 924 8080; e afepasajeros@adinet.com.uy; www.afe.com.uy) trains run four times a day (three times on Saturdays) to Sudriers via Peñarol, Toledo and Suárez; and five times a day Monday to Friday (four on Saturdays) to 25 de Agosto, one continuing to San José and one to San José and Florida, plus one only as far as Canelones.

GETTING AROUND

BY BUS An efficient bus network (www.montevideo.gub.uy/stm) reaches every corner of Montevideo, although there are no trams or metro. The system is being modernised, with smartcards replacing conductors; a card is already in use on some suburban buses, although you can still pay cash. The most useful innovation so far is the CA1 service, introduced at the end of 2008, with modern, low-emission, wheelchair-accessible buses with large baggage racks shuttling every 6–10 minutes between the Ciudad Vieja, the Centro and the Tres Cruces bus terminal [88–9 F1] (🕐 07.30–21.10 Mon–Fri, 08.00–14.00 Sat).

Drivers have no Formula One fantasies (and all wear seatbelts), unlike in neighbouring countries.

Buses start running between 04.35 and 06.15, and finish between 22.30 and midnight, with some services running hourly through the night. Any bus for Aduana, Ciudad Vieja or Ciudadela will get you to the Ciudad Vieja. The standard ticket or viaje común rose to P15 (US$0.65) at the start of 2009; it's valid for one hour, with one transfer on a bus of the same company that sold you the ticket. A viaje zonal, costing P8, is valid for most shorter journeys, including anything between the Ciudad Vieja, the Centro and Tres Cruces, and only on that one bus. Diferencial or metropolitano tickets, costing P20, are valid for express and longer-distance buses, or for two hours' unlimited travel; and it's P24 to the airport. Suburban buses use stops marked with a green 'S'.

There's free Wi-Fi on route D10, from the Centro (*Avenida 18 de Julio*) to the airport, with plans to extend this to other routes.

BY TAXI There are plenty of black-and-yellow taxis, either waiting at street corners or cruising, with reliable meters producing a figure that needs to be decoded from a laminated price sheet. Taxis are safe and affordable (though fares are higher late at night and at weekends); the only time you might want to agree the fare in advance is when heading for the airport. There's no need to tip, but rounding up a little bit is appreciated.

To call a taxi, phone Radio Taxi 141 (✆ *141*), Radio Taxi Cooperativa (✆ *2 311 1030*), Radio Taxi Scot (✆ *2 208 0810*) or Fono Taxi (✆ *2 203 7000*).

It's also possible to book a *remise* (car with driver), for day tours or a cheaper transfer to the airport – companies include Remises Montevideo (*San Jose 1226 bis;* ✆ *2 902 8844, 2 900 0015; 24hr* m *9962 8725;* e *remis@adinet.com.uy*), Independencia Remises (*Colonia 807;* ✆ *2 902 6766*), Remises Carrasco (✆ *2 606 1412; 24hr* m *9440 5473;* e *info@remisescarrasco.com.uy; www.remisescarrasco.com.uy*), Remises La Española (✆ *2 622 2323*), Remises Pocitos (*26 de Marzo 1269;* ✆ *2 707 1807*) and Remises Tres Cruces (✆ *2 401 8241*). *Remises* charge around US$10–12 per hour, or a little more if booked through a hotel or if going outside Montevideo department.

BY CAR Driving in Montevideo is easy and relaxed by Latin American standards, with the usual grid of one-way streets. The *ramblas* are usually the easiest way to get to the east and north of the city, with a speed of 75km/h allowed in places. Parking in the Ciudad Vieja and the Centro must be paid for Monday to Friday (⊕ *10.00–18.00*), with tickets bought from shops; there's a free day once a month, which causes a degree of chaos.

There are several 24-hour filling stations on Avenida Italia, one on Artigas at Echevería, and various others.

Car rental

🚗 **Americar** Sarandí 443 & Misiones; ✆ 0800 8339, 2 902 2949; 24hr m 9970 4289; e americar@ebicarmotors.com; www.ebicarmotors.com

🚗 **America Rentacar** 21 de Septiembre 2784 bis; ✆ 2 710 2886

🚗 **Avis** Avda Uruguay 1417; ✆ 1700, 2 903 0303; ⊕ 09.00–19.00 Mon–Fri, 09.00–13.00 Sat; Carrasco airport; ✆ 2 604 0334; e avis@avis.com.uy; www.avis.com.uy; ⊕ 24hrs

🚗 **Budget** Ellauri 350, Local 1; ✆ 2 712 2020; e budget@budget.com.uy; www.budget.com.uy

🚗 **Dollar** Ruta 101, Carrasco (200m from airport); ✆ 2 682 8350; 24hr m 9443 4937; e dollarpdp@adinet.com.uy; www.dollar.com.uy

🚗 **Europcar** Bvar Artigas 1875, Tres Cruces; ✆ 2 401 0575; 24hr m 9440 4570; Carrasco airport; ✆ 2 604 0350; e reservas@europcar.com.uy; www.europcar.com.uy

🚗 **Federal Car Rental** Paysandú 1570; ✆ 2 409 2737/2759, m 9644 3688; e reservas@federal.com.uy; Carrasco airport (Esso filling station); ✆ 2 682 4772; m 9618 3209; e aeropuerto@federal.com.uy; www.federal.com.uy

🚗 **Fedmik Rentacar** Avda Parque Roosevelt 67; ✆ 2 600 3765; www.fedmik.com

🚗 **Hertz** Guipuzcoa 404; ✆ 2 712 5000; ⊕ 09.00–19.00 Mon–Fri, 09.00–13.00 Sat; Carrasco airport; ✆ 2 604 0006, 2606 1137; e info@hertz.com.uy; ⊕ 07.00–23.00 daily; www.hertz.com

🚗 **Multicar** Asencio 1277, between Yí & Cuareim; ✆ 2 902 2555; m 9966 0959; ⊕ 09.00–19.00 Mon–Fri, 09.00–13.30 Sat; Colonia 1227, between Zapicán & Enrique Martínez; ✆ 2 204 0878; m 9430 7048; Francisco Bonilla (200m from Carrasco airport/Ruta 101); ✆ 2 682 2707; m 9966 0959; www.redmulticar.com

🚗 **Palermo Rentacar** Ramírez 1382; ✆ 2 908 7432; e info@palermorentacar.com.uy; www.palermorentacar.com.uy

🚗 **Power Rentacar** Avda Italia 3394; m 9436 0400; e franciscoperez@power-rent-a-car.com

🚗 **Rally Rentacar** Avda Brasil 2917 bis; ✆ 2 707 3910; e consultas@rallyrentacar.com.uy; www.rallyrentacar.com.uy

🚗 **Rentacar Del Río** Germán Barbato 1431, between Mercedes & Colonia; ✆ 2 908 4140

🚗 **Rentautos** Marcelino Sosa 2222; ✆ 2 203 7080; e rentautosmvd@hotmail.com

🚗 **Snappy Car Rental** Andes 1363, Local 17 & 18 de Julio; ✆ 2 900 7728, 2 901 6588; m 9966

0660; e gerencia@snappy.com.uy; www.snappy.com.uy

🚗 **Sudancar** Acevedo Díaz 1813, Tres Cruces; ✆ 2 402 6616/20; 24hr m 9962 7607; e info@sudancar.com.uy; www.sudancar.com.uy

🚗 **Thrifty** Bvar Artigas 2966, Tres Cruces; ✆ 0800 8278 (08.00–22.00 daily), 2 481 8170; e thrifty@thrifty.com.uy; Ruta 101, Carrasco (200m from airport); ✆ 2 682 4495; www.thrifty.com.uy

BY BICYCLE Cycling is relatively civilised in Montevideo, thanks to the courteous local drivers. In any case the best excursion is traffic-free, alongside the *rambla*, which stretches 22km along the seafront from the Escollera Sarandí to the Puente Carrasco. In its busier parts this has a segregated cycle track, while elsewhere cyclists and pedestrians (and a few rollerbladers) share the same space. There's a gravel track alongside the outer stretch of Avenida Italia; there are also quite a few cyclists on Ruta 5, the main dual carriageway north from Montevideo, both lycra-clad club riders and locals on shopper bikes.

There are few bike rental outlets; if your hostel or hotel doesn't offer bikes, try Uruguay Rent A Bike (m *9916 5213, 9947 3521*) which has a range of leisure, mountain and children's bikes and will deliver them to you, along with helmet and lock. They also offer tours. The Centro de Investigación y Promoción de la Bicicleta en Uruguay (*www.urubike.com*) is a pressure group which organises some group rides; in August 2009 they inaugurated a *bicipunto* at the Punta Carretas ANCAP station (*Rambla & Bulevar Artigas*), a sort of DIY maintenance/repair facility.

Bicicletería Sur (*Aquiles Lanza 1100 & Durazno;* ⊕ *09.00–13.00, 15.00–19.00 Mon–Fri, 09.00–15.00 Sat*) mostly undertakes scooter repairs, but does also offer bike rental for P20 per hour, although the bikes are not very sophisticated.

La Clínica de Bicicletas (*Maldonado 1701 & Magellanes;* ⊕ *09.00–20.00 Mon–Sat*) is good for repairs, and GT Bicycles (*Barreiro 3225, Pocitos*) is a good modern bike shop.

ORIENTATION

The **Ciudad Vieja** or old city of Montevideo sits on a peninsula south of the port. The financial district is here, and is very lively in the daytime, but the rest of the old city is now somewhat run-down and not particularly safe at night, although regeneration projects aim to turn this around, and the city's liveliest bars are also found here. Beyond Plaza Independencia [111 D2], and the landmark tower of the Palacio Salvo [111 D2], is the **Centro**, often described as 'downtown', a lively area of shops, offices and hotels on either side of Avenida 18 de Julio, the city's main axis. To the south are the residential districts of the **Barrio Sur** and **Palermo**, once home to the middle class (with some fine Art Deco houses) but now a poorer area with many Afro-Uruguayan residents. Beyond the Intendencia or Palacio Municipal (City Hall) [111 G2], 18 de Julio continues through Cordón, a mixed district of shops and apartments, to **Tres Cruces**, where the bus terminal [88–9 F1] sits opposite the start of Avenida Italia, the main highway east to the airport and the beach resorts. Just a few blocks east, this passes Parque Batlle [88–9 G1], site of the Estadio Centenario, the stadium built for the first soccer World Cup.

The bus terminal is also on Bulevar Artigas, leading north towards the north and west of the country and south to the headland of Punta Carretas, passing Parque

Rodó [88–9 F4] and the even more luxuriant golf club [88–9 F5]. On the coast to the east of Punta Carretas is **Pocitos**, a very agreeable residential area with plenty of good restaurants and pubs and enjoyable streetlife. There's a fine beach here [88–9 H4], lined with a row of uniform, middle-class apartment blocks; property isn't as expensive as in the more exclusive suburbs along the coast to the east, but here people actually walk to local shops and restaurants rather than driving everywhere. To the east are Buceo, Malvín and Punta Gorda, desirable suburbs with bungalows and villas nearer the waterfront, and denser housing inland. The city ends with Carrasco, its wealthiest suburb, handy for the airport and with some fine restaurants.

A riverside boulevard known as the Rambla runs for 22km along the shore of the River Plate, from the Escollera Sarandí, the breakwater that juts like a narwhal's horn from the end of the Ciudad Vieja peninsula, to the Puente Carrasco, the bridge that marks the end of the city (and of Montevideo department), although the coastline is built-up for a long way further east, beyond the resort of Atlántida. In the other direction the Rambla continues as a busy highway past the docks, brewery and oil refinery to the west and north of the country.

To the north of the centre, the Legislative Palace [88–9 D1] sits on a small hill in the **Aguada** district to the east of the modern railway station [88–9 C1] and the soaring modern Torre de las Communicaciones (Communications Tower) [88–9 C1]; beyond here are mainly poorer residential districts, surrounding the Prado, where the country's élite had first their weekend homes and then (once public transport was available) their permanent residences, in park-like gardens, many of which still exist. In addition, the Jardín Botánico (Botanic Garden), Parque del Prado (Prado Park) and Museo de Bellas Artes (Art Museum) are in this neighbourhood.

The city is not totally flat but it's still pretty easy to walk (or cycle) around, and there are no no-go areas (although a few places are less safe after dark – see page 109). The city's main squares all have two names, one official and one that is generally used because of a building or statue found there, eg: Plaza Constitución/Matriz, Plaza Independencia/Artigas, Plaza Fabini/Entrevero, Plaza Libertad/Cagancha and Plaza Treinta y Tres/Lavalleja (also known as Plaza Bomberos). The southern half of Calle Yaguarón is now Aquiles Lanza, but is still better known as 'Shaguarón'; and Cuareim is now Michelini. Building numbers are not matched to city blocks, ie: No 301 will probably not be on the corner of the third block up the street; *piso* means floor.

TOURIST INFORMATION

There's a tourist information office (✆ *2 604 0329/86*), run by Canelones department, at the airport, and an Uruguay Natural (Ministry of Tourism) office (✆ *2 409 7399*) at the Tres Cruces bus terminal.

In the Ciudad Vieja, there's a good municipal tourist information centre [88–9 F1] (*Rambla 25 de Agosto & Maciel, by the Mercado del Puerto;* ✆ *2 916 8434;* e *imminfotour@gmail.com;* ⊕ *daily 11.00–17.00*) next to the Museo del Carnaval. Across the *rambla* by the entry to the port, the Ministry of Tourism (✆ *2 188 5100*) has an information desk [111 B2] (✆ *1885 or 2 188 5111;* ⊕ *09.00–18.30 Mon–Fri; www.turismo.gub.uy, www.uruguaynatural.com*) in the former Depósito Santos warehouse. Inside the port there's also the Isla de Información y Servicios (*Cruise Service Island, open when cruise ships are in port*), with staff speaking English, Spanish and Portuguese.

In the Centro there's a municipal information kiosk [111 G2] (*18 de Julio at Ejido, in the foyer of the Palacio Municipal;* ✆ *1950 or 1830*) and one run by the Policía Turística [111 G2] (*in PLUNA airline office, Colonia 1021;* ✆ *2 901 9102, 2 403 0026*).

As in much of Latin America, many streets are named after dates, for example:

19 de Abril	The landing of the *Treinta y Tres Orientales* (33 Uruguayans) in 1825
18 de Mayo	The battle of Las Piedras in 1811, a crucial battle in the struggle for independence
25 de Mayo	The overthrow of the viceroy in Buenos Aires in the Semana de Mayo, 1810
19 de Junio	The birth of Artigas in 1764
18 de Julio	The swearing of the constitution in 1830
25 de Agosto	The declaration of Independence in 1825
21 de Septiembre	The *cabildo abierto* or open council of 1808

Other streets are named after places, mainly battlefields, such as **Ituzaingó** (an Argentine–Uruguayan victory over Brazil in 20 February 1827) and **Sarandí** (Lavalleja's victory over Brazil on 12 October 1825); the **Arenal Grande** was the stream on the north side of the Playa Agraciada (Lucky Beach) where Lavalleja (*El libertador*, as distinct from Artigas, *El procer*) landed with his 32 companions on 19 April

City maps can be bought for about US$5 at some news kiosks, but the standard free handout map will be fine for the area between the Ciudad Vieja, Pocitos and Tres Cruces (but not for the Prado).

WHERE TO STAY

LUXURY
Ciudad Vieja
⌂ **Radisson Montevideo Victoria Plaza** [111 D2] Plaza Independencia 759; ✆ 2 902 0111; e reservas@radisson.com.uy; www.radisson.com/montevideouy. In a great location right between old & new towns, this towering block is known for its fine restaurant on the 25th floor, with views over the harbour. It also has a huge foyer with pianist & original art, a fine ballroom, spa & a large casino. Rooms are spacious with all those 5-star fitments, & service is excellent. $$$$$

Centro
⌂ **Four Points by Sheraton** [111 G2] Ejido 1275 near San José; ✆ 2 901 7000; www.fourpoints.com/montevideo. Next to the Palacio Municipal & by far the best hotel in the Centro; clean modern styling with non-smoking rooms, indoor swimming pool & attractive café-restaurant. $$$$$

Punta Carretas
⌂ **Cala di Volpe** [88–9 G5] Rambla Mahatma Gandhi & Parva Domus; ✆ 2 710 2000; e hotel@hotelcaladivolpe.com.uy; www.hotelcaladivolpe.com.uy. A self-proclaimed boutique hotel (although a 12-storey tower doesn't really seem boutique-sized), this is in fact a good modern hotel, worth 4 stars in most parts of the world. Good views of the Río de la Plata. $$$$$
⌂ **Meliá Confort** [88–9 G5] Héctor Miranda 2361; ✆ 2 710 3800; e meliamvd@confort.com.uy; www.solmelia.com. On a quiet street near the Golf Club, this modern 4-star hotel is literally very cool, with chilly AC as well as black leather & brushed steel décor. Facilities include bar, restaurant, gym, sauna & hydromassage. Rates inc b/fast, parking, internet access & business centre access; & there's an overrated restaurant. $$$$$
⌂ **Sheraton Montevideo** [88–9 G5] Victor Soliño 349; ✆ 2 710 2121; e sheraton.montevideo@sheraton.com; www.sheraton.com. In a somewhat odd location near the pleasant residential district of Pocitos, this is your classic American luxury hotel with one of the city's best shopping malls attached. $$$$$

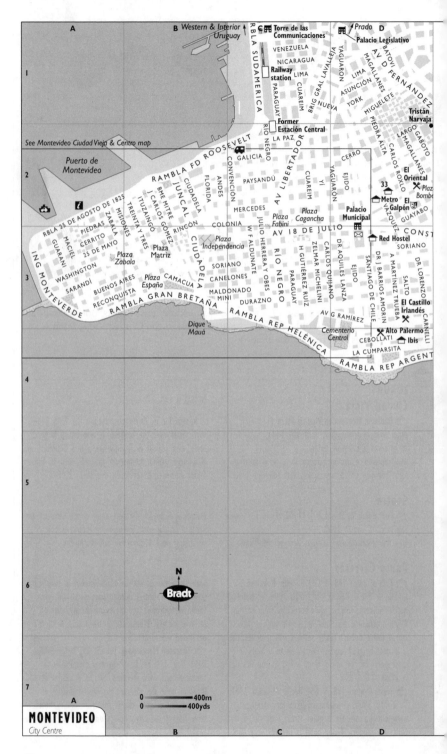

See Montevideo Ciudad Vieja & Centro map

MONTEVIDEO
City Centre

0 — 400m
0 — 400yds

N
Bradt

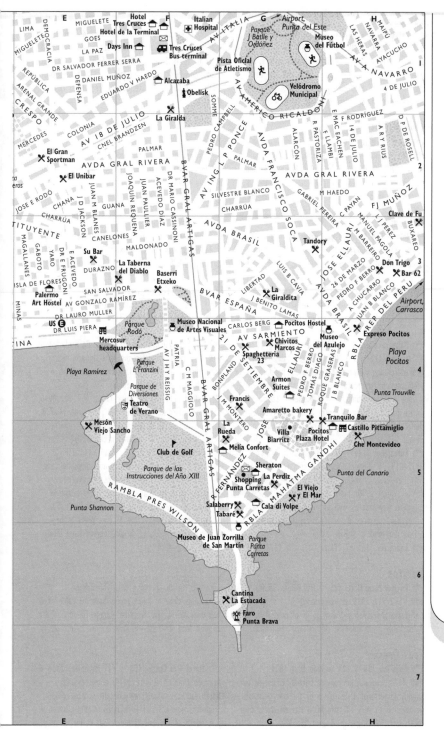

Carrasco

🏠 **Belmont House** [overview map] Avda Rivera 6512; ☎ 2 600 0430; e belmont@ belmonthouse.com.uy; www.belmonthouse.com.uy. In a swanky area nearer the airport than the city centre, this is the city's only luxury hotel that isn't part of an American chain. It has spacious lawns with

outdoor swimming pool, & gym, sauna & jacuzzi indoors, as well as a good restaurant, cocktail bar & salón de té. With only 24 rooms & 4 suites, as well as antique furniture & portraits by J M Blanes, this really does feel like a secluded retreat from city bustle. $$$$$

MID-RANGE
Ciudad Vieja

🏠 **NH Columbia** [111 D3] Rambla Gran Bretaña 473; ☎ 2 916 0001 e nhcolumbia@nh-hotels; www.nh-hotels.com. An excellent hotel, with views of the river & good restaurant, but alas in a bad area

– you may prefer taxis to walking. 3 computers in the lobby, Wi-Fi, 24hr room service, restaurant & 10 meeting rooms. $$$$

Palermo

🏠 **Ibis** [88–9 D4] La Cumparsita 1473; ☎ 2 413 7000; www.ibishotel.com. Not luxury but excellent value as you'd expect from this chain; handy for US

& German embassies. Rooms are AC, there's Wi-Fi & a 24hr bar with snacks, & buffet restaurant. B/fast not inc. $$$

Centro
Montevideo's midtown is home to many three- and four-star hotels (similar to European two- and three-star establishments), all built in the 1960s and 1970s in the same monolithic style, and lightly refurbished as a rule.

🏠 **Balmoral Plaza** [111 F2] Plaza Cagancha 1126 & San José 1121; ☎ 2 902 2393; e balmoral@ netgate.com.uy; www.balmoral.com.uy. A good, professionally run place with comfortable rooms, terrace with panoramic view & barbecue, sauna, gym, secure parking, business centre & meeting rooms. Buffet b/fast inc, & restaurant does a good lunch & dinner. $$$$

🏠 **Embajador** [111 F2] San José 1212; ☎ 902 0012/0193; e hotelemb@adinet.com.uy; www.hotelembajador.com. Newly refurbished, this is still a typical 1970s block, although rooms now have magnetic keycards as well as minibar, TV & AC. 8 suites have terraces, & there's multi-storey parking across the road. $$$$

🏠 **Lancaster** [111 F2] Plaza Cagancha 1334; ☎ 2

902 1054; www.lancasterhotel.com.uy. Particularly well sited (with its sister, the Hotel Iguazú, nearby), well refurbished with AC, flat-screen cable TV, free Wi-Fi & hair driers in all rooms. $$$$

🏠 **Oxford** [111 F2] Paraguay 1286; ☎ 2 902 0046; www.hoteloxford.com.uy. A friendly place with small & rather dated rooms & free but rather slow internet access. Good b/fast & teatime snack inc. $$$$

🏠 **Campoamor** [111 F2] Rondeau 1446 1st Flr; ☎ 2 902 2137; e reservas@hotelcampoamor.com; www.hotelcampoamor.com. The rooms have been renovated in fairly drab style, but bldg is still an Art Nouveau treasure, with the original lift still in place. Rooms AC with cable TV; free Wi-Fi to be installed soon. 'Artesanal' b/fast, sourced from local farms. $$$–$$

Pocitos

🏠 **Pocitos Plaza Hotel** [88–9 H5] Benito Blanco 640; ☎ 2 712 3939; e reservas@ pocitosplazahotel.com.uy; www.pocitosplazahotel.com.uy. Remarkably good value in this relaxed residential

area with beach, shopping & neighbourhood restaurants close at hand; rooms have AC, cable TV & hair-drier. Wi-Fi, gym & sauna, garage, friendly service & good food. $$$$–$$$

Tres Cruces

🏠 **Days Inn** [88–9 F1] Acevedo Díaz 1821; ☎ 2 400 4840; www.daysinn.com.uy. Friendly & decent but slightly impersonal 4-star place by the bus terminal; in addition to very effective AC it has electronic door locks, safes, Wi-Fi, garage & gym. $$$$

🏠 **Hotel Tres Cruces** [88–9 F1] Miguelete 2356 & Acevedo Díaz; ☎ 2 402 3474; e reservas@ hoteltrescruces.com.uy; www.hoteltrescruces.com.uy. Friendly, decent 3-star in a fairly modern tower just north of the bus terminal has coffee shop/confitería (⏲ *until 23.00 daily*) & free internet access in the lobby. $$$

🏠 **Alcazaba** [88–9 F1] Cassinoni 1669; ↘ 2 408 0701. A decent enough little 2-star just south of the bus terminal that offers rooms with private bath for the night, or P130/US$47 to wash & freshen up after an overnight journey. $$

Carrasco

🏠 **Best Western Pedro Figari** Rambla República de Mexico 6535; ↘ 2 600 8824;
e hfigari@hotelpedrofigari.com;
www.hotelpedrofigari.com. A relatively small red-brick place on the waterfront, this is a very decent place to stay within reach of the airport; rates inc a welcome drink, buffet b/fast, Wi-Fi throughout the hotel & business centre. $$$$

🏠 **Posada del Mar** Rambla Costanera & Tacuari; ↘ 2 601 2539; e visitalaposada@hotmail.com; www.posadadelmar.com.uy. An attractive red-brick

🏠 **Hotel de la Terminal** [88–9 F1] Goës 2377; ↘ 2 400 0264; e hoteldelaterminal@adinet.com.uy; www.hoteldelaterminal.com/english.html. On the north side of the bus terminal, this affordable little place has rooms with & without private bathroom. Some have Jacuzzis. $$

motel in well-kept gardens, this is a perfectly civilised place with 24hr room service. $$$

🏠 **Motel Dunas** Rambla Costanera & Piriápolis; ↘ 2 601 2209, 2 601 2336. The motels in this area are intended for couples trying to get away from the in-laws, or something a bit more illicit, but this still makes a decent enough stopover near the airport. Rooms with cable TV & jacuzzi, & there's an adequate cafeteria. $$

BUDGET Of the cheaper hotels, those in old family homes with rooms around a patio are far more pleasant than those in more modern multi-storey buildings, which are often airless and noisy.

Ciudad Vieja

🏠 **Posada al Sur** [111 B3] Pérez Castillano 1424 between 25 de Mayo & Washington; ↘ 2 916 5287; e info@posadaalsur.com.uy; www.posadaalsur.com.uy. A self-styled B&B, this estimable place feels more like a large shared apt. It exists to support sustainable & community tourism, working with local groups to offer tours of the deprived but very colourful Barrio Sur & Palermo districts of Montevideo, & in Rocha, Río Negro & Tacuarembó (see page 71). Big kitchen, laundry, internet access (inc Wi-Fi), roof terrace, & common room for activities such as Spanish or tango classes. From US$15 pp (room for 6), US$40 (dbl with

shared bathroom), US$45 (private bathroom), all inc good organic b/fast (*until noon*) plus sheets & towels. There's also a new & very cute wooden rooftop cabin, with dbl bedroom, kitchen, bathroom & living room, from US$65 for 2. $$$–$$

🏠 **Splendido** [111 D2] Mitre 1314; ↘ 2 916 4900; e splendidohotel@gmail.com; www.splendidohotel.com.uy. Formerly the Hotel Solís, now a self-styled 'backpacker paradise', this offers beds in 15 shared rooms right above some of the noisiest bars in Montevideo. Kitchen, internet access & cable TV. $$–$

Centro

🏠 **ITA** [111 F2] San José 1160; ↘ 2 901 3363. Basic 1-star hotel with internal light-well – all rooms have private bathroom & fan, but cost more with TV. $$

🏠 **Juncal** [111 G3] Durazno 1279; ↘ 2 908 7997. Cheap but adequate 1-star place; rooms with private bathroom, cable TV, fans & towel. $$

🏠 **33** [88–9 D2] Mercedes 1516; ↘ 2 409 7154. Very quiet budget hotel near Plaza de Bomberos; rooms, with private or shared bathrooms, come with fan, mirror & bedside light, though no TV. $$

🏠 **Colonia** [111 F2] Colonia 1168; ↘ 2 901 0390; e colonialhotel@gmail.com. A classic Belle Epoque bldg with rooms with & without bathroom, somewhat dingy & not very quiet; but prices are reasonable. $

🏠 **Florida** [111 D2] Uruguay 808; ↘ 2 900 3667; www.hotelflorida.com.uy. A classic 2-star hotel dating from 1901, rooms with & without private bathroom. A cafeteria serves b/fast (not inc), lunch & dinner. $

🏠 **Hospedaje del Este** [111 F3] Soriano 1137; ↘ 2 908 5495. A friendly family-run place with rooms with private bathrooms & cable TV plus use of kitchen & internet access. There are other decent *hospedajes* in nice old houses on Soriano either side of Paraguay. $

⌂ **Metro** [88–9 D2] Barrios Amorin 1440; ☎ 2 401 3451. A fine old-style 1-star with Belle Epoque exterior & Art Deco interior, with several skylit lobbies on 1st Flr, this has small rooms with & without private bathroom, all with cable TV. No food available. $

⌂ **Nuevo Ideal** [111 F3] Soriano 1073, Centro; ☎ 2 908 2913. Classic family-run *hospedaje* with rooms on 2 patios; rooms with shared bathroom are decent but fairly basic $

APARTMENTS

APARTMENTS For longer stays, perhaps on business or with a family, an apartment may be more convenient than a hotel.

⌂ **Apart-Hotel Bremen** [111 G3] Aquiles Lanza 1168, Centro; ☎ 2 900 9641, m 9449 9641; e hotel@bremenmontevideo.com; www.bremenmontevideo.com. In several houses on the block next to the office/reception (English & German spoken) are 15 apts of various sizes, nicely fitted out, decorated in pale blue & cream, with kitchen, CD player, TV in every bedroom, washing machine & internet cable. Prices from US$25/30/60 for 1/2/5 to US$85/90/110 (with terrace); monthly rates from US$500/600 sgl/dbl to US$1,850 for 1–3 or US$2,200 for 5. In the same block is the Bremen pub-restaurant (see page 99).

⌂ **Armon Suites** [88–9 G4] 21 de Septiembre 2885, Punta Carretas; ☎ 2 712 4120; e ventas@armonsuites.com.uy. Much slicker & more businesslike than the Bremen, this has lift, sauna, tiny swimming pool, PCs & Wi-Fi (all inc) together with buffet b/fast. Rates from US$92 for 2; w/end discounts.

HOSTELS

HOSTELS Montevideo has a good supply of backpacker hostels, mostly well located in the Centro. These are open all year, usually 24 hours a day, and are clean and safe, with lockers (bring a padlock) and English spoken. If you don't feel the need for networking with fellow travellers, free internet access and English-speaking staff, the cheapest hotels will give you a private room for the price of a dorm bed in a hostel. You'll get a simple breakfast in a hostel but not in a cheap hotel.

Ciudad Vieja

⌂ **Che Lagarto** [111 D2] Plaza Independencia 713; ☎ 2 903 0175; e montevideo@chelagarto.com; www.chelagarto.com. Offshoot of an Argentine chain of party-oriented hostels, this one is easy to find your way back to late at night, but rather noisy with buses & other traffic. There's a good range of rooms (book early to get your choice) from sgls, dbls, trpls & quadruples to dorms (some women-only & with bathrooms en suite) & family rooms, from US$12 pp (US$9 for 3 or more nights) inc b/fast, sheets & taxes. Common areas inc non-smoking, games & TV rooms, a pub, & a secret backyard; there's also a computer room plus free Wi-Fi, & a guest kitchen. Laundry service, bike rental & bike & luggage storage available.

⌂ **El Viajero Ciudad Vieja Hostel** [111 C2] Ituzaingó 1436; ☎ 2 915 6192; e info@ciudadviejahostel.com; www.ciudadviejahostel.com. Part of a small Uruguayan chain, this lively place near the cathedral is part of the Hostelling International network, with a mix of private rooms & 6- & 8-bed dorms, from US$14 pp (inc b/fast, sheets & taxes). There are family rooms & segregated male- & female-only rooms. 2 TV/DVD rooms, 2 kitchens, bar with meals & a new terrace with hammocks, barbecue & a view over the port. Free internet access (inc Wi-Fi), laundry service & bike rental, as well as Spanish & tango lessons. Other activities are provided daily, eg: pizza & *asado* nights, movies & live music at w/ends.

Centro

⌂ **Montevideo Hostel** [111 E3] Canelones 935 & W Ferreira Aldunate; ☎ 2 908 1324; e mvdhostel@montevideohostel.com.uy; www.montevideohostel.com.uy. Montevideo's original Hostelling International outpost, now over 30 years old, this is still a friendly backpacker place but slightly tattier & less hip than some newer hostels. The main hall is a partly roofed-in courtyard which can be noisy till midnight, although there is also a cellar bar with pool table, karaoke & musical instruments. A spiral iron staircase leads to a mezzanine with free PCs (free Wi-Fi too) & to a roof terrace with barbecue. There's a large kitchen, & laundry service. Bikes can be rented (& stored) here, & city tours are available (US$15 for half a day) as well as a day trip to Punta del Este (US$430). Dormitories are segregated (no private rooms). US$12 pp inc small b/fast, sheets & taxes.

🏠 **Planet Hostel** [111 F3] Canelones 1095 & Paraguay; ✎ 2 900 0733; e info@ planetmontevideohostel.com; www.planetmontevideohostel.com. A friendly smaller hostel in the Centro. Dorms are fairly small, almost cramped, without enough power sockets, & segregated by gender – each is named after a planet, with

appropriate décor. Beds are made daily, & good b/fast is inc, for US$13 pp, as well as free Wi-Fi, baggage storage & small kitchen.

🏠 **Red Hostel** [88–9 D3] San José 1406 & Santiago de Chile; ✎ 2 908 8514/16; e info@ redhostel.com; www.redhostel.com. The most stylish & laid-back of the Centro hostels, in a family home built in 1912 with central light-well, fireplace, large rooftop terrace with hammocks. Nicely restored, it's definitely red in colour (rather than referring to a *red* or network); the rooms are fairly spacious, with small balconies over the street, but bathrooms are somewhat cramped. There's free internet access inc Wi-Fi, plus smallish kitchen, bar & gym. US$14 pp in mixed dorm, inc good b/fast, sheets & towels.

East of the Centro

🏠 **Palermo Art Hostel** [88–9 E3] Gaboto 1010 between Isla de Flores & San Salvador, Palermo; ✎ 2 410 6519; e info@palermoarthostel.com; www.palermoarthostel.com. Seemingly more a party hostel than an art hostel, patronised more by boho South Americans than by tourists from the northern hemisphere. Stylishly designed, with 2 adjacent houses interconnecting in a mysterious manner, but there's not much real art in evidence, apart from live music at w/ends. The location is a bit odd, although handy enough for Playa Ramírez beach. B/fast & bedding inc (though not towels), for US$12 pp, & there's a guest kitchen, plus PCs & Wi-Fi. Bikes can be rented for P80/hr or P120/day, & Spanish, tango & candombé drumming lessons are offered.

🏠 **Pocitos Hostel** [88–9 G4] Avda Sarmiento 2641 & Aguilar, Pocitos; ✎ 2 711 8780; www.pocitos-hostel.com. In a nice old house in probably the most pleasant district of Montevideo, & run by a friendly gang of rugby-playing students, this hostel offers mixed-sex & women-only dorms with big cupboards & plenty of power sockets, plus twin & dbl rooms. There's free Wi-Fi, kitchen & a nice garden with barbecue, & they're converting the basement into a bar & DVD theatre for winter use – but mercifully there's no cable TV to take over the common spaces. For US$14 pp (US$16 w/ends) you get good b/fast & sheets, with towels for rent; bikes can also be rented (US$4 for 5hr). From the airport, bus DM1 will drop you on the far side of Avda España; from the bus terminal, bus 183 leaves you just a block away, at España & Avda Sarmiento.

CAMPING The only campsite within reach of Montevideo is the **Parque Municipal Punta Espinillo** (✎ 2 312 0667; ⊕ 1 Dec–15 Apr daily, all year w/ends & holidays), well to the west near Santiago Vásquez; it's 8km southwest on Camino General Basilio Muñoz from km20 of Ruta 1 (the exit for the Complejo Carcelario or prison). It has space for 70 tents (with electric lighting and hot water), cabins, barbecues and a stony little beach; there's a *parador* with restaurant & shop at the gate.

Camper-vans can stop at the ANCAP service station at Punta Carretas, where there's 24-hour security, or even on the sandy point immediately to the south, where there's much less traffic noise.

✗ **WHERE TO EAT**

LUXURY
Ciudad Vieja
✗ **Estrecho** [111 C3] Sarandí 460; ✎ 2 915 6107; ⊕ 11.00–17.00 Mon–Fri. The only seating at this cool contemporary place, open only for w/day

lunches, is at the long bar; the food is simple *cuisine moderne*, using fresh seasonal ingredients. **$$$$**

✗ **La Corte** [III C2] Sarandí 586; ☏ 2 916 0435; www.lacorte.com.uy, ⊕ 10.00–15.00 Mon–Fri. Near the cathedral on Plaza Constitución, this classy restaurant specialises in regional cuisine with a nouvelle touch. **$$$$**

✗ **Montevideo Sushi Osaka** [III D2] Bacacay 1319; ☏ 2 915 6010; ⊕ 12.00–15.00, 20.00–00.00

Centro
✗ **Arcadia** [III D2] Plaza Independencia 759; ☏ 2 902 0111; www.radisson.com/hotels/urumont/dinings, ⊕ 07.00–10.30 (to 11.00 Sun), buffet lunch 12.00–15.00 (from 12.30 Sat–Sun), 16.30–18.30, 19.30–00.00. On the 25th floor of the Radisson hotel, this is the best restaurant in the area & in particular a good bet for a less carnivorous meal. Nevertheless you pay an awful lot for the fine linen, the chandeliers & the views over the harbour. Starters inc *jamón crudo* (raw ham) US$18.50, soups US$6, salads US$7, pasta from US$12, steaks & fish from US$15. You can pay much more for specialities such as *costilla de cordero a la menta* (grilled rack of lamb with mint & garlic) or terrine of pheasant marinated in cognac. **$$$$$**

Punta Carretas
✗ **Francis** [88–9 G4] Luis de la Torre 502 & Montero; ☏ 2 711 8603; e francis@francis.com.uy; www.francis.com.uy; ⊕ 12.00–14.45 daily, 20.00–23.45 Mon–Thu, 20.00–00.45 Fri–Sat. The city's pre-eminent seafood restaurant, serving, for instance, grilled *chipirones* (grilled baby squid), stuffed pollock, seafood stew, 2 types of paella & sushi, as well as pasta & meats. **$$$$$**

✗ **La Perdiz** [88–9 G5] Guipúzcoa 350; ☏ 2 711 8963; e laperdiz2007@hotmail.com. Despite its name, 'The Partridge' in fact specialises in Basque fish dishes, as well as the standard *parrilla*, *milanesa* & pasta. Good choices include *chipirones*, seafood lasagne or *pescado a la bizkania* (pan-fried fish, perhaps salmon, sea bass or sole, in a tomato sauce with red peppers & parsley). Although handy for the Sheraton, this feels like a neighbourhood bistro (with a partially covered terrace) where everyone is greeted like an old friend. **$$$$$**

Carrasco
✗ **Café Misterio** Costa Rica 1700 & Rivera; ☏ 2 600 5999, ⊕ from 12.00 & 20.00 Mon–Sat. One of the trendiest places in town, serving sushi as well as modern Mediterranean-style cuisine, with an excellent wine list & desserts. Service seems to be better at lunchtime, whereas in the evening the see-&-be-seen element takes over. Prices are high at all times. **$$$$$**

✗ **Nuevo Garcia** Arocena 1587 & Otero; ☏ 2 601 8681, 2602 2703; ⊕ 09.00–02.00 daily. Business travellers who spurn airline food often come here to eat before or after flights, although some complain of bad service & the bar-like ambience. The *parrilla* is generally excellent (the baby beef is renowned) & there's also fish or pasta, with mediocre deserts to follow. **$$$$**

MID-RANGE
Ciudad Vieja
✗ **Cervecería Matriz** [III C3] Sarandí 582; ☏ 2 916 1582, ⊕ 08.00–24.00 Mon–Thu, until 02.00 Fri–Sat. A very modern diner-style place with efficient service & a wide range of dishes at pretty fair prices; try the *pizzetas* or the *revuelto gramajo* (scrambled egg with potato, onion & ham). **$$$**

✗ **Lo De Mané** [III C2] J C Gómez 1420, just north of Plaza Matriz; ☏ 2 916 7770/5835; ⊕ 09.30–17.30 Mon–Fri. This classy restaurant serves fresh, well-presented dishes (try *tarta de ratatouille*) at very reasonable prices – but only during the week. **$$$**

✗ **Rincón de Zabala** [III B2] Rincón 787; ☏ 2 915 1617; ⊕ 09.30–17.30 Mon–Fri. Known as RdZ ('erre-day-zayta'), this is a stylish place for lunch, aimed at financial types but very affordable for those working through the nearby museums. In addition to the inexpensive menu of the day there are sandwiches, & specialities such as *ternera* (veal), *zapallitos rellenos de ricota* (round squashes stuffed with ricotta cheese) & paella. Wi-Fi is available. **$$$**

Centro

El Fogón [111 F2] San José 1080; ☎ 2 900 0900; e elfogon@elfogon.com.uy; ⊕ 12.00–16.00, 19.00–01.00 daily. One of the most renowned *parrilladas* in town, & well placed for many mid-range hotels. It's well known to coach parties, but there are private rooms for them (or for you); it's also generally popular for late-night dinners. In addition to grilled beef, it offers seafood, pasta & salads, at very reasonable prices. There's covered parking nearby (*San José 1066*). $$$$

Euskal Erria [111 F2] San José 1168 1st Flr; ☎ 2 902 4374. Founded in 1912, the Basque Institute has a fine old-style restaurant, offering an excellent lunchtime *menú del día* with Basque-style garlic-heavy fish, pork or chicken; next to the restaurant is a *frontón* (handball court), battered but still in use. $$$$

Las Brasas [111 E2] San Jose 909; ☎ 2 900 2285; ⊕ 11.45–15.30, 19.30–24.00 daily. Famed for its steaks, this is a typical Uruguayan *parrillada*, serving good seafood alongside the grilled meat & vegetables. The style is casual but efficient, with the quality remarkably consistent. $$$$

Tannat [111 F2] San José 1063; ☎ 2 900 8127; www.tannatrestaurant.com; ⊕ 12.00–03.00 Tue–Sun. As the name implies, this is as much a wine-bar as a restaurant, but unexpectedly it serves sushi, as well as boar, lamb, risotto & pasta. It's a classy venue & one of the more expensive in this area. $$$$

Clube Brasileiro [111 E2] 18 de Julio 994, 2nd Flr; ☎ 2 902 4344, 2 908 7430. There's nothing especially Brazilian about the food here, but this makes a handy lunchtime stop, with a *menú ejecutivo* (executive menu) plus *chivitos*, pizzas, salads & other snacks. $$$

El Lobizón [111 F2/3] Michelini 1264; ☎ 2 901 1334; ⊕ 20.00–03.00 daily. A cosy cellar-pub, 'The Werewolf' offers attentive service & very reasonable prices. The meat is hardly the best in town, but the *revuelto gramajo* (scrambled eggs with potato, onions & ham) is renowned. The *tortilla gallega* (potato tortilla) & *pollo al ajillo* (chicken with garlic) are also excellent. To drink, *sangría* & *clericó* are house specialities. $$$

Locos de Asar [111 F2] San Jose 1065; ☎ 2 903 2120; www.locosdeasar.com. This place is 'Crazy about Grilling' as its name implies — it's one of the leading venues for *parrilla*, with the usual alternatives of fish & pasta; service is excellent, with English-speaking staff. $$$

Mesón Viejo Sancho [111 F2] San José 1229; ☎ 2 900 4063; ⊕ 12.00–15.00, 20.00–24.00 Mon–Sat, until 01.00 Fri–Sat. One of the Centro's classic restaurants for 3 decades, & seemingly never redecorated, the very attentive staff serve huge portions of filling food such as *kassler* (pork chops smoked then grilled) with *papas a la suiza* (rösti), steak, *milanesa* or chicken, followed by amazing desserts, & all at prices that hardly seem to have gone up since they opened. $$$

Ruffino [111 F2] San José 1166; ☎ 2 908 3384; ⊕ 12.00–15.00, 20.00–24.00 Mon–Fri, from 20.30 Sat, 12.00–15.30 Sun. A classic Italian restaurant, complete with red & white chequered tablecloths, serving homemade pasta & pizza, as well as steak, followed by desserts such as *profiteroli* or ice cream. $$$

La Vegetariana [111 F2] Yí 1369; ⊕ 11.30–15.30, 19.30–24.00 Mon–Thu, until 00.30 Fri–Sat, 12.00–16.00 Sun. A hot buffet of various overcooked veggies & pulses, this isn't the most welcoming of places, but if you're tired of pizza & pasta it's a healthy alternative. US$7 for all you can eat, or at lunchtimes you can pay US$9 per kilo. $$

Barrio Sur

Jacinta [111 F4] Carlos Gardel 1123; ☎ 2 908 2192; e casajacinta@montevideo.com.uy; ⊕ lunch & evening Tue–Sat, lunch Sun. In a beautifully restored house dating from 1880, with a large central patio in which they put on musical events & cabaret, as well as art shows; the food is a fine blend of traditional Uruguayan & modern Mexican cuisines. $$$

Pocitos and around

Baserri Etxeko [88–9 F3] Avda Julio Herrera y Reissig 957; ☎ 2 411 6895, 2 410 0262; www.baserricocinavasca.blogspot.com; ⊕ 12.00–15.00, 20.00–24.00 Mon–Sat. This highly regarded Basque restaurant specialises in fish & seafood, such as *kokotxas en salsa verde* (hake throat in green sauce) & paella. $$$$

Che Montevideo [88–9 H5] Rambla Ghandi 630; ☎ 2 710 6941; ⊕ 09.00–03.00 daily. Opposite the Castillo Pittamiglio (see page 128), with a great waterfront setting (& its own tiny beach), this is a place to come to for the view & atmosphere rather than the food, which is decent but slightly overpriced. They serve good-sized portions of fish, seafood & pizza, but it's probably best to come for lunch or an afternoon snack. $$$$

✗ **El Viejo y El Mar** [88–9 G5] Rambla Gandhi 400, Punta Carretas; ☎ 2 710 5704; ⊕ 12.00–16.00, 20.00–0100 daily. One of the best places in the area for fish, but there's good pasta & salads on offer too; service is poor, however. There's a nautical theme, with an old boat converted into the bar, & a terrace looking out to sea. $$$$

✗ **La Rueda** [88–9 G5] Miñones 452 & Joaquín Nuñez, Punta Carretas; ☎ 2 711 3214; ⊕ from 12.00 Tue–Fri, from 12.30 Sat–Sun, from 20.00 Tue–Sat. A promising new *parrillada* which is almost unique in Montevideo in allowing guests to bring their own wine (no corkage charge Tue–Thu; otherwise *descorche* costs P100/US$4). They do have a good wine list anyway, while the menu includes tapas such as sweetbreads with mushrooms & white wine sauce or langoustine brochettes, grilled meats such as baby beef, pork with teriyaki sauce, with rösti potatoes & vegetables, & excellent desserts such as chocolate fondue, pears in red wine, bread pudding & pancakes. $$$$

✗ **Salaberry** [88–9 G5] Zorrilla de San Martín 176, Punta Carretas; ☎ 2 711 1900; ⊕ from 19.00

Tue–Sat, 12.00–16.00 Sat–Sun. New, ambitious & already very popular (although there's no website yet & they don't yet accept credit cards), the service is very welcoming, with a bread basket & dips arriving rapidly. There's an excellent *parrilla*, as well as dishes like salmon ravioli, pork in cherry sauce or glazed chicken, & the splendid *tentación salaberry* (chocolate brownie with *dulce de leche* & cream) to finish. There's a limited but good choice of wine (served by the glass), & the prices are fair. $$$$

✗ **Tandory** [88–9 G3] Libertad 2855 & Massini, Pocitos; ☎ 2 709 6616; www.tandory.com; ⊕ lunch Tue–Fri, dinner Mon–Sat. Definitely not your normal curry-house, this is an upmarket place offering 'global fusion' cooking, with Chinese & Thai dishes as well as tandoori. $$$$

✗ **Cantina La Estacada** [88–9 G6] Camino El Faro, Punta Carretas (rear of the Punta Brava naval station); ☎ 2 710 0576, 2 712 1566. Behind the deceptively hippyish front, this is a very good seafood restaurant. $$$

✗ **Spaghetteria 23** [88–9 G4] Scosería 2584 & Franzini, Pocitos; ☎ 2 711 4986; www.spaghetteria23.com; ⊕ 12.30–16.00, 20.30–00.30 daily. A good local Italian place with a cosy patio out front. $$$

Elsewhere

✗ **Casa Violeta** Rambla Armenia 3667, Buceo; ☎ 2 628 7626; e cvioleta@adinet.com.uy; www.lacasavioleta.com; ⊕ from 12.30 & from 19.30 daily. A *parrilla* (actually inspired by Brazilian *churrascarias*) with a huge salad bar in the middle of the room, with good grilled meats, as well as fish, seafood & pasta, all served in a friendly, relaxed atmosphere, looking out over the *rambla* to the Plate. $$$$

✗ **Heming.Way** Rambla República de México 5535, Punta Gorda; ☎ 2 600 0121;

⊕ 09.00–02.00 daily. The food is decent enough (a fairly standard choice of beef, fish & pasta), but people come here mainly for the view. Set on a hillside, with a non-smoking terrace giving views along the coast to the city centre, this is one of the best places in town to while away the sunset hour. $$$

✗ **L'Italiano** Quivén, Puerto de Buceo; ☎ 2 622 7930. Near the Yacht Club, this is one of the best & most affordable seafood restaurants in town. $$$

BUDGET Two chains must be mentioned, as both are ubiquitous and excellent value.

✗ **Cervecería La Pasiva** This well-established chain has managed to acquire prime locations on every plaza in the city, inc Plaza Constitución, Plaza Independencia (next to the Palacio Salvo), Plaza Fabini, Plaza Cagancha, at 18 de Julio 1350 & Ejido by the Palacio Municipal, the Punta Carretas Shopping Centre & at Benito Blanco 920 & Avenida Brasil in Pocitos. Calling itself a *cervecería* or beer-hall, it's known above all for its *chivitos* (steak

sandwiches) & *panchos* (hot dogs), & more especially its mystery sauce (see page 65). It also serves burgers, steaks, salads & a wide range of pastas, all very reasonably priced. Some branches have Wi-Fi. $$

✗ **La Cigale** The ice cream equivalent of La Pasiva, also found in the city's main squares & shopping centres. Its success is well deserved, as these really are the best ices around. $

Ciudad Vieja The *Mercado del Puerto* [111 A2] (*www.mercadodelpuerto.com.uy*) is an unmissable market that shelters a variety of restaurants specialising in fish and, of course, *asado*. They are not cheap but are very popular with locals and tourists alike, especially at weekend lunchtimes. Inside, the market restaurants close early (around 17.30), while those outside have open-air terraces and a lively evening trade too; however, you should take a taxi home at night.

✗ **Cabaña Verónica** [III A2] Mercado del Puerto; \ 2 915 1901. Sitting at one of only 2 remaining *mostradors* or bars left inside the market is much more fun than sitting in yet another AC tourist restaurant, & you'll pay half the regular cover charge for bread, *chimichurri* sauce, olive oil & maybe a free glass of *medio y medio*. With the grill just feet away from you, the range of meats (from chorizo at US$3 to filet at US$15) is obvious, but there's also good pasta & seafood. $$$

✗ **Don Tiburón** [III A2] Mercado del Puerto; \ 2 916 4268. Very busy & commercial, but one of the classic Mercado del Puerto restaurants, famed for its huge portions of beef above all. It has an outdoor terrace & is open into the evening. $$$

✗ **El Palenque** [III A2] Perez Castellanos 1597; \ 2 917 0190, 2 915 4704; www.elpalenque.com.uy. Founded in 1958, this is one of the classic Mercado del Puerto restaurants, serving the usual range of *asado*, fish & pasta. It has an outdoor terrace & is open into the evening. $$$

✗ **Café de la Pausa** [III C3] Sarandí 493 & Treinta y Tres, 1st Flr; \ 2 915 3856; e cafelapausa@ hotmail.com; ⏰ 11.00–19.00 Mon–Sat. A pleasant café & bookshop, also selling newspapers, magazines & artworks. Snacks include *quesadillas* & pita sandwiches, as well as milkshakes & other drinks. $$

✗ **Las Misiones** [III C2] 25 de Mayo 449; \ 2 915 4495. Behind a beautiful green-tiled shopfront, dating from 1907, is a café-restaurant specialising in good straightforward business lunches. $$

Centro

✗ **Casa de los Chivitos** [III G2] 18 de Julio 1251. Not just a *chivito* (steak sandwich) joint, this also serves pizza (from US$1.30 to US$11!), pasta & fish (inc swordfish for US$8), & large glasses of wine. You can also use the Wi-Fi from across the road. $$

✗ **El Candil** [III F2] San José 1095; \ 2 908 8246. 'The Lantern' is a simple neighbourhood café-bar that's handy for some of the Centro's hostels & *hospedajes*. It serves pizzas, tortillas & other standards, & is good value, even if the service is a bit sluggish. $$

✗ **Manchester** [III E2] 18 de Julio & Convención; \ 2 900 4383. An old-school local diner that serves a Dagwoodesque *chivito*-with-everything for US$4. $$

✗ **El Copacabana** [III C3] Sarandí 454 & Misiones; \ 2 915 3205. A nice *cafetería*-restaurant, with a standard menu inc good *chivitos* & well-presented special coffees, served with a glass of fresh orange juice, whipped cream & cake. There's Wi-Fi, though only from 15.00. $$

✗ **Irazú Café Gourmet** [III D3] Juan Carlos Gómez 1315; \ 2 915 7434; e info@cafeirazu.com.uy; www.cafeirazu.com.uy; ⏰ 09.00–20.30 Mon, 09.00–21.30 Tue–Fri. A delightful new café, serving sandwiches, salads, juices, teas & Costa Rican coffee. There's free Wi-Fi. $$

✗ **La Catedral de los Sandwiches** [III C3] Sarandí 502; \ 2 915 7349; ⏰ 07.30–21.00 Mon–Fri, 07.30–16.00 Sat. As it says, the Cathedral of Sandwiches – not a London sandwich shop or a New York deli, but a classy café where you can have a sandwich plate or a salad, as well as a pastry, a soft drink or a beer. $$

✗ **Empanadas El Rincón** [III C3] Rincón & Zabala; \ 2 916 9367; also Gestido near Simón Bolivar, Pocitos; \ 2706 7525; ⏰ Mon–Fri. Eat in or out, with upmarket *empanadas* at just over US$1 each (or US$0.70 for sweet ones). $

✗ **Empanadas La Barca** [III C3] Reconquista 331 & Alzaibar; \ 2 915 4454; www.empanadaslabarca.com; ⏰ 08.00–24.00 daily; also Luis A. De Herrera 1245, Pocitos; \ 2 628 8282, 2 623 4495; Orinoco 4845, Malvín; \ 2 619 2230, 2 613 0923. No fewer than 46 types of excellent *empanadas*, to eat here or take away, or delivered to homes & offices. $

✗ **Mondo del Pizza** 18 de Julio 1105 & other locations. A friendly, cheap, high-turnover chain that serves not only pizza but lots of steak. $$

✗ **El Oriental** [88–9 D2] Magallanes & Colonia, Plaza de Bomberos. A *carrito* reputedly serving some of the best *panchos* (hot dogs) in town. $

✗ **Madison** [III D2] Andes 1403 & Colonia; \ 2 900 4074. A simple neighbourhood café-restaurant, not easily confused with the Radisson, just around the corner – here you'll get pizza, *milanesa* & other simple dishes, with friendly service & an English-language menu. $

✗ **Pizzeria El Gaucho** [III G2] 18 de Julio 1449 & Barrios Amorín; \ 2 900 3914; www.elgaucho.com.uy;

3

⊕ 08.00–01.00 daily. Despite the name, this really is an all-purpose eatery, open all day for everything from tea & toast to a full meal. But the small pizza really is small. There's free Wi-Fi. **$**
✘ **Tío Chef** [111 G2] Carlos Quijano 1334 near 18 de Julio; ✎ 2 900 0130. If you love real Chinese

food enough to ignore the dire décor & the doubts about kitchen cleanliness, this place serves great dim sum & chop suey at a great price. (There are a few other Chinese & Korean restaurants in Montevideo, all pretty cheap & basic.) **$**

Palermo
✘ **Su Lugar** [111 G4] Santiago de Chile 951 & Gonzalo Ramírez; ✎ 2 900 9988; ⊕ 10.00–02.00 daily. With a couple of wooden decks in front, an upstairs terrace, & high-ceilinged rooms decorated in rustic-modern style, this is an attractive place to enjoy homemade pastas, pizza & grilled meats &

cheeses. There's a wide range of salads in summer, & desserts are good too. **$$$**
✘ **La Taberna del Diablo** [88–9 F3] Gonzalo Ramírez 2051; ✎ 2 413 7543; www.latabernadeldiablo.com. Despite the name, this is a pleasant family restaurant, known for its *empanadas*; it also has Wi-Fi. **$$**

Pocitos and around There's a fascinating row of cheap restaurants (mainly take-aways) on José Marti, including **Empanadas** (✎ 2 706 8505); **Gago** (✎ 2 706 7876), serving Armenian dishes such as shwarma, shish, hummus, felafel and borek; **Parrillada La Tira** (✎ 2 706 6414), with a sit-down terrace; and **Hong Kong Chino** (✎ 2 706 9132).

✘ **Amaretto Bakery Café** [88–9 G4] 21 de Septiembre 2998 & Roque Graseras, Villa Biarritz; www.amaretto.com.uy; ⊕ 08.00–23.00 daily. All kinds of coffee, plus muffins, pastries, soups, salads, sandwiches, as well as live music on some w/end evenings. **$$**
✘ **Chivitos Marcos** [88–9 G4] Luis de la Torre 895 & Sarmiento, Punta Carretas; ✎ 2 710 7649; ⊕ until 01.00 Sun–Thu, until 03.00 Fri–Sat. Serving reputedly the best *chivitos* in town for over 20 years, this branch (near the Pocitos Hostel) is probably the handiest. Also at Luis A de Herrera 1186 & 26 de Marzo; ✎ 2 628 3512, 2 628 6326; Avda Italia 4675 & Troitiña, Malvín; ✎ 2 613 5535;

& Coimbra 5855 & Gral. Paz, Punta Gorda; ✎ 2 604 4562, 2 606 2827. Also deliveries. **$**
✘ **El Condór** Quivén, Buceo; ⊕ 24hrs. One of the best *carrito* stalls for *panchos* & *chivitos*. There's free Wi-Fi too! **$**
✘ **Medialunas Calentitas** 29 de Septiembre 2982, Pocitos; ✎ 2 7105045; ⊕ 24hrs; also at Luis A de Herrera 1191 & 26 de Marzo, Pocitos; ✎ 2 623 4799; & Arocena 1631 & Otero, Carrasco; ✎ 2 604 0559; www.medialunascalentitas.com. A chain of cafés specialising in *medialunas* or small croissants with a variety of great fillings, as well as sandwiches & cakes. **$**

NIGHTLIFE

BARS The *boliche Montevideano* developed out of the 18th-century *almacénes de ramos generales* (general shops) that also sold drinks, much as happened in small Irish villages, and became a bar that also sold foodstuffs, and nowadays meals. In many you'll still see glass-fronted display cases. Many of the most traditional *boliches* have gone, including the legendary Tupí Nambá, where Gardel had his own table facing Solís street. A project to boost interest in the remaining ones has produced a fine coffee-table book (see *Appendix 2* on page 337), and a leaflet promoting two dozen of the best ones.

There's a very thin dividing line between bars and restaurants, so that you can eat at some of the places listed here, or go to many restaurants just to have a drink.

Ciudad Vieja
✘ **Café Bacacay** [111 D2] Bacacay 1310 & Buenos Aires; ✎ 2 916 6074; ⊕ 09.00 to at least 02.00 Mon–Fri, from 10.00 Sat, closed Sun. Home to the

actors of the Teatro Solís for almost a century, this was bought by a German in 1995 & converted to a chic café-bistro. Its kitchen is now open non stop, serving dishes such as steak, goulash & chicken, as well as cappuccinos & other drinks.

✕ **Café Brasileiro** [111 C2] Ituzaingó 1447. Opened in 1877, this remains perhaps the classic Montevideo bar (frequented by writer Eduardo Galeano), a spacious room with Art Nouveau features & big windows that fail to overcome the dark wood panelling. Come here for coffee (or perhaps a *carajillo*, with rum), tea or hot chocolate, with croissants, toast or a sandwich; or to hear the live music on Thu or Fri evening.

✕ **El Pony Pisador** [111 D2] Mitre 1323 & 1326; ✆ 2 915 7470; www.elponypisador.com.uy; ⏰ 17.00–08.00 Mon–Fri, 20.00–08.00 Sat. A hectic late-night pub, split on both sides of the street, with live music at w/ends, serving passable pizzas, calzones & other snacks.

✕ **Fun-Fun** [111 D3] Ciudadela 1229; ✆ 2 915 8005; www.baarfunfun.com. Founded in 1895, this is known as Montevideo's historic tango-bar, where Gardel was inspired to sing unaccompanied in 1933 after sampling an *uvita*, a mixture of port & wine concocted by the bar's founder. Described as 'half Glasgow pub, half museum of life', it has moved several times, ending up in a faithful reconstruction in the former Mercado Central, with its original tin bar & an autographed photo of Gardel. There's live music Wed–Sat evenings & you can get snacks & pizzas.

✕ **La Crêperie** [111 D2] Mitre 1332; ✆ 2 915 9858; ⏰ from 11.00 Mon–Fri, 12.00–17.00 & from 20.00 Sat. Crêpes are available, but essentially this is one of a row of party-pubs, with tables on both sides of the Ciudad Vieja's liveliest street as well as in the wood-panelled interior.

Centro

✕ **Bar Iberia** [111 D1] Uruguay & Florida. In the 1980s this place sold more beer than any other Montevideo bar, thanks to some very thirsty Polish & Russian fishing crews; now it's a pleasant café-bar, serving *empanadas* & *panchos* as well as all the usual drinks.

✕ **Bremen** [111 G3] Aquiles Lanza 1150 & Maldonado; ✆ 2 903 2094; ⏰ from 17.00 daily. Montevideo's German pub, with good beer, well-loaded plates of German food, a very cheery atmosphere & a roof terrace.

✕ **El Gran Sportman** [88–9 E2] 18 de Julio 1803 & Tristán Narvaja. Located opposite the university, this bar (founded in 1892 & supposedly named after an English gentleman) has always attracted intellectuals such as Borges, as well as the Argentine rocker Charly García; but it's not really a drinking bar, more a place for a quiet coffee or a quick *chivito*

✕ **La Ronda** [111 D3] Ciudadela 1182; ⏰ from 12.00 Mon–Fri, from 19.30 Sat–Sun. Less noisy than the bars on Mitre & Bacacay, this is nevertheless very popular with the cool kids; sharing its owner with the next-door Cheesecake Records, it has walls covered with record sleeves & classic LPs playing (except after 22.00 Thu when there may be a poetry slam). Soak up the drink with a *masticable*, a sort of Mexican wrap.

✕ **Roldós** [111 A2] Mercado del Porto No 09; ✆ 2 915 1520. Founded in 1886 as a general store & converted into a proper bar in 1930, this Montevideo institution has always been associated with *medio y medio* ('half & half' – in fact 3 parts dry white wine & 1 part sparkling wine) that makes a great aperitif before an *asado* (although you should drink a fuller, smoother wine with the meat). Past customers include Enrico Caruso, Jean-Louis Barrault & Carlos Fuentes. In addition to the stand-up bar there's also a small seating area.

✕ **Tasende** [111 D3] Ciudadela 1300 & San José. Founded in 1931, this is one of Montevideo's classic *boliches* – legend has it that one president used to bring his cabinet here to relax tense meetings. It's a straightforward bar-restaurant, serving its unique style of pizza for over 75 years.

✕ **The Shannon** [111 D2] Mitre 1318; ✆ 2 916 9585; ⏰ 18.30–04.30 Mon–Fri, 19.00–05.00 Sat–Sun. An Irish pub on Montevideo's liveliest pub street, with a wide range of beers (although Uruguayans find it hard to understand why an Irish pub doesn't serve Irish coffee), with decent snacks available & live music, often semi-Celtic.

or pizza (although the lunchtime *menú ejecutivo* does offer more choices).

✕ **El Unibar** [88–9 E2] Eduardo Acevedo 1450 & Guayabos. To the rear of the university, this little place is a student bar par excellence; there's a small street-side terrace.

✕ **La Giralda** [88–9 F1] Bvar Artigas 1598 & Francisco Canaro; ⏰ 24hrs. Founded in 1943 (& claiming to have sold the first Coke in Montevideo), this has always been popular with staff from the nearby hospitals.

✕ **Montevideo Sur** [111 F3] Paraguay 1150 & Maldonado. An authentic pre-war shop/bar, still with its Art Deco furnishings & *azulejo* tiles, & lots of empty whisky bottles. Cold pies & *milanesas* are available, but it's probably best to stop for a drink & move on to eat.

✗ Su Bar [88–9 E3] Jackson 1151 & Maldonado. A traditional Spanish bar & also a good place for w/day lunch, serving dishes such as spinach crêpes &

Palermo

✗ El Castillo Irlandés [88–9 D3] Gonzalez Ramírez 1483 & Martínez Trueba; ☎ 2 413 7453; ⏲ 12.00–16.00, 20.00–00.00 daily, until 02.00 Fri–Sat. Not your normal Irish pub, but a friendly Uruguayan pub-*parrilla* with semi-industrial décor, a nice little garden at the rear & live music at w/ends.

Pocitos and Punta Carretas

✗ Bar 62 [88–9 H3] Barreiro 3301 & Chucarro; ☎ 2 707 3022; www.62bar.com; ⏲ from 10.00 daily. In the former terminal of the city's first trolley-bus line (route 62, in 1951), this is a lively bar (especially Sat nights) that also does good, if slightly pricey, food, with a *parrilla*, salmon teriyaki, sushi, & desserts that include a fine pear *tarte tatin*.

✗ Clave de Fu [88–9 H3] 26 de Marzo 1125 & Buxareo. The place to hear folk music, especially with a Brazilian flavour; live music from 22.00 at w/ends.

✗ Don Trigo [88–9 H3] Pereira 3201 & Berro. In 1939 the British minister Eugen Millington-Drake discussed the *Graf Spee* crisis here with the Uruguayan foreign minister (& spread rumours about the British ships just over the horizon); more recently it has been popular with art students, giving a bit of spice to an otherwise quiet traditional bar.

✗ El Pony Pisador José Iturriaga 3497 & Herrera; ☎ 2 622 1885; ⏲ from 20.00. A branch of the Ciudad Vieja disco-pub.

✗ Expreso Pocitos [88–9 H4] J Benito Blanco 956 & Brasil. In the Edificio El Mastil, one of the city's finest Art Deco buildings, this is a good, largeish café-restaurant (& *cocktelería-cafetería-sandwichería*) that's still at the heart of the local community.

milanesas. The attractive Taberna del Sol is on the same crossroads.

✗ Alto Palermo [88–9 D4] Barrios Amorin 949 & Ramírez; ☎ 2 900 0505. A decent neighbourhood *parrilla*-pizzeria. There's another branch up near the Palacio Legislativo (*Asunción 1450 & Hno Damasceno;* ☎ *2 924 1212;* ⏲ *09.00–24.00 daily, until 01.00 Fri–Sat*) that is more attractive but not very convenient.

✗ La Giraldita [88–9 G3] J Benito Lamas 2745 & E Muñoz. Opened in the early 20th century, this is one of the city's most attractive & best preserved shop/bars, with its brown wood bar, glass-fronted display cases & walls cluttered with posters.

✗ Tabaré [88–9 G5] Zorrilla de San Martín 152 & Tabaré, Punta Carretas; ☎ 2 712 3242; http://bartabare.com; ⏲ 20.00–01.00 Mon–Sat. Founded in 1919 as a shop & fishermen's bar, this survived to be listed in the 1990s by *Time* magazine as one of the world's 100 best bars, with pasta & bottles displayed in glass-fronted wooden cases; in 2003 it was refurbished & reopened with a restaurant upstairs. There are 2 small sidewalk terraces, & tango on Wed.

✗ Tranquilo Bar [88–9 H4] 21 de Septiembre 3000 & Roque Graseras, Punta Carretas; ☎ 2 711 2127; www.tranquilobar.com. Although only a few decades old, this is a typical Galician bar, favoured by actors & writers. With a small interior bar, the best place to be is on the largish terrace, where you can eat sandwiches or simple meals, inc a dish of the day or plates of cheeses or cold meats, each costing US$6. There's Wi-Fi.

TANGO Uruguayans are proud of their tango tradition (see page 312 on Carlos Gardel's roots), but in a quieter, less intense way than in Buenos Aires. Attempts to cash in a bit more include the Montevideo Tango Festival (*www.montevideotangofestival.com*), held at the Radisson Hotel in February.

To learn how to tango, head to **Tanguería Salu** [88–9 G5] (*García Cortinas 2398*) on a Saturday evening, or **La Crêperie** [111 D2] (*Mitre 1332;* ⏲ *18.30–20.00, summer 19.30–21.00*) on a Tuesday. There are also salsa lessons at **Academia Azúcar Para Ti** [111 F2] (*Paraguay 1279;* ☎ *2 908 9882, 9459 4628;* e *nando5982@hotmail.com;* ⏲ *until 21.30 Mon–Sat*). If you can tango a bit already, head to **Bar Fun-Fun** [111 D3] (*Ciudadela 1229*) or **Tango Joven** [111 G2] at the Centro Cultural Mercado de la Abundancía (*San José & Aquiles Lanza*); the dancing seems pretty poor to Buenos Aires tango snobs, but it's friendly and relaxed. There's also free open-air tango most evenings (*from 19.30*) on Plaza Fabini.

Dinner shows (featuring tango and *candombé*) are offered by **Cuareim** [111 F3] (*Zelmar Michelini 1079;* ◷ *21.00 Wed, Fri & Sat*), **El Milongón** [88–9 D1] (*Gaboto 1810;* ☎ *2 929 0594;* e *elmilongon@elmilongon.com.uy; www.elmilongon.com.uy;* ◷ *20.30 nightly*), **La Casa de Becho** [88–9 C1] (*Nueva York 1415;* ☎ *2 400 2717;* ◷ *22.30 Fri–Sat*) and **Tangombe** [88–9 E2] (*Rivera 1989 & Jackson;* ☎ *2 403 5682*).

DISCOS The liveliest pubs are on Mitre in the Ciudad Vieja; there's a selection of discos nearby on Rincón, including **Codigo** [111 D2] (*Rincón 626*); **Divina** [111 D2] (*Rincón 613 & Mitre;* ☎ *2 916 1841/4122;* ◷ *22.00 Fri–Sat*), with live bands, three dance floors and a smokers' room; **Plató 55 Night Ideology** [111 D2] (*Rincón 613*) and **Santos y Pecadores** [111 D2] (*Saints & Sinners; Rincón 740 & Ciudadela;* ☎ *2 908 4789;* ◷ *22.30 Fri–Sat*).

Other clubs and discos include: **Mariachi** [88–9 H3] (*Gabriel Pereira 2964;* ☎ *2 709 1600;* ◷ *22.00 Wed–Sun*), **New York** (*Mar Artico 1227;* ☎ *2 600 0444*), **Saideíra** [88–9 E3] (*Gonzalez Ramírez 1963;* ◷ *23.00 Thu, midnight Fri–Sat*) and **W Lounge** [88–9 F4] (*Rambla Wilson & Requena, Parque Rodó;* ☎ *2 712 1177*), playing techno downstairs and rock upstairs.

LIVE MUSIC Live bands can be heard in the various pubs and at **BJ** [111 E3] (*Banda Joven; Soriano 820 near Convención;* ☎ *2 908 5703;* e *gramonproducciones@gmail.com; www.bandajoven.com;* ◷ *22.00–05.00 daily*), **Espacio Guambia** [111 C2] (*25 de Mayo 591 & Gómez;* ☎ *2 916 3800: www.guambia.com.uy*) and **La Barracca** [88–9 E1] (*Muñoz 2049 & Defensa, Tres Cruces*). International touring bands are likely to play at the **Sala Zitarossa** [111 E2] (*Plaza Fabini, Avda 18 de Julio 1012;* ☎ *2 901 7303; www.salazitarrosa.com.uy; box office* ◷ *15.00–21.00 daily*), the open-air **Teatro de Verano** [88–9 F4] (*Rambla Wilson in south of Parque Rodó;* ☎ *2 712 4972; www.teatrodeverano.org.uy*) or the **Gran Teatro Metro** [111 F2] (*San José 1203 & Zelmar Michelini;* ☎ *2 902 2017; www.teatrometro.com; box office* ◷ *15.00–21.00 daily*), in addition to playing in pubs and bars (see page 98). There's no real listings magazine, but you'll get an idea of what's on from the *Guia del Ocio* (*www.guiadelocio.com.uy*) or the *Busca* newspaper's weekly *Galeria* supplement.

CASINOS The best of the state casinos (*www.casinos.gub.uy*) in Montevideo is the **Plaza Victoria Casino** [88–9 D2] (*Radisson Hotel, Plaza Independencia 759;* ☎ *2 902 0111/2155;* ◷ *from 14.00 daily*), which offers baccarat, blackjack, bingo, roulette (mainly for European visitors) and the ubiquitous slot machines. **Another** [111 G2] (*Avda 18 de Julio 1297 & Yaguarón;* ☎ *2 902 3065;* ◷ *09.00–05.00 Mon–Thu, non-stop Fri–Sun*) is similar to the Radisson but smaller. The city of Montevideo owns two historic casinos, in the Hotel Carrasco and the Hotel Parque, both small and very run-down but which should be refurbished soon.

GAY MONTEVIDEO A map of gay Montevideo is available at La Lupa Libros (*Bacacay 1318, Ciudad Vieja*) and online (*www.friendlymap.com.uy*). There's a new men-only gay B&B, **La Puerta Negra** [88–9 D3] (*Durazno 1525 & Salto;* ☎ *2 410 6554; www.lapuertanegragay.com;* $$$), owned by a Spanish–Italian couple, as well as the gay-friendly 'love hotel' **Hotel Marivent** (*Cipriano Miró 2969 between Apóstoles & Agaces;* ☎ *2 507 0725; www.marivent.com.uy;* $$).

Cruising spots include Plaza Libertad, the Mercado del Puerto, the Carreta statue in Parque Batlle y Ordóñez, the Rose Garden in the Prado Park, the Parque de Los Aliados near the *Obelisco*, and the Playa Turisferia beach just over the Arroyo de Carrasco into Canelones department.

Uruguay takes great pride in having the longest carnival season of any country, over 80 days long, although it has to be said that between the opening and closing parades the activities are largely confined to various open-air theatres and stages across Montevideo.

The prelude to *Carnaval* season, usually in February, is *Las Llamadas* ('The Calls'), a procession of close to 100 *comparsas* or *cuerdas* (*candombé* drumming groups) through the Barrio Sur and Palermo (see page 120). *Carnaval* itself begins with an even grander parade, when huge floats, giant puppets and groups of *murga* (see below) performers proceed for five hours along Avenida 18 de Julio, the city's main axis. The 40 days of Lent are occupied by performances on *tablados* or temporary stages in the various quarters of Montevideo and in the Teatro del Verano, the open-air theatre near Parque Rodó, where a competition is held to choose the very best acts.

Uruguay's *Carnaval* has various sources: in classical antiquity, the church calendar, Venetian carnival, the commedia dell'arte, and in the Bantu and Angolan Benguela cultures brought by African slaves. *Candombé* remains specially associated with the Afro-Uruguayan community, although the majority of drummers nowadays are of European descent (there are increasing numbers of female drummers, too).

Many slaves were brought from Africa to Montevideo after 1750, developing the habit of meeting to dance on the shore at weekends, gatherings known as tambos or tangos. These were restricted after 1808 by a fearful white population, but continued in a more discreet form. *Candombé* was first recorded in 1834 and then 1839, and was banned, although the Afro-Uruguayan population was in any case declining, due to assimilation and civil wars. The first drumming *comparsas* were founded in the 1860s by Afro-Uruguayans, and in 1876 a black-face *comparsa*, Los Negros Lubolos, was founded by a group of upper-class young white men. Imitating the Afro-Uruguayan groups, they were a great success at that year's *Carnaval* and paved the way for *candombé* to enter the mainstream of white Uruguayan culture. Even now, a white drummer is known as a *negro lubolo*.

☆ **Alexander** [111 D2] Plaza Independencia 846 & Avda 18 de Julio; ☏ 2 900 1929; ⏰ 01.00–07.00 Thu–Sat. A 3-floor disco in the basement of the Palacio Salvo.

☆ **Blue Cat Sauna Relaxation Center** [88–9 E1] Democracia 1811 & La Paz; www.saunabluecat.com; ⏰ 15.00–24.00 Mon–Wed, 15.00–02.00 Thu & Sun, 15.00–06.00 Fri–Sat; men-only except Thu & Sat

☆ **Cain Dance Club** [88–9 E1] Cerro Largo 1833 & Fernandez Crespo; www.caindance.com; ⏰ midnight–07.00 Fri–Sat. Montevideo's largest club, with 2 dance floors (techno & Latin), shows & a dark room.

☆ **Chueca** [88–9 F1] Brandzen 2712 bis, Tres Cruces; ☏ 2 402 9979; www.chuecamontevideo.com;

⏰ 21.30–02.00 Tue–Sun. A lounge-bar with drag shows Thu & Sun.

☆ **Ibiza** [111 F1] Rondeau 1493 & Uruguay; ☏ 2 901 7643; ⏰ midnight–07.00 Wed–Sun. Cruisey bar with dark room & drag queens. Strippers Thu, live bands Fri–Sun.

☆ **Il Tempo** [88–9 F3] Gonzalo Ramírez 2121, Parque Rodó; ⓜ 9938 6811, 9858 2300; ⓔ iltempopub@gmail.com; www.iltempodisco.com; ⏰ from midnight Thu–Sun. Gay-friendly disco.

☆ **Korpus Club** [111 E3] Herrera y Obes 1240 & Soriano; www.korpussauna.com; ⏰ 15.00–midnight Mon–Thu, 15.00–08.00 Fri/Sat, 15.00–03.00 Sun. Men-only sauna with bar & video room.

ENTERTAINMENT

TICKETS Ticket agencies include Cartelera (*www.cartelera.com.uy*) and Palacio de la Música at Punta Carretas Shopping Centre (*Local 136/137;* ☏ *2 711 1242*), Tres Cruces bus terminal (*Local 35;* ☏ *2 408 6925*), Avda 18 de Julio 1112 and Paraguay (☏ *2 902 1958*) and Portones Shopping Centre (*Local 262;* ☏ *2 601 7843*).

In the 20th century there was massive European immigration to Montevideo, with many poor immigrants living in the crowded *conventillo* tenements of Barrio Sur and Palermo, learning candombé drumming from their Afro-Uruguayan neighbours. Meanwhile the banner-twirling which has also become a major feature of Las Llamadas seems to have Basque origins. The most important *comparsas* (many of which survive today) were racially mixed, and blacks and whites contributed together to creating a wholly Uruguayan art form, which has seen its popularity grow steadily since the 1950s.

In 1958 the Las Llamadas procession was created as a separate event – the painter Ruben Galloza had wanted to revive the traditional Afro-Uruguayan celebrations between Christmas and Epiphany (a time when slaves were given more freedom) but an all-white municipal commission decided to add it to *Carnaval*. In the 1990s the drumming became even more popular, spreading into the middle-class suburbs of Pocitos, Buceo, and Malvín.

The other distinctive form of Carnaval is *murga*, a kind of musical theatre with bass drum, snare drum and cymbals backing up to 17 male singers with painted faces, colourful costumes and unique vocal harmonies. Each neighbourhood has its own troupe (also known as *parodistas*), developing a new show each year and performing on temporary stages across the city. With its roots in Cádiz, Spain, *murgas* had appeared in Montevideo by 1910 and soon became a central part of *Carnaval*, lampooning public figures and satirising current society and politics. Nowadays women and the young are increasingly involved, and latex and polyurethane have opened up new possibilities for masks and costumes, with more and more outlandish punk and SM features.

Montevideo's *Carnaval* is typically Uruguayan and has relatively little in common with the slick dance performances by the perfectly honed athletes of the Brazilian samba schools – despite the satire of the *murga* shows, the carnival as a whole has a sort of small-town innocence about it.

Even if you can't be in Montevideo for *Las Llamadas* or *Carnaval*, you'll learn a lot from visiting the Museo del Carnaval, near the Mercado del Puerto in Montevideo's old town (see page 122).

THEATRE

Teatro Solís [111 D3] Buenos Aires 652; 2 916 0908; www.teatrosolis.org.uy; box office 11.00–20.00 Mon–Sat, 15.00–20.00 Sun. Montevideo's main theatre, home of the Comedia Nacional & of opera, ballet & orchestral music. In the newly reopened west wing are a shop (15.00–20.00 Mon, 10.00–20.00 Tue–Sun) & the Allegro café (12.00–20.00 Mon, 10.00–20.00 Tue–Fri, 16.00–20.00 Sat–Sun, or until the start of performances).

Gran Teatro Metro [111 F2] San José 1211 & Michelini; 2 902 2017

Teatro Agadu [111 F3] Canelones 1122; 2 901 1855; www.agadu.org. Home to the Uruguayan Authors' Association.

Teatro Alianza Cultural Uruguay-Estados Unidos [111 F3] Paraguay 1217; 2 908 1953; www.alianza.edu.uy. The Uruguay–US cultural centre, often putting on English-language plays.

Teatro Anglo [111 G2] San José 1426; 2 901 8819. A centre for English-language culture, with 2 auditoria.

Teatro Circular [111 F2] Avda Rondeau 1388, Plaza Cagancha; 2 901 5952; e circular@ adinet.com.uy; box office 18.00–22.00 Tue–Thu, 18.00–24.00 Fri–Sat, 18.00–21.00 Sun. At the side below the Ateneo, this was the first theatre in the round in Latin America, founded in 1954.

Teatro del Centro [111 F2] Plaza Cagancha 1164; 2 902 8915

Teatro del Círculo [88–9 D3] Soriano 1710–24; 2 411 9719, 2 401 9719

Teatro El Galpón [88–9 D2] Avda 18 de Julio 1618; 2 408 3366; www.teatroelgalpon.org.uy; box office 18.00–21.00 Mon–Sat, 17.00–19.30 Sun. Perhaps the city's leading independent theatre, & newly refurbished.

Teatro El Tinglado [88–9 E2] Colonia 2035; 2 408 5362

🎭 **Teatro La Candela** [88–9 G5] José Ellauri 308 (Shopping Punta Carretas); ☏ 2 712 3227

🎭 **Teatro La Casa de los Siete Vientos** [88–9 E3] Gonzalo Ramírez 1595, Palermo; ☏ 2 419 2598

🎭 **Teatro del Notariado** [88–9 E2] Guayabo 1729; ☏ 2 408 3669. An outpost of the Comedia Nacional.

🎭 **Teatro Sala Verdi** [111 E3] Soriano 914; ☏ 2 901 7453. Recently refurbished, this houses an outpost of the Comedia Nacional.

🎭 **Teatro Stella d'Italia** [88–9 E2] Mercedes 1805 & Tristán Narvaja; ☏ 2 408 2649; box office ⊕ 16.00–20.00 Tue–Sun. Founded in 1895 & now housing the La Gaviota (Seagull) company, this is a National Historic Monument.

🎭 **Teatro Victoria** [111 E1/2] Río Negro 1479 between Mercedes & Uruguay; ☏ 2 901 9971. In a National Historic Monument.

Other cultural centres

Alliance Française Bvar Artigas 1229; ☏ 2 400 0505; www.alliancefrancaise.edu.uy. The French cultural centre, with frequent events & films (& the Café Sucré-Salé).

Ateneo de Montevideo Plaza Cagancha 1157; ☏ 2 900 0987; www.ateneodemontevideo.com. Montevideo's Atheneum, with art exhibits, free concerts & other events.

Centro Cultural de España Rincón 627; ☏ 2 915 2250; www.cce.org.uy; ⊕ 11.30–20.00 Mon–Fri,

11.30–18.00 Sat. A strikingly refurbished building with free avant-garde art exhibits & films.

Centro Cultural Lapido (Unión Latina) Avda 18 de Julio 948, 1st Flr; ☏ 2 307 4318

Goethe Institut Canelones 1524 & Salto; ☏ 2 410 5813; e info@montevideo.goethe.de; www.goethe.de/montevideo. The very active German cultural centre.

MUSIC Uruguay's leading **orchestra** is the Filarmónica de Montevideo, founded by the city in 1958; based at the Teatro Solís, it's now directed by Javier Logioia Orbe. The state broadcasting body SODRE also has an orchestra, although it's plagued by labour problems, and the Teatro Sodre [111 D2] (*at Mercedes & Andes*) is currently being rebuilt after being burnt down; currently they perform (from May to November) in the Auditorio Nelly Goitiño [111 E2] (*formerly Sala Brunet; Avda 18 de Julio 930 & Río Branco; ☏ 2 901 2850; box office ⊕ 15.30–21.30 Mon–Sat, 10.00–12.00, 15.00–20.00 Sun*).

CINEMA The first film was shown in Montevideo in 1896, and the first three cinemas opened in 1908. Since 1999 multiplexes have opened in the modern shopping centres, so that the cinema-going experience is now just the same as anywhere else in the world. Tickets start at about US$2, or US$4 in the multiplexes; they cost slightly more from Friday to Sunday and on holidays, and there are discounts for children and senior citizens in most cinemas. In April 2009 the 27th Uruguayan International Film Festival (*www.cinemateca.org.uy/festivales.html*) was held at the four Cinemateca screens and at the Casablanca cinema, with over 100 films of various kinds shown.

🎬 **Cine Casablanca** 21 de Septiembre 2838, Pocitos; ☏ 2 712 3795

🎬 **Cinemateca** Lorenzo Carnell 1311 & Constituyente; ☏ 2 418 2460, 2 419 5795; http://cinemateca.org.uy

🎬 **Cinemateca 18** Avda 18 de Julio 1280; ☏ 2 900 9056

🎬 **Cine Metro** San José 1211; ☏ 2 901 0772

🎬 **Cine Opera** Avda 18 de Julio 1710 & Magallanes; ☏ 2 403 1415

🎬 **Cine Plaza Libertad** Rondeau 1383; ☏ 2 901 5384

🎬 **Cine Universitaria** Canelones 1280; ☏ 2 901 6768; e cuniv@adinet.com.uy. With a video store too.

🎬 **ECU Pocitos** Chucarro 1036; ☏ 2 708 2957

🎬 **Grupocine** Ejido 1377; Shopping Punta Carretas, Ellauri 350; Torre de los Profesionales; all ☏ 2 901 4242; www.grupocine.com.uy; Colonia 1297 & Yaguarón; Avda Arocena 1660, Carrasco; ☏ 2 601 7992

🎬 **Hoyts Cinemas** Barreiro 3231 & Berro, Pocitos; Punta Carretas Shopping Centre, Ellauri 350; ☏ 2 707 3037; www.cineshoyts.com.uy

🎬 **Maturana** Avda Agraciada 3178; ☏ 2 203 3244

🎬 **MovieCenter** Luis A de Herrera 1290, Pocitos; ☏ 200 2511; Shopping Punta Carretas, Ellauri 350; ☏ 2200 2511; Portones Avenida Italia 5775; ☏ 2200 2511

SPECIAL EVENTS Summer starts on the first Friday of December (as a rule) with the annual **Museos en la Noche (Museums at Night)** event, the peg for a variety of free activities in museums, most of which stay open until midnight.

The **Noche de las Luces (Night of Lights)** is a massive firework display over the Pocitos *rambla* at 22.00 on the second Saturday of December (as a rule), preceded by a Disneyfied parade of Santa, the Three Kings and other figures. All traffic is halted from late afternoon and most of the 600,000 or so spectators walk in along the *rambla*.

In December or January the **Carrera de San Felipe y Santiago** (San Felipe y Santiago was the original name of the city of Montevideo) is a 10km race along the *rambla* from Carrasco to Pocitos.

Holy Week (Semana Santa or Semana del Turismo), the week leading up to Easter Sunday, is a time for many people to take a last few days on the beach, but it's also a busy time in the city, with the finish of the Vuelta Ciclista del Uruguay along Avenida 18 de Julio and the **Semana Criolla** (Countryside Week, more or less), hosted by the Sociedad Rural in the Parque del Prado. There are rodeos and *asados*, arts and crafts for sale and live music, and hordes of people, more from the countryside than the city, with special trains and buses coming in from all around. There's also a rodeo in Parque Roosevelt the same week, but the Rural show in the Prado is the main event, with quite staggering levels of horsemanship on display.

SPORTS The capital's, indeed the nation's, two leading **football** teams are Peñarol and Nacional (see page 36), both founded in the 1890s and based respectively at the Estadio Parque Central (in La Blanqueada) and the Estadio Centenario [overview map] (in the Parque Batlle). Matches between the two, known as *clásicos*, are always at the Estadio Centenario, the stadium built for the 1930 World Cup (although the Estadio Parque Central was in fact also used in that competition). Other Montevideo clubs include Liverpool, Danubio, Defensor Sporting, River Plate, Bella Vista, Central Español, Wanderers and Rampla Juniors, their names revealing both British origins and some influence from Buenos Aires. Peñarol is a suburb in northern Montevideo, home to the railway works where the club was founded, but their headquarters are now in the bright yellow Palacio Peñarol [88–9 D2] (*Cerro Largo 1411, between Minas and Magallanes, Centro*), with a covered arena that's used for boxing and other sports.

There are two **golf** clubs in the city, the better-known being the Club de Golf del Uruguay [88–9 F5], which occupies a large area of prime real estate in Punta Carretas (*Bvar Artigas 379;* ✆ *2 710 1721–5;* e *cgu@cgu.com.uy; www.cgu.com.uy*); laid out by the Scottish designer Alister MacKenzie in 1930, this seems like an exclusive private club but is technically a municipal course where guests are welcome and visitors can wander around on Sunday afternoons. It has an excellent restaurant, open to non-members except for Sunday lunch. The alternative is the Club de Golf del Cerro [overview map] (*west of the centre at Punta de Lobos;* ✆ *2 311 1305;* e *cgcerro@adinet.com.uy*). Established in 1905–10 by the owners of the Frigorífico Swift, it has a vintage clubhouse and a delightful course, lined with old native trees and with two of its 18 holes by the Plate, vaguely like a Scottish links. There's also one suburban course, the La Tahona Golf Club (*Ruta Interbalnearia km23.9, Camino de los Horneros 220, Lomas de Carrasco;* ✆ *2 684 0004;* e *latahona@latahona.com.uy*), founded in 1996 in Canelones department.

Also on the Canelones coast just east of the city is the Montevideo Cricket Club (*Ruta Interbalnearia km23.5, Solymar;* ✆ *2 696 4762; www.montevideocricketclub.com*), founded as the Victoria Cricket Club in 1842 and known for **rugby** as much as for **cricket**; in fact the MCC is the eighth-oldest rugby club in the world, and the first to be founded outside Europe. In 1878 it also introduced soccer to Uruguay (bizarrely, one of its leading players was called Henry Stanley Bowles). In 1874 some members also formed the Montevideo Rowing Club, and in 1894 others formed the Club de Golf del Uruguay in Punta Carretas.

The premises at Avenida 18 de Julio 1297 are shared with Maroñas (*www.maronas.com.uy*), which runs **horse-racing**, held at the Hipódromo Nacional (*Maroñas district*). Maroñas has other betting shops (with slot machines) in the Montevideo Shopping Centre [overview map] (*Avda Luis A de Herrera 1290;* ↘ *2 622 5055;* ⊕ *10.00–06.00 Mon–Thu, non stop Fri–Sun*), the Géant Shopping Centre [overview map] (*Avda Giannattasio & Avda La Playa;* ↘ *2 600 9282;* ⊕ *10.00–03.00 Sun–Thu, 10.00–04.00 Fri–Sat*) and the Sala Las Piedras [88–9 E2] (*Rivera 613;* ↘ *2 365 8700;* ⊕ *10.00–02.00 Sun–Thu, 10.00–04.00 Fri–Sat*). Races are held every Sunday and most Saturdays throughout the year, and on 6 January, whichever day of the week it is, when the country's premium race, the Gran Premio José Pedro Ramírez, is run.

SHOPPING

Uruguay is unusual in that most food, at least, is still bought from local grocery stores, but even so there are huge suburban malls and hypermarkets, and the city centre shops have felt the need to attract customers. So on the second Saturday of each month (*10.00–22.00*) the Encuentros Felipe y Santiago in the Ciudad Vieja offer tango shows, choirs and military bands. On the Día del Centro y Cordón, on two Thursdays a month, shops along Avenida 18 de Julio and nearby charge no IVA (ie: give an 18% discount). Avenida 18 de Julio is the traditional shopping district, although tourists are more likely to find what they want elsewhere.

LEATHERWARE The most obvious purchase for tourists, and transfers are provided from cruise ships to the main stores, Don Mario [111 C1] (*Piedras 641 & Mitre;* ↘ *2 916 2356; www.casamarioleather.com*) and Leather Factory [111 D2] (*Plaza Independencia 832;* ↘ *2 908 9541; www.montevideoleatherfactory.com*). They sell a great variety of men's and women's jackets, coats, trousers, belts and other items, in suede and sheepskin too. The Talabartaría [111 E1] (*Paysandú 1033*) is an authentic saddlery shop, selling tack for horses and boots, ponchos, *bombachas* and sombreros for their riders.

SEMI-PRECIOUS STONES Semi-precious stones such as agate and amethyst from the north of Uruguay are also popular, the main outlets being Van Der Brüin [overview map] (*Mantua 6886, Carrasco;* ↘ *2 600 3589;* e *bdv@gmail.com; www.vanderbruin.com.uy*), Mundo Mineral [111 C3] (*Sarandí 672;* ↘ *2 915 0194;* ⊕ *09.30–19.00 Mon–Fri*) and Amatistas Uruguayas [111 C3] (*Sarandí 604;* ↘ *2 916 6456*).

There's a wide range of crafts for sale in the Mercado de los Artesanos, on the ground floor of the former Mercado de la Abundancia [111 G2] (*San Jose 1312;* ⊕ *Mon–Sat*), including knitting and wood carvings; upstairs there's a choice of cheap eateries. There's a similar craft market in an arcade at Plaza Cagancha 1365 [111 F2], as well as some kiosks on the plaza.

FASHION Fashion in Montevideo is classical in style and beautifully made; some younger, more cutting-edge designers can be found in the Ciudad Vieja, such as ARA [111 B2] (*25 de Mayo 286;* ↘ *2 915 7981*), Imaginario Sur [111 B2] (*25 de Mayo 263;* ↘ *2 916 0383; www.imaginariosur.com*) and Ana Livni [111 B2] (*25 de Mayo 280;* ↘ *2 916 5076; www.analivni.com*), which claims to deal in Slow Fashion. Imaginario Sur also has a stylish café, selling Segafredo coffee, *licuados* (fruit drinks) and so on.

Manos del Uruguay (*www.manos.com.uy*) A women's co-operative producing fine knitwear (and yarns and wools for the likes of Ralph Lauren and Benetton); they have shops at San José 111 (✆ 2 900 4910) and Sarandí 668 (✆ 2 915 5345), both in the Ciudad Vieja, as well as the Montevideo Shopping, Punta Carretas Shopping [88–9 G5] and Portones Shopping malls. You'll pay about a third of what you'd pay abroad for their knitwear.

Hecho Aca [111 B2] (*Edificio Santos, by the port entrance on Rambla 25 de Agosto;* ✆ 2 915 4341; *www.hechoaca.com.uy*) 'Made Here' is a non-profit body also encouraging high-quality contemporary artisans. They have a shop in the Tourism Ministry, as well as in the Montevideo Shopping and Portones Shopping malls.

MARKETS It's well worth being in Montevideo for the **Sunday market** [88–9 E2] (*Calle Tristán Narvaja, opposite the university;* ⊕ *roughly 09.00–15.00*), where you can find fishing tackle, shoes, DVDs, posters, bookstalls, caged birds, kittens, rabbits, guinea pigs, hamsters and almost anything else, including cheese, fruit and vegetables. This is also a great place to see *cachila* trucks, which look as if they've struggled in from rural farms and probably won't make it back again. There's an antique market on Saturdays on Plaza Matriz [111 C2] (which spills over on to Sarandí, and may also take place on weekdays in the tourist season), with old postcards, photos and frames, gaucho trappings, watches, jewellery, *maté* gourds and lots of silver. There's a smaller clothes market in the Parque Juan Zorrilla de San Martín [111 G5] in the Villa Biarritz area of Punta Carretas until 15.00 on Saturdays, reappearing by the Parque Rodó castle [88–9 F3] on Sundays.

BOOKSHOPS Tristán Narvaja [88–9 E2] is also the main area for secondhand **bookshops** (which also open on Sundays, from around 09.00), such as Babilonia Libros (*No 1591*), Librería Montevideanos (*No 1617*), Finisterre Libros (*No 1635*), Arete Libros Usados (*No 1641*), Librería Latina (*No 1645*), Librería del Cordón (*No 1728*), Librería Rubén and Librería Horizonte (*No 1585*), Afrodita Libros (*No 1528*) and Tertulía (*Colonia 1802*). In the Ciudad Vieja there are a couple of fine old-style bookshops, Librería Oriente-Occidente [111 D2] (*Rincón 609*) and Librería Linardi y Risso [111 C2] (*J C Gómez 1435*). On the other side of the Ciudad Vieja, between the Teatro Solís and the Anglican church, La Pasionaría [111 D3] (*Reconquista 587*) is a stylish new design shop and bookshop with the excellent El Beso café (✆ 2 915 6852; ⊕ *10.00–19.00 Mon–Fri, 12.00–18.00 Sat*).

Next to the Palacio Salvo, the Librería Palace [111 D2] (*Plaza Independencia 842*) is a good general bookshop, and there are similar places nearby on Avenida 18 de Julio, such as MVD Books (*No 1261*) and Librería América Latina (*No 2089*). Sitio del Lector (*Avda 18 de Julio 1306*) also has branches in the Devoto hypermarkets at Portales, Sayazo and the Centro Comercial Geant. At the Teatro El Galpón [88–9 D2] (*Avda 18 de Julio 1618*), Libros Banda Oriental publishes and sells books on Uruguayan culture, and in the same place Auídiscos sells mainly folk and traditional Uruguayan music. Corazón al Sur (✆ 2 901 1714; *www.corazonalsur.com.uy*), in a kiosk above the Subte exhibition centre on Plaza Fabini, sells books, videos, CDs etc on Uruguayan art and culture, and plays tango music for dancing from about 19.30 nightly. Tamborilarte [88–9 E2] (*Rodó 1994 & Jackson*) sells *candombé* drums and carnival costumes.

FOOD SHOPPING In the city centre there are Disco, Ta-Ta, Micro-Macro and MultiAhorro **supermarkets**, with larger outlets such as Fresh Market, Devoto and Tienda Inglesa hypermarkets on major arteries such as Avenida Italia in the suburbs;

there's one Géant hypermarket (*Avda Giannattasio, Carrasco*). There are also the **malls** or Shoppings, which usually contain a supermarket or hypermarket (and a food court and cinemas): the main ones are Montevideo Shopping (*Luis A de Herrera 1290, Buceo*), Portones (*Avda Italia & Bolivia*), Punta Carretas [88–9 G5] (*Ellauri 350*) and above the Tres Cruces bus terminal [88–9 F1]. All are easily accessible, with Portones serving as a terminal for many buses out on Avenida Italia.

For other types of food shopping, one Montevideo speciality is the fresh **pasta shops**, which sell ready meals and are particularly busy on Sunday mornings (and close on Mondays to recover) – for some reason there are a lot of these in Pocitos, such as La Spezia [88–9 G3] (*Libertad & España*) and La Doménica [88–9 G3] (*Libertad 2935*), as well as Pastas Blanes [88–9 F3] in Parque Rodó (*Blanes 1000 & Salvador*), and Gente di Buon [111 F3] (*Soriano 929*) and Los Dos Leones [111 G3] (*Aquiles Lanza 1327*) in the Centro. Similarly, good **delis**, offering cheeses, meats, teas and so on, are mainly in Pocitos, including Deli Singer [88–9 G4] (*Scosería 2607*) and La Colonial [88–9 H3] (*Barreiro 3336 & Blanco; Vidal 755 & Perez*). For cheeses and other dairy products, you can also go to Talarcrem (*Avda Italia 4569; \ 2 613 8614; www.talarcrem.com*).

In the Centro, however, there are some small **health food shops**, such as Primer Centro de Ecología [88–9 E2] (*Tristán Narvaja 1612*), Madre Tierra [111 F2] (*Colonia 1327*), El Naranjo [111 G2] (*18 de Julio 2164*), Ecotiendas [111 G3] (*Maldonado 1390; www.ecotiendas.com.uy*), which also has a lunchtime café, and in the Ciudad Vieja Ecosol [111 D2] (*25 de Mayo 687 & Juncal; www.economia-solidaria-uruguay.org*), which sells food and also clothes, presents and crafts.

There are some specialised **wine shops**, selling both Uruguayan and imported wines. These include La Casa del Vino [111 B2] (*25 de Mayo 230*) and Arte Cuero y Vinos [111 B2] (*Pérez Castellano*) in the Ciudad Vieja, Cachi [111 E2] (*Herrera y Obes 1397 & Colonia*), four branches of Iberpark along Avenida 18 de Julio, La Cava [88–9 G3] (*Avda Brasil 2557 & Brito del Pino; www.lacava306.com.uy*), Las Croabas [88–9 G2] (*Rivera 2666 & Brito del Pino*), Las Duelas [88–9 G3] (*Bvar España 2511 & Obligado*) and Los Dominguez [111 F2] (*Paraguay 1400 & in Montevideo Shopping; www.losdominguez.com*). There are also the online retailers (*www.vinoacasa.com, www.vinosuy.com*).

MISCELLANEOUS Montevideo is, naturally, not the best place in South America for **camping and hiking gear**, but the Doite chain (*Avda 18 de Julio 1743 & Gaboto; Avda 18 de Julio 1237 & Yí; Montevideo Shopping, Portones, Punta Carretas & Tres Cruces shopping centres; www.doitestore.com*) is decent enough. Martín Pescador [88–9 E3] (*Kingfisher; Gonzalo Ramírez 1360 & Ejido; www.martinpescador.com.uy*) has fishing and camping gear. The place for **car parts** (*repuestos*) is on Galicia east of Libertad.

The best **photography** shop is the Fuji Center [111 G2] (*18 de Julio & Yaguarón*); there are other Fuji shops, which will all have black-and-white and slide film.

OTHER PRACTICALITIES

MONEY AND EXCHANGE There are plenty of ATMs (*bancomats*) all over town, especially along Avenida 18 de Julio and in the airport, port and bus terminal. The financial district, with the national headquarters of Uruguayan and international banks, is in the Ciudad Vieja, in the area of Cerrito and Misiones. Exchange offices (*cambios*) are located in this area (⊕ *Mon–Fri only*) and in places like the bus terminal (*also open Sat or Sat–Sun*), including Abitab, Indumex, etc.

COMMUNICATIONS The main post office (Correo) [111 C3] is at Sarandí 468 and Misiones, Ciudad Vieja (⊕ *09.00–18.00 Mon–Fri, 08.00–12.00 Sat*); the main branch in the Centro is in the side of the Palacio Municipal [111 G1] on Ejido (⏁ *09.00–18.00 Mon–Fri*); and the Pocitos branch [88–9 G4] is at 21 de Septiembre 2895 (⏁ *09.00–17.00 Mon–Fri*). There are useful branches with extended hours in the Tres Cruces bus terminal [88–9 F1] (⏁ *09.00–22.00 Mon–Sat, 10.00–22.00 Sun*), Montevideo Shopping (*Plaza de Servicios, Local 07;* ⏁ *10.00–22.00 daily*) and Punta Carretas Shopping [88–9 G5] (*Ellauri 350, Local 7;* ⏁ *10.00–22.00 daily*). There are also many *farmacías* in which you can buy stamps, although the Correo signs aren't obvious.

For international **courier service**, try Federal Express [111 D2] (*Juncal 1321, Plaza Independencia;* ☏ *2 628 0100;* ⏁ *10.00–13.00, 14.00–19.00 Mon–Fri; Avda Rivera 3528;* ⏁ *10.00–20.00 Mon–Fri*) or TNT (*Avda Italia 6878;* ☏ *2 600 1080;* e *tnt@tnt.com.uy*).

The telephone company Antel has **call centres** in Rincón 501 & Treinta y Tres, Ciudad Vieja (⏁ *09.00–18.00 Mon–Fri*); 18 de Julio 891, Centro (⏁ *08.00–23.00 Mon–Sat, 09.30–22.00 Sun*); García Cortinas 2408 and Ellauri (*near Punta Carretas Shopping;* ⏁ *09.00–19.00 Mon–Sat*); and elsewhere, with 24-hour *telecentros* at San José 1101 and the Tres Cruces bus terminal. Antel's *telecentros* are marked on the standard city map handed out at tourist information offices.

Internet access is available at numerous cybercafés, particularly in the Centro, eg: Cibercafé [111 E2] (*San José 1086*), Ciber Coloni@ [88–9 E2] (*Tristán Narvaja 1536 & Colonia*), Cyber [111 E2] (*Soriano 1083*), Cyber ya! [111 E2] (*Convención 1440 & Mercedes*), Internet Colonia [111 F2] (*Colonia 1325*), Maico Computers Cybercafé [111 F2] (*Paraguay 1331*), Tu Rincón Cyber [111 G1] (*Yaguarón 1465*) and 24 Internet/Calculo Comunicaciones [111 F2] (*Plaza Cagancha 1342*). There's no free Wi-Fi in the plazas, unlike the rest of the country, but it is available in the Tres Cruces bus terminal and shopping centre [88–9 F1], Punta Carretas Shopping [88–9 G5], the Buquebus ferry terminal [88–9 A2], the airport, most decent hotels and quite a few pubs and restaurants.

CRIME, SAFETY AND POLICE Generally, Montevideo is a safe friendly city, and you'll find it a relaxing place to explore on foot. Throughout the evening and even after midnight you'll see local women happily walking home from shops or friends' homes without worry. That said, there's a risk of mugging after dark in the further reaches of the Ciudad Vieja, beyond Calle Ituzaingó. This unfortunately includes the port and the Mercado del Puerto. Be prepared to take a taxi home but don't let this put you off. The Barrio Sur and Palermo have a similar reputation but are now much better; on the *rambla* in particular you'll find many families happily strolling well into the night. The one area that you should definitely avoid at night is El Cerro.

In the main tourist areas, such as the Peatonal Sarandí and Avenida 18 de Julio, you'll see Tourist Police in bright yellow tabards, whose main qualification is that they speak some English; they can be called on ☏ 0800 8226.

Police headquarters are at Carlos Quijano 1310 [111 G2], in the Centro. In the Ciudad Vieja the Primera Comisaria de Policía is at 25 de Mayo 230 [111 B3], immediately west of Pérez Castellano. For immigration issues and residence permits, the Dirección Nacional de Migraciones is at Misiones 1513 [111 C2] (☏ *2 916 0471, 2 916 0970;* e *secretaria@dnm.minterior.gub.uy; www.dnm.minterior.gub.uy;* ⏁ *09.15–14.00 Mon–Fri*), at the airport (☏ *2 604 0322/0161;* e *i02carrasco@dnm.minterior.gub.uy*) and the port (☏ *2 915 4253;* e *i01pmdeo@dnm.minterior.gub.uy*).

HEALTH The main hospitals are on Bulevar Artigas [88–9 F2] and on Avenida Italia [88–9 F1], near the Tres Cruces bus terminal. The best, private ones are the Hospital Británico [88–9 F1] (*Avda Italia 2420;* ☏ *2 487 1020;* e *info@*

hospitalbritanico.org.uy; www.hospitalbritanico.org.uy) and the Hospital Italiano [88–9 F1] (*Ospedale Italiano Umberto I; Bvar Artigas 1632;* ✆ *2 247 9717*). Nearby are the Hospital Pereira Rossell [88–9 F1] (*Bvar Artigas 1550;* ✆ *2 707 6667*) and the University of the Republic's Hospital de Clínicas [88–9 G1] (*Avda Italia s/n;* ✆ *2 480 1222, 2 487 1306; www.hc.edu.uy*), both more than adequate. The main children's hospital is the Hospital Pereira Rossell.

Ambulance services
✚ **SEMM** Bvar Artigas 870; ✆ 2 711 1111, emergency ✆ 159

✚ **SUAT** Avda Sarmiento 2570; ✆ 2 711 0711, emergency ✆ 133

✚ **UCM** Bvar Artigas 1958; ✆ 2 487 3333, emergency ✆ 147

WORSHIP
✝ **Iglesia Matriz (Roman Catholic Cathedral)** [111 C2] Plaza Constitución; ✆ 2 915 7018. Masses 12.00 Mon, 12.00 & 17.00 Tue–Sat, 11.00 Sun.

✝ **Iglesia Anglicana (Church of England)** [111 C3] Reconquista 522; ✆ 2 915 4037/9627; http://uruguay.anglican.org. Eucharist Sun 10.00 English/11.30 Spanish.

✝ **Iglesia Evangélica Luterana (German Lutheran Church)** [88–9 E3] Blanes 1116 & Durazno

✝ **Iglesia Metodista (Methodist Church)** Constituyente 1460; ✆ 2 418 4236; http://imu.org.uy. Sun 11.00.

✝ **Iglesia Apostólica Armenia (Armenian Apostolic Church)** [overview] Church of St Nerces Shnorhali, Avda Agraciada 2842; ✆ 2 209 0165. Sun 10.00; Cathedral of Nuestra Señora de Bzonmar, Avda 19 de Abril 3325, Prado; 11.00 Sun, 16.00 Mon–Sat.

✝ **Comunidad Israelita del Uruguay (Jewish Community of Uruguay)** [111 F3] Canelones 1084; ✆ 2 902 5750, 2 710 4396

✝ **Comunidad Sefaradi (Sphardic Community)** [111 B3] Buenos Aires 234; ✆ 2 915 4751, 2 916 1136

✝ **Nueva Comunidad Israelita (New Jewish Community)** [111 E3] Ferreira Aldunate 1168; ✆ 2 902 6620

✝ **Vaad-Hair synagogue** [111 F3] Canelones 828; ✆ 2 900 6106

✝ **Yavne syngaogue** [88–9 G3] Luis B. Cavia 2729/2800, Pocitos; ✆ 2 708 0100

✝ **Centro Islámico Egipcio de Cultura (Egyptian Islamic Cultural Centre)** [88–9 G3] Baltasar Vargas 1178, Pocitos; ✆ 2 708 5637

✝ **Centro Islámico (Muslim Centre)** [111 F2] Mercedes 1204; ✆ 2 903 6785; e jaiumi@adinet.com.uy

CITY TOUR

CIUDAD VIEJA The obvious place to begin a tour of the city is the **Mercado del Puerto** [111 B2], across the road from where ferry and cruise passengers emerge from the port. Although it's widely believed that this cast-iron structure, opened in 1868, was intended to be a railway station in Chile, this is an urban myth, as it was always planned to be a market here. The metalwork was, however, cast in the Union Foundry of Liverpool. In 1897 an iron fountain was added in the centre of the market, and a clock that was restarted in 1996 and is still going strong.

The 3,500m² market is now one of the city's prime tourist attractions, and a hub for *montevideanos* too, especially at weekends, when the many restaurants inside (see pages 96–7) are buzzing. There's no smoking inside, of course, but thanks to all the *parrillas* grilling away inside, the cloudy vaults could almost belong to a steam-era railway station after all. There are also restaurants outside, which remain open into the evening when the market itself is closed, and there are buskers and other entertainment, especially at weekends.

Alongside the Mercado is the Museo del Carnaval [111 A2] (see page 122); across the road is the massive Customs building [111 A2] (*Aduana*, 1923), and on its north side (passing a plaque put up by the Customs men in honour of the 1928 Olympic soccer team) the entry to the port. Show your ID here and you can go in to see an anchor of the battleship *Admiral Graf Spee* (see the box on pages 76–7) and

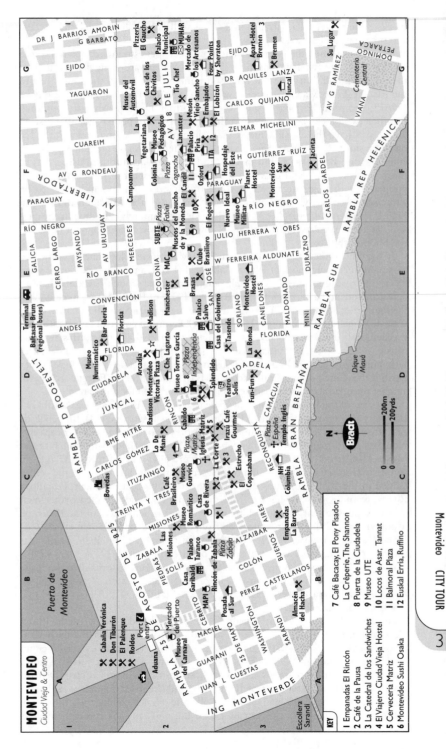

MONTEVIDEO
Ciudad Vieja & Centro

Puerto de Montevideo

Port entry
Aduana

KEY

1 Empanadas El Rincón
2 Café de la Pausa
3 La Catedral de los Sandwiches
4 El Viajero Ciudad Vieja Hostel
5 Cervecería Matriz
6 Montevideo Sushi Osaka
7 Café Bacacay, El Pony Pisador,
  La Crêperie, The Shannon
8 Puerta de la Ciudadela
9 Museo UTE
10 Locos de Asar, Tannat
11 Balmoral Plaza
12 Euskal Erria, Ruffino

its 27-tonne rangefinder, salvaged in 2004, as well as a small dockside steam crane and other bits and pieces.

The area around the Mercado has now been pedestrianised, including the stretch of Pérez Castellano south to 25 de Mayo; there are some decent shops at the northern end, but little but fast-food joints up the hill to the south. Just to the east, at 25 de Mayo 279, the new Museo de Arte Precolombino y Indígena (MAPI; see page 122) has taken over the former Defence Ministry building. Another two blocks brings you into the heart of a very poor residential district where you have the classic Ciudad Vieja sight of roads sloping down to the sea on three sides. To the west, Sarandí leads past the Cuartel de Dragones [111 A3] (the Dragoon Barracks, rebuilt in 1831 and now run-down but in use as part of the Maciel hospital) and down to the Escollera, a long breakwater that's very popular for fishing; the views of the harbour are a bit too industrial to be attractive. Nearby a very anonymous building houses the **Almacén del Hacha** [111 B3] (*Buenos Aires 202 & Maciel*), the oldest commercial building in the city; in 1794 a barman was killed with an axe by an Italian seaman, giving it its name, the Shop of the Axe.

In the other direction, Sarandí leads to Plaza Matriz (see below) and the cathedral, passing immediately south of **Plaza Zabala** [111 B3], a pleasant open space set at 45° to the road grid; there's a sizeable colony of *cotorras* (monk parakeets) here to entertain you, and a very grand bronze statue (1931) of Bruno Mauricio de Zabala, the founder of Montevideo. This was the site of the original Spanish fort, then of the Casa de Gobierno (Government House), which became a public library in 1816 and was demolished in 1880; the plaza was inaugurated in 1890. On the north side of the square is the splendid Palacio Taranco [111 B2], now the Museo de Artes Decorativas (see page 123), on the site of the city's first theatre, and a block further north is the church of **San Francisco** [111 B2], built in 1864 in Eclectic style (with a rather unusual steeple, finished in 1895) and now closed for restoration.

Just west of the Palacio Taranco, at 25 de Mayo 314, is the **Casa Garibaldi** [111 B2], now an outpost of the Museo Histórico Nacional (see page 124). Rincón leads east from Plaza Zabala, passing the Montevideo Waterworks Company's Neoclassical former offices on the corner of Zabala, and the main branch of the Museo Histórico Nacional in the **Casa de Rivera** [111 C2] at Rincón 437. A fairly simple two-storey building with a distinctive lighthouse-like tower in the centre (added in the 1850s), this was the home of Uruguay's first president, Fructuoso Rivera, from 1834 (he bought it from the family of a widow killed by her own slaves). Opposite it at Misiones 1399 is the former headquarters of the Banco de Montevideo (1929), and across the road from that the Bolsa de Comercio [111 C2] (*Stock Exchange; Misiones 1400*), a fine Modernist block built in 1936. To the rear (north) of the Casa de Rivera is the **Casa Montero** [111 C2] (*25 de Mayo 428*), a two-storey Neoclassical house that now houses the Museo Romántico (see page 123), another branch of the Museo Histórico Nacional. A block away at 25 de Mayo 500 the **Caja Obrera** [111 C2] (Workers' Bank; 1941) displays some fine reliefs by Edmundo Prati.

Another block east along Rincón from the Bolsa de Comercio is **Plaza Constitución** [111 C2], also known as Plaza Matriz because of the **cathedral** (*Iglesia Matriz;* ⊕ *09.00–19.00*) on its west side. This is not an especially grand basilica (it was built in 1790–1804 as the Baroque style was going out of fashion), but does have some nice tombs, including those of Juan Antonio Lavalleja, Dámaso Antonio Larrañaga and presidents Rivera and Suárez. There's a splendid Neorenaissance baptistry, with marble walls and plaster ceiling, just inside the main doors to the right – it's usually closed but you can look through the glass doors (it's always lit).

Around the fine fountain in the centre of the plaza there's an antiques market on Saturdays and often on other days too. On the south side of the plaza is a row of imposing buildings, notably the Club Uruguay, built in 1885–88 in the Historical Eclectic style; on the west side is the **Cabildo** or former City Hall [111 D2], a fine Neoclassical palace built in 1804. One of the city's few unaltered colonial buildings, it housed courts and a prison and is now a museum (see page 124). Just to its north, at Gómez 1390, is a striking Art Deco apartment block. On the north side of the cathedral is the **Museo Gurvich** [111 C2] (see page 124); on the north side of the plaza is an ugly government block housing on its ground floor the **Sala de Arte Carlos Federico Sáez** [111 C2] (⊕ *09.30–18.00 Mon–Fri; www.mtop.gub.uy/salasaez*) which puts on free shows of art and photography.

Two blocks south of the cathedral is **Holy Trinity Church** [111 C3], the Anglican cathedral (Templo Inglés), a fine Neoclassical edifice (with no steeple) that's now very tatty and in a run-down area. Built in 1844 close to the shore, it was moved inland in 1835 when the Rambla Gran Bretaña was built.

To the north of Plaza Matriz lies the financial district, the busiest part of the Ciudad Vieja in the daytime, and home to some good restaurants (mostly lunchtime only) as well as bank headquarters. A block north of the plaza at the junction of Gómez and 25 de Mayo is a spiky 'Flamboyant Neogothic' confection that was built as the Casa Gómez in 1870–85 but was never lived in; it now houses the Junta Departamental de Montevideo, the seat of the council for the department of Montevideo (not just the city). A block west of this, at 25 de Mayo 555, a striking Expressionist tower [111 C2] marks the Edificio Centenario (1930). Continuing three blocks north to the main road on the south side of the docks (*Rambla 25 de Agosto*), where the historic shoreline was, you'll reach the Parque Portuario, a new plaza of bare sun-baked white stone, and at its west end the **Bovedas** (Vaults) [111 C1], the remains of a series of 34 shellproof powder stores built in 1794–1807; one blew up in 1815, killing over 100 people. Most were demolished in 1926, but those that survived have recently been restored, along with the Neoclassical Casa de los Ximénez (1817), facing them at Rambla 25 de Agosto 580–86.

If you choose to loop back to the Mercado del Puerto from here on Cerrito, you'll pass the former Banco de Londres at Zabala 1486, a dilapidated Neoclassical pediment (1890) attached to the modern Lloyds TSB bank on Cerrito, the site of the Artigas family home at Zabala 1500, then the Banco de la República Oriental at Cerrito 351, a Neoclassical pile (built by Juan Veltroni in 1926–38) that in fact occupies the entire block. At Zabala 1469 the **Casa Lavalleja** [111 B2] is a plain two-storey colonial house, built in 1783 by Manuel Cipriano de Melo; bought in 1830 by Juan Antonio Lavalleja (then interim head of state), it was his home until his death in 1853. It's now owned by the Museo Histórico Nacional but is not open to the public. Across the *rambla* at the north end of Zabala you'll glimpse a warehouse by Eladio Dieste (see page 34), not very special architecture but recognisably in his style of undulating brickwork.

If you prefer to continue from Plaza Matriz towards the Centro, you can go along Rincón, passing the **Palacio Gandos** [111 D2] (now the Consorcio del Uruguay) at No 649 and the Centro Cultural de España [111 D2] at No 629 (see page 104). Built as an ironmongers in 1870, this has been beautifully refurbished around the original steel columns and covered atrium. The rear of the first floor is a *mediateca*, with free use of books, newspapers and films, and the front is a *café literaria*, very relaxing as the clients are all quietly browsing arty magazines.

Alternatively you can follow **Sarandí** from the Cabildo – this stretch was pedestrianised in 1995 and is busy with hippies selling the handmade jewellery that Uruguayans seem to need so much of, as well as art galleries and antique shops. To the right, Mitre and Bacacay, lined with restaurants and bars, are the city's busiest area at night. Opposite Bacacay, the **Edifico Pablo Ferrando** [111 D2] (*Sarandí 675*) is a beautiful Art Nouveau building (1917) with a huge area of window; it's now a bookshop. Next to it is the **Museo Torres García** [111 D2] (see page 125), dedicated to Uruguay's national painter and well worth a visit.

Just west, the **Puerta de la Ciudadela** [111 D2], dating from 1746, is all that remains of the citadel of Montevideo; it now marks the entry point from the Ciudad Vieja to **Plaza Independencia** [111 D2] and the Centro or New Town. A line of orange paint on the Plaza marks the outline of the Ciudadela, which was demolished in 1829–33, except for a few bits of wall still visible at the northwest corner of the plaza. (At the junction of Buenos Aires and Mitre, just west of the Teatro Solís, you can also see the remains of the Batería San Sebastían.) A public market grew up on the site of the citadel, which was known as Plaza Independencia by 1843; by the 1860s there was an even Doric colonnade (based on the Rue de Rivoli in Paris) all the way around the square, but this was largely lost when the square was expanded in 1877.

The **Teatro Solís** [111 D3], to the southwest of Plaza Independencia, is one of the city's chief landmarks and its cultural heart. Built in 1842–56, with lateral wings added in 1868–74 (originally housing the national museum and public library), it was very well refurbished in 1998–2008. The lyre-shaped hall has superb acoustics, and a new set of stairs connects all the floors, doing away with the original set-up that kept the rich patrons apart from those in the cheaper seats. The basement exhibition hall (⊕ *15.00–20.00 Tue–Sun*) shows varying displays of costumes, set designs and the like (there are also very nice toilets). Backstage tours (*16.00 Tue & Thu, 11.00, 12.00 & 16.00 Wed, Fri & Sun, 11.00, 12.00, 13.00 & 16.00 Sat*) cost US$1 in Spanish or US$2 in other languages; they are free on Wednesdays (in Spanish only).

In the centre of Plaza Independencia is the great bronze equestrian **statue of Artigas** [111 D2], the father of independent Uruguay, by the Italian sculptor Angelo Zanelli, erected in 1923. Beneath it (on the west side) the ashes of Artigas were installed in 1977 in a dramatically lit mausoleum, where two guards from the ceremonial Regimiento Blandengues flank the urn and the walls are inscribed with the key dates of his career. In June 2009 a controversial decision was taken to transfer Artigas's remains to the **Casa de Gobierno** [111 D2] (also known as the Palacio Estévez after its builder, and as the Edificio Independencia). This is the arcaded building on the south side of the plaza, built in 1873–74, which served as the seat of government from 1880 to 1985; it's now the *presidencia*, used only for protocol receptions and as a museum of the presidents (see page 125). After the end of the dictatorship, President Sanguinetti moved the presidency into the Ministry of Defence, out in the northern suburbs and now known as the Edificio Libertad.

The immensely ugly block between the Edificio Independencia and the Teatro Solís is the Torre Ejecutiva (Executive Tower – formerly the Palacio de Justicia), which was started in the 1960s, left as a steel frame for several decades, and finally handed over to the government in mid-2009, with the intention of bringing the presidency back to the city centre before too long.

THE CENTRO The Centro (New Town or midtown) is the commercial heart of the city, and to many Uruguayans and tourists it *is* the city. It was laid out after 1861, and by 1867 development had spread beyond the present Palacio Municipal into the Cordón area. The main axis is **Avenida 18 de Julio**, running from Plaza Independencia via Plaza Fabini (aka Plaza Entrevero) and Plaza Libertad (aka Plaza Cagancha) to the **Palacio Municipal** [111 G2] (aka the Intendencia) at Ejido. It's a busy shopping street and bus artery, and is also lined with superb Eclectic and Art Deco buildings.

The city's most recognisable landmark is the **Palacio Salvo** [111 D2], built in 1922–28 on the site of the Confitería la Giralda, the café where the very first tango, 'La Cumparsita', was performed in 1917. Originally a hotel, with a theatre in the basement (now a car park) in which Josephine Baker performed, it was converted into apartments in the 1960s. When it opened it was the tallest building in Latin America and the highest reinforced-concrete building in the world; another tower, the Palacio Barolo, was built in Buenos Aires at the same time, and the plan was to signal between the two with lights (as if radio had not been invented). In any case the curvature of the earth meant that the distance was just a bit too great for the scheme to work. Something like a gigantic space rocket dreamt up by Jules Verne, with four booster-rocket turrets strapped to the main tower, it should be ugly but manages to be loveable. There's a small display in the foyer, which is drab but lively, with residents coming and going.

On the other side of Avenida 18 de Julio, the **Palacio Rinaldi** [111 D2] (*Plaza Independencia 1356–58*) is a fine Art Deco apartment block (built in 1929) with beautiful reliefs on the façade. Buildings to look out for along the Avenida include the Jockey Club at No 857 (built in 1920 in Historical Eclectic style), the Edifico Lapido at No 948–50 (a splendid Expressionist apartment block, built in 1930), the Palacio Brasil at No 984–94 (built in 1919 in Historical Eclectic style) and the Palacio Uriarte de Heber at No 998–1000 (built in 1896–97 in Historical Eclectic style), now housing the museums of the Gaucho and of the Mint (see page 126). Across the road from this, on the south side of Plaza Fabini, is the Edificio Cine Rex, built as a cinema (but now a theatre) in 1928, in Historical Eclectic style.

Plaza Fabini [111 E2] was remodelled in 1964, with the sculpture of *El Entrevero* (The Brawl) by José Belloni installed in 1967; with its curving path, continuous benches and combined café-bus stop, it's regarded as one of the most successful pieces of urban design worldwide. Just north of the plaza at Herrera y Obes 1431 is the church of the **Immaculate Conception** [111 E2], established in 1858 after the Bishop of Bayonne sent priests to tend to the Basque community; a slightly odd Neoclassical building, with the organ behind the altar, it's still the centre of the city's Basque community.

Continuing up Avenida 18 de Julio, it's just two blocks (passing the Edificio del London-Paris, built in 1908 in Historical Eclectic style) to **Plaza Cagancha** [111 F2], also known as Plaza Libertad after the statue of Liberty (1866) atop a column in the centre of the avenue. On the south side of the plaza is the **Supreme Court** [111 F2], in the Palacio Piria at Gutiérrez Ruiz 1310 (in fact on the pedestrianised Pasaje de los Derechos Humanos or Human Rights Passage); built in 1910 in Historical Eclectic style, this was the town house of the property developer and alchemist Francisco Piria (see page 128–9 and 173). On the north side of the plaza is the Ateneo or **Athenaeum** [111 F2], built in 1900 in Historical Eclectic style as an arts centre; immediately on its east side is the Museo Pedagógico (see page 125), a Neoclassical mansion built in 1889.

Avenida 18 de Julio continues out of the square past the Edificio Sorocabana, built in 1925 in Historical Eclectic style, with a prominent tower on its leading corner. A block further east, the **Palacio Santos** [111 F2], a single-storey villa built in 1881–86 by President Maximo Santos, now houses the Ministry of Foreign Affairs (although most of the work is done in a modern block at the rear, well disguised by the slope of the street). Opposite is the former Confitería La Americana (*18 de Julio 1216–20*), a pleasantly asymmetrical Art Deco block built in 1937. On the next block to the east, the former building of the El Día newspaper, with its huge portico, faces the Edificio Café Montevideo, both built in the 1920s in Historical Eclectic style. On the next block, at Avenida 18 de Julio 1333, the **Palacio Díaz** [111 G2] (1929) is a spectacular Art Deco apartment block that tapers upwards into a tower like a miniature Empire State Building.

On the next block east, the **Palacio Municipal** [111 G2] or Intendencia (the City Hall) rises behind a small plaza at 18 de Julio 1352–60; built in 1936–41 (but not finally completed until 1968), it's an otherwise plain brick Modernist building with a grand loggia that's reminiscent of Norwich City Hall in England. In front stands what is supposedly one of only three good copies of Michelangelo's *David* in the world. In the spacious entry hall there are usually interesting exhibitions, as well as the Espacio Cultural Ciudadano (⊕ *10.00–16.00 Mon–Fri*), with exhibits of old postcards and maps of the city, and the Centro Municipal de Fotografía (⊕ *10.00–19.00 Mon–Fri, 09.30–14.30 Sat; www.montevideo.gub.uy/fotografia*), which puts on very good photography exhibitions in a small exhibition space at San José 1360, in the tunnel under the Palacio. The doors to the Sala Aquiles Lanza are early 20th-century replicas of the Puerta del Paraíso, Ghiberti's doors to the Baptistry of the Duomo in Florence, and there are also replicas of 13th- and 15th-century carvings from Chartres and Amiens cathedrals. In fact the MUHAR collection (see page 126), below the Palacio, largely consists of replicas of great artworks from all around the world.

CORDÓN Immediately east of the Palacio Municipal the main avenue splits on either side of the *Gaucho* **statue** [111 G2] (1927, by José Luis Zorrilla de San Martín), with Avenida 18 de Julio swinging slightly to the left and Constituyentes heading to the right towards Palermo and Parque Rodó. To the south of the statue at Constituyente 1460 is the city's **Methodist church** [88–9 D2] (1909), much like a Catholic church but with a style of steeple that's only possible with concrete.

Five blocks up Avenida 18 de Julio you'll pass **Plaza de los Treinta y Tres Orientales** [88–9 D2], better known as Plaza Lavalleja (because of a statue) or Plaza Bomberos (because of the imposing 1920s fire station on its north side, known as the Cuartel Centenario de Bomberos). It's two blocks further to the Lycée Français (1937) at Avenida 18 de Julio 1772 and the **Biblioteca Nacional** (National Library; 1937–55) at No 1790, their Neoclassical porticos echoing each other. Immediately beyond (opposite Tristán Narvaja, site of the Sunday market) is the main building of the Universidad de la República (now the Law Faculty; 1911); there are a few student bars and bookshops in this area, but not as many as you might expect.

Just to the east the Ministerio de Salud Pública (Public Health Ministry) stands across the avenue from a bright Neoclassical portico at Avenida 18 de Julio 1865, also used by the health service; just beyond, at the crossroads of Avenida Crespo, stand the modern Banco Hipotecario del Uruguay (Mortgage Bank of Uruguay) and the Dirección General Impositiva (Tax Office), beyond which it's another eight blocks of apartment blocks (with some nice Art Deco buildings) before the busy Bulevar Artigas and the **Obelisco** [88–9 F1], erected in 1938 in homage to the Constituyentes, those who drew up the country's constitution in 1830. The sculptures of Law, Liberty and Strength around the base of the 40m-high obelisk are by José Luis Zorrilla de San Martín. Just to the northeast of the obelisk, the **Hospital Italiano** [88–9 F1] is a beautiful arcaded building, built in 1890 by Luis Andreoni (also responsible for the Estación Central and the Club Uruguay).

Back on the west side of Artigas (beyond a crucifix and monument to John Paul II, the first Pope to visit Uruguay) is the **Tres Cruces bus terminal** [88–9 F1] (see page 81). The name comes from the wooden crosses commemorating three travellers killed by robbers here in the early 18th century; it's also where Artigas's *Instrucciones del Ano XIII* were debated (see page 15). Just north of the terminal, what looks like a mission church is actually the church of San Expedito, the chapel of the women's prison (*Acevedo Díaz 1923 & Miguelete;* ⊕ *14.00–17.00 Tue & Thu, 08.30–11.00 Sun, & 07.00–19.30 on 19th of each month*) – over 10,000 pilgrims come here on 19 April each year.

On the south side of the Hospital Italiano, Canning and Lord Ponsonby (named after the British diplomats who brought about Uruguayan independence) lead east to **Parque Batlle y Ordóñez** [88–9 G1], passing the residences of the British and American ambassadors, fine villas set in spacious gardens. Space for a park was allocated in 1907, and the French landscape designer Charles Thays started work in 1911; after World War I it was known as Parque de los Aliados, after the victorious allies, but was then named after Uruguay's greatest president. The park was only opened in 1934, after the first soccer World Cup. On the far side of the park is the **Estadio Centenario** (Centenary Stadium) [88–9 G1], built in a rush by Juan Scasso in 1929–30, and not actually ready for the opening matches of the World Cup. The world's first stadium built specifically for soccer, it was declared an International Historical Football Monument in 1980 and now houses the Museum of Football (see page 127). Built to mark the centenary of the adoption of the constitution, it accommodated 100,000 spectators (now 70,000) and had a 100m-high Homage Tower, built to display the spotlit winners' flag, which gives panoramic views. There are other sports facilities, such as a velodrome and an athletics track, in the park, and immediately beyond it on Avenida Italia the Hospital de Clínicas [88–9 G1], the city's largest public hospital. José Belloni's sculpture *La Carreta* (The Oxcart; 1934), in honour of the country's rural pioneers, is visible in the park from Avenida Italia.

NORTH TO THE PRADO From Plaza Fabini the broad Avenida del Libertador General Lavalleja runs northeast through the Aguada district to the massive Palacio Legislativo; it passes the historic **Estación Central** [88–9 C2], two blocks west of La Paz. Opened in 1897, this was controversially closed in 2003 when a much smaller modern terminal was opened about 500m to the north – passenger numbers on the already attenuated suburban service were far too low for the cavernous train shed of the Estación Central, but the remoter location of the new station was predicted to drive loadings down even further. The property developer bought the site at a low price on condition of converting the original station into a cultural centre, but this has not happened, and the building has fallen into a distressing state of decay, with homeless people sleeping behind the statues of George Stephenson, Volta, Papin and Watt in front of the building. In 2009 it was agreed that the tracks would be reconnected so that the port could handle containers on the station approaches.

Heading north from the Estación Central on Paraguay, you'll come to the modern station, and immediately north, the dramatic new **Torre de las Communicaciones** [88–9 C1], the tallest building in the country at 159m, recently renamed the Torre Joaquín Torres García. Built for the national phone company Antel by Carlos Ott, it has a *mirador* (viewing area) on the 26th floor (❭ *2 928 4417;* e *visitasguiadas@antel.com.uy;* ⊕ *15.30–17.00 Mon, Wed & Fri, 10.30–12.00 Tue–Thu*). There's also a small museum of telecommunications (see page 127), a multi-purpose hall and amphitheatre, and outdoor sculptures by Nelsón Ramos and Águeda Dicancro.

Three blocks south of the Palacio Legislativo at Avenida Libertador 1960 is the **Iglesia Sagrado Corazón (Sacred Heart Church)** [88–9 C1], a fairly grand but tatty Neoclassical structure with a new façade added in 1837 – this is where the Asamblea General Constituyente y Legislativa (the General Constituent and Legislative Assembly) met from February to April of 1829 to draft the new country's constitution.

The **Palacio Legislativo** (Legislative Palace) [88–9 D1], also known as the Congreso, sits on a small hill and makes a fine sight along Avenida Libertador, even if it can't really be seen from the heart of the city. It was designed by Vittorio Meano, who died a mysterious death before he knew he'd won the competition, leaving Cayetano Moretti and others to oversee construction, from 1908 to 1925. It's a massive Neoclassical pile with ornate decorations (largely by Italian artists) in white marble, granite, porphyry and basalt. On the lawns on the north and south sides are two matching pairs of Rodinesque sculptures (representing Law, Justice, the Sciences and Labour) by Giannino Castiglioni, who also designed the façades along with José Belloni and Gervasio Furest. Guided tours (⟍ 2 924 1783; e protocolo@parlamento.gub.uy; ⊕ 09.00, 10.00, 11.00, 12.00, 14.30, 15.30 & 16.00 Mon–Fri; US$3) take up to 1½ hours, and start on the north side. You'll begin by being led up into the huge Salón de los Pasos Perdidos (Hall of Lost Steps), where two guards in 19th-century uniforms flank the text of Uruguay's Declaration of Independence in the centre of the hall, beneath allegorical stained glass windows and Venetian mosaics of the arts and the sciences (by Giovanni Buffa), four plaster reliefs by Edmundo Prati showing key scenes of Uruguayan history, from the Grito de Asencio to Independence, and four reliefs of the national symbols by José Belloni on the ceiling. The floor and walls are composed of 52 types of Uruguayan marble, as well as granite and porphyry, with light fittings of bronze and Murano glass.

At the south end is the small Reception Hall, with two big and slightly lurid paintings by Manuel Rosé (on canvas, although they look like murals) and an almost photorealist depiction by Pedro Blanes Viale of the Swearing of the Constitution of 1830 (behind the text of the constitution itself, flanked by two more guards). At the other end of the central hall is the Fiesta Hall, with a Byzantine-style ceiling of wood and gold leaf by the Venetian Enrico Albertazzi. Here there are portraits of Lavalleja and Rivera by José Luis Zorrilla de San Martín, portraits of Rivera and Oribe and a Battle of Las Piedras by Rosé, and *Las Instrucciones del Año XIII* by Pedro Blanes Viale.

On one side of the central Salón de los Pasos Perdidos is the chamber of the Diputados, panelled in Italian walnut, and on the other that of the Senadores, in Paraguayan mahogany; tours are taken upstairs to view them from galleries. The 99 deputies sit facing a painting of Artigas meeting Rondeau during the second siege of Montevideo in 1813, by the French artist Fernand Laroche. The Senate chamber (with just 30 members) is a rather smaller semicircle, with a bust of Pallas Athena (goddess of wisdom) above the national shield.

Going up another flight (you'll also see the white marble caryatids around the exterior of the central lantern, and the sgraffito decoration of the four internal courts around it) is the Pompeian-style library. Also panelled in very dark wood, it has very tempting leather armchairs and bookcases with stained-glass doors, a copy of the *Venus de Milo* and in the centre of the room a maquette of the statue of Artigas by Angelo Zanelli now in the Plaza Independencia. A copy of every book by an Uruguayan author has to be deposited here, along with one at the Biblioteca Nacional, and it now contains close to 300,000 books. It's open to the public in the mornings, and in the afternoon to legislators only.

From the Palacio Legislativo, Avenida Agraciada heads northwest, roughly parallel to the shoreline, eventually crossing Bulevar Artigas, the main road to the west, and coming to the west side of the Prado, once an area of *quintas*, weekend homes for the city's most affluent citizens, and still an upmarket residential district. You'll pass the Armenian Apostolic Church of St Nerces Shnorhali (see *Montevideo overview map*, page 74) (*Avenida Agraciada 2842*), with a miraculous relief of St Gregory the Illuminator and, outside, a monument raised in 1975 to the victims of the 1915 genocide of the Armenians in Turkey. Typically, it has an altar raised on a proscenium stage (in the apse) but otherwise has a fairly anonymous interior.

Just north of the Armenian church, a statue of Joaquín Suárez stands in a road junction, from where Avenida Suárez runs north to the east side of the Prado Park; at No 3765 is the remarkably low-key presidential residence, next to the Castillo Soneira at No 3781, a mock castle incongruously set opposite McDonalds and Mondo del Pizza. Continuing north (now on Avenida Millán), you'll pass some fine villas, and at Avenida Millán 4015 reach the Museo de Bellas Artes (Museum of Fine Arts; see page 127), a typical large *quinta* with behind it the **Jardín Japones** [overview map] (🕐 *12.00–18.00 Wed–Mon; free*), an authentically Japanese garden fitted around the existing trees in 2001, including an *ishi-doro* stone lantern, a zigzag bridge, a tea house and a stone garden. Immediately to the north is the Arroyo del Miguelete, the only river flowing through Montevideo, alongside which a new park has been created.

Just south of the Museum of Fine Arts, Avenida Luis Alberto de Herrera leads west to the Prado via the Botanic Garden (see below) and east to the **Barrio Atahualpa** [overview map], Montevideo's best-known garden suburb, laid out in 1868. Three blocks east (at Cubo del Norte) you'll come to the Boliche de los Yuyos (the Pub of the Herbs, founded in 1906 and so called because of the herb-flavoured grappas it specialised in), with a fine Art Deco house opposite it, and then the Neogothic Capilla Jackson, built in 1870 for the same family that built the present Museo del Gaucho. Just to the east is the former Quinta de Larrañaga, built in 1830 by Dámaso Antonio Larrañaga (1771–1848), a priest who was very active in public and scientific life; its attractive grounds are now used by a youth sports organisation, but you're free to walk around. To the south of Herrera is the dull Plaza Atahualpa and the Quinta de Vaz Ferreira (1918), now hemmed in by suburban houses but once a larger estate where the philosopher Carlos Vaz Ferreira grew up as seemingly the only normal one among nine dysfunctional siblings. At the rear of the modern Farmacía Atahualpa (*Avda Millán 3701*) is the Pharmacy Museum (see page 128), founded in 1908 on the other side of the road.

To the west of Avenida Millán, Avenida Herrera leads swiftly to the northern gate of the Jardín Botánico (Botanic Garden; see page 128), although the main gate is to the south at Avenida 19 de Abril 1181; the River Plate, Montevideo Wanderers and Bella Vista soccer grounds are in this area too. Immediately beyond, you'll reach the Arroyo Miguelete and the Parque del Prado proper, famed for its Easter Week rodeo and cattle show, and for the Rosedal (Rose Garden), laid out in 1912 by the French garden designer Charles Racine. Turning left on to Avenida Delmira Agustín, on the south side of the *arroyo*, you'll pass the sculptural group of **Los Últimos Charrúas** [overview map] by Edmundo Prati, Gervasio Furest Muñoz and Enrique Lussich (1938), commemorating the four sad Charrúa *indigenas* (plus a baby born in France) who were shipped off to Paris to be exhibited and never returned (see page 16). Beyond it at the Plaza del Policía (on Avenida Agraciada) is *La Diligencia* (The Stagecoach), another sculpture by José Belloni (1952). This is the Paso del Molino, once the only crossing of the Miguelete and a prestigious resort in the 19th century. There are plenty of buses back to the city centre on Avenida Agraciada, but it's also interesting to walk some way south, past the Mauresque ex-cinema at Agraciada 3759 and the very grand quintas at No 3567 (now a Salvation Army retirement home), Capurro 980 and Agraciada (now the naval hydrographic and meteorological service), Agraciada 3451 (headquarters of the army's First Division), No 3423, and No 3397–3401 (formerly the Argentine embassy).

EL CERRO On the far side of the harbour, west of the Prado and across Highway 1 to Colonia, rises the distinctive Cerro de Montevideo [overview map], the 139m-high mount that gave Montevideo its name. Uruguay's oldest lighthouse was built here by Spain in 1802, surrounded in 1809–11 (after the British invasions) by a fort, from which the flag of the United Provinces was first flown, in defiance of Spain. In the Battle of El Cerro in 1826, Uruguayan troops led by Manuel Oribe drove off Brazilian forces. In 1860–64 it was used to quarantine victims of yellow fever, and then decayed until it was restored in 1931–39 and became a military museum. Turning off Ruta 1 and then following Gracia parallel to the shore, turn right up Viacara through the run-down residential area and then left at a small Che Guevara monument to the *castillo*. It's possible to take a bus (line 76, 125, 128 or 195) and then walk up from Gracia, but most people prefer to take a taxi, which will wait while you admire the museum and the view. Known since 1882 as the Fortaleza General Artigas, it's staffed by friendly soldiers who will point out where the *Graf Spee* sank, off Punta Yeguas.

Below the fortress to the southwest (beyond a newly refurbished stretch of *rambla* and the Playa Cerro bus terminal) lies the delightful Club de Golf del Cerro [overview map], with its vintage clubhouse, founded in 1905 as the Chimont (Chicago–Montevideo), a nod to the home of the owners of the Frigórifico Montevideo. The Frigórifico Montevideo, known as the Frigórifico Swift from 1916, is the meat-packing plant immediately to the south on Punta de Lobos. Just to the west is the Frigórifico Nacional, also American-owned; both were closed by 1978. El Cerro grew up as a settlement of immigrants attracted by the jobs in the *frigóríficos*, and the streets are named after their countries of origin, such as Poland, Portugal, France, England, Bulgaria and China.

THE EASTERN SUBURBS To the south of the Centro is the **Barrio Sur**, a poor residential district with many run-down Belle Epoque houses and a few Art Deco ones; this is the heart of the *candombé* culture, with *comparsas* often drumming in the streets on evenings and weekends. The only tourist sight in the area, other than the stroll along the *rambla* past the formerly British gasworks, is the **Cementerio Central** [111 G4] (*Central Cemetery; Gonzalo Ramírez 1302;* ⊕ *10.00–16.45 daily*), laid out in 1835. Its alleys are lined with grand tombs including those of the Pittamiglio family (on the way to the central chapel), Dr Washington Beltrán, a journalist and statesman, (just inside the gate to the right) and President Claudio Williman (in a large grey tomb on the diagonal alley to the left from the gate). The cemetery is also enlivened by its population of parakeets.

To the east of Ejido, running south from the Palacio Municipal, is **Palermo**, similar but with patches of gentrification, and a few bars and restaurants along Avenida Gonzálo Ramírez; No 1497 (now the Edificio Montserrat) was the home of the novelist Juan Carlos Onetti (see page 29). On the *rambla* is the US embassy [88–9 E4], an early Brutalist design by I M Pei (1959–68), but not too fortress-like. Two streets were closed by bollards in the 1990s, but after constant complaints they were opened up again in 2007, although it's still not possible to pass through and underneath the building as Pei intended. To the east is the **Parque Rodó** district, around the park of the same name, opened in 1901 and now named after the writer José Enrique Rodó, who died in 1917; there's a large monument to him (as well as statues of Confucius, Einstein and the playwright Florencio Sánchez), and a small castle by a lake that houses a children's library and is a venue for story-telling and puppet shows. On the east side of the park is the excellent **Museo Nacional de Artes Visuales** [88–9 F4] (see page 128). To the south is a fun-fair, and across the *rambla* is Playa Ramírez, the nearest beach to the city centre, popular for beach volleyball and soccer. Heading south, the *rambla* splits and passes either side of the open-air **Teatro del Verano (Summer Theatre)** [88–9 F4], venue of *candombé* and *murga* competitions during Carnaval.

The *rambla* swings around the Club de Golf del Uruguay, with various fishing clubs on the seaward side, as well as the Holocaust Memorial, to **Punta Carretas** [88–9 G6], the southernmost point of the city, jutting out into the River Plate. A dusty track leads south to the *faro* (*lighthouse; Punta Brava;* ⊕ *24hrs; US$0.70*), built in 1876. The final steps are steep and awkward and not at all Health & Safety-compliant. It's not very high (20m), but gives nice views east and west. The whole headland is pleasantly informal, with people driving out to fish and drink *maté*. Not far north of the *rambla*, the Punta Carretas prison, which was notorious during the dictatorship for its treatment of political prisoners (over 100 of whom broke out in 1971) reopened in 1995 after a very successful conversion into the Punta Carretas Shopping mall. The surrounding area of Punta Carretas has also been transformed, from a somewhat gloomy area to a desirable suburb with fine bars and restaurants. It's also home to the Juan Zorrilla de San Martín Museum (see page 128), in the poet/diplomat's lovely Andalusian-style home, and the truly eccentric Castillo Pittamiglio (see page 128).

The upmarket Villa Biarritz and Punta Trouville residential areas lie along the *rambla* as it leads back northwards to **Pocitos**, a livelier district with plenty of shops, bars and restaurants (a block or three inland from the *rambla*), and plenty of streetlife in and around them. Apartments here are not cheap, but it's not an exclusive area, so it's popular with young professionals and families; it also has a decent beach, longer but less sheltered than Playa Ramírez. This is lined with an almost unbroken line of eight- to ten-storey apartment blocks, leading some to describe this as Montevideo's Copacabana. The main arteries leading inland (to Bulevar Artigas) are Bulevar España and Avenida Brasil, with some fine Art Nouveau and Art Deco villas; the two blocks of Santiago Vásquez east of Brasil also have some fine old buildings, but otherwise Pocitos has been almost entirely rebuilt since the 1950s. At the junction of Avenida Brasil and J B Blanco, the Edificio El Mástil is one of the city's major Art Deco buildings.

To the east of Pocitos (beyond the Naval Museum – see page 129) is the **Buceo** district, with the Yacht Club Uruguayo and the Puerto del Buceo, a small harbour for yachts, sport-fishing boats and tours out to the **Isla de Flores**, 30km to the east (and 12km offshore), a quarantine island for slaves and later for immigrants and for mail (which was sterilised in an autoclave), and in the 1930s a prison for intellectuals and others opposed to the dictatorship of Gabriel Terra. On the highest point of the island stands a stumpy, Portuguese-style lighthouse – many ships were wrecked on the Banco Ingles (English Bank, once known as the *tragabarcos* or ship-eater), just to the east, but the authorities in Buenos Aires refused to allow the construction of a lighthouse because it would have attracted trade to the rival port of Montevideo; eventually a cunning treaty recognised Brazilian ownership of Rio Grande do Sul state in exchange for Brazil building a lighthouse here in 1828. There are still the remains of the first- and second-class hotels (reminiscent of the opening of *Little Dorrit*), through which passed almost 58,000 immigrants between 1871 and 1891; later a narrow-gauge railway was built to reach the isolation unit at the end of the island. The lighthouse is closed, but the island can be visited, mainly by birdwatchers (in about October some areas are closed in deference to nesting gulls).

Buceo owes its name ('Diving') to the many colonial wrecks along this shore which are still being discovered by divers; just east of the harbour (above the mosque-like Zoological Museum – see page 129) is the Buceo cemetery, opened in 1835, and now stuffed with ornate marble tombs decorated with allegorical angels and many more sculptures by Belloni, José Luis de San Martín, and many leading Italian sculptors. Perhaps the most famous resident is the *blanco* warlord Aparicio Saravia, buried in 1904. Alongside is the British Cemetery, where many merchants and engineers lie, as well as victims of the World Wars, including some killed in the Battle of the River Plate.

There's a succession of beaches, interspersed with rocky areas where cormorants and other birds feed, along the seafront of the quiet residential district of Malvín, before the Playa de los Ingleses and the minor protrusion of **Punta Gorda**, a more expensive suburb where people actually used to come for beach holidays from Montevideo. There's a pleasant viewpoint at the Plaza de la Armada (Navy Plaza), with a monument to those lost at sea on naval duty (representing man struggling against the sea), which may have a *hornero* (ovenbird) nest inside it. Immediately to the east, at Mar Antártico 1227, is the house of the engineer–architect Eladio Dieste (see page 34), a typically modest structure built in 1961–63 and largely hidden behind a brick screen wall.

From here the *rambla* continues past more beaches and fishing clubs (with cheap fried-fish restaurants) to **Carrasco**, the most upmarket of Montevideo's suburbs long before the presence of the airport made it even more desirable. Its focal point is the massive Belle Epoque Hotel-Casino Carrasco, opened in 1922 (having been left half-built throughout World War I) and now awaiting a major refurbishment from Hyatt or some similar chain. Immediately west of it is a squash club, while a few blocks north on Avenida Arocena is the Carrasco Lawn Tennis Club, where Davis Cup matches are held. There's a 'villagey' feel to this section of Arocena, although restaurants such as Nuevo García and Dackel are very expensive. The most recent developments along the *rambla* are in the minimalist white-cube style of José Ignacio (not otherwise seen in Montevideo), but one of the finest Art Deco buildings in the city is the peach-coloured **Hotel Riviera**, eight blocks west of the casino at Rambla México 6095 & 6 de Abril, sadly now only a *centro de eventos* and tea-room.

Just east of the casino, where Cartagena and Otero meet the *rambla*, the Carrasco Kite Center (*www.ckc.com.uy*) offers windsurfing and kite-surfing and has a nice bar over the beach, serving sushi, fish and pasta; another few blocks east the *rambla* passes the Escuela de Guerra Naval (Naval War School), with anti-aircraft guns and propellers mounted in front, facing the Playa Miramar. Immediately beyond is the Puente Carrasco, where the *rambla* crosses the Arroyo de Carrasco and leaves the city for Canelones department. Just north, Avenida Italia crosses the *arroyo* and splits, with Avenida Giannattasio continuing towards Punta del Este and Avenida de las Américas swinging left to the airport and Minas; both pass through the Parque Nacional Roosevelt, which is wholly planted with eucalyptus and of no conservation value. Nearby are the Bañados de Carrasco, wetlands with many waterbirds, though these are not currently safe to visit without a guide because of a number of illegal settlements.

MUSEUMS

CIUDAD VIEJA
Museo del Carnaval [111 A2] (*Carnival Museum; Rambla 25 de Agosto 218 & Maciel;* ℡ *2 915 0807; www.museodelcarnaval.org;* ⊕ *10.00–18.00 Tue–Sun, winter until 17.00, closed 22–25 Dec, 29 Dec–1 Jan, 6 Jan; US$2, or US$0.40 for Uruguayans, free Tue*) This is one of the best presented museums in Uruguay, with great examples of carnival costumes, masks and drums, coupled with detailed information on the origins and history of the event.

Museo de Arte Precolombino y Indigena (MAPI) [111 B2] (*Museum of Precolombian and Indigenous Art; 25 de Mayo 279;* ℡ *2 913 9360; www.mapi.org.uy;* ⊕ *12.00–18.00 Tue–Fri, 11.00–18.00 Sat; free*) One of the most exciting museum projects now under way in Montevideo, this opened in 2004 to show the refurbishment work in progress and a small portion of its collection. A palace built for the hugely ambitious Emilio Reus, director of the Banco Nacional, it was intended to be the Establicimiento Médico Hidro Termo Terápico. However, Reus died in 1891 at just 33, impoverished and broken by the banking crisis of 1890, and the building was used by a bank, then various government ministries, before being handed to the city in 2003. There's a two-floor atrium, and the main hall at the rear was a hot pool (with a proscenium stage). Currently the ground-floor exhibition is not huge, with *zoolitos* (animal-shaped carved stones) from Rocha, and other archaeological pieces from the Diaguita and Condorhuasi cultures of northwestern Argentina, and the Maya, Moche and Inca cultures. There are temporary shows provided by other institutions and a photography room, as well as an art shop.

Museo de Artes Decorativas (Palacio Taranco) [111 B2] (*Museum of Decorative Arts; 25 de Mayo 376; ✎ 2 915 6080; ⊕ 12.30–18.00 Mon–Sat, 14.00–18.00 Sun; free*)

On the site of the city's first theatre, La Casa de Comedias (1793), the mansion of the Ortiz de Taranco family was built in 1908–10 in the Historical Eclectic style by the French architects Charles Louis Girault and Jules León Chifflot, also responsible for the Petit Palais in Paris and the French embassy in Vienna. The Prince of Wales (later King Edward VIII) stayed here in 1925; the Acta de Montevideo, a treaty between Argentina, Chile and the Vatican to settle Argentine–Chilean frontier disputes, was signed here in 1979 and ratified in 1987 in the presence of Pope John Paul II. Beautifully kept, its fine furnishings and paintings now form the Museum of Decorative Arts.

The grand entrance leads to a Louis XV interior with Palladian loggias opening on to a small garden (sometimes open). There are paintings by the Spanish painters Sorolla y Bastida (1863–1923), Mariano Barbasán (1864–1924) – who worked, appropriately enough, in the Barbizon style – and Narciso Díaz de la Peña (1807–90), while Uruguayan art is represented by Juan Manuel Blanes. There are three pianos on the ground floor (one a Pleyel, transferred from the presidential residence in 2005). In the dining room are seven specially woven Aubusson tapestries and two lovely Art Nouveau vases.

At the top of the stairs (with their Art Nouveau banisters) is a painting of San Roque by José Ribera (1588–1656) and a portrait by Sorolla y Bastida of Señora de Signorini (1887); otherwise the upper floor is much less ornate than the ground floor, with a pair of Edmundo Prati busts in the library, some fine marble fireplaces and parquet flooring. Staff tend to keep the upper floor closed, but it's worth a look if you can persuade them to allow you upstairs.

Museo Histórico Nacional (Casa de Rivera) [111 C2] (*National Historical Museum; Rincón 437 & Misiones; ✎ 2 915 1051; www.museohn.org.uy; ⊕ 11.00–17.00 Mon–Fri, 12.00–17.00 Sat; free*)

Once the home of Uruguay's first president, this is now the museum's main branch, with a collection ranging from pre-Columbian stone weapons and ceramics to portraits of colonial and Independence-era figures, as well as Lavalleja's armchair, Admiral William Brown's (creator of the Argentine navy; 1777–1857) bureau and barometer, and a leather chair owned by both Artigas and Juan Zorrilla de San Martín. You'll learn something of the country's history, but it's best to have some previous knowledge, or to refer regularly to this book's history section.

Museo Romántico [111 C2] (*25 de Mayo 428; ✎ 2 915 5361; www.mhn.gub.uy; ⊕ 11.30–16.45 Mon–Fri; free*)

A two-storey patrician home known as the Casa Montero, this was built in 1782 for Bernardo de la Torre (who had his shop on the ground floor) and taken over in 1831 by Antonio Montero, who made it one of the most luxurious homes in the city. In 1896 the first cinema in Uruguay was set up here in the Salón Rouge. In 1962 it became part of the National Historical Museum, displaying patrician living quarters of the second half of the 19th century.

The rooms open to the public are upstairs, around the attractive patio with its unusual octagonal balcony and classical marble statues and basin. There are portraits by Juan Manuel Blanes and the little-known but very decent Cayetano Gallino; the dining room has late-19th-century furnishings including the table and chairs of Alfredo Vásquez Acevedo (1844–1923), politician and rector of the University of the Republic, and the silverware used by his son Jacobo Varela Acevedo (1876–1962) when he was ambassador to the USA. Elsewhere are six portraits by the French-born Amadeo Gras (1805–71), with fans and other accessories, the dress worn by Ninon Vallin (1886–1961) as Massenet's Manon (on tour with Caruso), an Egyptian-style desk and bureau owned by two presidents, the bedroom furniture of President Maximo Santos (1847–89) and other furniture owned by his bitter rival Julio Herrera y Obes (1841–1912).

Casa Garibaldi [111 B2] (*25 de Mayo 314;* ⊕ *11.00–17.00 Mon–Fri; free*) Giuseppe Garibaldi (1807–82), exiled from Italy because of his revolutionary activities, lived in this house from 1841; the following year he married his Brazilian lover Anita Ribeiro da Silva, and they had four children by 1847. Initially working as a maths teacher and commercial agent, in 1842 he was placed in command of the Uruguayan fleet and raised an 'Italian Legion' to support Rivera's Colorado government against Oribe's Blancos, backed by the Argentina dictator Juan Manuel de Rosas. He and his men wore gaucho ponchos and sombreros, with the red shirts that later became their trademark when they fought for Italian independence. Adopting guerrilla tactics on land and sea, he was very successful in harrying the Oribist forces; his capture of Colonia, Isla Martín García and Gualeguaychú in 1845 opened up the Río Uruguay, and in 1846 he defeated Oribe twice near Salto. However, in 1848, the Year of Revolutions in Europe, he led his Italian Legion to fight for the freedom of their homeland.

The house was built in 1830 around two patios hung with vines; the Garibaldis lived to the right of the entry to the first patio, with a small kitchen to the rear (opening on to the second patio). It became a museum in 1957. There's a display of documents, garments, medals and engravings evoking Garibaldi's heroic career.

Museo Gurvich [111 C2] (*Ituzaingó 1377;* ↘ *2 915 7826; www.museogurvich.org;* ⊕ *10.00–18.00 Mon–Fri, 11.00–15.00 Sat; P30, free Tue*) Next to the cathedral on Plaza Constitución, this building has seen a good modern internal conversion to house a small art shop and coffee shop as well as display space for José Gurvich's paintings (see page 32). Upstairs there's also a changing display of works by his teacher Joaquín Torres García and other pupils.

Cabildo [111 D2] (*Old City Hall; J C Gómez 1362, Plaza Constitución;* ↘ *2 915 9685;* e *museocabildo@correo.imm.gub.uy;* ⊕ *12.30–17.30 Tue–Fri & Sun, 11.30–16.30 Sat; free*) In the two courtyards of this fine colonial edifice are displays on colonial shipbuilding and the like; upstairs (passing a statue of Artigas by José Luis Zorrilla de San Martín halfway up), you'll find a great display of historical maps and prints (some by English artists William Heath and Edward Burney, and by Conrad Martens, who came here to join the *Beagle* as official artist) to the right, together with pistols and rifles and replicas of *peinetones*, the elaborate 18th-century women's headdresses. There's also a *Mater Dolorosa* brought from the Canary Islands with the first settlers. On the other side are the Assembly Room (with fairly antique furniture) and a long tiled gallery with furniture, chandeliers and some very miscellaneous paintings.

Museo Joaquín Torres García [111 D2] (*Sarandí 683;* ☎ *2 916 2663; www.torresgarcia.org.uy;* ⊕ *09.30–19.30 Mon–Fri, 09.00–18.00 Sat; donations from US$1*) Another good modern conversion, preserving the fine staircase. There's an art shop and bookshop downstairs (with some of Torres García's wooden toys, and a colour catalogue in English for just US$6). On the first floor there's a good video and biographical information, and some of his works up to the 1930s (similar to Mondrian and van Doesburg but never quite as good). The second floor shows the development of Universal Constructivism, in works that are more individual and more interesting. Outside, at the junction of Sarandí and Bacacay, is a reproduction of his mural, *Pax in Lucem*.

THE CENTRO

Museo Numismático [111 D1] (*Numismatic Museum; Florida & 25 de Mayo;* ⊕ *10.00–16.00 Mon–Fri; free*) In the ugly Banco Central tower (sign in and leave ID at the downstairs entry) there's a display of Uruguayan money (from the first coins, issued in 1840), with banknotes from before and after the reform of 1975, when P1,000 became P1. There's also a collection of notes from Africa and elsewhere, and on the mezzanine an amusing collection of piggybanks and a display on the destruction of old notes.

Museo de la Casa del Gobierno [111 D2] (*Edificio Independencia, Plaza Independencia;* ⊕ *10.00–17.00 Mon–Fri; free*) In the former seat of government (to 1985), there's now a display on the nation's presidents. It's well presented, starting with Fructuoso Rivera's coach on the first floor landing, and continuing with lots of swords, medals, busts, portraits and death-masks, not forgetting Venancio Flores's stuffed dog, but it doesn't provide much historical narrative. There's no need for ID, but you will have to leave any bags at the entrance.

Museo Militar [111 F3] (*Military Museum; Soriano 1090 & Paraguay;* ⊕ *10.00–17.00 Sun, Wed–Fri, 09.00–12.00 Sat; free*) The former Italian Hospital was built in 1858, to an Italian Renaissance design, but when the money ran out it was given to the army, serving as a military hospital (1865–70) and then offering university courses for women; it became the Military Museum in 1981. The main patio is now the Sala de Uniformología, displaying figures in historic uniforms; other rooms show prehistoric arrowheads, displays on Artigas and his campaigns, the Guerra Grande of 1843–51, the War of the Triple Alliance of 1865–69, and finally a room on peace-keeping – Uruguay had around 2,000 troops each in Mozambique and Angola in the 1990s, and more recently a thousand or so in the Democratic Republic of the Congo and in Haiti. Uruguay contributes more troops to the UN per head of population than any other country.

There are also military museums at El Cerro (see page 119) and in the forts of San Miguel and Santa Teresa in Rocha (see pages 243 and 240).

Museo Pedagógico [111 F2] (*Museum of Education; Plaza Cagancha 1175;* ☎ *2 902 0915; www.crnti.edu.uy/museo;* ⊕ *16 Dec–14 Mar 08.00–12.00 Mon–Fri, rest of year 09.00–19.00 Mon–Fri; free*) Bigger and (slightly) better than you might expect, this museum displays lots of old teaching aids, especially for the sciences, as well as a *gorro de burro* (dunce's hat with donkey ears). It also looks at the history of education in Uruguay from the opening of the first free school in Montevideo in 1809, with emphasis on the reforms of José Pedro Varela in the 1870s and 1880s, when teacher training was introduced for the first time, and compulsory, free and secular primary education laid the foundations for a democratic modern society.

Museos del Gaucho y de la Moneda [111 E2] (*Museums of the Gaucho and the Mint; 18 de Julio 998 & Herrera y Obes;* ↘ *2 900 8764; www.brounet.com.uy;* ⊕ *10.00–17.00 Mon–Fri; free*) In the Palacio Heber, built in 1896–97 by the French architect Alfred Massüe and now owned by the Banco de la República, these two museums share a delight in silver – the Museo de la Moneda has a very dated display (in Spanish only) of money, including ancient Chinese bronze 'coins', colonial gold pieces, the first Uruguayan coins from 1840 (in copper, then later silver) and notes from 1887, as well as commemorative medals. Upstairs, the Gaucho Museum displays silver *maté* gourds and *cuchillos* (knives), massive carved bulls' horns, stone bolas wrapped in leather (a small one held in the hand and two larger ones), lassos, branding irons, pistols, spurs and stirrups, men's and women's costumes, and a row of five full-size model horses in harness – a pretty good collection, although not very well displayed. In addition, the Espacio Cultural Banco República shows temporary art exhibitions.

SUBTE – Centro Municipal de Exposiciones [111 E2] (*under Plaza Fabini;* ↘ *2 908 7643; http://subtemvd.blogspot.com;* ⊕ *15.30–21.00 Tue–Sun; free*) A municipal space for changing art exhibitions, often with a political or avant-garde tinge.

Museo de Historia del Arte (MUHAR) [111 G2] (*Museum of the History of Art; Ejido 1326;* ↘ *2 908 9252;* ⊕ *12.00–17.30 Tue–Sun, until 21.00 Thu; free*) In the corner of the City Hall, this large collection contains a few original pieces but is mostly plaster replicas of great works of art (mainly sculptures, as well as ceramics and jewellery) from all the world's ancient cultures, a very refreshing antidote to a Eurocentric view of culture. Near the entrance you'll see copies of the *Winged Victory of Samothrace*, Donatello's *St George* and *David* and a Della Robbia majolica, among others; one floor below you'll see copies of Greek sculptures such as the *Apollo Belvedere*, rather fewer Roman ones, a Khmer Buddha, Persian, Hittite, Assyrian and Egyptian carvings, and an authentic 3rd-century Gandhara Buddha. In the lower level are replicas from Mesoamerican cultures, such as a basalt Aztec calendar; ceramics, gold and crystal heads from pre-Columbian Mexico; original 8th- to 12th-century pieces from Costa Rica including a jaguar *metate* and gold votive jewellery; Mayan ceramics and jade; ceramics and stone from pre-Incan Peru, Bolivia, Ecuador and northwestern Argentina, authentic Uruguayan shaped stones, 12,000–9,000 years old (and bird-shaped ones 3,300–2,200 years old), as well as pottery from the *litoral* of the Río Uruguay that's 4,500–2,500 years old. It's all well displayed, with quite a bit of information, all in Spanish.

Museo de Arte Contempóraneo (MAC) [111 E2] (*Museum of Contemporary Art; 18 de Julio 965, 2nd Flr;* ↘ *2 900 6662;* ⊕ *14.00–18.30 Mon, 14.00–20.00 Tue–Sun; free*) A small space, putting on temporary shows with a few pieces of contemporary Uruguayan art on permanent display at the rear.

Museo del Automóvil Club del Uruguay [111 G2] (*Museum of the Automobile Club of Uruguay; Colonia 1251 & Yí, 6th Flr;* ↘ *2 902 4792;* ⊕ *14.00–19.00 Tue–Sun; free*) At the rear of the ACU petrol station, take the lift by the offices to the sixth floor, where you'll see a fine collection of vintage cars, starting with a Belgian Delin manufactured in 1899, the oldest car in Uruguay, and a pair of Clement Bayard & De Dion Boutons from 1904, and others including a 1923 Model T Ford, three Model A Fords, Armstrong Siddeleys from 1948 and 1950, a 1955 Renault Frégate, various Packards, Cadillacs and Chevrolets from the 1950s and 1960s (with jet fighters on the bonnet), a Ferrari and an E-Type Jaguar. You'll also see the trophies won by Hector Suppici Sedes, the Uruguayan racing driver killed in a crash in Chile in 1948.

Museo UTE [111 E2] (*Museum of the State Electrical Company; Herrera y Obes 1322, just south of Plaza Fabini;* ☎ *2 908 5262;* ⊕ *09.00–15.00 Mon–Fri; free*) The museum of Usinas y Transmisiones Electricos (formerly Usinas y Telefonos del Estado, State Power Stations and Telephones) has a small but well-displayed collection of vintage ammeters and other gear, as well as information on the first electric lighting in Montevideo (in 1886) and later hydro-electric schemes. There's not much to it, but it's something to see on a Monday.

NORTHERN MONTEVIDEO
Museo de las Telecomunicaciones [88–9 A1] (*Museum of Telecommunications; Guatemala 2097 & Paraguay;* ☎ *2 928 4124;* ⊕ *09.00–18.00 Mon–Fri; free*) If you're visiting the viewpoint in Montevideo's highest building you might as well pop in to this small collection of old phones, including the first magnetic card phones in Uruguay (1988) and the first mobile telephone (cellphone; 1991). A couple of rescued murals by Joaquín Torres García (done in 1944 for the Hospital St-Bois in Colón, in Montevideo's northern suburbs) are also here, with another in the reception area of the main tower.

Museo del Fútbol [88–9 G1] (*Museum of Football; Avda Ricaldoni s/n, Parque Batlle y Ordóñez;* ☎ *2 480 1259; www.museodelfutbol.com.uy;* ⊕ *10.00–18.00 Wed–Fri, 09.00–14.30 Sat–Sun; P60 or US$3*) This museum, in the Estadio Centenario, by the tower opposite the Medical Faculty, is a couple of minutes' walk from the bus-stops on Avenida Italia.

A fine film (made for FIFA by a British team in 2004, with a good tango soundtrack) covers the achievements of the Uruguayan soccer team at the Olympics (their matches in the 1928 Amsterdam games were relayed by telegram and loudspeakers to huge crowds in Plaza Independencia) and then the first World Cup in 1930 (with clips of very bad colour film). The architect Juan Scasso only had eight months to build this stadium, the first built specifically for soccer, and in fact the first game of the first World Cup had to be played at the Pocitos stadium.

There's a display on José Leandro Andrade, the 'black marvel' of the 1930 team, the only Uruguayan player in FIFA's Hall of Champions of the greatest players of the 20th century (announced in 2000), on the basis that he was the game's first iconic figure (he also led a *comparsa* of *candombé* drummers, although that's not mentioned here). There's also material on Obdulio Varela of Albion FC, captain of the 1950 team; general Olympic mementoes, a photo of Westminster School cloisters (the 'cradle of football'!) and Maradona's shirt; in addition to the permanent museum there are temporary exhibits.

Museo Municipal de Bellas Artes Juan Manuel Blanes [overview map] (*Juan Manuel Blanes Municipal Museum of Fine Arts; Avda Millán 4015, Prado;* ☎ *2 336 2248; www.montevideo.gub.uy/museoblanes;* ⊕ *12.15–17.45 Tue–Sun; free*) A typical *quinta* with beautiful gardens (as well as the Japanese Garden to the rear – see page 119), this doesn't contain a great deal of art, taking at most half an hour to visit. There's one gallery dedicated to the pretty academic paintings of Juan Manuel Blanes, some of them enormous, including a ceiling mural of the *Eternal Father and Four Evangelists* (c1884). The collection also includes oils and drawings by Pedro Figari and works by Pedro Blanes Viale, Rafael Barradas, Raúl Cabrera and other

Uruguayan artists, which may not be on display, depending on what temporary shows are on.

Jardín y Museo Botánico [overview map] (*Botanic Garden and Museum; Avda 19 de Abril 1181, Prado;* ⌇ *2 336 4005; www.montevideo.gub.uy/botanico;* ⊕ *07.00–17.30 daily; free*) The Botanic Garden was founded in 1902 and is laid out on either side of an imaginary Equator, with northern hemisphere flora to the north, and southern to the south, in theory – in fact there are eucalyptus trees to the north, and a nice avenue of oaks to the south. In any case it's a delightful, well-tended garden, with over 1,000 species planted in its 13ha, and most plants are decently labelled; there are also plenty of parakeets and other birds. Opposite the south gate is the Botanic Museum (⊕ *09.00–17.00 Mon–Fri; free*), with samples of rocks and minerals, slices of tree trunks and displays on recognising seeds and basic flower parts.

Museo de la Farmacia [overview map] (*Pharmacy Museum; Avda Millán 3701, Barrio Atahualpa;* ⌇ *2 336 3534;* ⊕ *shop hours*) At the rear of the modern Farmacía Atahualpa are the cabinets, bottles, emulsifier, autoclave and mortars of the original pharmacy, as well as old advertisements and photos, and an interactive multi-lingual touch-screen.

EASTERN MONTEVIDEO
Museo Nacional de Artes Visuales [88–9 F4] (*National Museum of Visual Arts; Julio Herrera y Reissig s/n;* ⌇ *2 711 6054/6124; www.mnav.gub.uy;* ⊕ *14.00–19.00 Tue–Sun; free*) It's always worth checking out the shows at this museum, also known as the Museo Parque Rodó. The first room houses 11 portraits by Juan Manuel Blanes, not especially good but he does at least show ugly people without prettification. The main spaces house temporary shows which may include works by Joaquín Torres García, Cúneo, Saéz, the brothers Nerses and Ohannes Ounanian, and Europeans such as Delaunay, Arp, Chagall, Klee, Balla, Picasso, Braque, Léger, Gris, Cézanne, Manet, Delacroix and Daumier – although these are usually in store. Modern sculptures stand in the gardens and in the central strip of the road outside.

Museo de Juan Zorrilla de San Martín [88–9 G6] (*J L Zorrilla de San Martín 96;* ⌇ *2 710 1818;* ⊕ *14.00–18.00 Mon–Fri, 14.00–19.00 Sat–Sun; free*) The poet and diplomat Juan Zorrilla de San Martín had this white Andalusian-style villa built in 1904, set in peaceful gardens with fountains, and expanded in 1921. Now there's also a café, a shop and an air-conditioned modern display room. The ground floor is open as a museum, with his personal effects and furnishings, including the contents of the room in the Ciudad Vieja in which he died. You'll also see his private oratory – he was strongly Roman Catholic, fathering 13 children and negotiating with Rome to have an archbishopric in Montevideo. Zorrilla de San Martín was a traditional patrician, filling his house with Spanish paintings, but as a poet he created Uruguay's 'national myth' and established the country's Latin American identity.

Museo del Azulejo [88–9 H4] (*Museum of Decorative Tiles; Cavia 3080, Pocitos;* ⌇ *2 709 6352;* e *museodelazulejo@adinet.com.uy;* ⊕ *10.15–15.45 Tue–Sun; free*) A small house with a collection of over 3,000 tiles, the great majority made in Desvres in northern France between 1840 and 1900. There are also a few colonial Spanish tiles, some very basic hand-painted 19th-century tiles from Maldonado, and 20th-century European tiles, as well as many photos of church domes and bars – almost every major Uruguayan church has a tiled dome.

Castillo Pittamiglio [88–9 H5] (*Rambla Gandhi 633, Pocitos;* ↘ *2 712 0284;* ⊕ *only for guided visits Thu 16.00, closed for most of Jan–Feb; US$2*) The most eccentric building in Montevideo, built in 1933 by the architect and alchemist Humberto Pittamiglio (1887–1976), is now occupied by the Uruguayan Association of Private Property Developers, who allow weekly tours, except when the offices are closed for summer holidays. Pittamiglio left the Castillo to the city when he died, but his 150,000 books, Murano chandeliers and mirrors, and other furnishings had all vanished by the time the city took possession.

Entering from the *rambla* (which didn't exist when the house was built – the original entry is now part of the Montecristo restaurant, to the north at Francisco Vidal 638), you go upstairs to a reception room, then up a narrow staircase to the reading room, with a fireplace of walnut (the alchemist's wood) and a mandala; around it are claustrophobic passages, offering alternative routes through the house. The décor is mostly wood, with elements of Art Nouveau and Arts and Crafts styles; but you'll see various symbols portraying aspects of man's journey to understanding and the transformation of metals and of society. The original unrestored bathroom is worth a look before you go out to the internal terrace, below the Tuscan-style tower, where you'll see a beautiful relief of the goddess Diana with a hound. Overlooking the entrance and the beach is a circular room below the ship's prow and replica of the *Winged Victory of Samothrace* that will have caught your attention from the *rambla*. Beneath is a circular room with a square in a circle in the ceiling, and a Templar cross hidden under the table, the room with the most energy in the building.

Museo del Arma de Ingenieros [overview map] (*Museum of Military Engineering; Aduana de Oribe, Rambla Armenia 3975 & Riveros;* ↘ *2 622 1480; www.ingenierosmilitares.org.uy;* ⊕ *14.00–17.00 Sat–Sun; free*) In an old brick building on the *rambla* west of the Zoological Museum, this displays the usual rifles and so on plus tools and models of fortifications, and also more contemporary displays on de-mining, for instance.

Museo Zoológico [overview map] (*Zoological Museum; Rambla República de Chile 4215;* ↘ *2 622 0258;* ⊕ *11.00–17.00 Tue–Sun; free*). This mosque-like building was constructed in 1930–33 as the Café Morisco, but this soon failed and the building was used as an oceanographic station, and then from 1956 as the Zoological Museum. It's in good condition, but the tower (or minaret) is not open. The left-hand side of the building is full of stuffed birds, almost all Uruguayan and reasonably well labelled; to the right are mammals and other types of animals.

Museo Naval [overview map] (*Naval Museum; Rambla Charles de Gaulle & Luís Alberto de Herrera;* ↘ *2 622 1084;* ⊕ *08.00–12.00, 14.00–18.00 Fri–Wed; free*) At the terminal of bus routes 116 and 185 (to Pocitos), the naval museum has dated displays of which only those on the Battle of the River Plate are likely to interest tourists. There are maps and photos, a uniform from the *Graf Spee* and the dress uniform of Admiral Sir Henry Harwood, then a commodore in command of the British ships. One of the *Graf Spee's* secondary 150mm guns was placed outside the museum in 1997. There are also displays on the Uruguayan sail training vessel *Capitán Miranda*, a three-masted schooner that sails around the world with naval cadets and samples of Uruguayan foodstuffs and wines, and on the 1993–94 Around The World race which stopped in Punta del Este both outbound and inbound.

SOUTHERN URUGUAY

MONTEVIDEO

Viñedo
los Vientos

Viña Varela
Zarranz

Bodegas Carrau

Bodega
Santa Rosa

Bodega
Castillo Viejo

Bodega
Marichal

Casa
Filgueira

Antigua Bodega Stagnari
Vinos Finos
H Stagnari

Bodega
Bouza

Bodega de Lucca

PANDO

TOLEDO

LAS
PIEDRAS

LA PAZ

CANELONES

SANTA LUCÍA

SAN JOSÉ

Juanicó

Progreso

El Colorado

Parador
Tajes

Aguas
Corrientes

Suárez

Santa Rosa

San Jacinto

Solís de
Mataojo

Atlántida

Ciudad de la Costa

Pinar

Solymar

Montevideo Airport
(Carrasco)

Punta del Este

Jaureguiberry

Santa Lucía
del Este

Biarritz

INTERBALNEARIA

Santiago Vásquez

Playa Pascual

Kiyú

Minas

Florida

Colonia

N

Bradt

25km

25 miles

4

Southern Uruguay

The area around Montevideo is densely populated by Uruguayan standards, but will seem fairly empty to most tourists, apart from the semi-continuous strip of resorts along the coast, especially to the east of Montevideo. Closest to Montevideo is Canelones department, with fairly small mixed farms (producing vegetables for the capital), rather than the huge *estancias* further into the country's interior, and with small vineyards that produce the bulk of the country's wine. To the north and west are Florida and San José departments, largely given over to dairy farming, and to the northeast (inland from Maldonado department, covered in *Chapter 5*) is Lavalleja department, whose capital, Minas, is an easy excursion from Montevideo, although the further parts of the department are clearly part of the interior.

CANELONES DEPARTMENT: WEST

The department of Canelones (named not after a type of Italian pasta but after the *canelon* tree) is also known as the *comuna canaria*, many of its earliest settlers having come from the Canary Islands. Later it attracted Spanish and Italian immigrants, very religious by Uruguayan standards, especially to the area known as El Santoral in the centre of the department, where many of the villages are named after saints. The department has 65km of coastline, most of it east of the capital, and over 160 vineyards and wineries.

The main road through the department is Ruta 5, heading north from Montevideo to Durazno, Tacuarembó and Rivera; starting at the port as Rambla 25 de Agosto, it's a good dual carriageway that passes El Cerro, splits from Ruta 1 (which leads west to Colonia) at km7, meets the new Ruta 102 to the airport at km17, and passes junctions to the small towns of Las Piedras, La Paz and Progreso at km19.5, km20 and km26.5. Plans for a Museo del Vino – Wine Museum – in Las Piedras were launched in September 2009; it is to be in the Parque Tecnológico Canario, on Ruta 67 at Elías Regules. At km37.5 you'll pass the Bodega Juanicó, perhaps the country's best-known winery (see page 145), and at km43 the dual carriageway ends at the junction to the town of Canelones, 45km from Montevideo.

CANELONES The town of Canelones is fairly nondescript but pleasant enough to visit. It was founded in 1774 as Villa Guadalupe. Here the first independent government of the Banda Oriental was set up in 1813, and the Uruguayan flag was unfurled for the first time in 1829. There's nowhere to stay, although this would make a logical base for winery tours.

Getting there Frequent buses from Montevideo and elsewhere leave you at the Plaza 18 de Julio, where the cathedral stands on the south side, a standard Neoclassical building with blue and white *azulejos* on the exterior of its dome, and

CANELONES

Florida

0 ———— 200m
0 ———— 200yds

N

Bradt

CARLOS GARDEL

DR CRISTÓBAL CENDÁN

MARTÍNEZ MONEGAL

JULIO BRUNERAU
● Ta-Ta supermarket
LUIS ALBERTO BRAUSE

W FERREIRA ALDUNATE

CAMINO MELGAREJO

JAVIER DE VIANA

TERESA CABANA DE MORENO

RAMÓN VÁZQUEZ VARELA

MARÍA STAGNERO DE MUNAR

LUIS ALBERTO DE HERRERA

FROILÁN VÁZQUEZ LEDESMA

CALLE C
CALLE B
CALLE A

R5

PATRIA

LAURELES

INSTRUCCIONES

FCO SOCA

DR BALTASAR BRUM

HÉCTOR MIRANDA

TOLENTINO GONZÁLEZ
● Complejo Cultural
BROU

GRAL APARICIO SARAVIA

R11

ESSO ⛽ i

Atlántida

R BARRIOS

Santa Lucía

R11

DR TOMÁS BERRETA

Cathedral JOSÉ ENRIQUE RODÓ
COPSA ● ✝ ● CITA

JOSÉ G ARTIGAS

Old Cat ✕
Pizzería
Casa Juan
Spikerman ☕

JOAQUÍN SUÁREZ

JUAN ZORRILLA DE SAN MARTÍN
♪

DR FRANCISCO LAVANDEIRA

AV EDUARDO MARTÍNEZ MONEGAL

Zoo 🐘
Museo
Arqueológico
Taddei

JOSÉ MARTI

CAMINO NACIONAL CARLOS CIGLIUTTI

JOSÉ BATLLE Y ORDÓÑEZ

TREINTA Y TRES

FLORENCIO SÁNCHEZ

FRUCTUOSO RIVERA

ACUÑA DE FIGUEROA

HERMENEGILDO MELO

C CÁMERA

JOSÉ MARTI

R64

CAMINO DR B FUSTER

CNO A LAS BRUJAS

J ROSA GIFFUNI

MARÍA ÁLAMO DE SUÁREZ

R5

Montevideo

a clean blue and white interior too. You'll also notice the bishopric on the west side of the plaza, and the Monument to the Flag in the centre.

The COPSA bus company (for Montevideo, Santa Lucía, Atlántida and Costa Azul) has an office a block south of the plaza (*Batlle y Ordóñez;* ☏ *33 22379;* ⊕ *06.00–20.30 Mon–Fri, 06.00–13.00 Sat*), although you should buy tickets on the bus. CITA (for buses to Montevideo, San José and Florida) has an office on the south side of the plaza (*Rodó 373;* ☏ *33 23001;* ⊕ *06.45–21.00 Mon–Fri, 06.45–14.15, 15.30–21.00 Sat, 17.30–21.00 Sun*); three Turil buses a day to Durazno, Tacuarembó and Rivera also call here.

Tourist information The departmental tourist office (which doesn't know much about the town but is very knowledgeable about the region) is in the Complejo Cultural Lumiere (*Batlle y Ordóñez 621* ☏ *33 22288*), immediately north of the plaza. It's probably better to try the Tourist Information Centre (*Avda Martínez*

Monegal & Héctor Miranda; ☏ *33 26989; www.canelonesturismo.gub.uy),* five blocks east of the plaza, just west of the junction of Ruta 5 and Ruta 11.

✘ Where to eat Perhaps the best place to eat is the Old Cat Pizzería, opposite the COPSA office on Batlle y Ordóñez.

Other practicalities On the north side of the plaza you'll find the post office, Antel and the Banco República. There's Wi-Fi internet on the plaza, but it's very weak. The Ta-Ta supermarket and hospital are on either side of a small plaza seven blocks north of the centre at Calle Brause (where buses to and from the north stop).

What to see and do There are a couple of less-than-exciting museums in the town. The **Museo Arqueológico Taddei** *(east end of Joaquín Suárez;* ⊕ *10.00–18.00 daily; free)* – named after Professor Antonio Taddei (1908–95), who played first division soccer before turning to archaeology in 1940 – has a pretty poor display of relics of Uruguay's earliest cultures. The **Casa Juan Spikerman** *(Treinta y Tres & Juan Zorrilla de San Martín;* ⊕ *09.00–16.00 Tue–Fri; free),* three blocks south of the plaza, has very fancy Neogothic décor on an otherwise ordinary house, and a garden with a cart and a printing press parked in it. Named after one of the Treinta y Tres, it's the departmental history museum, with a mish-mash of items on display.

Immediately north of the archaeological museum there's a small **zoo** (⊕ *12.00–18.00 Tue–Fri, 10.00–18.00 Sat–Sun & holidays)* with domestic and introduced species and few interesting wild animals.

The Teatro Eslabón, just south of the plaza on Batlle y Ordóñez, the Teatro Politeama, just east of the plaza on Berreta, and the Complejo Cultural Lumiere, a striking Art Deco former cinema immediately north of the plaza at Batlle y Ordóñez 621, may offer distraction.

At km53.5 on Ruta 5, 7km north of town, the Represa Canelon Grande is an artificial lake with a campsite that's a popular place for local people to come for a swim on hot days. At km64 a very long bridge over the Río Santa Lucía marks the boundary with Florida department, a good birdwatching location with plenty of *monte* (native woodland).

RURAL TOURISM IN CANELONES

The Dirección de Desarrollo Turístico (Tourism Development Office) of Canelones has some interesting projects to develop rural tourism.

On the second Sunday of each month they put on a tour *(bookings* ☏ *33 22288;* m *9533 1157;* e *paseoporelrincon@hotmail.com, turismo@imcanelones.gub.uy)* of vine-, fruit- and flower-growers in the southwestern corner of the department, known as the Rincón del Colorado. One family produces fruit and flowers such as fuchsias, another makes wine and grows lemons and mushrooms. Lunch is provided by a rural women's group. The trip leaves from the Sociedad de Fomento Rural de Rincón del Colorado at Ruta 48 km8.5, where there's also a bar and shop (at km7.8 you can buy homemade Mamboretá jams and liquors, at km8 La Cueva del Art sells artworks and at km10 there's horseriding at Cabaña El Viraro – ☏ *36 77788).* A tourist information centre is under construction at the junction of Ruta 36 and Ruta 48, on the edge of El Colorado.

On the third Sunday of each month they also have a tour *(bookings* ☏ *33 22288;* m *9947 5515;* e *senderosantalucia@hotmail.com)* of similar places to the northeast of Santa Lucía, including the Filgueira winery (see page 147).

WESTERN CANELONES

Santa Lucía To the northwest of Canelones, 61km from Montevideo where Ruta 11 crosses the Río Santa Lucía into San José department, is Santa Lucía, a quiet historic town founded in 1782 as Villa San Juan Bautista. It's best known for the **Quinta Capurro** (❧ *33 46137; ⊕ 10.00–19.00 daily, winter until 17.15*), a country house built in 1870–73 that has preserved its historic charm. The 9ha walled park is delightful, with plants brought from Europe and Asia, including magnolia, camellia, wisteria, bamboo and a 120-year-old *Agathis robusta* (Queensland kauri). The *quinta* is at the northern end of Calle Roosevelt, five blocks from Plaza Berreta, also well planted with pines, palms and camellias.

Five blocks west of the plaza on Rivera is the **Casa de Cultura 'Casa de Rodó'**, the slightly Moorish house (built in 1871) in which the writer José Enrique Rodó (see page 28) spent his first nine years, and which now houses a small museum of local history (⊕ *07.00–21.00 Mon–Fri, 08.00–20.00 Sat–Sun; free*). It's another five blocks to the municipal park by the river, beyond the railway station (which has a few trains a day to Montevideo via Canelones); the riverside beaches are very popular for swimming.

Where to stay Facing the station is the Hotel Oriental (*Batlle y Ordóñez 99;* ❧ *33 46276;* e *hoteloriental@gmail.com; $$*), opened in 1872 as Uruguay's first tourist hotel. Many distinguished people took holidays here, including José Enrique Rodó, José Pedro Varela, Carlos Gardel and Argentine presidents Domingo Sarmiento and Juárez Celman, and President Máximo Santos actually took it over and ruled Uruguay from here for the summer of 1885–86. It's been beautifully restored, with antique furniture but modern comforts, and fine home cooking. On the eastern edge of town is the Hotel Lamas (*Ruta 11 & Diego Lamas;* ✆ *33 47130; $$*).

On the south side of Ruta 11, just west of the bridge over the Río Santa Lucía, are a tourist information centre (✆ *33 49803*) and the Camping Cristóbal Colón (✆ *33 49803*), with electric lighting and hot water.

Aguas Corrientes One of the most interesting sights in western Canelones is the **Museo del Agua** (*Museum of Water;* ✆ *1952 1601;* ⊕ *by appointment*) in Aguas Corrientes, 7km south of Santa Lucía on Ruta 46, where a British-built purification plant, opened in 1871, took water from the Río Santa Lucía and fed it into Montevideo's drinking water supply. It's perfectly preserved, with its Babcock & Wilcox boilers and Worthington pumps still in place. You'll visit Casa Uno (House No 1) on Avenida del Parque in the centre of the village, and also the inlet valves near the river, beyond the filtration beds. There is a campsite here, at the riverside Club Náutico, where you can rent canoes; paddling down the river from Santa Lucía or Aguas Corrientes to the Parador Tajes makes a delightful day out, a distance of 11km or 32km in total.

Also on the east bank of the Río Santa Lucía, 21km south as the canoe follows the river, is the **Parador Tajes**, the Italian-style mansion that Máximo Tajes built when he became president of Uruguay in 1886. It's maintained by the army and houses a Museum of Arms and Uniforms (✆ *33 03641;* ⊕ *10.00–18.00 Sat–Sun; free*), mainly displaying flags and uniforms of the Artiguista period. There's also a viewpoint with views of the river and wetlands, and paths through 60ha of woodland. There's also a campsite (with electric lighting and wash-blocks), a restaurant, and the Puerto Jackson beach and canoe rental. The army currently levies a charge of US$1 per car to enter the whole site, but this is controversial and may be removed.

Below here the Río Santa Lucía, swollen by the waters of the Río San José, becomes much wider and is navigable by larger boats, although there are increasing numbers of islands; fishing is very popular here.

WINERIES OF URUGUAY

The first vines in Uruguay (probably Muscat table grapes) were planted near Colonia by 1688, and wine was soon being produced for domestic consumption, as well as for Communion. In the 1870s, after the Guerra Grande, the country was stable and both agricultural investment and immigrants began to flood in. From 1880 the government began to offer incentives to the wine industry. New varieties of grape, such as Tannat (see the box on page 142), Folie Noire and Gamay Noire began to be planted, and in 1883 the first vintage was produced of what might be called 'fine wine', ie: something better than rough table wine. The pioneers of fine winemaking in Uruguay were the Basque Pascual Harriague, who established a vineyard near Salto in 1870, and Francisco Vidiella, a Catalan who set up a winery in Colón (now in Montevideo's northern suburbs) in 1874, as well as Francisco Piría (see page 173). In fact the Tannat grape was initially known in Uruguay as Harriague, and Folie Noire as Vidiella or Peñarol, while Gamay Noire, planted in the Carrasco area of Montevideo from 1880, was known as Borgoña.

In 1903 the Viticulture Law (still largely in force) gave the state considerable powers over the industry, which continued mass-producing rough table wines for much of the 20th century. These were semi-sweet whites and rosés and rough reds, largely produced from hybrid grapes giving high yields per hectare.

The process of 'conversion' to a modern, higher-quality industry began in the early 1970s, with consultants brought from France and California, and the start of a programme of replanting with cloned, virus-free rootstocks. In 1988 the government set up the National Institute of Winemaking (INAVI), which works to improve the industry, for instance by researching which grape varieties are most suited to Uruguay's soils and microclimates, and through marketing and training. A 1991 study by Californian experts decided that Uruguay should concentrate on Tannat, and with government help most vineyards started growing it. The area planted with vines has shrunk from 120,000ha to 8,500ha but is now producing far better wines, at higher prices than bulk table wines. Production is around 95 million litres per year, with 10 million litres exported (40% to Brazil, 10% to the USA, 8% to Canada, 5% to Switzerland, 4% to the UK and 3% each to Germany, Benelux, Poland, Russia and Mexico). Most of the exports are of fine wines, while most domestic consumption (33 litres per year, the tenth-highest level in the world) is of bulk table wines, often sold in *demijuanas* (demijohns) of five litres.

Most of Uruguay's wineries being near the sea, their weather is changeable and wine making is challenging, with varying results (2002, 2004 and 2007 were particularly good years). The main problem is that humidity brings disease. Cabernet grapes, which ripen late (perhaps after the autumn rains have come), can struggle, with skill and care required. White wine grapes and Merlot do well but Malbec, so common in Argentina, is virtually unknown here. Similarly, the Rioja grape Tempranillo likes drier climates, but does well enough in Uruguay. Pinot Noir is not common in Uruguay, but with cool nights it can produce delicate complex wines. In the last 40 years the average alcohol level of Uruguayan grapes has risen from 10% to 12% (though still slightly lower than French and Californian grapes); hotter weather should benefit Merlot in particular (and Tannat–Merlot blends may become very successful). Winemakers are also experimenting with less traditional varieties such as Petit Verdot and Albariño.

Increasingly, as harvest draws near, the grapes are not just checked daily for polyphenol and tannin levels, but are tasted and the colour of the pips examined, in a move from purely chemical analysis to an 'organoleptic' approach. It's expensive, but given the family-sized scale of the industry the boutique approach is the only way for Uruguay's industry to go – the entire country produces less wine than Chile's giant Concha y Toro. These very different vintages and the small size of the wineries mean that there will never be many Uruguayan wines in northern hemisphere supermarkets (although production levels are sufficient for the more specialist wine shops). This small scale also works in favour of wine tourism, as tastings are often accompanied by the winemaker or a member of the immediate family, giving special personal insights.

Each winemaker works in his own way with the local environment, and each vineyard has its own character. Pesticides are not widely used but spraying of some is compulsory, so there is no certified organic wine production. Grapes are generally picked by hand and efforts are increasingly made to reduce the amount of handling, using gravity rather than pumping where possible to move the wine. In most vineyards cement tanks have been fitted with epoxy linings, but for white wine in particular chilled stainless steel tanks are becoming more important. Most fine wines are stored in oak barrels for a year or more, although some white wines are unoaked.

Virtually all of Uruguay's 280 or so wineries are small, family-run private businesses, and 10 or 20 go out of business every year, having failed to change with the times; however, those that have adapted are doing very well. Fourteen of the most export-oriented wineries have formed an association called Los Caminos del Vino – Bodegas Familiares del Uruguay (*Wine Roads – Family Wineries of Uruguay;* m *9914 9662; www.uruguaywinetours.com*), and visits can be arranged to these (they have good websites and can easily be contacted by phone or email). Almost all are in Montevideo and Canelones departments (though two have outposts in Salto and Rivera), but new wineries are appearing in Colonia and in particular Maldonado. The wineries near Montevideo are mostly close to Ruta 5 and it's easy to visit three or more in a day by car; the welcome is warm and an English-speaking guide can usually be provided. A tasting of three or four wines, with snacks and a tour of the winery, costs US$15; with a barbecue lunch it costs US$40–60. A few of the larger wineries have restaurants, but most tastings will be accompanied by cold meats and cheese or homemade *empanadas*. The larger wineries, close to Ruta 5, host groups from cruise ships in Montevideo harbour, and are also popular for weddings and other events.

Alternatively, you can take a Senderos del Tannat (Tannat Trails) tour organised by **Cisplatina Viajes y Turismo** (*Bvar España 2189, Montevideo;* \ *2 409 9107,* m *9963 1547;* e *senderosdeltannat@cisplatinauruguay.com; www.cisplatinauruguay.com; 5–6hr tour US$61, inc transport & English-speaking guide; tours Jan–Feb 14.00 Tue & Thu, 09.00 Sat, Apr–Dec 09.00 Tue, Thu & Sat*). Private custom tours can be arranged with Lares Tours (*W Ferreira Aldunate 1341, Montevideo;* \ *2 901 9120,* m *9959 2009;* e *info@lares.com.uy; www.larestours.com*) who offer the Tannat Experience day-tour as well as two- and three-day tours combining the Colonia and Montevideo areas, with visits to wineries and cheese-makers. Robertson Wine Tours (*The Penthouse 1202, Vázquez Ledesma 2865, CP 11200, Villa Biarritz. Montevideo;* \ *2 711 3032,* m *9434 5144; www.robertsonwinetours.com; from US$575 pp inc everything except accommodation*) and Daniel Reyes (*Colonia 892 Of, 601, Montevideo;* \ *2 902 2054;* e *reservas@danielreyes.com.uy*) offer upmarket tours of Argentine and Uruguayan wineries.

In addition to tours and tastings, wineries are increasingly putting on harvest festivals (January for white wine and February/March for red) and pruning festivals (Festival de la Poda) in mid-August. The members of Los Caminos del Vino open to the public for El Día de la Vendimia, probably on the first Saturday of March.

THE WINERIES There are two fine wineries in Montevideo's northern suburb of Villa Colón. On the Plaza Colón (reached by buses such as the D5, 4A, 40, 130, 169 and 174) is a statue of Francisco Vidiella (see page 135), as well as a branch of La Pasiva. Just north is a church by Eladio Dieste (see page 34) and then on the left of the main road north to La Paz and Las Piedras, the Bodega Santa Rosa.

Bodega Santa Rosa (*Avda César Mayo Gutiérrez 2211;* \ *2 320 9921;* e *export@ bodegasantarosa.com.uy; www.bodegasantarosa.com.uy*) One of the country's larger and more historic wineries, Santa Rosa was founded in 1898 by Juan Passadore, who was responsible for introducing European grape varieties such as Cabernet Sauvignon, Merlot, Sauvignon Blanc and Pinot Blanc to Uruguay, and was important in the mid 20th century, exporting to the United States, and also producing grappa until the government set up a monopoly. It also made the sparkling white wine for Roldos *medio y medio* (see page 99) for 40 years before parting company with them. The bodega is now run by the founder's great-grandson (who speaks good English and handles tours for foreigners). Sparkling white wine is still a speciality (with around 80% of the domestic market), and they still produce a tiny amount of table wine, supplied in 3-litre bottles to a few favoured restaurants, as well as cider for New Year's Eve. However, this is now a thoroughly modern producer of fine wines, with grapes grown in Las Violetas, 17km away in Canelones department, and processed here largely by gravity rather than pumping, and using ozone rather than chlorine for cleaning; they've used screw-tops for many years.

Below the winery, the cellars are cavernous, with massive 19th-century oak tanks from Nancy, two of which are still in use (though most of the wine is made in epoxy-

4

lined concrete tanks). There's a *museo* where old machines and bottles are displayed, with a nice small tasting area. You can also see the Champenoise process for making sparkling wines, including an old German cooling machine. For up to 100 people, tastings can be organised with an *asado* and a live tango and *candombé* show.

Chardonnay, Pinot Noir and Pinot Blanc grapes for sparkling whites are harvested a couple of weeks early for greater acidity, sugar and yeast are added and the wine is bottled with a crown cap and kept in the cellar for up to 16 months, where 30,000 bottles are riddled (rotated a quarter-turn) in eight hours and then turned back the other way for a period of 30 days. This gathers the sediment of dead yeast in the neck; this is placed in ice water and opened, and the frozen plug of sediment is blown out by the pressure inside the bottle, after which it is topped up with some sugared Chardonnay and corked and sealed. Their best sparkling white is Le Fond de Cave (known as Le Chef de Cave for export), with 60% Pinot Noir and 40% Chardonnay kept for 16 months to produce the smallest of bubbles. The Brut Sauvage is all Chardonnay (10% of it spending a year in a French oak *barrique*), with a surprising amount of fruit colour and aroma, something like a Veuve Cliquot but only costing US$10! The (non-sparkling) Sauvignon Blanc Reserva, made in traditional Sancerre style by a visiting French oenologist, is also excellent, with no wood taste, moderate acidity and excellent structure.

The red wines are also excellent, including the fruity Cabernet Sauvignon and Merlot Reservas and the Cabernet Clásico, which is one of Uruguay's best-selling wines (a blend of Cabernet Sauvignon and Cabernet Franc, with a touch of Tannat). The Tannat Reserva is smooth and clean and not too tannic (with just 30% aged for a year in French oak), while the Tannat del Museo Gran Reserva (in fact 20% Merlot) is much softer, with plenty of fruit and subtlety. It is great with cheese and pasta but a tad light for rich meat like game. The Merlot del Museo Reserva is smooth and fruity, while the Juan Bautista Gran Reserva (60% Tannat, with Merlot and Cabernet Sauvignon) is young and wooded.

Bodegas Carrau (*Avda César Mayo Gutiérrez 2556;* ⟍ *2 320 0238/8948;* e *info@ bodegascarrau.com; www.bodegascarrau.com*) Across the road just to the north, Bodegas Carrau is one of the country's largest and most progressive winemakers, although like Santa Rosa they grow their grapes elsewhere. Juan Carrau Sust arrived in Uruguay in 1930 (his family having made wine in Catalunya since 1752) and helped Santa Rosa boom in the 1930s and 1940s (introducing champenoise-style sparkling wines to Uruguay). His son Juan Carrau Pujol ran Santa Rosa for 25 years before going independent, setting up a vineyard in Brazil and then in 1975 Vinos Finos Juan Carrau, using an old winery here in Colón and growing grapes on 24ha (now 35ha) at the Castel Pujol vineyard in Las Violetas.

In 1972, following a study by the University of California at Davis that identified the Brazil–Uruguay border area as ideal for growing grapes for fine wines, he planted vines in Cerro Chapeu, near Rivera, the highest vineyards in Uruguay at over 300m. Initially the grapes were trucked south to Colón overnight, but in 1998 a striking modern winery was opened at Cerro Chapeu, built into the hill to allow the wine to be moved by gravity rather than pumping. With well-drained sandy soils and a stable continental climate, their best grapes are grown here, with low yields to produce a more concentrated taste, the wine still being moved south for blending and bottling.

The aim has always been to produce fine wines for export. Today Carrau produces a million bottles a year, with around 40% exported to 30 countries (roughly a quarter of Uruguay's exports).

Carrau marketed the first 100% Tannat Reserva in 1979. In the last decade, with government support, they began a project to study Tannat's genetic variations (as part of Uruguay's cultural heritage) and produce a more authentic standardised stock; you'll be shown a small test plot of century-old Tannat clones. The Amat line is judged by experts such as Hugh Johnson as Uruguay's best Tannat, being hand-picked at Cerro Chapeu, kept in new oak barrels for 20 months, bottled without filtering and kept for another year in the cellar; it's well worth laying down for many years. The Bodegas Carrau Tannat de Reserva, which spends a year in French oak and a year in the bottle, is also excellent, with lovely soft tannins. The Ysern Tannat is a blend of wines from Las Violetas and Cerro Chapeu, aged in oak for 20 months, fantastic value for money. There's also an Ysern Cabernet Sauvignon (60% from Cerro Chapeu) that's aged for 12 months in year-old French oak. The Tannat Rosé Saigné is made with hand-picked grapes from Las Violetas, and the Vivent fortified Tannat, with rich raspberry and sultana flavours, is soon to be added to the range.

The 1752 Gran Tradición Juan Carrau Pujol range is made from the best Tannat, Cabernet Sauvignon and Cabernet Franc grapes of each vintage, kept in new French oak barrels for 18–20 months and then aged in the bottle for a year; the Tannat is a 50-50 mix of grapes from Cerro Chapeu and Castel Pujol, with a complexity and maturity that make it worth keeping for up to 20 years. The Tannat Juan Carrau is, unusually, made with grapes from Las Violetas only and is very good, with earthy soft tannins. There are also plenty of younger wines, mostly aged in oak for about six months, that won't keep for so long but offer a more affordable taste of what can be done.

On the white side, the Bodegas Carrau Sauvignon Blanc Sur Lie has been produced specifically for North American tastes; fermented in temperature-controlled stainless steel tanks, it's aged for six months with the lees, or yeast sediments, and is soft and juicy with lightly spicy flavours. Castel Pujol is Carrau's most popular brand in the domestic market – the Sauvignon Blanc, kept in steel tanks for six months, is more conventionally smooth but more citric than the usual Sauvignon Blanc – excellent with fish or desserts. One of the more interesting wines is the single vineyard Vilasar; some of the Nebbiolo vines planted at the start of the 20th century were identified at the end of the century as Marzemino, one of the best red varieties from the Trentino in northern Italy, and this is now produced as a blend of 90% Nebbiolo and 10% Marzemino. The Sust (named after Juan Carrau Sust, who introduced the champenoise method to Uruguay in 1930) sparkling wines are 75–80% Chardonnay blended with Pinot Noir, and fermented in the bottle at 12°C for 18 months; it's dry and indeed rather austere in taste.

Guided tours and tastings are available from Monday to Friday (⊕ 09.00–15.00; about 90mins), when a wine shop is also open. Groups of four or more can also arrange to have tastings with cold meats and cheeses (2½ hrs, also possible Sat mornings), or a full meal (Mon–Sat). Tuesdays may be busy with school groups (sampling grape juice rather than wine). In an extension to the 1887 house you'll see some nice historical photographs and documents relating to the family's history.

Bodegas Bouza (Camino de la Redención 7658 bis; \ 2 323 4030; e visitas@ bodegabouza.com; www.bodegabouza.com) Turning west off Ruta 5 at km13.5, it's about 1km to Bodegas Bouza, one of the best organised wineries for visits. Despite being in Montevideo department it's delightfully rural, at the headwaters of the Arroyo de Melilla, with paperbark, cork and Brazilian araucaria trees on the lawns. In 2001 Montevideo businessman Juan Luis Bouza bought a run-down winery (built in 1942) here, and a vineyard just north in the Las Violetas region of Canelones, installed state-of-the-art equipment and now produces a modest 80,000 bottles a year, mostly for restaurants and wine shops, and half exported. Using parcel vinification (hand-picking and processing of just one small plot at a time, with very detailed record-keeping), and small tanks (including three of French oak), remarkably good results are produced.

In addition to the inherited Tannat, Merlot and Chardonnay, Bouza has planted rarer varieties such as Tempranillo and Albariño (a Galician white-wine grape planted for the first time in Uruguay in 2001).

The product range includes standard and premium lines of Tannat, Merlot, Tempranillo, Chardonnay and Albariño. There's an unoaked Chardonnay (produced only for the British market and for blending) as well as a blend produced 60% in stainless steel tanks and 40% in French oak, for the Uruguayan and other export markets. The Albariño (60% oaked) is lovely, with good acidity and a long finish. Other unique blends are the Tempranillo–Tannat, the elegance of the Tempranillo (60%) given strength and acidity by the Tannat (40%), and Monte Vide Eu, a blend of 50% Tannat, 30% Tempranillo and 20% Merlot, all kept in oak for 14 months.

Bouza's Tannat may in fact contain a large proportion of Merlot, kept in oak for 9–14 months. Although the superb Tannat Parcela Única wines are unblended, kept for just six months in new French oak barrels, and bottled without filtering, with mature fruits and spices, the tannin gives structure but no more.

Since the 2008 harvest, Bouza has made a Tempranillo Rosé, macerated for 12 hours and kept for three months over the vine leaves before being put into oak barrels. There are also grappas of Tempranillo, Merlot and Albariño, made in very small batches with an old French still.

The winery is open daily (not Wed in winter) from 11.00 to 16.00, with tastings until 18.00 (*tour US$9, US$19 inc tasting*). There's a very good restaurant (☉ *12.00–15.30 daily, booking essential at w/ends*), serving vegetables and Hampshire Down sheep raised at the bodega. About once a month on average, this serves a cruise group of 80–100 people, but usually it's peaceful enough.

An old railway carriage is being restored to provide two bedrooms, and more accommodation is planned (a simple dinner and breakfast will be provided).

Another of Bouza's interests is *cachilas* or classic cars – a barn houses a collection of superbly restored models such as four Model T Fords (one red, with metal spokes, as opposed to the near-compulsory black, with wooden spokes), a Willy's Jeep, Škodas and Alfa Romeos, BMW and Raleigh motorbikes, and a Messerschmidt three-wheeler. There are tours of the collection at 11.00 and 16.00 daily, and some are driven around outside on Saturdays.

Antigua Bodega Stagnari and Vinos Finos H Stagnari Continuing north up Ruta 5 to km20 and heading west for a couple of kilometres (on a fairly rough road), you'll come to the two Stagnari vineyards, originally all one but now split between the older and younger generations of the Stagnari family, which has been making wine since 1880 in Italy, and since 1928 in Uruguay. First is the **Antigua Bodega Stagnari** (*Santos Lugares, La Paz;* ✆ *2 362 2137;* e *info@antiguabodegastagnari.com.uy; www.antiguabodegastagnari.com.uy*), where Merlot is grown on a soil of decomposed pink granite; Syrah, Tannat, Sangiovese, Cabernet Sauvignon, Sauvignon Blanc and Chardonnay are all grown nearby at Riberas de Santa Lucía.

The standard wines are the Del Pedregal range (aged in oak barrels for six months), with the better Prima Donna wines (in oak for around eight months) and then the new Osiris Reserva Tannat and Merlot at the top, their only 100% single varietals. These are aged in American oak barrels for 12–15 months to give complexity and a balance of fruit and wood. In the Del Pedregal range there's a Tannat, a Merlot, a Cabernet Sauvignon, a Tannat–Merlot (60%–40%, full and fruity for those who find Tannat too strong alone) and even a Tannat–Merlot–Cabernet blend. There's also a Del Pedregal Rosé, which is pure

Merlot (a relatively common choice in Chile, if not elsewhere). As for white wines, there's the Del Pedregal Chardonnay (aged in oak for just three months), and the Prima Donna Sauvignon Blanc, both fresh and easy-drinking wines.

Tastings cost US$15 (for three or four wines), or US$30 with lunch – there's no restaurant as yet, but a good meal can be laid on. The philosophy is to connect personally with visitors and show the winery as a family business, and questions are welcomed.

More or less across the road is **Vinos Finos H Stagnari** (*Santos Lugares;* ☎ *2 362 2940;* e *lapuebla@adinet.com.uy; www.hectorstagnari.com*), set up by Héctor Stagnari in 2000. All the vines were planted by him, the first in Uruguay to be planted at a density of 10,000 vines per hectare, thus producing under 1kg per plant, but with more concentrated sugar. Héctor also set up microplantations all over Uruguay, trying to determine the best place to grow the Tannat grape, ending up at Nueva Hesperides, just outside Salto and very close to where Pascual Harriague first planted Tannat in Uruguay – daytime temperatures reach 40°C, falling to 20°C at night, ideal conditions for developing sugars and alcohol. The wine is all made here, in a high-tech new winery with temperature-controlled 10,000-litre stainless steel tanks. Volumes are relatively low, and only 20% is exported, with most of the wine sold through hotels, restaurants and the more upmarket supermarkets such as Tienda Inglesa. Although no table wines are made here, since 2002 fine wine has been sold to restaurants in two-litre bottles with plastic corks at a similar price to table wine.

The Daymán 'Castel La Puebla' Tannat, with grapes from Salto aged for a year in French oak and then two months in American oak, was voted world champion red in Ljubljana in 2006. However, the Tannat Viejo is even better (well balanced, with a big nose, soft tannins and a chocolatey finish), and the Dinastía (90% Tannat, aged in French oak for 14 months, and only made in small quantities) was the 2007 world champion. The Premier Tannat is younger and a bit heavy on tannins but is remarkably good value if you can lay it down for a couple of years. There are also some good Cabernet Sauvignons, and a Syrah, with grapes from Salto, young and moderately light.

Grapes for white wines (Chardonnay, Viognier, Gewurztraminer and Moscatel d'Alejandria) are grown at La Puebla in Canelones department. They're distinctive for Uruguayan whites, very aromatic and with well-balanced acidity (like white Burgundy). The Chardonnay de Virginia (created for Héctor's wife) is full and fruity, especially compared with other Uruguayan Chardonnays, and doesn't seem as young as it is, with a good body. Their only oaked white wine is the Dinastía Blanco (90% Chardonnay). The Blush Moscatel d'Alejandria (pink from a touch of Tannat) is sweet and very perfumed, with good balance and fruit.

Since around 2007, tourists have been welcomed. For tours in English (*US$16, with four wines & cold meats & cheese*) you should call at least a day ahead; an excellent *parrilla* is available for groups. There's a choice of an air-conditioned tasting room (decorated with award certificates) or a larger room with a view over the vineyards (nicely lit up at night). The style is more modern and technological than at Antiguo Stagnari, with oenologists who will happily talk chemistry with you.

Bodega De Lucca (*Ruta 48 km13.1, El Colorado;* ☎ *2 367 8076;* e *reideluc@ adinet.com.uy, deluccawines@adinet.com.uy; www.deluccawines.com*) Turning west off Ruta 5 at km32, you'll come in 13km to the Bodega De Lucca, where the mercurial Reinaldo De Lucca has been growing grapes (first planted by his grandfather in 1906) for a long time, starting to replant his vines and modernise his business around 1990. While very proud of his degrees from Montevideo, Penn State and Montepellier and his experience abroad, he also feels very much in touch with this land and climate, where no irrigation, fertilisers or insecticides are needed (though minimal use of

TANNAT

The grape that is, rightly or wrongly, always associated with Uruguay is Tannat, originally from the Madiran region of southwestern France, near the Pyrenées, and therefore known to the Basques who came to Uruguay in the 19th century and played a major role in starting its winemaking industry. In 1870 one of them, Pascual Harriague, planted Tannat vines near Salto in the northwest of the country, and in 1876 Francisco Vidiela planted them in Colón, now in Montevideo's northern suburbs. As early as 1877 Tannat (then called Harriague) was known as the 'Uruguayan grape', and in the late 20th century it became associated with the country's resurgent wine industry. Winemakers have used Tannat as Uruguay's calling card, even more than Chilean winemakers have used Carménère, and most visitors to Uruguay will want to try it. In fact it is quite hard to avoid as it's used a lot, being very productive, ripening late and coping well with frost. It produces large, tight bunches of smallish grapes which are easy to pick, an important consideration as harvesting in Uruguay is almost always done by hand (unusually, its leaves begin with three lobes and then develop two more). It produces a full-bodied, deep red-black wine that's fruity and a bit smoky.

However, there is a problem. Tannat is known for its very high tannin levels (the name is no coincidence), a consequence of the grape's thick skin, and on its own Tannat can be just too much for many people. Historically this has happened when the summer has been wet or the grapes have not ripened fully, or when it's been aged for too long in poor barrels; good management is vital. In France it has always been used mainly as a blending grape, and the rules of the Madiran *appellation* require Tannat to be blended with Cabernet Sauvignon, Cabernet Franc or Fer. It is also blended with Manseng and Courbu Noir, but blending Tannat with Merlot has been particularly successful in giving softer, fruitier wines. Tannat's high acidity allows it to be aged in oak barrels for up to 20 months to soften the tannins and bring out its flavour, and it benefits further from bottle aging (up to six years) and from decanting before serving. French rosés made with Tannat are allowed to macerate or steep for only a short time, to stop the wine becoming too tannic. The technique of micro-oxygenation was introduced in Madiran in 1990, with oxygen being bubbled through fermenting Tannat, to soften the wine's tannins.

In Uruguay, Tannat has been bred to be less acidic and tannic but with higher alcohol levels and more complex fruit tones. Some winemakers blend these modern clones with grapes from the 'old vines' descended from the original French cuttings; both types of Tannat are often blended with fruitier grapes such as Merlot or Cabernet Sauvignon. Some of these blends work immensely well; in addition fortified and distilled Tannats (like port or brandy) are now appearing and seem to be very successful. With luck, the days of people having to add ice or soda to their Tannat to make it drinkable are over. Indeed, *Financial Times* wine writer Jancis Robinson chose a 2006 Uruguayan Tannat as one of her 30 choices for Christmas, perhaps because it goes so well with chocolate.

Tannat has now spread from Uruguay to Argentina, Chile, California and Australia; in the last five years most vineyards in Mendoza, Argentina, have taken to adding 5–10% Tannat to their Malbec, an amount that doesn't have to be shown on the label. In California it's used in Meritage (or Bordeaux-style) wines and also blended with Cabernet Franc, Sangiovese and Syrah grapes.

Around 25% of Uruguay's vineyard area is now planted with Tannat, mostly in Canelones and elsewhere in the south. However, in recent years it's been found to do even better in the north, and new vineyards are being established near Salto (where Tannat was first planted in Uruguay) and Rivera.

fungicide can't be avoided). In a hilly area on either side of the Arroyo El Colorado, his four vineyards have shallow, well-drained soils that still store enough water for the dry growing season, and the relatively humid climate is similar to Burgundy without producing the over-ripe fruit of Argentine vines. Speaking of fruit, you'll be given melon with your Marsanne, as well as peaches, plums, strawberries or whatever else he sees as the right match, rather than meats and cheeses.

For red wines Reinaldo grows mainly Merlot, Tannat, Syrah, Cabernet Sauvignon, Cabernet Franc and Sangiovese; and for whites Sauvignon Blanc, Chardonnay, Marsanne and Rousanne. His best wine may be the Syrah, produced mainly for export, with 20% Tannat and Marsanne; it's well structured and balanced, with elegant tannins, and subtle, complex floral aromas with a bit of spice. The Merlot is well structured and full-bodied with round tannins and a complex aroma of nuts, toasted almonds and hints of tobacco. The Cabernet Sauvignon is very elegant, with ripe fruit on the nose, notes of liquorice and aromatic hints of ripe red peppers. The Tannat is a bit heavy, with very ripe concentrated fruit and velvety tannins. The Río Colorado is a blend of the best Cabernet Sauvignon, Tannat and Merlot.

On the white side, the Marsanne (probably the only Marsanne made in Uruguay) is exotic, with an elegant structure and long finish. The Sauvignon Blanc is well balanced, with lots of ripe fruit and good acidity. A Viognier will soon be released too.

Tastings are usually conducted by Reinaldo himself, who will tell you everything about pairing wine and fruit, particularly to bring out the wine's erotic potential. He's highly entertaining, but also very knowledgeable and serious about his craft.

Bodegas Castilo Viejo (*Ruta 68 km24, Las Piedras;* ↘ *2 368 9606;* e *directorio@ castilloviejo.com; www.castilloviejo.com*) On the less hilly eastern side of Ruta 5, Bodegas Castillo Viejo is 3km north of Las Piedras on Ruta 67. Founded in 1927 on a very small scale, another 150ha were bought in the cooler terrain of San José department in the 1960s, although purely for the production of table wines. Since 1982 the winery has been run by the third generation of the Etcheverry family, who started to modernise from 1986, with classic French grape varieties grown on V-shaped Open Lyre trellises (then almost unknown in South America), to expose the grapes to light and air. They benefited from the skills of a New Zealand consultant who subsequently married into the family, helping them to produce clean tangy Sauvignons Blancs. They're also known for their old-vine Cabernet Franc, including a rosé. They produce over a million litres a year, half of it bulk table wine; of the fine wine, 75% (especially white wine) is exported, with sales to 22 countries including less obvious ones such as Poland and Iceland.

The Catamayor ('Good Tasting') brand includes the entry-level Clásico range, with young (unoaked) Sauvignon Blanc, Chardonnay, Cabernet Franc, Merlot and blends of both of these last two reds with Tannat, as well as a Tannat that's aged in oak for ten months and in the bottle for six months; these are all full of fruit and colour but well balanced. The Catamayor Reserva range, aged in oak for 6–10 months, includes Tannat, Tannat–Cabernet Franc, Merlot and a lovely Viognier; and the Vieja Parcela Reserva de la Familia line includes Tannat and Cabernet Franc, both oaked for ten months (but needing to be aged in the bottle for a year or so after purchase), and a Sauvignon Blanc of which 5% is aged in new French oak barrels for concentration and persistence. In 2005 the El Preciado Primer Gran Reserva wines were released – they're generic blends of red (largely Cabernet Franc) and white (mainly Viognier), but top quality, with 8% of the red and 65% of the white aged in oak for a full 15 months. There's also the Hasparren Brut sparkling wine.

Tourism is important to them – there's no charge for tastings, but these tend to end in people buying their better wines (though at lower prices than in the shops). It's well set up, starting with a video in the old cellar, and one of the three siblings who run the business is usually in attendance. It's possible to have lunch, the usual *asado*, with grilled vegetables and a dessert. You can also arrange to visit the San José vineyard for a relaxing day in the country, with bikes or a tractor and trailer to take visitors to a viewpoint and then at 19.30 an *asado*, before watching (or helping with) the grape-picking, which – perhaps uniquely in the world – takes place only at night.

Pizzorno Wines (*Ruta 32 km23, Canelón Chico;* ✆ *2 368 9601;* e *info@pizzornowines.com; www.pizzornowines.com*) Just south of Castillo Viejo (and employing the same New Zealand consultant), Pizzorno Wines was founded in 1910 and is now run by the founder's grandson, Carlos Pizzorno. His wife Ana is a doctor who's researching the benefits of moderate red wine consumption in preventing cancer of the colon (linked to Uruguay's meat-rich diet). Like most wineries in this area it has moved successfully from mass-production table wine to crafting fine wines. They've done so well that they are the only Uruguayans to get a wine into a British supermarket (the 2005 and 2006 Merlot–Tannat, described as well structured, supple and smooth in the mouth, soft but full of flavour and deliciously smoky, underpinned by soft tannins, and available at Waitrose, admittedly hidden among the Argentine wines). The 2004 Tannat Reserva is superb, if a bit 'international' in style, with complexity and concentration, and smoky plum and ripe blackberry fruits. There's also an unoaked Tannat, a little rougher but still fine, and a Tannat–Merlot, also unoaked, which works well. There's also Cabernet Sauvignon, and a Reserva red (60% Tannat, 30% Cabernet Sauvignon, 10% Merlot) that in a good year is well integrated, with smoky fruits and soft tannins, but may need time to mature in other years.

There's an excellent Sauvignon Blanc, with touches of citrus and vanilla and good acidity (and a Sauvignon Blanc Reserva launched in 2009), and a sparkling Chardonnay, with 10% Sauvignon Blanc, that's light and refreshing but without much depth.

Visitors are welcome with 48 hours' notice, and a new cellar, tasting room and shop are under construction.

Bodega Pisano (*Ruta 68 km29, Progreso;* ✆ *2 368 9077;* e *pisano@adinet.com.uy; www.pisanowines.com*) To the north of Las Piedras, just short of Progreso, Bodega Pisano is Uruguay's leading exporter of fine wines by value, selling to 38 countries. Their wines are in fact pretty pricey, but that's not a problem as every bottle of their deliberately limited production (about 350,000 bottles) is soon sold. Founded in 1924, the winery is now run by the fifth generation, three brothers who all believe in small-scale production, with hand-picking of high-density/low-yielding vines and simple equipment with limited chilling and use of new oak barrels.

Tannat is a speciality, the headliner being the Axis Mundi Premium Tannat, which costs no less than £70 a bottle in Britain but may actually be worth it; having spent a massive 30 months in French oak it has massive power and concentration. The Arretxea blend of Tannat and Cabernet Sauvignon (40% each) with Merlot, aged in French oak for a year, has complexity, elegance and well-defined spices; there's also an Arretxea Tannat–Petit Verdot. The core range of reserve varietals is called Reserva Personal Familiar (RPF; The Family's Personal Reserve); the Tannat has intense colour and complex concentrated tannins with long robust fruit and spice. The RPF line also includes Merlot, Cabernet Sauvignon, Petit Verdot and Pinot Noir, and the white Chardonnay.

At the budget end of the range, the Cisplatina Tannat–Merlot (60%–40%) is a good everyday blend; the Río de los Pájaros Tannat and Merlot–Tannat are a bit more complex. There's also a Río de los Pájaros Tannat–Syrah–Viognier, very purple with spicy aromas and toasty fruits. They also produce the light, fresh Brut Negro sparkling Tannat, and the extraordinary Etxe Oneko fortified dessert wine, something between a port and an amarone, made from late-harvested Tannat.

They've also planted Syrah and Moscato Giallo, although these are not yet in production; Sangiovese has been tried but wasn't a success here.

On the white side, there's superb Torrontés (which usually does best in arid high-altitude parts of Argentina, rather than in relatively humid Uruguay) in the affordable Río de los Pájaros and Cisplatino lines, and the Fabula Late Harvest Viognier–Torrontes, a sweet dessert wine full of soft peach and honey flavours. In 2006 the Arretxea Lyrios was launched, a white blend to match the red Arretxea, with Chardonnay, Viognier and Riesling all aged separately for 18 months before blending and bottling.

Establicimiento Juanicó (*Ruta 5 km37.5, Juanicó;* `\` *33 59725,* m *9484 7482;* e *visita@juanico.com; www.juanico.com*) The biggest and most successful of Uruguay's family wineries is right on Ruta 5 (and the 34th parallel), 6km south of the town of Canelones. The Establicimiento Juanicó was built in 1755 as a farm. In 1820 it was bought by Francisco Juanicó, who began planting vines and about 1840 built some fine brick cellars, declared a national historical monument in 2009. Still in use, it's claimed that this is the oldest continuously operating winery in South America.

The winery ended up in the hands of the state, which supplied the Free French forces with beef during World War II. Unable to repay the debt in cash, in 1946 the French government built a modern winery like a concrete flying saucer, a state-of-the-art complex with gravity-fed processing, although now run from a 21st-century computerised control room. In 1979 the winery was bought from the government by the Deicas family, who set about transforming it with new techniques and new grapes (especially the 'noble' Bordeaux varieties), and a change from quantity to quality, cutting yields from 25,000kg/ha to between 2,000 and 12,000. Relaunched as a producer of fine wines in 1984, it began exporting and winning medals in the 1990s. The Don Pascual brand (named in honour of Pascual Harriague, who introduced the Tannat grape to Uruguay and founded the country's wine industry) was launched in 1996, and is now found in most of the country's restaurants. Indeed the brand is so omnipresent that a careless guidebook writer might assume that many restaurants are named Don Pascual.

In 1999 Juanicó set up the first Uruguayan joint venture with a French winery, Château Pape Clement (owned by the Magrez family of Bordeaux) to produce a high-quality Tannat called Casa Magrez; these vines are on a separate, far smaller vineyard nearby, and the intention is to set up a separate winery here too.

Juanicó now produces over five million litres of wine a year and supplies 30% of the domestic market; in fact 70% of the production is still table wine (mostly made from grapes bought in from other growers). It's immensely impressive that so much wine is mass-produced here at the same time as small batches of genuinely world-class wines. The vines at Juanicó are managed 'semi-organically', being sprayed against Botrytis fungus but otherwise managed naturally, encouraging natural predators to control insects, and with all seeds and stalks being composted. They're planted at a high density, with up to 8,000 vines per hectare, but with only two bunches per plant, to give highly concentrated sugars. Laboratory analysis and tasting show the precise moment for picking (by hand, naturally). Although the vineyard is at only 45m altitude, temperatures can range between 35°C by day and 18°C by night, ideal for boosting sugar and alcohol levels.

The Don Pascual range (exported under the name Bodegones del Sur, with labels showing Uruguayan Constructivist art) includes the single varietal reds Tannat, Merlot, Petit Verdot, Cabernet Sauvignon, Cabernet Franc and Pinot Noir and Marselan; Tannat–Merlot and Shiraz–Tannat blends; and the whites Chardonnay, Viognier and Tempranillo. Marselan (a cross between Cabernet Sauvignon and Grenache) was developed in France in 1961 and has been used here since 2002; it's partly oaked, but displays less tannin and less fruit than you might expect, and goes well with heavy pasta, meat and cheese. Tempranillo is the only non-French grape grown here, used mainly in a rosé.

The Don Pascual Tannat Reserva is young but excellent, with fruit, spice and leather shining through the sharp complex tannins, and a long finish. There's also the Tannat Roble, aged for a year in American oak, with softer tannins and better structure. The Pinot Noir Reserva is not bad, with sweetish fruit and a slightly thin finish; likewise, the Cabernet Sauvignon Reserva, partly aged in oak for balance and structure, has plenty of acidity and alcohol but can be a bit cloying and needs time to open up. The Petit Verdot Roble, also aged in oak, is a fine Bordeaux-style wine that goes well with game, duck and pheasant.

Among the more limited range of whites, the Sauvignon Gris, Marselan and Viognier Reservas are fine, but the Viognier works better as an oak-aged blend with Chardonnay, with good acidity and light fruits plus hints of ginger. There are also two sparkling whites, the Cuvée Castelar Extra Brut and Brut Reserva, also blends of Chardonnay with just 10% of Viognier, light, acidic and very dry.

The premium wines, under the Familia Deicas name, include the Cru Garage Tannat (*garage* being a Bordeaux term for a small winery) – one of the best Tannats you could hope for, with intense inky-black fruit with toffee and chocolate, and superb structure – and the Preludio blends. The red blend is composed of Tannat (40%), Cabernet Sauvignon, Cabernet Franc, Merlot, Petit Verdot and, since 2002, precisely 2% of Marselan, all from the best plots of old vines, aged in oak for 22 months. It's quite superb, as is vouched for by its presence on the wine list of the very prestigious Fat Duck run by Heston Blumenthal in Bray, and the many prizes it has won. The Preludio Blanco, almost as good, is 95% Chardonnay, with Sauvignon Blanc and Viognier, also aged in oak for length and structure, with luscious, buttery fruit and good acidity. The small amounts of varietal wines made for blending in Preludio, but not used, are bottled as Single Barrel Limited Editions.

Also in the Familia Deicas range is the Botrytis Noble Cosecha Tarde, the late harvest dessert wine (like a Sauternes) that's blended from Sauvignon Blanc, Sauvignon Gris, Gewurztraminer, Petit Grain and Rossesse grapes, picked right at the end of the season when the 'noble rot' fungus has taken hold.

Finally, also in the Familia Deicas range, the Licor de Tannat is a port-style fortified wine that's full of fruit and almost syrupy-sweet, and excellent with Stilton-type cheeses (not easily found in Uruguay). Historically, cognac was also produced at Juanicó, and there are still Ugni Blanc vines here, but none is made now.

Turning off Ruta 5, a dirt track winds through the beautifully tended vineyards and past the railway station (used by occasional charter trains for cruise groups) to the winery. Tastings are held in a lovely red-brick hall (built by the British in the 1860s). Below this are the original cellars, built in about 1840 and still in use, where you'll see some Art Nouveau stained glass rescued from Montevideo's legendary Tupi Nambi bar; there's also plenty of contemporary art on show. Visits are very professionally managed, with a tour of the vineyard, winery, cellar and historic buildings. There are three *cachilas* (vintage cars) under a thatched roof, and you might see a *lagarto overa* (tegu lizard) on the lawn, or some of the 120 species of birds recorded here (a large part of the estate is still woodland). Tastings start at

US$10 with four wines; you can try up to eight wines, or choose cold meats and cheeses, *empanadas* or a full lunch, usually the classic *asado* with a huge salad and dessert. Naturally you can buy wines in their shop too.

Bodega Marichal (*Ruta 64 km48.5, Etchevarría;* ☎ *33 21949;* e *info@marichalwines.com; www.marichalwines.com*) Turning west from Ruta 5 at km39, it's almost 7km to Bodega Marichal, a relatively small winery founded in 1910 and now run by the third and fourth generations of the family. It's one of the nicest to visit, thanks to the charming Juan Andrés Marichal, who handles all English-speaking visits, as well as to the food laid on by 'Granny Teresita'. They have 50ha of vines here, on gentle slopes with semi-permeable soils that almost never need irrigation. White grapes (Chardonnay, Semillon and Sauvignon Blanc) account for 30% of production and Tannat for about half of the remainder; there's also Merlot, Pinot Noir, Cabernet Franc and some experimental varieties. No less than 70% of their fine wines are exported, to Europe, Brazil and Barbados.

The Pinot Noir, grown on a hill enjoying cool breezes at night, has done well on its own (with 70% kept in oak for 11 months) and also in a very unconventional blend with Tannat that has the delicacy of Pinot but the body and colour of Tannat. Pinot Noir is even blended with Chardonnay to give a delightful, buttery, light-red wine with good cherry fruit. The Reserve Collection Tannat (with 65% kept in oak for 11 months and then aged in the bottle for a year) needs to be decanted or given time to open up, but then works very well, with some spice on the nose and a long finish; a Grand Reserve Tannat was launched in 2009, after a full 18 months in oak.

The Cabernet Franc is used for a young unoaked rosé, and there's an excellent fresh Chardonnay, made without malolactic fermentation. The Blanc de Noir, made of Pinot Noir with 35% Chardonnay and kept in oak for just three months, is very creamy, and excellent with food.

Tastings cost from US$15 (for three wines with cold meats and cheese) to US$25 (five wines with cold meats, cheeses and homemade *empanadas*), or US$45 with an *asado*. Booking is essential, except for the Día de la Vendimia (Harvest Festival) in early March and the Dia del Patrimonio (Heritage Day) in October.

Bodega Casa Filgueira (*Ruta 81 km7, Cuchilla Verde;* ☎ *33 46438;* e *info@bodegafilgueira.com; www.bodegafilgueira.com*) Turning off Ruta 5 at km47, north of Canelones town, and going to the end of Ruta 62 and a little bit to the left, you'll come to Bodega Casa Filgueira. A little out of the tourist mainstream, this is a friendly and modern place that built a new winery and started making fine wines only in 1998 (although the family has been making wine here since 1927). Vines are trained on Open Lyre stands and replaced every eight years; the grapes are hand-picked early in the morning, and processed in chilled stainless steel tanks. Tannat vines cover 40% of the 45ha area, followed by Cabernet Sauvignon, Cabernet Franc, Merlot, Pinot Noir and, most recently, Sauvignon Gris.

The Clásico range of young wines (to be drunk within a year) is aged only in the bottle, for between two and eight months. The Reserva and Reserva de la Familía ranges include Tannat, Merlot, Cabernet Sauvignon and Chardonnay, all aged in French oak barrels for between 8 and 15 months to give structure and complexity to go with their intense fresh aromas. At the top end are the Premiun Merlot (oaked for 15 months) and Sauvignon Gris (aged in the bottle only, for eight months); Casa Filgueira is the first winery in Uruguay to tackle the rare Sauvignon Gris (or Grigio) variety, and claims to account for 5% of world production already.

Visits are welcome with 48 hours' notice (⊕ *10.00–15.00 Mon–Sat*). You'll see the vines, winery and cellar, and taste the wines either with cheese and snacks or with an *asado* lunch and salad.

4

Viña Varela Zarranz (*Ruta 74 km29, Suárez;* \ *2 364 4587;* e *info@ varelazarranz.com; www.varelazarranz.com*) Between Ruta 7 and Ruta 8, to the northeast of Montevideo, Viña Varela Zarranz is an historic estate entered along an avenue of century-old olive trees; grand araucarias, casuarinas, eucalyptus and other trees stand in the park.

Diego Pons – banker, senator and ambassador to Italy – bought this estate in 1888 and entertained politicians including Julio Herrera y Obes, José Batlle y Ordóñez, Claudio Williman and Baltasar Brum in his Italianate mansion. He planted French vines here and in 1892 built the winery and cellar, with winemaking equipment from Italy and massive oak vats from Nancy in France. In 1944 the estate was bought by brothers Ramón and Antonio Varela, who had founded the Viticultores Unidos del Uruguay (VUDU) co-operative winery in 1933. Ramón married María Zarranz, and their four sons in time took over the business. Since 1986 the third generation has been in charge, bringing in new investors to set up Viña Varela Zarranz as fine-wine makers alongside VUDU, which continues to produce table wines.

With 60ha of vines here and another 50ha at Cuatro Piedras on the far side of Ruta 5, they've steadily replaced old vines with healthy new French stock, now growing on Open Lyre stands, for greater exposure to light and air. In addition to the traditional Tannat (20% of the total), Merlot, Cabernet Franc, Cabernet Sauvignon, Chardonnay and Sauvignon Blanc, they've added unusual varieties such as Muscat de Frontignan, Muscat de Ottonel, Bourboulenc, Marsanne and Viognier. New technology includes machines to gently remove the grapes from the stalks, low-pressure pneumatic presses, chilled stainless steel tanks and bottling with inert gas. Table wine, which accounts for about 94% of production (c2.5 million litres a year), is made in far bigger tanks than the fine wine, without chilling, and is bottled (with plastic corks) in Tetrapaks, 1.5- or 2-litre bottles, or demijohns of up to 10 litres.

White wines, all unoaked, include a delicate Sauvignon Blanc, Chardonnay and the only Muscat Petit Grain made in Uruguay – this is dry (despite first impressions on the nose) and smooth, with citric aromas and good fruit. There's also an unoaked Cabernet Sauvignon rosé. The María Zarranz sparkling champenoise (a blend of Viognier, Marsanne, Bourboulenc and Chardonnay) was introduced in 2008; young, fresh and fruity, it's aimed at the domestic market.

Among the red wines, there's an unoaked Cabernet Franc–Tannat (young and plummy, although it will age well); the others are all aged in oak barrels, although the Cabernet Sauvignon only gets a month and 40% of the regular Tannat gets two months. The Tannat Reserva is aged in oak for six months, and there are three premium Tannats, the Roble (aged for ten months) and the Crianza and 150 Años Teatro Solís, which spend a year in French and American oak, giving lots of concentrated fruit with smoky notes, and good structure with smooth tannins. The Guidaí Detí (Charrúa for 'Three Moons') is a premium blend of Tannat (55%) Cabernet Sauvignon (25%) and Cabernet Franc (20%), all fermented separately, then blended and kept in oak for 14 months; it's full of black fruits and rounded tannins, with good structure and complexity.

Visits are available, mostly for small groups (it's a bit far from the port for cruise groups, although it is the handiest winery for the airport). Tastings for up to 30 are held in the atmospheric original cellars, although a barn is being converted for bigger events. Regular tastings cost US$20, or around US$50 for lunch (for groups of ten or more; smaller groups can have *empanadas*); with luck the impressive sommelier Magdalena Américo will lead you through the sampling. You'll see French oak barrels dating from 1903, holding about 10,200 and 16,900 litres, now used only for storing table wine rather than ageing.

Viñedo de los Vientos (*Ruta 11 km162, Atlántida;* ✆ *37 21622,* 📱 *9937 2723;*
e *info@vinedodelosvientos.com; www.vinedodelosvientos.com*)Finally, at the eastern end
of Canelones department, Viñedo de los Vientos is a delightfully offbeat place that
is, however, totally serious about winemaking. Pablo Fallabrino is a surfer dude
whose family has been growing grapes here since 1947. He loves the land, and its
150 bird species, managing it as sustainably as possible, with only low-impact
fungicides and minimal amounts of organic fertiliser. You'll see plenty of flickers
and horned beetles busy controlling insect pests. He also goes with his instincts as
a winemaker, with some very interesting choices of grapes and blends; he tends to
blend during the fermentation process, rather than making varietal wines and
then blending them.

Most of the original vines have been replaced by virus-free stock from France
and South Africa (there's still some Ugni Blanc, which is sold for table wine). Now
there's Tannat, Cabernet Sauvignon, Ruby Cabernet, Trebbiano, Gewurztraminer,
Moscato Blanco and Chardonnay, and Pablo is planting Nebbiolo and Dolcetto,
which should work well as a blend with Tannat. Just 4km from the sea, there's
plenty of wind and humidity, so the vines are trained high above the ground for
ventilation. Pablo built the winery in 1998, before which the grapes were sold for
blending as table wine; even now, about 40% goes for blending.

The standard white wine is Estival (60% Gewurztraminer, 30% Chardonnay,
10% Moscato Blanco), which is very quaffable with or without food. There's also
the fine Blanc de Bianco (80% Chardonnay, 10% Trebbiano, 10% Viognier), aged
for six months in French oak over the spent yeast (*sur lie*); it has lots of rounded,
light fruit flavours. The standard Tannat is young and light but very approachable,
with more fruit than you'd expect and hints of oak and smoke. The Eolo Gran
Reserva is 80% Tannat (with Ruby Cabernet), aged for a year in French oak, and
very good. Pablo also makes a Ripasso di Tannat, fermenting Tannat for a second
time over leftover Tannat skins, producing a rich, dry, raisiny wine a little lighter
than an Amarone. Alcyone is a Tannat dessert wine (sold by the half-bottle),
fortified with brandy and full of velvety fruit, chocolate, honey and vanilla.

Midway between Montevideo and Punta del Este (and under half an hour from
Carrasco airport), the winery sees a certain number of tourists, as well as locals
calling in to fill up their jugs. Tastings, costing US$8 with four wines, should be
booked 24 hours ahead. You can also book the Antipasto Special (*US$22 for two*),
with fine snacks accompanying the four wines, or a four-course meal with four
matching wines (*US$40 each, with a minimum of four people*) – Pablo's partner
Mariana is a superb cook!

Other wineries Other wineries worth visiting include **Alto de la Ballena** in
Maldonado (see page 201), and Los Cerros de San Juan in Colonia (see page 256).

Granja Aripuca (*Ruta 103 s/n, Canelones, north off the Interbalnearia at km55.5;* ✆ *37
37024,* 📱 *9441 0108;* e *aripuca@adinet.com.uy; www.aripuca.com.uy*) Aripuca is
somewhat tourist-oriented, with horseriding available and a country restaurant,
but also makes some decent Tannat, Pinot Noir, Cabernet Sauvignon and
Gewurztraminer, as well as a fortified *licor de Tannat.*

La Cruz (*Ruta 5 km117, La Cruz, Florida;* ✆ *35 02115*) La Cruz is the only certified
organic winery in Uruguay and is probably also the country's oldest winery, founded
in 1887. Some Tannat vines and French oak vats, brought here in 1903, are still in
use. Of the 60ha of vineyards, 20ha are organic, producing a dry velvety Malbec; it's
also certified sugar-free and thus suitable for diabetics. They also grow Nebbiolo,
Merlot, Tannat, Pinot Noir, Muscat d'Hamburg and Sauvignon Blanc. There's a

Pinot Noir–Folie Noir sparkler, and in 2009 they're releasing a white wine made from Arriloba grapes (a cross of Sauvignon Blanc and Raffiat de Moncade). They have a small museum and tasting room; call a day ahead.

Ariano Hermanos (*Ruta 48 km15, El Colorado;* \ *2 364 5290, 2 365 2066;* e *arianohnos@cs.com.uy; www.arianohermanos.com*) Just beyond the Bodega De Lucca, Hermanos is one of the larger, established family wineries, but doesn't offer tastings and visits. Founded in 1929, it has vineyards in Canelones and Paysandú departments and produces 1.5 million litres of wine a year, 60% of it table wine. They produce good Merlot, Cabernet Franc, Tannat, Muscat Ottonel (an Alsace-style white that's ideal with desserts) and Chardonnay, and blends of Tannat with Cabernet Franc, Merlot, Syrah and Cabernet Sauvignon, mostly aged in oak barrels for around six months.

Viñedos y Bodegas Bartora (*Ruta 5 km39, Las Violetas, Canelones;* \ *33 28831,* m *9933 6782;* e *bodegabartora@adinet.com.uy*) Just north of Juanicó, this winery welcomes visits by appointment.

Vinos Finos Beretta (*Camino La Renga 2443, Melilla;* \ *2 322 7503;* e *turismo@ vinosfinosberetta.com, folgtberetta@montevideo.com.uy; www.vinosfinosberetta.com*) Founded in 1911, Beretta welcomes visitors by appointment, with snacks or lunch available. With three vineyards around the Melilla region of Canelones, they grow Merlot and Syrah in particular.

Buzzone y Sciutto (*Camino Guerra 6950, Punta de Rieles;* \ *2 514 5722;* e *bys@ internet.com.uy; www.bys.com.uy*) Founded in 1888, Sciutto works closely with university consultants and also grows grapes in Durazno and at Cerro Chapeu, Rivera. They produce good Tannat as well as sparkling and fortified wines; 90% of production is table wine for the demijohn market.

Bodega Gimenez Mendez – Plaza Vidiella (*Battle y Ordoñez 165, Canelones;* \ *33 20307;* e *sgonzatto@plazavidiella.com; www.gimenezmendez.com*) Produces a million litres a year of table wine, plus fine Tannats (including a fortified Licor de Tannat), and the young and fresh Las Brujas Cabernet Sauvignon and Suavignon Blanc.

Monte de Luz (*Ruta 23 km125, Mal Abrigo, San José;* \ *2 369 1855;* e *contact@leda-sa.com; www.vignobles-lesgourgues.com*) The French-owned de Luz is at 150m, close to the Sierras de Mahoma. Half the vineyard is planted with Tannat and the rest with Cabernet Sauvignon, Cabernet Franc and Syrah. They produce fruity young varietals and oaked Reservas. Nearby is the **Finca Piedra** (see page 160), which also produces a nice Tannat.

Traversa Vinos Finos (*Avda Pedro de Mendoza 7966, Las Piedras;* \ *2 222 0035;* e *bodega@traversahnos.com*) and **Bodega Juan Toscanini e Hijos** (*Ruta 69 km30, Canelón Chico;* \ *2 368 9696;* e *info@toscaniniwines.com; www.toscaniniwines.com*) are two of Uruguay's biggest wineries, producing large quantities of table wine as well as fine wines.

FLORIDA DEPARTMENT

From Canelones, Ruta 5 continues north as a 90km/h single carriageway towards Durazno and Rivera, near km73 passing the junction of Ruta 76 west to the town of 25 de Mayo – after 10km, Ruta 5 passes **Paso Severino**, where the

FLORIDA DEPARTMENT

OSE water utility has a recreation centre at a dam that attracts over 1,000 people on sunny weekends. There are swimming pools, sports and boating facilities, barbecues, a restaurant and accommodation (↳ *33 09033/5;* **e** *pasoseverino@ ose.com.uy;* $) with both shared and private bathrooms. There's also good native forest here for birdwatching. A bus runs from Florida at 10.00 on Sundays, returning at 19.30.

FLORIDA The town of Florida is 50km north of Canelones and 100km from Montevideo, making it the last convenient stopover if you're heading towards the capital. Founded in 1809, and now a quiet provincial town of just over 30,000 inhabitants, it had its moment in the limelight when a provisional government was set up here on 14 June 1825, and the Assembly of Representatives declared Uruguay's independence on 25 August (see page 15).

Getting there Just north of km95, Ruta 5 crosses Ruta 56, which leads west past Parque Robaina and the Piedra Alta to the centre of town, but buses continue up Ruta 5 past km97 to run south past the Piedra Alta railway station (where 0-6-0 steam locomotive No 3 is preserved) to the bus terminal, just west of the main Plaza Asamblea.

By train There's one train a day (*Mon–Fri; 2 on Sat*) from Montevideo; the Piedra Alta station is more convenient than the Florida terminal, west of the centre.

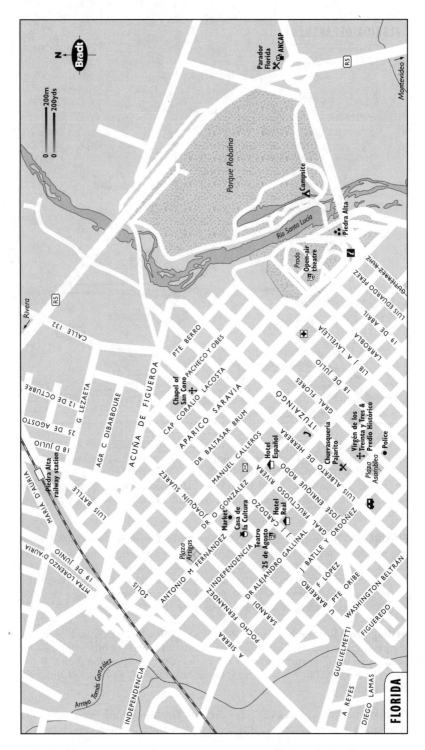

FLORIDA

By bus From the terminal at Battle y Ordóñez and Herrera, CITA runs frequent buses to Montevideo (see page 82); services north to Durazno are run by Bruno Hermanos, CTTM and Turismar. A COOM bus leaves at 15.00 daily for Minas and Punta del Este; COAA and OPAC run six services in all east to Chamizo, Casupá and Cerro Colorado (also known as Alejandro Gallinal), for connections on Ruta 7 to Melo.

Tourist information The Centro de Información Municipal is at Gutiérrez Ruiz & Saravia, at the corner of the Prado park (🕾 35 21738; e *floridaturismo@ adinet.com.uy; www.imf.gub.uy*).

🏠 Where to stay

🏠 **Hotel Real** Independencia 627; 🕾 35 22498; e hotelreal@adinet.com.uy. Has larger, nicer rooms with cable TV, AC & internet access, although rooms at the front can be noisy. $$

🏠 **Hotel Español** Rodó 360 & González; 🕾 35 22262; e hotelesp@adinet.com.uy. This more economical option was built in 1926 & is in excellent condition, with a garage, Wi-Fi, rooms with cable TV & AC, but no lift; b/fast costs US$2 extra. $$–$

🔺 **Campsite** 🕾 35 27395; ⏰ all year. Located in the Parque Robaina, east of the centre before the Ruta 5 bypass. It's in thick native forest, although the area is too busy for there to be much birdlife. $

✖ Where to eat
There's a limited choices of eating places, beyond the fast food joints on the main drag, Independencia.

✖ **Churrasquería Pajarito** Ituzaingó between Gallinal & Independencia; ⏰ 11.30–15.00, 20.30–00.30 daily. A bit of a party place, but serves good grilled meats & has AC & Wi-Fi. $$

✖ **Parador Florida** Junction Ruta 5 & Ruta 56; 🕾 35 23359. $$

✖ **Confitería del Centro** Independencia 645. Serves snacks & cakes. $

Other practicalities

Banks There are ATMs on the north side of Plaza Asamblea and along Independencia.

Communications The post office is in the MultiAhorro supermarket (*Rivera 3320; ⏰ 09.00–17.00 Mon–Fri, 08.00–12.00 Sat*). Antel's *telecentros* are at Fernández 564 & Ituzaingó (⏰ *09.00–20.00 daily*) and Independencia 749 (⏰ *07.00–23.00 Mon–Sat*). There's public Wi-Fi on Plaza Asamblea and the Prado, and a good signal at a school on Fernández between Rodó & Herrera.

Emergency services The **Hospital Florida** (🕾 35 22109/2119) is at Baltasar Brum & Lavalleja, towards the Prado. The **police** (*Flores 509;* 🕾 352 3301/2) are on the south side of Plaza Asamblea.

Markets The municipal market is at Fernández & Barreiro; supermarkets include MultiAhorro (*Rivera between González & Calleros;* ⏰ 08.00–22.00 daily), Ta-Ta (*Independencia 666, north of Rodó;* ⏰ 08.00–21.00 Mon–Sat, 08.30–13.30, 16.00–21.00 Sun) and the Supermercado San Cono (*opposite the bus terminal at Herrera & Batlle, and at Fernández & Barreiro*).

What to see and do Plaza Asamblea, busy with noisy, small, pale-green *cotorras* (parakeets), is immediately east of the bus terminal; on its east side is the cathedral of the **Virgén de los Treinta y Tres**. In the usual Neoclassical style, it was built in 1887–94, although the towers were left unfinished. The interior walls were totally covered with rather uninspired paintings in 1931. The large organ at the west end, installed in 1935, is one of the best in South America, and the bronze doors are by the sculptors José and Stelio Belloni. On the altar (dating from 1898) is a small spotlit statue of the Virgin, a copy of Our Lady of Luján, to which the Treinta y Tres lowered their flag and pledged their loyalty; now the Virgén de los Treinta y Tres is honoured with a festival on the second Sunday of November, including a choral festival in the cathedral.

On the north side of the cathedral is the **Predio Histórico** (*Historic Site; Ituzaingó & Gallinal*), where the Sala de Representantes, meeting in the rancho of Don Basilio Fernández, declared Uruguayan independence on 25 August 1825. Later a school, it was destroyed in 1864 in the Guerra Grande and now there is just a commemorative plaque on the site.

The Casa de Culture (*Barreiro 420*) houses a library and a small historical museum; nearby is the Teatro 25 de Agosto (*Independencia 787*), built as the Cine Nelson in 1945.

Just northeast of the centre, the **chapel of San Cono** (*Rodó 150 & Lacosta*), built in 1955, has a relatively modern exterior but a gaudy interior with murals of the 12th-century saint's miracles. To the rear of the altar is an amazing display of ex-voto offerings from the faithful in search of divine help, including bikes and motorbikes, many *quinceaño* dresses (worn by girls for their 15th birthday parties, when they supposedly reach adulthood) and lots of foreign banknotes, watches, rings, pearl necklaces and the like. On 3 June each year the statue of San Cono is taken in procession to the plaza and back, and up to 20,000 people come to pray for help with lotteries and gambling, Cono's speciality.

Five blocks southeast from here along Lacosta is the **Prado**, a park overlooking the Río Santa Lucía Chico (a minor branch of the main river) which was laid out in 1910 and last remodelled in 1981, with sculptures, exotic flora, a summer theatre and the Parador Piedra Alta restaurant. At the southern end of the Prado, by the road bridge across the river to the Parque Robaina and Ruta 5, is the **Piedra Alta (High Rock)**, actually just a couple of metres high, where the Declaration of Independence was read to the people; there are lots of plaques and a monument with the text of the declaration.

ESTANCIAS IN FLORIDA DEPARTMENT

San Pedro de Timote (*Between Ruta 6 & Ruta 7;* \ *310 8086–88,* m *9961 4110;* e *centraldereservas@montevideo.com.uy, info@sanpedrodetimote.com; www.sanpedrodetimote.com;* $$$$$) Perhaps the most historic and upmarket of Uruguay's tourist *estancias*, Timote is in the Cuchilla Grande range 14km from Cerro Colorado – definitely a countryside hotel rather than a working ranch. It was part of the first and most important of Uruguay's Jesuit *estancias*, Nuestra Senora de los Desamparados (c100,000ha in size), founded in the 1740s and when the Jesuits were expelled in 1767. The present *estancia*, a mere 30,000ha in area, was founded in 1854 by Pedro Jose Jackson, and later owned by the Hebers and the Gallinals, some of the country's leading ranching families. In the late 1990s a *hotel de campo* (rural hotel) was established here, run since 2008 by Sacramento Management, one of the country's leading hotel management companies. Beautifully restored in colonial style, you can see the Jesuits' chapel, the library and a patio decorated with 1930s Spanish majolica tiles. There are 30 bedrooms, with open fireplaces and contemporary if rather conventional décor. You can walk in the 50ha park, swim in the outdoor heated swimming pools, take carriage rides, go fishing, visit the farmyard and above all go horseriding, although there's less scope for working with gauchos than on other *estancias*. You can also play soccer, volleyball, tennis, basketball, and pelota, as well as pool, table-tennis, mini-soccer table and other board games.

Other estancias Other tourist *estancias* nearby include: Parada Arteaga (*Ruta 7 km142;* ☏ *310 8086,* **m** *9961 4110*), Estancia Tornero (*Ruta 6 km121;* ☏ *336 4164, 350 2169;* **e** *matildev@adinet.com.uy*), Estancia Doña Yita (*Ruta 6 km137;* **m** *9962 4973;* **e** *estanciayita@movinet.com.uy*) and Estancia Ingá (*Ruta 6 km171.5;* ☏ *360 7138;* **e** *mmurgate@hotmail.com*). Closer to the town of Florida are La India (*Camino La Macana km4;* ☏ *352 3883,* **m** *9935 5396*), with a menagerie and archaeological collection, and Estancia El Ceibo (*15km northeast from Ruta 5 km97.5;* ☏ *352 3393,* **m** *9912 5761; www.elceibo.com.uy*).

SAN JOSÉ DEPARTMENT

Ruta 1 westbound (to Colonia) splits from Ruta 5 at a flyover junction at km7 and crosses the Río Santa Lucía (from Montevideo department to San José department) at km21, where the village of **Santiago Vásquez** lies below to the right. Traffic on Ruta 1 stops at a toll and continues westwards, but there's an older metal bridge to the right which is open to bicycles and other traffic; buses from Montevideo's Baltasar Brum terminal come here too.

Santiago Vásquez was founded in 1878 around a slaughterhouse, well placed at the mouth of the river, and was also a resort for the citizens of Montevideo. It was prosperous until the 1940s but was then left isolated by new roads.

On the east side of the village is the **Parque Zoológico Lecoq** (*Avda Luis Batlle Berres s/n;* ⏱ *09.00–17.00 Wed–Sun; US$1.80/car w/ends only*), a zoo which has recently reopened after fire damage. It has native fauna kept in newly planted native woodland, exotic fauna kept in pretty decent conditions and organised by their continent of origin, and new aviaries with over 140 species of birds. There are also trails into the *humedales* (wetlands) of the Río Santa Lucía, a protected ecosystem with lots of native plants and waterfowl. In fact there are over 20,000ha of wetlands around the mouth of the Río Santa Lucía that can also be explored by boat, horse and bicycle; from the village, Silvestre Ochoa leads east to Avenida de los Deportes, alongside a *pista de regatas* (rowing lake, which also gives good views of birds), and loops right around the back of the zoo to Camino los Camalotes. By the River Plate a couple of kilometres west on Ruta 1, the Reserva Nacional Playa Penino is another good spot for birding, with over 200 species nesting in the area.

The Centro de Visitantes de la Comisión de Humedales is on La Guardia s/n, opposite the Club Alemán de Remo (German Rowing Club); free walks are led by rangers on weekends and holidays.

The Parque Municipal Parque Espinillo (*8km southwest on Camino General Basilio Muñoz from Ruta 1 km20, the exit for the* complejo carcelario *or prison;* ⏱ *w/ends & holidays, 1 Dec–15 Apr daily*) is the only **campsite** within reach of Montevideo. There's space for 70 tents (with electric lighting and hot water), cabins, barbecues and a stony little beach. At the gate is a *parador* with restaurant and shop.

Along the San José coast there's a string of minor beach resorts. The Río de la Plata is muddy and semi-salty here, and the surf is poor, but the beaches are popular with local people in summer. At km32 of Ruta 1 there's a turning to Playa Pascual, a small beach resort with restaurants and cafés but no hotels. From Libertad, at km50, a minor road heads north to Rincón de Buschental, on the Río Santa Lucía, where the Complejo Buschental (☏ *34 05230;* **e** *complejobuschental@gmail.com*) comprises a *parador* (with restaurant and rooms) and dock, with canoes to rent, as well as the Cabañas Santa Esmeralda. At km54 the Restaurant El Campo (☏ *34 54714;* ⏱ *to 18.00, to midnight Sat*) makes a decent stop-off for *parrilla* or pasta, and at km61 a paved road runs south for

4

14km to the larger beach resort of Kiyú, known for hang-gliding and fishing; there's camping here at the Parador Chico (↘ 34 57078) and about 1km south in Vista Mar.

At km67 there's a flyover where Ruta 3 turns north for San José, Paysandú and the *litoral*; continuing on Ruta 1, the Estancia Turística Don Joaquín (*km94.5;* ↘ 34 92007; www.donjoaquin.com) offers horseriding, boating, cycling and walks in 600ha of native forest. There's a heated pool and a new spa; double rooms cost US$180, cabins cost US$65 per person, and a day's activities, with lunch and tea, costs US$45 per person.

At km96 (90 minutes from Montevideo), at the junction of Ruta 1 and Ruta 11, immediately before the boundary with Colonia department, is Ecilda Paullier, a small village known for cheese-making, with a couple of roadside restaurants; 17km south by an unmade road is Boca del Cufré, another small beach resort with accommodation at Casapuerto (m 9933 2102) and camping (↘ 34 09344). At the mouth of the Arroyo del Cufré, it's a good location for fishing.

SAN JOSÉ Founded in 1783, San José – 93km from Montevideo, and capital of the department – was settled by families from the Galicia, Castille and León regions of Spain. In 1811 José Artigas's cousin Manuel Artigas was killed in the battle of San José, when Spanish forces were defeated by those fighting for independence, and the town became known as San José de Mayo (so its citizens are known as *maragatos*). In 1828 the Asamblea Constituyente y Legislativa (see page 16) met here to draw up the new nation's constitution, adopted nationwide in July 1830. In 1856 San José became a city, and is now capital of the department and a prosperous commercial and agricultural centre with a population of around 36,000.

Getting there

By car Coming from Santa Lucía on Ruta 11, there's a toll at km81 (from Ecilda Paullier). There's a long bridge across the Río San José at km53 and then you enter San José by Avenida Herrera. Coming up from Ruta 1, Ruta 3 bypasses San José to the west, so you'll come in from the other end of Avenida Herrera.

By bus Frequent CITA buses from Montevideo's Baltasar Brum terminal (about 34 a day via Ruta 1 and 10 via Santa Lucía and Canelones; US$3.50) arrive at the terminal on Bentancur y Artigas (↘ 34 26863); COTMI also has roughly hourly services from Montevideo. Buses to Montevideo pick up passengers a block north of Avenida Herrera, those via Canelones on Oribe and others on Espínola. Agencia Central has five buses a day (from Montevideo) to Trinidad, three continuing to Paysandú. Three COTMI buses continue to Cardona, to the northwest, as well as two SOMAR/Don Pepe services as far as Mal Abrigo. To the southwest, SOMAR/Don Pepe runs four services (three at weekends) to Boca del Cufre, and Comsa run four a day to Kiyú and three to Colonia Suiza.

By rail Two blocks east of the terminal on Bentancur is the railway station, which now sends out just one train a day to Montevideo, except on Sundays (US$2). There are plans for a cultural centre in the station, including a railway museum and craft studio.

Tourist information There's a tourist information centre (*25 de Mayo;* ↘ 34 28452; ⊕ *summer 09.00–18.00 daily*) on the northeastern corner of the main square, Plaza Treinta y Tres Orientales. There's also a craft shop here, and on weekdays they can open the Teatro Macció, immediately to the west (see page 159).

SAN JOSÉ

600m
600yds
0
0

Montevideo
by Rutas 11 & 5

Río San José

Bradt

N

R11

Montevideo
by Rutas 3 & 1

Trinidad, Paysandú,
La Caleta, Picada de Varela

Colonia, Sierras de Mahoma,
Ruta 11

Parque Rodó

Hostería
del Parque

El Ombú

R3

R3

R GÓMEZ
HOLANDA
C GARDEL
ASOCIACIÓN RURAL
COLONIA
AVDA ITALIA
HAITÍ
URUGUAY
COLOMBIA
COSTA RICA
CAMAGUA
CHANÁ
MÉXICO
PERÚ
AVDA MANUEL A RODRÍGUEZ
QUEGUAY
SUIZA
ECUADOR
CANELONES
FRANCIA
REPÚBLICA
H SANTOS FLORES
ESPAÑA
SALTO
CERRO LARGO
GRAL LAVALLEJA
A PAN
DE BENGOA
EMILIO FRUGONI
C LARRIERRA
MONS DI MARTINO
GRAL MANUEL ORIBE
DR BECERRO
18 DE JULIO
BATLLE Y ORDÓÑEZ
ASAMBLEA
Plaza
Artigas
Plaza
Zorrilla
HERRERA
CAP E VIDAL
AVDA LUIS A DE
FCO CANARO
AVDA BRASIL
ELLAURI
JAIME ZUDÁÑEZ
LARRAÑAGA
25 DE MAYO
TREINTA Y TRES
ARTIGAS
Hotel
Centro
ITUZAINGÓS
DR A ESPÍNOLA
Plaza
4 de Octubre
Museo Varela
Café Medio Punto
Cathedral-basilica
Treinta y Tres
Orientales
SEMI-PEATONAL
Market
Club San José
Teatro Maccio
Museo
Departamental
Hospedaje
San Carlos
Police
Station
Obelisk
Detomasi
monument
Railway
station
BENTANCUR
SAN SALVADOR
CHARRÚA
C MARIN
AVDA LARRIERRE
PASO DEL REY
GUAYABOS
LAS PIEDRAS
INSTRUCCIONES
25 DE AGOSTO
ASENCIO
ARTIGAS
Quinta de
Hornos
C MARIN
RINCÓN
COLÓN
SARANDÍ
ANSINA
LUIS BATLLE BERRES
ZORRILLA DE SAN MARTIN
F ACUÑA DE FIGUEROA
P MONTAGNE
AVDA GRAL RIVERA
ATILIO PELOSSI
DR E CIGANDA
W FERREIRA ALDUNATE
DR A ESPÍNOLA
R MASSINI
CAP VIDAL
FCO ESPÍNOLA
FCO DONATO
LAURA CORTINAS
AVDA MANUEL D RODRÍGUEZ
P VARELA
AVDA P VARELA
MA ESPÍNO
LAURA CORTINAS

🏠 Where to stay

🏠 **Hotel Centro** 25 de Mayo 407; ☎ 34 23901; www.hcentro.com. The only accommodation in the centre is the fairly modern Centro, 2 blocks south of the plaza. It has AC rooms with internet access, but no lift; there's a fairly simple b/fast & a 24hr cafeteria. $$$

🏠 **Hosteria del Parque** Ruta 3 km92.5; ☎ 34 22339; www.hosteriadelparque.com.uy. Just inside the Parque Rodó, on the northwestern edge of town, is this good 3-star place, with a nice magazine-strewn lobby, shaded parking, a swimming pool & AC rooms with internet access; there's a good buffet b/fast included. $$$

🏠 **Hospedaje San Carlos** Bengeo 541; ☎ 34 22604.The San Carlos is the town's only cheap place & it's unwelcoming. Near the museum. $$

🏠 **Picada de Varela** 2km north, Ruta 3 km95; ☎ 34 28452. There's also 'camping' on the north side of the zoo in Parque Rodó, which is intended for day use but might be usable overnight. Free.

✘ Where to eat

✘ **Club San José** 25 de Mayo 550; ☎ 34 26344. Probably one of the town's best restaurants, & certainly the most convenient, the San José is located on the east side of the plaza. It serves standard fare in a rather old-school ambience. $$

✘ **Café Medio Punto** Treinta y Tres 402 & Larreñaga; m 9674 1598; ⏲ from 10.00 Mon–Sat, Jan from 19.30. Back in the centre, this stylish *cafetería-confitería*, has art hanging on the walls & organises cultural events. $$

The other good restaurants are *parrillas* out north by Ruta 3:

✘ **El Ombú** Ruta 3 km93 & Artigas; ☎ 34 27715. The thatched Ombú is on the way to the Hostería del Parque (see above), which itself has a good restaurant. $$

✘ **La Caleta** 2km north on Ruta 3; ☎ 34 30637. It's worth the journey from town to this rural grill. $

Other practicalities

Banks There are plenty of ATMs; to change money go to Cambio San José (*25 de Mayo 560*) on the east side of the plaza.

Car rental Cars can be rented from Gol Rentacar (*Vidal 758;* ☎ *34 29907,* m *9987 4066;* e *golrentacar_sj@hotmail.com*). There are several 24-hour petrol stations near the junction of Ruta 3 and Ruta 11.

Communications Antel's *telecentro* is at Colón & Ciganda (⏲ *09.00–21.00 daily*); there should be Wi-Fi on the plaza but it may have 'problems', and in any case the incessant pop music on the plaza may drive you away. The post office (*25 de Mayo 683;* ⏲ *09.00–17.00 Mon–Fri, 09.00–12.00 Sat*) is two blocks north of the plaza.

Markets The Mercado Municipal (*Asamblea 676, east of the plaza*) is a proper food market. It's across the road from the Supermercado Italia (⏲ *07.30–12.30, 14.30–22.00 Mon–Fri, 07.30–13.00, 15.00–22.00 Sat, 07.30–13.00 Sun*). There's also a Micro-Macro a block south (*Sarandí & Ciganda;* ⏲ *08.00–21.30 Mon–Sat, 08.30–13.00, 16.30–21.30 Sun*).

What to see and do The **Cathedral-basilica**, on the south side of the plaza, was built in 1857–75, in a pretty grand Neoclassical style with eight Doric columns of Carrara marble from Italy and chandeliers of Murano glass. The marble main altar and baldacchino, also on eight Corinthian pillars, are by the Catalan sculptor Domingo Mora; there's a grander marble altar in the chapel of the Holy Sacrament, to the left. The modern frescoes of St Joseph in Glory in the central dome and the reliefs of the Four Evangelists on the pendentives are by Lino Dinetti (1951–54).

On the north side of the plaza is the **Teatro Macció**, opened in 1912, a grand Eclectic edifice which claims to be the second most important theatre in the country; certainly all of Uruguay's leading actors have appeared here, as well as singers of the stature of Carlos Gardel.

A block to the north is the **Museo Departamental** (*Bengoa 493 & Treinta y Tres; ⊕ 15.00–18.00 Mon–Fri, 18.00–21.00 Sat–Sun & holidays*), partly in a colonial house (built in 1806) from the *mirador* of which Artigas directed the battle of San José in 1811. It has some displays on local history, some old furniture and art, and a good art collection, including works by Torres García, Figari, Barradas, Cúneo, Serrano and Carmelo de Arzadun, as well as some foreign works. Unusually for Uruguay, it has a museum shop, where you can buy T-shirts and other souvenirs. The city's other museum is the **Museo Varela** (*Varela 267, just south of Avda Herrera;* m *9431 5200; ⊕ 09.30–12.00, 15.00–19.00 Tue–Sun; free*), a small cottage commemorating the 'last gaucho poet', Wenceslao Varela (1908–97), with personal belongings including traditional gaucho items that he collected from his youth.

Six blocks north of the plaza, just east of the bus terminal at 25 de Mayo & Avenida Rodríguez is a short but quite stylish obelisk, commemorating the battle of 1811, and three blocks east, at the end of Avenida Larriera, a monument set up by the Aero Club del Uruguay in honour of pioneer aviator Ricardo Detomasi, who died in a crash in San José in 1915. Three blocks north of the obelisk, on the west side of Leandro Gómez, the **Quinta de Hornos** is one of the oldest houses in the city, now preserved and used mainly for weddings and other events; but the gardens and some farm buildings are worth a visit.

To the northwest of the city by the junction of Ruta 3 and Ruta 11, the Parque Rodó is a pleasant place to spend a hot afternoon, with grills and play areas, but its zoo has some of the smallest cages in any Uruguayan zoo and the animals seem to have lost the will to live. Alternatively, you can go 2km north on Ruta 3 to the Picada de Varela, where there's a summer-only *parador* (✆ 4342 8452) with open swimming pools and beaches on the Río San José, both very popular in hot weather.

THE SIERRAS DE MAHOMA In the northwestern part of San José department, on Ruta 23 towards Mercedes, the Sierras de Mahoma is a low range of hills better described as a 'sea of stone', with its exposed rocks that appear to have been beaten by a shower of meteorites into weird formations such as the Turtle, the Waterfall and the Three Brothers. The rocks are intrusive granite with some metamorphic ectinites on the edges; few cows wander up here so unusual plants flourish, including orchids, mosses, *Tillandsia* epiphytes, *Echinopsis* cacti and other specialised plants. Birds include cardinals, mockingbirds, monjitas, white woodpeckers, blue-and-yellow tanagers, pampas finches, sharp-tailed streamcreepers and masked ducks, and foxes are common.

This area has an almost iconic status for Uruguayans, partly owing to the strange aura of its unusual rocky formations, and partly because Artigas passed through here during the Exodo del Pueblo Oriental (see *Chapter 1*, page 15), camping at the so-called Casa de Piedra (Stone House) formation.

On the northwestern flank of the Cuchilla de Mahoma (part of the Cuchilla Grande Septentrional or Great Northern Range, the Sierras cover an area of 20km² and rise to a maximum of just 178m above sea level, with an average of 140m. They can be explored on foot, by horse or even on a bike – you'll be quite exposed to the sun, so take water and suncream.

Getting there
By car The entry to the Sierras is 37km from San José at km126 of Ruta 23 (131km from Montevideo), where a track leads to the right to the Posada Sierras de

Mahoma (see below). There's a gate here (☉ *08.00–20.00 daily*) at which you'll have to pay about US$2 – except on the 25th of each month, when there's free access for pilgrims to a shrine to the Virgén del Rosario de San Nicolás. You can book a guide by calling m 9934 0345.

By bus Three COTMI buses from San José to Cardona pass the entry, and two SOMAR/Don Pepe services run as far as Mal Abrigo, the village at km123.

Where to stay and eat

🏠 **Posada Sierras de Mahoma** m 9934 0345, 9934 2220; e sierrademahoma@adinet.com.uy; www.sierrasdemahoma.com. Meals & accommodation available & there's a paddock with goats, sheep & even a fallow deer for the delight of school groups. $$

🏠 **Finca Piedra** \ 34 03118; www.fincapiedra.com. This French/English-owned ecotouristic *estancia* is much nicer & visible on the hill to the right just beyond the village of Mal Abrigo; the gate is at km125, where buses will drop you off. With 1,000ha (including 20ha planted with Tannat & other vines & now producing a very palatable wine), horseriding (with 27 horses, mostly *criollos*) is a core activity here, both in the Sierras & helping the gauchos work with the 500 Hereford cattle & 300 Corriedale sheep. The excellent restaurant uses the *estancia's* own vegetables, eggs, milk & meat (beef, pork &

lamb). There's a new jacuzzi, outdoor swimming pool, table tennis, pool table & other games, & even a soccer pitch – the owners are keen to attract sports teams & other groups, with facilities for groups in a converted barn. Packages include 3 days of riding (30–40km/day, from US$250) & 5 days riding to the River Plate (with 2 nights camping, from US$360).

Their Casco Viejo was actually only built c1950 & recently extended. There's a living room with an open fire, library, cable TV & a computer with internet access. Rates are US$85/130 sgl/dbl for a deluxe room, or US$80/110 with separate (but still private) bathroom, with b/fast; FB costs US$65 pp in the cheapest rooms, US$155/220 in the superior rooms & US$175/270 in deluxe rooms. They have 4 cheaper rooms, aimed more at the backpacker market, at US$20 pp with b/fast.

CANELONES DEPARTMENT: EAST

Following the *ramblas* east from Montevideo and crossing the Arroyo de Carrasco in Canelones department, you'll continue through a succession of beach resorts/mid-range suburbs – incorporated in 1994 as the Ciudad de la Costa – including **Solymar** (Sunandsea), where the Museo del Pan (*Bread Museum; Avenida Márquez Castro & Gestido km24.3;* ☉ *summer 16.00–20.00 Fri–Sun & holidays, winter 10.00–18.00; US$1*) is worth a brief stop – it doesn't exactly cover all the wonderful worldwide variations of bread, but does a fair job of showing how the traditional Uruguayan loaf was produced, with old mills and ovens.

In **Pinar**, just beyond Solymar at km30.5, the Proyecto Karumbé has a marine turtle breeding centre (☉ *summer 10.00–20.00 Tue–Sun, winter Fri–Sun & holidays 10.00–18.00; US$1.80*), worth a visit if you're not going to their main station in Rocha (see page 241). There are frequent buses from Montevideo's Baltasar Brum terminal to Solymar and Pinar.

Just east of Pinar the main highway to Punta del Este (the Ruta Interbalnearia), coming from Montevideo via the airport, merges with the coast road and Avenida Giannattasio, and continues towards Maldonado. There's a toll at km34, immediately east of the Arroyo Pando, then the road runs through pine forest, with resorts such as Salinas on the right. At km44 there's a turning to the right to El Águila (see page 163) and 1km later the main turning into **Atlántida**, at the junction with Ruta 11 from Canelones town (see page 131).

Continuing east, the Interbalnearia crosses the Arroyo Solís Chico at km51.5 and gives access to the strip of coastal resorts known as the Costa de Oro (Gold Coast); to the right at km60 (an hour from Montevideo by direct bus) is Guazú Vira (or

Guazubirá), where there's a hide for birdwatching, and where you can also see migrating southern right whales and false orcas in October and November. At km70.5 is the small resort of Biarritz, where the Posada-Restaurant Biarritz (*Calle 6;* ☎ *37 88968,* 📱 *9915 6795;* ℯ *biarritz@internet.com.uy; www.posadabiarritz.com.uy;* $$$ *during summer,.* $$ *rest of the year*) is a small hotel by the sea with a classy restaurant serving meats, seafood and homemade pastas as well as Asian dishes such as Thai chicken and chop suey, with wines from Bodegas Carrau. Nearby, the beaches of Santa Lucía del Este and Jaureguiberry can have good surf, attracting crowds from Montevideo when conditions are right. At km80 the highway crosses the wide Arroyo Solís Grande and enters Maldonado department (see *Chapter 5*) at a toll and summer-only tourist office.

ATLÁNTIDA The main beach resort of Canelones department is somewhat misnamed, as the Río de la Plata only gives way to the Atlantic at Punta del Este. The first hotel opened here in 1913; in 1956 the great Chilean poet Pablo Neruda, returning from exile in Italy, met secretly here with his last wife Matilda Urrutia (however, the museum dedicated to him is now closed). The town does have a sizeable permanent population, and is noted for its active participation in Las Llamadas (see page 27), with 18 drumming *comparsas*.

Getting there Frequent buses (operated by Cutcsa and COPSA, from Montevideo's Baltasar Brum terminal) take about an hour to reach Atlántida, continuing east to Parque del Plata and La Floresta.

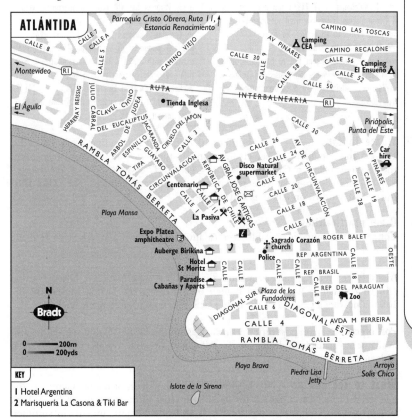

Tourist information Heading south on Ruta 11 (Avenida Artigas) for half a dozen blocks, you'll find the church of the Sagrado Corazón (fairly modern, and attractive enough); turning right at the roundabout here, it's just over one block to the very helpful Tourist Information Centre (*Calle Roger Balet & Calle 1;* ☎ 37 23104/ 26122; e *turismo@imcanelones.gub.uy; www.canelonesturismo.gub.uy;* ⊕ *08.00–22.00 daily in season*).

Where to stay In the centre, Calle 11, one block from the *rambla*, has been closed to traffic north of Calle 20, forming a *microcentro*, a pedestrianised zone of restaurants, bars and craft stalls. The town's main hotels are immediately north of the pedestrianised zone, notably:

⌂ **Argentina** Calle 11 & 24; ☎ 4 37 22414/21728; e info@hotelargentina.com.uy; www.atlantida.com.uy/ hotelargentina. A decent newish 3-star place with AC rooms & a covered swimming pool. No Wi-Fi. $$$$

⌂ **Centenario** Calle 11 & 24; ☎ 37 22451/22021; e htl.centenario@hotmail.com. Older than the Argentina, but reasonably spruced up. Has AC rooms & a covered swimming pool. No Wi-Fi. $$$$

⌂ **Hotel Colonial** ☎ 37 21818. Just north, at Artigas & Circonvalación, is this oversized suburban house; an adequate mid-price alternative. No Wi-Fi. $$$

⌂ **Hotel St Moritz** ☎ 37 28946; www.hotel-saint-moritz.com. Just to the south across from Argentina, the newly modernised Moritz has a garden with swimming pool & barbecue; rooms all have balconies. $$$

⌂ **Auberge Birikina** Rambla Mansa & Argentina; ☎ 37 28462; e fermajoyroma@yahoo.com.ar; http://auberguebirikina.blogspot.com, www.atlantida.com.uy/birikina. No longer a youth hostel & does not offer shared rooms; nevertheless it's a decent budget option, especially since the introduction of free Wi-Fi. $$

⌂ **Paradise Cabañas y Aparts** ☎ 37 21573; e paradise@adinet.com.uy; www.paradise.com.uy. A block further south, between Brasil & Paraguay roads, Paradise has 'VIP' cabins & apartments with kitchens, Wi-Fi, a spa & swimming pool. $$

⋏ **Camping El Ensueño** ☎ 37 23467, m 9966 8427; e psiconando@hotmail.com. A simple, friendly campsite with cabins & tents under eucalyptus trees, with rough old concrete picnic tables. $

⋏ **Camping CEA** Antel Employees Club; ☎ 37 24171. Nearer Ruta 11 on Avenida Pinares is this a posher, more formal place. $

Where to eat There's a good choice of restaurants, including a branch of **La Pasiva**, and two *heladerías* (ice cream shops) in the *microcentro*. Immediately south, the **Marisquería La Casona** (*Balet & Chile;* ☎ 37 20800/21571; e *lacasonasrl@ hotmail.com*) is a popular fish restaurant with a large terrace. The **Tiki Bar**, immediately north on Chile, is a lively pub.

Other practicalities
Car rental Car rental is available from Atlántida Rentacar (*Calle 38 between 18 & 20;* ☎ 37 21312).

Markets For buying your own food, the handiest supermarket is Disco Natural (*Artigas & Calle 24*). There's a branch of the upmarket Tienda Inglesa on the Interbalnearia (*at Calle 11*) – the only place in town with free open Wi-Fi.

Post office The main post office is on Artigas south of Calle 22, but stamps are also available at Farmacía Rodríguez in the *microcentro*, opposite a *cambio* (⊕ *09.30–23.00 daily in season*).

What to see and do A block south of the Tourist Information Centre is the sheltered Playa Mansa, famed for its sunsets. Just to the right is the ExpoPlatea beachfront amphitheatre, used for bands and other entertainments in summer.

Opposite this is the Art Deco former Hotel Planeta Palace, built in 1940–41; now used as apartments, it's still a very striking sight, like a beached ocean liner.

From here it's a 25-minute walk west (turn left off Zorrilla de San Martín on to Carlos Roxlo, and it's 300m further, just off the edge of the tourist map in the Villa Argentina area) to **El Águila** (*The Eagle;* ☺ *summer 09.00–19.30, winter 09.00–18.00; free*), a bizarre viewpoint over the beach that was built in 1945 by the local builder Juan Torres for the Neapolitan-born Natalio Michelizzi, developer of the Hotel Planeta Palace and the casino behind it. Michelizzi asked for a small room (4m square) in which to read and paint, with a niche for a statue of the Virgin; then he asked for a bigger space in which to entertain friends, and Torres produced this eagle's head (as well as a mock ship below, now washed away by the sea); a narrow corridor leads to stairs up into the head and a platform atop the beak. A kilometre to the west is the gay beach known as the (ex-)playa de la Boya.

Turning left along the *rambla* from Calle Roger Balet, it's five blocks to a headland where you'll find the yacht club and a viewpoint. The Rambla Tomás Berreta continues east along the shore past the Piedra Lisa jetty, known for its fishing. Just beyond this, Avenida Circunvalación leads three blocks north to the small and unexciting **zoo** (☺ *10.00–20.00 daily; free*), which has mainly exotic species such as goats, deer, llama, guinea fowl, ostrich, peacock and golden pheasant, as well as seals and parrots.

It's also worth heading 4km north to Estacíon Atlántida (*Ruta 11 km161*), where Eladio Dieste (see page 34) built the **Parroquía Cristo Obrera** (*Church of Christ the Worker;* ☺ *15.00–18.00 Sat*) in 1957–58, just south of the railway crossing. It's one of his best designs, its curved brick walls and roof magically meeting with a tolerance of just 5mm, while the broad façade is free-standing. Inside, hidden openings direct light to the altar and a wooden statue of Christ by Joaquín Torres García's pupil Eduardo Díaz Yepes. To the right is the bell-tower, with a spiral staircase of bricks cantilevered on steel rods.

Another 4km north, at Ruta 11 km157, the **Estancia Renacimiento** (☏ *37 02021;* m *9910 8597;* e *cabren@netgate.com.uy; www.estanciarenacimiento.com.uy*) offers free entry all year to its 500ha, with opportunities to feed farm animals and enjoy tractor, horse and sulky rides; there's a shop and a restaurant serving solid traditional food.

Between the beachside suburbs of Parque del Plata and La Floresta is the Arroyo Solís Chico, where the riverside *rambla* is very popular at full moons. On the *rambla* at the far end of La Floresta is an open-air sculpture park by another creek, the Arroyo Sarandí. The church of the Virgén de las Flores (Virgin of the Flowers) houses a statue of the Virgin brought from Italy in 1917, the focus of fervent Marian pilgrimages.

LAVALLEJA DEPARTMENT

Named Minas after its capital and main town, until 1927 when it was renamed after the father of Uruguayan independence, Lavalleja is the hilliest department in Uruguay and thus one of the most scenic. Although the hills are not amazingly high, they are quite steep, with some fine canyons. As Darwin said in 1832, 'The country was rather more hilly, but otherwise continued the same; an inhabitant of the pampas no doubt would have considered it as truly alpine'. Nowadays the north of the department is ranching country, with Hereford cattle, sheep and pigs, while the south is more agricultural; near Minas are some quarries and cement plants, including the most modern cement plant in the Mercosur countries.

Ruta 8 leads northeast from Montevideo to Minas; leaving the city it's a tediously slow drive, with lots of speed humps, and it's far easier to go via Carrasco airport and take the road that joins Ruta 9 1km before the small town of Pando (at km31). The suburbs end here and the going is faster, bypassing Soca and crossing the Arroyo Solís Grande to reach Solís de Mataojo, the first town in Lavalleja department, 80km from Montevideo. At km91 you can turn right on Ruta 81 for 10km to reach the Aguas Blancas dam in the Sierras del Abra de Zabaleta, where the water of the Arroyo Mataojo is used to irrigate fruit farms; nearby are a Tibetan Buddhist temple and a municipal campsite (37 09121; all year) with electric lighting, hot water, barbecue grills and a shop. You can fish and watch birds, as well as the wild goats that roam the hills.

The country gets hillier, with some eucalyptus plantations; the old road is still alongside the modern highway for much of the way, giving cyclists a quieter alternative. At km109.5, two hours by bus from Montevideo, is a junction in the middle of the fields, with the Virgin of Verdún and accompanying radio masts on a hill to the northeast; it's about 500m right to the old Ruta 8 and the entry to the **Parque Salus**. Since 1892 Salus mineral water, filtered through the rocks of the Sierra de Coronilla, has been bottled here; the waters are supposedly protected by a mythical puma, hence the name of the spring, the Fuente del Puma. In 1936 the company also began to make Patricia beer, now Uruguay's favourite, with the same mineral water. In 2000 the Salus company was bought by the multinational company Danone, whch sold the brewery on to the equally global Inbev.

A palm-lined avenue leads to the brewery, behind which, 1.2km from the gate, is the Parador Parque Salus (✆ *44 31652/3;* e *paradorsalus@dedicado.net.uy;* $$$$), a fairly upmarket hotel with just 14 air-conditioned rooms, a swimming pool and a good restaurant. It's another 3km along a dusty unpaved road to the bottling plant, where you should continue up to the right for 700m to the rangers' house and plant nursery (which distributes native plants free to schools and the like), opposite a viewpoint over the bottling plant. The road loops to the left to the far side of the plant, passing the Vieja Carpintería, a corrugated iron shed that now houses an interpretation centre, with information on local flora and fauna, and advice on recycling your mineral water bottles. At the end of the road, steps lead down past magnolias and Ceiba (*palo borracho*) trees to the Fuente del Puma, where cups are provided for you to sample the Salus mineral water that pours into the bottling plant at a rate of 200,000 litres per day.

You might be forgiven for thinking that the whole park is planted with introduced eucalyptus trees, but in fact they only cover the central 370ha of a total 1,300ha. The rest is typical *monte serrano* (though damaged by a fire in 2004), with birds such as pava de monte (dusky-legged guan) remarkably easy to spot. As yet there are no paths into the native area (although these are planned), but a dirt road does continue from just after the rangers' house to a disused quarry. There are open hills to the south and east, but these are likely to be planted with eucalyptus at some point.

A bus runs from the plaza in Minas via the bus terminal to the brewery every two hours (from 06.20), returning on the odd hour from 07.00 to 21.00.

Ruta 8 continues past a couple of cement plants and the turning (at km114) to Cerro de Verdón (390m; named after a pioneer called Berdom); a track leads to the statue of the Virgen de la Inmaculada Concepción (Virgin of the Immaculate Conception) on a sort of arched tripod atop the peak. Since 1901, thousands of pilgrims have come from Montevideo and further afield to worship here every 19 April. A road leads halfway up, after which there's a path lined with shrines and the Stations of the Cross. From here it's 5km down into Minas.

MINAS Minas, capital of Lavalleja department, with a population of 38,000 *minuanos* (just over half the department's total population), is a pleasant country town, although it gets pretty hot, being set in a bowl of hills. Founded in 1784 as Villa Concepción de las Minas, its name refers to the gold mines along the Arroyo San Francisco. This was as far inland as Darwin came in Uruguay: 'Las Minas…is seated on a little plain, and is surrounded by low rocky mountains. It is of the usual symmetrical form; and with its white-washed church standing in the centre, had rather a pretty appearance.'

Tourist information Regular buses from Montevideo (some continuing to Treinta y Tres, Melo or Río Branco – see page 82) arrive at the terminal at Treinta y Tres and Sarandí, where there's also a tourist information office (✆ *44 29796;* ⊕ *07.00–19.00 daily*) as well as a baggage store (⊕ *06.00–24.00 daily*). COOM also operates buses west to Florida and south to San Carlos, Maldonado and Punta del Este, and to Pan de Azúcar and Piriápolis. Tourist information is also available in the Paseo de Artesanos (⊕ *15.00–21.00 Mon–Fri, 10.00–21.00 Sat–Sun*), just east of the Hotel Plaza.

Where to stay The main hotels are on the main Plaza Libertad, two blocks southeast of the terminal.

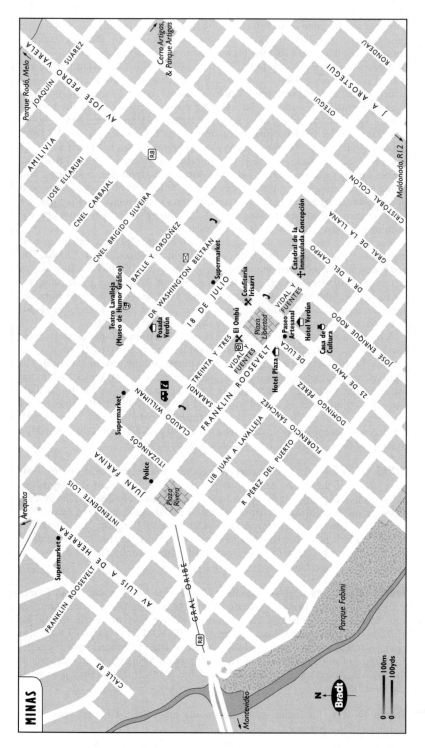

MINAS

Cerro Artigas, & Parque Artigas ↗

Parque Rodó, Melo ↗

RONDEAU

J A AROSTEGUI

OTEGUI

AMILIVIA

JOSE ELLARURI

CNEL CARBAJAL

CNEL BRIGIDO SILVEIRA

R8

CRISTOBAL COLON

Maldonado, R12 ↗

GRAL DE LA LLANA

J BATTLE Y ORDÓÑEZ

DR WASHINGTON BELTRÁN

Teatro Lavalleja (Museo de Humor Gráfico)

Posada Verdún

18 DE JULIO

Supermarket

R A DEL CAMPO

Confitería Irisarri

Catedral de la Inmaculada Concepción ✝

El Ombú

Plaza Libertad

VIDAL Y FUENTES

Paseo Artesanal

VIDAL Y FUENTES

Hotel Verdún

Casa de Cultura

JOSE ENRIQUE RODO

TREINTA Y TRES

SARANDI

FRANKLIN ROOSEVELT

DE LUCA

Hotel Plaza

25 DE MAYO

DOMINGO PÉREZ

CLAUDIO WILLIMAN

ITUZAINGÓS

Supermarket

FLORENCIO SÁNCHEZ

Police

JUAN FARINA

Plaza Rivera

LIB JUAN A LAVALLEJA

INTENDENTE LOIS

R PÉREZ DEL PUERTO

Arequita ↗

Supermarket

FRANKLIN ROOSEVELT

AV LUIS A DE HERRERA

GRAL ORIBE

R8

CALLE 83

Montevideo ↗

Parque Fabini

N

Bradt

0 ___ 100m
0 ___ 100yds

166

☗ **Hotel Plaza** Roosevelt 639 & Pérez; ✆ 44 22328; e hplaza@adinet.com.uy; www.geocities.com/hotelplazaminas. Another 3-star place but more modern (although it doesn't have a lift); 2 rooms have Wi-Fi & balconies looking over the plaza, while others can use a computer at reception. $$$

☗ **Hotel Verdún** (25 rooms) 25 de Mayo 444 & Roosevelt; ✆ 44 20910/20219; e hverdun@adinet.com.uy; www.hotelverdun.com. A nicely modernised 3-star with AC rooms, a swimming pool, parking & Wi-Fi. $$$

☗ **Posada Verdún** (16 rooms) Washington Beltrán 715; ✆ 44 24563; e posadaverdun@hotmail.com. The cheapest option is the friendly Verdún 2 blocks north of the plaza, with rooms with cable TV & private bathrooms. $$

✗ **Where to eat** Outside the hotels, there's not a great choice of places to eat. At the northwestern corner of the plaza, **El Ombú** (*Pérez & Treinta y Tres*) is a friendly pizzería-*parrillada*, although it only offers café food until 21.00; it also has a good *heladería* at the rear, and Wi-Fi. There are two other pizzería-*parrilladas* on the east side of the bus terminal. The most notable food outlet in town is the famous **Confitería Irisarri** (*Treinta y Tres 618;* ⊕ *09.00–22.00 daily*), a Belle Epoque *patissería*-café on the northeastern side of the plaza that has been serving *alfajores, damasquitos, yemas* and other sweet things since 1898 (with Art Deco additions).

Other practicalities

Communications Antel has three *telecentros*, at Treinta y Tres & Sarandí, opposite the bus terminal, and at Treinta y Tres 589 (*both* ⊕ *08.00–20.00 Mon–Fri, 08.00–13.00, 16.00–20.00 Sat*) and at Washington Beltrán & Rodó (⊕ *09.00–19.00 daily*). There's free Wi-Fi on the main plaza. The post office is at Washington Beltrán 612 (⊕ *09.00–17.00 Mon–Fri, 08.00–12.00 Sat*).

Healthcare The Farmacía Garmendía-Sabia is on the plaza at Treinta y Tres 630.

What to see and do Plaza Libertad is an attractive square, with fine palm trees, fountains and a statue of Lavelleja, raised in 1902 for the 77th anniversary of his great victory at Sarandí by Juan Manuel Ferrari; this was both the first equestrian statue in Uruguay and the first bronze statue cast in Uruguay. To the southeast of the plaza, across the road from the Hotel Verdún, the Jefatura de Policía (police headquarters) dates from 1897 and is in very good condition; just north of it a short road leads to the **Catedral de la Inmaculada Concepción**, a Neoclassical edifice built in 1892, and modernised in 1966. It's unusual in being set back from the plaza, and surprisingly long, with a dome halfway along the nave providing plenty of light. At the east end of the south aisle is a simple Neoclassical chapel with an unusual altar in a sort of Arts and Crafts style.

The house in which Lavalleja was born in about 1786 is now incorporated in the **Casa de Cultura** (*Lavalleja 572, between Rodó & 25 de Mayo;* ⊕ *07.00–19.00 Mon–Fri, 15.00–19.00 Sat, 13.00–19.00 Sun; free*), two blocks south of the cathedral. It incorporates several museums. The Museo del Gaucho y del Indio displays the usual round stones for *boleadoras*, arrowheads, lance-heads, carved cow-horns, some fine silverware and some very rusty Independence-era swords, a late-19th-century poncho, and some lance pennants bearing *divisas* or mottos from the Guerra Grande. The Museo Eduardo Fabini commemorates Uruguay's leading composer (see page 26), born in Solís de Mataojo in 1882; on show are scores and various personal effects, such as a huge *maté* gourd and *bombilla*, his violin, pedal harmonium and two guitars, and portraits of Fabini by Manuel Espinola Gómez (a protégé who also came from Solís de Mataojo), by Alessandro Métalo Gibert and by Pedro Blanes Viale (see page 31), the latter showing Fabini and a friend playing the organ outdoors. Alas, you won't hear his music playing here.

Lavalleja's birthplace, known as the Casa de Ramona de la Torre (after his mother, the only resident of Minas to follow Artigas on the Exodus of 1811), consists of a couple of rooms under a new concrete roof in the courtyard; you'll see his ceremonial sabre and some uniforms, guns and bayonets. Also at the rear of the Casa de Cultura is the Museo de la Ciudad, stuffed with all kinds of artefacts such as hats, fans, musical instruments, an Edison voice-recorder, a Victrola record-player, and a chestnut-roasting trolley disguised as a steam locomotive. There are also rooms dedicated to the local writers Santiago Dossetti (1902–81) and Juan José Morosoli (1899–1957, who left school at ten, worked in a café, became a journalist and ended by writing successful novels that gave a sympathetic portrait of the lives of the people of rural Uruguay). There's also a theatre here, as well as a library and temporary exhibition spaces.

A block northeast of the Posada Verdún is the **Teatro Lavalleja** (⏰ *12.00–18.00 daily; free*), a striking pile by Cayetano Buigas, a Catalan Modernist of the school of Gaudí, although this is not externally obvious. The drab interior is apparently similar to the Liceo of Barcelona and the Teatro Colón in Buenos Aires; the building is being restored for its centenary in 2009. It now houses the **Museo del Humor Gráfico**, a collection of cartoons and caricatures which are quite good and varied, though not very well displayed. The star turn is Julio E Suárez (1909–65), Uruguay's most distinguished cartoonist, who created his character Peloduro in 1933 as a vehicle for political satire. In the lobby you'll also see six statues by José Belloni (see page 32) and his son Stelio.

One of the attractive features of Minas is that you can see hills at the end of the streets in all directions, and the city is also ringed by parks, which all have picnic facilities and playgrounds. The closest to the centre is the **Parque Fabini**, beside the Arroyo San Francisco by Ruta 8 to Montevideo. To the east is Parque Artigas, with a hilltop statue of Artigas by Stelio Belloni that's supposedly the largest equestrian statue in the world. Raised in 1974, it's 10m high plus a plinth of almost 8m, and consists of 150 tonnes of concrete; it's possible to drive up to the statue and viewpoint of Cerro Artigas. To the northeast, by Ruta 8 to Melo, the Parque Rodó is the largest of Minas's parks, with a rose garden, municipal swimming pool and **zoo**, which houses a motley collection of animals such as llamas, lions, tigers, monkeys, boars, foxes and goats, and birds such as vultures, eagles, caracaras, owls, jays, cardinals, hooded siskins, herons, ducks and black-necked swans. There's also a fine display of plant life. The cages are clean and spacious enough, but this is mainly a zoo for children

Parque Rodó is the venue for the Minas y Abril festival, named after a song and held in aid of the local hospital. Over a weekend in mid-April, up to 30,000 people enjoy a combination of music, displays of clowning and of gauchos' riding skills. This is followed on 19 April by the pilgrimage to the Virgin of Verdún (see page 165).

AROUND MINAS Just 3km southeast of the centre of Minas (following Roosevelt, then Bonilla), the Represa OSE is a dam built in 1934 by the OSE water utility, with a 33ha park that's popular for family picnics and for fishing (for bagre and tararira). At km347.5 on Ruta 12, 20km south on the road to Maldonado, the **Parque de Vacaciones Sierra de Minas** (✆ *44 23788;* e *parquerecepcion@ ute.com.uy*) is owned by UTE-Antel, the state telecommunications and electricity companies. There's a classy Parque de Vacaciones (*160 rooms;* ✆ *44 30000; www.parquedevacaciones.com.uy;* $$) with conference facilities, as well as the Complejo San Francisco de las Sierras (✆ *44 21105;* e *sanfranciscodelassierras@hotmail.com;* $$), which has cabins. The 479ha park is also open to day visitors (*US$1*), with open and covered swimming pools, other sports facilities and playgrounds, all in beautifully tended grounds; there's a plant nursery, a petting farm and horseriding. There's a good restaurant plus the Parador Los Quinchos, where you can enjoy a *parrilla*. COSU buses run here from Minas, especially at weekends and holidays, and COOM buses to Maldonado will leave you at the entrance. Both these parks lie on the Arroyo San Francisco, which also runs along the west side of Minas (past the Parque Fabini) – there's good birding along the stream.

Just north of Cerro de Verdún, 8km northwest of Minas, the **Valle del Hilo de la Vida** is a narrow valley where over 100 circular stone towers (up to just 1.2m in height) stand on a slope, seemingly oriented to the sun. They may be over a thousand years old and have not yet been excavated or investigated professionally. The land is owned by a friendly couple who welcome visitors at weekends (**m** *9966 3084; US$4*) and are keen to acquaint Uruguayans with the idea that their country has an unknown history that long predates the arrival of European colonists. You'll need to turn north at km346 of Ruta 12, towards Florida.

One of the most popular excursions from Minas is to **Cerro Arequita**, 10km north on the road to Santa Lucía and Polanco. There's a riverside beach below the 230m-high granite hill (painted by Blanes Viale and others), and one of the few caves in Uruguay that can be visited. A COSU bus leaves from bay 1 at the Minas terminal (*3 daily, extra departure w/end afternoons; US$1, day return US$1.25*), running via the long-closed railway station before picking up the signed route along Avenida Flores. Most people get off, laden with folding seats and picnics, at the Parque Arequita, 12km (25 minutes) from Minas just before the bridge over the Arroyo Santa Lucía, where there's a riverside beach (*lifeguards in summer 13.00–19.00 Tue–Sun*), picnic tables, a restaurant and a small shop, as well as a campsite (see page 170).

About 500m before the campsite, by a small school, signs point east (right) to the Isla de Ombues (at least 500m away, although the sign reads 300m) and the **Gruta Colón** (Columbus Cave). An unpaved track leads along the flank of the hill for 800m to the Mirador Arequita restaurant (✆ *44 02731;* **e** *grutaarequita@ hotmail.com; www.complejoarequita.com*), a modern building set at the top of a field, looking out across the *llanura* (plain) that stretches west all the way to Colonia. You can buy tickets here for hour-long tours of the cave (⊕ *10.30–17.30 daily; US$2.50*), which start with a rather tedious introduction making as much as possible of what's only an averagely interesting cave, before walking up the hill and then into the cave. You'll go down metal stairs which Health & Safety officers would definitely not approve of, but you only need to be vaguely fit and mobile to visit the cave.

The cave was formed in the Cretaceous period, 144–100 million years ago (at the time of the break-up of the super-continent of Gondwana), of 300 million-year-old rocks. It was 'discovered' in 1873, although of course it had long been known by the indigenous people, who called it Araicaihuita (Water of the High Rocks of the Caves). There are two chambers, of which you'll visit the main one, 57m long, 19m wide and 9m high, and inhabited by millions of bats. There's also an unusual blind white cricket here that feeds on the bat droppings. For more information on wildlife and the environment, consult the Grupo Ecológico Arequita, which has offices in the Minas bus terminal (⊕ *07.00–13.00 Mon–Fri*) and at Domingo Pérez 570 (✆ *44 23916*).

Halfway back to the road there's space for a few cars, and a path across a field to the foot of the Cerro. Going up into the trees, you'll come in a couple of minutes to the Sendero de los Ombues, a path around the country's second largest *isla* (grove) of ancient and weirdly contorted ombú trees. Following a tiny path steadily up to the left, you'll come in five minutes to the limit of the trees and in a couple of minutes more reach the flattish top of the Cerro. In fact it comprises two main hills, Cerro Arequita and Cerro Arequito Chico (also known as Cerro de los Cuervos or Vulture Mountain), separated by a gully from which a steam flows into Río Santa Lucía, plus the lower Cerro de Iriarte. Nowadays you'll find cowpats up here, but in the mid 19th century access was a little harder and it served as a refuge for combatants in the Guerra Grande. Even so, there's no invasive flora here and this is a good place to study native plants. There are guided walks to the *cima* (summit) at 11.00 and 16.00 daily in summer, as well as full moon walks.

There are two **campsites** here, where you can sleep in tents or cabins. The Camping Municipal Parque Arequita (✆ *44 02503, 44 29796;* ⊕ *all year;* $) is divided into Zona A (*day use US$1 pp, tents US$1.30 pp*) by the bridge, and the classier Zona B (*tent pitches with electricity US$2 pp, 6-person cabañas with/without private bathroom, 2-person mini-cabañas without bathroom;* $), with a swimming pool. Horseriding is available from the Zona B gatehouse in summer (⊕ *15.00–21.00 Mon–Fri, 11.00–21.00 Sat–Sun; US$3/hr*); call m 9446 3682 to ride on Sundays or holidays in winter. You can cut across the fields on foot directly from here to the cave.

Alternatively, 2km beyond the cave is Camping Laguna de los Cuervos (✆ *4440 2746;* ⊕ *all year; camping US$2/2.50 pp without/with electricity, 5-person cabañas with bathroom from US$26, 2-person cabañas without bathroom from US$9;* $).

Continuing northeastwards from Minas, Ruta 8 is a fast modern road through rolling country with some rocky outcrops (the old road runs parallel and is largely usable by mountain bike). Turning right at km125, an unpaved road leads 10km south to the **Parque Salto del Penitente** (✆ *44 03096;* e *parquepenitente@ adinet.com.uy; www.saltodelpenitente.com;* ⊕ *09.30–19.30 daily; US$1*), where a waterfall drops 60m from the Sierra del Carapé. The falls are very dramatic after rain, but can dry up in summer, but the area has now been developed as an adventure tourism centre, with horseriding, hiking, birdwatching, bathing pools and a native plant nursery. At weekends you can try 'canopy', a 190m-long Tyrolean or zip-wire ride over the waterfall (*US$7*); or 'rappel', abseiling down 20–50m (*US$9*). The fairly new **Parador El Penitente** houses a restaurant specialising in lamb and wild boar, and there's a refuge and a rustic campsite ($).

There's also the 'panoramic' road to Parque Salto del Penitente, a much rougher 8km road starting at km139.8 (20 minutes from Minas by bus); turning left off this road after 2km, Avenida Bernasconi leads over a low pass to Villa Serrana, but it's better to continue on Ruta 8 to the main entry at km145. **Villa Serrana** (Mountain Town) was laid out in 1945–50 by architect Julio Vilamajó (see page 34) as a new kind of settlement in harmony with nature. In a bowl between the sierras del Penitente and de Carape, with a reservoir, market gardens and orchards, he built over 100 thatched houses of local stone and wood. Many are now in a poor state – although there was a revival after the arrival of electricity. People mostly prefer to visit rather than to live here. One recent development has been the arrival of a Buddhist temple and yoga centre. The conservation NGO Probides is working at Villa Serrana, to enhance the habitat for the many native birds.

Uruguay's first **youth hostel** (m *9922 6911, 9962 4098;* e *info@ villaserranahostel.com; www.villaserranahostel.com;* $) opened here in 1958, and is still going strong – the oldest youth hostel still in operation in South America – a tiny, very simple thatched cottage which makes a great place to spend a day or two riding horses and relaxing in nature. The hostel consists of a snug lounge (with a fireplace and DVD player; there's no TV reception here), one four-bed room and four two-bed rooms (one of them just a platform up a ladder), as well as sofas and mattresses on the floor; sheets and blankets are supplied. There's a kitchen, and a barbecue in the garden, but water is often in short supply; you may have to buy water from the nearby shop-bar to cook with. The garden is delightful, with epiphytic orchids hanging from the trees and hummingbirds and parkeets visiting.

There's a COSU bus from Minas (⊕ *09.00 & 15.30 Tue & Thu only*) which goes into Villa Serrana and will leave you at the hostel; alternatively, any bus from Montevideo towards Melo will drop you at the junction at km145 (23km from Minas). From there an unpaved road leads across a valley – forking right past some rocky outcrops – (about 2km from the highway) to the simple, affordable Hospedaje Familiar La Olla (✆ *44 02799,* m *9937 9113; $$*) – and on for almost another kilometre to a police post; the youth hostel is a couple of hundred metres to the left on Calle Molle.

Just beyond the hostel an attractive house is available to rent (m *9918 0970*). Where the road more or less ends you can turn right on Carobá to two hosterías, La Calaguala (✆ *44 02955,* m *9938 7519; Montevideo* ✆ *2 200 2842;* e *lacalaguala@ adinet.com.uy; www.paysandu.com/lacalaguala; $$$*) and La Fortaleza Hostería (m *9961 3564; Montevideo* ✆ *2 708 1740; $$$*). Both have swimming pools and offer good filling food and contacts for horseriding. La Fortaleza has the best views over Villa Serrana, and also boasts a collection of hundreds of witch dolls, which might put you off your food in the otherwise charming restaurant and salón de té.

From the police post the main route, Avenida Vilamajó, drops steeply (past a kiosk where you can buy drinks or arrange horseriding) to the low Stewart Vargas dam. Immediately before the dam, Calle Coronilla leads left to the Cabañas del Lago (✆ *44 25212,* m *9984 0094;* e *minadeoro@adinet.com.uy; $$*), 500m away. Camping is allowed by the dam (although there are no toilets or water supply), and there are opportunities here for horseriding. Continuing up the hill on the far side you'll see classic but very dilapidated Villa Serrana houses such as the Mesón de las Cañas and then (100m to the right) the Ventorrillo de la Buena Vista, originally a restaurant with great views across the valley but now almost ruined, its thatched roof covered with moss. Beyond this the road continues towards km139.8 on Ruta 8.

Continuing up Ruta 8, it's a five-minute drive from the Villa Serrana turning to the start of Ruta 13 (at km150.5), leading to Aiguá and Rocha (see page 221). Ruta 8 continues through pretty empty cattle country to the tiny towns of Mariscala (*where you can eat and sleep at the Parador El Rancho,* ✆ *44 92082*), Pirarajá and José Pedro Varela (*where the simple Hotel Patrón is right on the plaza at Podestá 668;* ✆ *45 59138; $$*). Bypassing the centre, Ruta 8 immediately crosses into Treinta y Tres department (see page 323) at km258.

5

Eastern Uruguay

The southeastern departments of Maldonado and Rocha, along the Atlantic coast, are known for their beaches – with very developed resorts in Maldonado, above all Punta del Este, and much wilder ones to the east in Rocha – but they also have some interesting countryside. The wetlands of Rocha are internationally important bird habitat, and the highest hills in Uruguay are not far inland from Punta del Este.

MALDONADO DEPARTMENT

Entering Maldonado department at km80 of the Ruta Interbalnearia, there's a toll with a small tourist office (summer only). At km83 there's a turning to the coastal route to Piriápolis, but it's better to stick to the main highway unless you want to go via the beaches of Solís (still home to Anglo-Uruguayan descendants of British railway workers) and Bella Vista. Ruta 9 joins from the left just before the junction at km86 to the Sierra de las Ánimas (see page 181) to the north; to the south you'll see the obvious Pan de Azúcar, with a huge cross and antenna on top (see page 181). At km94.5 (75 minutes by bus from Montevideo) there's an interchange with Ruta 37, leading north to the town of Pan de Azúcar (see page 181) and south to Piriápolis.

PIRIÁPOLIS This small town has an interesting history and makes an enjoyable and genuinely Uruguayan place to enjoy the beach when Punta del Este is packed with partying Argentines.

History This area has been inhabited for close to 13,000 years, judging from arrowheads found just west of the present town at Playa Verde and Playa Hermosa; there are also traces of a Charrúa cemetery on Cerro del Toro.

The modern history of Piriápolis began in 1890 when the property developer Francisco Piria (1847–1933) established it as his own private town – he owned the roads, the utilities, the stone quarries, everything. As an alchemist (taught by a Jesuit uncle, it seems), he is supposed to have laid the town out on mystical lines, oriented to springs and water courses below the Hill of the Bull (an alchemical figure) – but it's also inspired by the French resort of Biarritz, with its promenade and Belle Epoque hotels. Piria planted large numbers of eucalyptus trees to hold the sand dunes in place, and some 200ha of vineyards, taking Uruguayan soil to France in which to bring the vines back. He promoted his wines by writing as an anonymous critic in a newspaper he happened to own, and also tried selling *cognaquina*, a medicinal blend of cognac and quinine. In 1897 he completed his castle (see page 180) and in 1905 the first permanent hotel; in 1913 he built a narrow-gauge railway to Pan de Azúcar, where there was a main-line station (the Interbalnearia highway came only in the 1950s). He also built a port in 1916, with

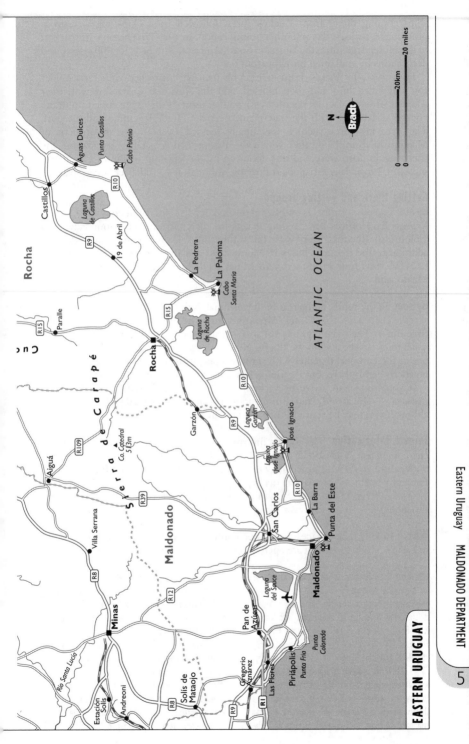

EASTERN URUGUAY

Rocha

ATLANTIC OCEAN

Aguas Dulces
Punta Castillos
Cabo Polonio

Castillos
Laguna de Castillos
19 de Abril

La Pedrera
La Paloma
Cabo Santa María

Paralle

Laguna de Rocha

Rocha

Garzón
Laguna Garzón
José Ignacio
Laguna José Ignacio

Alguá
Co. Catedral 513m

Maldonado

Serra de Carapé

Villa Serrana

San Carlos
La Barra
Punta del Este

Maldonado
Laguna del Sauce

Minas

Pan de Azúcar

Gregorio Aznárez
Piriápolis
Punta Fría
Punta Colorada

Las Flores

Solís de Mataojo

Andreoni
Estación Solís

Río Santa Lucía

20km

20 miles

ships coming direct from Buenos Aires, followed by a 7km-long waterfront promenade, parks, walks and other beautification. In 1929 Piria began construction of the Hotel Argentino, the largest in South America, with beds for 900 guests, and decorations by craftsmen brought from Italy.

However, after Piria's death in 1933 his manager quarrelled with Piria's older son and killed him and then himself, and the sons also quarrelled with their adopted sister (in fact Piria's mistress), so that most of the estate ended up in the pockets of lawyers, with the state taking over the Hotel Argentino and the port. The decaying infrastructure was finally handed over to the department of Maldonado from 1974, after which the Parque Municipal La Cascada and the Camping El Toro were laid out, followed by the opening of Piria's Castle as a museum. Nowadays Piriápolis is thriving, although it's a laid-back sort of place.

Getting there and getting around

By bus The bus terminal is on Niza at the end of Misiones; Buquebus and Colonia Express have offices here, selling tickets for their ferries from Montevideo and Colonia to Buenos Aires, with bus connections from Piriápolis included. In addition to the frequent buses to Montevideo and Punta del Este (see page 82), COOM runs four buses a day to Minas, and there are hourly local buses to Maldonado.

By boat To the south, at the rear of the terminal, is the large Plaza Artigas and then, across Tucumán, the Hotel Argentino and the waterfront Rambla de los Argentinos. The main commercial area is just to the left (east), beyond which the *rambla* curves southeast to the Puerto Nuevo; there are some fishing boats working out of the harbour, together with some sailing yachts, mostly with owners in the northern hemisphere, but the Buquebus ferries no longer use the port.

If you happen to arrive by yacht from abroad, you should call on Customs (*Aduana*; ☏ 43 20038) and Immigration (*Migración*; ☏ 43 20555) at the port, although you may be sent to Punta del Este airport.

Tourist information The tourist information centre (*on the rambla just east of the Hotel Argentino*; ☏ 43 25055; ⊕ 10.00–18.00 daily) is helpful, and also has public phones and an ATM. Immediately to the west is another office run by the Liga de Fomento business association (*www.piriapolistotal.com*; ⊕ 12.00–18.00 Mon–Thu, 12.00–17.00 Fri, 13.00–19.00 Sat), in a wing of the school colony (the former Hotel Piriápolis).

🏠 **Where to stay** The cheapest hotels open only for the peak season (mid-December to Easter), while those that are open for longer have a wide seasonal range in prices.

🏠 **Apart-Hotel Terrazas de San Franciso** Rambla de los Ingleses & Rawson; ☏ 43 27153; www.terrazasdesanfrancisco.com. Something a little different, this hotel has AC apartments with kitchens & Wi-Fi; it's just east of the town on the Playa San Francisco. $$$$

🏠 **Hotel Argentino** Rambla de los Argentinos s/n; ☏ 43 22791; e reservas@argentinohotel.com; www.argentinohotel.com.uy. The town's classiest place to stay was founded by Piria as a centre for thalassotherapy (treatments with seawater); you can still have massages with seaweed extracts or bathe in the saltwater pool. There's also a casino, an international restaurant & a big traditional bar that hosts afternoon tea & a Saturday night dinner-dance. Although well modernised, it still has the original lifts, staircase & stained glass, & the corridor leading to the casino is lined with historic photos & posters — well worth a look even if you're not staying here. $$$$

🏠 **City Hotel** Rambla de los Argentinos & Freire; ☏ 43 22522; e cityhotelpiriapolis@gmail.com; www.cityhotelpiriapolis.com. An adequate fallback option; rooms have cable TV, fan & frigobar. $$$$

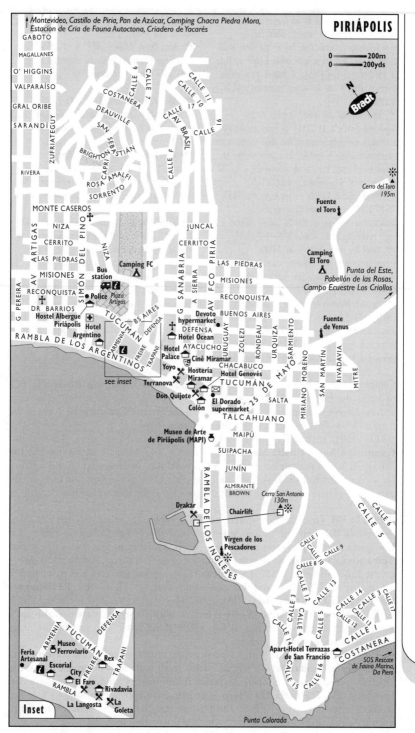

PIRIÁPOLIS

↑ Montevideo, Castillo de Piria, Pan de Azúcar, Camping Chacra Piedra Mora,
Estación de Cria de Fauna Autoctona, Criadero de Yacarés

GABOTO
MAGALLANES
O' HIGGINS
VALPARAÍSO
GRAL ORIBE
SARANDÍ
RIVERA

COSTANERA
DEAUVILLE
SAN SEBASTIÁN
BRIGHTON
ROSA CAPRI
AMALFI
SORRENTO

CALLE 6
CALLE 7
CALLE 11
CALLE 10
CALLE 17
AV BRASIL
CALLE 16
CALLE F

0 ━━━ 200m
0 ━━━ 200yds

N

Bradt

Cerro del Toro
195m

Fuente
el Toro ⚱

MONTE CASEROS ✝
NIZA
CERRITO
LAS PIEDRAS
MISIONES
RECONQUISTA
DR BARRIOS

AV ARTIGAS
SIMÓN DEL PINO
NIZA
G PEREIRA

JUNCAL
CERRITO
LAS PIEDRAS
MISIONES
RECONQUISTA
BUENOS AIRES

G SANABRIA
A SIERRA
AV FCO PIRIA

Camping
El Toro
⛺

Punta del Este,
Pabellón de las Rosas,
Campo Ecuestre Los Criollos

Camping FC ⛺

Bus
station 🚌

Police ●
Plaza
Artigas

Fuente
de Venus

Hostel Albergue
Piriápolis ✚
Hotel
Argentino

TUCUMÁN
ARMENIA
FREIRE
DEFENSA
TRAPANI
BS AIRES

Devoto
hypermarket

DEFENSA ✝
Hotel Ocean 🏠
AYACUCHO

URUGUAY
ZOLEZI
RONDEAU
URQUIZA

DE MAYO
MIRIANO MORENO
SAN MARTÍN
RIVADAVIA
MITRE

RAMBLA DE LOS ARGENTINOS

Hotel
Palace
Yoyo ●

Ciné Miramar ⚙
Hostería
Miramar

CHACABUCO
Hotel Genovés
TUCUMÁN

see inset

ℹ

Terranova ✕
Don Quijote ✕
Colón

El Dorado
supermarket

☒
SALTA

SARMIENTO
2,5

TALCAHUANO

Museo de Arte
de Piriápolis (MAPI) ⚙

MAIPÚ
SUIPACHA
JUNÍN

ALMIRANTE
BROWN

RAMBLA DE LOS INGLESES

Cerro San Antonio
130m

Drakar
✕
☐

Chairlift

Virgen de los
Pescadores

CALLE 6
CALLE 5

CALLE 1
CALLE 9
CALLE 8 10
CALLE 12
CALLE 13
CALLE 14
CALLE 3
CALLE 17
CALLE 5
CALLE 12
CALLE 13
CALLE 1

Apart-Hotel Terrazas
de San Francisco

COSTANERA

CALLE 14
CALLE 16
CALLE 15
CALLE 1

SOS Rescate
de Fauna Marina,
Da Piero

Punta Colorada

Inset

ARMENIA
TUCUMÁN
DEFENSA

Museo
Ferroviario ⛫
Feria
Artesanal
●
ℹ
Escorial
City
El Faro ☐
RAMBLA
La Langosta ✕

FREIRE
TRAPANI
Rex ⛫
Rivadavia ✕
La
Goleta ✕

🏠 **Hotel Colón** Rambla de los Argentinos 950 & Piria; 🕿 43 22508; e colon@adinet.com.uy; www.hotelcolonpiriapolis.com. One of the nicer small hotels, it was built in a half-timbered style by Piria in 1910; there's lovely tiling & stained glass inside. Open all year, it has an indoor swimming pool, Wi-Fi & cable TV. $$$$

🏠 **Hotel Escorial** (52 rooms) Rambla de los Argentinos 1290; 🕿 43 22537; e hotel_escorial@hotmail.com; www.hotelescorial.com. Next to the tourist information centre is this Art Deco jewel worthy of Miami Beach that's been nicely refurbished; it has 52 en-suite rooms & a swimming pool. $$$$

🏠 **Hotel Genovés** Rambla de los Argentinos 1050; 🕿 43 22505; e hgenoves@adinet.com.uy; www.hotelgenoves.com. Has AC rooms, covered & open swimming pools, jacuzzi & Wi-Fi. $$$$

🏠 **Hotel Rex** Freire 968; 🕿 43 22543; e correodelrex@adinet.com.uy; www.hotelrex.com.uy. A simpler Art Deco place that has a lift, free internet & Wi-Fi. $$$$

🏠 **Hostería Miramar** Rambla de los Argentinos 1082; 🕿 43 22544; e info@hosteriamiramar.com; www.hosteriamiramar.com. On the seafront, the Miramar is open all year & boasts a panoramic solarium & beach service, & also has shaded parking

& Wi-Fi, as well as the Restaurante-marisquería Don Quijote (see below). $$$

🏠 **Hotel Ocean** Sanabria 1009; 🕿 43 22554; e pirocean@adinet.com.uy. An affordable 3-star that's open longer than some; there's parking at the rear. $$$

🏠 **Hotel Palace** Sanabria 990; 🕿 43 23040; e psagario@viajescontinental.com. Near Hotel Ocean is the similar Palace, but with a shorter season. $$$

🏠 **Hotel Rivadavia** Rambla de los Argentinos & Trápani; 🕿 43 22532; e rivacol@adinet.com.uy. This seafront hotel is airily simple (with fans rather than AC) but has undergone a stylish refurbishment & has Wi-Fi. $$$

🏠 **Hostel Albergue Piriápolis** Simón del Pino 1106-36; 🕿 43 20394; e informes@hostelpiriapolis.com; www.hostelpiriapolis.com; closed May–Aug. A good old-style youth hostel, somewhat institutional but with plenty of space. It's definitely not a party hostel, & you'll get a good night's sleep. There are rooms with 2, 3 & 4 beds, a large patio with parrilla, laundry space, a kitchen, a TV room & bikes for rent. A bed costs from US$10 including b/fast (08.30–10.30). $

Camping There are two campsites in Piriápolis: the **Camping Piriápolis FC**, opposite the bus terminal (*Misiones & Niza;* 🕿 43 23275; e *piriapolisfc@yahoo.com;* ⏱ *Nov–Easter*), with space for 800 tents and 15 chalets; and **Camping El Toro**, in the Parque Municipal behind the Fuente de Venus (*Avda 25 de Mayo;* 🕿 43 23454; ⏱ *Dec–Mar*), attractively planted with pines and eucalyptus trees. There's also **Camping Chacra Piedra Mora** (*Ruta 37 km3.8;* 🕿 43 24057; ⏱ *all year*) towards the Pan de Azúcar, a pretty place with thatched buildings, swimming pool and facilities for soccer, volleyball and basketball; camping costs US$4 per person, and there are six *minicabañas*. There are also beach campsites not far to the west in Las Flores.

✖ **Where to eat** There are various restaurants with pleasant waterfront terraces along the *rambla* between the Hotel Argentino and the Hotel Colón, including **La Langosta** (*Trápani*), a better than average seafood restaurant that does a fine paella; **Terranova** (*Sanabria*), serving the full range of *chivitos*, pizzas, *parrilla* and a three-course lunch menu at US$7; **La Goleta** (*Sierra*), good for steak and pasta, with a set menu at US$7.50; and on the other side of Sierra the **Restaurant-marisquería Don Quijote** (⏱ *Dec–Apr*), which offers seafood including a fine paella. A block inland, **Yoyo** (*Sanabria & Tucumán*) is a stylish place that also has a sidewalk terrace and specialises in fish and seafood while also serving the usual range of meats, pastas and pizzas.

At the north end of the port, a nice thatched building houses the **Restaurant-marisquería Drakar**, which has affordable fresh seafood. The **snack bar** at the chairlift (see opposite) is open 24 hours in summer. Pushing on to Playa San Francisco, the **Trattoria Da Piero** is an attractive spot specialising in fish and seafood, as well as pasta; a little further east they have their own lobster farm, raising Australian red-claw lobsters, which is interesting to visit.

Afterwards, or indeed at any time, you could sample the ices at the **Heladería El Faro,** on the *rambla* at Freire.

Other practicalities

Communications The Antel *telecentro* is on Barrios just east of Plaza Artigas (☉ *09.00–18.00 daily*), and there's free public Wi-Fi access on the plaza. The post office is near the south end of Avenida Piria near Tucumán (☉ *08.00–18.00 Mon–Fri, 09.00–12.00 Sat*).

Emergency services For health problems, the *policlínica* is across the road south of the youth hostel (*Simón del Pino & Barrios*), and the police station is immediately north of the hostel (*Simón del Pino & Reconquista*).

Markets There's a fairly large El Dorado supermarket on Avenida Piria at Salta (opposite the Moto-Park bike rental shop), and a Devoto hypermarket four blocks north on Piria at Buenos Aires; on Saturdays there's a market on Plaza Artigas.

Entertainment Films are shown at the Cine Miramar (*Rambla de los Argentinos 1124 & Sierra;* ✆ *43 20600;* ☉ *Fri–Sun*). Horseriding on the Cerro del Indio is on offer from the Campo Ecuestre Los Criollos (*take Calle Ayacucho opposite Fuente de Venus and then the track towards Punta Colorada;* m *9917 0168*).

The best known annual event is the **Paella Gigante** in mid-December, when 4,500 people share a paella cooked up from 300kg of rice, 100kg of vegetables, 500kg each of seafood and chicken and 200kg of pork.

What to see and do Piriápolis has a fine sandy beach. with just one red-brick apartment tower just west of the centre; other buildings are all very low-rise. The beach is sheltered from the Atlantic waves, and has a gentle slope that's very safe for children. Alongside Calle Armenia, on the east side of the Hotel Argentino, the **Museo Ferroviario** (☉ *summer 17.00–21.00 daily*) is home to a rusted narrow-gauge steam locomotive, a goods wagon and carriage and other decaying bits of railwayana. Across the road at the rear of the Hotel Argentino is the circular **Pabellón de las Rosas (Rose Pavilion),** ordered by Piria from the Eiffel company in France as a banqueting hall. Walking southeast along the *rambla*, you'll pass the Feria Artsanal (craft market) and fine Art Deco edifices such as the Hotel Escorial (see opposite), as well as Piria's Gran Hotel Piriápolis (1905, now a school colony) and Hotel Colón (1910). Crossing Avenida Piria and heading inland, the Casa Lorenzo Piria, a mini-castle which was the home of Piria's son, houses MAPI, the **Museo de Arte de Piriápolis** (*Avda 25 de Mayo 843;* ✆ *43 22375;* e*museopiriapolis@ hotmail.com;* ☉ *summer 18.00–21.00 daily*), which houses a different art exhibition every summer.

Avenida 25 de Mayo continues to the **Fuente de Venus (Fountain of Venus),** a pool surrounding a circular classical temple that's a copy of one at the Villa Parravicini near Milan in Italy; to the north is an attractively landscaped park (with children's playground), with a road winding up past the campsite to the Fuente del Toro. This is another fountain (of alchemical importance to Piria), with water flowing from the mouth of a life-size bronze sculpture of a bull by Antoine Bourdelle, one of Rodin's best students; it weighs three tonnes and was shipped from Paris by Piria. The Cerro del Toro was badly affected by a fire in January 2009.

To the south by the harbour, the statue of Stella Maris, also known as the Virgen de los Pescadores (Virgin of the Fishermen), was brought by Piria from Italy. The western end of Cerro San Antonio was cut away to make room for the road and port, but there is now a **chairlift** (*aerosilla;* ☉ *winter 10.00–19.00 Thu–Sun & holidays,* *summer 10.00 till late daily; US$3*). Cerro San Antonio was known as Cerro de los Ingleses (Hill of the English), but after a chapel to St Anthony of Padua was built on top, together with a road in 1952, it gradually became known by its current name.

The Rambla de los Ingleses continues around Punta Fría to the Playa de los Ingleses, home to a small British colony at the start of the 20th century. At its eastern end is the rocky Punta Colorada, popular with local fishermen, on the sheltered side of which you'll find **SOS Rescate de Fauna Marina** (🌂 *43 20011*, m *9433 0795*; e *sos-faunamarina@adinet.com.uy; US$2; see Punta del Este overview map*), a rescue and rehabilitation centre for marine wildlife. Since 1993 they've been looking after sea lions, Magellanic penguins and other stranded and injured creatures, and now have four saltwater pools, other enclosures and a small shop.

If you (or your children) are interested in captive wildlife, there's also the **Criadero de Yacarés** (*Caiman Breeding Centre;* m *9968 7136; www.yacares.org;* ⊕ *10.00–sunset daily in summer, Sat–Sun in winter; US$2*), 600m north from km86 of the Interbalnearia, to the west of Piriápolis. Here they breed the *yacaré overo* (*Caiman latirostris*), threatened by hunting, and the tortuga morrocoyo (*Trachemys dorbignyi*) or Orbigny's slider, a water turtle threatened by the pet trade.

On the other side of town, three blocks west of the Hotel Argentina, Avenida Artigas heads straight inland as Ruta 37 to Pan de Azúcar; it's eight blocks to the Parque La Cascada, created in 1979. There's no waterfall (although the Arroyo Cascada flows through), but it's a pleasant creekside park with barbecues, play areas, thatched shelters and a snack bar. There's car parking a couple of blocks north of the entrance beyond Rivera. The road rises to a roundabout immediately beyond Piria's Neo-Romanesque hilltop church (which was never consecrated and is now roofless and semi-ruined) and heads into the countryside (Goscopar bus No 27 to Pan de Azúcar takes this road, leaving the terminal at 25 minutes past the hour).

At km4.8 the **Castillo de Piria** is about 300m up a tree-lined drive to the right (east). This is Piria's home, completed in 1897 by the architect Aquiles Monzani and opened to the public in 1979 as the Museo Parque Municipal Castillo Fransisco Piria (⊕ *10.00–17.00 Tue–Sun; free*). It's somewhat fortress-like, with its Ghibeline battlements, but far too symmetrical. To the left inside the front door is a small chapel, and to the right space for temporary art shows and odds and ends such as old bibles and a phone exchange. Upstairs, a tiled corridor gives access to seven rooms (including two bedrooms), containing mock-medieval furniture, some very average paintings and three pianos. There's a brace of Turkish shields, helmets, axes and maces, and a view to the church and the sea. It's worth a stop if you're passing, but not worth a special trip. A plaque commemorates a visit in around 1901 by the poet Julio Herrera y Reissig, whose congenital heart defect, aggravated by typhoid fever, left him unable to travel further from Montevideo than Piriápolis and Buenos Aires.

In the park you'll see a fine Canary Islands dragon tree (*Dracaena draco*), and a little *glorieta* (summer house). Behind the castle is a very ruined railway carriage, as well as the Pueblo Andaluz (Andalusian Town), built as a set for a TV series and now in ruins.

It's another 1km north (passing a smaller castle that was the house of Piria's mistress) to the **Estación de Cria de Fauna Autoctona** (*Native Fauna Breeding Centre;* 🌂 *43 23468;* ⊕ *07.00–19.00 daily; free; see Punta del Este overview map*), also known as the Parque Municipal Cerro Pan de Azúcar, which is well worth a visit. Set up when the area was replanted with native species after a fire in 1980, a track and side-paths lead through the woodland to various enclosures housing many different kinds of birds (including ducks, egrets and other waterbirds, owls, screamers, seriemas, caracaras, vultures and dusky-legged guans) as well as slider turtles, yacarés, capybaras, wild cats, opossums, raccoons and otters, and at the end, pampas deer.

You'll also see wild tegu lizards (*Lagarto overo*) lurking in the undergrowth. The circuit ends at the reptilarium, with snakes and other cold-blooded beasts; you can also turn uphill to a viewpoint and some *pinturas rupestres* (indigenous rock paintings). Back by the entry you can find refreshments at the Parador Drago (m *9417 8136;* e *paradordrago@adinet.com.uy*), which sells *chivitos*, pizzas, ice cream and other snacks; there are also picnic tables, a play area and a craft shop run by a rural women's co-operative.

You can also start here to hike up **Cerro Pan de Azúcar (Sugar Loaf Mountain)** (*see Punta del Este overview map*), the third-highest hill in Uruguay at about 390m, and probably the most popular hike in the country. From the Breeding Centre a track turns into a steep path, taking between 90 minutes and two hours to the top, following red paint marks, first through eucalyptus trees and then bare hillside.

On the summit is a 30m concrete cross that can be seen from miles around. Erected in 1938, it was designed by the sculptor Juan Zorrilla de San Martín (who had died in 1931). A spiral staircase leads up inside the main shaft to the arms, where there are *miradors* giving a panoramic view that's not very different to that from the base of the cross.

It's another 3km to the cloverleaf interchange with the Interbalnearia, on the far side of which is the small town of **Pan de Azúcar**, founded in 1874 and known mainly for its Museo al Aire Libre (Open Air Museum), consisting of murals dotted around town. Most are nothing special, but there is one by Carlos Páez Vilaró, painted in 1980, just east of the junction of Ruta 9 and Ruta 60, south of the centre. Buses to Rocha pass along Ruta 9; there are no bus offices here but they'll pick you up by the roadside, although there may well be standing room only.

ECOTOURIST *ESTANCIAS* There are several places in the hillier country north of the Ruta Interbalnearia that offer family-friendly outdoor activities. The best known is the **Paseo Sierra de las Ánimas** (*km86 of the Interbalnearia;* m *9441 9891; www.sierradelasanimas.com;* ☉ *summer, Easter & Carnaval 09.00–sunset daily, rest of year on w/ends depending on the weather; US$2*). Cars have a 600m drive in but pedestrians have a shorter path (get off the bus at the Parador Los Cardos). A very basic campsite is available. There are walks to the Cerro de las Ánimas (formerly known as the Mirador Nacional) or to the Cañadón de los Espejos, a dramatic little gorge with pools and waterfalls, each taking three hours (round trip), or five hours as a combined circuit. The Cerro de las Ánimas is, at 501m, the second-highest peak in the country, and was much visited by the indigenous inhabitants, as well as by Artigas and by Darwin, who wrote:

> On the summit of the mountain there were several small heaps of stones, which evidently had lain there for many years. My companion assured me that they were the work of the Indians in the old time. The heaps were similar, but on a much smaller scale, to those so commonly found on the mountains of Wales.

Immediately east, the **Estancia Bellavista** (*km87 of the Interbalnearia;* ☏ *43 81201,* m *9438 2387;* e *estanciabv@adinet.com.uy; www.estanciabellavista.com.uy;* ☉ *all year*) offers horseriding and birdwatching walks, has a *hostería* and *salón de té*, and can arrange *asados* for groups of up to 60.

Just west, the **Estancia El Centinela** (*6km from km87 of Ruta 9;* ☏ *49 02262;* e *centinela@todouy.com;* ☉ *all year*) specialises in horseriding, although you can also hike, or swim or canoe in the river. There's also a swimming pool outside the adobe house full of antique furniture, where the owners serve lunch and tea.

Finally, the luxury **Posada Kururu** (*6km from km82 of Ruta 9;* ☏ *2 901 8821; www.kururu.com.uy;* $$$$$) has eight beautifully designed rooms and offers full board (with four meals including wine) and horseriding, canoeing and hiking on colonial routes such as the Camino Real. Good-quality Trek mountain bikes are available, and there's a swimming pool; TV and internet are available in a separate building.

PIRIÁPOLIS TO PUNTA DEL ESTE From Pan de Azúcar the Interbalnearia (Ruta 93) swings southeast to run between the Laguna de los Cisnes (Swan Lake) and the coast; at km113.3 it passes Punta del Este's airport, crosses the Arroyo El Potrero, flowing out of the Laguna del Sauce, and at km116 reaches the Chihuahua roundabout. Immediately to the west is Playa Chihuahua, which has been Uruguay's main naturist beach (with a popular gay section at the right-hand end) since the 1960s, although it was strictly illegal then.

It's less than a kilometre on to the Solanas roundabout, with a supermarket, 24-hour petrol station and various pizza stands and the like lining the road. Immediately to the right, Playa Solana is shallow and sheltered, and particularly popular from late afternoon until sunset. There are often glamorous yachts anchored here in the summer. The Playa Portezuelo area, immediately southeast, was laid out by the Catalan architect Antonio Bonet (1913–89), a disciple of Le Corbusier, who also designed several fine buildings here. The long, low former Hostería Solana del Mar and adjacent Casa Berlingieri (both built in 1946) are perhaps the best of the few Corbusieresque buildings in Uruguay, with their flat roofs and succession of arches, together with his own house, the more minimalist Casa Rinconada.

From the Portezuelo flyover, Avenida Lussich runs inland to the Arboretum and Museo Lussich (see page 200), the Camping Internacional Punta Ballena (see page 191) and the Tambo Lapataia (see page 200); the Interbalnearia climbs sharply up to the Punta Ballena (Whale Point) ridge, with a viewpoint accessible by eastbound traffic and the turning south to Carlos Páez Vilaró's Casapueblo (see page 199). Dropping back to near sea level, there's a turning south to Las Grutas, caves which once housed bars and discos but since the 1990s have been protected. The tiny half-hidden beach is still very popular, with *paradores* such as El Chiringo offering food and drink on the beach. Soon you enter the coastal sprawl of Punta del Este, starting with new apartment blocks by the small Laguna del Diario to the north. At *parada* (numbered bus stop) 24, where Avenida España turns north to the older, more historic town of Maldonado, there's a tourist information office by the beach. Buses from Montevideo follow the seaside Rambla Williman for a bit longer before looping up to the Maldonado bus station, 110 minutes from the capital; otherwise follow the *rambla*, lined with hotels and apartment blocks, to Punta del Este, set on the low peninsula that marks the end of the Río de la Plata.

PUNTA DEL ESTE Not only Uruguay's premium beach resort but Argentina's as well (there being no decent beaches anywhere near Buenos Aires), Punta del Este is a strange mix of surfers, party animals, celebrity spotters and curious tourists wondering why the others spend their holidays in such an overpriced madhouse. In fact it's only a madhouse for about three weeks a year, covering the New Year holiday and the two following weekends, when every Argentine celebrity has to be seen at several obligatory parties here every night, with paparazzi chasing them from one to another and world-class DJs charging US$30,000. At other times, although Punta is still more expensive than other resorts along the coast, you might be able to see some reasons why it's worth it.

The heart of Punta del Este is the eponymous peninsula (an island for most of the last 20 million years) that marks the boundary between the Río de la Plata and the Atlantic Ocean, 134km east of Montevideo; just inland is the town of

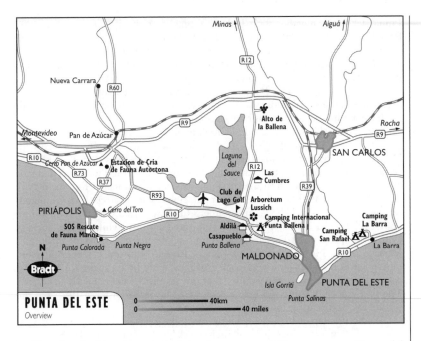

PUNTA DEL ESTE
Overview

| 0 | 40km |
| 0 | 40 miles |

Map labels: Minas, Aiguá, R12, Nueva Carrara, R60, Alto de la Ballena, Rocha, Montevideo, Pan de Azúcar, R9, SAN CARLOS, R9, R10, Cerro Pan de Azúcar, Estación de Cría de Fauna Autóctona, R73, R37, Laguna del Sauce, R12, Las Cumbres, R39, R93, PIRIÁPOLIS, Cerro del Toro, R10, Club de Lago Golf, Arboretum Lussich, Camping Internacional, Camping La Barra, SOS Rescate de Fauna Marina, Aldilá, Camping Punta Ballena, Camping San Rafael, Casapueblo, Punta Colorada, Punta Negra, Punta Ballena, La Barra, MALDONADO, R10, Isla Gorriti, PUNTA DEL ESTE, Punta Salinas, N, Bradt

Maldonado, the historic capital of the department of the same name. Punta del Este now sprawls along the coast both east and west of the peninsula, with rows of modern apartment blocks lining the waterfront *rambla*; this heavily built-up strip ends just beyond La Barra, 10km east, which is where the best surfing and the best bars and clubs are, and where many of the hottest stars rent houses for the summer. The richest and highest-ranking celebrities mostly stay much further east, towards José Ignacio, although this is often counted as 'Punta del Este' for these purposes.

There's always a breeze, so even the hottest days are bearable, while even summer evenings may require an extra layer. The sea is warmest in February and March, but the weather is better in January.

History The peninsula and the sheltered haven on its western side were 'discovered' by Juan Díaz de Solís in 1516. There have been many shipwrecks along this coast: in 1812 the Spanish barque *El Salvador* was wrecked near what is now *parada* 8 of the Playa Mansa, with only 116 of the 800 on board surviving. It was carrying 500 soldiers, who would probably have allowed Spain to win the battle of El Cerrito, near Montevideo, on New Year's Eve of 1812, and the history of Uruguay might have been rather different.

A tiny fishing settlement was established by Francisco Aguilar in 1829, followed in 1835 by salt pans set up by the American Luis Burmester for preserving beef. In 1860 a lighthouse was built on what was then known as Punta Salinas. From 1880 Antonio Lussich (1848–1928, who ran a salvage company and wrote Uruguay's first gaucho stories) and Henry Burnett (1845–1927, the British vice-consul and Lloyd's insurance agent) devoted themselves to planting pine and eucalyptus trees to stabilise the sand dunes that lined this coast and made it largely unfit for settlement. By 1897 the people of Maldonado were building summer houses on the coast, initially at La Aguada, the present *parada* 24 of the Playa Mansa, west of Punta del Este, where a jetty had been built in 1890 (functioning until 1968). In 1907 the first hotels were built on the peninsula (then known for the first time as

Eastern Uruguay **MALDONADO DEPARTMENT**

5

183

Punta del Este), together with bathing cabins near the present port. In 1909 President Claudio Williman visited, and in 1911 mixed bathing was permitted. The resort's development really took off after World War I, with electric lighting from 1916 (only in summer until 1919), water-skiing from 1920, a church consecrated in 1922, and many new hotels and other developments. The main street, Avenida Gorlero, was laid out in 1918 and named after the first mayor of Maldonado department (1909–13). Punta was seen as very 'fast' and liberated compared with the more traditional resorts close to Montevideo.

It was General Perón's decision in 1955 to allow Argentinians to travel abroad again that started Punta del Este's modern fame and prosperity. It soon vied with Havana as the hottest destination in the hemisphere, and has been very busy in summer ever since, its population rising to close to half a million every January. There was an annual Festival Internacional de Cine de Punta del Este from 1951 to 1958, revived in 2006; this has brought global stars such as Yves Montand, Jeanne Moreau, Anita Ekberg, Yul Brynner, Rita Hayworth, Marcelo Mastroianni, Gina Lollobrigida and more recently Antonio Banderas, while figures such as Prince Philip, Princess Diana, Sarah Ferguson, the royal families of Spain and Monaco, Pablo Neruda, Jorge Luis Borges, Rudolf Nureyev, Pamela Anderson, Simon Le Bon and Naomi Campbell (snapped nude by a paparazzo) have also passed through. In the 1960s South American summits were regularly held here. The first Queen of Punta del Este was crowned by Sacha Distel in 1967, and the second the next year by Tony Curtis.

The dictatorship of 1973–84 had little effect, the generals allowing it to carry on as a social safety valve (and they and their wives liked to come and play bridge and tennis here), but since the return of democracy it has become far more open and inclusive. The early 21st century boom brought glitzy new developments, such as Aqua (*parada 19, Playa Brava; www.aqua.com.uy*), by Uruguayan 'starchitect' Rafael Viñoly, the penthouse of which sold for US$7.3m, as well as a planned US$60 million investment by Donald Trump.

Getting there

By air The modern airport (*PDP; www.puntadeleste.aero*), 24km west at Laguna del Sauce, has at least one flight a day from Buenos Aires (with PLUNA), and many more at weekends in summer, as well as from Brazil and Chile.

Airline companies

✈ **Aerolíneas Argentinas** Galería Santos Dumont, Local 2, Avda Gorlero between calles 30 & 31; ☎ 42 559777, 42 444343; e pdpcbar@ aerolineas.com.uy; ⊕ summer 09.00–22.00 daily, rest of year 10.00–12.30, 14.30–18.00 Mon–Fri, 10.00–14.00 Sat; call centre ☎ 4054 86527; ⊕ 09.00–21.00 daily

✈ **American Airlines** Calle 24 & Calle 27, Local 3; ☎ 2 916 3929; ⊕ 10.00–14.00, 17.00–21.00 Mon–Sat
✈ **Gol** Punta del Este airport; ☎ 42 559777 ext 300
✈ **PLUNA** Avda Roosevelt, parada 9; ☎ 42 490101, 42 492050; ⊕ 09.00–17.00 Mon–Sat; call centre ☎ 2 401 5000; ⊕ 09.00–19.00 daily
✈ **Sol** Punta del Este airport; ☎ 42 210053, 2 601 2072; m 9550 1119

Airport transport From the airport it's easiest to get a taxi (around US$30), although buses do pass on the main highway half a kilometre to the south. Hourly local buses from Maldonado to Pan de Azúcar and Piriápolis pass the airport; buses to Montevideo, though faster, cost a lot more and may be reluctant to take a booking for such a short journey.

From Montevideo's Carrasco airport, it's possible to catch a regular bus to Punta del Este (see page 79). Private transfers (*car for 4, US$160–170; minibuses for 15,*

US$200) are available for with Taxi Aeropuerto (📞 *2 604 0323, 2 604 0188; www.taxisaeropuerto.com*) or Transfers Lema (📞 *42 236052,* m *9435 7375; www.transfers.com.uy*).

By bus The bus terminal is on the site of the former railway station (which operated only from 1930 to 1983), right at the neck of the peninsula where Avenida Artigas runs into Gorlero. There are frequent buses from Montevideo (see page 82), COOM goes at 09.00 to Minas and Florida, and COT goes twice a day to Rocha, Punta del Diablo and Chuy. Local buses go to Piriápolis, Maldonado, San Carlos and José Ignacio. International buses from Montevideo to Brazil call here, and ferry companies run buses to connect with their boats from Montevideo and Colonia to Buenos Aires. In the terminal are a café, telephone/internet, office, left luggage (🕒 *09.00–23.00 daily*), exchange desk and tourism office (📞 *42 494042*) – not to be confused with the Buquebus Turismo office opposite.

By cruise ship Punta del Este is a regular stop for cruise liners (about one ship a day on average in season); there's no dock but passengers are brought ashore by boats to the new teardrop-shaped double-decker La Pastora pier. This is at the Terminal de Cruceros (*parada 3, Playa Mansa, just north of the peninsula by the Conrad Resort and Casino*), which has toilets and a waiting area for 300 passengers.

Ferry companies For bookings from Montevideo/Colonia to Buenos Aires.

🚢 **Buquebus** Avda Gorlero & Calle 32; 📞 42 484995; 🕒 10.00–22.00 daily. Punta Shopping, level 1, Local 104; 🕒 10.00–22.00 daily. Buquebus Turismo, bus terminal; 📞 42 488380; 🕒 10.00–18.00 Mon–Fri, 10.00–14.00 Sat, summer from 09.00

🚢 **Colonia Express** bus terminal, c/o COPSA; 📞 42 421975; 🕒 04.30–23.30 daily
🚢 **Seacat Colonia (Ferrylineas)** Avda Gorlero & Calle 31, Galería Sagasti; 📞 42 442820; e agencias@ferrylineas.com.ar. Bus terminal, Local 9; 📞 42 493892

Orientation Like most of the Uruguayan resorts, Punta del Este is divided into a *brava* (wild) side and a *mansa* (calm) side, with crashing surf on the *brava* side, facing the Atlantic to the east, and family-friendly beaches on the *mansa* side, on the estuary of the Plate to the west (very popular at sunset). The peninsula itself is largely rocky, although there are tiny patches of sand, and a large harbour on the west side. A dual-carriageway *rambla* runs along the coast in both directions, with locations along it indicated by numbered bus stops (*parada*) – eg: parada 11, Playa Mansa. On the peninsula itself roads have both names and numbers, eg: Avenida Gorlero is also Calle 22 (although the numbers are not always obvious). The first part of the peninsula is the main commercial area, with fairly high modern buildings, while south of the port, around the lighthouse and church, there are only older buildings with a maximum of four storeys.

Getting around
By bus Lots of local buses (some very smoky) run between Punta del Este (some running south as far as Calle 7) and Maldonado, mostly running via either Punta Shopping or Rambla Williman (Playa Mansa), Las Delicias and Avenida España. Routes 1 and 24 continue north to the small town of San Carlos (see page 218) for connections to Rocha department.

By taxi Taxis wait at various locations, eg: the bus terminal, the Conrad Resort and Casino, and by a small obelisk (📞 *42 441123*) at the south end of Avenida Gorlero.

By car All the major companies can be found just south of the bus terminal.

🚗 **Allcar** Galería Mejillón, Local 9, Calle 31 (Inzaurraga) between Avda Gorlero & Calle 20; ☏ 42 480000, 📱 9445 5885; www.allcarrental.com.uy

🚗 **Avis** Avda Gorlero & Calle 31 (at rear of casino); ☏ 42 442020; ⊕ 09.00–21.00 daily. Also at Punta del Este airport; 24hr ☏ 4244 2020; www.avis.com.uy

🚗 **Brisas Rentacar** Galería El Mejillón, Local 001, Calle 27 near Avda Gorlero; ☏ 42 491490

🚗 **Dollar** Avda Gorlero 961; ☏ 42 443444; e dollarpdp@adinet.com.uy; www.dollar.com.uy; ⊕ summer 10.00–19.00 daily, rest of year 10.00–13.00 daily, 15.00–19.30 Mon–Sat. Also at Punta del Este airport; ☏ 42 559550; 24hr 📱 9443 4937

🚗 **Europcar** Avda Gorlero & Calle 30 (Las Focas); ☏ 42 495018, 24hr 📱 9443 7273; e punta@ europcar.com.uy. Also at Punta del Este airport; ☏ 42 495017; www.europcar.com.uy

🚗 **Federal Car Rental** Calle 31 (Inzaurraga) & Avda Gorlero; ☏ 42 449489, 24hr 📱 9620 9427; e punta@federal.com.uy

🚗 **Hertz** Calle 31 (Inzaurraga) between Avda Gorlero & Calle 20; 24hr ☏ 42 489775/8; ⊕ 09.00–13.00, 15.00–19.00 daily. Also at Punta

del Este airport; ☏ 42 559032; ⊕ 07.00–24.00 daily. Punta Shopping, Avda Roosevelt, parada 7; 📱 9964 0202; ⊕ 10.00–20.00 daily, mid-Dec–mid-Mar until 22.00

🚗 **InterAutos** Calle 28 (Los Meros) near Avda Gorlero; ☏ 42 446869; 24hr 📱 9444 0420

🚗 **José Garrido** Avda Gorlero & Calle 32; ☏ 42 486800; e info@josegarrido.com; www.josegarrido.com

🚗 **Localiza** Apolo Shopping Center, Calle 29 (Las Gaviotas) & Avda Gorlero; ☏ 42 449489; www.localiza.com.uy

🚗 **Multicar** Apart-Hotel Punta del Este, Avda Gorlero 860 near Calle 28; ☏ 42 443143, 📱 9444 3868; www.redmulticar.com; ⊕ 09.00–19.00 Mon–Fri, 09.00–13.30 Sat

🚗 **Punta Car** Avda Artigas facing the bus terminal; ☏ 42 482112; www.puntacar.com.uy

🚗 **RentAutos** Calle 27 & Avda Gorlero; ☏ 42 446363/4; e rentautospunta@hotmail.com

🚗 **Thrifty** Paseo Ancal, Local 002, Avda Gorlero & Calle 30; ☏ 42 447462, 0800 8278; e puntadeleste@thrifty.com.uy; ⊕ 08.00–22.00

🚗 **Win Rentacar** Avda Roosevelt, parada 13½; ☏ 42 483004

By bike Bikes are available at many hotels and hostels, or they can be rented at Amalfi Sports (*Calle 24 & Calle 27*; ⊕ *10.00–13.00, 15.00–22.00 Mon–Sat*), DW Service (*Bvar Artigas & Chiverta*; ☏ *42 491749*, 📱 *9444 0812*; e *dwservice@ movinet.com.uy*; *www.dwservice.com.uy*), Rueda Cycles (*Avda Artigas & Lenzina*; ☏ *42 486732*) and Zap (*Calle 28 between Avda Gorlero & Calle 24*; ☏ *42 441899*). The main roads outside the peninsula often have parallel cycle tracks, but you'll need to pay attention to their idiosyncratic features.

DW Service offers bike tours of Punta (*summer 09.00 & 20.00 daily*). The best bike shop for buying bikes, parts or spares is probably Trek Punta del Este (*Avda Roosevelt & Londres*; ☏ *42 480906*; e *trekpunta@adinet.com.uy*; *www.trekpunta.com*; ⊕ *10.00–20.00 Mon–Sat, 15.00–20.00 Sun, winter closed Wed*).

Tourist information There are various tourist information offices. Those at the bus terminal (☏ *42 494042*), on Plaza Artigas (☏ *42 446510*) in the centre of the peninsula, at *parada* 24, Playa Mansa (☏ *42 230050*) and a temporary office at the port (☏ *42 448685*; ⊕ *summer only*) are run by the Municipio de Maldonado (☏ *42 220847*; e *dgturismo@maldonado.gub.uy*; *www.maldonado.gub.uy*) and are open 08.00–midnight in January and February. The Liga de Fomento business association has a helpful office just west of the terminal by the Playa Mansa (☏ *42 446519*; ⊕ *summer 08.00–22.00 daily*), which also offers internet access. The national Ministry of Tourism, Uruguay Natural, also has an office (*Gorlero 944 between calles 29 & 30*; ☏ *42 441218*; ⊕ *10.00–18.00, later in summer*). Useful websites include www.vivapunta.com and www.quehacemoshoy.com.uy (What Shall We Do Today?).

Local tours Reputable tour companies include the following.

Alvaro Gimeno bus terminal, Local 8; ↘ 42 490570; e gimeno@adinet.com.uy; www.alvarogimenoturismo.com
Jetmar Viajes Chalet Paicha, parada 21, Playa Mansa; ↘ 42 492222; www.jetmar.com.uy

Maldonado Turismo Galería Mejillón, Calle 32 (La Angostura) 641; ↘ 42 495504/5; e maldonado@maldonadoturismo.com; www.maldonadoturismo.com
Turismo Top Calle 29 (Las Gaviotas) & Avda Gorlero; ↘ 42 448373/7; e turismotop@adinet.com.uy

Where to stay There's no end of hotels in Punta del Este, of course, including some of the best and most expensive in Uruguay. They are all amazingly expensive in early January, merely expensive from then until Easter, and really quite affordable the rest of the year. All are open year-round unless indicated otherwise.

Villas To do things properly, you might consider renting your own villa by the week or month through a company such as Terramar (*Ruta 10 km161, La Barra;* ↘ *42 770707;* e *labarra@terramar.com.uy. Saíz Martínez, José Ignacio;* ↘ *44 862525;* e *joseignacio@terramar.com.uy;* $$$$$).

Hotels
Luxury

Aldilá (14 rooms) Rinconada Alta, Punta Ballena; ↘ 42 579202; e aldila@adinet.com.uy; http://posadaaldila.com. A small luxury lodge by one of the most prestigious beaches, each room has a terrace & sea views (& spectacular sunsets), antique-style furniture & carpets, hydro-massage showers & Wi-Fi. There's a gym & sauna, bicycles, lift, infinity pool with wet bar, indoor bar & restaurant, & business centre. It claims to be gay-friendly, but children under 12 are not accepted. $$$$$

AWA Pedragosa Sierra & San Ciro, parada 5; ↘ 42 499999; e reservas@awahotel.com; www.awahotel.com. A flashy new boutique hotel, 1.5km north of the bus terminal, this has microcinema, swimming pool, spa (e spa@awahotel.com) & bistro with wine cellar (↘ 4249 7777; e reservas@life-bistro.com; www.life-bistro.com) with live music Fri & Sat, & Mediterranean food such as sole in mustard with tabouleh, chicken risotto, rib-eye beef, ceviche & salads. $$$$$

Conrad Resort & Casino (296 rooms) Rambla Williman, parada 4; ↘ 42 491111; e conradpe@conrad.com.uy; www.conrad.com.uy. The huge casino parachuted in from Las Vegas to just north of the bus terminal (& operated by Vegas giant Harrah's) offers tasteless luxury in 296 rooms & 30 suites, all with terrace. $$$$$

La Capilla Viña del Mar & Valparaíso, San Rafael, parada 12, Playa Brava; ↘ 42 484059, free ↘ 0800 8101; e capilla@punta.com.uy; www.lacapilla.com.uy. One of Punta's more established celebrity boltholes, even though the Roma Amor Italian restaurant isn't world-class, rooms are not huge & there's Wi-Fi only in the lobby. The gardens, however, are big, with a sizeable outdoor pool. The bars & *salón de té* are open 24hrs in summer. $$$$$

Las Cumbres Ruta 12 km3.9, Las Cumbres de La Ballena; ↘ 42 578689; e hotel@cumbres.com.uy; www.cumbres.com.uy; ⊕ Jun–Apr. Calling itself a Hotel-Art & Spa, this is fairly handy for the airport (across the Laguna del Sauce) but 4km from the nearest beach, which seems to suit many of the rich & famous. Nevertheless it promises sea views, thanks to the winding road that brings you to the *cumbre* (summit). Beautifully designed & fitted-out, & frequently voted one of the best hotels in South America, it's a wonderful place to relax, with just 28 rooms. $$$$$

L'Auberge Avda del Agua & Carnoustie, Parque del Golf, parada 19, Playa Brava; ↘ 42 482601; e lauberge@laubergehotel.com; www.laubergehotel.com; ⊕ Dec–Mar, rest of year Sat only. Around a fortress-like water tower, built in 1947, with a legendary tea room that serves truly decadent waffles with *dulce de leche*, honey or jam (Punta's high society still gathers here from 17.00), this is a elegant 5-star hotel, with rooms in the tower itself added in 1981. $$$$$

Serena Rambla Williman, parada 24, Las Delicias; ↘ 42 233441; e serenahotel@adinet.com.uy; www.serenahotel.com.uy. Uniquely, this modern hotel is on the seaward side of the *rambla*, & has full beach service as well as a pool (with bar). With its all-white décor, it feels more like José Ignacio than Punta del Este. But it has to be said that it is

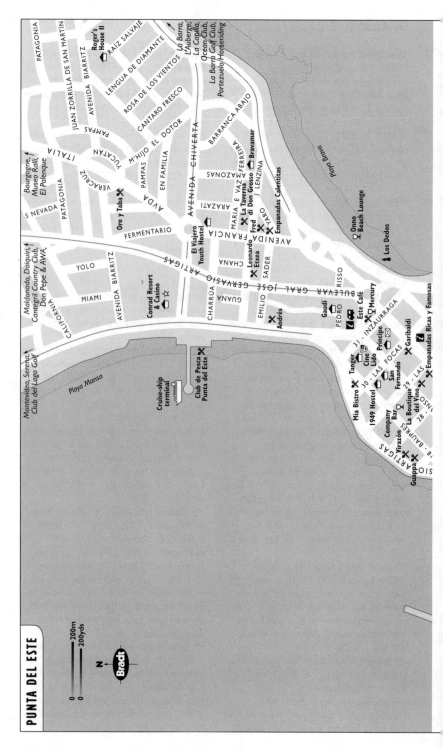

PUNTA DEL ESTE

0   200m
0   200yds

Bradt

N

Montevideo, Serena;
Club del Logo Golf

Bourgogne, ▲
Museo Ralli;
El Palenque

Maldonado, Daiquiri; ▲
Cantegril Country Club,
Don Pepe & AWA,

PATAGONIA

JUAN ZORRILLA DE SAN MARTÍN

AVENIDA BIARRITZ

LENGUA DE DIAMANTE

RAÍZ SALVAJE

Roger's
House II

La Barra,
L'Auberge,
La Capilla,
Ocean Club,
La Barra Golf Club,
Portezuelo Horseriding

ROSA DE LOS VIENTOS

CÁNTARO FRESCO

ITALIA

PAMPAS

YUCATÁN

M'HIJO EL DOTOR

EN FAMILIA

PATAGONIA

VERACRUZ

Oro y Taba

AVDA.

AVENIDA CHIVERTA

BARRANCA ABAJO

S NEVADA

FERMENTARIO

ARRAZATI

MARÍA E VAZ FERREIRA

La Taverna
di Don Grosso

Bravamar

CALIFORNIA

YOLO

MIAMI

AVENIDA BIARRITZ

Conrad Resort
& Casino

CHARRÚA

GUANÁ

JOSÉ GERVASIO ARTIGAS

CHANÁ

EMILIO

SADER

El Viajero
Youth Hostel

FRANCIA

AMAZONAS

YARO

Fred
Leonardo ✕ Etxea

J LENZINA

Empanadas Calentitas

Playa Brava

Cruise-ship
terminal

Playa Mansa

Club de Pesca
Punta del Este

Andrés

Gaudí

PEDRO

BULEVAR

RISSO

Este Café
Mercury

INZAURRAGA

Onno
Beach Lounge

Los Dedos

Mia Bistro

Tánger

Cine
Lido

30 - LAS FOCAS

1949 Hostel

San
Fernando

Príncipe

31 -

Garibaldi

Company
Bar

Virazón

La Boutique
del Vino

29 - LAS

Empanadas Ricas y Famosas

ARTIGAS

18 - BAUPRÉS

28 -

Guappa

188

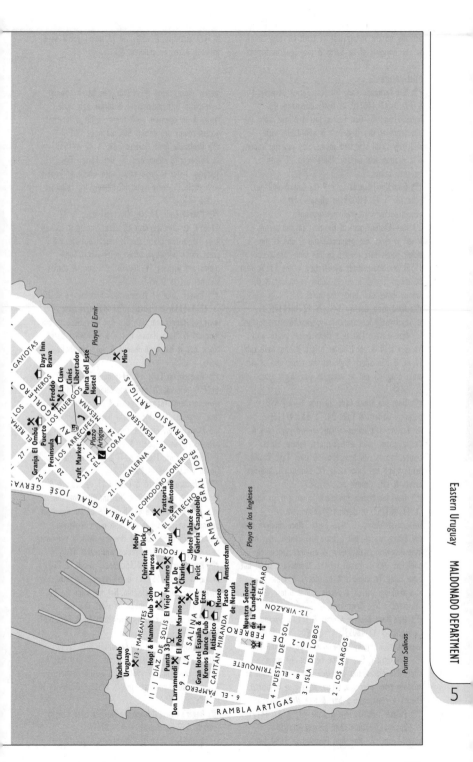

Playa El Emir

LOS GAVIOTAS

Days Inn
Brava

Miró

LOS REMEROS

LOS GORLERO

Freddo
La Clave

Cinés
Libertador

Punta del Este
Hostel

AV. GORLERO

LOS MUERGOS

MESANA

25 - EL REMANSO

Granja El Ombú
Puerto
Península

LOS ARRECIFES

Plaza
Artigas

GRAL JOSÉ GERVASIO ARTIGAS

20

Craft Market

22

23 - EL CORAL

24

26 - PESALSERO

RAMBLA GRAL JOSÉ GERVASIO

21 - LA GALERNA

19 - COMODORO GORLERO

Trattoría
da Antonio

EL ESTRECHO

RAMBLA GRAL JOSÉ

Hotel Palace &
Galería Casapueblo

Azul

Playa de los Ingleses

Moby
Dick

Chivitería
Marcos

El Viejo Marinero

FOQUE

14 - EL

17

Lo De
Charlie

Petit
Amsterdam

Museo
Paseo
de Neruda

Yacht Club
Uruguayo

13

MAREANTES

Hop! & Mamba Club Soho

11 - J. DIAZ DE SOLÍS

Punta 33

Don Larramendi

El Pobre Marino

Gure-
Etxe

Gran Hotel España &
Kronos Dance Club

Atlántico

CAPITÁN MIRANDA

Nuestra Señora
de la Candelaria

5 - EL FARO

12 - VIRAZÓN

FEBRERO

9 - LA SALINA

10 - 2

8 - ELSOL

4 - PUESTA DEL SOL

3 - ISLA DE LOBOS

2 - LOS SARGOS

7 - EL PAMPERO

6 - EL TRINQUETE

RAMBLA ARTIGAS

Punta Salinas

189

actually on the wrong side of town for easy access to the hotspots of La Barra & José Ignacio. Service is very attentive, & with just 32 rooms you'll need to book early; no children. $$$$$

Mid-range

⌂ **San Fernando** Calle 30 (Las Focas) between 18 & 20; ⏳ 42 440720; e hotelsanfernando@ hotmail.com; ⏲ Oct–Easter. Just 3 blocks from the bus terminal, this is decent & affordable, with relatively small standard rooms plus superior rooms, & a rooftop sun terrace. There's one PC with internet access. $$$$$–$$$$

⌂ **Gran Hotel España** Calle 9 (La Salina) 660 near Calle 10; ⏳ 42 440228; e ghespana@ adinet.com.uy; www.granhotelespana.net; ⏲ Nov–Easter. South of the port (as far as the buses go down the peninsula), this is one of the oldest hotels here (owned by the same family since 1959), but substantially modernised in the 1980s, with AC rooms. There's a decent public restaurant, & the Kronos dance club below the hotel. $$$$$–$$$

⌂ **Azul** Avda Gorlero 540; ⏳ 42 441117; e reservas@hotelazul.com.uy; www.hotelazul.com.uy; ⏲ Nov–Easter. This is a clean bright place with friendly staff & good buffet b/fast. Rooms have cable TV, AC & hair-driers. Right at the south end of the main drag, it's not as noisy as you might fear. $$$$

⌂ **Days Inn Brava** Calle 28 (Los Meros) 590, between Gorlero & Calle 24; ⏳ 42 447116; e daysbrava@adinet.com.uy; www.daysinn.com. A decent chain hotel, with business centre, fitness centre, indoor swimming pool & Days Café. Rooms aren't huge but have cable TV, hair driers, internet access & safe deposit box. $$$$

⌂ **Days Inn Mansa** Rambla Williman s/n, parada 3; ⏳ 42 484353; e daysinn@adinet.com.uy; www.daysinn.com; ⏲ Nov–Easter. More modern than the Brava branch, but a little less central, this has a fitness centre, small indoor & outdoor swimming pools, as well as beach service. Rooms are small but have cable TV, minibar & hairdriers, & some are non-smoking. There's a decent buffet b/fast, & you can have a free newspaper. $$$$

⌂ **Don Pepe** Bulevar Artigas & Scasso, parada 14, Cantegril; ⏳ 42 480535; e info@ hoteldonpepe.com.uy; www.hoteldonpepe.com.uy; ⏲ Nov–Easter. One of the best of the more affordable places, this has spacious gardens with an outdoor pool, plus spa, sauna, aqua-gym & jacuzzi. There's a restaurant & bar, & free Wi-Fi. $$$$

⌂ **Palace** Avda Gorlero & Calle 11; ⏳ 42 441919; e jdlpunta@hotmail.com, palacepunta@ hotmail.com; ⏲ Nov–Apr. Founded in 1890 but largely dating from the 1940s, this has a colonial-style patio with palm trees & surprisingly wide lawns & an open-air pool. There's a lift & internet access; rooms are decent but not huge. $$$$

⌂ **Peninsula** Avda Gorlero 761; ⏳ 42 441533; e hotpenin@yahoo.com; ⏲ Oct–Easter. This 3-storey 3-star is good value, with simple AC rooms with cable TV; there's one PC offering free internet access. $$$$

⌂ **Puerto** Calle 27 (Los Muergos) 626; ⏳ 42 444692; e olmosgervasio@adinet.com.uy. A friendly little family-run place, this is simple but clean & great value (although b/fast costs extra). Some rooms are without TV, but all have fans, & there's internet access & Wi-Fi. $$$$

⌂ **Tanger** Calle 31 (Inzaurraga) between 18 & 20; ⏳ 42 441333; e contacto@hoteltanger.com; www.hoteltanger.com; ⏲ Oct–Apr. Very close to bus terminal & Playa Mansa, this is a somewhat dated block, but it has both indoor & open-air rooftop pools. $$$$

⌂ **Amsterdam** Calle 14 (El Foque) 759; ⏳ 42 444170; reservas@hotelamsterdampunta.com; www.hotelamsterdampunta.com. A reasonably modern (but somewhat coach-partyish) hotel with views over the Playa de los Ingleses, this has both open-air & covered swimming pools & sauna with gym, as well as bikes to rent. There's Wi-Fi & a PC in the lobby. Closed for a week in May. $$$

⌂ **Atlántico** Calle 10 & Calle 7 (2 de Febrero & Miranda); ⏳ 42 440229; e hatlanti@adinet.com.uy. Just a block from the lighthouse (& as far down the peninsula as buses go), this is a quiet & decent 3-star that's open most of the year, with a swimming pool & apts as well as rooms with cable TV. $$$

⌂ **Bravamar** Lenzina & Amazonas, parada 2, Playa Brava; ⏳ 42 480559; e hotelbravamar@gmail.com; www.hotelespuntadeleste.com. Not far from the bus terminal (but on the mainland side), this has affordable pleasant rooms with both AC & fans, Wi-Fi & cable TV. $$$

⌂ **Principe** Calle 20 (El Remanso) 938; ⏳ 42 440351; e smap65@hotmail.com; ⏲ Oct–May. A modern block in the 1960s, this is still comfortable & fair value. Rooms are simple & clean & service is friendly. $$$

⌂ **Roger's House II** Juana de América near Biarritz (parada 6, Playa Brava); ⏳ 42 482696; e rogerhouseuruguay@hotmail.com. A guesthouse that attracts surfers & backpackers, this is a comfortable suburban house with bunks in 6 mixed dorms, shared kitchen, barbecue & bar at the bottom of the garden. Surfing lessons can be arranged. $$$

Budget Almost all the hotels on the peninsula have three stars; there are just two with two stars – both, fortunately, very decent little places. There are more cheap hotels in Maldonado (see page 204).

🏠 **Gaudi** Pedro Risso s/n; 🖂 42 494116; e info@hotelgaudi.com.uy; www.hotelgaudi.com.uy. A friendly place next to the bus terminal. Ideal for late arrivals & early departures. 1st floor rooms have AC, 2nd floor rooms do not; all have cable TV. There's a PC for internet access plus Wi-Fi. $$$$$–$$$

🏠 **Petit** Calle 9 (La Salina) 717; 🖂 42 441412. At intersection of Calle 10 & 2 de Febrero, , in a quiet area 2 blocks from the lighthouse, this is a classic mid-20th-century house with lawns & swimming pool, decently modernised with Wi-Fi & AC. $$$

Hostels There are three backpackers' hostels in Punta del Este, as well as others in Maldonado (see page 204), La Barra (see page 209) and Manantiales (see page 209).

🏠 **Punta del Este Hostel** Los Arrecifes (Calle 25) 544; 🖂 42 441632; e puntadelestehostel@ hotmail.com; www.puntadeleste hostel.com; ⊕ Dec–Apr; b'fast 09.00–11.00. Just off Plaza Artigas, Punta del Este's official HI hostel is a once-pleasant villa converted into a cramped hostel, with mixed & single-sex dorms, lockers, very few electric sockets, & broken-down bikes. There's free internet access with two PCs & Wi-Fi, as well as TV & a DVD player, a kitchen & board games. $$
🏠 **1949 Hostel** Corner Las Focas & Baupres (calles 30 & 18); 🖂 42 440719; e info@hostel1949.com; www.1949hostel.com. Just 3 blocks from the terminal, this is cramped & lively – sleep is not guaranteed. Kitchen, bar, lockers & 30mins free internet (or unlimited but slow Wi-Fi) are included. $$
🏠 **El Viajero Brava Beach Hostel** 🖂 42 480331; e info@elviajerobravabeach.com; www.elviajerobravabeach.com. Opened in late 2009 by the successful El Viajero chain, this is 3 blocks from the terminal & has dorms & private rooms plus internet, & surfboard & bike rental. $$

Camping There are campsites within reach, none particularly close to the centre of Punta del Este. Two are on the Punta side of the bridge at La Barra: **Camping La Barra** (*Camino Saravia & Batlle, El Placer;* 🖂 42 489279, 42 441533; $) and **Camping San Rafael** (*1km west on Camino Saravia, a short walk north from parada 29;* 🖂 42 486715; *www.campingsanrafael.com.uy;* ⊕ *Nov–15 Mar; US$16 for 2 with tent, 4-person cabañas with private bathroom US$50–65;* $). West of Punta del Este are two more: **Camping Internacional Punta Ballena** (*Camino Lussich km2, Portezuelo;* 🖂 42 578902, 42 578978; e *campunta@adinet.com.uy;* *www.campinginternacionalpuntaballena.com;* ⊕ *Nov–Easter; US$6–8/p tent, motorhome US$6.50–8.70, cabañas from US$48–59 for 4 people to US$60–76/8 for 8 people;* $) and **Camping Cardenal Azul** (*Ruta Interbalnearia km117.5, Sauce de Portezuelo;* 🖂 42 578178; $).

✘ **Where to eat** Fish is the thing here, especially *brótola* (Brazilian codling), which you'll find on many menus. The reliable **La Pasiva** chain, serving excellent *chivitos* (steak sandwiches), is here too. There are also many *paradores* (beachside diners), which are local institutions, especially for sunset drinks and snacks.

✘ **Bourgogne** Avda del Mar & Pedragosa Sierra, La Brava & El Bosque (on border of El Bosque & Brava beach zones); 🖂 42 482007; e bourgogn@ adinet.com.uy. An elegant French restaurant that also serves superb beef in classic Uruguayan style; some consider this the best restaurant in South America. It's also one of the most expensive. $$$$$

✘ **Club de Pesca Punta del Este** Parada 3, Playa Mansa; 🖂 42 485060; ⊕ all year. Between the Conrad & the cruise jetty, this serves the best fish in town (try the merluza), as well as snacks, sandwiches, salads, omelettes, steaks, & pastas with a good range of sauce options. The waterside deck more than compensates for the plastic furniture. $$$$$

✗ **El Viejo Marinero** Calle 11 (Solís) 739 between calles 12 & 14; ☎ 42 443565; e elviejomarinero@hotmail.com; ⏰ summer daily for lunch & dinner; rest of the year w/ends only. Run for 25 years by the Marrero family, this friendly, unstuffy place serves the Uruguayan Riviera's best paella & grilled fish (such as *corvina* & *brótola*), as well as fine *mejillones a la provenzal* (Provençal mussels) & *chipirones a la plancha* (small squid). $$$$$

✗ **Fred** Avda Francia & J Lenzina, parada 2; ☎ 42 499347; www.fred.com.uy; ⏰ summer lunch from 12.00, dinner from 21.00 daily, rest of year lunch from 12.00 w/ends & holidays, dinner from 21.00 Fri–Sat. A new restaurant with a Norwegian chef, offering a unique fusion cuisine, including a tasting menu of 6 small but complex dishes (allow plenty of time for this). It's expensive but well worth it. Service is excellent, though the black-&-white décor is not to all tastes. $$$$$

✗ **Gure-Etxe** Calles 9 & 12; ☎ 42 446858, 42 447233/35. A nice uncomplicated place specialising in Basque fish & shellfish dishes, as well as steaks & omelettes. $$$$$

✗ **Lo de Charlie** Calle 12 (Virazón) 819 between calles 9 & 11; ☎ 42 444183; ⏰ summer lunch & dinner Wed–Mon, rest of the year Thu–Sun. One of Punta's most renowned (& priciest) restaurants, Charlie's Place is a little bistro with an open kitchen. It's in a small house where you can eat on the front veranda or indoors in a room brightly decorated by Carlos Páez Vilaró. It specialises in Mediterranean food, especially seafood, such as paella, sautéed *chipirones* (small squid), fish such as *brótola* with polenta or stingray with a saffron sauce, as well as ravioli & other pastas, with good desserts such as tiramisu to follow. $$$$$

✗ **Andrés** Parada 1, Playa Mansa; ☎ 42 481804; ⏰ Dec–Feb daily lunch & dinner; Mar–Nov Sat–Sun lunch, Thu–Sat dinner. On the waterfront terrace, excellent steaks & grilled meats, fish & soufflés are served at very reasonable prices. $$$$

✗ **Don Larramendi** Calle 8 between calles 9 & 11; ☎ 42 448037; ⏰ summer daily, rest of the year Thu–Sun. A very unpretentious & affordable but excellent Basque restaurant that specialises in fish & seafood, especially *brótola*, *cazuela* (fish stew), *kokotxas* (hake throat) & *chipirones* (small squid). You'll probably want to sit on the terrace, but the interior is also attractive, & the service is excellent. $$$$

✗ **El Palenque** Avda Roosevelt, parada 6; ☎ 42 494257/60; e puntadeleste@elpalenque.com.uy. Facing the Punta Shopping mall, this is an offshoot of the *parrilla* restaurant in Montevideo's Mercado del Puerto, & is reputed to serve the best red meat in town. It also serves fish & seafood, inc *paella especial* with chicken, goat & rabbit. It's big, noisy & a bit pricey. $$$$

✗ **Garibaldi** Gorlero & Calle 30; ☎ 42 447714, m 9957 1418; e garibaldi@adinet.com.uy; ⏰ summer only, 08.00–02.00 daily. Unashamedly for tourists who want to see & be seen on the main drag, a decent & affordable Italian place, serving good lasagne, gnocchi & potato ravioli with bacon, as well as b/fast. $$$$

✗ **Guappa** Rambla Artigas between calles 27 & 28; ☎ 42 440951; ⏰ 09.00–02.00 daily. With an AC restaurant on the inland side of the *rambla* & a terrace on the other side looking out to Isla Gorriti, this is not a gourmet restaurant but delivers good food, eg: pasta with seafood, *kassler* (pork chops smoked, then grilled), salads, as well as the usual meats, fish & *chivitos*, coffees & snacks. You pay for the setting, but it's not excessive. $$$$

✗ **Hop!** Rambla Artigas between calles 10 & 12; ☎ 42 446061; ⏰ summer only. In the strip of trendy bars by the port, this is not a gourmet place but serves decent food in a lively atmosphere, including sushi, seafood lasagne & chicken with rice & mushrooms, with a fair choice of pizzas & wines. Also houses Mambo Club (see page 194). $$$$

✗ **La Boutique del Vino** (LBDV) Calle 29 (Las Gaviotas) between Gorlero & Calle 20; ☎ 42 447929; www.boutiquedelvino.com. A very stylish new wine & tapas bar, offshoot of a successful Buenos Aires establishment. $$$$

✗ **La Clave** Calle 27 between Gorlero & Calle 24; ☎ 42 448518; www.laclaverestaurant.com; ⏰ all year. With a relatively limited menu of steak & *milanesa*, fish of the day, seafood risotto, seafood omelette, pizzas & *chivitos*, this is more focused on music, with live jazz or tango on Fri, Sat & Sun evenings. $$$$

✗ **Leonardo Etxea** Lenzina just east of Avda Artigas, parada 2, Playa Brava; ☎ 42 493723; ⏰ 12.00–16.00, 20.00–01.00 daily. 'Leonardo's House' is a traditional Basque restaurant, in a quiet location just north of the bus terminal. Seafood is the speciality, of course, with pastas as an alternative. $$$$

✗ **Mia Bistro** Calle 18 (Baupres) between calles 30 & 31; ☎ 42 449240; ⏰ summer 09.00–14.00 daily, winter Wed–Sat & holidays. Near the Playa Mansa & the bus terminal, this is a stylish place for lunchtime wraps with an Asian flavour, *chivitos* & sushi. $$$$

✗ **Oro y Taba** Avda Italia facing Plaza Mexico, parada 3½; ☎ 42 495789/90. An upmarket *parrilla*

left   Enjoy long lazy lunchtimes, Colonia (JH/Corbis)

below   Tile-work street-sign, Colonia (DLO/Corbis)

bottom   Colonia is Uruguay's oldest town and its *Barrio Histórico* boasts superb single-storey 18th-century cottages (B/Dreamstime) page 252

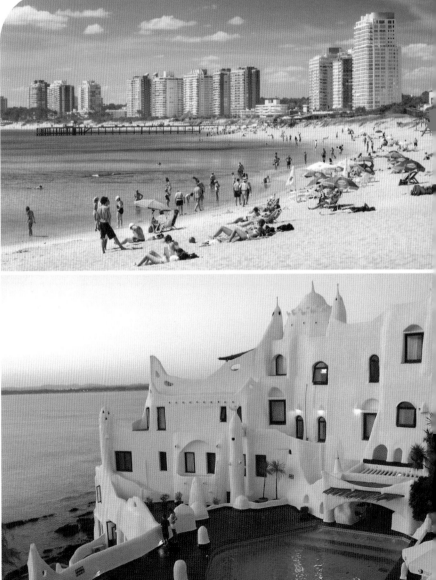

Uruguay is home to more cattle than men, so *gauchos* (ranchers) and their traditions are thriving (YD/Alamy) page 39

top **Grey brocket deer**
(J&CS/FLPA) page 7

above **Paca are nocturnal
and good swimmers**
(FL/FLPA) page 8

right **Capybara – the world's
largest rodent** (ML/FLPA)
page 7

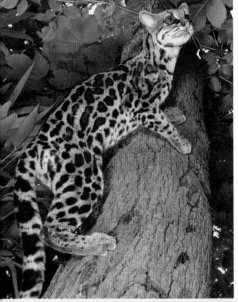

above   Crab-eating fox: they do, in fact, eat crabs, as well as lizards (J&CS/FLPA) page 7

left   The margay is a solitary, nocturnal cat native to Central and South America (TW/FLPA) page 7

below   The saliva of the vampire bat contains anticoagulants which stop the host's blood clotting, thereby allowing the bat to feed longer (M&PF/MP/FLPA) page 8 top right   Spotted tinamou are incredibly common in pasture land (NB/FLPA) page 10

above   Turkey vultures are gregarious and roost in large groups (PL/FLPA) page 10

right   Greater rheas look very similar to ostriches (KW/MP/FLPA) page 10

below right   The ovenbird, or *hornero*, is named after the rounded mud nests it builds in trees and on fence posts (J&CS/FLPA) page 10

below   The southern lapwing is Uruguay's national bird (NB/FLPA) page 10 *above* Southern right whales are most easily recognised by the callosities on their heads (HM/MP/FLPA) page 10

left Elephant seals are so-named after the males' proboscis (SE/MP/FLPA) page 9

below The sperm whale has the largest brain of any animal (FN/MP/FLPA) page 9 (also serving seafood), not very different to the nearby El Palenque but rather cheaper. **$$$$**

✗ **Virazón** Rambla Artigas & Calle 28 (Los Meros); ☎ 42 443924; www.virazon.com.uy; ⏰ daily. With a terrace by the Playa Mansa just north of the port, this is a great place for fish, including good sushi & sashimi (mostly in 5-person servings); also late b/fast, coffees, salads & excellent *chivitos*. **$$$$**

✗ **Yacht Club Uruguayo** Rambla Artigas & Calle 8; ☎ 42 441056; e yacht@adinet.com.uy; ⏰ 11.00–16.00 & from 20.00 daily. Not to be confused with the Yacht Club de Punta del Este, in the port, this is a local institution, run by the Idiarte family for 15 years. The fish is good, especially the paella, but salads are unexciting; prices are fair for the quality & location. **$$$$**

✗ **Chivitería Marcos** Rambla Artigas between calles 12 & 14; ☎ 42 449932. The best place in town for Chile's national snack, with added beachfront views. **$$$**

✗ **El Pobre Marino** Calle 12 (Virazón) near Calle 11 (Solís); ☎ 42 443306; ⏰ till 01.00+. This *rotisería-marisquería*, serving fish, seafood, grilled meats & pastas, is far less trendy & overpriced than those by the port immediately to the north, & has friendly, relaxed service. Take-aways available. **$$$**

✗ **Granja El Ombú** Calle 27 (Los Muergos) 626; ☎ 42 444692; e olmosgervasio@adinet.com.uy. An unpretentious & very affordable *parrilla*, serving the usual grilled meats as well as fish (eg *brótola*) & spinach crêpes. **$$$**

✗ **La Taverna di Don Grosso** Lenzina 443 near Avda Francia, parada 2, Playa Brava; ☎ 42 496851; www.tavernagrosso.com; ⏰ 12.30–16.00 & from 20.30 daily. An authentic trattoria that may serve the best pasta in Punta, although the kitchen seems to be a bit erratic. Seafood pastas are a speciality, & there's also fish, shellfish & pizzas, as well as

good tiramisu. Rather cheesy live music Wed in summer. Not expensive. **$$$**

✗ **Miró** Rambla Artigas & Calle 27, Playa El Emir; ☎ 42 449380; www.mirorestobar.com.uy; ⏰ from 10.00 daily. A lively Resto–Music–Bar serving b/fast, sandwiches, the usual pizza, pasta, fish & steak, plus stir-fries & sushi, all at reasonable prices. Big screens show music & pop videos (not too loud) during the day & after midnight there's dancing to 'pop-house', disco, Latino hits & oldies. **$$$**

✗ **Trattoria da Antonio** Gorlero 572 between calles 17 & 19; ☎ 42 449770; ⏰ all year. Relatively cheap & cheerful for the location, this is a very Italian place, with good cannelloni with meat or vegetarian filling, other pastas, gnocchi, fish, & pizza & *faina* from a wood-fired oven; deliveries available. **$$$**

✗ **Daiquiri** Rambla Williman, parada 19, Playa Mansa; ☎ 42 226451. One of the best beachside *paradores*, which rather strangely specialises in fondue. **$$**

✗ **Este Café** Calle 31 (Inzaurraga) & Angostura; ⏰ all day (in season only). Just southwest of the bus terminal, this is a stylish café with excellent sandwiches, cakes, muffins, coffees, juices & shakes, & Wi-Fi. **$$**

✗ **Freddo** Gorlero & Calle 27; also Calle 20 between 29 & 30; ⏰ summer only. An Argentine chain selling the best ice cream in town; long queues all evening. **$$**

✗ **Empanadas Calentitas** Avda Francia between Lenzina & Yaro, parada 2, Playa Brava; ☎ 42 482567; ⏰ all year. Excellent *empanadas* for food on the run. **$**

✗ **Empanadas Ricas y Famosas** Calle 29 (Las Gaviotas) between Avda Gorlero & Calle 20; ☎ 42 447599; & Pedragosa Sierra & San Francisco, parada 5, Playa Mansa; ☎ 42 494066; ⏰ 10.00–02.00 daily. Founded as a grocery in 1946, this is now famous for its 26 varieties of excellent *empanadas*; you can also call for free deliveries. **$**

Entertainment and nightlife The bars and nightclubs of Punta del Este set the musical fashions of the season for Brazil and Argentina as well as Uruguay, and CDs are in great demand. The epicentre is La Barra (see page 210), with famed venues such as Buddha Bar and Tequila; you can get there by bus or taxi, but it's also quick and easy for girls in particular to hitch a ride – being Uruguay, there's no great risk.

Note that in January people (Argentines in particular) have a nap when it gets dark and eat around midnight. Bars and clubs only get really lively around 04.00, and it'll be broad daylight when many people head home. By March things are much quieter, with little happening except at weekends (although Easter is again a lively time).

One key element in Punta's revival was the 1997 opening of the **Conrad Resort and Casino** (see *Where to stay*), largely to cater for Brazilians, who are unable to gamble at home. A huge chunk of Las Vegas has been parachuted in to Punta; you expect to see Elvis impersonators, Céline Dion and Californian college kids, or perhaps a software developers' convention. Being Uruguay, however, you get the Copacabana Show (*US$15*), the Conrad Dolls shaking it all about, Julio or Enrique Iglesias, fashion shows and book readings. In fact, from April to December the Conrad provides locals with a remarkable range of cultural events (and decent restaurants) when the town is otherwise dead. There's a mural by Carlos Páez Vilaró at the top of the escalators from the southern entry.

There's also the Casino Nogaro (*Avda Gorlero & Calle 31;* ❧ *42 441918*), a more straightforward wallet-emptying operation, with 200 slot machines, three blackjack tables, four Punto Banco tables and six roulette tables.

♀ **Company Bar** Calle 29 (Las Gaviotas) between calles 18 & 20; ❧ 42 440130; e companybar@ netgate.com.uy; ⊕ summer daily from brunch time (serving pasta, fish, meat & snacks), rest of the year from midnight Fri–Sat. There's live music here daily in summer, plus Wi-Fi & a smokers' terrace.

♀ **Kronos Dance Club** Edificio España, below the Gran Hotel España, calles 9 (La Salina) & 10 (2 de Febrero); m 9915 4529; e kronosdance@ hotmail.com; www.kronosdance.com

♀ **Mercury** Gorlero 1045 & Calle 31; ⊕ nightly, but only really lively at w/ends. A small gay dance bar. Staff & clientele are friendly, but there are some men there who'll cost more than the price of a drink.

♀ **Moby Dick** Rambla Artigas; ❧ 42 441240. One of the longer-lasting bars on the jumping strip of the *rambla* by the port.

♀ **Ocean Club** Barrio San Rafael, parada 12, Playa Brava; ❧ 42 484869; www.oceanclub.com.uy. In a modern 1-storey bldg, a series of large rooms with teak floors & large chandeliers serve as one of the hottest upmarket dance clubs of the moment. There are themed (ie: sponsored) events with top DJs

throughout the summer, & the beachside patio hosts afternoon lounge sessions.

♀ **Onno Beach Lounge** parada 1, Playa Brava; ❧ 42 497289 Just north of the Hand in the Sand (see *What to see*), this is a restaurant–pub with Wi-Fi, serving the usual range of fish & steaks, then turning up the salsa from 23.00.

♀ **Mambo Club** Rambla Artigas between calles 10 & 12; ❧ 42 448956. Well-established nightclub with dinner shows (*nightly Jan & Feb*) with live music & dancers; also hosts events such as Miss Universe Uruguay. Food & service are acceptable, drinks very overpriced. Also houses Hop! (see page 192).

♀ **Punta 33** Calle 11 (Solís) between calles 8 & 10; ❧ 42 447719. An offshoot of a bar in Paraty (the Brazilian equivalent of Colonia), this is a new bar-restaurant just south of the port, in an older house with palms in the garden. In summer there are live bands, mostly playing covers & Brazilian hits, & a dance floor that's packed until dawn.

♀ **Soho** Rambla Artigas; ❧ 42 447315; http://sohopuntadeleste.com. At the port, this is a long-established dance bar that also serves good food (especially fish) & cocktails.

Entertainment There are two cinemas in downtown Punta del Este: the five-screen **Cines Lido** (*Calle 20 & El Remanso & Calle 31;* ❧ *42 440911*) and **Ciné Libertador** (*Avda Gorlero & Calle 25, on north side of Plaza Artigas;* ❧ *42 444437*), both open only Friday to Sunday out of season. There's also the Hoyts multiplex (❧ *42 492196;* ⊕ *all year*) in the Punta Shopping mall.

The Orquesta Municipal de Maldonado performs open-air evening concerts in many locations in January and February. There's always plenty going on at the Conrad Resort and Casino (*www.conrad.com.uy*), and other venues include the Teatro Sala Cantegril (*Avda Roosevelt, parada 16;* ❧ *42 223211*), Teatro de la Galería Sagasti (*in casino at Avda Gorlero & Calle 31;* ❧ *42 444111*) and Arcobaleno Convention Centre (*Parada 16, Playa Mansa;* ❧ *42 224822*).

Events At weekends in January in particular there's a constant succession of glitzy events in Punta del Este, including Harley Davidson motorcycle rallies, sailing regattas and motor racing (which closes part of the Playa Brava *rambla*). The Punta del Este International Jazz Festival (*www.festival.com.uy*) takes place in mid-January, a big carnival parade usually in late February and the Festival Internacional de Cine de Punta del Este film festival in mid-April. There's also the Creamfields electronic music festival on the second Saturday of January, at Parque El Jagüel

(Avda Saravia, near the campsites west of the La Barra bridge). The free Punta Rock festival takes place at the same place on the first weekend of March. The Que Hacemos Hoy (What Shall We Do Today?) website (*www.quehacemoshoy.com.uy*) is a good source of further information.

Shopping There's a surprising variety of designer stores on Calle 20 (El Remanso) and the intersecting Calle 29 (Las Gaviotas), including Louis Vuitton, Tommy Hilfiger, Gap and Banana Republic. **Magma** (*Calle 20 between calles 27 & 28;* ❧ *42 441273*) sells Argentine clothing lines such as Jazmín Chebar, Rhapsodía and María Vásquez. There's also the self-described 'Design District' on Avenida Italia, including a Versace outlet. For crafty souvenirs and the authentic beach boho-chic look, it's better to look at street markets such as the one on Plaza Artigas, or boutiques in La Barra.

For upmarket craftwork, go to **HechoAca** (*Galeria Comercial, Hotel Conrad;* ❧ *42 486168*) or **Manos del Uruguay** (*Punta Shopping, midway between Punta and Maldonado;* ❧ *42 495822*). You can buy work by Carlos Páez Vilaró at his Galería Casapueblo (*Solís 720, under the Hotel Palace*) – not just his original (and expensive) paintings but also prints, ceramics and a big book in English and Spanish on Casapueblo. Otherwise the best place for art is La Barra, where there are many galleries (see page 211).

An Uruguayan speciality is amethyst and agate, from the northern border region; the place to buy this is **Van Der Brüin** (*at the junction of calles 20 & 27;* ❧ *42 443434;* **e** *bdv@gmail.com; www.vanderbruin.com.uy*).

Punta Shopping (*Avda Roosevelt, parada 7, east of Bvar Artigas, between Punta del Este & Maldonado; www.puntashopping.com.uy*), near the Cantegril country club, is a rather futurist mall, designed by Carlos Ott, with shops (⊕ *10.00–23.00 daily, until midnight Fri–Sat*), a Tienda Inglesa supermarket (⊕ *08.00–24.00*), a *plaza de comidas* or food court (⊕ *10.00–24.00*) and the Hoyts multiplex cinema (see opposite).

Other supermarkets include **Devoto** (*Avda Roosevelt, parada 11, Barrio Cantegril*), Disco (*Avda Gorlero & Calle 17; Avda Italia, parada 5 & Pedregosa Sierra*), El Dorado (*Calle 9/La Salina & Calle 12; Gorlero 630 & Calle 29/Gaviotas*).

For good Uruguayan wines, try **La Boutique del Vino** (see *Where to eat*) or Grand Cru (*Torre Amadeus, Avda Roosevelt, parada 7;* ❧ *42 498980; www.grandcru.com.uy*).

There's a surprising number of bookshops along Gorlero (clearly not all the bodies lying on the beaches have switched their brains off), notably Libros Libros (*just south of Calle 29/Las Gaviotas*). There's also **Mundo Mac** (*Gorlero 996;* ❧ *42 448255*), if you need a new iPod, by the casino.

Other practicalities

Banks In summer banks are all open around 15.00–20.00, with more normal hours the rest of the year. There are plenty of ATMs, especially along Gorlero.

$ **ABN Amro** Avda Gorlero 907; ❧ 42 444050; Avda Roosevelt, parada 11; ❧ 42 491650

$ **American Express** c/o Turisport, Edificio Torre Verona, Avda Gorlero & Calle 21; ❧ 42 445500; **e** turisport@turisport.com.uy; ⊕ 11.00–17.30 Mon–Fri

$ **BBVA** Avda Gorlero 630 between calles 19 & 21; ❧ 42 444060, 42 443553

$ **BROU** Avda Gorlero & Calle 25; ❧ 42 441802, 42 441930

$ **Citibank** Avda Gorlero & Calle 21; ❧ 42 444841

$ **Credit Uruguay** Avda Gorlero & Calle 25; ❧ 42 448044/6/7

$ **HSBC** Avda Gorlero & Calle 28; ❧ 42 444773/4

$ **Itaú** Avda Gorlero 644; ❧ 42 445556, 42 446298

$ **Nuevo Banco Comercial** Avda Gorlero 705; ❧ 42 441801/4; Avda Roosevelt, parada 14, Local 8–9; ❧ 42 488412

$ **Republic National Bank of New York** Avda Gorlero & Calle 28; ❧ 42 444770/2

$ **Santander** Avda Roosevelt, parada 16; ❧ 42 491887/8

Exchange offices

$ Aeromar Edificio Santos Dumont, Avda Gorlero 965 between calles 30 & 31; ↘ 42 443440; ⊕ 10.00–18.00 Mon–Sat

$ Cambio Uruguay Rambla Artigas & Calle 8; ↘ 42 448537; ⊕ from 08.30 daily; Torres del Triángulo, Francia & Lenzina, parada 2, Playa Brava; ↘ 42 497458; ⊕ from 09.00 daily

$ Gales Avda Gorlero between calles 30 & 31; ↘ 42 446571

$ Indumex Gorlero & Calle 28; ↘ 42 444172; Punta Shopping; ↘ 42 492078

$ Viaggio Gorlero & Calle 31; ↘ 42 445325

Communications The post office (*Avda Gorlero 1035;* ↘ *42 493691;* ⊕ *10.00–18.00 Mon–Fri, 10.00–15.00 Sat; summer until 22.00 Mon–Sat*) is just south of the bus terminal. Antel has *telecentros* on Plaza Artigas at the junction of calles 24 and 25 (⊕ *09.00–23.00 daily*) and at Pedragosa Sierra & Francia, north of the Conrad.

For courier service, go to DHL Express (*Edificio El Monarca, Local 5, Avda Gorlero & Calle 21;* ↘ *42 441725*) or UPS (*Galería Torre Verona, Local 31; Avda Gorlero & Calle 21;* ↘ *42 442263*).

Crime, safety and police Punta del Este is largely crime-free, which no doubt helps visitors from Buenos Aires and Brazil to relax. The occasional high-profile burglary is usually (rightly or wrongly) blamed on Argentine gangs following their targets from Buenos Aires.

Useful telephone numbers

Police ↘ 911 or 42 224401/2; at the port, ↘ 42 441971

Fire ↘ 42 223777, 42 223111

Marine rescue ↘ 42 442683

For **Immigration** issues, the Inspectoría de Migración is at Ventura Alegre 727 & Sarandí in Maldonado (↘ *42 237624*) and at the airport (↘ *42 559137;* e *i13laguna@ dnm.minterior.gub.uy*).

Health The nearest public hospital is in Maldonado (*Continuación Ventura Alegre;* ↘ *42 225889/90*). There are plenty of *farmacías* in Punta, especially along Avenida Gorlero:

✚ Campus Avda Gorlero 920 near Calle 29; ↘ 42 444444

✚ Farmashop Avda Roosevelt, parada 10; ↘ 42 486927

✚ Font Edificio Vanguardia, Rambla Williman, parada 1.5; ↘ 42 482923

✚ Ituzaingó Avda Gorlero & Calle 19; ↘ 42 441819

✚ La Pastora Avda Francia & Lensina; ↘ 42 483132

✚ Las Delicias Avda España, parada 27; ↘ 42 225966

✚ Maria Amelia Avda Gorlero 685; ↘ 42 443082

✚ Menafra Calle 28 near Calle 20; ↘ 42 446888

✚ San Roque Punta Shopping, Local 239–41; ↘ 42 492236/38

Laundry Punta Wash has two branches (*Calle 24; Sierra west of San Francisco;* ⊕ *10.00–20.00 daily*). Espumas del Virrey (*Calle 28 near Calle 18;* ↘ *42 445255*) will wash, iron and do small repairs.

Activities

Watersports Naturally Punta del Este is ideal for just about any watersport, from swimming to kite-surfing, parasailing and waterskiing, but the most popular and the easiest to try for yourself is probably surfing, practised all along the Playa Brava (the beach facing the Atlantic) and the coast to the east of Punta del Este. The real centre of surfing in the region is La Barra (see page 212). You can rent boards from many shops, as well as these schools:

El Emir Surf School Playa el Emir; m 9988 5935; escuelaelemir@gmail.com; www.escuelaelemir.com
El Templo del Surf Edificio Opus Alpha, parada 3½, Playa Brava; ☎ 42 481388; www.sunvalleysurf.com; ⏰ 11.00–17.00 daily

Zorba parada 5, Playa Brava; m 9990 3090; e escuelazorba@gmail.com; ⏰ 08.00–20.00 daily
Escuela de Surf H2O parada 30, Playa Brava; m 9966 6813, 9968 7554; e escueladesurfh2o@yahoo.com.es; http://h2oescueladesurf.com

Lessons cost around US$25, or US$85 for five days. A local speciality is Flesh wetsuits, hand-cut in Punta del Este (*Avda Gorlero & Calle 25;* ☎ *42 445892; www.fleshwetsuits.com*).

There's good **scuba diving** on over 50 wrecks near Punta del Este; operators include Paul Díaz of Punta Divers (☎ *42 487103,* m *9442 4463;* e *p-divers@multi.com.uy*) and Mariano Boyadjian (☎ *42 252971,* m *9927 6372;* e *buceo@punta.com.uy*).

Fishing is very popular, as it is all along the Uruguayan coast, with anglers on the beaches and boats leaving from the port. The very detailed *Mapa de Pesca Deportiva* should be available at tourist offices and the Club de Pesca Punta del Este (*parada 3, Playa Mansa*). Burriqueta, pescadilla and lisa are present all year; from September to March/April there are also *corvina blanca, corvina negra, lenguado* and *cazón* (a small shark).

If you plan to stick to the beach, remember that there's no topless sun-bathing here (but no-one seems unhappy with this). Watch out for jellyfish (*medusas*), particularly Portuguese men-of-war, which appear occasionally when prolonged dry weather reduces the flow of water from the Río de la Plata. **Beach volleyball** happens on the Playa Mansa at paradas 7, 9 and 10.

Golf Golf clubs include the Cantegril Country Club del Uruguay (*Avda San Pablo s/n;* ☎ *42 482121/6/7;* e *golfccc@adinet.com.uy; www.cantegril.org.uy*), founded in 1947; the Club del Lago Golf (*Ruta Interbalnearia km116.5;* ☎ *42 578423/4;* e *lagogolf@adinet.com.uy; www.lagogolf.com*), a testing American-style course opened in 1983 with a five-star resort; and the La Barra Golf Club (*Ruta 104 km2.5, Camino al Golf, Manantiales;* ☎ *42 774440;* e *info@labarragolfclub.com*), opened in 1994 with computerised watering.

Horseriding Horseriding both along the beaches and inland, is very popular, as is polo. Portezuelo Horseriding (*Interbalnearia km116, Laguna del Sauce;* m *9737 1619*) offers riding on the Portezuelo beach, west of Punta, including sunset rides. Huellas (m *9961 5094; www.huellascabalgatas.com*) offers full-moon rides on the beach, and longer rides, eg: from La Pedrera to the Laguna de Castillos with a local historian (*around US$22–50/day inc B&B*). Riding clubs include the Club Hípico Burnett (*Parque Burnett, Calle Tauro s/n, Camino a la Laguna, parada 32½, Playa Mansa;* ☎ *42 237292;* e *secretaria@hipicoburnett.com; www.hipicoburnett.com;* ⏰ *summer 09.30–18.30 daily, rest of the year Tue–Sun*) and the Club Hípico Cantegril (*Avda Aparicio Saravia & Tacuarembó;* ☎ *42 220560;* e *hipico@cantegrilcountryclubpe.com; www.cantegrilcountryclubpe.com*).

Spectator sports The main venue for polo is the Medellín Country Club (*Ruta 10 km176;* ☎ *42 449342, 42 774520,* m *9990 3011;* e *rbusquet@medellinpoloclub.com.ar; www.medellinpoloclub.com.ar;* ⏰ *early Dec–Feb*), with six fields in a 1,500ha estate near José Ignacio.

In early January in particular there are lots of sporting events, such as the Punta Sevens rugby tournament (*http://ur7s.com/tournaments/sevendepuntadeleste*), the most prestigious in South America (though it's actually in Maldonado); the San Fernando 10K run from Maldonado to the peninsula; polo at the Medellín Country Club; pro-am golf and the International Classic Sport Car rally.

What to see and do Being a beach resort, there's not much to see here other than beaches and their occupants; the one museum is of interest mainly as a temple to bad taste. One unusual feature of beaches along this coast are whale-watching towers, allowing tourists to view migrating right whales from March to October.

To the west of the peninsula, the Playa Mansa is largely patronised by Uruguayan families, while the Playa Brava, to the east, is popular with Argentines. Some hotels attempt to stake out private beaches but by law all Uruguayan beaches are open to all. On the west side of the peninsula itself, a wooden boardwalk leads north from the bus terminal to the cruise ship terminal (near the Conrad Resort and Casino), and is being extended further north to parada 5. There's also, rather bizarrely, a totem pole just north of the Liga de Fomento tourist office, west of the bus terminal.

The broad promenade continues around the peninsula, busy with power-walkers and flanked by the busy Rambla Artigas. At the west end of Calle 23 (El Coral) are two ship's anchors and a short boardwalk leading to a *glorieta* (viewing pavilion), where you may spot cormorants, oystercatchers and miscellaneous wading birds. Immediately south is the port, which has three or four working fishing areas, where sea lions wait in the water for fish guts or lie hauled out. There are plenty of fish restaurants here, mostly fairly downmarket although one or two are pretty good. On the inland side of the *rambla* are some very lively all-night bars. You'll see some pretty fancy motor yachts here in high season. Just south of the port at Solís (Calle 11, also known as Avenida de las Palmeras) 720, under the Hotel Palace, the **Galería Casapueblo** houses a display of work by Carlos Páez Vilaró (see page 32), the artist behind Casapueblo (see opposite). You can buy ceramics, prints and books as well as original paintings; influenced in a relatively shallow way by Picassso and Matisse (you'll see the ubiquitous photo of him with Picasso), he's as much a great publicist as a great artist.

Nearby, the **Museo Paseo de Neruda** (*Calle 12/Virazón near Calle 9;* \ *42 484826;* ⊕ *20.00–22.00 Thu–Sun; voluntary donation*) is open for guided tours of a collection of manuscripts, books, personal objects and photos of the great Chilean poet Pablo Neruda, who lived in Atlántida in the early 1950s. There are also films, readings and other events.

Beyond the port in the Altos del Puerto quarter, buildings are restricted to a maximum of four storeys to avoid blocking the lighthouse, and this area has the feel of a quiet suburb, with few striking or modern houses. Rusty walkways lead to tiny islets on the rocky west side of the headland, where you'll see more waders and other birds. Jogging around the headland is popular, past the Plazoleta Gran Bretaña at its southern tip, with a helipad and the rusty anchor of HMS *Ajax*, commemorating the Battle of the Plate. This point, known as Punta Salinas, is the southernmost point of Uruguay and marks the northern end of the imaginary line from Punta Rasa (Argentina) drawn in 1857 to mark the end of the Río de la Plata (River Plate). At the highest point, a couple of blocks inland, the **lighthouse** (*faro*) stands on a grassy plaza; originally raised in 1858 on the Isla de Lobos (see page 202), it was moved here in 1860 and rebuilt in 1923. The light, 44m above sea level, has a range of 11 nautical miles. It's possible to climb the 25m-high tower, but it depends on whether the personnel are free.

Also on the plaza is the church of **Nuestra Señora de la Candelaría (Our Lady of Candlemas)**; built in 1909–11 and rebuilt in 1942–50, it's not unattractive and a pleasant refuge on a hot day. To the east is the Playa de los Ingleses (British Beach), not really much of a beach, and beyond the rocky Punta del Vapór (with an image of Nuestra Señora de la Candelaría) the Playa El Emir (the Emir's Beach – named after Emin Arslan, an exiled Turkish noble, who built a house here in 1920). It's one of the country's busiest surfing spots, with powerful left- and right-hand waves, and sheltered from winds from the southwest. Just inland is Plaza Artigas, where the statue of the father of the country seems to be leaning backwards, kept upright only by the weight of his nose. The plaza is being re-landscaped; on its northern and eastern sides are the modern structures of the Feria Artesanal or craft market, busy with shoppers until late at night (⊕ *winter 12.00–20.00, summer until 02.00*).

The main commercial zone of Avenida Gorlero runs from Plaza Artigas to the Paseo de las Américas, with the bus terminal to the left and the start of the Playa Brava to the right. Here you'll see the striking concrete sculpture of the **Dedos** (Fingers), known to English-speakers as 'The Hand in the Sand', created in 1981 by the Chilean Mario Irrarazabal. It's become an iconic image of Punta del Este, but on the grassy road islands there are half a dozen other steel or concrete sculptures (by Gyula Kosice, Enio Iomo, Hernán Jugiari, Edgard Negret, Francisco Matos and Waltercio Matos), which are always overlooked. Immediately beyond is Playa La Olla, with good surf (up to 2m high) that can start to break 200m offshore. The Rambla Lorenzo Batlle Pacheco continues along the Playa Brava, with some striking apartment blocks on the inland side, and some older villas surviving between them. Beyond parada 10, the upmarket Barrio San Rafael (named after a Spanish frigate, wrecked here in 1765) was laid out by Giovanni Veltroni and is a shameless mix of thatched cottages, mock-Tudor houses and Modernist white cubes.

A kilometre or so inland (about 15 minutes' walk from the nearest buses on Avenida Roosevelt, or half an hour from the Conrad), the **Museo Ralli** (*Los Arrayanes & Los Platanos, Barrio Beverley Hills;* ❧ *42 483476; www.rallimuseums.org; ⊕ Jan–Feb 17.00–21.00, Mar–Apr & Oct–Dec 14.00–18.00 Sat–Sun, May–Sep closed; free*) is the perfect art museum for the kind of town that thinks Salvador Dalí is a great artist. It's a temple to bad art (mainly Surrealism and excessive Realism), although there's no doubt that plenty of money has been spent on the huge collection. There's a Modigliani in the sculpture patio, as well as *Eve* by the Colombian Fernando Botero.

AROUND PUNTA DEL ESTE
Casapueblo (❧ *42 578611, 42 578485;* **e** *casapue@adinet.com.uy; www.carlospaezvilaro.com; www.clubhotel.com.ar;* $$$–$$) Some 11km west of Punta del Este, Casapueblo is one of the area's compulsory sights thanks to its cultural importance, its visual impact and stunning setting, and the sundowner drinks and snacks you can have here. As a hotel, however, it's overpriced and just too eccentric and awkward. It's a huge house-sculpture that the artist Carlos Páez Vilaró began with his own hands in 1960 (when there were no roads and no electricity here), around a shack he was then living in. It grew into a studio, then a house that could accommodate friends (with a room sometimes added for a particular guest), and then a sizeable hotel and a monument to his self-importance. Visitors have included Lech Wałęsa, Placido Domingo, Bo Derek and Astor Piazzolla.

The whitewashed concrete structure climbing up the cliffside was partly inspired by the mud nests of Uruguay's *horneros* (ovenbirds) but has overtones of Mykonos, Gaudí's Barcelona, Hundertwasser's Vienna and Malian mud mosques. In the words of CPV, 'I call it my habitable sculpture … the result of my personal war against the right angle.' Staying in one of the 70 different rooms, small and sunny and with stunning views out over the bay, still feels like staying in a guestroom at a friend's beach cottage, although the dark, twisting, tunnel-like passages undermine this effect somewhat, as do the poor breakfast and service.

Virtually at the end of the Ruta Panorámica, a 2.5km scenic loop road built in 1978 along the crest of Punta Ballena, it's easiest to come by car or on a tour from

Punta del Este. Visitors enter at the top of the building and then take a tiny old lift down to level –9, where there's a terrace bar by an open-air swimming pool. There's no entry fee, but as you arrive you'll have to pay a minimum US$3 towards drinks and snacks, which are not at all overpriced, though service can be slow (*snack bar* ⊕ *10.00–23.00, restaurant* ⊕ *08.30–11.00, 12.30–15.30 & 20.30–23.00*). The terrace is a great spot to enjoy the best sunsets in the area, as is the viewpoint at the end of the Ruta Panorámica. There are some pieces of art by CPV, and a small museum on a upper floor (⊕ *till sunset daily*). Overnight guests also have use of a covered pool with hydromassage, sauna, solarium and gym.

Arboretum Lussich (❋ *42 578077;* e *arboretumlussich@maldonado.gub.uy; www.www.maldonado.gub.uy/casona.php;* ⊕ *mid-Dec–Easter 08.00–20.00 daily, rest of the year 08.00–18.00 w/ends & holidays; free*) The Arboretum Lussich has the biggest collection of trees in Uruguay, although most of the 400 foreign and 70 native species are unlabelled. From the Portezuelo flyover (15km from Punta del Este, at km120 of the Interbalnearia), reached by Linea 21 midibuses heading for Solanas and Piriápolis (15 minutes from Maldonado terminal, 30 minutes from Punta), it's 300m uphill on the road north towards Lapataia.

The Ballena (Whale) ridge was first settled in 1755. In 1896 Antonio Lussich (see page 183) bought 1,800ha, continuing his self-imposed task of planting trees to stabilise the coastal sand dunes (and bringing birds to populate the new woodland), and building himself a house on the ridge. He first planted native tamarisks, eucalyptus, pines and locust trees to provide windbreaks, then araucaria, oak, cypress, cedar, walnut, maple, lime, fir, birch, cork oak, camphor, magnolia and many others, as well as cacti and bamboos.

In 1979, 182ha were handed over to the departmental government to be opened to the public, with another 10ha added in 1990. The entrance is at the top of the ridge, with a small museum in Lussich's house to the left (there's a smaller area also open to the public across the road to the right). There are photos of Lussich and his family, and of the early years of forestation, a few of the books he wrote, and upstairs a collection of tiles, similar to that of the Museo del Azulejo in Montevideo (see page 128) but more spacious. There are a few Catalan tiles from the 18th and early 19th centuries, but most are from Desvres in northern France.

Continuing past the house, a track leads north to a *glorieta* (viewpoint) on the first hilltop, and continues to a watchtower (marked *prohibido subir*, but there's nothing to actually stop you climbing up); you'll have to return the same way.

It's worth continuing along the road for 3km to **Nonno Antonio** (*Camino Lussich & Paseo Marrero;* ❋ *42 241664; www.nonnoantonio.com.uy*), which produces perhaps the best cheeses in Uruguay, including mascarpone, gorgonzola and reblochon. Having been a near-secret for some years, they have just recently opened a shop at the dairy.

Tambo Lapataia (*Camino Lussich, 4km from Ruta Interbalnearia km128 (parada 45);* ❋ *42 220000, 42 236288;* e *info@lapataiapuntadeleste.com; www.lapataiapuntadeleste.com;* ⊕ *summer 10.00–21.00 daily, rest of the year until 20.00*) Tambo Lapataia, formerly known as Estancia El Sociego, is a very popular tourist *estancia*, a dairy farm where children can pet and bottle-feed young farm animals and then enjoy pancakes with the farm's wonderful *dulce de leche*, and other dairy products. There are free guided tours, including to the cheese and *dulce de leche* plants, as well as tours in open carts. Horseriding is available, and you can walk on four trails; 113 species of birds have been recorded so far on the 45ha property, and there's also a native plant nursery. There's live jazz daily at 'pancake hour' (late afternoon), and one of the country's leading jazz festivals, Festival Internacional de Jazz de Punta del Este (see page 194), is held here in mid-January, in an open-air amphitheatre. The property is owned by Princess Laetitia d'Arenberg, who was born in 1941 in Lebanon (to a Belgian father and French mother) and came to Uruguay at the age of ten; she's been very successful in business, for instance owning the Mitsubishi franchise.

Alto de la Ballena (*Ruta 12 km16.4, Maldonado;* m *9424 0365; www.altodelaballena.com*) One of Uruguay's most impressive start-up wineries is Alto de la Ballena, which certainly indicates that Maldonado has a promising future as a winemaking region. Álvaro Lorenzo and his wife Paula Pivel were high-flying MBAs (he was also a member of Congress from 2004 to 2010) but decided to follow their passion and create a boutique winery. Their research identified southeastern Uruguay as ideal for dry wines, with sea breezes and temperatures of 30°C when it's 35° or 40° in Canelones and the interior. They planted 8ha from 2001 on, and began making wine using equipment at other wineries; since 2008 they've had their own winery and the results are even better than before. They're producing 30,000 bottles a year, and aim to increase that to 50,000, exporting 20,000 soon.

Almost half the area is planted with Merlot, with Tannat, Cabernet Franc and half a hectare each of Syrah and Viognier. They make a unique and very successful Reserva of Tannat (85–90%) and Viognier, and also blend up to 20% Viognier with their Syrah. The spicy, plummy Merlot Reserva is excellent too, spending a year in French oak. The entry level line includes a clean, well-balanced Viognier, a Merlot–Cabernet Franc–Tannat blend (with half the Merlot aged in French oak, but still a young wine overall with lots of tannin) and a rosé (60% Cabernet Franc, 40% Tannat, so like a light red wine); they may also add a Cabernet Franc.

Turning south off Ruta 9 at km127 on to Ruta 12 (from Minas to Maldonado), the vineyard is 16km from the sea, with iron-rich soil of oxidated grey granite with schist and quartz. Some of their land is too rocky to plant, but it's a haven for wildlife (with lots of field flickers) and has great views out across the Laguna del Sauce. Tastings are on a hilltop deck (although a tasting room and restaurant are under consideration), where 90-minute visits tend to stretch to two hours or more as people relax in hammocks to enjoy the breeze and the vista.

There's a fairly lengthy approach along a dirt track to the vineyards and the hilltop tasting room, with stunning views. Small groups come mainly from Punta del Este's hotels, and can buy wines for US$9 a bottle, or US$19 for the reservas (which sell for US$40–50 in Punta's restaurants); there's an extra charge for a selection of wonderful cheeses from Nonno Antonio (see opposite).

A visit here can be combined with birdwatching and the nascent Ruta del Olivo (excellent olive oil is already being produced in this area): contact Circuito Sierra de los Caracoles (m *9643 2662;* e *info@ sierradeloscaracoles.com; www.sierradeloscaracoles.com*).

Isla Gorriti and Isla de Lobos Just 1.5km offshore, and reached by frequent boats from the port, **Isla Gorriti** is known for its beautiful sandy beaches (used for fashion and glamour shoots) and for fishing. In 1531 a cross was raised, below which captains left messages for other ships; pirates and other mariners used it as a haven for many years. Originally known as Isla Maldonado, it was renamed after Captain Francisco Gorriti, imprisoned in 1771–73 for refusing to pay his share of the expenses of a war against the indigenous peoples. Fortified by the Spaniards, it was bombarded by the British navy in 1806; ironically HMS *Agamemnon* (the ship on which Nelson wooed Lady Hamilton, and which fought at Trafalgar in 1805) was wrecked just northeast of the island in 1809 and is now a popular dive site. In 1827 Brazilian troops dug in on Isla Gorriti and the peninsula, but soon left for

Montevideo. In 1832 the *Adventure*, accompanying the *Beagle*, was repaired on the beach. Planted with pines in the mid 20th century, its trees are now lit up at night. Two kilometres long and 1km across, the island has two beaches, Playa Honda to the west and Puerto Jardín to the northeast. So many people bring get-away-from-it-all picnics here that it's actually very crowded in high season. You can see the ruins of the Spanish battery of Santa Ana, and at the southern tip of the island the *faroleta* (little lighthouse). Boats (*US$9 round trip*) leave every half-hour from 08.00 to 19.00, returning from 10.15 to 19.00.

It's 12km further (*2hr round trip; US$70*) to **Isla de Lobos,** named after the 'marine wolves' (ie: sea lions) which live here, and when you arrive you can't actually land. Said to be the world's biggest sea lion reserve, introduced species such as rabbits have been eliminated and landing is allowed only with a special permit; nevertheless the boat trip is well worth making. The sea lions breed here and come into the harbour of Punta del Este in search of fish scraps; they're also happy to approach boats. There's a total of around 200,000 sea lions and southern fur seals here, plus elephant seals in winter. It's also easy to see two species of petrels from the boats, and possibly albatrosses, especially after stormy weather.

A lighthouse was built here in 1857–58, but was moved to Punta del Este in 1860 so as not to disturb the sea lions, which were 'harvested' commercially. However, there were still so many wrecks here and on the rocks offshore that the present lighthouse was built in 1907. At 59m above the ground (and 66m above sea level), it's the highest lighthouse in the Americas. It was built this high in order that the light would only be seen at sea and not on the island, again to avoid disturbing the sea lions.

Boat operators, who also offer fishing for shark and other fish, include:

Calypso Charters Rambla Artigas & Calle 21; ↘ 42 446152, m 9444 3600; e info@calypso.com.uy; www.calypso.com.uy

Dimar Tours Local 1A, Puerto Punta del Este; ↘ 42 444750; m 9441 0899; e reservas@ dimartours.com.uy; www.dimartours.com.uy
Samoa ↘ 42 446166, 42 448955; e crucerosamoa@adimet.com.uy

MALDONADO The name of the town (and the department) is thought to be based on *mar de ao*, Guaraní for 'sea lion', rather than for Francisco Maldonado, who was supposedly sent by Cabot to explore inland in 1527 and never returned. In 1755 Joaquín de Viana founded the town, which soon became the second city of Uruguay. The town's inhabitants are known as *fernandinos* after Ferdinand VI, king of Spain when the town was founded. In 1806 Maldonado was captured by the British, who left in early 1807 to take Montevideo. In June 1810 a *cabildo abierto* (open council) was the first to support the *primer cabildo* established in Buenos Aires on 25 May 1810. The Brazilians again captured the town in 1827; Lavalleja failed to drive them out but they too soon marched on to Montevideo.

In July 1832 the *Beagle* arrived with Charles Darwin, who spent ten weeks in the area, travelling inland as far as Aiguá and Minas, collecting what he called 'all my treasures from Maldonado' and beginning to formulate the ideas that were to lead to his theory of evolution. He wrote:

I stayed ten weeks at Maldonado, in which time a nearly perfect collection of the animals, birds, and reptiles, was procured... It is a most quiet, forlorn, little town; built, as is universally the case in these countries, with the streets running at right angle to each other, and having in the middle a large plaza or square, which, from its size, renders the scantiness of the population more evident. It possesses scarcely any trade; the exports being confined to a few hides and living cattle. The inhabitants are

AV J A LAVALLEJA

GUTIÉRREZ RUÍZ

0 ⬛⬛⬛ 200m
0 ⬛⬛⬛ 200yds

JOSE PEDRO VARELA

N

ROMAN BERGALLI

Bradt

DR JUAN T EDYE

VENTURA ALEGRE

B ARAUJO

Museo Regional
Mazzoni

Hotel
Isla Gorriti

ITUZAINGÓ

San Carlos

Hotel
Catedral

Hotel
Le Petit

Sumo
Evolution

AV AIGUÁ

Hotel Colonial

FLORIDA

Lo de Ruben
El Tranco

Plaza
San Fernando

San Fernando
Plaza Hotel

Wha? Patio-Bar

25 DE MAYO

Bambara

Hotel 25 de Mayo

Hostel del Patio

Colección de Pinturas y
Escultura Nacional

Museo Vivo
del Títere

Café del
Conservatorio

Cuartel
de Dragones

RAFAEL PÉREZ DEL PUERTO

Plaza Torre
de Vigia

Macro Salud &
Oca Blanca

Casa de la Cultura &
Museo San Fernando
de Maldonado

ARTURO SANTANA

19 DE ABRIL

TREINTA Y TRES

Museo de Arte
Americano Maldonado

3 DE FEBRERO

3 DE FEBRERO

Jazz Café

Piriápolis

JUAN LEDESMA

HONDURAS

ENRIQUE BURNETT

BELICE

HOLANDIA

MARTINICA

Empanadas
Ricas y Famosas

1900

DINAMARCA

SAN JOSÉ

Punta del Este

IPIRANGA
AVENIDA JOAQUIN DE VIANA
SOLIS
ZELMAR MICHELINI
SARANDÍ
ROMAN GUERRA
RINCÓN
SAN CARLOS
SANTA TERESA
GUAVIRA
PARQUE ALICIA
25 DE MAYO
JOSE DODERA
18 DE JULIO
AV ESPAÑA
AV FRANKLIN DELANO ROOSEVELT
LA CAÑADA
JONES
MELVIN ANTÁRTIDA
MALVINAS
FORMOSA
FCO ACUÑA DE FIGUEROA
SUECIA
SUIZA
NORUEGA
AV CÓRDOBA

San Carlos

Eastern Uruguay MALDONADO DEPARTMENT

chiefly landowners, together with a few shopkeepers and the necessary tradesmen, such as blacksmiths and carpenters, who do nearly all the business for a circuit of fifty miles round. The town is separated from the river by a band of sand-hillocks, about a mile broad; it is surrounded, on all other sides, by an open slightly undulating country, covered by one uniform layer of fine green turf, on which countless herds of cattle, sheep, and horses graze. There is very little land cultivated even close to the town. A few hedges, made of cacti and agave, mark out where some wheat or Indian corn has been planted.

Bizarrely, on Darwin's 200th birthday, 12 February 2009, a volunteer at the Cambridge Zoology Museum rediscovered a tinamou egg that he had collected in

Maldonado – it was damaged because he packed it in too small a box, but it is the only surviving egg that he collected.

Now Maldonado is part of the sprawling Punta del Este conurbation, but still has its own small-town character and some relaxing places to eat and sleep.

Getting there

By bus Buses arrive at the terminal on Avenida Roosevelt and Sarandí, seven blocks south of the plaza; virtually every bus to and from Punta del Este calls here, and there are a few extra services north to Treinta y Tres (with EmTur). Lots of local buses link Maldonado and Punta del Este, mostly running via either Punta Shopping or Avenida España, Las Delicias and Rambla Williman (Playa Mansa); some continue north to the small town of San Carlos (see page 218) for connections to Rocha department. Northbound, these run up Dodera, a block west of the plaza; southbound, they use Rincón, two blocks east of the plaza (stopping almost at the Hostel del Patio). Linea 20 buses go from the terminal past the airport to Pan de Azúcar.

Local bus timetables are displayed in the IMM Informes window, and there is a left luggage counter (⊕ *06.15–20.30 daily*). Tickets for Colonia Express services to Buenos Aires can be booked at the COPSA desk (⊕ *04.30–23.30 daily*).

Tourist information Tourist information is available at the terminal and through the Informes Municipal de Maldonado (📞 *42 223333;* e *informes@maldonado.gub.uy; www.maldonado.gub.uy*).

🏠 Where to stay

There's a very limited range of hotels in Maldonado, open all year and not oriented solely to holidaymakers.

🏠 **San Fernando Plaza Hotel** 25 de Mayo 810 & 18 de Julio; 📞 42 242410; www.sanfernandoplazahotel.com. This is the best place in town, a newly refurbished 4-star on the plaza. It's nicer inside than out, with attractive public areas, especially the bright, well-lit b/fast room. Rooms aren't huge but have AC, flat-screen TV, minibar & Wi-Fi, & there's a lift. Rates inc good, big b/fast. $$$$

🏠 **Hotel Colonial** 18 de Julio 841 & Florida; 📞 42 223346. 2-star place on the plaza. $$$$

🏠 **Hotel Le Petit** Upstairs in Galería Marco de los Reyes, Sarandí & Florida; 📞 42 223044. Has AC rooms with cable TV. $$$

🏠 **Hotel Catedral** Florida 830 & 18 de Julio; 📞 42 242513; e hotelcatedral@adinet.com.uy. 2-star place on the plaza. $$$

🏠 **Hotel Isla Gorriti** Michelini 884, just south of Izutaingo; 📞 42 245218. Simple 1-star hotel. $$$

🏠 **Hotel 25 de Mayo** 25 de Mayo 851 & Dodera; 📞 42 220573. Simple 1-star hotel. $$$

🏠 **Hostel del Patio** Rafael Perez del Puerto 678 & Roman Guerra; 📞 42 221052; e hosteldelpatio@gmail.com; www.hosteldelpatio.com. The best backpackers' hostel in the area – far nicer than those in Punta del Este – del Patio's reception is in an antiques shop & there are spacious rooms upstairs around a 3-sided patio. Also has a kitchen, dining room, lounge with cable TV & PC (& Wi-Fi throughout). There are shared rooms for up to 8 people with large individual lockers & private rooms for 2. A good b/fast is included (09.00–12.30). $$

✖ Where to eat

✖ **El Tranco** Santa Teresa 820 between 25 de Mayo & Florida; 📞 42 220370; e info@eltranco.com; ⊕ 12.00–16.00, 20.00–02.00; winter closed Tue. In addition to parrilla & fish of the day, El Tranco specialises in Greek food such as musaka, keftedes (meatballs) & berenjenas (aubergines). This is one of the classier options on this busy strip. $$$$

✖ **1900** Acuña de Figueroa & Suiza; 📞 42 232966; e 1900@adinet.com.uy. Near the bus terminal (with easy on-street parking), this is a good parrilla, with a salad bar, in a pleasant, modern, AC setting. It also offers jazz & cocktails. $$$

✖ **Bambara** 25 de Mayo 711 (just west of Román Guerra); 📞 42 249938; ⊕ daily. This new parrilla, whose owner spent 4 years in London, offers great value with no cover charge (but 3 sauces with bread or biscuits offered), huge portions & low prices. There's good meat & pasta, a rear patio & Wi-Fi. $$$

✗ **Lo de Ruben** Santa Teresa 846 & Avda Aiguá; ✎ 42 223059; e loderuben@adinet.com.uy; ⏱ 12.00–17.00, 20.00–04.00 daily. You may have to wait for a table at this local institution, which serves grilled meats swiftly & exactly as you requested them. You can also order grilled vegetables & provolone cheese, pasta or fish, all at very reasonable prices. There are only basic salads, but desserts are good, & you can bring your own wine for US$4. $$$

✗ **Oca Bianca** Román Guerra 714 between Pérez del Puerto & Santana; ✎ 42 220957. With more than 40 types of pizza as well as pasta & fish, this is a good option for a cheap & cheerful meal. $$$

✗ **Café del Conversatorio** Paseo San Fernando; ✎ 42 220478. In the delightful patio of the music college on the south side of the plaza, this pleasant cafetería–sandwichería offers 'Coffee & Art', plus live music w/end evenings. $$

✗ **Jazz Café** Ledesma between Acuña de Figueroa & Sarandí; ✎ 42 233042; www.jazzcafe.com.uy; ⏱ 08.00–22.00 daily. A lively modern place with jazz videos, Wi-Fi & good coffees, wines, snacks & cakes. $$

✗ **Macro Salud** Guerra 736, south of Pérez del Puerto; ✎ 42 222695; ⏱ Mon–Sat lunch & evening. A friendly little health-food café, selling cooked meals by weight as well as diabetic desserts & products for coeliacs. $$

✗ **Sumo Evolution** Sarandí & Florida; ✎ 42 223959. This youth-oriented place serves chivitos, milanesas, burgers, pizza & pasta. It's a bit chain-like but has AC. On the northeastern corner of the plaza, it's a great spot for people-watching. $$

✗ **Wha? Patio-Bar** Santa Teresa 813 near 25 de Mayo; ✎ 42 251656; www.hostalsantateresa.net. With a hostel next door, this is a lively place, with live blues & jazz music nightly, a wood fire in winter & a patio for summer, with vegetarian food, waffles & pancakes, & Wi-Fi. $$

✗ **Empanadas Ricas y Famosas** Acuña de Figueroa between Suecia & Holanda; ✎ 42 248488; ⏱ 10.00–02.00 daily. Founded as a grocery in 1946, this is now famous for its 26 varieties of excellent empanadas; you can also call for free deliveries. It's handy for the bus terminal. There are also 2 branches in Punta del Este. $

Entertainment The theatre at the Casa de Cultura (Pérez del Puerto & Sarandí; ✎ 42 231786, 42 237808; e dgcultura@maldonado.gub.uy; ⏱ summer 08.00–14.00 daily, rest of the year 10.00–16.00) stages plays, music, dance, comedy and other events. The Club de Teatro Fernandino (25 de Mayo 828), opposite the Cuartel de Dragones, is a small theatre that puts on good plays year-round. There are also concerts and exhibitions at the Azotea de Haedo (Bvar Artigas & Mercedes; ✎ 42 223288; ⏱ 10.00–16.00 daily), the little summer house of President Haedo.

Shopping Isabel Fonseca wrote in the Sunday Times that 'the city of Maldonado is one of the great ironmongery capitals of the world…a wholesalers' paradise, with a large shop that sells only hinges, and an enormous emporium called Todo Goma, or Everything Rubber'. Todo Goma is at Florida 670, if you need it, and there are plenty of supermarkets in the centre of Maldonado, including El Dorado (between 18 de Julio & Dodera), immediately north of the plaza (the branch at 25 de Mayo & Román Guerra, a block east of the plaza, deals in home furnishings and the like), Ta-Ta (25 de Mayo & Rincón), two blocks east of the plaza, Disco (Avda Roosevelt & Michelini) and Macro Mercado (Bvar Artigas & 3 de Febrero).

Other practicalities

Banks There are ATMs at Banco República (Florida 774; ⏱ summer 15.00–20.00 Mon–Fri, rest of year, 09.45–14.45 Mon–Fri), on the north side of the plaza, and on Sarandí a block south of the plaza. You can also change money at Cambios Bacacay (just west of the plaza at Florida 803 & 18 de Julio) and Cambios Maiorano (Dodera & Florida).

Communications The main post office is at 18 de Julio 965 (⏱ 09.00–18.00 Mon–Fri, 09.00–12.00 Sat). Antel's main call centre (Florida & Avenida Joaquín de Viana; ⏱ 09.00–19.00 daily) is four blocks west of the plaza; there's a more convenient call centre but with shorter hours on the north side of the plaza (🕓 *09.00–18.00 Mon–Fri (summer until 23.00), 09.00–13.00 Sat*). There's free Wi-Fi on the plaza, although it's not a great signal.

Emergency services The police are at 25 de Mayo 95 (📞 *42 224401; www.policiamaldonado.gub.uy*). There are two hospitals (*Continuación Ventura Alegre;* 📞 *42 225889/90; Avda Roosevelt & Avda España;* 📞 *42 222860*).

Laundry There's a laundry at 25 de Mayo & Rincón (🕓 *09.00–13.00, 15.30–19.30 Mon–Sat*).

What to see and do The town's central plaza is modern, with very little shade, but there are some attractive colonial buildings around it. On the west side of the plaza, the cathedral of San Fernando, built between 1801 and 1895, is a plain Neoclassical structure. However, it has a grand altar by Antonio Veiga (born in Vigo, Spain, in 1845), completed after eight years' labour in 1872; it was taken to Buenos Aires to be displayed at the Continental Exposition of 1882, where it won two awards but then was held by Customs in Montevideo. In 1890 it was sold to the state to pay storage costs, and was given to Maldonado. Veiga himself installed it in 1894, and in 1896 the Baroque Virgin of Santander (from the *Ciudad de Santander,* wrecked off the Isla de Lobos) was added. The effect is not overwhelming as it's not overloaded with gold.

Off the southwestern corner of the plaza, the **Cuartel de Dragones** (barracks of the Blandengues Dragoons, 1774–97) houses the Museo Didáctico Artiguista (🕓 *10.00–23.00 daily; free*), commemorating Artigas's joining the regiment of Blandengues here in 1797. Entering from the south (Pérez de Puerto, west of 18 de Julio), the first room has material on Artigas, and the second has busts of the Liberators of the Americas (13 of them, including George Washington), a model of the barracks and prints of independence-era uniforms. In the southeastern corner is the chapel, now empty.

On the north side of the barracks (with entries both from the barracks and from 25 de Mayo) is the excellent **Colección de Pinturas y Escultura Nacional** (*Collection of Uruguayan Paintings and Sculptures;* 🕓 *10.00–18.00 Wed–Sun; free*). This houses many sculptural studies by José Belloni (1882–1965), including ones for Montevideo monuments such as *La Diligencia* (The Stagecoach, in the Prado), the Rodó monument (in Parque Rodó) and a funerary monument for the Gorlero family (in the Central Cemetery). They're impressive, but they seem of Rodin's age rather than the mid 20th century. The Argentine cement heiress Amalia Lacroze de Fortabat has given substantial donations, including self-portraits by José Cúneo and a painting by Pedro Blanes Viale. In the other wing are sketches by Antonio Pena (1894–1947) and José Luis Zorrilla de San Martín, as well as a bust of his father Juan Zorrilla de San Martín, and another Pedro Blanes Viale painting, of the Cerro de Arequita. There are also good sketches and models by Federico Moller de Berg (1900–91) for sculptures of Artigas and of Victory, works by Edmundo Prati and Rafael Barradas, and a case of commemorative medals.

A block east, in the same building as the Casa de la Cultura, the **Museo San Fernando de Maldonado** (*Sarandí & Pérez del Puerto;* 🕓 *15.00–21.00 daily*) consists of two rooms used for temporary shows of contemporary art, but it's a pleasant setting with very nice patios.

On the south side of the plaza is the **Museo Vivo del Títere** (*Puppet Museum; Paseo San Fernando, 25 de Mayo & Sarandí;* 🕓 *10.00–16.00 Wed–Sun; free*) – follow the mosaic line upstairs to the museum door. This displays puppets from around the world, including an Italian Pinocchio, Czech and Romanian puppets, one of Gardel from Uruguay, and Turkish, Burmese and Javanese shadow puppets. There are also 8th-century Toltec and pre-Inca dolls, and German porcelain, as well as puppets made by classes here in winter (when occasional shows are staged).

A block north of the plaza, the **Museo Regional Mazzoni** (*Ituzaingó 789, east of 18 de Julio;* ↘ *42 221107;* ☉ *summer 16.00–22.00, winter 13.00–19.00 Tue–Sun; free*) is housed in an atmospheric late-18th-century house with 12 rooms and two exuberantly vegetated internal patios. The home of Professor Francisco Mazzoni (1883–1978), it houses an entertainingly diverse collection, with lots of dark wood furniture and glass-fronted cabinets containing, for instance, Masonic regalia and voting urns, guns, family photos and portraits, a few sad stuffed animals and the usual indigenous stone weapons (*bolas* and *rompacabezas*). In the room dedicated to Henry Burnett (see page 183) you'll see his telescope and certificates from Lloyd's and from King George V, the latter conferring the Order of the British Empire on him. There's the odd Páez Vilaró painting, Blanes's painting smock and boots, and a pretty average collection of woodblock prints and other art. Beyond the garden is a room with temporary exhibits of art or photography.

Two blocks west of the barracks is the Plaza Torre del Vigía, surrounded by suburban bungalows and centred on the **Torre del Vigía** (Watchtower), built in 1801 to watch for ships at sea. Just to the southeast, the red-painted house of William Burnett now houses the **Museo de Arte Americano Maldonado** (*Treinta y Tres 823 & Dodera;* ☉ *summer 18.00–22.00 daily; free*), founded in 1973 by Jorge Páez Vilaró (1922–98; brother of Carlos) to house his collections of pre-Columbian and contemporary Latin American art. Temporary exhibitions are also staged here, as well as concerts in the garden.

To the east of town, buses pass the Cachimba del Rey (Royal Well), a not particularly attractive monument on 3 de Febrero just east of Bulevar Artigas; it was the town's main source of water from its foundation until around 1873.

LA BARRA AND MANANTIALES As opposed to the rather sterile strips of mega-villas to either side, La Barra seems like a real seaside resort, with lots of bars, shops and streetlife. It was never a fishing village, but developed as a resort for the people of San Carlos, the first hotels appearing in the 1920s. Nowadays this is the resort of choice for hip fashionistas (above all at New Year), with the best bars in the Punta del Este area, playing the coolest tunes, and the best displays of surfer dudes and bikini babes on the beaches. It's the St Tropez to Punta's Cannes. On a Saturday morning in summer it's totally gridlocked with cruising cars and motorbikes.

Getting there A ferry crossed the Arroyo Maldonado from 1912 until 1936, when a wooden bridge was built; in 1965 Lionel Viera designed the famous *puente ondulado* (undulating bridge) now named after him. Something like a pair of giant speed humps, this was simply the cheapest way to span the river, but it has become the iconic image of La Barra (inspiring a poem by Neruda). An identical bridge was built alongside in 1999, providing two lanes in each direction, and the original bridge was rebuilt in 2005–10.

There are regular midibuses (*routes 14 and 22; every 20 minutes until midnight*) to La Barra from Punta del Este's terminal, although they tend to just drive through rather than pulling into a bay. There's also a cycle track along the *rambla* of the Playa Brava.

Orientation and tourist information From the bridge you reach the excellent Museo del Mar (see page 212). The main Ruta 10 turns sharply right, past the striking, modern Edificios Delamar (by far the tallest buildings here) to a brief one-way section of road past the ANCAP station and a few shops. Then the road swings left at a summer-only **tourist information office** (☉ *09.00–21.00 daily, Jan–Feb until 22.00*), staffed by helpful students, and follows the coast, lined with bars,

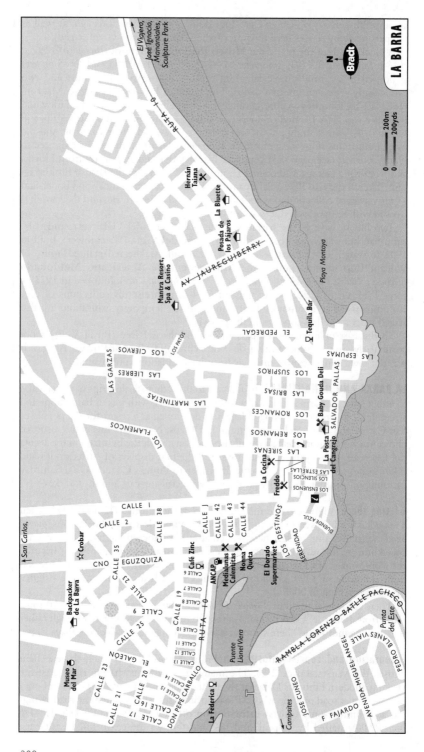

LA BARRA

N

Bradt

0 ——— 200m
0 ——— 200yds

El Viajero,
José Ignacio,
Manantiales,
Sculpture Park

RUTA 10

Hernán
Taiana

Posada de La Bluette
los Pájaros

AV. JAUREGUIBERRY

Mantra Resort,
Spa & Casino

Playa Montoya

LOS PATOS

LAS GARZAS

LOS CIERVOS

LAS LIEBRES

LAS MARTINETAS

LOS FLAMENCOS

Tequila Bar

EL PEDREGAL

LOS SUSPIROS

LAS BRISAS

LOS ROMANCES

LOS REMANSOS

LAS SIRENAS

Baby Gouda Deli

SALVADOR PALLAS

La Posta
del Cangrejo

LAS ESPUMAS

La Cocina

LAS ESTRELLAS

Freddo

LOS SILENCIOS

LOS ENSUEÑOS

CALLE 1

CALLE 2

CALLE 38

CALLE J

CALLE 42

CALLE 43

CALLE 44

DUENDE AZUL

SERENIDAD

LOS DESTINOS

Crobar

CNO. EGUZQUIZA

CALLE 35

Café Zinc

ANCAP

CALLE 6

Medialunas
Calentitas

Nonna
Queta

El Dorado
Supermarket

Backpacker
de La Barra

CALLE 23

CALLE 9

CALLE 7

CALLE 8

CALLE 19

CALLE 10

RUTA 10

San Carlos,

Museo
del Mar

CALLE 25

EL GALEÓN

CALLE 11

Puente
Lionel Viera

CALLE 21

CALLE 17

CALLE 20

CALLE 16

DON PEPE CARBALLO

CALLE 15

CALLE 13

CALLE 14

La Federica

Campsites

RAMBLA LORENZO BATLLE PACHECO

JOSE CUNEO

F FAJARDO

AVENIDA MIGUEL ANGEL

PEDRO BLANES VIALE

Punta
del Este

208

restaurants and art galleries. This soon ends at Playa Montoya, perhaps Punta's most stylish beach. From here a dual carriageway and parallel cycle track continue east for a kilometre or so to **Manantiales**, where high-ranking Argentine politicians and others rent houses.

Entering Manantiales you have Bikini Beach on your right, aptly described as 'less a fleshpot than a fleshcauldron'. There's also plenty of silicon on view here, it must be said. It's also a surfing beach, known for its consistent waves; the surfers have the beach to themselves in the mornings, and it only really becomes a social scene after about 16.00, when the Buddha Bar's DJ starts to crank out tunes.

Where to stay Most of La Barra's and Manantiales's summer residents rent houses. There's one backpackers' hostel in each resort & some luxury hotels, but nothing in the middle market. Two of Punta del Este's campsites are just across the bridge (see page 191).

Mantra Punta del Este Resort, Spa & Casino Ante Millat, Ruta 10 km162, parada 48, Montoya; 42 771000; www.mantraresort.com. The only rival to the Conrad, with a luxury spa & casino, not to mention cinema, boutique shops, art gallery, restaurants & wine-bar. Modelled on a Mediterranean village, sprawling down a hillside, Mantra is divided into 2 parts, the lively Plaza (open to outsiders) with restaurants, bars & casino, & the quieter hotel area, with 100 minimalist white rooms. The Zafferano restaurant serves innovative Mediterranean cuisine, & you can also eat at the more casual Indigo restaurant with salad bar, pizza & *parrilla*, or the poolside La Piscina Café. Most local buses run up Avda Jaureguiberry & turn around just east of the Mantra; guests can use golf-carts to reach the hotel's section of the Playa Mantra, with attentive service. Catamarans, jet-skis, fishing & whale-watching are all available. $$$$$

Posada de los Pájaros Calle 10 & 5, parada 48.1, Montoya; 42 772181; e info@posadadelospajaros.com.uy; www.posadadelospajaros.com.uy. Modern villa in the white-cube style with sweeping lawns & a swimming pool, this boutique place has just 16 rooms & impeccable service. $$$$$

Las Dunas Hotel & Spa de Mar Ruta 10 km163½, Manantiales; 42 771211; e lasdunas@adinet.com.uy; www.lasdunas.com.uy. Glitzy, very expensive spa & resort near Bikini Beach, with 72 rooms, each with glazed terrace & ocean view. There's an AC pool with a glass roof as well as an outdoor pool & paddling pool, plus gym, spa, sauna, hydromassage & tennis courts. It's actually quite quiet & not too tacky. $$$$$

La Posta del Cangrejo Los Remansos & Salvador Pallas, La Barra; 42 770021; e alaposta@adinet.com.uy; www.lapostadelcangrejo.com; all year. With just 30 rooms, an outdoor pool & a good

French restaurant looking out across the Playa de la Barra (& patronised by the likes of George Bush Snr & Julio Iglesias), this has a sort of country-house style, with soft sofas & softly-spoken welcoming staff. $$$$$

La Bluette Ruta 10, parada 49, Manantiales; 42 770947; www.hotellabluette.com. One of the most exclusive hotels in Punta del Este, very affordable Mar–Sep but remarkably pricey in high season. It's a 2-storey ochre colonial-style bldg that's more like a home than a chic boutique hotel. Each room is individually designed, with private terrace. $$$$$

Backpacker de La Barra Calle 9, La Barra; 42 772272; e backpacker@vivapunta.com; www.backpackerdelabarra.com. Calle 9, a very nice residential street that quickly becomes rural, leads north from parada 40 (Galería del Paseo), just east of the bridge, to the hostel about 1km from the main road. Very bright & multicoloured, this is the only budget option here (though prices double to US$30 in the first half of Jan) & you'll need to book. Open only for pre-booked groups Mar–Nov. It's a nice place, with lots of greenery & a swimming pool. Standard dorms have 8 beds, & there are 4-bed rooms for US$10 pp extra. There's a kitchen, barbecue, TV/DVD, 2 computers & Wi-Fi; bikes can be rented. $$

El Viajero Ruta 10 km164.5, Manantiales; 42 774427; e info@manantialeshostel.com; www.elviajerohostels.com; Nov–Apr. On the edge of the woods just 500m from Bikini Beach, this is a slightly Casapueblo-esque white house with swimming pool, open-air bar & barbecue, & terraced gardens. Indoors there's a kitchen, TV room, Wi-Fi, mixed & women-only dorms, & dbl & trpl rooms. It's aimed at international travellers, with an emphasis on surfing in the daytime (lessons available) & hitting the bars & clubs at night. Bikes are available for rental, & horseriding can be arranged. $$

✕ Where to eat La Barra has some excellent and very pricey restaurants. If you want *chivitos*, *empanadas* or other snacks, head for the area near the ANCAP filling station.

✕ Cactus y Pescados 1er bajada a Playa Bikini (First road leading down to the beach), Manantiales; ☎ 42 774782. A popular Mediterranean-style restaurant (serving the usual range of grilled meats, fish, pasta & pizza), not too overpriced for the excellent location; there's Wi-Fi. $$$$$

✕ Hernán Taiana Ruta 10 km162.5, parada 49½, Manantiales; ☎ 42 771356; www.hernantaiana.com. A cool little bistro with simple seasonal fare where the main attraction is the wine list; they're also known for their narancello: like limoncello 'an Italian lemon liqueur mainly produced in Southern Italy', but made of tiny local oranges. $$$$$

✕ Nonna Queta Restaurant–Bar–'Slow Food' Ruta 10 & Camino al Cerro, La Barra; ☎ 42 770524/1409; ⏱ 18.00–23.00 Fri, 12.00–16.00, 20.00–24.00 Sat, 12.00–16.00 Sun. Taking very seriously the rules of the Slow Food movement, with all ingredients sourced locally & cooked only when ordered, the open kitchen here produces superb, largely Mediterranean-style, dishes such as risotto, wild salmon with sauce béarnaise, guacamole with tiger prawns, duck breast, & a tower of grilled vegetables, cheese & *jamón crudo* (raw ham). The desserts are also excellent, as is the service (it's true, you may have to wait a while). The wine list is limited, but you can bring your own. $$$$$

✕ O'Farrell Ruta 10 km164.5, Manantiales; ☎ 42 774331; www.ofarrellrestaurant.com; ⏱ Dec–Feb from 19.00 daily, Easter & holiday w/ends 13.00–16.30, 20.00–24.00 Sat–Sun. On the road to the Viajero hostel, though catering to a different market, this offshoot of a Buenos Aires restaurant is one of the best in the area, & very expensive. It offers a modern Mediterranean cuisine with seasonal ingredients & a Mallmanesque (see page 218) emphasis on wood fires & smoking. Fresh fish is a staple, or try the rack of lamb (*costillar de cordero*) with a Malbec sauce; there's also a tasting menu

with matching wines. It's in a stylish modern house with sofas, director's chairs & other cool furnishings. From the bar there's a nice vista out towards the beach, but the interior rooms are shady & without much of a view. Service is excellent, & there's a very long wine list, quite a few by the glass (they also work as wine merchants). $$$$$

✕ La Cocina Las Sirenas, just north of Ruta 10, La Barra; ☎ 42 772462; e restaurant-lacocina@adinet.com.uy; ⏱ Fri–Sat dinner, Tue–Sun lunch. A small place with excellent service & a changing menu of simple seasonal dishes (just a couple of choices for each course). Not overpriced for the location. $$$$

✕ Baby Gouda Deli Ruta 10 km160.9 & Los Romances, La Barra; ☎ 42 771874; e babygouda@adinet.com.uy; ⏱ summer 11.00–02.30 daily. One of the hippest places to see & be seen, & the food's good too. The open kitchen produces a wide range of salads, sandwiches & wraps, pasta & desserts, to be eaten indoors or on the terrace looking out over the beach. There's Wi-Fi, & sometimes belly-dancing in the evening. $$$$–$$

✕ No Me Olvides Ruta 10 km164, Manantiales; ☎ 42 775154, 42 775531. A simple pizza-*parrilla* with a large wood-fired oven, wooden seats, wooden tables. The pizzas are good & affordable. $$$$–$$

✕ Freddo Ruta 10 & Las Sirenas, La Barra; ☎ 42 770120; ⏱ high season only. An Argentine chain selling the best ice cream in town. $$

✕ Medialunas Calentitas Ruta 10, Palmas de La Barra, La Barra; ☎ 42 772347; www.medialunascalentas.com; ⏱ summer 24hrs/day. The original branch of the 'Hot Croissants' chain (now also in Montevideo & Punta del Este), selling croissants with & without fillings (such as *dulce de leche*), cakes, *empanadas*, milkshakes & coffees. There's live music in the late afternoon in summer, & you can eat at picnic tables outside. $

Entertainment and nightlife

♀ Buddha Bar Bikini Beach, Ruta 10 km160. Covered beach bar that serves fine sushi & cocktails. A DJ cranks out the coolest music on the coast from about 16.00 but the party only really gets going towards midnight, when celebrity supermodels such as Naomi Campbell & Gisele Bundchen may pass through. More realistically, you may find a sponsored fashion event or glamour shoot.

♀ Café Zinc Ruta 10 & Calle 6, La Barra; ☎ 42 770626; ⏱ 10.30–19.00, until 18.00 Wed, until 20.00 Fri–Sat. In a corrugated iron shed with lots of antique junk for sale, the quite stylish café seems a bit of an afterthought, but it does have Wi-Fi.

☆ Crobar Camino Egozuiza km1. On the road north to San Carlos, this outpost of a hip Buenos Aires nightclub brings in top-rank techno DJs & attracts the hip crowd from Montevideo & further afield at w/ends late Nov–late Feb. Nothing happens until well after midnight, & frankly the dance floor is somewhat warehouse-like.

♀ **La Federica** Sobre el arroyo, La Barra; ☎ 42 772698. A simple bar in a lovely location by the river, immediately northwest of the bridge.

♀ **Tequila Bar** Ruta 10 & Calle 15; ☎ 42 771922. Season after season, this is the hottest dance club in Uruguay, perhaps because of a strict door policy that allows only the best lookers in. Once in, you'll find a small lounge with just 1 floor & cosy booths, & not much action until about 03.00. Music including vintage electronica & Latin & global beats. Cocktails can cost US$20, & there's a minimum age of 23 for men, 21 for women.

Shopping For practical purchases such as food your best bet is the El Dorado supermarket (*Ruta 10 near Calle Los Destinos, south of ANCAP petrol station*). There are smaller *supermercados* on Ruta 10 in Manantiales and on Calle 7 in La Barra.

For fun stuff, there's an array of boutiques including in La Barra Daniel Curto (leather and suede), Diablito (CDs, surfer clothes and trainers), Lanas del Este (knitted sweaters), Kosiuko (trendy clothing, belts, shorts, purses for men and women, and vintage denim; *http://kosiuko.com*) and No Se (eclectic art, antiques and home accessories), and, in Manantiales, Kallalith (silver jewellery), Manga Rosada (reversible embroidered Brazilian bikinis), Piramide (sequinned and embroidered bags and sandals) and Velas de La Ballena (perfumed candles).

This is also the best place in Uruguay to buy art and photographs, with many cool **contemporary art galleries**. The Arte en La Barra event involves all the galleries opening from 20.00 to midnight every Friday night in January, with a free bus shuttle between them. Between the ANCAP petrol station and the tourist information centre, the Paseo Real de la Barra is a small group of galleries, including the B&W photographer Roberto Fernández Ibañez (*Local 23;* ☎ *42 602297; www.robertofernandez.com.uy*). At the other end of La Barra near Playa Montoya, the Galería Sur (*parada 46, La Barra;* ☎ *42 772014; www.galeriasur.com.uy;* ⊕ *Dec–Mar 11.00–24.00 daily*) is a modern space selling works by Torres García, Gurvich, Figari, Barradas and Blanes Viale, as well as the Brazilian Portinari, the Chilean Matta and a range of contemporary artists. It takes its name from the Escuela del Sur, inspired by Torres García's comment, 'Nuestro Norte es el Sur' (Our North is the South), turning a map of Latin America upside down.

Other galleries in La Barra include Grupo Taller Jones Vicente (*Ruta 10 km160.5;* ☎ *42 484618*), Atelier José Etchepareborda (*Duende Azul & Ruta 10 km160.5;* ☎ *42 771974; www.etchepareborda.com*) and Chelsea Gallery (*Ruta 10 km161, parada 45;* ☎ *42 526560*). Taller Elina Damiani (*Ruta 10 & Los Silencios;* ☎ *42 772103; www.elinadamiani.com*) shows the rather naïf works (sailing ships, birds, cats, fruit and the like) of this self-taught Uruguayan. Nearby are Adrián Martínez Bojko (*Calle de Las Estrellas;* ☎ *42 77269; www.martinezbojko.com*) and Oscar Rocha Atelier (☎ *42 771970*), and the Atelier Aguiló-Abal (*calles 4 & 1;* ☎ *42 772855; www.arteuy.com.uy/aa/ee.htm*). The Lasarte Gallery (*Ruta 10, parada 46;* ☎ *42 771112; www.mercedeslasarte.com*) shows the excellent Post-impressionist/Expressionist works of Mercedes Lasarte.

In Manantiales there's the Atelier Vásquez (*Ruta 10 & Maldonado;* ☎ *42 774939; www.vasquez.com.uy*), the Galería del Paseo – Arte Contemporáneo (*Ruta 10 & 18 de Julio, km164;* ☎ *42 775860*) and the Atelier Marizú Terza (*Calle Pan de Azúcar;* ☎ *42 775240*).

Other practicalities

Banks The only ATM in La Barra is at the casino in the Mantra Resort. There's a branch of the Banco República north of the ANCAP petrol station, which will exchange cash, as will Cambio Maiorano (*Ruta 10 & Duende Azul;* ☎ *42 771080*), opposite the tourist information office. Also here is Punta Viaje (✆ *42 245831;* ⏲ *10.00–18.00 Thu–Mon*), where you can book tickets with PLUNA or Buquebus.

Car rental You can rent a car at La Barra Rentacar (✆ *42 772511*) just west of the tourist information centre, the Dollar agency in an estate agency nearby at Duende Azul or Punta Car (*Ruta 10 & Calle 15;* ✆ *42 772194*).

Internet For phone and internet service there are *locutorios* on Ruta 10 just west of Baby Gouda and by the tourist information centre at Calle Los Ensueños.

Laundry Opposite the El Dorado supermarket is the Mr Lav laundry (⏲ *09.30–17.00 Mon–Sat*).

Taxis For a taxi call Taxi La Barra or Taxi Manantiales (✆ *42 771122*).

What to see and do Other than the beach-life, the bridge, the shops and the art galleries, the main sight is the large and very interesting **Museo del Mar** (*Museum of the Sea;* ✆ *42 771817;* e *museodelmar@gmail.com; www.museodelmar.com.uy;* ⏲ *summer 10.30–20.00 daily, rest of the year 10.30–17.00 Mon–Thu, 10.30–19.00 Fri–Sun; US$4*), 1km north of the bridge on Calle El Galeón and easily spotted by the large blue shark in front. Opened in 1995, this has grown to fill a warehouse-scale building, with lots of whale skeletons (up to 15m in length) as well as a 6m manta ray, lots of stuffed birds (all found dead of largely natural causes) and a bathing machine. There's not a lot on actual ships (other than a room for the kids on pirates) but there's lots of material on wildlife and on the social history of Uruguay's beach resorts. The music is good too, and the staff are very helpful.

Another option is the **Fundación Atchugarry** (*Ruta 104 km4.5, El Chorro, Manantiales;* ✆ *42 775563; www.fundacionpabloatchugarry.com;* ⏲ *summer 11.00–23.00 daily; free*), displaying the amazingly delicate abstract marble sculptures of Pablo Atchugarry, as well as temporary exhibitions which may feature locally big names such as Octavio Podestá. A 15ha park displays a variety of modern sculptures in metal, concrete, marble and other materials. It's signposted 'Parque de Esculturas' from Ruta 10 km165.

Activities Surf shops include Sun Valley Surf (*Ruta 10 km160, Complejo Koby VIII, Local 1;* ✆ *42 772451*), next to Baby Gouda. For surfing lessons, ask here or call Bagus School (✆ *42 774646;* e *alfonso_fermin@hotmail.com*).

EAST OF MANANTIALES Ruta 10 continues along the coast east of Manantiales, via **Punta Piedras**, where houses worth US$1.5 million overlook the virtually empty beach that stretches from here east to José Ignacio. It costs about US$100,000 to rent the best ones for the month of January – no problem for the likes of supermodels Naomi Campbell, Eva Herzigova and Valeria Mazza, Argentine tycoon Eduardo Constantini or Prince Albert of Monaco. The architectural style is consistently Modernist – cool white cubes with great expanses of glass, in contrast to the catholic mix of styles in Punta and La Barra. In 2008 Michael Caine's daughter Natasha and her husband created the Villalagos gated development, with 13 *chacras* or plots (of close to 5ha, each with villa and infinity pool) surrounded by lakes and woods. There are many more *chacra* developments along the coast to the east, with prices rising spectacularly in the early years of the century before global recession pushed them down.

There are also small *balnearios* (beach resorts) such as Balneario El Chorro and Balneario Buenos Aires, where you'll see signs for houses to rent at far lower rates than the luxury villas. Beyond km168 the developed strip (with a lot of speed humps) gives way to dunes and pine trees, with the Pueblo San Vicente to the left at km170, a planned development begun in 1959 and revived in 2002, which has a highly regarded restaurant, Pueblo San Vicente (❦ *42 775100; www.pueblosanvicente.com*). At km174.5 there's the surprising sight of ANCAP oil tanks on the left and a buoy for discharging tankers a couple of kilometres offshore.

At km180 (30km from Punta del Este) the road crosses a bridge over the outflow from the Laguna José Ignacio, where you may see flamingos and remarkable numbers of crabs. At km183 it reaches a petrol station and roundabout with José Ignacio 2km to the right; the road to the left leads to Pueblo Garzón (see page 218) and Ruta 9, while Ruta 10 continues for 7km (newly paved) to **Laguna Garzón.** This passes the vaguely medieval gate towers of the Laguna Escondida development at km184½, then at km185.1 the modern greeny-blue shark metal sculpture marking the turning to the Posada Azul Marino (see page 215) and the very cool Marismo and Namm restaurants (see page 216), hidden in the forest. The road ends at km190½ at the slipway to the free ferry (⊕ *08.00–12.00, 14.00–18.00 daily*), a raft on a cable (moved by a boat tied alongside with an outdoor motor) that can take cars and small vans across the mouth of the lagoon. There are remains of an unfinished bridge here, and there's talk of building a bridge again, causing property prices on the far side of the lagoon (a currently isolated part of Rocha department) to soar. Here on the west bank are a windsurfing school (see page 217) with a small café, and a few huts selling drinks, snacks and fresh fish. There are flamingos, herons, ducks, swans and other waterbirds to be seen on the lagoon.

JOSÉ IGNACIO The small fishing village of José Ignacio has recently been transformed into one of the world's most chic and exclusive holiday destinations, with boutique hotels (and absolutely no budget accommodation), superb restaurants and an array of stunning modern houses. In summer the traffic jams are mad, but from March to November this is still a remarkably peaceful fishing village. The sandy roads, empty beaches, hand-painted wooden signs and boho-chic style are key to its success, studiously avoiding the Miami Beach-style high-rise development of Punta del Este.

The first couple of weeks of January are fairly manic, with parties sponsored by brands such as Lacoste and Chivas Regal, with catering by Francis Mallman (see page 218) and music by the likes of Brazilian singer Bebel Gilberto, in beachfront tents or at the La Huella restaurant. Otherwise there's a 02.00 curfew and there are no discos – it's not far to the clubs of La Barra. It's a great place to let your children loose to roam and make friends with other kids.

In any case this is a place of great and subtle beauty, set on a rocky headland with the usual *brava* and *mansa* sides, and the quintessential lighthouse on the point. Set between two lagoons totalling 4,000ha, this is a paradise for birdwatchers (even the streets are named after birds), and from March to October southern right whales are easily seen from the point. Horseriding, cycling and walking are ideal ways of getting into nature here.

The village is named after a José Ignacio who built a slaughterhouse on the headland, an easy location for rounding up cattle. The lighthouse was built in 1877 and in 1917 the first streets were laid out as a small fishing village grew up. The coastal Ruta 10 only reached José Ignacio when the outlet from Laguna José Ignacio was bridged in the 1980s; until then access was by a dirt road from Ruta 9, well to the north. This direct link to Punta del Este and La Barra transformed José Ignacio, unleashing a property speculation boom that is set to be repeated to the east if and when the Laguna Garzón bridge is built. This is merely the latest phase

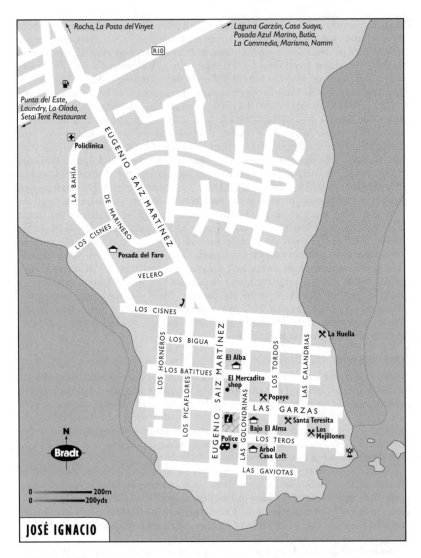

Rocha, La Posta del Vinyet

Laguna Garzón, Casa Suaya,
Posada Azul Marino, Butia,
La Commedia, Marismo, Namm

R10

Punta del Este,
Laundry, La Olada,
Setai Tent Restaurant

Policlínica

EUGENIO SAIZ MARTÍNEZ

LA BAHÍA

DE MARINERO

LOS CISNES

Posada del Faro

VELERO

LOS CISNES

LOS HORNEROS

LOS BIGUA

EUGENIO SAIZ MARTÍNEZ

El Alba

La Huella

LOS PICAFLORES

LOS BATITUES

El Mercadito
shop

LOS TORDOS

LAS CALANDRIAS

Popeye

LAS GOLONDRINAS

LAS GARZAS

Santa Teresita

Bajo El Alma

N

Los
Mejillones

LOS TEROS

Police

Bradt

Arbol
Casa Loft

LAS GAVIOTAS

0 ————— 200m
0 ————— 200yds

JOSÉ IGNACIO

of a process that began when the Carrasco bridge, just east of Montevideo, was built in 1951. First a few high-society families from Montevideo and Buenos Aires built summer homes here, but it was only in the 1990s that Argentine TV star Mirtha Legrand, Latina pop star Shakira (and boyfriend Antonio de la Rúa, son of a former Argentine president) and British writer Martin Amis and his Uruguayan wife Isabel Fonseca began to give the village a wider reputation. It was only in 2006 that luxury style magazines began to tout José Ignacio as the coolest place in the world to go for the southern summer. It's usually compared with the Hamptons on Long Island (the summer refuge for the rich and famous of New York).

Now many people worry about runaway development along the coast, although upmarket projects such as Laguna Escondida (200 lots with houses by Carlos Ott, being built just east of José Ignacio by Cuban-American tycoon Jorge Pérez, the man who turned Miami around) and the Setai (immediately west of the roundabout on Ruta 10, with a lodge, ten rental villas and 40 villas) will not immediately lead to high-rise sprawl. The global recession has already led to the suspension of other projects such as Barrancas de San Ignacio, a 98ha development by the Laguna José Ignacio.

Getting there From Montevideo COPSA runs three buses a day to José Ignacio in summer (*US$8*), as does COT (via Montevideo airport), all calling at Maldonado and Punta del Este too. It's often more convenient just to take the next bus to Punta del Este and change there for the local *micro* (bus)14 which runs nine times a day from bay 2 to José Ignacio, taking about 50 minutes. There are also four modern Machado buses a day from San Carlos via La Barra.

Orientation and information Buses terminate on Los Teros, by the police office on the south side of the wide grassy plaza. At the plaza's northwestern corner is a tourist information centre that is open late into the evening in January but cannot be relied on otherwise. There's limited information online at www.jose-ignacio.com.uy.

To the west, Los Teros leads to a slipway on the Playa Mansa where are a few fishing boats usually lie drawn up below a small shrine; to the east it leads to the lighthouse, where good boardwalks lead to the beach and nearby craft stalls. The *faro* (lighthouse), built in 1877, is 25m high (32m above sea level, with a range of 14 nautical miles), with 122 spiralling steps, but is not usually open to visitors. Along the shoreline you'll see granite boulders, small cacti, salt-resistant waxy-leaved plants and hummingbirds.

A sign at the entrance to the village reads 'The only thing that moves fast here is the wind', and there is a speed limit of 25km/h throughout the village.

Where to stay There's no campsite and no backpacker accommodation in the neighbourhood, although you may see a few *alquilo* signs, for houses and cabins to rent, by the main road to the west.

Arbol Casa Loft Los Teros, just east of the plaza; ℘ 486 2278; bookings Buenos Aires ℘ +54 11 4803 1113; e arbol@curiocitytravel.com; www.arbolcasaloft.com; ⏲ all year. Expensively simple & elegantly rustic, this discreet assemblage of white cubes including 1 loft, 4 suites & an apt (with open-air shower). All rooms are spacious, with heated floors, flat-screen TV, CD players, Wi-Fi, minibar & electronic safe, handmade candles & flowers. A swimming pool is tucked away in the beautifully manicured subtropical garden; there's also an honesty bar & games room with pool table. The friendly staff can arrange cars, tours, massages or horseriding. $$$$$

Casa Suaya Ruta 10, km186.5; ℘ 486 2750; Buenos Aires ℘ +54 11 5983 1622; Los Angeles ℘ +1 323 468 0200; e info@casasuaya.com; www.casasuaya.com. Aimed at those who want luxury, seclusion & an empty beach, this was created in the dunes 3.5km east of the village by the Argentine-American restaurateur Adolfo Suaya, who founded the Gaucho Grill, the Lodge & Geisha House in Los Angeles. The stone-walled suites are furnished fairly minimally but are cosy with open fireplace, kitchenette & balcony giving views of the ocean & of fantastic clear night skies. They come with cable TV, Wi-Fi & own-label toiletries. Bicycles are available, & horseriding can be arranged nearby. New blocks are being added, & the excellent Butiá restaurant (see below). which opens on to an infinity pool, is being joined by a new bar-restaurant. $$$$$

Posada Azul Marino 300m north from Ruta 10 km185.1; ℘ 486 2363; www.azulmarino.com.uy. Established as a relaxed & unpretentious private home offering B&B accommodation, a branch of Montevideo's classic La Commedia restaurant opened here in 2009 – although being on the same road as the ultra-chic Naam & Marismo restaurants you'd probably have managed fine anyway. You'll almost certainly need a car to go anywhere else. It's a classy Modernist house with 6 dbls & 3 suites (for up to 4), all with private deck or balcony (the best suite has a 40m² terrace with hot tub), sharing 4 common rooms with TV & DVD player, & a bar-restaurant. There's free Wi-Fi & a swimming pool. $$$$$

Posada del Faro Calle de la Bahía & Timonel; 486 2110; www.posadadelfaro.com; Jul–Apr. The best boutique hotel in the village itself, with Mediterranean hacienda-style rooms looking out over a small swimming pool (with in-pool bar, underwater stools & floating candles) to the Playa Mansa &, far in the distance, the towers of Punta del Este. The 12 rooms are individually designed but essentially all white, & TV-free (but with Wi-Fi). Service is excellent but unobtrusive, not disturbing the peace & tranquillity. B/fast is provided (from 09.00) & dinner in winter (when guests would otherwise have to drive to Punta). $$$$$

La Posta del Vinyet Chacras de Medellín; 480 6136; e info@lapostadelvinyet.com; www.lapostadelvinyet.com; mid-Sep–mid-Apr. The most delightful place to stay, a 4-bedroom romantic hideaway on a *chacra* development 4km north of José Ignacio, with stunning views from the huge living room over the infinity pool & Laguna José

Ignacio to the ocean. The 5ha of native parkland are beautifully laid out with benches & paths. Rooms have AC, cable TV, Wi-Fi, safe, fridge & kettle. It's all beautifully designed & managed with rescued doors, chandeliers & the like, own-label toiletries & lavender sprigs placed on beds & towels at turndown time. Everything's well organised to preserve the tranquillity, with no pets or under-16s allowed. $$$$$

Bajo El Alma Golondrinas & Garzas, just east of the plaza; 486 2098. The owners of this boutique shop (there was also a restaurant of the same name, but that has closed) have a couple of rooms to rent on a B&B basis, with a small kitchenette. $$$$

El Alba Los Battues, west of Las Golondrinas; 486 2088. 3 rooms to rent, with a deck & barbecue; perfectly comfortable, but as close as José Ignacio gets to a budget option. $$$$

✗ Where to eat
Fish is the thing here, of course, but a local seaweed is a speciality, cooked mainly in omelettes (*omeletta de algas*). Beachside *paradores* serve slow-motion lunches through the afternoon, and dinner in the coolest places doesn't get going before 22.00. With a reservation and a very full wallet, it's well worth the expedition from here to Pueblo Garzón (see page 218).

✗ Butia Ruta 10 km185.5; 486 2751; www.casasuaya.com; 09.00–01.00 daily. The restaurant of the Casa Suaya hotel, this is run by Uruguayan chef Clo Dimet, who has a successful restaurant in São Paulo. It serves Mediterranean-style cuisine with fish, chicken, lamb & beef cooked in the wood-fired oven or grilled. Specialities include *corvina negra* (sea bass) baked with glazed onions, *chipirones* (small squid) & squid with sweet pepper. The style is very relaxed, with some poolside tables & some in a thatched hut, lit by torches & the pool's underwater lighting. The El Brasero bar-restaurant has recently opened here, offering cheaper, simpler food such as steaks. $$$$$

✗ La Commedia 300m north from Ruta 10 km185.1; 486 2363, m 9910 8868; www.azulmarino.com.uy. The summer branch of a Montevideo restaurant which opened in January 2009 at the Posada Azul Marino, this serves b/fast, brunch-style lunch with gourmet sandwiches & salads, tapas, grilled sea bass, lamb, crab ravioli or seafood risotto. There are plans to bring in a DJ for a sunset spectacle. $$$$$

✗ La Olada Balneario La Jacinta; 486 2745; summer from 20.30 daily. In the very non-

touristy village 2km west (*enter at km181.5 on Avda Hector Soria, take 2nd right*), this is a real find, the restaurant that opens first every season & stays open longest, & serves remarkably fine food in what seems to be the chef's front room & porch. The wooden furnishings, candles & earth oven give a deceptively bohemian feel. Typical meals include sweetbreads with provolone cheese followed by lamb (from the family farm) with ratatouille, homemade pasta or seaweed risotto, with a *dulce de leche* flan to finish. $$$$$

✗ Marismo Ruta 10 km185.1; 486 2273; mid-Dec–Feb from 22.00 daily. Turning off the Laguna Garzón road at the sign for the Posada Azul Marino, you'll head into the forest for a few hundred yards until someone with a torch waves you in to a car park. This ultra-chic restaurant is totally alfresco, with candles on wooden tables around a bonfire. The menu is short but delicious, with tender slow-braised lamb a speciality. It's not too expensive, but credit cards are not accepted. $$$$$

✗ Namm Ruta 10 km185.1; 486 2526; mid-Dec–Feb from 22.00 daily. In a wooden hut in the forest, near Marismo, the equally trendy Namm (run by the owner of Montevideo's Café Misterio) serves sushi, grilled meats & fusion cuisine, in a magical atmosphere with lanterns & soft cushions. $$$$$

✘ **Setai Tent Restaurant** Ruta 10 km182; m 9563 0767. As part of its campaign to get planning permission for the luxury Setai resort, this restaurant was created in a large Moroccan-themed tent by the Playa Mansa. In a sort of Oriental-Zen setting, there's a wide range of dishes, all well presented. $$$$$

✘ **La Huella** Los Cisnes, Playa Brava; ☎ 486 2231/2279; www.paradorlahuella.com; ⏰ lunch Fri–Sun, from 1 Dec daily; dinner mid-Dec–Mar. Great food in a wonderful setting, & the place to eat (& people-watch) in José Ignacio – it's best to reserve, although there will be a queue all afternoon. It's a beachfront *parador* that seems casual but is actually very precisely run, with a simple menu of grilled or stewed fish, squid, langoustines, mussels, sushi or pizza. There's a good choice of vegetarian dishes such as polenta &

spinach with blue cheese. The bar is well stocked, & there's good music with a suitably relaxed vibe. You can come for a leisurely lunch or coffee in your swimsuit, sip clericó with the sunset, or enjoy a candle-lit dinner. $$$$

✘ **Los Mejillones** Los Teros & Las Calandrias; ☎ 486 2018. With a panoramic terrace near the lighthouse, this serves seafood (including seaweed omelettes), b/fasts, teas, coffees & cakes, in a relaxed family atmosphere. $$$

✘ **Popeye** Tordos & Garzas; ⏰ Dec–Easter. A friendly diner that serves good *chivitos* as well as seafood paella, seaweed ravioli, pasta & gnocchi. $$$

✘ **Santa Teresita** Las Garzas between Golondrinas & Tordos; ☎ 486 2004. Known as the birthplace of the seaweed omelette, this small restaurant in one of the village's older houses has long since been left behind by the trendy modern restaurants, but serves adequate fish, seafood & pizza. $$$

Other practicalities

Healthcare For health care, there's a *policlínica* (⏰ 09.10–11.55 Mon–Fri) to the west of Sainz Martínez, just south of the Ruta 10 roundabout.

Laundry There's a laundry and internet place on Calle Albatros in the Balneario La Jacinta (*inland from Ruta 10 km181.5;* ☎ 486 2421).

Markets For basic foodstuffs there's El Mercadito (*Saiz Martínez, immediately north of the plaza*), with a *farmacía* alongside. There's also La Pulpería/Carnicería Manolo (*north end of Las Golondrinas*).

Shopping Upmarket boutiques include El Canuto (*Los Cisnes, Playa Mansa*), including sundresses by Uruguayan designers and shoes, and Bajo El Alma (*Golondrinas & Garzas*), selling sarongs and silky tops. The classiest shop of all is the very minimalist Tierra y Vino (*Los Tordos & Las Garzas;* ☎ 486 2550), which looks more like a sculpture gallery than a wine shop.

Taxis For a taxi call (24 hours) ☎ 486 2173, m 9981 5643, or for a *remise* ☎ 486 2225.

Activities

Surfing Surfing is the main sport here, with ideal conditions when the *pampero* is blowing from the southwest, when waves can reach 2m; for lessons call m 9910 6707.

At Laguna Garzón, 7km east, Laura Moñino, sub-champion (ie: runner-up) at the South American windsurfing championships, offers windsurfing and kite-surfing lessons and also has a Hobie Cat dinghy – contact Laura Kite & Windsurf (☎ 486 2060, m 9442 0704; e laumonino@hotmail.com).

Water-skiing Water-skiing is banned on the *lagunas* but a 700m-long artificial lake has been created 9km north of José Ignacio on Camino Sainz Martínez (leading to Ruta 9) at Lassarena Club de Ski (m 9926 5483; e info@lassarena.com; www.lassarena.com).

Horseriding Horseriding is very popular, with various operations along Ruta 10 east of José Ignacio – first is Cabalgatas (*entre el Campo & el Mar, 600m north;* m *9995 6262*), then the recommended Haras Godiva (*km187½;* ꕦ *480 6112*).

PUEBLO GARZÓN

The town of Garzón, 42km (largely unpaved) north of José Ignacio and 70km from Punta del Este (about an hour and US$60 by taxi), was founded in 1892 by Fermín de León, at a ford on the road to Rocha where governor Vicente Garzon had a ranch. It had a population of over 2,000 until the granite quarries and railway closed in the 1960s, when it fell to around 200. Since then it has looked like a classic western ghost town (without the tumbleweed rolling down the main street), although there is more work nowadays, processing trees from local plantations.

The station is still there, along with the church, school and town hall on the plaza with its old palm trees, but on a corner of the plaza the old general store is now a five-star boutique hotel with just five rooms, and perhaps the most prestigious restaurant in the country.

The Argentine star chef Francis Mallman (born Francisco, to an Uruguayan mother), who owns the prestigious Restaurant 1884 (Mendoza, Argentina), Patagonia Sur (Buenos Aires) and Patagonia West (Westhampton, New York), created a restaurant called Los Negros in José Ignacio back in 1977, when it really was known only to those far ahead of the trends. It became legendary, partly because of the cast-iron boxes which he used as both cooking utensils and serving dishes. As José Ignacio filled up and became, to Mallman's mind, more affluent, crowded and less interesting, he began looking for somewhere new to set up a small luxury guesthouse, and at the start of the century moved to Garzón, which he describes as *el Uruguay de adentro*, authentic backcountry Uruguay.

The **Hotel & Restaurant Garzón** (*11km north from Ruta 9 km175;* ꕦ *410 2811;* e *info@restaurantegarzon.com; www.restaurantegarzon.com;* $$$$$) has just five smallish rooms, with boho-rustic décor, lots of cushions on the floor, oversized candelabras and claw-foot bathtubs. They also have free Wi-Fi and slightly thin walls, and there's an attractive patio, garden and swimming pool. But all that really counts is the food, and the jaw-dropping room rates do include full board (breakfast, lunch, tea and dinner, including wines from Finca Anita in Mendoza) as well as laundry, bikes, horseriding and sulky rides. The cooking is bold and simple, based on the traditional *inferniello* (little hell) technique of cooking between two wood fires on iron griddles that are also used to serve the food at the table. There's also a wood-fired oven for baking breads and desserts. Mallman's best-known dishes include chicken in a salt crust, lamb in a mustard-and-thyme crust, duck breast with Malbec sauce and potatoes, endives and tomatoes, and grilled steak with *chimichurri* sauce (olive oil, parsley, oregano and garlic), along with corn *humitas*, baked peaches with Iberian ham and hazelnut, leeks vinaigrette with eggs and anchovies, and pears in Tannat sauce.

You can also dip into Mallman's collection of around 3,000 volumes of poetry (including Neruda, Lorca and Mayakovsky), as well as books and magazines in Spanish, English, French and Portuguese. Mallman gives free cookery classes for local 6- to 14-year-olds, and 90% of the staff are from the village.

SAN CARLOS

Immediately south of Ruta 9, the unassuming little town of San Carlos was founded in 1763 by Viceroy Pedro de Ceballos (1715–78), first viceroy of the River Plate in 1776, and largely settled by Portuguese families. Famous *carolinos* include Colonel Leonardo Oliveira (who captured the Fortaleza de Santa Teresa from Brazil in 1826), Father Antonio Vidal (president in 1880–82 and 1886) and Mariano Soler (1846–1908, the first Archbishop of Montevideo). With a population of 25,000, it's now the main agricultural centre of Maldonado department. It's a cheap place to spend the night if you want to experience authentic small-town Uruguay rather than the madness of Punta del Este. It also has a good zoo, as well as a poor museum.

Getting there

By car San Carlos is 15km and 20 minutes north of Maldonado, following Ruta 39 (dual-carriage for most of the way) through attractive open country and wetlands.

By bus Codesa buses run from Punta del Este and Maldonado to San Carlos every 15 minutes through the day, and every 30 minutes in the evening. These leave you near the terminal, where you can connect with buses from Montevideo to Rocha. COT's two daily buses from Punta del Este to Rocha also call here. COOM and EmTur run north to Minas and Treinta y Tres. The bus terminal is on Avenida Rodó immediately west of the main north–south road, Avenida Andrés Ceberio; Plaza 19 de Abril, a block to the east and a block north, is a secondary one, with the main Plaza Artigas six blocks further east along 18 de Julio.

Where to stay There are only a couple of places to stay, both absurdly cheap. On the south side of the bus terminal is the decent **Hospedaje Terminal** (*Avda Rodó 1115;* ☎ *42 668011; rooms with private bath & cable TV, or with shared bathroom, US$2 pp*). Slightly better rooms are on offer at the **Hospedaje Uruguay** (*25 de Agosto 1053 & Avda Ceberio, a block north of the terminal;* ☎ *42 669463; rooms with bathroom & cable TV US$3 inc b/fast*). On the southeast corner of Plaza Artigas at 19 de Julio 663, Hotel 18 is currently closed and for sale.

Where to eat There are various places to eat around Plaza Artigas, including the Bar Colonial *cafetería-sandwichería* north of the church, the bigger better Plaza Café restaurant-pizzería on the northwestern corner of the plaza, and the *cafetería-pizza-parrilla-heladería* Messano diagonally opposite. On the southwestern corner of the plaza the Nuevo Grieco restaurant-pizzería is a bit less of a bar.

Other practicalities

Banks There's an ATM at the Banco República (*corner of Oliveira on the east side of Plaza Artigas*).

Communications A weak Wi-Fi signal is available on Plaza Artigas. The post office is in a *farmacía* by the Maldonado bus stop, immediately east of the bus terminal.

Emergency services The San Carlos hospital (*Avda Ceberio 519;* ☎ *42 669043, 42 669519*) is southwest of the centre.

Markets The most convenient supermarket is the El Dorado (*Avda Ceberio & Rincón*), with others at Sarandí 873 and at 25 de Agosto & Sarandí.

What to see and do On the west side of Plaza Artigas you'll find the church of San Carlos Borromeo (1792–1801), with a simple colonial-style façade and plain white brickwork inside. Next to it is a radio station in an Art Deco former cinema. On the southeastern corner of the plaza, La Garita is a tiny turret, a replica of one at the Fortaleza de Santa Teresa in Rocha, erected in 1953 to commemorate Leonardo Oliveira and other *carolinos* who fought for independence.

From the north side of the plaza, Treinta y Tres leads three blocks east to the riverside Teatro Municipal de Verano, the open-air theatre where *carnaval* parades are held in the second half of February. A footbridge leads across to the Parque Municipal Cayetano Silva, named after the son of a black slave (1868–1920) who moved to Argentina and became famous there for composing the army's March of San Lorenzo. There's also a road bridge (leading to Ruta 9) a block to the north; about half a kilometre to the east of the bridge a road leads south to the stadium, the **Parque Medina zoo** (⏱ *to sunset Tue–Sun; free*) and 12km away, La Barra.

The zoo is quite large and well kept, but a bit old-fashioned. In an area of 14ha (once the Medina family estate) it houses around 600 animals of 48 species, mainly native and African (including lions and various monkeys). South American animals include llamas, pumas, foxes, boar (introduced for hunting), carpinchos (capybaras), *guazuvirá* (grey brocket deer), birds including vultures, parrots, jays, rheas and flamingos, and snakes. There's also a large grassy area with picnic tables, barbecues and drinking water, as well as a souvenir kiosk.

A block south from the east side of Plaza Artigas is the **Museo Histórico Regional** (*Reyles & Oliveira;* ⏱ *09.00–19.00 Tue–Sat, 13.00–19.00 Sun, summer 09.00–23.00 Tue–Sat; free*), which seems to be reorganising its small collection of indigenous and pioneer oddments; there are also temporary art shows here. Built in 1782, this was the Spanish commander's house.

CERRO CATEDRAL The highest point in Uruguay is Cerro Catedral (513.7m), although the Cerro de las Ánimas, at 509m, was thought to be the highest until 1973. An almost traffic-free dirt road passes within a couple of hundred metres of the summit, making it an easy hike, with some excellent birdwatching along the way.

Just north of San Carlos, main roads meet at a roundabout at km138 of Ruta 9 (Montevideo–Chuy) and km20 of Ruta 39 (Punta del Este–Aiguá). Continuing northwards, the scenery gets rockier, with lots of *chirca* scrub, as the road winds up to km56 and then down. Three EmTur buses a day (Maldonado–Treinta y Tres) come this way and will set you down at km67.5, by a radio mast to the west and a dirt road to the east signposted to Villa El Cordillera and La Laguna. Hiking east from here, you'll drop a bit to a broad valley, with a ridge of almost equally high tops ahead – it's easy to see why it took so long to identify Cerro Catedral as the highest point. This is all open farmland at first, with some eucalyptus trees and agaves, as well as horneros, flickers, teros, doves, swallows and vultures. After an hour you'll drop and swing right at the gate of Establecimiento Villa del Cordillera. After crossing a creek you'll climb again to the entry to the **Posada de Campo La Laguna** (m *9442 3136; www.posadadecampolalaguna.com*), 6km to the left, after about 40 minutes (8km from the road). It's possible to stay here (by reservation), a different experience to most tourist *estancias* in the flatlands. Horseriding and guided walks are available, and there's a stream with tranquil pools and plenty of birdlife, as well as margay cats. Day visits are possible as well as overnight stays with full board.

Another 15 minutes on the dirt road brings you up on to a plateau with pools of water and big views back to the west. There are cattle here as well as teros, kestrels and other birds. In another 20 minutes (about 2½ hours from the road) you'll come to a sign reading 'Cerro Catedral', with an obvious small pile of stones where you can climb the fence to the right, or squeeze through. It takes a couple of minutes to reach the highest point in Uruguay, where a survey point bears its former name, Cerro Cordillera. There's a small outcrop on the flank of the summit that looks vaguely like cathedral spires.

It's tempting to explore along the ridge north and south, but when you're ready to continue the dirt road drops into a valley with much more birdlife, including tijeretas (fork-tailed flycatchers) and other flycatchers and tyrants, field flickers, teros, doves, partridge and brown-and-yellow marshbirds. After 40 minutes you'll pass a farm and will then need to turn left at a junction, bringing you in about half an hour to the unpaved Ruta 109 from Rocha to Aiguá. There are no buses on this road, and not much traffic, but you should get a ride eventually. Alternatively, walk back from Cerro Catedral to Ruta 39.

Aiguá is a small town, bypassed by Ruta 8 between Minas and Treinta y Tres; 2km from the town at Ruta 39 km90, the Stella Maris farm (✆ 44 06127; ⊕ all year) offers agroturismo, guided walks, horseriding, cart-rides and farm activities. There's simple accommodation for six, or day visits are possible.

ROCHA DEPARTMENT

Ruta 9 continues east from San Carlos in pleasant park-like country with lots of trees. At km143½ Ruta 104 leads south to Manantiales (see page 207), and at km160.8 another dirt road heads south to José Ignacio (see page 213). At km175½ a police post and school mark the turning north to Pueblo Garzón (see page 218), and 2km further east the highway crosses the Arroyo Garzón into Rocha department, with a toll post just beyond. At km187 a road leads south to the isolated stretch of Ruta 10 between lagunas Garzón and Rocha, and at km205 another road leads 5km south to the *zona de playa y pesca* (beach and fishing zone) and the *puerto de las botes* (boat harbour) on the north shore of Laguna de Rocha. At km206 (68km from the San Carlos junction, one hour by bus) is another roundabout, with a tourist information office, petrol station and 24-hour supermarket and *parador*, where you can turn left into the town of Rocha, capital of the department of the same name.

Rocha is one of Uruguay's most attractive departments, with its long, empty coastline, windswept sandy beaches separated by rocky points, inland lagoons – formed when the sea rose at the end of the last Ice Age – with plentiful birdlife, and rolling interior dotted with Butia palms. This is the area that Prince Charles particularly asked to see on his 1999 visit to Uruguay. The largest grove of ombú trees in the country grows beside the Laguna de Castillos.

From around 4,000 years ago, large mounds known as *cerritos* (up to 40m in diameter and 7m in height) were constructed in the coastal area – not, as was assumed, burial mounds, but the sites of villages created as the climate changed and marshlands dried out. The border with Brazil moved to and fro across this area in the 18th and 19th centuries, with many skirmishes and raids, delaying settlement and development; now it is largely occupied with cattle ranching. In the 1940s future resorts were designated along its 180km Atlantic coast and divided into lots on paper, but no money was forthcoming to build anything. Then some totally unplanned settlements, such as Aguas Dulces and Cabo Polonio, appeared, with cabins being built on public land without permission, and no services whatsoever – not even road access in the case of Cabo Polonio. In 1990 the department began to regulate these developments, in order to boost tourism but without losing what makes the department special. Property speculation is moving along the coast from Punta del Este and José Ignacio into Rocha, betting on a bridge being built at Laguna Garzón. Some huge private houses are being built here, notably one of 2,300m² by Microsoft Vice-President Ralf Harteneck.

In 1976 the **Bañados del Este** (Eastern Wetlands) Biosphere Reserve was designated by UNESCO, encompassing various existing nature reserves and historic monuments including the Santa Teresa and San Miguel forts, Cabo Polonio and lagunas Rocha and Garzón (12,500km² in total, in five departments). This also became a Ramsar wetlands reserve in 1982, but is not yet part of the Sistema Nacional de Areas Protegidas (SNAP), the new national system of protected areas, and there are not enough environmental controls on development, particularly given the increase in rice farming. Habitats include seashore, dunes, lagoons, inland marshes, palm swamps, grassland, gallery forest and hilly *bosque serrano*, supporting at least 75% of the bird species found in Uruguay; in Rocha you can easily see 60 or more species in a day. These include austral migrants that breed in Patagonia and then move north, nearctic migrants, especially shorebirds, that winter here (in the southern summer) and neotropic migrants that breed here and fly north for the winter. The brackish coastal lagoons are South America's most important coastal site for American golden plover, while grasslands provide breeding habitat for several threatened capuchino seedeaters (*Sporophila* spp.). In addition 60% of Uruguay's mammal species are found here, including carpincho (capybara), paca, otter, guazu-birá and pampas deer, and marine mammals such as sea lions and cetaceans.

The non-profit body Probides (*Programa de Conservación de la Biodiversidad y Desarrollo Sustentable en los Humedales del Este; Ruta 9 km205, Rocha;* ✆ 47 25005/28021; e *probides@probides.org.uy; www.probides.org.uy*) produced the management plan for the Bañados del Este in 2000 and now manages the Laguna de Rocha, working closely with local fishing communities.

ROCHA The town of Rocha was founded in 1793, basically by accident: a group of settlers from Asturia in northern Spain were heading for Patagonia, but their ship was forced to put in to Maldonado. It was named after the Argentine Luis Rocha, who issued permits for the slaughter of cattle here at the time. Now it's a typical quiet market town with a population of 26,000 (of a total of 70,000 in the department). It calls itself the Uruguayan capital of *maté* and hosts the Fiesta Nacional del Maté in early December, with gauchos and carts riding into Plaza Independencia at midday on Sunday with sprigs of the medicinal herb.

Getting there, orientation and information The departmental tourism office (*junction of Ruta 9 & Ruta 15;* ✆ 47 29728, 47 23100; e *turismorocha@adinet.com.uy; www.turismorocha.gub.uy;* ⊕ 10.00–18.00 *Mon–Fri*) is on the southeastern edge of town. From here José Batlle y Ordóñez leads northwest into the town, continuing as Ruta 109 to Aiguá; turning left on 25 de Agosto it's four blocks to Plaza Independencia, the leafy central square.

By bus The bus companies COT, Cynsa and Rutas del Sol all have offices on the southwestern side of Plaza Independencia, where taxis (✆ 47 27870) also wait. All bus services from Montevideo to Chuy and La Paloma (see page 82) call here, as well as COT's two daily buses from Punta del Este to Chuy and local services to La Paloma and La Pedrera.

⌂ **Where to stay** There are just a few fairly simple but central places to stay.

⌂ **Hotel Trocadero** 25 de Agosto & 18 de Julio; ✆ 47 22267. Just east of the plaza, this 1970s-style 3-star has some AC rooms (US$5 extra). $$$

⌂ **Hotel Arrarte** Ramírez 118 & 25 de Mayo; ✆ 47 26756/24597; e arrarte@hotmail.com. On the southwest side of the plaza, this nice old-style place is traditional & not tatty; there's parking & a buffet b/fast is included. $$

⌂ **Hotel Municipal** 19 de Abril 87; ✆ 47 22404. Just southeast of the plaza, this quiet & very friendly 2-star hotel has clean simple rooms, some with cable TV; a decent b/fast is included (07.00–10.00). $

✖ **Where to eat** Likewise, the choice of restaurants is limited, but all are on or close to Plaza Independencia. Near the bus offices on the southwestern side of the plaza,

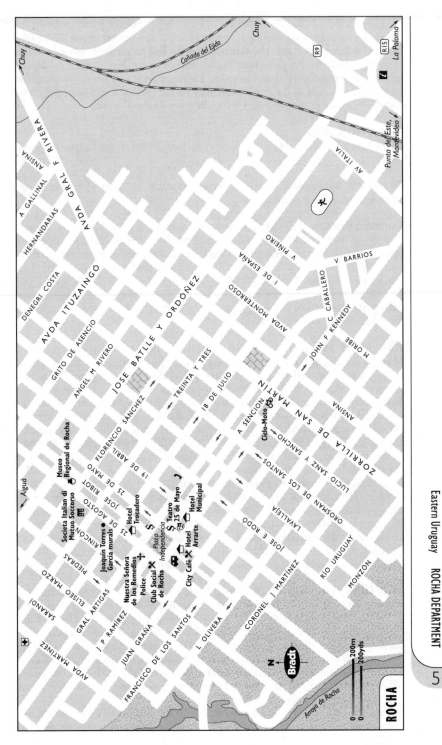

ROCHA

Chuy

Cañada del Ejido

Chuy

R9

R15

La Paloma

Punta del Este, Montevideo

AV ITALIA

V PIÑEIRO

V BARRIOS

I DE ESPAÑA

AVDA MONTERROSO

JOHN F C CABALLERO

M ORIBE

ANSINA

A GALLINAL

HERNANDARIAS

AVDA GRAL F RIVERA

ANSINA

AVDA ITUZAINGÓ

DENEGRI COSTA

GRITO DE ASENCIO

ANGEL M RIVERO

JOSÉ BATLLE Y ORDÓÑEZ

FLORENCIO SÁNCHEZ

TREINTA Y TRES

18 DE JULIO

A SENCIÓN

ZORRILLA DE SAN MARTÍN

LUCIO SANZ Y SANCHO

OROSMAN DE LOS SANTOS

LAVALLEJA

JOSE E RODÓ

Ciclo-Moto

19 DE ABRIL

25 DE MAYO

JOSÉ RIBOT

25 DE AGOSTO

RINCÓN

PIEDRAS

ELISEO MARZO

GRAL ARTIGAS

J P RAMÍREZ

JUAN GRAÑA

FRANCISCO DE LOS SANTOS

L OLIVERA

CORONEL J MARTÍNEZ

RÍO URUGUAY

MONZON

Museo Regional de Rocha

Societá Italian di Mutuo Soccorso

Joaquín Torres García murals

Nuestra Señora de los Remedios

Police

Club Social de Rocha

City Café

Hotel Trocadero

Plaza Independencia

Teatro

25 de Mayo

Hotel Arrarte

Hotel Municipal

SARANDÍ

AVDA MARTÍNEZ

Aiguá

N

Bradt

200m
200yds

0

0

Arroyo de Rocha

the **City Café** is a bar-café which serves a basic range of steaks, pastas and the like; there's a *salón comedor* upstairs with a more peaceful atmosphere, but it'll probably be open at lunchtime only. The **Club Social de Rocha** on the north side of the plaza is an attractive Art Deco building, as marked by its Deco Lounge restaurant and bar, the more formal option in town. There are some tiny but enjoyable **cafés** on Paseo Vaz Mendosa, the refurbished alley on the southeastern side of the plaza, and the Féola ice cream shop on J P Ramírez just south of the plaza.

Other practicalities

Banks Banco República and Banco Comercial have ATMs on the eastern corner of the plaza.

Bike repair Bike and motorbike parts are available at Ciclo-Moto Repuestos (*Ramírez & Zorrilla de San Martín*).

Communications Antel's call centre is nearby (*19 de Abril 116 near Artigas;* ⊕ *09.00–19.00 Mon–Sat*). There's free public Wi-Fi on Plaza Independencia, which you can use near the windows of the City Café. The Cyber Space internet centre is on the traffic-calmed southeast side of the plaza. The post office is east of the plaza (*18 de Julio 2085 near 19 de Abril;* ⊕ *09.00–17.00 Mon–Fri, 08.00–12.00 Sat*).

Emergency services The public hospital (✆ *47 22608*) is on Avenida Martínez, to the left off Ruta 109 towards Aiguá.

What to see and do On the northwestern side of the plaza is the church of **Nuestra Señora de los Remedios**, founded in 1794, remodelled in 1956 and now pretty unattractive, with a very plain Neoclassical interior and a spotlit Virgin and Child above the altar. At the southwestern corner of the plaza are the single-storey Belle-Epoque **Teatro 25 de Mayo** (reopened in 2007) and the Art Deco-style Primero Agosto cinema. Going northeast from the plaza on 25 de Agosto you'll see two Constructivist murals by Joaquín Torres García in front of the Teacher Training Centre (*25 de Agosto 131*), then the ornate Società Italiana di Mutuo Soccorso (*Italian Mutual Aid Society; Treinta y Tres 1985*). A block further, beyond the duller Sociedad Española de Socorros Mutos (*Spanish Mutual Aid Society; 25 de Agosto 149*), is the very missable **Museo Regional de Rocha** (*25 de Agosto 162 & Sánchez;* ⊕ *08.00–13.45 Mon–Fri; free*). Its old-fashioned displays feature ancient bones, *bolas* and *rompacabezas*, material on local children's author Constancio Vigil, the landing of a flying boat on the Laguna de Rocha in 1945 by Lionel de Marmier (inaugurating the Paris–Buenos Aires service), and a local man who served in the French Foreign Legion in World War II. The end room contains swords, uniforms, old phones, harnesses and a carriage for taking prisoners from court to jail.

LA PALOMA From the junction of Ruta 9 and Ruta 15, on the southeastern edge of Rocha, it's 28km to La Paloma, the most developed beach resort in Rocha and one of the most popular with the surfing community. A lighthouse was built on the rocky headland known as the Cabo Santa María in 1874, followed by a port at the start of the 20th century. In 1936 the Sociedad Cabo Santa María was set up, led by Nicolás Solari (a prosperous merchant in Salto), to construct a new resort, designed by Carlos Gómez Gavazzo (1904–87), who had worked in Le Corbusier's office in Paris. It's a very pleasant low-rise development, but there are few actual Corbusieresque buildings.

The port (north of the resort, protected from the Atlantic by a long mole), has become one of the Uruguayan navy's main bases, and there are currently plans to build a major new port with a pipeline and a rail link to southern Brazil. This would take ships with a draught of up to 24m, double what's possible in Montevideo. However, it would seriously compromise the country's fastest-growing centre of tourism. For the last couple of years, La Paloma has been totally packed out with school-leavers and students for the first two weeks of January – it's said that up to 20,000 young people come here, 10 or 12 to a house, although they don't seem to sleep much, with all-night parties everywhere.

Getting there, orientation and information Ruta 15 crosses Ruta 10 5km north of La Paloma, and 2.5km further on passes La Aguada, site of the most popular student campsite. After another 2km through pine woods you suddenly arrive at La Paloma's bus terminal, separated from the resort by a row of trees. Walking ahead (southwest) you emerge on Avenida Paloma by the police station. Turn left towards the centre; just beyond the Hostel Ibirapitá (on the right) and craft market (on the left) are a roundabout and petrol station, with a tourist information centre (*www.lapaloma.net*) on the traffic island.

By bus There are reasonably frequent local buses between Rocha and La Paloma in summer, as well as through services from Montevideo (see page 82), and one or two from Chuy. Bus companies are in the terminal. For tickets to Buenos Aires, Buquebus (*Avda Solarí north of Avda del Navío;* ⊕ *10.00–19.00 Mon–Sat, 09.00–14.00 Sun*) is in the only tall building in town.

By taxi There are two taxi co-ops, both at the bus terminal: Central de Taxis (↘ *479 6710, 479 8064*) and Radio Taxi (↘ *479 8664,* ⊞ *9927 9625*). There's also Swan Rentacar (⊞ *9957 9336*).

Where to stay There are quite a few mid-range hotels spread around the rather suburban area west of the centre. Most young people who flock here in January stay in the campsites and *cabañas* just north of La Paloma, but there are a couple of hostels. There are also *alquilo* signs around the resort, advertising houses and cabins for rent.

Hotels

Portobello Tres Marías near Foque, Los Botes; ↘ 479 6159; www.hotelportobello.com.uy; ⊕ mid-Dec–Feb. In a quiet area 2km west of the centre, on Playa Los Botes (also known as Playa Anaconda or Solari), this has 46 rooms for up to 4 people, all opening on to the sea & garden. Sports facilities & bicycles are available. $$$$– $$$$

Bahía Avda del Navío & Sol; ↘ 479 6029; e hbahia@montevideo.com.uy; www.elbahia.com.uy; ⊕ all year. Just off the main drag, this 3-star place is a classic 1936 edifice but well modernised, with clean, bright rooms, cable TV, Wi-Fi & a decent restaurant. There are dbl & trpl rooms plus superior rooms with balconies & better bathrooms. $$$$

Tirrenia Avda de Navío between Leo & Piscic; ↘ 479 6230; e adriadi@adinet.com.uy; www.htirrenia.com. A smallish 3-star with 7 rooms with fan & 7 with AC, as well as apts for up to 7 people, all with cable TV & frigobar. Free umbrellas & deck chairs available on the beach. $$$$

Cabo Santa María Avda Solari between Sirio & Titania; ↘ 479 6004; e cabosantamaria@redfacil.com.uy; www.cabosantamaria.com; ⊕ all year. The grandest hotel here, built in 1980 to house a casino (now only slot machines; ⊕ *daily in summer, w/ends from 20.00 the rest of the year*), this is a rambling pile of a place near the lighthouse, 1km from the bus terminal. Rates inc buffet b/fast in summer & continental b/fast the rest of the year. At the rear of the hotel there are apts & bungalows with kitchenettes. $$$

Perla del Este Adonis between Apolo & Júpiter; ↘ 479 6078; e hotelperladeleste@adinet.com.uy. By the sea just north of the lighthouse, this 3-star place looks like a rather run-down apt block, but is open when most others in the area are closed. Cable TV, shaded parking & buffet b/fast inc. $$$

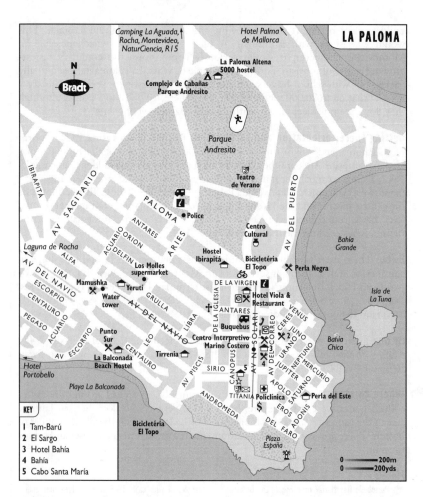

LA PALOMA

Camping La Aguada,
Rocha, Montevideo,
NaturCiencia, R15

Hotel Palma
de Mallorca

La Paloma Altena
5000 hostel

Complejo de Cabañas
Parque Andresito

N

Parque
Andresito

Teatro
de Verano

Police

Centro
Cultural

Laguna de Rocha

Hostel
Ibirapitá

Bicicletéria
El Topo

Perla Negra

Bahía
Grande

Los Molles
supermarket

Mamushka

Yerutí

Hotel Viola &
Restaurant

Isla de
La Tuna

Water
tower

Buquebus

Bahía
Chica

Punto
Sur

Centro Interpretivo
Marino Costero

Tirrenia

Hotel
Portobello

La Balconada
Beach Hostel

5

Playa La Balconada

Policlínica

Perla del Este

KEY

1 Tam-Barú
2 El Sargo
3 Hotel Bahía
4 Bahía
5 Cabo Santa María

Bicicletéria
El Topo

Plaza
España

0 ———— 200m
0 ———— 200yds

Yerutí Grulla near Aries, La Balconada; ☎ 479
6235, m 9969 5707; e yaruti@adinet.com.uy;
www.hotelyeruti.com. An attractive Modernist bldg
with a balcony all around the upper floor, this has
22 rooms with cable TV & fans; service is excellent.
$$$

Palma de Mallorca La Aguada; ☎ 479 6739;
www.hotelpalmademallorca.com.uy. About 3km north
of La Paloma, on one of the main surfing beaches,
this resort-style place has an indoor pool, beach

service, children's games room, video room, tennis
courts & bikes, & offers a fine buffet b/fast, as well
as free coffee 24hrs/day. However, it's a bit run-
down & overpriced. $$

Viola Solari near Antares; ☎ 479 6020;
e hviola@adinet.com.uy. On the main drag close
to the tourist information centre, this is clean &
simple, with fans in rooms, & PCs with internet
access. There's also a decent restaurant serving fish
& pasta. $$

Hostels

Hostel Ibirapitá Avda Paloma s/n; ☎ 479 9303,
m 9996 0869; e hostelibirapita@hotmail.com;
www.hostelibirapita.com; ⏰ all year. Just 5mins from
the bus terminal & the beach, this friendly place has
rooms around 2 interior patios behind the
shopfront-style reception, where new arrivals are

given a Google Map tour of the area. There are
men-only, women-only & mixed rooms with 4–10
beds, & rooms for couples. Fairly poor b/fast inc
(09.00–11.00) & a kitchen is available, as well as
a PC, Wi-Fi, cable TV, laundry service, bike rental &
surfing lessons. $$

La Balconada Beach Hostel Playa La Balconada at rear of Punto Sur restaurant; m 9419 8686, 9920 5423; e info@labalconadahostel.com; www.labalconadahostel.com; ⏱ all year. Cooler & more stylish than the other hostels, this is virtually on La Balconada beach, 10mins walk from the terminal. It has shared rooms for 4 & 6, plus dbls, with kitchen, internet access (Wi-Fi & a PC) & open-air bar. B/fast inc. $$

La Paloma Altena 5000 Hostel Parque Municipal Andresito; ☎ 479 6396; e lapaloma@hosteluruguay.org; ⏱ all year. A small thatched place in the Parque Andresito campsite, with 6-bed dorms for men & women, this is the cheapest hostel in La Paloma; it's also the least clean. Continental b/fast inc. A kitchen is available, as well as internet access. $

Camping

Complejo de Cabañas Parque Andresito Ruta 15 km1.5; ☎ 479 6081; e complejoandresito@adinet.com.uy. In the woods between the terminal & the port, there are 3 sizes of *cabaña*, all with cable TV. On the west side is a so-called *zona de camping*, with pretty basic facilities (⏱ Dec–Mar). $$–$

Camping La Aguada Ruta 15 km2.5; ☎ 479 6239; e complejolaaguada@hotmail.com; www.complejolaaguada.com; ⏱ all year. With tent space & *cabañas*, this is packed with students in high season & probably not a lot of sleeping takes place. Buses stop outside, & there are barbecues, electrical sockets & a laundry. $

✗ Where to eat

✗ Bahía Avda del Navío & Sol; ☎ 479 6029; www.elbahia.com.uy. A long-standing restaurant serving a standard range of fish, steaks, chicken & pasta, as well as some salads. $$$

✗ Punto Sur Playa La Balconada; ☎ 479 9462; ⏱ Dec–Easter. You pay for the ideal beachfront location, but service is good & food is well presented; the menu is limited but this is the perfect spot for a bit of seafood at sunset. $$$

✗ El Sargo Mercurio & Ceres; ☎ 479 7922. Across the road from the Bahía, this is a lively pizza & fish restaurant that's excellent value. $$

✗ Mamushka Avda del Navío & Acuario; m 9946 0538; ⏱ all year. On the roundabout right by the OSE water tower, this is quite a stylish café-bar that has Wi-Fi & hosts live bands. $$

✗ Perla Negra Avda del Puerto. A lively resto-pub at the rear of the ANCAP petrol station near the Bahía Grande, with a disco (*from 01.00*); go for the action, not the food. $$

✗ Tam-Barú Avda del Navío & Sol. Excellent ice cream. $$

✗ Viola Solari near Antares; ☎ 479 6020. At the top of the main street, this has a good choice of fresh fish, as well as pasta & gnocchi. $$

Entertainment and nightlife La Paloma, and La Aguada in particular, has changed rapidly from a family-oriented resort to one dominated by youth, at least in the first half of January. Now up to 8,000 people a night head for the discos (*US$4*) in the woods between the port and La Aguada. These get going around midnight and close only at 08.00, when the party continues with dancing to car stereos for another hour or two. The best disco is said to be Pogo, followed by Arachanes and Hippie. A row of *carritos* opposite the discos sells hot dogs from 07.30. The noise and disruption may oblige the discos to be moved north to the junction of Ruta 10 and Ruta 15.

Some of the bar-restaurants listed above have live bands in summer and stay open late; other bars are along Avenida Solarí and Calle de la Virgen. The Perla Negra caters to the older generation, playing hits from the 1960s to 1990s.

The Cine La Paloma (☎ 479 7022; ⏱ Dec–Mar; US$5) is just south of the casino.

Other practicalities

Banks Banco República (*Avda Solari & Titania*), with an ATM, is handily placed opposite the casino. Two exchange offices are Cambio Nelson (*Avda Solarí south of Antares; ⏱ Jan–Feb 08.00–22.00 daily, rest of the year 09.00–20.00 Mon–Sat*) and Cambio Maiorano (*Avda Solarí & Avda Del Navio; ⏱ 09.00–19.00 Mon–Sat, 09.00–13.00 Sun*).

Bike hire The Bicicletería El Topo is on Calle de la Virgen just west of Avenida Solarí; there's also the Taller de Bicicletas (⏲ *09.00–13.00, 15.00–19.00*), a very basic shed opposite the police station on Avenida Paloma, near the terminal.

Communications The post office (⏲ *11.30–18.00 Mon–Fri*) is next to the casino. The Antel *telecentro* is on Avenida Solarí north of Avenida del Navio (⏲ *09.00–18.00 daily*). There's an internet café by the Hotel Viola on Avenida Solarí, and Cyber del Navio and the Barahona Cafetería-Cyber, both on Avenida El Navio east of Avenida Solarí.

Healthcare There's a 24-hour pharmacy just southwest of this junction, and a *policlínica* (✆ *479 6060*) on Avenida Solarí between Sirio & Titania. And on the subject of health issues, there are plenty of dropped kerbs for wheelchairs here, thanks to Rotary.

Markets There are two supermarkets on Avenida Solarí: Los Jardines, at the roundabout at its north end, and El Dorado (⏲ *08.00–21.30 Mon–Thu, 08.00–22.00 Fri–Sat, 08.30–21.00 Sun*) at Sirio, opposite the casino. To the west at Delfín and Aries (south of the terminal) the Los Molles supermarket is also pretty good. Just south of the Hostel Ibirapitá, Pastas Oggi (*Avda Paloma;* ⏲ *summer daily, rest of the year 09.30–13.00 Sat, 09.00–14.00 Sun*) sells ready-made meals (largely pasta) to heat up in your *cabaña*. A good bakery is Don Dante (*Antares & De le Iglesia*).

Activities Surfing is the main sport here, with beaches that face south and east on either side of the headland. To the south, the Los Botes or Anaconda beach often has waves up to 150m long and 2m high; to the east the La Aguada beach is 7km long (stretching to La Pedrera) but gets crowded in summer as it's popular with Brazilian surfers. The webpage www.surfinglapaloma.com/nomenclaturadepicos.htm gives details of breaks on every beach here. Surf shops are on Avenida Solarí, including Peteco Surf Shop (**m** *9962 6726;* **e** *petecosurf@adinet.com.uy*), south of Sirio, and Surfshop (*at junction of Avda Solarí & Avda del Navio*). The H2O Surf School (**m** *9970 7314*) is at the Peteco Surf Shop, and the Escuela de Surfing La Paloma (**m** *9917 3078; www.surfinglapaloma.com*) is at Playa Los Botes.

Just west of the lighthouse, Playa La Balconada has particularly clear water and is popular with swimmers. To the east, canoes can be rented in the sheltered and very attractive Bahía Chica. Tiny Isla de la Tuna can be reached by swimming for about 20m.

What to see and do In the central reservation of Avenida Solarí just south of Avenida del Navio, the skeleton of a southern right whale sits in front of the **Centro Interpretivo Marino Costero** (*Coastal Marine Interpretative Centre;* ✆ *479 8318; www.occ.org.uy;* ⏲ *Jan–Feb 20.00–24.00 Mon–Fri, rest of the year 20.00–24.00 Fri–Sat*) of the Organización para la Conservación de Cetáceos (OCC; Organisation for the Conservation of Cetaceans). Some of their excellent (Spanish-language) posters are on display in the windows, while there's another whale skeleton inside, with other information on whales and dolphins, and very enthusiastic staff.

In early October each year the OCC organises the Semana de la Ballena Franca Austral (Southern Right Whale Week), including the National Day of the Whale, with many activities for schoolchildren in particular, here and in Piriápolis, Punta del Este and elsewhere. Between March and October migrating southern right whales rest along Uruguay's Atlantic coast, on their way to and from breeding around Patagonia, and they may come within 200m of the shore. There's a whale observation platform in Costa Azul, immediately north of La Aguada, but they can also be seen from Cabo Santa María by the lighthouse. The OCC also organises whale-watching weekends (*US$140 pp, min 5, inc transfers from Montevideo & 2 nights FB at Hostel Ibirapitá*).

It's well worth taking a trip to the **Laguna de Rocha**, an hour's walk west along the beach (10km by road), where you can see almost the only black-necked swans in Uruguay (up to 15,000 of them), as well as flamingos, and a total of 220 recorded bird species. Covering 72km^2, this is semi-fresh water, with an outlet to the sea opening in winter. Travel agencies can arrange for fishermen to take you out in boats. In any case you can see plenty of birds around the port, including green-barred woodpeckers, great grebes, neotropic cormorants, kelp gulls and oystercatchers.

At the southern end of Avenida Solarí is the *faro* or **lighthouse** of Cabo Santa María (⊕ *summer 08.00–sunset daily, rest of the year w/end & holiday afternoons; US$0.70*), opened in 1874 after the first attempt to build a tower ended in 1872 in a collapse that killed 15 workers. It's nicely set up, with red and green navigation lights beside the path from the gate to the door, and, on the beach to the south, hourposts that work as a sundial with the lighthouse as the gnomon.

The church at the west end of Antares is bare and barn-like, but a cool refuge on a hot day; mass is said at 19.00 'almost every day'.

NaturCiencia (*Ruta 15 km7.2, heading towards Rocha;* ☎ *479 9065;* e *naturciencia@ adinet.com.uy;* ⊕ *Dec–Apr 11.00–20.00 daily, May–Nov 11.00–18.00 w/ends & school holidays; US$2.20*) is a *museo de ciencias interactivo* (interactive science museum). In addition to walk-in kaleidoscopes, trick mirrors and other fun stuff including magnetic black sand, there's a collection of skulls of over 100 mammals and birds, an olive ridley turtle shell and various strange plants. There are also disabled toilets, a play area and a souvenir shop.

LA PEDRERA From Ruta 15, 5km north of La Paloma, Ruta 10 runs east to La Pedrera, La Paloma's more bohemian little sister. The name means 'stony place' and it feels rather Cornish, especially when the wind is blowing and the surf is rolling. It's currently very popular with the arty crowd, with new cafés and architect-designed houses appearing, but it's hardly José Ignacio as yet, and there's still plenty of wildlife, including woodpeckers and tegu lizards crossing the sandy roads. Surfing is great here, but only for those with experience; on the south side of the village, Playa del Barco (Boat Beach) has deep water and consistent breaks up to 2m high, but the remains of wrecked ships lie half-buried in the sand. Immediately below the cliffs at the end of Avenida Principal, El Desplayado (The Beachless) has perfect waves up to 2m high that run for up to 200m.

Getting there Some Rocha–La Paloma buses, some starting in Montevideo (see page 82), make the ten-minute detour to La Pedrera, leaving you in the centre by the OSE water tower. From here Avenida Principal, jammed solid with traffic in January, leads southeast to finish at the cliff-top *rambla*. Turning left (north) here brings you down to the beach, where new white-cube houses are appearing. You can loop back to the water tower; turning right, you'll swing around to some wooden sculptures just south of Avenida Principal.

For bus tickets, COT (☎ *479 2164;* ⊕ *10.00–18.00 daily*) is on Avenida Principal just east of the water tower, and Cynsa (⊕ *13.00–17.00 daily*) is on the same road close to the junction with Ruta 10.

⌂ **Where to stay** There's not a lot of budget accommodation here, other than campsites and hostels.

🏠 **Hotel La Pedrera** ☎ 479 2001; e hpedrera@
adinet.com.uy; www.hotelesderocha.com; ⊕ mid-
Aug–mid-Jul. A 4-star hotel incorporating a seawater
thermal spa (with indoor & outdoor pools), this is
not the most stylish or up-to-date (there's only
limited internet access), but rooms do have AC as
well as cable TV. US$90/2 $$$$$

🏠 **Appart-Hotel Terrazas de La Pedrera** ☎ 479
2102/2197; www.terrazasdelapedrera.com; ⊕ all
year. Opened in 1999, this upmarket apt-hotel has
an open-air swimming pool & an excellent
restaurant. Apts have kitchen, balcony, satellite TV &
Wi-Fi; there are also several PCs downstairs as well
as a pool table & a telescope for watching the sea.
$$$$

🏠 **Hotel Posada del Barco** ☎ 479 6152;
e posadadelbarco@adinet.com.uy;
www.hotelesderocha.com; ⊕ all year. With a terrace
facing the Playa del Barco, this friendly, arty place
has a *cafetería*, *salón de té* & restaurant serving
good seafood & lamb. $$$$

🏠 **El Viajero La Pedrera Hostel** m 9996 2495;
e informes@lapedrerahostel.com;
www.lapedrerahostel.com; ⊕ Dec–Apr. This brand-
new hostel is in a quiet location 500m from the
beach & 150m from Avda Principal. There are men-
only & women-only dorms only plus private dbls

with bathroom & balcony, as well as a kitchen,
barbecue, a wooden porch & garden with hammocks,
free internet access, & bike & surfboard rental;
surfing lessons can also be arranged. $$$–$$

🏠 **Cabañas Las Lunas** ☎ 479 209, m 9969 2882;
e laslunaslapedrera@hotmail.com; ⊕ all year. In a
tranquil location a block south of the water tower,
there are 4 thatched cabins here for up to 6
people, with cable TV & barbecue. $$

🏠 **Hostal El Tucán** ☎ 479 2978, m 9429 8019.
One block south of the water tower, this is an
immaculate white Modernist house with small, clean
rooms & a microwave but no real kitchen, & no
b/fast. There's a pleasant garden with sunbeds. $$

🏠 **Posada Hostel La Casa de la Luna** Ruta 10
km230; m 9460 2271, 9446 9300; e recepcion@
lacasadelaluna.com.uy; www.lacasadelaluna.com.uy;
⊕ Dec–Mar. At Punta Rubia, 2km east of La
Pedrera, this is the most stylish place to stay here.
They'll pick you up from the bus & also run you
down to the bars in La Paloma. There's a kitchen &
barbecues, laundry facilities, cable TV & internet
access. Bikes, books & DVDs are available, as are
kite-surfing lessons (see below). Beds US$15 (US$20
Jan–Feb) in 12-person dorms, US$20 (US$25) in 4-
bed rooms, US$25 (US$30) in dbls; camping is
possible for US$10 (US$15). B/fast inc.

Camping There are campsites off Ruta 10 between La Aguada and La Pedrera (and
at Punta Rubia), including **Camping PP** (*km226.5;* ☎ *47 97328,* m *945 1904;*
e *kimli123@adinet.com.uy;* ⊕ *Dec–Easter*), 500m from the beach & 2km from La
Pedrera. It has shaded tent spaces, picnic tables, barbecues, electric sockets, soccer
and volleyball pitches, restaurant, bar, shop and TV room.

🍴 **Where to eat** Along Avenida Principal there are a couple of *panadería-confiterías*
where locals gather early in the morning – Empanadas San Telmo serves tasty
snacks – and there are a couple of ice cream shops and some snack bars.

🍴 **La Pé** Avenida Principal, Posada El Torbellino;
☎ 479 2122; ⊕ Dec–Easter. In a walled garden 3
blocks from the *rambla* (with very few tables
indoors), this is one of the best new restaurants here,
with a wide-ranging menu based on seafood, including
sole, paella or langoustines in a sort of teriyaki
sauce, as well as a vegetable tower or *jamón crudo*.
Desserts are excellent, & there's a good wine list as
well as house wine by the jug. $$$$$

🍴 **Perillan** Avda Principal & Rambla; m 9622
7683, 9954 6410. The cliff-top location is fantastic
at lunchtime, while in the evening there's music, low
lighting & a great atmosphere. The menu focuses on
seafood, with a grilled fish of the day, *brótola* &
shellfish risotto, all fresh & well-presented. $$$$$

🍴 **Fulano** Playa del Barco; m 9550 1728. A decent
pub-restaurant with a great view of the beach &
surfers, although the service & presentation do not
live up to the interesting dishes such as fish roll, leg
of lamb & *civias de algas* (seaweed fritters). $$$$

🍴 **Lajau** m 9992 2091. Just north of the water
tower, in a garden with its own mini-golf course,
this friendly place serves a menu based on what is
available on the day, perhaps shellfish tapas, fresh
fish or pasta. $$$$

🍴 **Los Girasoles** ☎ 479 2197. The Provençal-styled
restaurant of the Appart-Hotel Terrazas de La
Pedrera serves a great buffet b/fast, as well as
lunch, tea & dinner, featuring fish & seafood, & local
specialities such as seaweed fritters with a butia

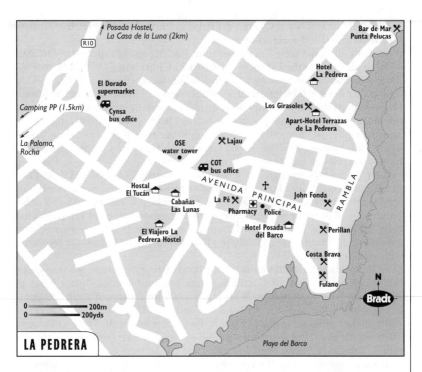

LA PEDRERA

Playa del Barco

sauce. Service is very prompt & prices are reasonable. **$$$$**

✗ Bar de Mar Punta Pelucas ☎ 479 2206; www.puntapelucas.com. Just beyond the end of the road to the northeast of the resort, this is a classic beachfront bar with a large deck that serves cocktails, crêpes & cakes. There's also a *cabaña* available to rent. **$$$**

✗ Costa Brava Rambla; ☎ 479 2051. A simple but decent seafood restaurant almost on the headland, with a view over miles of beach to the north & east. **$$$**

✗ John Fonda Rambla; m 9626 5497. A tapas bar, in a great position but without a terrace so rather a waste. **$$$**

Entertainment With so many cool kids and crazy artists here, there are quite a few interesting festivals: Vox y Pop on the first weekend of January, the Festival de Cortometrajes (*Short Film Festival;* ☎ 2 708 2174; *www.lapedrerashortfilmfestival.com*) on the second weekend of January, the biggest and best Desfile de Carnaval (Carnival Parade) on the Uruguayan coast, and the Jazz Festival at Easter.

Other practicalities The El Dorado supermarket is at the junction with Ruta 10. There is no bank or ATM here. There's a pharmacy and a police office opposite the little church on Avenida Principal.

Activities For surfing lessons, contact the Escuela de Surf La Pedrera (m *9974 4783; www.escueladesurflapedrera.com*), who charge US$20 for a lesson or US$100 for five classes or three days, and can also provide accommodation. The Posada Hostel La Casa de la Luna (see *Where to stay*) offers kite-surfing courses, with seven 90-minute classes (initially on Laguna de Rocha and then the ocean) costing US$300.

CASTILLOS In the 30-odd kilometres between La Pedrera and Cabo Polonio ten *balnearios* were designated in the 1940s, but none were developed beyond a few

5

houses at Punta Rubia and Oceanía del Polonio. Nowadays this stretch of Ruta 10 is partly unpaved and sees no bus services.

Virtually all traffic takes Ruta 9 east from Rocha, passing a turning at km220.5 which leads south to the **Estancia Turística El Charabón** (✆ *470 2403,* m *9912 7345;* e *gsbarbaro@elcharabon.com; www.elcharabon.com;* ⊕ *all year*), a 950ha working farm with around 650 Hereford cattle, 500 Hampshire Down sheep and 30 horses. Horseriding is the main activity here, including working with the cattle or a day ride to La Pedrera for a gallop along the beach. There's good birdwatching, or you can just enjoy the tranquillity and the big views over the surrounding plains. There's a swimming pool, Wi-Fi and satellite TV. There are nine air-conditioned rooms, and rates include four excellent meals each day.

Ruta 9 continues through 19 de Abril (km235, with fuel, food and drink) and passes the Parque Eólica Loma Alta, 16 wind turbines on a hill to the north; this was Uruguay's first windfarm, opening in 2008 ahead of UTE's in the Sierra de los Caracoles (16km north of San Carlos), which got more publicity. Loma Alta has been known for its herd of Polled Hereford cattle, and is now diversifying into olive-growing. From around km246 you'll see the Laguna de Castillos to the south, with sand dunes beyond.

At km260 there's a small tourist information centre at the turning into the sleepy little single-storey town of **Castillos**, where you may have to change buses to reach Cabo Polonio or Valizas. With barely 7,000 inhabitants, it's still the third-largest town in Rocha. Rutas del Sol, COT and COTEC share an office at Ferrer 1201, on the northwest corner of Plaza Artigas, where taxis wait. There's not much shade on the plaza, but there is a weak Wi-Fi signal (which works inside the bus office), a statue of Artigas (raised in 1966) and on the west side a modern church with some murals inside. It's two blocks east to the Banco República (*Ferrer & Pintos*), with an ATM, and another block to the Cynsa bus office (*Ferrer 1404*). There's an Antel call centre (*19 de Abril 7 & Treinta y Tres;* ⊕ *09.00–18.00 Mon–Sat*).

The Hotel A Mi Gente (✆ *475 7273; www.hotelamigente.com.uy;* $$$) is at Lavalleja 1235, between Ferrer and 19 de Abril, east of the plaza. La Strada (*19 de Abril 1375 & Pintos;* ✆ *47 57717;* ⊕ *12.00–16.00, 20.00–24.00 Thu–Sun;* $$$) is a good new restaurant. This is not a place for a quick *chivito*, but for shrimp risotto, fish of the day with polenta, lamb or spaghetti with chicken pesto, all well done and very affordable.

AGUAS DULCES Turning right just after Castillos at km261.5, it's 10km to the **Estancia Guardia del Monte** (✆ *470 5180, 475 9064;* e *guardiam@adinet.com.uy; www.guardiadelmonte.com*), one of the most attractive and historic ranches that's open for visitors. Named after an old Spanish guardpost, the single-storey colonial house dates from 1785 and has a dining room like a *pulpería* or rural shop-bar, and in the kitchen a massive Danish cooking range salvaged from a shipwreck in 1884 and still in use. It's just 250m from the Laguna de Castillos, and you can swim, canoe or fish, as well as riding horses through the shallows and across the plains dotted with palms. You may see black-necked swans, spoonbills, egrets, herons or ducks, and can also visit the fascinating Monte de Ombúes (see page 237). The 1,000ha spread is a working ranch, with just a few rooms for guests; however, day visits are possible, including a slap-up lunch (starting with a taste of *licor de butia* or butia palm syrup).

From the southeastern exit from Castillos, Ruta 16 runs south to the coast. You'll see plenty of palm trees, but largely on the road verges because cows eat the young shoots elsewhere. It's hard to believe that in colonial times the *palmares de Rocha* grew too thick and close for people to get through. Turning left after 9.5km, it's a couple of kilometres more to the tiny settlement of **Aguas Dulces**, a very laid-back resort with an unplanned jumble of bungalows close together, and a nudist beach (Playa La Sirena, about 2km east). Most visitors stay in rented houses and cabins, enjoying seafood and butia palm fruit, but there are various other options. Midway between the junction and the beach are the **Camping Aguas Dulces** (\ *470 5874; $*) and the **Aguas Dulces Resort Club** (\ *475 2235; m 9987 5699; http://aguasdulcesresortclub.com; $$$$*), an attractively landscaped development of *cabañas* around a large swimming pool, with a bar (and pool table) and a *parrilla* restaurant. The *cabañas* have a full kitchen, cable TV, indoor fireplace and a porch with outdoor barbecue; breakfasts and transfers are available.

Buses stop on the main Avenida Los Palafitos, a couple of blocks inland from the beach, turning around to return to the main road. Two blocks south of Avenida Los Palafitos on the *rambla* is the Complejo Los Arinos (\ *475 2161, m 9987 2504; www.complejoarinos.com; restaurant on seaward side, 6 apts on inland side; $$*). Other accommodation options can be found on the excellent website www.aguasdulces.com.uy (there's also a Spanish-language blog at http://aguasdulcesherald.blogspot.com).

BARRA DE VALIZAS Buses return to the Aguas Dulces junction and head west on another isolated section of Ruta 10 for 5km to the start of a dirt road leading 4km south to Barra de Valizas, a similarly bohemian resort to Aguas Dulces, with stunning empty beaches that stretch for ever. Buses continue on Ruta 10 to the Arroyo de Valizas (for boats to the Monte de Ombúes; see page 237) and the turn-off for Cabo Polonio at km264 (see page 235) and then return to enter Barra de Valizas. You'll arrive in the centre of the village, with thatched wooden shacks serving as bars, food stores and rental cabins; there are plenty of hippies here, selling the usual beads and jewellery, as well as families in summer. In the evenings people hang out, playing guitars and singing by candlelight; many houses have no electricity and there are no street lights (and thus great night skies). However, in 2009 there were protests at plans to install street lights. Many of the shops and cafés open only for the summer season, but houses can be rented very cheaply so there are various alternative types here through the winter. There are plenty of free-range animals, and everyone seems to have a dog or three.

The main road, Calle Aladino Veiga, ends by the beach at the Plazoleta Fragata Leopoldina Rosa (named after a ship wrecked here in 1842), from where sandy tracks lead left to Aguas Dulces (6km along the beach) and right past a pond to the Arroyo Valizas. On the far side of the stream lie 40km² of **sand dunes**, the last significant remnants of the dunes that lined the whole of this coast from over 4,000 years ago until pines and other trees were planted from the end of the 19th century. They abut the granite Cerro Buena Vista (50m high), which marked the end of the Spanish–Portuguese border from 1750 to 1777; in 1752 a boundary stone was placed at the foot of the hill and can still be seen. Valizas is also associated with the French pirate (really more of a leather smuggler) Etienne Moreau, who bought the hides of stolen cattle from indigenous inhabitants from 1717 until he was shot in a skirmish with government troops here in 1720.

Tourist information Local tourist information is available from Punto G (*G Spot;* ⊕ *Dec–Feb*), a charming café/museum/cyber-centre by the small lagoon a block southwest from the main street. The museum is a collection of fossils and indigenous objects picked up in the dunes and elsewhere over the last few decades; on Tuesdays and Thursdays they show a children's news programme outdoors at 20.00 followed by a free film at 21.00. You'll also find some information online at www.portaldevalizas.com.uy.

There are almost no services here, and certainly no ATM or anywhere to exchange money – the nearest ATMs are in Castillos and Rocha.

🏠 **Where to stay** Most people stay in rented houses or cabins – you'll see hand-painted *alquilo* signs, or you can ask at Punto G or in other shops. In peak season you should book something in advance though **Casas en Valizas** (m *9910 3607;* e *casasenvalizas@adinet.com.uy; www.casasenvalizas.com*). Most *cabañas* consist of just a bedroom, sitting room and kitchenette, with a water pump and often no electricity, for US$25–40 a week in season; in winter a house can cost under US$80 a month.

🏠 **Posada Eirete** ☎ 475 4011, m 9929 6600; e mariabelosoeirete@hotmail.com; http://posadaeiretevalizas.webs.com. The nicest place in the village, Eirete is run by an artist. It's composed of with thatched cottages with 6 shared rooms combining rustic charm & modern comforts (including internet access), & organic food from local producers (the restaurant is open to all). $$$

🏠 **La Comarca de Valizas** Near the junction with Ruta 10, 1.8km from Barra de Valizas; m 9917 7004, 9967 5460; e lacomarcadevalizas@gmail.com; www.lacomarcadevalizas.com.uy; ⊕ all year. An *estancia* house, built in 1900 & opened in 2006 as a *posada de campo* or country inn with camping. With its large bedrooms it's ideal for families who want to let their children run free, but it is open to all. The living room has a fireplace made of granite slabs & a wooden door from a wrecked ship; the former *pulpería* (rural shop) is now the dining room, serving largely their own organic products. On relatively high ground, with native trees such as ombúes, it has good views of the sea, dunes & lagoon. Horseriding is available, as well as free transfers (every 2hrs) to the beach. $$$–$$

✗ **Hostel La Duna** Carretero 685, 3km from the centre; ☎ 475 4045; www.hosteluruguay.org/valizashostel.html; ⊕ Nov–Apr. Affiliated to Hostelling International, has 58 beds (but is often full in summer), with kitchen, barbecue, TV & games rooms. $

It's possible to **camp** in the centre of the village, either in a yard with about 50 tentfuls of people sharing one toilet, or in any other yard where you make friends with people renting a *cabaña*.

✗ **Where to eat** There's excellent food at Punto G (see page 233), all with fresh local fruits and no artificial colorants, including homemade ice cream (with flavours such as butia, mburucuya, pitanga, *dulce de leche*, lemon and mint, and honey orange and ginger), cakes and desserts, toasted sandwiches, smoothies, coffees and teas. Quite a few other places serve local seafood, beer, *milanesas* and pizzas.

CABO POLONIO Cabo Polonio – named after Joseph Polloni, captain of the *Nuestra Señora del Rosario*, wrecked here in 1752 (and not after a ship called the *Polonio*) – is one of the most alluring destinations in Uruguay for backpackers and others in search of isolation and tranquillity. It's a headland much like Punta del Este, La Paloma and José Ignacio, with *brava* and *mansa* sides; the Playa Sur (or Playa La Ensenada) offers surfers a great variety of waves, thanks to its constantly moving sandbanks, and the Playa de la Calavera (Beach of the Skull, to the east – so called because of the cattle slaughtered here by the indigenous people) is the only beach on the whole coast which faces east and northeast. The beaches are always virtually empty, and to the southwest you can walk all the way to La Pedrera, seeing little more than a few shanties and shipwrecks.

This has been a *monumento natural* within the Bañados del Este biosphere reserve since 1976. In July 2009 it was declared a Protected Area, with hunting, mining and other damaging activities prohibited and tourism more tightly regulated. The legendary squatter settlement here – a collection of shacks and cabins that have sprung up on the point near the lighthouse – will not be removed or interfered with, but there are plans for a reception centre at the main road, with café, shop, ticket offices for jeep access (see opposite) and a ranger station and information centre. The government is taking a very restrained approach to tourism, realising that while mega-complexes like Punta del Este have their place, there's a need for diversity, and places like this are sought out by many. Cabo Polonio is developing in any case, and what was until recently a fishing village with a few hippies in summer shacks, and no fresh water or electricity (except for the lighthouse), is now a permanent settlement (population 88) with half-decent accommodation and seafood restaurants, some with generators or solar panels. The scene is a bit druggy in summer, but most people are just getting high on the solitude and natural beauty of the endless beaches of perfect sand.

There's been considerable over-grazing, and you'll still find cows in the unlikeliest places, looking for scraps of grass among the dunes which are the natural habitat of snakes, rodents and burrowing owls. Sea lions (*lobo marino de un pelo*) and fur seals (*lobo fino de dos pelos*) breed on the three rocky islets about a kilometre off the point, spending a lot of time on the point as well. It's quite normal to find dead seal pups on the beach after storms, as there's less shelter on these islands than, for instance, on Isla de Lobos. There are also otters, whales, dolphins, at least seven species of crabs, plus mussels, sea anemones, sponges, starfish, Darwin's toad, sea slugs, over 40 species of seaweed, and birds up to the size of petrels and albatrosses.

Information is available online at www.cabopolonio.com

Getting there

On foot or horseback From the Plazoleta Fragata Leopoldina Rosa in Barra de Valizas, a sandy track leads to the right for about half a kilometre past a pond, reaching the beach at the Arroyo Valizas, where a boat is usually waiting to ferry you across to the south side of the river (*US$1*). The *arroyo* is not deep but it's wide and fairly fast, and wouldn't be easy to wade.

Once across, it's about 7km to Cabo Polonio by the direct route across the dunes, or 9km if you follow the coast around Punta Castillos Grande. If you don't fancy the hike, you can do it on horseback – contact A Caballo a Polonio (↘ *470 5386*, m *9963 5441*; e *elparaiso@cabopolonio.com*), based at the Estancia Turística El Paraíso (*Ruta 10 km274.5*; ↘ *470 5266*), where there's a child-friendly collection of turkeys, peacocks, Asian pheasants, carpinchos and boars.

Taking the direct route, you should head up the highest dune, for the views as much as anything – inland you'll see a couple of shacks and scrubbier land with rock outcrops and some cows, while to the south is the rocky headland. Dunes stretch ahead for about 3km – head southwest as well as you can, and keep just to the left of the forest when you see it on a ridge ahead. Passing through the trees you'll come at once to a nice grassy place with views to the lighthouse of Cabo Polonio and the rocky islets and reefs to the east. Going down towards Cabo Polonio, you'll soon find a faint 4x4 track, ending up on the beach which is usually good firm going. It takes about two hours to hike from the Arroyo Valizas to the Cabo Polonio Hostel.

By 4x4 Cabo Polonio has no road access. The main way in is on 4x4 trucks which shuttle along a sandy track from km264½ on Ruta 10. Buses from Rocha and Castillos for Aguas Dulces and Barra de Valizas come this far before turning around (there are no buses from La Paloma; a taxi from Castillos will cost about US$15), and there's shaded parking here for cars and motorbikes. Until recently there was just one beat-up truck that made the journey when its owner saw fit; now there's a fleet of big jeeps with open seating on the back, with ticket booths (*US$7 return*) for competing services, and a regular sequence of departures.

Operators are El Canario (m *9987 5622*), El Cachorro (☏ *470 5263,* m *9987 5302*) and Safari del Cabo (☏ *470 2099,* m *9987 3705*). The 7km journey takes about 30 minutes of rocking and rolling, on a wide track through pine trees and then following the coast for the last kilometre or so. This hurdle filters out most day trippers, although in fact it's perfectly easy to come for the day if you have accommodation elsewhere.

🏠 Where to stay All liable to be closed out of season.

🏠 **Hostería La Perla** Playa de la Calavera; ☏ 470 5125, m 99921037, 9987 1017; ⊕ all year. Near the point, this has tiny en-suite rooms, some with sea views, others just with skylights, & a decent restaurant; b/fast inc. There's a generator & hot water, & service is good. $$$$

🏠 **Posada Mariemar** ☏ 470 5164, 470 5241, m 9987 5260; e mariemar@cabopolonio.com; ⊕ all year. A very normal-looking place near the point that doesn't altogether fit in here, but open for 40 years, with 6 comfortable rooms (all with bathroom & hot shower) & its own generator, good restaurant & waterfront terrace. $$$$

🏠 **Hostal del Cabo** Playa de la Calavera; ☏ 682 4900, m 9930 7870; e hostaldelcabo@cabopolonio.com; ⊕ mid-Dec–Feb & Easter. Small A-frame with shared rooms with 3, 5 & 6 beds, 3 bathrooms, kitchen & electric lighting. B/fast extra. $$

🏠 **Posada de los Corvinos** Playa de la Calavera; m 9856 5966; e posadadeloscorvinos@cabopolonio.com; ⊕ all year. A pink house 300m from the centre of the settlement, this has 3 dbls (1 with private bathroom) & 1 shared room with 4 beds (& individual lockers), kitchen & living room with wood stove (as well as solar power). There's a shared bathroom as well as an outdoor shower with solar-heated water. Books, games & guitars can be borrowed, there's a kitchen & free tea & coffee in the morning. B/fast is extra. $$

🏠 **Posada Santa Maradona** m 9418 9556; e posadasantamaradona@cabopolonio.com. Where the 'road' enters the settlement, there's a dbl & 2 4-bed rooms here, but on hot summer nights they're just as likely to take everyone off to sleep in the dunes or the forest. A kitchen is available, but at w/ends there's usually a shared meal of roast lamb or pasta with their homemade bread. $$

🏠 **Posada y Parador La Cañada** Playa Sur; m 9955 0595, 9997 2410; e posadalacaniada@cabopolonio.com. A friendly little guesthouse by the 'road' in to the Cabo (the trucks will drop you off here), with shared rooms, battery lighting, kitchen, games & toys, & fishing tackle; good meals are available. $$

🏠 **Cabo Polonio Hostel** Playa de la Calavera; m 9900 0305, 9944 5943; e cabopoloniohostel@hotmail.com; www.cabopoloniohostel.com. A 3-room wooden shack that's better inside than it seems outside, simply furnished & quite comfortable. The Argentine owner Alfredo is a trained chef who cooks up superb fresh fish by candlelight; b/fast inc. There are 4-bed dorms & a dbl room. $$–$

✖ Where to eat There's no gourmet cooking here but the fish is as fresh as could be, and you can also enjoy the local speciality of *buñuelos de algas* (seaweed fritters).

✖ **Hostería La Perla** Playa de la Calavera; ⊕ all year. Near the point, with a wooden terrace that's almost in the sea, this is a nice friendly spot for seafood & good simple salads, with desserts such as pancakes with *dulce de leche*. $$$$

✖ **Posada Mariemar** Right on the point, a good restaurant that looks too decent for Cabo Polonio, serving fresh fish, scampi, meats & *buñuelos de algas*. $$$$

✖ **Don Trigo** With a prime location right on the point, this could be on the waterfront of any little fishing port, serving good fresh fish, scampi & *buñuelos de algas*. $$$

✖ **La Golosa** On the main track through the settlement, this restaurant-tearoom-café serves good food in the garden or the more hippyish interior (no shoes). The menu includes hummus, tabouleh, stir-fried vegetables, crêpes, pizza & *feijao golosa* (Brazilian black beans). $$$

✖ **El Boliche de Chiche** A friendly little place serving fine lamb, pizza & pasta. $$

✖ **La de Joselo** The *grappamiel* honey liqueur slips down here in the vine-shaded bar until the owner brings out Pancho, his pet penguin, who got stranded here one winter & never left, like so many of Cabo's residents. $$

What to see and do The lighthouse, built in 1881–84, is 26m high (40m above sea level) and is open at weekends and on holiday afternoons – although you can probably visit at any time if you ask nicely.

Through the *posadas* and hostels it's possible to arrange horseriding (*about US$75/day*), along the beach, through dunes and to the wetlands of the Arroyo Valizas. There are also boats which will take you out for half an hour to watch the sea lions.

Monte de Ombúes At km267 of Ruta 10, 3km east of the start of the trail to Cabo Polonio, boats leave from the bridge over the Arroyo Valizas to the Laguna de Castillos and, on its east shore, the Monte de Ombúes (ombú forest). On the hour-long boat ride you'll see plenty of birds such as ducks, cormorants, gulls, herons, ibis, storks, kingfishers and teros, and perhaps even wood-rails, coscoroba swans, southern screamers or flamingos.

Ombúes grow along a 25km stretch of the lakeshore, but the main grove consists of about 100 of these odd trees with their stumpy trunks and seemingly random branches. In fact it's unclear whether the ombú is actually a tree or an overgrown bush – in addition to its weird shape, it has soft flaky wood that falls apart like a croissant, so that it gradually becomes hollow inside. This makes it hard to calculate their age by the normal technique of counting rings, but it seems that many of these trees are 500 – possibly as much as 800 – years old. It also means that they are not strong and can easily be blown over by a storm – hence their development in groves.

Laguna de Castillos, including the Monte de Ombúes, is one of the best-run areas within the Biosphere Reserve, with a very active ranger (❭ *470 5191*) and a popular junior rangers programme (Pequeños Guardaparques Castillos). The area is closed from March to December.

PUNTA DEL DIABLO Ruta 9 continues northeast from Castillos, through an area of small *estancias* where you'll see ñandues (rheas) roaming. At km280.5 a dirt road leads a couple of kilometres to the right to **La Esmeralda**, a very isolated spot with a campsite at La Esmeralda Resort (m *9961 8602;* ⊕ *Dec–Easter*) and the Cabañas del Sol (❭ *470 5005;* e *info@cabasol.com; www.cabasol.com;* $$), with cabins for two or four people, with or without kitchen.

After passing through low flat country beside the Laguna Negra (17,500ha), just after km298 (91km from Rocha) you'll come to the turning to Punta del Diablo, a slightly more upmarket and international version of Barra de Valizas. A partly paved road leads south for 4km to this colourful fishing village that over the summer months becomes a funky surfers' resort, although its sandy beaches are never in the least crowded.

There are good fish restaurants and bars in the village, and the beaches are beautiful in both directions. The east-facing Playa del Rivero (or Playa Pescadores) has waves up to 2m in height, and easy surfing when the wind is from the southwest. Beyond the Punta del Rivero, to the northeast, the Playa Grande continues for miles, past the Parque Nacional Santa Teresa. The Playa de la Viuda faces south-southeast and has powerful multi-peak waves, forming large barrels in the shallow shoals. This is where affluent Argentines and Brazilians are building modernistic new houses similar to those in José Ignacio. But there's none of the *chacra* development that is so big there, nor any real estate agents. The roads are all sand, some impassable, and there are lots of happy free-range dogs looking to adopt you for a few hours.

At the south end of the Playa Pescadores, where fishermen unload their boats and stalls sell fresh fish, a path leads east past a craft market on to the rocky point, with sea anemones in rock pools. There's no lighthouse here, but there's a small

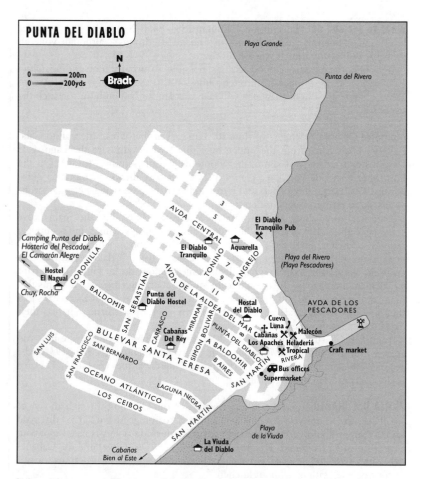

PUNTA DEL DIABLO

0 ——— 200m
0 ——— 200yds

Bradt

N

Playa Grande

Punta del Rivero

AVDA CENTRAL

3
5

Camping Punta del Diablo,
Hostería del Pescador,
El Camarón Alegre

El Diablo
Tranquilo Pub

El Diablo
Tranquilo

Aquarella

TONINO

7

Hostel
El Nagual

CORONILLA

Chuy, Rocha

CANGREJO

Playa del Rivero
(Playa Pescadores)

9

11

A BALDOMIR

SAN SEBASTIAN

AVDA DE LA ALDEA DEL MAR

Punta del
Diablo Hostel

Hostal
del Diablo

AVDA DE LOS
PESCADORES

CARRASCO

Cabañas
Del Rey

MIRAMAR

SIMON BOLIVAR

PUNTA DEL DIABLO

Cueva
Luna

Cabañas
Los Apaches

Malecón

Heladería

BULEVAR SANTA TERESA

SAN LUIS

SAN FRANCISCO

SAN BERNARDO

A BALDOMIR

B AIRES

Tropical

RIVERA

Craft market

OCEANO ATLÁNTICO

LAGUNA NEGRA

SAN MARTIN

Bus offices
Supermarket

LOS CEIBOS

SAN MARTIN

Cabañas
Bien al Este

La Viuda
del Diablo

Playa
de la Viuda

light with a very naff statue of Artigas and the text of his letter to Bolívar about respecting the Uruguayan flag.

For further information and accommodation see the excellent website www.portaldeldiablo.com.uy.

Getting there Many buses heading for Chuy (some from Punta del Este, as well as Montevideo; see page 82) drive down the access road to drop passengers off. There are no shuttle services back up to Ruta 9, so a rental car can be useful for visiting the Parque Nacional Santa Teresa and other sights. Alternatively you can borrow bikes or hike or ride horses along the beach.

Where to stay Less liable to be closed out of season.

Aquarella calles 5 & 12; ℡ 477 2400, m 9451 0000; e aquarella.puntadeldiablo@gmail.com; www.portaldeldiablo.com. A 5-star apart-hotel with apts with AC, cable TV & Wi-Fi, as well as a spa-jacuzzi, swimming pool & bar, & a restaurant that probably offers the finest dining in town. $$$$$

La Viuda del Diablo San Martín, Playa de la Viuda; m 9864 0792; www.laviudadeldiablo.com. The chic new place to stay in the dunes west of the point, & run by an Argentine interior designer, the 'Devil's Widow' is a posada-resto & beach-bar with 9 rooms with jacuzzi & floor-to-ceiling windows.

There's an excellent little restaurant & service is faultless. $$$$

🏠 **Hostal del Diablo** Avda Central; ✆ 477 2667, 479 7741; e hdiablo@adinet.com.uy; ⏰ all year. An attractive 2-storey thatched bldg around a garden, with 16 en-suite dbls, a 10-person *cabaña*, swimming pool & TV lounge. $$$$

🏠 **Hostería del Pescador** Bvar Santa Teresa km2; ✆ 477 2017, m 9877 2704. An attractive place in a fairly tranquil location with 16 rooms for up to 6, & restaurant, swimming pool & pool table. $$$$

🏠 **El Diablo Tranquilo** Avda Central, north of Tonino (Calle 12); ✆ 477 2647; www.eldiablotranquilo.com; ⏰ all year. For many people, visiting Punta del Diablo is synonymous with staying in this beautifully designed boutique hostel, which has become a destination in itself thanks to its owners, Americans Brian & Heidi. Opened in late 2007, it's built around a large thatched hall with sofas & an open fireplace in the reception area downstairs. On the mezzanine level there are computers, a foosball table & a somewhat cramped kitchen. Accommodation is in mixed or women-only dorms, private rooms for 1, 2 or 4, or 2 suites with private bathroom (& bathrobes), fireplace & balcony with hammock. There are also 28 newly added beds at the beachfront pub (see below), including 4 penthouses. Staff are a great source of information on the neighbourhood, & can arrange hiking or horseriding along the beach & into the Santa Teresa National Park, or surfboard rental (*US$15/hr, US$20/day, wetsuit US$10/15*) or lessons (*US$15/hr*). $$$

Cabañas Most South American visitors stay in *cabañas*, which are easily available on the spot (*about US$40-60 for 2 or 3, US$70+ for 6*); look for *alquila* signs. You can also try the two-storey thatched cabins at Cabañas Los Apaches (*San Martín;* ✆ *477 2040;* e *enavarron@mixmail.com*), Cabañas Bien al Este (*Playa la Viuda;* ✆ *479 2102,* m *9984 9062;* e *info@bienaleste.com.uy;* ⏰ *all year*) or Cabañas Del Rey (*Bvar Santa Teresa & Miramar;* ✆ *477 2025*). Vilasar de Mar (✆ *477 2641,* m *9947 5061;* e *agrestepuntadeldiablo@hotmail.com*) promises gay-friendly *cabañas* 80m from the sea.

Hostel

🏠 **Hostel El Nagual** Bvar Santa Teresa km1, parada 2; ✆ 477 2009, m 9982 4164; e hostelelnagual@gmail.com; www.hostelnagual.com; ⏰ early Dec–Easter. On the main road into the village, this is an older more basic hostel with dorms & rooms with 2, 3 & 6 beds, 4 clean bathrooms & a kitchen. There's a common room with cable TV inside & hammocks in the large patio outside, where there's also room for a few tents, if you arrive in time. Free bikes are available. $$

🏠 **Punta del Diablo Hostel** Sarandi & Ciudad de Rocha; ✆ 477 2655, 477 2151; www.puntadeldiablohostel.com; ⏰ mid-Dec–mid-Apr. Behind the supermarket at parada 2 of the access road, this is an HI-affiliated hostel with shared dorms & camping space, kitchen, TV lounge, free internet & free use of bicycles. $

Camping

⛺ **Camping Punta del Diablo** Bvar Santa Teresa km2.5; ✆ 477 2060, 474 5040; e campingpuntadeldiablo@yahoo.com.ar; ⏰ all year. A pleasant wooded site with 175 pitches & *cabañas*, electricity, barbecues, bar, restaurant, laundry & shop, huge swimming pool, & hourly shuttles to the village. In season it can become a crowded tent city.

✖ Where to eat

✖ **El Camarón Alegre** Ruta 9 km298; ✆ 477 2263, 477 2055; e camaronalegre@hotmail.com; www.portaldeldiablo.com.uy/elcamaronalegre; ⏰ all year. This ordinary pink house, about 80m from the Punta del Diablo junction with Ruta 9, is a temple to Slow Food & regional Rochense cuisine. Specialities include *siri* (crab), *centolla* (king crab), seaweed ravioli, shellfish salad, *cazuela* (fish stew), *gatuzo* (a small shark), sole, *jabalí* (boar) & the always excellent 'Elizabeth's choice'. Desserts include *chajá* (see page 66), apple pancakes with a caramel sauce or a sublime *butiá* mousse. Service is friendly & enthusiastic, prices are very reasonable, & the only flaw is the poor state of the toilets. $$$$$

✖ **El Diablo Tranquilo Pub** calles 5 & 10; ⏰ from 12.00 daily. On the beach a couple of blocks from their hostel, this stylish place serves excellent food & is also a great place for an afternoon drink, an evening pub session or a full-moon party. Dishes include salads, grilled fish of the day, grilled meats & pasta, with crumble or cheesecake to follow. They have good Uruguayan wines &, amazingly, 3 types of draught Mastra beer from Uruguay's only craft brewery. **$$$$**

✗ **Cueva Luna** Avda de los Pescadores, just north of the craft market. The liveliest place to have a few beers & play some pool. **$$$**

✗ **Heladería Tropical** Rivera. An ice cream shop handily placed by the bus offices. **$**

Other practicalities

In practical terms, the centre of Punta del Diablo is the end of San Martín, where buses pull up and Cynsa and Rutas del Sol have ticket offices. There's also a police office and the La Barca supermarket (*closed in winter*). In high season you'll find a couple of internet places dotted around, as well as bakeries and cafés. There's no ATM or exchange office – bring plenty of cash.

Surf boards can be rented just below near the craft market. Surfing lessons (*about US$15/hr*) and horseriding can be arranged through your accommodation, as well as birdwatching by Laguna Negra and volunteering at the Karumbé Project (see *La Coronilla*, see opposite).

PARQUE NACIONAL SANTA TERESA

At km302 of Ruta 9 a cloverleaf junction gives access to Laguna Negra to the west and the Parque Nacional Santa Teresa to the east. The national park is based around the historic Fortaleza Santa Teresa, although the entry is further north at km306. Between the volcanic Cerro Rivera (at the southern end of the national park) and Cerro Verde (at the northern end) is an area of native parkland with plenty of palm trees and native birds. It's dotted with campgrounds and is very popular in summer, especially with Brazilians. It's well set up and maintained, with some good boardwalks and birdwatching *miradores*.

Tourist information

From km302 an avenue of palms leads to a junction with the so-called Capatacia to the left, where some colonial buildings house the park's offices (*www.parquesantateresa.com.uy*; ⊕ *07.00–18.00 daily; free*). Buses call here, and Rutas del Sol have a ticket office. There's also a supermarket, a restaurant, an Antel phone office and, nearby, a 19th-century glasshouse.

Where to stay

Camping Santa Teresa (❑ *477 2101/3*; e *cdosepae@adinet.com.uy*; ⊕ *early Dec–Easter*; $) has spaces for 2,500 tents and 1,200 caravans, as well as 18 *cabañas*; electricity and barbecues are provided, and it's all very cheap and full of young people. In fact the park and campsite are managed by the army, who are friendly but not always the most efficient at telling you where to pitch your tent. Choose your site with care: La Moza, at the northern end of the park, is full of partying surfers in summer, while Cerro Chato is quieter.

What to see and do

From the Capatacia, tracks lead to the camping sites, east to the Playa del Barco and north to the fort via the *pajarera* (aviary), which houses various colourful birds and also monkeys and rabbits. There are ducks in a nearby pond, where you might also see an otter. Elsewhere in the park you may see axis deer (*Axis axis*), introduced from South Asia, as well as plentiful *cotorras*, swallows, field flickers and semi-wild cattle. Ñandúes (rheas) can wander in to the campsites, and whale-watching is possible in season on the coast.

Fortaleza Santa Teresa (⊕ *10.00–19.00 daily; US$1*) Construction of the Fortaleza Santa Teresa was begun in 1762 (on St Teresa's Day, 15 October) by the Portuguese Colonel Tomás Luis Osorno. It was captured by Ceballos in 1763 and completed by the Spaniards. In 1826 it was definitively captured from Brazil by Colonel Leonardo Olivera (1793–1863), and was held by the *blancos* during the Guerra

Grande. It was very run-down by 1919 when President Baltasar Brum visited, and was restored in 1927–31.

Opposite the entry to the fort is the Posta del Viajero restaurant, and a small cemetery. Inside the fort's buildings you'll see lots of mainly 18th-century uniforms (mostly in prints), guns and pikes, and the forge and kitchen. In the sacristy are ceramic medicine jars, healthcare being part of the chaplain's role; there's also a Bible with onionskin pages. Some cannon dating from 1813 stand on the ramparts, from where there's a view over Laguna Negra.

Getting there Buses will tend to assume you want the Capatacia, but you can ask to be dropped at km306, from where it's about 1km to the fort, turning right at the first junction. To the left, the road continues to a statue of Colonel Oliveira and a national park gate, from where pedestrians can continue to the Punta de la Moza beach and campsite, at the northern end of the park. It's tempting to walk to the park's southern part from Punta del Diablo, but it's not easy to know where to turn inland from the beach – it's easier to take a bus to the fort (heading towards Chuy) and walk the 6km back to Punta del Diablo.

Surfing Surfing is very popular (especially with Brazilians at Mardi Gras). Playa del Barco and Pesqueros de Playa Grande are good. Playa La Moza, to the north is one of the best in Uruguay, with right-hand waves 500m long from about 300m off the beach. There's a beach-bar here, the only one in the area, where you can also rent surfboards. Playa Cerro Chato, near the centre of the park, is partly sheltered from the wind, and always busy with campers from the nearby site.

From the junction at km302 a road also leads east to **Potrerillo de Santa Teresa**, on the north shore of Laguna Negra, where there's a biological station run by Probides (*Programa de Conservación de la Biodiversidad y Desarrollo Sustentable en los Humedales del Este;* ☎ *470 6028,* 📱 *9987 0622; www.probides.org.uy*), with an exhibition including indigenous relics. You can take tours in 4x4 vehicles and boats, to see birds, carpinchos and the *cerritos* or mounds left by the indigenous people.

LA CORONILLA Ruta 9 passes the Aduana La Coronilla (where there's no real Customs check) at km311 and crosses the Canal Andreoni, built to irrigate the rice plantations in the interior; 3km later buses pull into the village of La Coronilla, a small beach resort that's also known for its fishing. It's of interest to tourists mainly because of the **Marine Turtle Centre**, run by a group called Karumbé (*Avda Giannattasio km30.5 & Roma, Montevideo;* 📱 *9861 4201, 9991 7811;* e *karumbemail@ gmail.com; www.karumbe.org*), which welcomes volunteers to help with its work of protecting marine turtles (the green turtle, *Chelonia mydas*; loggerhead turtle, *Caretta caretta*; olive ridley turtle, *Lepidochelys olivacea*; and leatherback turtle, *Dermochelys coriacea*).

Cerro Verde, just south on the edge of the Parque Nacional Santa Teresa, is an important feeding area for juvenile green turtles, many of which die after being caught in fishing nets. Cerro Verde became Uruguay's first Coastal-Marine Protected Area in 2007, and is part of the Sistema Nacional de Areas Protegidas (SNAP), the new national system of protected areas. There are also various dolphins, sharks, seabirds and sea lions here, as well as migrating right whales in season. Karumbé ('turtle' in Guaraní) runs works with local fishing people and holds many public events including turtle festivals and turtle camps, when children help with tagging and rehabilitation of stranded turtles. The Karumbé field station is on the beach in La Coronilla, and volunteers are welcome to help with cooking and cleaning, as well as caring for turtles, monitoring the local fishing industry and working with researchers.

Information on accommodation is available online at www.lacoronilla.com.uy. Hotels, including the Costas del Mar (✆ 474 2781) and Rivamare (✆ 476 2986; e hotalrivamare@hotmail.com), are to be found about half a kilometre north of the town centre. For Camping La Coronilla (✆ 474 2877, 476 3150; ⊕ mid-Dec–Easter) turn off Ruta 9 at km314.5; it has plenty of space, with electric lighting, barbecues and a shop. COT and Rutas del Sol both have ticket offices on the main street, Fernández, where there's also a police station and policlínica.

CHUY Ruta 9 continues northeastwards through more park-like country, passing the turning to Barra del Chuy (see page 244) at km331 and reaching the Aduana Chuy at km336, where the main road swings right to bypass the town and proceed directly into Brazil. Buses swing left on to Artigas, into the centre of the little border town of Chuy, 2km north and 340km from Montevideo (five hours by bus). The Uruguayan and Brazilian border posts are respectively 2km and 3km from the actual border, and people can move freely in the area between them, including Chuy and its Brazilian twin, Chuí. Buses will stop at Customs (Aduana) for you to have your passport stamped, but only if you ask – otherwise you'll have to hike back. There's a tourist information office here (✆ 474 4599).

The centre is tiny, soon giving way to unpaved residential roads. There's no bus terminal, with bus companies using their offices near the plaza, which is on Artigas a block south of Avenida Internacional, the wide boulevard that runs along the border. This area is dominated by 'free shops', ie: duty-free stores, as well as a casino (⊕ 14.00–01.00 Tue–Thu, 14.00–02.00 Fri–Sat) on the Uruguayan side. Prices in the free shops are posted in US dollars, but you can pay in Uruguayan or Brazilian currency, and can of course import the goods freely into either country.

Getting there For buses to Montevideo (see page 82) as well as La Paloma and Punta del Este, Cynsa, Rutas del Sol and COT are all on the block of Oliveira between the plaza and the border; some buses also call at Barra del Chuy. Expreso Chago (Avda Brasil at San Miguel, near Hotel Internacional) has slower services to Montevideo via Lascana Aiguá and Ruta 8.

Where to stay There's not a great choice of hotels (though there are more in the beach resort of Barra del Chuy; see page 244); see www.chuynet.com/guia/hoteles.htm for information.

⌂ **Hotel Alerces** Laguna de Castillos 578, just off Artigas; ✆ 474 2260; e alerces@adinet.com.uy. Rooms are not huge but are light & clean. Use of swimming pool & PC or Wi-Fi inc. B/fast costs extra. $$$

⌂ **Nuevo Hotel Plaza** On the plaza at Artigas & Arachanes; ✆ 474 2309; e hoteplplaza@hotmail.com; www.hotelplaza.chuynet.com. The best hotel in town, a relatively grand 3-star. There's also the El Mesón del Plaza restaurant (see below). $$$

⌂ **Hotel Internacional** (25 rooms) Avda Brasil 679; ✆ 474 2153, 474 2055; e hotel@adinet.com.uy. Some rooms have AC. $$

⌂ **Hospedaje Atlántico** Oliveira 211, 150m south of the plaza; ✆ 474 2575, m 9987 7015. US$9 for basic room with no window & shared bathroom; some rooms have external windows & TVs. No b/fast, but it's friendly & adequate. $

Where to eat There are several pizza-parrilla restaurants near the plaza, including **Javier** (on the plaza at Arachanes), **Jésus** (Oliveira & Brasil) and **Las Leñas** (Artigas between Brasil & Arachanes), which is the liveliest of the three and also serves sweet pizzas, with dulce de leche or chocolate. The **Restaurant-cafetería El Mesón del Plaza** at the Nuevo Hotel Plaza is a bit quieter and more formal, although it hits no gastronomic heights.

Other practicalities

Banks The Banco República (with ATM) is at Artigas & Ventura, on the east side of the plaza; exchange offices include Gales (*Avda Brasil & Artigas;* ⊕ *08.30–18.00 Mon–Fri, 09.30–12.00 Sat*).

Communications The Antel *telecentro* (⊕ *08.00–22.00 Mon–Sat, 09.00–17.00 Sun*) is on Laguna Merín just west of Artigas; the post office is a block and a half further south, in an obscure shopfront on Artigas (⊕ *09.00–15.00 Mon–Fri, 08.00–13.00 Sat*). There's free public Wi-Fi on the plaza.

Consulate There is a Brazilian consulate (*Tito Fernández 147 & Laguna Merín;* ❱ *474 2049;* e *chubrcg@internet.com.uy;* ⊕ *08.30–12.30 Mon–Fri*) and an office of the Inspectoría de Migración (*Aduana, Ruta 9 km336;* ❱ *474 2072;* e *i08chuy@ dnm.minterior.gub.uy*).

Markets The El Dorado supermarket is on the south side of the plaza next to El Mesón del Plaza.

What to see and do

Fortín de San Miguel (⊕ *summer 10.00–19.00 daily, rest of the year Fri–Sun; US$1*) Chuy's only attraction is the Fortín de San Miguel, an 18th-century fort 6.5km west on Ruta 19. Construction was begun by the Spanish in 1734 and completed by the Portuguese in 1737 to observe Spanish military movements, rather than as a major defensive site. Smaller (and more attractive) than Santa Teresa (see page 240), it was built of compacted stone rather than masonry. It was already in ruins when captured by the Spanish in 1763; by 1927 it was in a very bad state but was then very well restored and became a Monumento Nacional (with a surrounding *reserva de flora nativa*) in 1937.

The fort is managed jointly by the army and Probides, and is in very good condition. You can walk around the Vaubanesque ramparts, with cannons and viewpoints, as well as the original toilets (not in use), on the outside wall. The buildings inside are labelled with their original functions but now house mannequins in military uniforms, as well as 18th-century kitchen equipment and so on. There are toilets opposite the gate.

Nearby are the Campo Santo (cemetery) and barn-like buildings housing the Museo Criollo (Rural Museum) and Museo Indígena (Museum of Indigenous Life). The former is mainly a surprisingly varied collection of carts and carriages, while the latter displays arrowheads, mortars, *bolas, rompecabezas, ornolitos* and other examples of worked stoneware, as well as a model of a *toldo* (leather shelter), and preserved insects.

A signed path leads from the road a few hundred metres to the Guardia Perdida (Lost Guardpost), a tiny sentry post in a partially walled-in gap under a rock – not very interesting in itself, but the path leads on in good native woodland to a field and the road from the museum to the low wooded hill of Cerro Picudo. In addition to palms, cacti and other native flora, there are birds including cotorras, jays and raptors.

Getting there Occasional buses run from Chuy to 18 de Julio, not far beyond the fort, although you'll have to pay the minimum fare of just over US$1. If you're driving or cycling, turn left at the border on to Avenida Internacional, which looks like a dual carriageway but is two separate roads, Avenida Brasil on the Uruguayan side and Avenida Uruguay on the Brazilian side. Only the Uruguayan road continues, with border markers on the right separating it from huge rice paddies on the Brazilian side. At km8 (from Ruta 9; about 6km from the town) the road crosses the Arroyo San Miguel on two longish bridges, at the far end of which is a highways maintenance depot. Behind this, bizarrely, is a *mirador de aves* (birdwatching hide) looking over the wetlands – only about 50m from the road but a good place to bring children. There is a good photographic guide to the birds of the area, with Spanish, English and scientific names.

Just west beyond a Customs (*Aduana*) checkpoint, an asphalt road leads up through attractive native trees and loops right around the back of the fort; on foot it's easier to walk up to the left as soon as you see the fort. What seems to be a moat is actually just a pool with a drawbridge over it.

Barra del Chuy Returning 6km towards Montevideo, an unpaved road turns south at km331 and runs through rice paddies for 7km to the beach resort of Barra del Chuy. It's a rather exposed beach which can yield good surfing. Just before the centre of this very scattered settlement is the **Complejo Turístico Chuy** (❋ 474 9425, 474 8113; e turchuy@adinet.com.uy; www.complejoturisticochuy.com; ⊕ all year), with a Parque de Aguas (thermal pools), large campsite, 14 *cabañas* and a hostel. The Hostal del Camping ($$$) is a fine big wooden building, built in 2000, with rooms for two, three and four plus family suites (all with private bathroom), with a TV room and wood-burning stove. The bungalows and cabins are in a quiet area, away from the campsite but near enough to the pools; they cost from US$57 for four in the low season, and some duplex *cabañas* have air conditioning. The campsite ($) has 150 pitches, with electricity and barbecues.

About 100m to the east along the main access road, the **Complejo Los Orozco** (❋ 474 9047, m 9923 1905; e orozco8@adinet.com.uy; www.losorozco.com; $$) also has *cabañas* and bungalows; they also offer free Wi-Fi.

Into Brazil Ruta 9 passes around the east side of Chuy, becoming BR-471 in Brazil. You'll need to clear Uruguayan Immigration and Customs at the Aduana, 2km short of town, and the Brazilian equivalent at the Policía Federal post nearly 3km towards Pelotas. Buses will stop as long as you ask, and the procedures don't take long.

In Chuí, Brazil (or Brasil as it's written locally, of course), there are more hotels, but they cost more than in Uruguay. The Rodoviario (bus terminal) is on Rua Venezuela, two blocks from the border and a block to the right (east) from Avenida Argentina, the continuation of Artigas. Buses run from Chuí to Pelotas (*6–7 daily, US$15, 4hr*), Rio Grande (*07.00 & 14.00, 5hr, US$12*) and Porto Alegre (*12.00 & 23.30, 7¾ hrs, US$33–40*).

6

Western Uruguay

Some two and a half hours and 177km west of Montevideo, across the rich dairylands of San José and Colonia departments, and an hour by ferry from Buenos Aires, the town of Colonia is a magnet for tourists. Beyond here the border follows the Río Uruguay northwards past the towns of Fray Bentos, Paysandú and Salto to the border with Brazil. This *litoral* (riverside region) is a prosperous area, with forestry and citrus plantations expanding fast, but there are also large areas of wetlands that are home to a wide variety of birds and other wildlife. This area also produces some of the world's most beautiful sunsets. Beyond Paysandú is Uruguay's hot-springs district, with lots of spas providing enjoyable stopovers year-round.

COLONIA DEPARTMENT

Buses from Montevideo's Tres Cruces terminal have a smooth run on Ruta 1, now largely dual-carriageway, past Santiago Vásquez (see page 155) and the turning to San José (see page 156). Beyond Ecilda Paullier there's a toll at km107 as the highway enters Colonia department after 1½ hours.

NUEVA HELVECIA AND COLONIA VALDENSE These two towns, settled by Swiss colonists in the 1850s and 1860s, are known for their (frankly rather bland) cheeses. There's the odd antique shop and Swiss-themed restaurant, but both villages look rather like American suburbs, with comfortable bungalows on wide lawns. Colonia Valdense holds a cheese festival in mid-November and Nueva Helvecia (also known as Colonia Suiza) holds a Bierfest in mid-December.

Tourist information is available in Colonia Valdense at the Centro Artesanos Ciudad Jardín (↘ *55 88412*).

Getting there Buses heading for Ruta 2 and Mercedes turn at km118 to Nueva Helvecia, 5km to the north. Most buses for Colonia detour through Colonia Valdense, just south of Ruta 1 at km121.

Where to stay In Nueva Helvecia, the **Hotel Nirvana** (*Avda Batlle y Ordóñez;* m *9554 4081;* $$$$$) is pretty comfortable. The **Granja Hotel Suizo** (*Federico Fischer 355;* ↘ *55 44002;* e *granjahotelsuizo@adinet.com.uy; www.hotelsuizonuevahelvecia.com;* $$$), founded in 1872, offers a swimming pool and Swiss food. Just beyond, at km123.5, a road leads south to the Blancarena (White Sand) **campsite** (↘ *58 72110;* ⊕ *Dec–Easter*). The small towns of Rosario and Juan Lacaze, to the north, each have a couple of simple hotels.

COLONIA Colonia del Sacramento was founded in 1680 by Manuel Lobo, governor of Rio de Janeiro, to be a Portuguese rival to Buenos Aires, directly across the River

Western Uruguay   COLONIA DEPARTMENT

6

245

WESTERN URUGUAY

Plate. Fought over by Spain and Portugal for almost a century, it was known as *la manzana de la discordia* (the apple of discord). In 1763 it was also attacked by the British, whose ship the *Lord Clive* was sunk and her officers hung in the plaza. In 1750 Colonia was awarded to Spain, but Portuguese settlers resisted the handover until the Spanish captured the town in 1777, ratified by the Treaty of San Ildefonso in 1778.

In 1807 the British again tried to capture Colonia. In 1818 the Portuguese seized it from pro-independence Artiguistas, and in 1826 a squadron under Admiral Guillermo (William) Brown drove off what were now Brazilian ships and bombarded the town but was unable to capture it. Until 1828, when the Brazilians left, this was a centre for smuggling (backed by the British) into Buenos Aires. In 1836 its population was just 762, plus 166 in Real de San Carlos. Colonia continued to be in the wars, being bombarded by an Argentine squadron in 1842, captured by Garibaldi and an Anglo-French force in 1845, and taken again by Oribe and the *blancos* in 1848.

Darwin visited in 1833, describing:

> ...a fine grass country, but which is very poorly stocked with cattle or inhabitants ...
> The town is ... strongly fortified, but both fortifications and town suffered much
> from the Brazilian war. It is very ancient, and from the irregularity of the streets and
> the surrounding groves of old orange trees and peaches had a pretty appearance.

After the Guerra Grande, Colonia was at last free to develop as a port and regional centre, with frequent ferries from Buenos Aires. The opening of bridges across the Río Uruguay at Paysandú (1975) and Fray Bentos (1976) removed a lot of the freight that had passed through Colonia. In compensation the government began a programme to restore Colonia's historic buildings, culminating in the old town's being added to UNESCO's World Heritage List in 1995.

Today, there are many boutique hotels and chic restaurants in old Portuguese houses, and many houses are owned by Argentines. The restoration work has been well done, and regulations about not altering façades have been strictly observed. Tourism is the main industry, but there's a nice sideline as a location for filming adverts and historical movies. Colonia is famed as an unspoilt and tranquil historic town; it's certainly quiet but isn't nearly as picturesque as your average French or Italian village, or as Paraty in Brazil. Nevertheless, it is very busy at weekends, and restaurants are crowded and expensive.

Getting there

By bus The bus terminal (*Avda Roosevelt & Manuel Lobo*) is immediately north of the port, just east of the old town. It houses a tourist information desk, ATM and exchange office, car rental and a phone/internet office. Buses to Montevideo are frequent enough (see page 82) that if you arrive from Buenos Aires and go to the terminal in the morning, you'll have no problem booking a bus for the afternoon; there's no need to call ahead from Argentina. Many of these buses connect to Rosario and Nueva Helvecia, and Compañía Omnibus Colonia also runs frequent local buses there and elsewhere. Nossar go to Durazno (*3/day*), Berrutti to Carmelo and Nuevo Palmira (*11/day, w/ends 4–6/day*), a couple continuing to Mercedes, and Chadre all the way up the *litoral* route to Mercedes, Fray Bentos, Paysandú, Salto and Bella Unión (*05.40 & 14.30 daily*).

By ferry A new ferry terminal opened in 2009, with ATMs, toilets and a cafeteria. There are tourist information offices by the exit for cars (east of the bus terminal) and by the pedestrian exit (to the west at Calle Mendez). Luggage

COLONIA
New Town

can be stored at the port (free with a ticket to or from Buenos Aires). The ferry companies all have ticket offices at the port: Buquebus (↳ *52 22950/23030*), Colonia Express (↳ *52 29676*; ⊕ *1hr 45min before each departure to 30min afterwards*) and Seacat Colonia (↳ *52 22919*; ⊕ *07.30–19.00 Mon–Sat*). Colonia Express are also in the bus terminal (↳ *52 29677/8*; ⊕ *10.00–19.00 Mon–Fri, 10.00–16.00 Sat, 10.00–12.00 Sun*).

Getting around The cobbled streets of the centre are largely car-free; most locals ride scooters, but visitors can rent golf-carts if they don't want to walk or cycle. A local bus runs up and down Flores. Bus A runs every 15 minutes from Flores to Real de San Carlos, 5km north around the bay, which was built a hundred years ago as a tourism development and still boasts a few hotels and museums.

Car rental

🚐 **Avis** bus terminal; ↳ 52 29842; e avis@avis.com.uy; www.avis.com

🚐 **Budget** bus terminal; ↳ 52 29841; e budget@budget.com.uy; www.budget.com.uy

🚗 **Dollar** Flores 234; ☎ 52 29805, 24hr m 9443 4937; e dollarpdp@adinet.com.uy; www.dollar.com.uy

🚗 **Europcar** Avda Artigas 154 & 18 de Julio; ☎ 52 28454, m 9850 0922, 24hr m 9622 2828; e reservas@europcar.com.uy; www.europcar.com.uy

🚗 **Hertz** Port; ☎ 52 29851; m 9441 5243; Radisson Hotel, Washington Barbot 283; ☎ 52 29851; www.hertz.com

🚗 **Mariño Sport Rent a Car** Florida 419; ☎ 52 30073, 52 30608; e colonia@mariniosport.com; www.mariniosport.com

🚗 **Moto Rent** Ceballos 223; ☎ 52 22266, 52 29665. Rent motorbikes & dune buggies. These are also available from Punta Car & Thrifty.

🚗 **Multicar** Manuel Lobo 505 & Rivera; ☎ 52 24893, m 9444 7500; e colonia@redmulticar.com; www.redmulticar.com

🚗 **Rentacar Daymán** Manuel Lobo 319; ☎ 52 26285, 52 21285, m 9952 2278; www.rentacardayman.com

🚗 **Punta Car** 18 de Julio 496 & Rivera; m 9461 9858; Florida s/n; ☎ 52 22353, m 9960 9643, 9852 2522; www.puntacar.com.uy

🚗 **Thrifty** Flores 172; ☎ 52 22939; Florida 415; ☎ 52 21936; e colonia@thrifty.com.uy

🚗 **UruCar** Florida s/n; ☎ 52 28889

🚗 **Viaggio Rentacar** Avda Roosevelt & Rivera, opposite bus terminal; ☎ 52 22614, 52 22929; 24hr m 9865 5325

Tourist information The most convenient tourist office is the Centro de Informes del Barrio Histórico (*Portón de Campo, Manuel Lobo;* ☎ *52 28506*), run by the Corporación Turistica Departamental de Colonia. Guided walks of the historic centre (*11.00 Thu–Sun, 15.00 Mon–Sat; US$5*) leave from here when it's dry. Colonia department's tourist office is at Rivera & Flores (☎ *52 26141, 52 23700;* e *turismo@colonia.gub.uy; www.colonianet.com;* ⏰ *08.00–19.00 Mon–Fri, 10.00–18.00 Sat–Sun*), together with the Cámara Hotelera y Turística de Colonia (☎ *52 27302;* e *camhotel@adinet.com.uy; www.hotelesencolonia.com*), which has information on hotels including availability. The national tourist office is at the port (☎ *52 24897*).

🏠 **Where to stay**
Hotels

🏠 **Days Inn Resort Casa del Sol** Ruta 1 km170; ☎ 52 26383; www.daysinncasadelsol.com. Much nicer than you might expect, with sizeable AC rooms, gym, indoor & outdoor pools & a restaurant-*parrilla*. It's by the highway 5km towards Montevideo (bikes are available). $$$$$

🏠 **Hotel La Misión** Misiones de los Tapes 171; ☎ 52 26767; e lamision@adinet.com.uy; www.lamisionhotel.com. A very stylish place right in the heart of the historic district, in a refurbished 19th-century house with lots of exposed stonework; AC rooms, Wi-Fi, & good buffet b/fast. $$$$$

🏠 **Hotel Sheraton** Continuación de la Rambla de Las Américas s/n, 7km north beyond Real de San Carlos; ☎ 52 32021; e reservas.colonia@sheraton.com; www.sheraton.com/colonia. Calling itself a 'golf & spa resort', a good base for those who like predictable 5-star megahotels. In addition to the golf course, it's right on the beach. The Sendero Areniscaleads in 50m to a pool with waterbirds. $$$$$

🏠 **Posada Plaza Mayor** del Comercio 111; ☎ 52 23191–3; e hmayor@adinet.com.uy; www.posadaplazamayor.com.uy. A boutique 4-star in the heart of the historic district, combining an 18th-century Portuguese rancho & a mansion built in

1860, with flower-bedecked patio & a famous fountain by local ceramicist Ariel Chape. 12 historic rooms on the ground floor, 2 new ones upstairs with sea views. All have AC & cable TV, but there's Wi-Fi only in the *cafetería*, lobby & business centre. $$$$$

🏠 **Radisson Hotel & Casino** Washington Barbot 283; ☎ 52 30460; www.radissoncolonia.com. Behind a very cool & unobtrusive modern exterior, this has indoor & outdoor swimming pools, jacuzzi, sauna & gym; the 60 rooms have AC & Wi-Fi. $$$$$

🏠 **Hotel Beltrán** Flores 311; ☎ 52 26260; www.hotelbeltran.com. A classy place, dating from 1873 (making it the country's second hotel) but now thoroughly modern, with AC & Wi-Fi in all rooms, & a fine restaurant. $$$$

🏠 **Posada del Ángel** Washington Barbot 59; ☎ 52 24602; www.posadadelangel.net. In a lovely older house & garden near the harbour, this has 11 rooms with AC throughout, swimming pool, sauna & gym. $$$$

🏠 **Posada del Gobernador** 18 de Julio 205; ☎ 52 23018; e posadadelgobernador@adinet.com.uy. A classy 4-star with just 15 AC rooms, swimming pool & 'ancient reading lounge'. $$$$

Posada del Virrey España 217; 🞜 52 22223; www.posadadelvirrey.com. Right in the World Heritage district, this beautifully restored historic house has AC rooms for 2, 3 or 4 as well as suites with jacuzzi. There's free internet access & Wi-Fi in the public areas of the hotel. $$$$

Posada Don Antonio Ituzaingó 232; 🞜 52 25344; www.posadadonantonio.com. One of the larger central hotels, with 37 rooms & spacious gardens with outdoor swimming pool, this is a nice blend of historical & modern, with AC & Wi-Fi. $$$$

Posada Manuel de Lobo Ituzaingó 160; 🞜 52 22463; www.posadamanueldelobo.com. In the former

Hotel Oriental, a large 19th-century colonial house with patio & garage, this has AC rooms & a suite with jacuzzi. $$$$

Hotel Posada Casa Los Pinos Washington Barbot 191; 🞜 52 31470; e casalospinos@adinet.com.uy. http://posadacasalospinos.com. Very good value, just a block from the World Heritage district. Free Wi-Fi & a snack bar. $$$

Hotel Posada del Río Washington Barbot 258; 🞜 52 23002; e hdelrio@adinet.com.uy. A nice family-style 2-star place around a patio, with AC, cable TV & a filling b/fast inc. $$$

Hostels There are three hostels, open all year and usually busy with international backpackers.

El Viajero Colonia Hostel & Suites Washington Barbot 164; 🞜 52 22683; e info@ elviajerocolonia.com; www.elviajerocolonia.com. The liveliest & most stylish of Colonia's hostels, this nicely refurbished house has AC rooms, kitchen & barbecue, free internet access with PCs & Wi-Fi, & bikes for rent (US$7/day). $$

Hostel Colonial Flores 440; 🞜 52 30347; e hostelling_colonial@hotmail.com. There's nothing colonial about this building between the casino & La Pasiva. It looks like a 1980s shopfront but inside is a pleasant patio with rooms around it for up to 9 (mixed & women-only), as well as private rooms, all with shared bathrooms, free Wi-Fi & PCs, kitchen,

barbecue & TV/DVD lounge. HI members pay 15% less & have b/fast inc. Bikes are available free, but are mostly broken; horseriding can also be arranged. $$–$

Hostel El Español Manuel Lobo 377 between Suarez & Lavalleja; 🞜 52 30759; e elespanio@ adinet.com.uy. A homely brick single-storey house dating from the 19th century, this has dorms with en-suite bathrooms for 6 & 8 (US$9), dorms for 4 with shared bathroom (US$7.40), dbls with/without bathroom (US$15/20). HI members pay 10% less. B/fast US$2. There's a kitchen, barbecue & TV/DVD room, as well as free internet & bikes. $

Camping The nearest campsite to Colonia is the Camping Brisas del Plata (🞜 52 02207; ⊙ Dec–Easter; $), 6km west on a dirt road from San Pedro, itself 11km north of Colonia on Ruta 21 at km189. It's pretty simple but popular with lovers of fishing.

✖ Where to eat

✖ Club de Yachting y Pesca Santa Rita s/n; 🞜 52 22197. With a rooftop restaurant & a harbourside terrace, this is one of the nicest places in town to eat fish, although it also serves steak & pasta. There's a 10% discount for cash. $$$$$

✖ La Casa de Jorge Páez Vilaró Misiones de los Tapes 65; 🞜 52 29211. An art gallery & restaurant opposite the Viceroy's house, this nice colonial-style building displays the modern paintings of Carlos Páez Vilaró's less famous brother. The restaurant serves well-presented steak, fish & pasta, as well as crêpes, indoors & in a nice garden; there's also Wi-Fi. $$$$$

✖ Mesón de la Plaza Vasconcelos 153; 🞜 52 24807; e mplaza@adinet.com.uy; www.mesondelaplaza.com;

⊙ 12.00–15.00, 20.00–23.30 Mon–Fri, until 01.00 Sat–Sun. Opposite the Casa del Gobierno on Plaza Manuel Lobo, this is perhaps Colonia's finest restaurant. In a beautifully restored house, with a patio & 2 fine rooms on either side, you can choose from a long, classy menu including salmon, fondue, lamb ragout, ravioli in squid ink & typically Uruguayan desserts. The wine list & service are also excellent. $$$$$

✖ Bianco y Negro Flores 248 & Ituzaingó; 🞜 52 22236, m 9952 4129; www.bynrestojazz.com.uy; ⊙ 11.30–15.30, 19.30–01.00 Thu–Tue. A restojazz, with live music (summer from 22.00 daily, the rest of the year Fri–Sat). The food is unexciting (the usual parrilla, pasta & so on) &

overpriced, but it's a nice spot for a drink if you want to listen to music (*US$3 cover charge*). **$$$$**

✕ Casagrande Misiones de los Tapes 143, opposite the Plaza Menor; ✎ 52 28371; ⏱ from 11.00 daily. This has one of the nicest terraces for daytime drinks & snacks, & serves reasonably decent lunches & dinners, though at a price that reflects the location. **$$$$**

✕ Del Carmen Washington Barbot 283; ✎ 52 30460; ⏱ 07.00–24.00 daily. The restaurant/lounge bar of the Radisson Hotel, this is a quiet & refined setting for fairly pricey food & drink. **$$$$**

✕ El Drugstore Vasconcelos 179 & Portugal; ✎ 52 25241; e eldrugstore@yahoo.com; ⏱ 12.00–01.00 daily. Facing the church, this is the funkiest place to eat in town, with lots of vegetarian & Japanese choices; the interior is attractive & the pavement seating is pleasant too. No credit cards. **$$$$**

✕ Lobo Restaurante Comercio & de la Playa; ✎ 52 29245; www.loborestaurante.com; ⏱ 12.00–16.00 daily, from 20.00 Thu–Sat. A very stylish place that serves up tapas as well as the standard steaks & pasta – come here for the rooftop terrace rather than for gourmet cuisine. **$$$$**

✕ Pulperia de los Faroles Misiones de los Tapes 101 & Comercio; ✎ 52 30271; e pulperiadelosfaroles@hotmail.com; ⏱ 12.00–24.00 daily. An attractive place with its brick-lined interior or seating outside on the plaza, this serves simple food, cooked well, including fish & pasta as well as good salads & interesting vegetarian options (eg: pumpkin fritters). Desserts include great meringues. Sometimes there's live music, & prices are not unreasonable for the location. **$$$$**

✕ Restaurant del Club Atlético Barrio Sur 18 de Julio 267; ✎ 52 24451. A very decent but totally non-touristy place, serving snacks, fish, chicken, meats & pasta. **$$$$**

✕ Sacramento Comercio & La Playa; ✎ 52 29245. Fab food served in a postmodern setting, including excellent steak, lamb with polenta chips, fish, salads

& desserts. Wine available by the glass. Live music Fri–Sat nights. **$$$$**

✕ El Portón Flores 333; ✎ 52 25318; e parrilladelporton@hotmail.com. A simple, cheerful *parrilla* with semi-industrial décor that's a good place to feed a family, with *chivitos*, pizza, pasta & fish as well as grilled meats, all very affordable. **$$$**

✕ El Torreón Flores 19; ✎ 52 20823. Below a fairly ugly modern tower, the waterfront terrace is the place to drink *clericó* & eat anything from *chivitos* to pasta, paella or ice cream. **$$$**

✕ La Bodeguita Comercio 167; ✎ 52 25329; ⏱ from 19.30 Tue–Sun, from 12.00 Sat–Sun. Great pizza, inc vegetarian options, & *faina*. There's outdoor seating & it's all cheap. **$$$**

✕ Los Dos Reales Dr Carlos Martínez 96; ✎ 223 0694. The best place to eat in Real de San Carlos (other than the Sheraton), serving homemade pastas, *parrilla* & snacks in a nice old house, well restored, not far beyond the bullring. **$$$**

✕ Mercosur Flores 252 & Ituzaingó; ✎ 52 24200; ⏱ from 09.00 daily. An uncomplicated, touristy place that serves good *chivitos* & Uruguayan approximations of Swiss cuisine such as polenta, *agnolotti* (stuffed pasta), *tortilla a la suiza* (a sort of omeletty version of *rösti* with cheese & onion) or cheese fondue. **$$$**

✕ Patrimonio San José 111; ✎ 52 24254. A lounge bar & restaurant with standard *parrilla* & grilled fish, as well as vegetarian dishes, on a pleasant terrace with Wi-Fi. **$$$**

✕ Viejo Barrio Vasconcellos 169; ✎ 52 25399; ⏱ 12.00–15.00, 20.00–24.00 Thu–Tue. Facing the church, this serves simple, traditional food – meat, fish & pastas – at very reasonable prices. The waiter is a bit mad but highly entertaining. **$$$**

✕ La Amistad 18 de Julio 448 & Mendez; m 9454 1596. Near the port, this non-touristy place serves good *chivitos*, vegetarian pasta, pizza & fish at half the price you'd pay in the historic district. **$$**

Shopping For craft shopping, the Feria Artesanal is on Fosalba at Suárez, with permanent stalls provided by the municipality; for more expensive items, including clothing, try the Paseo del Sol (*at intersection between Comercio and de la Playa*), Plaza Menor and Almacen La Carlota (*Calle Real*) and Santolina (*de la Playa 132*). For leather goods, look for Casacuero (*Paseo del Sol, Comercio 158;* ✎ *52 28997;* e *casacuero@movinet.com.uy*); and for knitwear Manos del Uruguay (*Flores 89;* ✎ *52 21793;* e *malvon_colonia@yahoo.com*).

The most convenient supermarket is Económico (*Flores 1730 near Washington Barbot;* ⏱ *08.30–22.00 Mon–Sat, 09.00–13.30, 17.30–22.00 Sun*). For wines and cheeses head for Granja Naturalia (*Flores 437, opposite Hostel Colonial*).

Other practicalities
Banks There are ATMs along Flores, and at the port and bus terminal. Shops and restaurants will accept Argentine pesos, US dollars and, often, Brazilian reals and euros. Exchange offices include Cambio Colonia (*at the port; & Flores 401 & Lavalleja; ⊕ 09.00–18.00 Mon–Fri, 09.00–13.00, 15.00–18.00 Sat, 10.00–13.00 Sun*) and Cambio Dromer (*Flores 350 & Suárez*).

Communications The post office faces the plaza at Lavelleja 226 (⊕ *09.00–17.00 Mon–Fri*). Antel's *telecentros* are at Flores 429 (⊕ *09.00–19.00 Mon–Sat, 10.00–18.00 Sun*) and Flores 172 (⊕ *09.30–21.00 Sun–Thu, 09.30–22.00 Fri–Sat*). There's free public Wi-Fi on Plaza 25 de Agosto.

Consulate For visa issues, the Inspectoría de Migración is at 18 de Julio 428 (🕿 *52 22126, 52 26105;* e *i07colonia@dnm.minterior.gub.uy*). The Argentine consulate is at Flores 209 (🕿 *52 22093, 52 22086;* e *conccolo@adinet.com.uy;* ⊕ *13.00–18.00 Mon–Fri*).

Emergency services The public hospital is near the terminal at 18 de Julio 462 (🕿 *52 22994, 52 22945*). To contact the police call 🕿 109 (emergency) or 52 23348; the Policía Turística are very visible patrolling the historic district and have an office on the south side of the Plaza 25 de Agosto on Flores.

Activities and entertainment The Teatro y Centro Cultural Bastión del Carmen (*Rivadavia 223;* 🕿 *52 27201;* ⊕ *10.30–21.00 Tue–Sun*) puts on art exhibitions and theatre performances.

Colonia's best beach is said to be the Playa Ferrando, 1km east of the port, a pleasant site with woods along the shore, and a restaurant. There are also beaches along Avenida Costanera, north of central Colonia, with bars and *paradores*, but they're less attractive with the road alongside.

One of the best of Uruguay's few golf courses is at the Sheraton Golf and Spa Resort, on the north side of Real de San Carlos (*Continuación de la Rambla de Las Américas s/n;* 🕿 *52 29000*).

What to see and do From the port and bus terminal, Florida leads west past the former railway station (across the tracks from the tourism and car rental offices is the former locomotive roundhouse, to become a cultural centre); just before reaching the old city wall, turn right to the Centro de Informes del Barrio Histórico (see *Tourist information*). Immediately west of this is the **Portón de Campo** (Country Gate), built in 1745 by the Portuguese and rebuilt in 1968–71 (bronze nails in the wall mark the level above which it is a reconstruction). Continuing into the walled town (and the UNESCO World Heritage District), the Plaza Mayor (or Plaza 25 de Mayo) opens in front of you, a long square planted with *palo borracho*, figs, palms, cycads, jasmine and bougainvillea, with cotorras and swallows flying about. To the left the **Calle de los Suspiros** is the most photographed street in Uruguay, a short traffic-free lane leading down to the Plate that is essentially unchanged from the 18th century, with its cobbles and central drain, and single-storey cottages on either side.

Just beyond this on the south side of the Plaza Mayor is the best of Colonia's museums, the Museo Portugués, in an 18th-century Portuguese house, and at the western end of the plaza are other museums, the Casa Nacarello, the ruined Casa del Virrey (see *Museums*, page 255) and the Museo Municipal. To the left are the ruins of the convent of San Francisco Xavier, built in 1683 and burnt down in 1793; the *faro* (lighthouse; US$0.60) was built on its ruins in 1855–57. At 27m it's

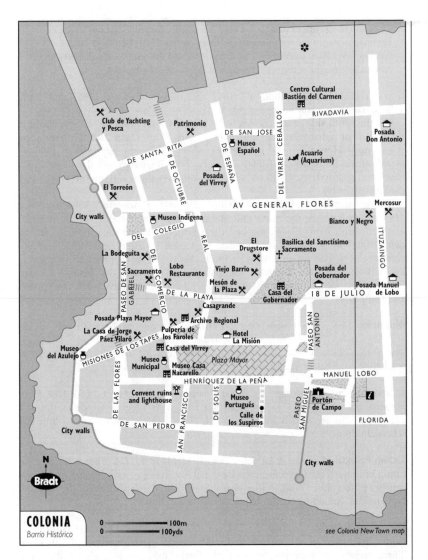

COLONIA
Barrio Histórico

0	100m
0	100yds

see Colonia New Town map

higher than the Faro Punta Brava in Montevideo, but the stairs are better. You can just make out the towers of Buenos Aires on the horizon, to the left of the leftmost islet (with a navigation light on it).

From the *faro* head west on San Pedro to the headland, where you can still see traces of the Bastión de San Pedro de Alcántara, built in 1723. Following the shore north (with sandy patches between rocky points and reeds) you'll come to the former Bastión de Santa Rita (1736) at the end of Avenida General Flores, the main street. To the north is the yacht club and the long jetty of the marina, and two blocks to the east an older jetty built in 1866 and reopened in 2001.

Going a few blocks up Flores and then south on Vasconcelos, you'll come to the **Basilica del Sanctísimo Sacramento** (Basilica of the Holy Sacrament), the oldest in Uruguay, built in 1680, rebuilt in 1695–99 and 1808–10 and destroyed in 1823. As Darwin put it:

The church is a curious ruin; it was used as a powder magazine and was struck by lightning in one of the ten thousand storms of the Río Plata. Two thirds of the building was blown away to the very foundation, and the rest stands a shattered and curious monument of the united powers of lightning and gunpowder.

It was rebuilt between 1836 and 1842 and restored between 1957 and 1995, although with its plain white exterior and interior it's not especially attractive.

On the south side of the church is the Plaza Manuel Lobo, an attractive park at the heart of what was the Portuguese fort. The **Casa del Gobernador** (Governor's House), ruined by the Spanish in 1777, was excavated in 1990–93 (some of the finds are on display in the Archivo Regional) and the foundations have been restored, with walkways through and over them and interpretative signs (in Spanish only).

To the north of Flores at Ceballos 236 is the Acuario (Aquarium; see *Museums*, below). At the north end of Ceballos by the harbour, the Bastión del Carmen, built in 1722–48, marked the northern end of the city wall. It was demolished in 1859 but its foundations are still visible near the 38m-high chimney of a soap factory, built in 1880, that went bankrupt when its owners lost a lawsuit with an Argentine company. Now it houses the Teatro y Centro Cultural Bastión del Carmen (see page 252), with an attractive waterside garden and sculpture.

Museums The town's museums are managed collectively, with one ticket (*US$2, from Museo Municipal, Museo Indígena or Museo Portugués; http://museoscolonia.blogspot.com*) valid for all of them for a week. All are open at weekends (and Easter Week), closing on different weekdays.

Acuario (*Aquarium; Ceballos 236; www.acuario.com.uy;* ⊕ *14.00–18.00 Wed–Mon, summer until 21.00; US$1*) This houses a tank with 12 glass windows through which you can see mainly indigenous fish. There's also an interactive centre for schoolchildren.

Archivo Regional (*Misiones de los Tapes 115;* ⊕ *11.15–16.45 Thu–Tue*) A Portuguese house built by 1750, this houses the Regional Archives (including some mid-19th-century watercolours) and archaeological finds from the excavation of the Casa del Gobernador, including bottle shards, ceramics and bones.

Museo Casa Nacarello (*Comercio 67;* ⊕ *11.15–16.45 Wed–Mon*) This little Portuguese *rancho*, bright red on the outside and whitewashed inside, was restored in 1993. Three rooms are equipped with simple furnishings (some replicas) from the period when it was built (c1790), and you can also see the kitchen.

Museo del Azulejo (*Museum of Decorative Tiles; Misiones de los Tapes 104;* ⊕ *11.15–16.45 Fri–Wed*) There's not a lot to see in the three rooms of this very modest Portuguese house from the mid 18th century. Restored in 1987, it houses a small collection of tiles that belonged to Jorge Páez Vilaró, mostly the standard ones from Desvres in northern France (see page 128), as well as some very early Uruguayan tiles, dating from 1840.

Museo Español (*Spanish Museum; San José 152*) This museum, built as the Casa de Don Juan de Águila in 1720 and rebuilt in 1840 in Neoclassical style, presents the history of the Spanish colonial period; there are also modern paintings by Jorge Páez Vilaró. It was closed for repairs in 2009.

Museo Indígena (*Museum of Indigenous Life; Comercio & Flores;* ⊕ *11.15–16.45 Fri–Wed; guided visits 13.30 & 16.00 Sat–Sun*) Upstairs in this townhouse is a private collection of Charrúa grinding stones, arrowheads (a few from Chubut in Argentina), ceramics and some miscellaneous minerals and fossils.

Museo Municipal (*Municipal Museum; Plaza Mayor 77;* ⊕ *11.15–16.45 Wed–Mon*) Built in 1795 and rebuilt in 1835 with a simple Neoclassical façade, the so-called Casa Almirante Brown (although it never in fact belonged to Admiral Brown, the father of the Argentine Navy) was the town's original museum, opening in 1951. Outside are three rusty cannon, and in the first room a few indigenous ceramics, *bolas* and *rompacabezas*. The second room has some fascinating material on the Real de San Carlos development (fliers for bullfights, *banderillas*, stirrups and crockery) and the third is a former kitchen with pots and also models of ships. The fourth and fifth rooms house furniture, a clavichord and harp, fans, guns and a very detailed timeline (in Spanish) of national and local history until 1931, including the arrival of the railway in 1901 and the first bus from Montevideo in 1925 (with six passengers, taking at least ten hours). Upstairs there's more furniture, a palaeontology room with a huge Glyptodon shell (from the bay off Real de San Carlos) and a fine Lestodon skeleton, and a room of stuffed birds and butterflies. There's usually no access to the garden, with a whale skeleton, a statue of Brown and some models of prehistoric beasts.

Museo Portugués (*de la Peña 180;* ⊕ *11.15–16.45 Thu–Tue*) Built for the Ríos family in about 1720, this was opened as a museum in 1977, incorporating an annexe built by the Spanish in 1792. Reorganised by the Gulbenkian Foundation in 1997, it is now the best presented of Colonia's museums, with replicas of furniture, Chinese porcelain, tableware, uniforms, *azulejo* tiles and portraits of Portuguese monarchs of the period, as well as real guns. Downstairs are rooms on the Portuguese Discoveries, with excellent reproduction maps of the voyages to Africa and Asia, and a room on slavery, abolished in 1813 in the United Provinces (including Uruguay) and only in 1888 in Brazil.

Real de San Carlos Avenida Costanera leads 5km north around the bay to Real de San Carlos, a tourism development built in 1910 by the Argentine immigrant Nicolás Mihanovich. Sadly his hotel and casino lost its business when the Argentine government levied punitive taxes on ferries. The *hipódromo* (horse-racing track, opened only in 1942) survives, facing the *frontón* (pelota courts), but everything is very run-down. The **Plaza de Toros** (bullring), at the inland end of Avenida Mihanovich, is fenced off; it closed down when Uruguay banned bullfighting in 1912. On its north side is a collection of railway carriages where a museum is under construction, with a reproduction signal-box. To the southeast of the bullring, Río del la Plata leads to the **Museo de Naufragios y Tesoros** (*Museum of Shipwrecks and Treasure; Roger Balet & Calle de los Argentinos;* m *9445 5133;* e *museonaufragios@hotmail.com;* ⊕ *10.00–13.00, 18.30–22.30 daily; US$1*), fun for kids with a replica 18th-century pirate ship and a pirate cave, but also with material rescued by divers from the wreck of the Spanish frigate *Nuestra Señora de Loreto*, which sank off Montevideo in 1792. The next project is to explore the British ship *Lord Clive*, sunk off Colonia in 1763 (see page 247).

Bus A runs every 15 minutes from Flores to Real de San Carlos, but it's more pleasant to cycle along the *costanera* (waterfront esplanade)

Excursions Just east of Colonia, **Bodega Bernardi** (*Ruta 1 km171.5 Laguna de los Patos;* ✆ *52 24752; www.bodegabernardi.com;* ⊕ *late Dec–late Mar 09.00–12.00,*

15.00–19.00 Mon–Sat, rest of the year 09.00–12.00, 14.00–17.30 Mon–Sat, 10.00–14.00 Sun; free) is known for its grappas but does make wines too. Founded in 1892 and still run by the same family, they have been open for guided visits and tastings since 2000 and are now a very popular destination.

At the small settlement of San Pedro (Ruta 21 km189, 11km north of Colonia) you can turn west to the Camping Brisas del Plata (see page 250) or east for 5km to the **Estancia Los Tres Botones** (**** *52 02163*, **m** *9952 2868*; **e** *los3botones@ adinet.com.uy*), where you can take horse-and-cart rides, learn about farm work and then of course tuck into the product of that work. A little further, 3km west from km192, **Villa Celina** (**** *52 02486*, **m** *9976 9098*; **e** *villacelina@adinet.com.uy*) is similar, with visits to the *tambo* (dairy), and cheeses and jams for sale.

After km193 a sign points left to the site of the battlefield of San Pedro, where British and Spanish forces fought in 1807. This was discovered by chance in 2005, and is the only Napoleonic battlefield in South America that is undisturbed, yielding lots of buttons and bullets for archaeologists. It was a minor victory for the British, outnumbered but armed with modern Baker rifles. In 2007 a small monument was set up to commemorate the bicentenary of the battle, but there's nothing else to see.

At km198 an asphalt road leads west to the **Parque Nacional Anchorena**, the former estate of the Argentine Aarón de Anchorena (1877–1965), given to him by his mother on condition he gave up flying. He left the half-timbered house and a park of 1,370ha to be the holiday home of the president of Uruguay; now it's used for meetings with the likes of presidents Lula and George W Bush, but is open to the public at other times (*tours: 10.00 & 14.30 Thu–Sun; US$1.40*). Beyond the visitor centre is a small lake, a chapel and a 75m-high tower built by Anchorena in honour of Sebastian Cabot, who may have landed here in 1527, from which you can see as far as Buenos Aires when conditions are clear. There are attractive gardens and a park with axis deer and wild boar introduced by Anchorena.

Passing the small settlement of Paso de la Horqueta and a bridge over the Río San Juan, a road leads west from km213.5 for 7km to **Los Cerros de San Juan**, the oldest vineyard in Uruguay. It was founded in 1854 by the Lahusen family from Germany, who established a cattle ranch and general farm as well as the winery. It became a self-contained community of 900 people, with two schools, a bakery, laundry and shops. This continues today to a certain extent, the farm supplying bread and meat to the restaurant, which doubles as a tasting room. It's all been lovingly restored; tours are available Monday to Saturday but must be booked in advance (**** *2 481 7200*; **e** *info@loscerrosdesanjuan.com.uy; www.loscerrosdesanjuan.com.uy/english/cerros.htm;* ⊕ *08.00–17.00 Mon–Fri, Sat can probably be arranged*). An *asado* lunch can be provided.

This was the first Uruguayan winery to plant Cabernet Sauvignon (in 1971) and has now released an organic Cabernet Sauvignon. Other grapes are Merlot, Tannat, Tempranillo, Pinot Noir, Riesling, Sauvignon Blanc, Chardonnay and Gewürztraminer. They have four main lines, from the cheap San Juan Fiesta (introduced in 1975) and the San Juan Crianza table wines to the oaked reserve wines of Cuna de Piedra and Maderos lines; there's also the fortified Soleado wine.

From km224 of Ruta 21 (47km from Colonia), it's 10km west to **Conchillas**, a hidden jewel that's largely as it was a century ago. The British firm C H Walker & Co Ltd established a quarry here in 1887, to provide sand and stone for the construction of a modern port in Buenos Aires, and built a company town as well. After 1911 David Evans, a former ship's cook, settled here and built up a big import–export business. There are streets of identical stone houses, as well as warehouses, a hotel (closed), a formerly Anglican church and a cemetery. The port (and beach) are 7km further south. Now a National Monument, it's a quiet place where old men drink *maté* and ancient *cachila* cars sit by the kerb, still in daily use. There are plans for a paper pulp mill nearby at Punta Pereira, and a luxury hotel (*www.hoteldeloeste.com.uy*).

A local bus meets passengers from Colonia–Carmelo buses on Ruta 21. A tourist information office and a small museum can be found in the Casa de Cultura on Calle David Evans.

CARMELO Carmelo prides itself on being the only town founded by Artigas, on 12 February 1816, although he simply granted land to allow a nearby settlement to move from a rather swampy site. In fact its recorded history goes back to c1611 when Hernandarias (Hernando Arias de Saavedra, governor of Asunción) landed cattle near the mouth of the Arroyo de Vacas. Now the second largest town in Colonia department, with a population of 22,000, it's a quiet place that serves as a port for ferries from Argentina and offers a couple of delightful places to stay nearby. There are some historic relics and a couple of wineries to visit.

Getting there
By ferry Small but modern ferries (pedestrians only), jointly operated by Cacciola Viajes and Trans Uruguay (see pages 49 and 50), sail here twice daily from Tigre, north of Buenos Aires, arriving at a small terminal on the Rambla de los Constituyentes, in the centre of town. It's a pleasant trip through the Paraná Delta, full of birdlife. From Carmelo there are minibus connections for ferry passengers to Colonia and Montevideo. Ferry tickets to Tigre can be bought at Constituyentes 263 (✆ *542 7551*), across the road from the terminal; if you're taking the one at 04.00 the security guard will probably let you wait in the terminal from around midnight.

By bus In addition to direct buses to Montevideo (see page 82), there are services to Colonia with Berrutti (also to Mercedes at 06.55 and 13.00), and Chadre's two *litoral* services, all the way to Bella Unión via Mercedes, Fray Bentos, Paysandú and Salto. The Agencia Central (Chadre/Sabelin) bus office is on the south side of Plaza Independencia at 18 de Julio 411 (✆ *542 2987;* ⊕ *03.00–04.00, 06.00–23.30 daily*); Berrutti is two blocks south at Uruguay 337 (✆ *542 2504;* e *berruttiturismo@ adinet.com.uy; www.berruttiturismo.com*).

Just east of the port Ruta 21 crosses the Arroyo de Las Vacas (at km252.6) on a picturesque swing bridge (Puente Giratorio), the first in the country and still hand-cranked; 88m long, it was built in Germany and assembled in 1912 by Juan Smith.

Getting around Plaza Independencia is the place to look for taxis. Cars and golf-carts can be rented from Thrifty (*19 de Abril 241;* ✆ *542 2939*), just north of the swing bridge. Urucar is at 19 de Abril 143 & Solis (✆ *542 2008,* m *9854 2542;* e *info@urucar.com.uy*). At 19 de Abril 225 bikes can be rented for US$1.50 per hour.

Tourist information The town's tourist information centre is in the Casa de Cultura, home of revolutionary hero Ignacio Barrios (*19 de Abril 246;* ✆ *542 2001;* e *ciudadcarmelo@adinet.com.uy; www.ciudadcarmelo.com*). However, there's a private bike-rental shop and information office across the road (*19 de Abril 225;* ✆ *542 5389*) which is more likely to be open.

⌂ Where to stay
⌂ **Hotel Playa Seré** Tabaré 2971; ✆ 542 6302/3; e hotelplayasere@hotmail.com; www.hotelplayasere.com, Next to the casino, this is a spiffy, new ranch-style single-storey place, with AC & free Wi-Fi throughout. $$$$$

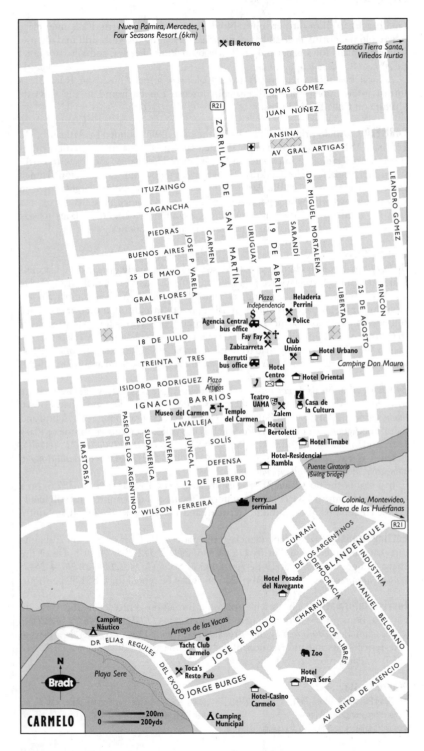

Nueva Palmira, Mercedes,
Four Seasons Resort (6km)

✕ El Retorno

Estancia Tierra Santa,
Viñedos Irurtia

TOMAS GÓMEZ

JUAN NÚÑEZ

R21

ANSINA

AV GRAL ARTIGAS

ZORRILLA DE SAN MARTÍN

ITUZAINGÓ

CAGANCHA

PIEDRAS

BUENOS AIRES

25 DE MAYO

GRAL FLORES

ROOSEVELT

18 DE JULIO

TREINTA Y TRES

ISIDORO RODRIGUEZ

IGNACIO BARRIOS

LAVALLEJA

JOSE P VARELA

CARMEN

URUGUAY

19 DE ABRIL

SARANDI

DR MIGUEL MORTALENA

LEANDRO GÓMEZ

LIBERTAD

25 DE AGOSTO

RINCÓN

Plaza
Independencia

Heladería
Perrini

Agencia Central
bus office

Fay Fay

Zabizarreta

Club
Unión

● Police

Hotel Urbano

Camping Don Mauro

Berrutti
bus office

Hotel
Centro

Hotel Oriental

Plaza
Artigas

Teatro
UAMA

Zalem

Casa de
la Cultura

Museo del Carmen

Templo
del Carmen

Hotel
Bertoletti

Hotel Timabe

Hotel-Residencial
Rambla

Puente Giratorio
(Swing bridge)

PASEO DE LOS ARGENTINOS

IRASTORSA

SUDAMERICA

RIVERA

JUNCAL

SOLÍS

DEFENSA

12 DE FEBRERO

WILSON FERREIRA

Ferry
terminal

Colonia, Montevideo,
Calera de las Huérfanas

R21

GUARANÍ

DE LOS ARGENTINOS

DEMOCRACIA

BLANDENGUES

INDUSTRIA

Hotel Posada
del Navegante

CHARRÚA

DE LOS LIBRES

MANUEL BELGRANO

Camping
Náutico

Arroyo de las Vacas

Yacht Club
Carmelo

🐾 Zoo

DR ELIAS REGULES

DEL EXODO

JORGE BURGES

JOSE E RODÓ

Toca's
Resto Pub

Hotel
Playa Seré

N

Bradt

Playa Sere

Hotel-Casino
Carmelo

AV GRITO DE ASENCIO

CARMELO

0 ———— 200m
0 ———— 200yds

⛺ Camping
Municipal

Hotel-Casino Carmelo Avda Rodó s/n; ℡ 542 2314; e airemar@adinet.com.uy; www.hotelcasinocarmelo.com. A 4-storey block in the beach area with 2 swimming pools, this has 85 rooms of 3 sizes (all with cable TV) plus AC suites. $$$

Hotel-Residencial Rambla Uruguay & 12 de Febrero; ℡ 542 2390, 542 6386; e carmeloramblahotel@adinet.com.uy; www.ciudadcarmelo.com/ramblahotel. Nicely located by the river, this has tired but affordable rooms in various categories, from económico, standard (with AC), preferencial & superior (with AC & balcony) to suites with AC, balcony & kitchenette. $$$

Hotel Timabe 25 de Abril 10 & Solís; ℡ 542 5401; e timabe@adinet.com.uy; www.ciudadcarmelo.com/timabe. A fairly new & decent 3-star behind a single-storey Neocolonial façade. $$$

Hotel Urbano Sarandí 308; ℡ 542 2224; www.hotelurbanocarmelo.com. The most modern place in the centre, with services inc free internet access. $$$

Hotel Bertoletti Uruguay 171; ℡ 542 2030. Dated but cheap & functional, with 25 rooms with private bathrooms. $$

Hotel Centro Uruguay 370; ℡ 542 4488; e hotelcentro@ciudadcarmelo.com; www.ciudadcarmelo.com/hotelcentro. Calling itself a 3-star hotel, this has dated but adequate rooms, plus a honeymoon suite with jacuzzi. $$

Hotel Posada del Navegante Avda Rodó 383; ℡ 542 3973, m 9936 2281; e posadadelnavegante@hotmail.com; www.geocities.com/posadadelnavegante. Near the yacht club & casino & 200m from the Playa Seré, this attractive place has just 8 rooms. $$

Hotel Oriental 19 de Abril 284 (no tel). An adequate hospedaje-type place, although rooms do have private bathrooms. $

A couple of places just outside Carmelo deserve to be mentioned separately:

Estancia Tierra Santa Costa de las Vacas; ℡ 540 2331, m 9954 3607; www.estanciatierrasanta.com; closed Feb–Mar, May–Aug. This American-owned working ranch makes a delightful spot to relax, watch birds (with at least 50 resident species) or ride Karen's fine criollo & Arabian horses. The Tuscan-style farmhouse, with parts dating from 1830, has been lovingly restored & a guest wing added, with a veranda giving on to 3 beautifully decorated rooms with huge bathrooms & Wi-Fi (but no TV). From US$365, inc 2 superb meals, lots of drinks, & use of bicycles & horses. $$$$$

Four Seasons Resort 7km northwest at Ruta 21 km262; ℡ 542 9000; e reservations.bue@fourseasons.com; www.fourseasons.com/carmelo. This is a one-off, a truly luxurious resort that flies guests in from Buenos Aires in a private plane & has little interest in travellers passing through Carmelo. Furnished with Southeast Asian antiques, including a 12th-century stone relief from Java & a front door commissioned from Balinese woodcarvers, it feels something like a Bariloche mountain chalet transposed to Bali – very odd! The luxury is astonishing, starting with being met at Carmelo's grass airstrip with a towel soaked in eucalyptus essence. There's an unheated outside pool & an indoor infinity pool & spa, & an excellent restaurant. Duplex suites & bungalows, from US$195. There's also what's meant to be the best golf course in South America (℡ 542 9047; e golf.uru@fourseasons.com), plus polo & horseriding facilities. $$$$$

Camping Across the swing bridge to the south, west at once on Avenida Rodó, and right to the northern end of the beach, the **Camping Náutico** (Dr Elías Regules s/n; ℡ 542 2058; $) is for visiting yachties but will take others as long as there's space. Just south of Avda Rodó by the beach, the **Camping Municipal** (no tel) is free and usually unstaffed; it has toilets, electric lighting and cold showers. On the north side of the river, the **Camping Don Mauro** (east end of Ignacio Barrios; $) is run by the Hotel-Residencial Rambla (see above), and you should enquire there first.

✕ Where to eat

✕ **El Retorno** Avda Paraguay 426 & Avda Italia; ℡ 542 7425; www.elretornorestopub.com; ⏲ 11.30–15.30 & from 20.00 Wed–Sun. A pub-restaurant at the north end of Zorrilla de San Martín, serving pizza & parrilla, with free Wi-Fi. $$$

✕ **Fay Fay** 18 de Julio, on Plaza Independencia; ☎ 542 4827. A standard *parrilla* with seating outside for people-watching. **$$$**
✕ **Club Unión** 19 de Abril 330; ☎ 542 2079. A classic small-town club restaurant, serving traditional dishes in a traditional way. **$$**
✕ **Toca's Resto Pub** Avda Rodó s/n; ☎ 542 2649. A lively pub-restaurant for the beach crowd, with AC. **$$**

✕ **Zabizarreta** 18 de Julio, on Plaza Independencia; ☎ 542 4827. A good option for *parrilla*, pasta or just a snack. **$$**
✕ **Heladería Perrini** 19 de Abril 440, on Plaza Independencia. The best ice cream. **$**
✕ **Zalem** 19 de Abril 225; ☎ 542 5735; ⏱ 21.00–03.00 Wed–Sat. A bar-pizzeria with a pool table. **$**

Other practicalities

Banks ATMs can be found on the west side of Plaza Independencia; you can also exchange money at Cambio Lenga (*19 de Abril 300*).

Cinema The Teatro UAMA at Uruguay 220 functions mainly as a cinema and was recently refurbished. Built in 1928, it's surprisingly big, with three U-shaped galleries.

Communications The post office is at Uruguay 360 (⏱ *09.00–17.00 Mon–Fri*). Antel's phone centre is at Barrios 349 & Uruguay (⏱ *09.00–20.00 Mon–Sat, 10.00–18.00 Sun*). There's internet access at Cato's Ciber Club (*25 de Abril 110*) and Cyber New Generation (*Uruguay 373*).

Emergency services The police station is on the east side of Plaza Independencia. The main hospital sits across the north end of Uruguay on Bulevar Artigas. The Inspectoría de Migración is at Solis 578 (☎ *542 2461, 542 2433*).

Markets The main food shop is Supermercado Durand (*Flores & 19 de Abril; ⏱ 08.00–12.30, 15.30–21.30 Mon–Fri, 08.00–12.30, 16.30–21.30 Sat*).

What to see and do Five blocks north of the ferry terminal on the south side of Plaza Artigas (where a statue of Artigas was unveiled on the centenary of the town's foundation in 1916), the **Museo del Carmen** (*Ignacio Barrios 208 & José Pedro Varela; ⏱ 09.00–11.00, 14.00–18.00 Mon–Fri, usually closed in Jan*) is a pretty amateurish museum of local history. It was built in 1847 as a school, alongside the Templo del Carmen, the town's main church (built 1830). Three blocks east is the Casa de Cultura (*Ignacio Barrios & 19 de Abril*), which may have more interesting displays. Three blocks south down 19 de Abril is the famous swing bridge (see above); on its south side is a memorial to Atilio François (1922–2007), the town's greatest sporting hero, known as El León de Carmelo, who won the Vuelta Ciclista del Uruguay three years running in 1946–48 and came fourth at the 1948 Olympics in London.

Turning right immediately south of the bridge, Avenida Rodó leads past the Rowing and Yacht clubs, with yacht moorings along a 600m stretch of the river, to the Playa Seré beach, with restaurants and bars. Just south of Avenida Rodó are the casino and a small zoo, with goats, peacocks and so on.

AROUND CARMELO Ruta 21 continues towards Colonia; turning left after 13km on to Camino Teniente Juan de San Martín, it's 4km to the ruins of the **Calera de las Huérfanas** (Lime kiln of the Orphan Girls), built as a Jesuit mission in 1740, with the lime kiln added in 1744. Established by the Colegio de Belén in Buenos Aires, it was administered by Juan de San Martín, future father of the Liberator of Argentina, Chile and Peru, José de San Martín, after the Jesuits were expelled from the Spanish empire in 1767. In 1777 the Sisters of Charity moved here from Buenos Aires, setting up a home for orphaned girls. In 1833 Darwin visited the quarry to study the rocks, and then passed through the 'straggling thatched town' of Arroyo Las Vacas (now Carmelo) to stay the night with an American who ran a lime kiln at Puente Camacho, just beyond Carmelo. Continuing beyond the Calera and turning left after 2km, it takes about 40 minutes by bike to reach Estancia Tierra Santo. There's not a lot left to see other than the roofless remains of the red-brick chapel, but it's an evocative site with plenty of birdlife.

Also on Camino Teniente Juan de San Martín is the Bodega Zubizarreta (\ 542 3080; mzubiza@adinet.com.uy), which offers wine tasting with advance reservations.

Uruguay's largest vineyard by area is 2.2km east of central Carmelo. **Viñedos Irurtia** (*Avda Paraguay;* \ *542 2323, 3355;* e *turismo@irurtia.com.uy; www.irurtia.com.uy*) was founded in 1913 and has been run since the 1950s by Dante Irurtia, who has also been a senator, although his children now manage most of the operation. Carmelo has an ideal microclimate for wine-growing because of the warm water flowing out of the Río Uruguay, with warm days and cool nights, plus well-balanced and drained soils. Growing a wide variety of French grapes including Tannat, as well as some Nebbiolo, Riesling and Gewurztraminer, they produce a lot of bulk wine plus fine wines, including the Reserva del Virrey Malbec, a unique variety of Malbec in Uruguay. There's also a late harvest Botrytis Gewurztraminer, a sparkling champenoise and grappas, from Pinot Noir, Tannat and Gewurztraminer grapes. You can also see goats, kept for cheese-making, and *ñandues* (rheas), kept for meat. Tastings are held in the fine brick cellars (⊕ *08.00–12.00, 13.30–17.30 daily; free, or US$11–14 for a plate of cheeses and breads or for premium wines*).

To the northwest on Ruta 21, beyond the Four Seasons Resort (see *Where to stay*), the **Puente Camacho** (Camacho Bridge) crosses the Arroyo de las Víboras (Stream of Vipers) near the original site of Carmelo. Built in 1858 with five stone arches, it was the first of its type in Uruguay. To the left are the Puerto Camacho marina and the Posada Camacho hotel and restaurant, very popular with affluent Argentines who come across by speedboat from Tigre. At km263 the **Estancia Narbona** is the oldest unaltered building in Uruguay (although the chapel is largely ruined), built in 1732–38 by Juan de Narbona, a Buenos Aires builder, and later named after his son-in-law and heir Francisco Martín Camacho. Four kilometres further on, the Finca & Granja Narbona (\ *540 4778;* e *narbona@ adinet.com.uy*) produces wines and cheeses and offers a couple of very comfortable rooms. There's a good restaurant specialising in pasta, and a shop selling their wines, as well as sparkling champenoise, grappa and *grappamiel* (with honey) and olive oil.

Just upstream of the mouth of the Río Uruguay, **Nueva Palmira** (founded in 1831) is a small port earmarked for expansion as an outlet for paper pulp, Brazilian iron ore and Bolivian exports. There's not much to see beyond the Museo Municipal (*Lucas Roselli 1130*) and Punta Gorda, just south, where the Río Uruguay becomes the Río de la Plata.

There not much reason to come here, unless you arrive by boat. Currently Líneas Delta Argentinas sail once daily from Tigre to Nuevo Palmira, leaving early in the morning and returning from Uruguay in the afternoon, with connecting buses to and from Colonia (see page 247). Bus services between Colonia and Mercedes are provided by Berrutti (*Artigas 1130;* \ *544 6181;* e *berruttiturismo@adinet.com.uy; www.berrutturismo.com*). Chadre has a couple of services a day from Montevideo via Colonia that continue north to Mercedes, Fray Bentos, Paysandú, Salto and Bella Unión. The best place to stay is the Posada del

Cabo (*Varela & Avenida Artigas;* ☎ *544 8095; www.posadadelcabo.com*). There's also the one-star Hotel Centro (*Artigas 822;* ☎ *544 6075*) and the Camping Náutico Las Higueritas at the yacht harbour (*Dársena Higueritas;* ☎ *544 6368*). The Inspectoría de Migración is also at the Darsena Higueritas (☎ *544 6553*). There are ATMs, and you can change money at Cambio Lenga (*Artigas 1028*).

SORIANO DEPARTMENT

Soriano is one of Uruguay's most historic departments, where the first European settlement, the Jesuit mission of Santo Domingo de Soriano, was founded in 1624 on Isla Vizcaino. This was soon shifted to the mainland, eventually moving four times before settling on the site of the present Villa Soriano. Artigas triggered the movement for independence from Spain with the Grito de Asencio (27 February 1811), 11km south of Mercedes, and the capture of Mercedes and Santo Domingo de Soriano (also known as Villa Soriano) the next day. The department also played a major role in the Cruzada Libertadora (Crusade of Liberation), starting on 19 April 1825 when Lavalleja and Oribe crossed the Río Uruguay and landed at the Playa de la Agraciada. A couple of days later they met Rivera at Monzón, agreeing to overcome their rivalry to unite against Brazil.

Nowadays Soriano is a prosperous agricultural region. Its northern boundary is the Río Negro, which flows right across the country and into the Río Uruguay just below Villa Soriano. Both rivers are known for their fine sandy beaches, their islands and backwaters, and the many opportunities they give for boating and camping. There are plenty of large and tasty fish such as dorado, *boga, tararira, bagre, pejerrey, surubí* and *mojarra*. There are also wild boar and deer in sizeable numbers, having been introduced to Anchorena and then escaped.

Ruta 2 runs from Montevideo to Mercedes, passing through the farming towns of Cardona and José Enrique Rodó. Coming from Nueva Palmira on Ruta 21 you'll pass **Playa de la Agraciada** soon after entering Soriano. The beach is still popular, and a small pyramid marks the spot where the 33 Orientales landed in 1825. Juan Manuel Blanes stayed at a nearby *estancia* (or ranch) while working on his painting of the landing. There's a *parador* and campsite (open all year) here.

DOLORES At km321 on Ruta 21, midway between Nueva Palmira and the departmental capital of Mercedes, this small town is the heart of Uruguay's wheat-growing belt. It's the jumping-off point for the even smaller and quieter Villa Soriano, Uruguay's oldest settlement, although there's little to see in either. Dolores itself (Nuestra Señora de los Dolores del Espinillo in full) was only finally moved to this site on the Río San Salvador in 1801, having failed to establish itself in several other locations.

The riverside *rambla* is the town's best feature, with thick gallery forest on the far side, and nice parks to left and right of the six blocks that constitute the waterfront; Plaza Constitución and the business centre is over 1km south.

Getting there and around Bus offices are on the plaza: Agencia Central (Chadre/Sabelin) (*Dr Puig 1653 & Artigas;* ☎ *534 2700;* ⊕ *08.00–23.30*, Intertur (*Artigas & Asencio*) and Berrutti (*Asencio 1671;* ☎ *534 4179*). Sabelin and Intertur go to Montevideo, Chadre from Colonia to Fray Bentos, Paysandú, Salto and Bella Unión, and Berrutti to Carmelo and Colonia. An ancient bus shuttles occasionally from the plaza to the *rambla*, going north on Puig and returning south on 18 de Julio.

Tourist information The nearest there is to an information office is the Centro de Interpretación Lacán Guazú (*Asencio 991*), in the same building as the Museo Histórico and Museo Regional de Agricultura, a block from the *rambla*.

Where to stay and eat A good new hotel is under construction by the river, but until then the only option is the friendly **Hotel Cris** (*Puig 1693 & Schuster;* \ *534 3235;* e *crishotel@hotmail.es;* $$), which has rooms with cable TV and breakfast; rooms with AC cost substantially more. There's a **campsite** (\ *534 2703;* $) on the shady Península Timoteo Ramospe, immediately to the west on the *rambla*, which has hot showers, barbecues, a cafeteria-bar, swimming and a boat-launch.

More or less the only place to eat is the **Asociación La Agropecuaría** on the south side of the main plaza.

Other practicalities
Banks There's an ATM opposite Intertur on the south side of the plaza, and Cambio Iberia (*Asencio1606*) is on the west side of the plaza.

Communications There's free Wi-Fi on Plaza Artigas (between Puig and Asencio, three blocks from the river, not on the main Plaza Constitución), as well as a British-style green letterbox made in Montevideo in 1897.

Markets There are supermarkets on the west side of the plaza and at Puig y Vásquez, two blocks south.

What to see and do On Plaza Constitución is José Zorrilla de San Martín's *Monumento a la Libertad*. On the east side of the plaza is the Neoclassical church **Nuestra Señora de Dolores (Our Lady of Sorrows)**, its red-brick exterior never finished. To the north on the corner of the plaza is the Torre de Reloj (clocktower), built in 1904 because the church tower was not ready to hold the clock as planned. It's also worth noting the Templo Evangélico Valdense (Waldensian Protestant church), built in 1934 at Vásquez & Varela. On the other side of town, by the river, are the two museums mentioned above (see *Tourist information*), and just to the west, before the tiny port, an old steam crane and a statue of Garibaldi by Edmondo Prati (1957).

The town's big event is the Fiesta de la Primavera (Spring Festival) in the second weekend of October, when thousands of people come to see the town decked out in spring flowers, as well as the usual procession and dances.

VILLA SORIANO The sleepy village of Santo Domingo de Soriano, known as Villa Soriano, is the successor to the first European settlement in Uruguay, founded in 1624 by the Jesuits on Isla Vizcaino, as a mission to the Chaná natives, and moved here in 1708.

There are no buses on the direct Ruta 95 from Mercedes to Villa Soriano; instead buses from Mercedes to Dolores drop passengers at a junction 3km north of Dolores (km323), where they are soon collected by a rattletrap bus from Dolores to Villa Soriano, about 20km northwest.

At the entrance to the village there's a massive timbó tree (planted in 1904), where the road splits into the only two asphalted streets, Lavalleja and Cabildo, leading through the village to the long wooden jetty on the Río Negro. Plaza Artigas sits between them, three blocks before the river, with the **Capilla de Santo Domingo**, built in 1797, on its south side; inside is an articulated wooden Christ made by a Chaná craftsman.

A block south of the chapel, the brightly painted Casa de las Máscaras (*Cabildo and Ituzaingó*) is almost hidden by ceramic masks hanging from nails; these were made of sand and cement by the late 'Don Paco' Juan Artega, and are good for amusing children. Almost opposite is the Casa de Marfetán, built in 1805 and housing the **historical museum** (⏲ *08.00–12.00, 15.00–19.00 daily*). Around a patio with an old cistern are rooms displaying a ragtag collection of Mylodon (giant sloth) bones, Glyptodon (giant armadillo) bones and shell, indigenous arrowheads, *bolas* and ceramics, 19th-century lamps and a carriage, rusty guns and bayonets, and lots of really bad paintings of historical scenes. At the rear through the office are coins and banknotes, ancient adding machines and moveable type. It's really not worth the detour, although the Artigas family history could be interesting: in 1790, when he was 26, the father of the nation married his first wife Isabel Sánchez (aged 30, from Villa Soriano), who was descended from a Chaná *cacique*. Their four children were born at the Solar de Artigas, two blocks east of the museum. In 1811 Spanish ships shelled Villa Soriano, trying to capture Artigas (who was then in Mercedes) and were driven off by local heroes.

Along Cabildo are various very tatty 19th-century houses, including the *Aduana* (Customs, in the former Hotel Olivera) opposite the jetty, the Casa de Alessio opposite the museum, and the Casa de Galarza, once home of a Colorado leader. Opposite this is a small park, at the rear of the museum, where two thatched cabins constitute the municipal motel. If you want to stay here you'll have to contact the Junta Local (*Cabildo, facing the plaza;* ✆ *530 4144*), and bring your own food; you should also ask before putting up a tent here. There are also a couple of houses to rent (*alquila*) in the village.

There's no beach or other obvious holiday attractions, but Uruguayans, including President Tabaré Vásquez, do enjoy fishing here for dorado, boga, tararira and bagre. It's also known for birdwatching, with wetlands and gallery forest – start with the riverside road to the right from the jetty (to the Parque Municipal La Islita), or go west on Asencio from the Casa de Alessio.

MERCEDES The capital of Soriano department, Mercedes was founded in 1788 and is now a city of around 40,000 with an attractive setting on the Río Negro, with over 2km of waterfront gardens and promenades that are astonishingly lively until midnight. It is also home to one of the best art galleries in the interior of Uruguay.

Mercedes has a lively carnival, known for the drag queens (*travestis*) who come from all over Uruguay, and one of Uruguay's best jazz festivals, Jazz a la Calle (*www.jazzalacalle.com*), in the second week of January, with free gigs on street corners and in the historic area known as Manzana Veinte (Block Twenty).

Getting there Ruta 2 from Montevideo passes close on the east side of town on its way to Fray Bentos and the international bridge to Argentina. There's a busy modern bus terminal, 13 blocks south of the river, with services to Montevideo and up and down the *litoral*.

From the main Plaza Independencia it's nine blocks south (and uphill) to the **bus terminal** (*Don Bosco 734 between Artigas & Colón*). Converted from an army barracks, it's a good modern place, but the attached shopping centre was burnt out in January 2009. All the bus companies are here: Agencia Central (✆ *53 21717;* e *mercedes@agenciacentral.com.uy*), Berrutti (✆ *53 25033*), Bonjour (✆ *53 26449*), CAUVI/Interutr (✆ *53 22046*) and CUT/Bus de la Carrera (✆ *53 23766*).

Tourist information The tourism office (*Detomasi 415, between Cassinoni & 19 de Abril;* ✆ *53 22733; www.soriano.gub.uy;* ⏲ *09.00–17.00 Mon–Fri*) is in Manzana Veinte, facing the Isla del Puerto. Look for the 'Oficina de la Juventud' sign.

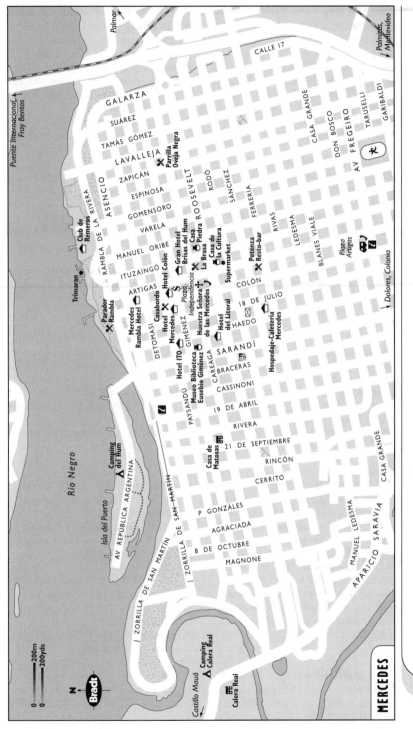

Western Uruguay SORIANO DEPARTMENT

6

265

MERCEDES

N

0 ——— 200m
0 ——— 200yds

Bradt

Río Negro

Isla del Puerto

Camping
del Hum

AV REPUBLICA ARGENTINA

Castillo Mauá

Camping
Calera Real

Calera Real

J ZORRILLA DE SAN MARTÍN

J ZORRILLA DE SAN MARTÍN

Puente Internacional,
Fray Bentos

Palmar

CALLE 17

Palmitas,
Montevideo

GALARZA

SUÁREZ

TAMÁS GÓMEZ

LAVALLEJA

Parrilla
Oveja Negra

ZAPICÁN

ESPINOSA

GOMENSORO

VARELA

MANUEL ORIBE

ITUZAINGÓ

ASENCIO

RAMBLA DE LA RIVERA

Club de
Remeros

Trimaran

Parador
Rambla

ARTIGAS

Mercedes
Rambla Hotel

DETOMASI

Casabordo
Hotel
Mercedes

GIMÉNEZ

PAYSANDÚ

Hotel ITO

Museo Biblioteca
Eusebio Giménez

CAREAGA

CASSINONI

19 DE ABRIL

RIVERA

Casa de
Matosas

21 DE SEPTIEMBRE

RINCÓN

CERRITO

P GONZÁLES

AGRACIADA

8 DE OCTUBRE

MAGNONE

Hotel Colón

Gran Hotel
Brisas del Hum

La Brasa Piedra

Plaza
Independencia

Nuestra Señora
de las Mercedes

Hotel
del Litoral

HAEDO

SARANDÍ

BRACERAS

ROOSEVELT

RODÓ

SÁNCHEZ

Casa
del Hum

Casa de
la Cultura

Supermarket

COLÓN

18 DE JULIO

Hospedaje-Cafetería
Mercedes

Dolores, Colonia

FERRERÍA

RIVAS

LEDESMA

BLANES VIALE

Potenza
Resto-bar

Plaza
Artigas

CASA GRANDE

DON BOSCO

AV FREGEIRO

TARUSELLI

GARIBALDI

CASA GRANDE

MANUEL LEDESMA

APARICIO SARAVIA

Where to stay

Gran Hotel Brisas del Hum Artigas 209; ☎ 53 29794; e info.mercedes@granh.com; www.granh.com. On the plaza, this is the most modern & stylish hotel in town, with swimming pool, sauna & gym, parking in the courtyard, & AC rooms with cable TV, minibar & cable TV. There are data sockets in the bedrooms but the only Wi-Fi is in the public areas downstairs. A good b/fast is served in the Don Peperone chain restaurant next to reception. $$$$

Mercedes Rambla Hotel Avda Asencio 728; ☎ 53 30696; e mrh@adinet.com.uy; www.mercedesramblahotel.com.uy. The best in town until the Brisas del Hum appeared, this is still very nice, with a trim garden, although staff could be friendlier. There are 25 suites with AC, but Wi-Fi only in public areas. $$$$

Hotel Colón Colón 169; ☎ 53 24720/1. A fine Belle Epoque frontage with 40 rooms behind, this has AC rooms, a good b/fast, & a PC in the lobby. $$$

Hotel ITO Haedo 184; ☎ 53 24919. A pleasant family hotel with some unwarranted pretensions, but decent rooms with private bathroom, cable TV & frigobar. B/fast US$2.50 extra. $$

Hospedaje-Cafetería Mercedes Sánchez 614; ☎ 53 23804. Excellent value, simple but friendly, with rooms with either private or shared bathroom. $

Hotel del Litoral Haedo 262; ☎ 53 24872, m 9916 5201. In a nice older house, this has large rooms all with AC & cable TV, a garden with barbecue, & a PC in the lobby. $

Hotel Mercedes Giménez 659. A simple place that's pretty fair value, with rooms with TV & shared or private bathrooms; no b/fast. $

Hostel The only hostel-style accommodation is at the **Club de Remeros** (*Rowing Club; de la Rivera 949 & Gomensoro;* ☎ *53 22227;* e *remeros@adinet.com.uy;* $), which is aimed at sports groups but may be available. They have six-bed rooms with shared bathrooms.

Camping There are three campsites nearby. The simple **Camping del Hum** (Hum meaning the Río Negro) on the Isla del Puerto (*Avda República Argentina; contact the tourism office,* ☎ *53 22733;* ☉ *mid-Dec–Easter;* $) is reached by a narrow bridge with manually operated traffic lights from the *rambla* just west of the centre, with a beach, a bar and picnic tables. There's also the **Camping Calera Real** (*Camino Tuya, 1km west on the Arroyo Dacá;* ☎ *53 21239;* $), also by the water, and the **Club Pescadores Biguá** (*Ruta 2 km281;* ☎ *53 21779;* e *contacto@clubbigua.com; www.clubbigua.com;* $), a fishing club at the north end of the bridge across the Río Negro, with shaded beachfront plots and no fewer than 52 grills with tables and benches, as well as a shop.

Where to eat

CasaBordo Paysandú 654; ☎ 53 29817, m 9994 7900; e casabordo@adinet.com.uy; ☉ 21.00–01.00 Tue–Sun. French-owned restaurant & wine bar with a creative menu adapting traditional French cuisine to Uruguayan tastes & materials – great food at a very low price. $$$

Club de Remeros Mercedes de la Rivera 949 & Gomensoro; ☎ 53 21520; e remeros@ adinet.com.uy. At the city's rowing club (also offering tennis, table tennis & basketball); you can eat well in the restaurant or on the excellent riverfront terrace. $$

La Brasa Careaga 780; ☎ 53 30136. Just east of the plaza, this serves simple but filling homemade pasta & snacks. $$

Parrilla Oveja Negra Lavalleja 178 & Giménez; ☎ 53 22649. A nice rustic-style *parrilla*, also serving pasta, at reasonable prices. $$

Parador Rambla Rambla Costanera & 18 de Julio; ☉ 12.00–15.30, 20.30–00.30 Tue–Sun, until 01.00 Fri–Sat. A nice thatched place by the river that serves *parrilla*, pastas & snacks, & is a great spot for a sunset drink. $$

Potenza resto-bar Artigas 426; ☎ 53 28893. A bar-pizzeria that's lively & cheap. $

Other practicalities

Banks There are ATMs at the bus terminal and around the plaza; you can also change money at Cambio Maiorano (*Colón 255;* ☉ *08.30–19.00 Mon–Fri, 08.30–12.30, 15.30–18.30 Sat*).

Car rental Cars can be rented from Avis (*Colón 260;* ☎ *53 24794,* **m** *9817 0015*), Mariño Sport Rent a Car (*c/o Detomasi, Artigas 100;* ☎ *53 20863,* **m** *9855 4670; www.mariniosport.com*), Multicar (*Mercedes Tomás Gómez 363;* ☎ *53 25324,* **m** *9553 5421; www.redmulticar.com*) or Rentacar Daymán (*Rodó 1033;* ☎ *53 24612, 4327,* **m** *9973 4638; www.rentacardayman.com*). Hertz are in Fray Bentos, with an agency here at GeoTour (*Giménez 701;* ☎ *53 28281;* **e** *geotour@adinet.com.uy*).

Cinema The Casa de Cultura, in the former Masonic Temple (1892), shows some interesting films; the Cine Rex (at the rear of the Gran Hotel Brisas del Hum) is closed and the Teatro Municipal is currently being refurbished.

Communications The post office is at Rodó 650 & 18 de Julio (⊕ *09.00–17.00 Mon–Fri, 08.00–12.00 Sat*). There's free Wi-Fi on Plaza Independencia but, bizarrely, it requires a password – ask at the tourism office, or ask the Gran Hotel Brisas del Hum if you can use theirs. There's no Wi-Fi yet at the terminal. Antel has call centres at Roosevelt 681 (⊕ *09.00–20.00 Mon–Sat, 10.00–18.00 Sun*) and Roosevelt 730 and the terminal (*both* ⊕ *09.00–22.00 Mon–Fri, 09.00–13.00, 18.00–22.00 Sat–Sun*).

Consulate For visa issues, the Inspectoría de Migración is at 18 de Julio & Roosevelt (☎ *53 22528;* ⊕ *09.15–14.30 Mon–Fri*).

Emergency services The Sanatorio CAAMS (*Sánchez 62;* ☎ *53 22313*) has an emergency clinic.

Markets The main supermarket downtown is Ta-Ta (*Artigas & Rodó;* ⊕ *08.00–22.00 daily*); there's also a MultiAhorro at the bus terminal. Casa Piedra (*Ituzaingó & Roosevelt;* ⊕ *08.30–12.00, 14.30–19.00 Mon–Fri, 08.00–12.00, 16.00–19.00 Sat*) is a classy crafts shop diagonally opposite the Casa de Cultura.

What to see and do On the south side of Plaza Independencia, four blocks south of the *rambla*, the cathedral of **Nuestra Señora de las Mercedes (Our Lady of Mercies)** was consecrated in 1868 on the site of the first church, established in 1788 by Padre Manuel de Castro y Careaga. It's Neoclassical, with a fairly striking façade and a simple interior except for the gilded wooden altar, carved in Buenos Aires.

Three blocks west of the plaza, the **Museo Biblioteca Eusebio Giménez** (*Giménez & Sarandí;* ⊕ *Jan–Feb 07.30–13.30 Mon–Sat, rest of the year until 18.30; free*) houses one of the best art collections outside Montevideo. Eusebio Giménez (1850–1933) was born on this site but his parents were forced to move to Argentina on account of their politics, and he grew up to be the dean of Buenos Aires's notaries, leaving money in his will for a library and an art gallery here. The ground floor opened in 1935 and the rest in 1945, and Education Minister Victor Haedo (born in Mercedes) donated paintings. There are lots of kitsch sculptures in the ground-floor foyer, leading to spacious galleries upstairs. There are a few European paintings, most notably the *Dead Christ* by Martin da Udine (better known as Pellegrino da San Daniele; 1467–1547), probably the only Renaissance painting in Uruguay. It's lovely, and has an interesting frame with ivory insets. There's also a Neoclassical portrait of a lady by José de Madrazo (1781–1859), court painter of King Fernando VII of Spain.

There are many Uruguayan paintings, including four very different ones by Pedro Blanes Viale (born in 1878 in Mercedes, near the Casa de Cultura at Roosevelt and Artigas), a Romantic work of 1898, two portraits, and a very Fauvist painting from 1924, two years before his death. There are also charming sketches on newspaper of cats and snakes. Four of the five main exponents of Planismo (see page 31) are displayed here – Rafael Barradas, Pedro Figari, José Cúneo and Carlos Federico Sáez (born in Mercedes in 1878).

Four blocks west, the **Casa de Matosas** and adjacent Panadería Matosas (*Careaga 337 & Rivera*) are locally famed for their Gaudiesque decoration, though it's more riotous and less tasteful than Gaudí.

The waterfront Rambla de la Rivera continues west past the bridge to the Isla del Puerto, to the former port (where some old rail lines are still visible), now being redeveloped for yachts, with three new pontoons. There's a wash-block across the road near the Surubí Club, a very friendly fishing club in what was the town's first permanent school. This is the historic Manzana Veinte, including the house in which Garibaldi lived in the 1840s. Avenida Asencio continues west by the water to the more open Parque Guernika, dotted with eucalyptus trees and a few picnic tables, east of the Arroyo Dacá. A new road (unsurfaced) loops around by the stream to join the west end of Careaga at the Puente Dacá (Bridge over the Dacá). On the far side of the bridge are the ruins of the Calera Real (Royal Lime Kiln), built by the Jesuits in 1722; the small building with a tin roof is actually their chapel, with four large kilns to the south by the stream. This is the oldest industrial site in Uruguay, and there's talk of creating a Museum of Industry.

Camino Tuya continues from the Calera Real to the **Castillo Mauá** (⊕ *07.00–21.00 daily; free*), a kilometre or so west, which was built in 1857–62 by the Brazilian Baron Mauá (born Irineu Evangelista de Sousa; 1813–89), a self-made banking and railway magnate who played a huge role in Brazil's development but eventually over-reached himself and went bankrupt in 1875.

The estate is open to the public and the 3ha park is a favourite place for weekend strolls and picnics. There's a small zoo, to the right just inside the entry, with goats and a few interesting birds. A winery was established here in 1892, but the property was taken over by the Intendencia (Departmental government) of Soriano in 1961 and remains municipally owned, producing 450,000 litres of table wine in 2008, as well as olive oil and sheep's cheese. Vinos Mauá (⊕ *Mon–Fri, mornings Fri & Sat*) is on the left-hand side of the castle-like main building. To the right is the Museo Paleontológico Alejandro Berro (⊕ *11.00–17.00 daily; free*), which has one of the country's best collections of bones and shells of extinct megafauna such as mastodons, Megatherium, Lestodon, Glassotherium and 25 species of Glyptodon, as well as a dinosaur egg. It's larger and more didactic than the Colonia museum but in dated 1980s displays, with much of the collection in store. They hope to post a digital catalogue online and perhaps even to expand upstairs in the largely empty castle, although there's also talk of building a modern hotel to the rear.

Boating is naturally very popular; motorboats shuttle across to the Playa Los Arrayanes, on the north shore of the river, and many people go across by canoe too. The trimaran *Capitán Dinamita V* (✆ *53 28281*, m *9953 1254*), which can land at any beach, carries 28 passengers on plastic seats and has a simple bar with music. The Intendencia has built a modern catamaran, *Soriano 1*, which will carry groups of up to 50; moving at up to 80km/h, it will be able to reach Villa Soriano in under a hour and continue to Dolores, with passengers returning by bus. The hope is to put on a regular scheduled trip at weekends, as opposed to charters; contact the tourism office for details.

Heading east from Mercedes on Ruta 14, beyond the interchange with Ruta 2, it's 4km to a left turning to the **Estancia La Sirena** (✆ *53 02271*, m *9910 2130*; *www.lasirena.com.uy*), a delightful, historic ranch near the river, 10km to the north. Founded in the mid 18th century, the house was a virtual fortress in the lawless 1820s. It was sold to Bernardino Rivadavia, who had been first president of

Argentina but then went into exile, who built the current house (in 1830) but soon sold it. Now the house is surrounded by huge eucalypti full of cotorra nests, with views west as far as Fray Bentos. Near the river is gallery forest with algarrobo trees over 800 years old, and lots of birdlife (129 species in all).

The wonderfully hospitable Bruce family created one of the first tourist *estancias* in Uruguay, while also raising Hereford cattle and collecting tennis cups. There are two bedrooms in the main house with the kitchen and dining room, and six new rooms in a converted barn, with fans but no air conditioning or TV. There is Wi-Fi, or you can ask to use the PC. It can seem like being sucked into an endless family holiday, with horseriding in the morning, followed by lunch and a siesta, then boating on the Río Negro, then perhaps sundowners on a sandbank and an *asado*. With luck Lucía will get out her guitar and teach you the gaucho version of *Blue Moon*. Waterskiing and Finnish massages are available, and they hope to offer two-day canoe trips from the Palmar dam and four-day horseback trips. Day rides are included, for US$100 per person full board (on a double basis).

Continuing east on Ruta 14, at km33.5 there's a turning to **Villa Darwin**, about 30km north. Darwin stayed for a few days on an *estancia* just to the north, studying the geology of the cliffs by the Río Negro; he also acquired the skull of a Toxodon (an extinct giant armadillo). There's a small granite obelisk to him overlooking the river, but there's a movement to return the village to its earlier name of Sacachispas ('striking sparks', a gaucho term for knife-fighting).

Turning left on to Ruta 55, it's 15km to **El Palmar** (72km from Mercedes), a village built for workers at the Represa Constitución, one of the biggest hydro-electric dams on the Río Negro (opened in 1980). You can take a dull tour, but it's far more popular for fishing (for dorado), boating and swimming. The simple Camping del Palmar (✆ 53 21611; *US$1 pp*) is at km14, at the southern end of the village. Going through the village (dotted with sculptures made of recycled metal at summer camps) to a headland on the lake, you'll find the Complejo del Palmar, incorporating a hotel (✆ 53 02153/6; *from US$15 pp, inc b/fast but without AC*) with a swimming pool and simple rooms that are excellent value, and large tegu lizards in the garden. It's not exactly scenic, but very restful. Down the dirt road to the former ferry below the sluices, there's good fishing downstream and *monte nativo* woodland with plenty of birdlife. There's another campsite 45km away on the south side of the lake, at the Parque Bartolomé Hidalgo on Ruta 3.

RÍO NEGRO DEPARTMENT

The Ruta 2 bridge (shared with a disused railway) crosses the Río Negro into Río Negro department. There's a turning to the Los Arrayanes beach at the north end (km281), then a toll, and at km286 a monument on the site of the battle of Rincón in 1825, the first clash in the war for independence from Brazil. By a red rock at km288.2 (about 700m after the junction to Paysandú) a dirt road leads left to the **Estancia Casa Piedra** (m *9968 5204, 9989 7713*; e *casapiedra@ adinet.com.uy*; $$$$), by the river near Isla Pichón, a house built in the local red stone as a relay post for cattle drives to Fray Bentos. There's plenty of native forest here (with a 400m path along the river) and it makes a lovely spot to stay for a day or two, fishing, boating and watching birds. It's a longish way off the main road but they'll pick you up in Mercedes (it's also possible to arrive by catamaran). There are four new en-suite rooms in a new building in the same style as the original house, as well as an events hall and viewing tower. Bed and breakfast costs US$70 for two or US$80 for full board, and one night with two days of activities cost US$100.

FRAY BENTOS To Uruguayans Fray Bentos is known largely for its international bridge to Argentina and the blockades that have kept it closed as a result of Argentine dislike of the Botnia paper pulp mill, close to Fray Bentos. To the British, however, Fray Bentos is synonymous with corned beef, and happily the Anglo meat-packing plant has reopened as an industrial heritage museum.

Deep water and woodland attracted wood-cutters and charcoal-burners, plus José Hargain, an Argentine merchant who opened a shop and bar, and the British entrepreneur Richard Bannister Hughes, who set up a meat-salting business. Established as Villa Independencia in 1857, the town was renamed in 1900 after Friar Benedict, a hermit who lived in a cave at Bahía Caracoles, about 20km downstream. After the meat plant closed in 1979 there followed a period of stagnation, but now it's a city of over 23,000 *triperos*, with new prosperity from the Botnia mill (see the box below).

The great Argentine writer Jorge Luis Borges, who always loved Uruguay, had relatives in Fray Bentos and even claimed to have been conceived there. The title character of the wonderful *Funes the Memorious* was from Fray Bentos, and he mentioned the town in *El Aleph* too.

Getting there and around

By car Coming from Montevideo or Mercedes on Ruta 2 and turning left at km301.8, it's 9km to Fray Bentos, or 7km straight on to the international bridge and Argentina. From the ANCAP station at km308 there are speed humps until the road splits into

---

BOTNIA

Towards the end of the 20th century large areas of woodland were planted in Uruguay with the aim of producing biofuels. However, when it was noticed that certain varieties of eucalyptus grow at a rate of 1cm per day (3.5m per year) the multinational forestry companies quickly took an interest.

In 2003 a subsidiary of Shell sold 80,000ha of eucalyptus plantations in Uruguay to the Finnish company Botnia, which began planning a new paper pulp plant in the area. Although they apparently looked in Argentina and elsewhere, they soon settled on a site outside Fray Bentos, near the international bridge to Gualeguaychú in Argentina's Entre Ríos province, from where pulp would be sent downriver for shipping to Europe. In December 2005, a World Bank study concluded that the factory would have no harmful effects and a year later the WB's International Finance Corporation approved a US$170m loan.

Opened in November 2007, the billion-dollar Botnia plant uses the latest chlorine-free technology and produces almost no pollution. However, the citizens of Entre Ríos, the Argentine province across the river, familiar only with their own filthy chlorine-spewing plants, refused to believe this and protested vehemently against the project, blockading the international bridge since November 2006 (although they are happy to take bribes to allow certain vehicles to cross). This was backed by the then governor of Entre Ríos, Jorge Busti, an old-style Peronist caudillo who provided the *asambleístas* (pickets) with facilities such as toilets and a TV room, and even paid them a wage – rumour has it that he bought land which he presumed Botnia could be persuaded to buy for their plant, and decided to take revenge when they refused to get involved in his corrupt dealings. In May 2006 Argentine president Néstor Kirchner came to a rally in Gualeguaychú to support the blockade, the day after Argentina filed a formal complaint at the International Court of Justice in The Hague, claiming that Uruguay had ignored the Uruguay River Treaty's requirement for both countries to consult on any project that could affect the river, and that pollution would affect Argentina.

Avenida 18 de Julio (the main street, inbound) and Avenida Rincón (outbound). The bus terminal is between these two roads at Varela, from where it's four blocks to Plaza Artigas and five more to the main Plaza Constitución, between 25 de Mayo and Treinta y Tres Orientales and four blocks short of the river. A faster route in is the Carretera Puente-Puerto, a bypass (with parallel cycle track) leading from near km306 of Ruta 2 to the port and former train station immediately north of the centre.

The 5.4km-long Puente Internacional (International Bridge) Libertador General José de San Martín, 9km east of the town, opened in 1976. It usually carries 5,000 lorries per month and a third of the tourists entering Uruguay. However, it has been blockaded by Argentine protestors since the Botnia paper pulp plant, just west of its southern end, opened in 2007. It will probably reopen sometime in 2010.

By bus The bus service from Mercedes is frankly very poor, with only about a dozen buses a day, many in the evening. From Montevideo there are eight buses a day, taking 4½ hours. The main bus company is CUT, with offices on the Plaza Constitución (*Avda 25 de Mayo 2263;* ✆ *56 27598;* ⊕ *08.00–12.00, 14.00–18.00 Mon–Fri, 09.00–12.00 Sat*) and the bus terminal (*Avda 18 de Julio & Varela;* ✆ *56 22618*).

Car rental
🚗 **Avis** Avda 18 de Julio 1227 & 25 de Mayo; ✆ 56 20322, 📱 9617 0004; e fraybentos@avis.com.uy; ⊕ 09.00–19.00 Mon–Fri, 09.00–13.00 Sat

🚗 **Dollar** Rincón & 25 de Mayo; ✆ 56 28300; e dollarfb@adinet.com.uy

Blockades on the crossings to Paysandú and Salta, in other Argentine states, were quickly lifted after courts threatened to send in the army; but the Gualeguaychú blockade is still in place as of March 2010. The Argentine government, now led by Néstor's wife President Cristina Fernández de Kirchner, has gradually distanced itself from this kind of vigilante action as an instrument of foreign policy, but still feels unable to actually reopen the bridge. Tourism in Entre Ríos has been badly hit by the blockade and the state's new governor, Sergio Urribarri, also wants to end the blockade but seems to be powerless. By January 2009, even Néstor Kirchner was calling for the blockade to be lifted, denying that he'd ever supported it. This was not enough for Uruguay, which blocked Kirchner's appointment as chair of Unasur, the Union of South American Nations, to Argentine fury.

Since the plant opened in late 2007, environmental monitoring (including by the World Bank) has shown no evidence of pollution, but the so-called *Asamblea Ambiental de Gualeguaychú* (Environmental Assembly of Gualeguaychú) has refused to accept this evidence. The Uruguayan government has been firm in its support for Botnia; the protestors thought they would soon bring Uruguay's tourist industry to its knees, but their compatriots have continued to flock to Punta del Este and elsewhere. Argentina seems likely to lose its case at The Hague (probably early in 2010), and at some point the blockade will have to be called off.

Argentines claim that Uruguay has simply sold out to big business, as Botnia and its suppliers are responsible for increasing Uruguay's GDP by 1% and its workforce by 1.5% (or 12,000 new jobs); Botnia has also created some useful nature reserves near the Río Uruguay. The Uruguayan government is unrepentant, and is keen to see another plant built nearby, proposed by the Spanish Grupo Ence; in October 2009 this was taken over by Stora Enso of Finland and Arauco of Chile, who confirmed the following month their plans for a US$2 billion pulp plant nearby. This should create around 3,000 jobs and boost GDP by another 2%. Stora Enso and Arauco also became Uruguay's largest private landowners, with 250,000ha of eucalyptus plantations.

6

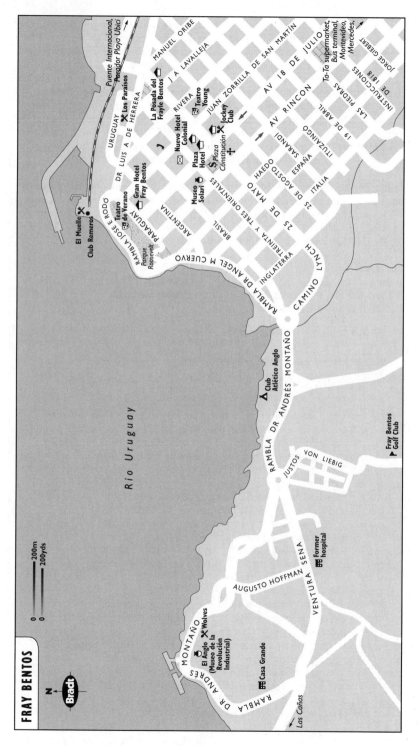

FRAY BENTOS

N

0 ——— 200m
0 ——— 200yds

Río Uruguay

Puente Internacional, Pescador Playa Ubici

URUGUAY

DR LUIS A DE HERRERA

RAMBLA JOSÉ E RODÓ

PARAGUAY

El Muelle ✕ Club Remeros

Teatro de Verano
Gran Hotel Fray Bentos

Parque Roosevelt

ARGENTINA

MANUEL ORIBE

J A LAVALLEJA

La Posada del Frayle Bentos
✕ Los Paraísos

RIVERA

Teatro Young

Nuevo Hotel Colonial

Museo Solari

Plaza Hotel
$ Plaza Constitución

JUAN ZORRILLA DE SAN MARTÍN

AV 18 DE JULIO

Jockey Club ✕

AV RINCÓN

25 DE AGOSTO

DE MAYO

HAEDO

SARANDÍ

ITUZAINGÓ

ESPAÑA

ITALIA

TREINTA Y TRES ORIENTALES

BRASIL

INGLATERRA

19 DE ABRIL

LAS PIEDRAS

INSTRUCCIONES DE 1818

JORGE GIEBERT

Ta-Ta supermarket, Bus terminal, Montevideo, Mercedes,

LYNCH

CAMINO

RAMBLA DR ÁNGEL M CUERVO

▲ Club Atlético Anglo

RAMBLA DR ANDRÉS MONTAÑO

JUSTOS VON LIEBIG

▶ Fray Bentos Golf Club

VENTURA SENA

AUGUSTO HOFFMAN

Former hospital

MONTAÑO

El Anglo (Museo de la Revolución Industrial)

✕ Wolves

Casa Grande

RAMBLA DR ANDRÉS MONTAÑO

Las Cañas

Bradt

272

Hertz Treinta y Tres Orientales 3162; 24hr ☎ 56 27770, 📱 9948 1111; e hertzfraybentos@maderal.com.uy; ⏱ 09.00–13.00, 15.00–19.00 Mon–Fri, 09.00–13.00 Sat

Multicar Zorrilla 1483; ☎ 56 23316, 📱 9588 5767, 9430 7069; e faviopolaskiarcioni@hotmail.com; www.redmulticar.com

Thrifty Avda 18 de Julio on the plaza; ☎ 56 22082; ⏱ 09.00–13.00 Mon–Fri

Tourist information There's a tourist information office (☎ 52 28369) at the bus terminal.

Where to stay
Hotels

Gran Hotel Fray Bentos Paraguay 3272 & 18 de Julio; ☎ 56 20566; e info.fraybentos@granh.com; www.granh.com. The best hotel in town, with modern AC rooms with cable TV & internet access (& Wi-Fi in the public areas), plus swimming pool, gym & sauna; the restaurant is less good. $$$$

Jockey Club 25 de Mayo 3262; ☎ 56 22258. A good mid-range place. $$$

La Posada del Frayle Bentos 25 de Mayo 3434; ☎ 56 28541/2; e posadadelfraylebentos@grupocarminatti.com; www.grupocarminatti.com. An attractively restored colonial house with patio & fountain, pool table & garden with 2 swimming pools. Rooms have AC, fans & cable TV. $$$

Plaza Hotel 18 de Julio & 25 de Mayo; ☎ 56 22363, 3815; e pzahotel@adinet.com.uy, plazahotel@grupocarminatti.com; www.grupocarminatti.com. On the plaza, with a casino, this can be a bit noisy but is a decent mid-range place. Rooms have AC, fans & cable TV. $$$

Nuevo Hotel Colonial 25 de Mayo 3293 & Zorrilla; ☎ 56 22260. A fine budget option with large rooms (with fans) round a patio; a decent b/fast costs US$2 extra. $$

Parador Playa Ubici Continuación Wilson F Aldunate; ☎ 56 24915. Simple rooms at a nice family-type place (ie: with lots of kids running around) 3km east of town, with a view to Botnia & the international bridge. $$

Camping There are campsites on either side of the town and at the beach resort of Las Cañas, 8km south.

Club Atlético Anglo Rambla Cuervo s/n; ☎ 56 22787. By the bay on the road out to El Anglo, this newly restored site has simple but decent facilities. $

Playa Ubici Continuación Wilson F. Aldunate; ☎ 56 24915. At the parador of the same name, 3km east

of town (1km from km311 of the Carretera Puente-Puerto), this isn't the most convenient site but has a nice waterfront setting, with views of the Botnia plant & the international bridge. $

Where to eat

Los Paraisos Brasil & Inglaterra; ☎ 56 27996, 📱 9956 3072; e losparaisos1@gmail.com.uy; ⏱ 11.00–15.00 & from 19.00 daily. An excellent parrilla, also serving seafood, pasta, fondue & salads. There's AC, Wi-Fi & an open-air terrace. $$$

El Muelle Club Remeros, Rambla Costanera; ☎ 56 22873. The rowing club has a friendly, simple restaurant & bar. $$

Jockey Club 25 de Mayo 3262; ☎ 56 22258. A pretty average parrillada. $$

Wolves Parque Industrial Municipal, Barrio Anglo; ☎ 56 23604. A nice little pasta place in the former staff club at El Anglo. $$

Other practicalities

Banks There are ATMs around the plaza and at Banco República (*25 de Mayo & Lavalleja*), and two exchange offices, Cambio Nelson (*Avda 18 de Julio & Young*) and Cambio Dromer (*Avda 18 de Julio 1511 & Treinta y Tres*). Antel has a *telecentro* at Zorrilla 1133 (⏱ *09.00–19.00 Mon–Sat, 10.00–18.00 Sun*).

Bike repair Bike repairs can be tackled at Rincón and Florencio Sánchez.

Communications The post office is at Treinta y Tres 3271 (⊕ *08.30–17.00 Mon–Fri, 08.00–12.00 Sat*). There's free Wi-Fi in the bus terminal.

Consulate The Inspectoría de Migración is at Zorrilla 1303 (☎ *56 22302;* e *i09fraybentos@dnm.minterior.gub.uy*) and at the international bridge (☎ *56 22687*). There's an Argentine consulate on the north side of the plaza (*Avda 18 de Julio 1225;* ☎ *56 23310/23225;* e *consarfb@adinet.com.uy;* ⊕ *08.00–13.00 Mon–Fri*).

Markets The most convenient supermarket is Ta-Ta (*Avda 18 de Julio 1625, between Young & Beaulieu;* ⊕ *08.00–21.30 daily*).

What to see and do The cast-iron *kiosco* (bandstand) in the centre of Plaza Constitución, raised in 1902, is a copy of one at the Crystal Place in London and has become a symbol of the town. The grand but battered building on the east side of the plaza is the Junta (local council), while the lovely Neoclassical building on the north side, built in 1879 as a Mutual Aid Society for immigrants, is the **Museo Solari** (⊕ *09.00–15.00, 16.00–22.00 daily, Jan closed Mon & Tue afternoon*). Luis Solari, born in Fray Bentos in 1918, studied art in Montevideo and Paris, lived mainly in the US from 1967 to 1988, and died in Montevideo in 1993. His style is generally naïve, with fantastical subjects, often with animal heads or masks. There are also temporary shows here. The Banco Comercial, on the west side of the plaza, is a less grand Neoclassical pile, as is the church to the south, which has a pleasant interior with a low coffered ceiling. A block northeast of the plaza at 25 de Mayo & Zorrilla de San Martín, the splendid **Teatro Young** is where Juan Zorrilla de San Martín gave his last public speech in 1931.

Avenida 18 de Julio and parallel streets end at Paraguay, beyond which is a small park around an open-air theatre, facing over the riverside *rambla*, with the former train station and port to the right. To the left, Rambla Cuervo leads west to the Barrio Anglo, the residential area laid out in 1887 for the Liebig plant's managers. At the entrance a monument by a *palo borracho* tree is a reproduction of the Liebig stand at the 1885 Food Fair in Paris. Turning left at the monument, Justus von Liebig leads up to the Fray Bentos Golf Club (☎ *56 22427;* e *dalgorta@adinet.com.uy, ainovales@jetmar.com.uy*), the oldest golf club in Uruguay. The nine-hole course, among old native trees, was designed by Dr Alister MacKenzie in 1928 and has now been beautifully restored for use by Botnia's expatriate managers. The little clubhouse, built to mark King George VI's coronation in 1937, is a period piece, with plaques recording the sporting feats of the mainly Scottish staff of El Anglo. The Río Negro Tennis Club is also here.

Turning right down at the monument, the *rambla* leads to the gate of El Anglo, now the **Museo de la Revolución Industrial** (*Museum of the Industrial Revolution; www.anglo.8m.com, http://sites.google.com/site/fraybentosmuseoanglo;* ⊕ *09.00–19.30 daily, later on summer w/ends & holidays; US$1*). A guided tour (*10.00 & 15.00 Mon–Sat; US$1.40*) is essential if you want to see the parts of the site not yet fully open to the public. There's parking by the jetty, now disused but with two cranes built in Rodley, near Leeds, still standing at its end. To the left is the *cámara fría* (cold store), a massive concrete block with the word ANGLO still visible, painted across its face. This was more or less the last part of the complex to be built, in 1921–23 and 1926; 400m long by 100m wide, with 70km of ammonia gas coolant pipes, it could hold 18,000 tonnes of frozen meat. Like modern Uruguayan wineries, the process was designed to be gravity-aided, with the *corrales* and slaughterhouse at the highest point and the carcasses finally rolling into the cold store hanging on hooks on an open-air overhead conveyor.

It was Justus von Liebig (1803–73), the 'father of organic chemistry', who invented concentrated meat extract around 1840, but with some 30kg of meat needed for 1kg of extract, it was too expensive to produce in Europe. George Christian Giebert, a German engineer working on railways in Uruguay, spotted the potential for using the meat of cattle raised for leather. In 1865 he sent his first 800kg of extract to Europe and followed it to London in search of investment. The same year the Liebig Extract of Meat Company was formed, a British- and Belgian-owned multi-national based in London, and in 1866 a plant was set up in Fray Bentos. This was one of the first companies to use modern marketing techniques, and by 1875 the plant was producing 5,000 tonnes of extract per year.

A cheaper meat extract called Oxo was introduced in 1899 (Bovril, with added flavourings, was produced from the 1870s in Argentina). In 1887, once canning technology had advanced, the Liebig company started to produce corned beef and then canned tongues and steak-and-kidney pies. Immigrants from over 60 countries flooded here, with over 25,000 people having worked at the plant since 1863. In 1883 the first electric lighting in Uruguay was installed here (using coal imported from Britain!).

The plant's record year was 1890, when 208,890 animals were killed (and almost half of Britain's meat came from the southern hemisphere). In subsequent years the plant's products were used by Henry Morton Stanley, Captain Scott, Florence Nightingale, Alcock and Brown, and on the British Everest expeditions (and by the first men on the moon, according to Jules Verne), and were crucial to the British war effort of 1914–18. (One of the early British tanks was code-named Fray Bentos because its crew were 'meat in a can'.)

Big changes came with refrigeration, and major expansions of the factory in 1921–23 and 1926–29. However, the company over-reached itself and in 1924 was sold to the British firm Vesteys, after which the plant came to be known as El Anglo. It was the British who discovered a market for 'every part of the cow but the moo', including hooves, hair, bones, even bile stones (for the French perfume industry). At its peak the plant processed 2,000 or more cows a day as well as 6,000 lambs, pigs and turkeys. It played a big role in World War II, with fruit and vegetables being canned as well as meat (16 million tins of corned beef were exported in 1943, with an animal processed every five minutes).

Fray Bentos had fewer links with North America, feeding the military only in the Korean war. After this there was no investment and the plant's fortunes declined. Its famous pies have been made in Britain since 1958, and British entry into the Common Market meant the end of special trading links with Uruguay. The plant was given to the Uruguayan government in 1971; it closed in 1979, reopening as a museum in 2005. Meanwhile, corned beef is again being produced in Fray Bentos, by the Brazilian company Marfrig, although rights to the Fray Bentos brand are owned by Unilever.

Cattle were killed by a hammer to the head, then slid into the *matadero* or *plaza de faena*, where they were hooked on to the conveyor belt and systematically skinned, gutted and deprived of each internal organ in turn until the bare carcasses rolled into the cold store. For many the most interesting part of the visit is the *sala de maquinas* or machine hall, with huge boilers, turbines and generators produced in places like Derby and Stoke-on-Trent, as well as ammonia compressors from Bradford and a gantry crane from Loughborough. This machine hall is visible from the museum hall through a window which may become the entry to a walkway. Outside there's also a Merryweather fire pump, all scarlet paint and shining brass, built in 1893.

The main hall of the museum has some excellent displays, all in Spanish, on both technology and social history, including early posters and packaging. You can also see the offices, with a central hall that once rang with the clatter of the typewriters that still sit on the ranks of clerks' desks. There's also a chemical laboratory full of flasks and retorts; on the same site is the LATU lab, testing outflows from the Botnia plant – it would be very appropriate if a viewing gallery could allow visitors to see this too, as part of the museum's search for contemporary relevance. Also on the site is the Museo de los Puentes (or the Museo Puentes de Integración y Innovación – the Bridges of Integration and Innovation Museum), a tribute to Ponce Delgado, the local engineer who built the International Bridge and two others in the area; however, there are not enough staff to open it.

The road continues on around El Anglo; heading back into the Barrio Anglo you'll soon come to the Casa Grande (Manager's House, built in 1868), where Robert Baden-Powell spent a night in 1909. It has a spectacular garden. An asphalt road to the right continues downriver to a viewpoint and the *aduana vieja* (old Customs post), which is in fact a small cottage. There are lots of loose horses and cattle which, rather bizarrely, can be seen wandering into El Anglo itself. There's good birdwatching here, with both *monte nativo* and eucalyptus trees. The road eventually continues to the beach resort of Las Cañas, but this is best reached by the main road.

Las Cañas From the centre of Fray Bentos, Camino Batlle runs past the new Barrio Botnia (with modern homes for Botnia's executives) and continues southwest for 8km to the beach resort of Las Cañas. Normally a quiet little place, at summer weekends it can have a temporary population of 10,000 or more, many coming from Argentina to enjoy its safe beach.

Getting there and information A bus comes here from Fray Bentos (*09.00 & 14.00 Sat & Sun, returning 12.00 & 20.00, daily in summer; US$1*). There are two entrances to the resort, with an information booth at each.

Where to stay The **Camping Las Cañas** (✆ *56 22224, 22148;* e *lascanas@ adinet.com.uy;* ⊕ *15 Dec–15 Mar & Easter;* $) has space for 3,000 tents, mostly at the southern end of the resort. Just inside the northern entrance is the very attractive thatched **Hotel Sol de Las Cañas** (*Calle 1/de los Crespines;* ✆ *56 27433, 22124;* e *leonsol@adinet.com.uy; AC rooms, each with both dbl & sgl beds, & cable TV;* $$). To the right are the Playa El Paraíso – and the El Paraíso sector of the campsite, much quieter than the main site, in a very natural setting with lots of native trees right down to the beach. There's a shop and showers here, as well as a natural amphitheatre. Swinging left, there are a few blocks of thatched bungalows and *posadas*, and then (beyond the jetty and Restaurant Punta Bahía) the large area of native woodland that comprises the main campsite. There are shops, *parador* restaurants, craft stalls and a polyclinic. The remoter southern end is the **Camping Los Pescadores** ($) or Fishermen's Beach, where you can indeed buy fish from the fishermen.

At the northern end of the campsite, just south of Calle 7, is the **Motel Municipal** (✆ *56 22224;* $) with very simple bungalows, next to the Parador El Entorno, a decent restaurant. Some good places to sleep near the beach in the central area are the **Posada del Barranco** (✆ *56 27109; www.delbarranco.com;* $$) and **Posada del Naranjo** (✆ *56 26285;* e *pnaranjo@adinet.com.uy;* ⊕ *all year;* $$), which has nice thatched *cabañas*. One block inland is **Bungalows Sol y Luna** (*Calle 8/de los Boyeros;* ☎ *56 23872;* $$).

FRAY BENTOS TO PAYSANDÚ Within Río Negro department, the *litoral* of the Río Uruguay north of Fray Bentos is largely undeveloped wetlands and gallery forest, with plenty of large riverine islands, an area famed for its hunting and fishing but more recently known to birdwatchers and other nature lovers. There are over 200 species of birds, as well as reptiles (14 species), amphibians (eight), mammals (30, including perhaps the very occasional visit by a puma or maned wolf) and many insect and butterfly species. There are also amazing sunsets. An area of 17,496ha has been designated the **Parque Nacional Esteros de Farrapos y Islas del Río Uruguay (Backwaters of Farrapos and Islands of the River Uruguay National Park)** – and a Ramsar site – but only on paper, and Argentines in particular still cross the river to hunt here.

From km287½ on Ruta 2 an unpaved short cut heads north to Ruta 24 towards Paysandú. (Buses heading north continue towards Fray Bentos to just short of km298, at the Parador La Víbora, an excellent restaurant at the junction of Ruta 24 and a road north to M'Bopicuá, where there's a wildlife reserve and another pulp mill project.) Heading up Ruta 24, at km9 is the junction with the short cut from Mercedes, and at km17 a pond where you'll often see spoonbills.

Nuevo Berlín At km20½ of Ruta 24 there's a junction to Nuevo Berlín, 9.5km west. The village was founded in 1875 by German settlers invited to work on the Estancia Nueva Melhem, just to the north, the birthplace of modern farming in the Plate region. It now has around 3,000 inhabitants.

Turning left as you enter, you'll pass the *policlínica* and police station to reach the Playa El Sauzal by the jetty, *Prefectura* (harbourmaster), *Aduana* (Customs) and the Parador El Sauzal restaurant (m *9911 1659*). Also here is the Moteles Municipales, four very simple and clean rooms for four people each; contact the Junta Local (*18 de Julio & Treinta y Tres;* ☎ *568 2049;* ⏰ *08.00–14.00;* $) about this or about camping here. A better place to stay, facing the river three blocks to the right, is the Posada Don Sebastián (☎ *568 2281,* m *9627 7113;* $$–$), with rooms for up to eight people with private bathrooms, TV, fridge and fan; there's a *parrilla*, or meals can be provided, including breakfast (not included in the cost).

The best starting point for boat trips into the islands of the national park (*about US$20*) is the Junta Local. The Festival desde la Costa is held usually on the third weekend of January, with folklore and other acts.

Plama's rural bus service from Fray Bentos to the farming town of Young runs via Nuevo Berlín. A minibus meets some Mercedes–Paysandú buses at km20½ to shuttle passengers in to Nuevo Berlín.

Young Ruta 24 continues north, reaching the Tres Bocas junction at km54, an hour by bus from either Mercedes or Paysandú. There's an ANCAP service station here with shop, coffee machine and hot water for *maté*, but no *parador*. Ruta 25 leads 27km east to Young (pronounced 'Jung'), centre of one of the richest agricultural districts in the country, now also known for its polo players, especially the Stirling family. Some of the surrounding villages, including Colonía Ombú, 12km southeast on Ruta 3, are German-speaking Mennonite colonies, their culture reinforced by German TV and radio received by satellite or internet. Claldy (*Compañía Lactea Agropecuaria Lecheros de Young; www.claldy.com.uy*), on the outskirts of Young at km311, is one of the country's leading dairy co-ops.

There are several adequate hotels, including the Casa Nuestra (*Ruta 3 immediately north of Ruta 25: Montevideo & Rincón;* ☎ *567 2371;* $$). Five blocks further east on Ruta 20 (18 de Julio) is the town centre, with a 2-6-0 steam locomotive preserved on a plinth opposite the former station, the church, a cinema and a supermarket. At the Junta Local you can ask for tourist information. There's a campsite 20km southeast (*Ruta 3 & Paso de las Piedras;* `\` *567 3031/2744;* $), where there's a kilometre-long riverside beach, hot showers, barbecues, restaurant, café and shop, as well as *cabañas* with private bathrooms.

On Ruta 3, Young sees a dozen buses a day between Montevideo and Paysandú, as well as local buses to Fray Bentos.

San Javier Continuing up Ruta 24 from Tres Bocas, it's 11km to the crossroads at Tres Quintos, with the scattered Mennonite settlement of Gartental to the right and San Javier 13km to the left (west) on the Río Uruguay. Settled by Russians of the rather odd New Israel sect in 1913, this village of around 2,000 people is now the main jumping-off point for ecotourism in the national park.

The New Israel sect believed in the existence of a living God, who was declared in 1891 to be Vasili Lubkov (1869–1937). It spread across much of southern Russia, attracting official persecution. In 1912 representatives of the Batlle y Ordóñez administration visited Russia to encourage emigration, and the next year two ships brought Lubkov and 580 followers to Montevideo, and on 27 July 1913 to Puerto Viejo, 5km north of San Javier. By 1914 the community numbered about 2,000, living largely in isolation from Uruguayan society and with all property handed over to Lubkov, who enforced tight control. In 1926 Lubkov made the mistake of returning to Russia, where he was imprisoned in Siberia (and finally shot under Stalin in 1937). He was succeeded here by Andres Poiarkov, then Miron Gayvoronsky, and the community gradually opened up. Uruguay's military government burned all the Russian books they could find and arrested some of the community. Today about 85% of the population is of Russian origin.

There are also Mennonite communities nearby, who came from East Prussia after 1948 (fleeing from the Russians, ironically), and about 100 Russian Old Believers, 3km north in Colonia Ofir, who came from Brazil in the 1960s.

As you enter the village on Artigas, the Sala Cultural Pobeda ('Victory' in Russian) is on the right just before the main crossroads with Calle Lubkov. The small Museo de los Inmigrantes is here, with interesting photos and documents of the Russian community; however, it may move to the former Cooperativa shop, just across Lubkov. Next to the Cooperativa on Artigas is the Galpón de Piedra (Stone Store), built without cement in 1914 when each family brought two cartloads of stone; there are plans for this to become the national park's visitor centre. Alongside is the community's flour and oil mill, built in similar style to the *galpón* but enlarged in concrete in 1945, and now abandoned.

Beyond this is an area of parkland by the Río Uruguay, with a slipway and jetty. Turning left at the *Prefectura* (harbourmaster's house) on the Paseo de los Inmigrantes, you'll see two tombs to the left under a large eucalyptus tree. These belong to Natalia Gregorivna Lubkova, Lubkov's wife, and Maxim Lavrentievich Shevchenko, the group's 'apostle'.

Following the Paseo to the end of Lubkov and turning left you'll come at once to the Casa Blanca, built in 1860 as the *casco* (main house) of the Estancia Montserrat. This was where the Lubkovs and Shevchenko lived, and it is being restored to house the **Museo de la Diáspora Rusa** (*Museum of the Russian Diaspora; http://museocasablanca.blogspot.com;* ⊕ *weekends only*), with Lubkov's office and desk, an icon and furniture left by Princess Ekaterina Romanova (who lived in Montevideo until her death at 92 in 2007), and various pictures and documents (not only about the community in San Javier).

A block inland from the Casa Blanca, on 18 de Julio south of Artigas, the **Sabrania** ('Assembly' in Russian) is the very simple, white worship hall (with 'Novi Izrael' in Cyrillic on the front wall). Built after Lubkov's departure (until then the community had met in the Casa Blanca), it's open on Sunday afternoons, when older members of the community meet to sing the old hymns – there's no spiritual leader now and the community seems very much in tune with secular Uruguay. A block north beyond Artigas on Plaza Libertad are the large *matrioshka* dolls that appear in almost every picture of San Javier.

To the south of San Javier there are riverside cliffs and gallery forest with wetlands to the east, then another line of cliff and forest – it's ideal for exploring by horse, but you can also walk (in about three hours, if you're busy watching birds) along the river to the Arroyo Farrapos. Watch out for the spiky acacias near the start; unfortunately cows are still being grazed on islands in the national park, spreading acacia seeds there. It's also possible to take a boat, the *Manuelita II*: ask at the Junta Local (✆ 569 2108) or *Prefectura*.

There's no accommodation in San Javier (but some basic options in Puerto Viejo; see below). The only place to eat is the Centro Bar, also known as Elsa's (*Artigas & 18 de Julio; ⊕ from 0700 daily*), which serves basic pizza. There's also a bakery (*Lubkov & Colón*) where you can buy Russian *pirogis*. Right at the other end of the village, La Casita Mujer Rural (*San Julián & Golovchenko, by the exit to Ruta 24*) is a women's co-op that sells great jams and craftwork. Diagonally opposite the *matrioshkas* at the northwestern corner of Plaza Libertad are the Junta Local, post office, Antel call centre and the Maxim Gorki cultural centre. The Banco República, opposite the Museo de los Inmigrantes on Artigas, doesn't have an ATM but will give advances on Visa cards.

The Fiesta del Girasol, on the Saturday before Easter, celebrates the introduction of the sunflower (for cooking oil) in 1913. The anniversary of Lubkov's release from prison is celebrated on 31 May. On 27 July, the anniversary of the Russians' arrival at Puerto Viejo, there's a huge feast with 2,000 lamb shashlik kebabs cooked, with honey-flavoured *kvaas* to drink.

Buses between Mercedes and Paysandú run up Ruta 24, most going via Fray Bentos and a few via San Javier. The Sabelin bus company has an office by the Casa Blanca (⊕ *07.30–11.30, 15.30–19.30 Mon–Sat*).

Puerto Viejo Heading north, Calle Lubkov becomes Camino Vladimir Roslik (in honour of the last victim of the dictatorship). Taking two left turns you'll come to Puerto Viejo, where the Russians first landed. In the village there's a memorial, some old millstones and a jetty, and an attractive, busy campsite (✆ 569 2146; ⊕ *Dec–Apr*), with 280 sites spread over 5ha. The Resto-Pub Zona Zero (✆ 569 2235) runs the Moteles Municipales ($$), six simple *cabañas* on a terrace with four beds, bathroom, fridge and fan. There's a noisy Saturday night dance in Puerto Viejo, which goes on until 05.00 in summer; you might not get much sleep.

The road to Puerto Viejo is asphalted, but there's no bus. You can take a taxi from San Javier, or follow the footpath along the river for about 2km from calles Fray Bentos and Colonia Ofir.

PAYSANDÚ DEPARTMENT

You can return to Ruta 24 either via Tres Quintos, or by continuing north past the San Javier turning to km81½; another 2km north you'll leave Río Negro and enter Paysandú department across the long Arroyo Negro bridge, with birdwatching possible in monte espinilla (spiney woodland) on the north side.

6

At km86.5 you can turn right to **Estancia La Paz** (↘ *72 02272,* m *9972 1513;* e *awyaux@adinet.com.uy; www.estancialapaz.com.uy;* $$$$), 5km to the east on a dirt road that leads to km336 of Ruta 3. This was one of the first tourist *estancias,* and is still one of the best. It was founded in 1856 by Richard Bannister Hughes, owner of a meat-salting business at the future Fray Bentos, who introduced Durham cattle and wire-fencing. In 1956 it was bought by the Belgian Pierre Wyaux, whose daughter still runs the estate. You'll pass a Protestant church built by Hughes in 1873, based on one in Liverpool, with lovely Arts and Crafts-style stained-glass. The main house, built in 1863, has been lovingly restored, and has a swimming pool, tennis court and spa with jacuzzi and sauna. The nine guest rooms are not huge but are nice, with air conditioning, heating and Wi-Fi. Activities include riding, hunting, canoeing on the Río Uruguay and star-watching; gourmet tourism is also a feature, with fine local food and a shop selling their own preserves and pecans. A room for two costs US$88, but watch out for extra charges.

PAYSANDÚ Uruguay's second-largest city, with around 115,222 *sanduceros,* Paysandú is a river port and a centre of the meat-processing industry (together with leather and wool). Founded in 1749, the city was bombarded in 1845 by Garibaldi's squadron of British, French and Uruguayan ships and captured in 1846 by Rivera. The Third Defence of Paysandú came in 1864–65 when General Leandro Gómez heroically resisted Brazilian forces, who shelled the city from land and river; when they finally captured it the city centre was in ruins. With industrial development came international immigration, and the city still has Swiss, Belgian, German, Russian and Ukrainian communities. There are some worthwhile museums in Paysandú, as well as practical services.

Getting there
By car Coming from the south, Ruta 24 and Ruta 3 meet at km94 and km355 respectively. Ruta 3 bypasses Paysandú to the east and at km370 crosses Ruta 90 (from Guichón), which leads west to the city centre as, successively, avenidas Italia, Argentina, España, 18 de Julio and Brasil.

By bus The bus terminal is six blocks south of the main Plaza Constitución at Zorrilla de San Martín & Artigas. There are a least a dozen buses a day from Montevideo to Paysandú, by three routes. Sabelin offers three services via Trinidad (Ruta 3 – the fastest option) and two via Mercedes (Ruta 2), as well as two via Colonia, Dolores and Fray Bentos, which continue to Salto and Bella Unión. Copay has four a day (via Trinidad) and Cynsa/Nuñez has two a day.

From Mercedes Chadre runs four services to Paysandú, but from Fray Bentos there are just two a day with Chadre plus an early-morning service with Plama via Nuevo Berlín and Young. There are also four buses a day (two on Sundays) run by Vittori between Young and Paysandú. There are five or six buses a day between Paysandú and Guichón, four a day (two on Sundays) continuing to Tacuarembó.

To the north, Agencia Central runs seven buses a day to Salto (two continuing to Bella Unión), Alonso runs three (via Guichón), and Nuñez and Quebracho two each. A Copay bus leaves for Rivera at 04.00 except on Sundays. Copay also run two or three international buses to Concepción del Uruguay and Colón, both in Argentina, where they usually just fail to make proper connections to Rosario, Córdoba, Paraná and Santa Fe. There's also a bus run by the Brazilian company Ouro e Prata (*www.viacaouroeprata.com.br*) on Friday afternoons to Sao Gabriel and Porto Alegre, returning on Sundays.

Getting around Plaza Constitución, at the end of Avenida España, marks the centre of the city, from where Zorrilla de San Martín leads to the large bus terminal, six blocks south. The port is at the west end of Avda Brasil, to the north of which parks and beaches are being developed into an increasingly attractive recreational zone, with the Artigas bridge to Colón in Argentina at its northern end. Note that there's a Bulevar Artigas running north–south and a Calle Artigas running east–west.

There's a charge for car parking in the city centre (*12.00–18.00 Mon–Fri*).

Car rental

🚗 **Avis** Leandro Gómez 1087 bis & 19 de Abril; ☎ 72 32037, 24hr m 9817 0006; e paysandu@ avis.com.uy

🚗 **Dollar** Treinta y Tres Orientales 956; ☎ 72 25070; e gonzapu@adinet.com.uy

🚗 **Multicar** Leandro Gómez 1325, between Varela & Mauá; ☎ 72 40464, m 9572 2276; www.redmulticar.com

🚗 **Punta Car** Leandro Gómez 1170; ☎ 72 28777; www.puntacar.com.uy

🚗 **Rentacar** Daymán Argentina 2082; ☎ 72 34973, m 9931 5855; www.rentacardayman.com

Tourist information The Oficina de Turismo (*Avda 18 de Julio 1226 bis;* ☎ *72 26220;* e *turismo@paysandu.gub.uy;* ⊕ *08.00–20.00 Mon–Fri, 10.00–20.00 Sat, Sun & holidays*) is on the south side of Plaza Constitución, on the site of the city's first church. There's another office (*Avda de los Iracundos;* ☎ *72 29235;* e *plandelacosta@paysandu.gub.uy;* ⊕ *08.30–21.30 daily, until 14.00 24 & 31 Dec, closed 25 Dec & 1 Jan*) to the north near the beach, between the Museo de la Tradición and the amphitheatre.

Where to stay

🏠 **El Jardín** Montevideo 1085 between Uruguay & Charrúas; ☎ 72 23745; e reservas@ hoteljardin.com. Opened at the end of 2008, this nicely converted house has 9 AC rooms with flat-screen TV, Wi-Fi (& a PC), attractive garden & good buffet b/fast. $$$$

🏠 **Mykonos** 18 de Julio 768; ☎ 72 28201, m 9972 7743; e mykonos@adinet.com.uy. A rather slick & chilly 3-star place with 26 rooms with AC, cable TV, hair drier, frigobar & safe, as well as 2 suites. Buffet b/fast incplus business room & Wi-Fi. $$$$

🏠 **Lobato** Gómez 1415; ☎ 72 22241; e hotellobato@adinet.com.uy. A very decent, modern place with AC rooms & Wi-Fi; no credit cards. $$$

🏠 **Hotel La Posada** Varela 566 & Solís; ☎ 72 27879; e laposada@adinet.com.uy. A nice enough 2-star hotel, which is listed in places as an HI-affiliated hostel, but it is definitely not. Handy for the bus terminal. PC & Wi-Fi, & buffet b/fast inc. $$

🏠 **La Casona del Centro** Zorrilla de San Martín 975, Plaza Constitución; ☎ 72 22998, m 9524 2868; e lacasonadelcentro@paysandu.com. Family home with bunks fitted into bedrooms, some huge, with private bathroom, AC & cable TV. $$

🏠 **Plaza** Gómez 1211; ☎ 72 33545; e hotelplaza@adinet.com.uy. A block south of Plaza Constitución, this is a good mid-range hotel with AC rooms, Wi-Fi, laundry & garage; no credit cards. $$

🏠 **Rafaela** Avda 18 de Julio 1181; ☎ 72 24216; e rafaela@paysandu.com. A bit tired but adequate & reasonable value, with AC rooms. $$

🏠 **Sarandi** Sarandí 931; ☎ 72 23465. Behind the black glass front lies a simple little hotel, some rooms with AC, some with fan, all with bathroom & cable TV. $$

🏠 **Concordia** Avda 18 de Julio 984; ☎ 72 22417. An old-style 1-star hotel, with a choice of simple rooms with or without private bathroom, all with cable TV. $

🏠 **Hospedaje Sosa** Sarandí 1039 & Montevideo (no tel). A friendly family-run place with both private & shared rooms. $

Camping The **Camping Municipal** is in the Parque Guyunusa, north of the yacht club at the west end of Henderson. It's very simple, without showers, and is always

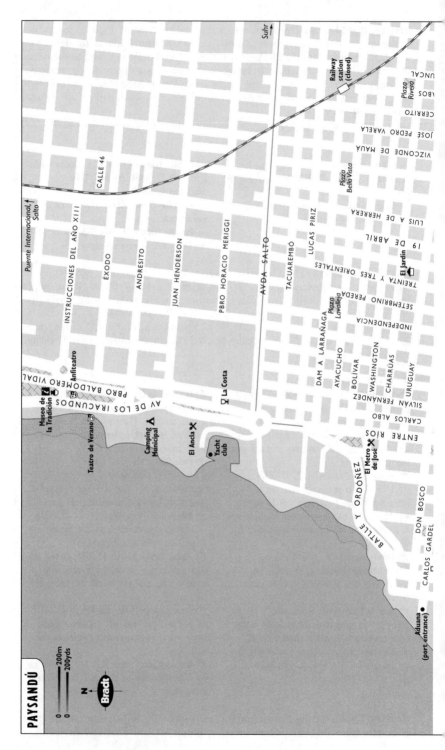

PAYSANDÚ

N

Bradt

0 ——— 200m
0 ——— 200yds

Puente Internacional, Salto

CALLE 46

INSTRUCCIONES DEL AÑO XIII

ÉXODO

ANDRESITO

JUAN HENDERSON

PBRO HORACIO MERIGGI

AVDA SALTO

TACUAREMBÓ

LUCAS PIRIZ

TREINTA Y TRES ORIENTALES

SETEMBRINO PEREDA

INDEPENDENCIA

DAM A LARRAÑAGA

AYACUCHO

BOLIVAR

WASHINGTON

CHARRÚAS

URUGUAY

SILVÁN FERNÁNDEZ

CARLOS ALBO

ENTRE RÍOS

DON BOSCO

CARLOS GARDEL

BATLLE Y ORDÓÑEZ

PBRO BALDOMERO VIDAL

AV DE LOS IRACUNDOS

Museo de la Tradición

Anfiteatro

Teatro de Verano

Camping Municipal

El Ancla ✕

La Costa

Yacht club

El Metro de José ✕

Aduana (port entrance)

Suhr

Railway station (closed)

Plaza Rivera

UNCAL

IBOS

CERRITO

JOSÉ PEDRO VARELA

VIZCONDE DE MAUÁ

Plaza Bella Vista

LUIS A DE HERRERA

19 DE ABRIL

El Jardín

Plaza Lavalleja

282

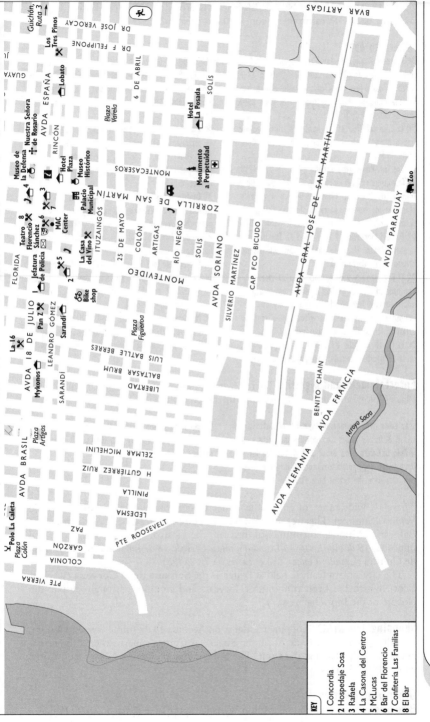

KEY

1. Concordia
2. Hospedaje Sosa
3. Rafaela
4. La Casona del Centro
5. McLucas
6. Bar del Florencio
7. Confitería Las Familias
8. El Bar

open for day use and barbecues. Electricity is provided only from Friday 22.00 to Monday 02.00. To camp there, contact the tourism office.

✗ Where to eat

✗ **El Ancla** Rambla de los Iracundos s/n; ✆ 72 40911; e hguedes@adinet.com.uy; ⏰ from 12.00 & 20.30 daily. Just north of the yacht club & handy for the campsite, this lively spot serves good pasta, fish & snacks. $$$

✗ **La Casa del Vino** 19 de Abril 876. This wine-bar half a block south of Sarandí has been here since 1886. $$$

✗ **Los Tres Pinos** Avda España 1474; ✆ 72 41211; e lostrespinos@adinet.com.uy; ⏰ 11.30–15.00 & from 19.00 Mon–Sat, 11.30–15.00 Sun. A versatile place serving parrilla, pasta (& ñoquis), fish & seafood. $$$

✗ **Bar del Florencio** 19 de Abril 930. The bar of the fantastic Teatro Florencio Sánchez, this still has its ornate 1870s décor. $$

✗ **El Bar** Herrera 955, 1 block west of Plaza Constitución; ✆ 72 37809; e elbaresotracosa@ adinet.com.uy. Traditional bar with plenty of atmosphere & live music at w/ends; good spot for b/fast & for drinks throughout the day. $$

✗ **La 16** 18 de Julio 833; ✆ 72 41711; e la-16@adinet.com.uy; www.paysandu.com/la16;

⏰ 12.00–15.00, 20.00–24.00 Mon–Fri, until 01.30 Sat, 12.00–15.00 Sun. Serving both Chinese & Italian food, inc parrilla, pasta & fish, this is a friendly, efficient place with reasonable prices; AC rooms & patio terrace. $$

✗ **Pan Z** 18 de Julio 950 & Pereda; ✆ 72 29551; e pizzeriapanz@adinet.com.uy; ⏰ 12.00–15.00 & from 20.00 daily. A cheap & cheerful place for pizza, pasta, parrilla & chivitos, with a streetside terrace. $$

✗ **Confitería Las Familias** 18 de Julio 1152 & Herrera; ✆ 72 22181; e paysandu@ postrechaja.com; www.postrechaja.com. The home of Paysandú's famous chajá dessert. You can also gets hot dogs & similar snacks here. $

✗ **El Metro de José** Entre Ríos 1139 & Washington; ✆ 72 35038; e elmetro@adinet.com.uy; ⏰ from 19.00 daily. A stylish place for pizza (by the metre), parrilla, pastas, chivitos & snacks. $

✗ **McLucas** Leandro Gómez 1050 & Montevideo; ✆ 72 29610; ⏰ 20.00–23.30 daily. A take-away with over 20 types of empanada, all excellent. $

Entertainment and nightlife There's a group of lively disco-pubs near the port on Plaza Colón, and also to the north by the beach.

♀ **La Costa** Avda Costanera s/n, north of Avda Salto. A stylish & trendy music bar opposite the yacht club.

♀ **Polo La Caleta** Avda Brasil 259 & Avda de los Deportistas; www.pololacaleta.com. A bright red disco pub, alongside the bright blue Pub Blue.

♀ **Suhr** Avda Wilson Ferreira Aldunate 2103; www.suhr.com.uy. A lively pub that serves pizzas & snacks.

There's a wide range of cultural activities throughout the year at the Teatro de Verano (Summer Theatre) and Anfiteatro (Amphitheatre), both of them by the Balneario Municipal (municipal beach); the Teatro Florencio Sánchez (see opposite; *19 de Abril between Leandro Gómez & Avda 18 de Julio*) and the tatty Casa de Cultura (*Leandro Gómez 852 & Berres;* ✆ *72 22398*).

The city's main festival, held at Easter, is the **Semana de la Cerveza** (Week of Beer), which has been running for 45 years and continues strongly despite the closure of the Norteña brewery.

Shopping The MAC Shopping Center is on Avenida 18 de Julio between Herrera, Leandro Gómez and 19 de Abril; the SuperStar Centro supermarket at the rear is better than the Ta-Ta at the front. The Sol craft shop (*Leandro Gómez 659*) is just east of Plaza Artigas.

Other practicalities

Bike hire A good bike shop is Milton Wynants Sport Bike (*Sarandí 952 & Pereda*).

Communications The post office is at 18 de Julio 1052 & Montevideo (⏰ *09.00–17.00 Mon–Fri, 08.00–12.00 Sat*). Antel's *telecentros* are at Herrera & Avda 18 de Julio and Montevideo 875 & Sarandí (*both* ⏰ *09.00–19.00 Mon–Sat, 10.00–18.00 Sun*) and opposite the terminal at Zorrilla de San Martín 645 (⏰ *06.30–23.30 Mon–Thu, 06.30–23.00 Fri–Sat, 07.00–23.00 Sun*). There's a very weak Wi-Fi signal on Plaza Constitución and a much better one on Plaza Artigas, as well as at the MAC Shopping Centre (see opposite).

Consulate The Inspectoría de Migración is at Independencia 940 (☏ *72 24997;* e *i12paysandu@dnm.minterior.gub.uy*) and at the International Bridge (☏ *72 25105*).

Emergency services The hospital (*Montecaseros 520 & Avda Soriano;* ☏ *72 24836*) is near the bus terminal. Police headquarters are at Leandro Gómez 1039 (☏ *72 26471*), facing the Argentine consulate (*Leandro Gómez 1034;* ☏ *72 22253;* e *cpays@ adinet.com.uy;* ⏰ *10.00–13.00 Mon–Fri*).

What to see and do On the east side of Plaza Constitución, the **cathedral of Nuestra Señora de Rosario** was built in 1873 in a pretty grand Neoclassical style, with frescoes over the ceiling and elsewhere, and a large altar. The organ above the entry was built in 1906 and restored in 1997. In front of the cathedral sits a bell cast in 1689 at one of the Jesuit missions to the north of Paysandú and donated by Fructuoso Rivera to commemorate his capture of the city. In the centre of the square is a statue of Leandro Gómez, the brave (and suicidal) defender of Paysandú, above the underground Museo de la Defensa (⏰ *08.00–12.45 Tue–Sun in theory, but usually closed*); you can look through the glass at the urn holding Gómez's ashes.

Two blocks south of the plaza, the grand Neo-Baroque Palacio Municipal stands nearly opposite the **Museo Histórico** (*History Museum; Zorrilla de San Martín 874;* ⏰ *08.00–12.45 Mon–Sat; free*) in the so-called Casa del Espíritu. Built in 1890 as a girls' orphanage, it became a museum in 1989. With some captions in English and a file with information in Braille, it covers local history in a broad sweep from the arrival of humans around 10,000 years ago (leaving rough stones and arrowheads) to the 19th century. Also on display are a large well-made Guaraní burial urn from the Arroyo Negro sands, the first map of Paysandú (1749), copies of English watercolours of Paysandú (1846) and a good model of the city centre after its capture in 1865 by Brazil, together with photos, a flag, cannonballs and rusty swords. Another room displays Lavalleja's pistol, and 19th-century items such as a theodolite, a typewriter, an organ and bedroom furniture.

Two blocks west, the Teatro Florencio Sánchez (*19 de Abril between Leandro Gómez & Avda 18 de Julio*), built in 1876, is Uruguay's oldest theatre outside Montevideo. Behind a 20th-century façade, it has an auditorium with three galleries, red plush seats and fine plasterwork; you should be able to look inside as long as it's not in use. A block west, the Jefatura de Policía (*police headquarters; Leandro Gómez 1039 & Montevideo*) was built in 1860 and survived the siege; it houses a Museo Policial (Police Museum), currently closed because of flooding.

Eight blocks west along Avenida 18 de Julio, Plaza Artigas has attractive trees on its southern half, but only flagpoles on its sun-baked northern half. It's another five blocks to Plaza Colón, heart of a pretty drab area with some disco-pubs. Immediately beyond is the *Aduana* (Customs) gate, which you can go through to visit the port. Here are rail-mounted Belgian cranes, and picnic tables with benches. A disused rail track leads north past a former railway shed to the Playa Park (Park Beach) and a long jetty, now closed off. To the right an obelisk with municipal-toilet tiling at its base commemorates Artigas's landing in 1811 to join the struggle for independence. Just beyond this is the yacht club, a nice little port with a smaller antique crane, and a couple of restaurants. Beyond the campsite, the start of the Balneario Municipal (municipal beach) is marked by craft stalls, the Teatro de Verano and the bigger, more modern Anfiteatro.

Immediately north of the Anfiteatro is the **Museo de la Tradición** (Museum of Tradition; ④ *08.00–12.45, 16.00–20.45 daily except Christmas & New Year; free*), with displays of archaeology, weapons (including Swiss target-shooting rifles), a school and a model of a *pulpería* (rural shop). There's also good material on gaucho culture, the *chajá* dessert, the Norteña brewery (now closed) and other local industries, and Los Iracundos (a Beatlesesque sextet from Paysandú who became 'the most famous band in Hispanic America', making their début at the Teatro Florencio Sánchez in 1961). It's nicely landscaped, with lots of labelled native trees and plants, and there are modern sculptures in the park immediately north.

The cemetery, east of the bus terminal, is now known as the **Monumento a Perpetuidad** (*Monument to Perpetuity; Montecaseros between Artigas & Soriano;* ④ *08.00–18.45 Tue–Sun except Christmas & New Year; free*), worth a look for its seriously ornate sculpture (since 1881). Continuing south on Montecaseros past the hospital and five longish blocks further, beyond Avenida Paraguay, the Parque Municipal houses the **Zoo** (④ *summer 07.00–21.00 daily, winter 08.00–18.00; free*), with 82 species of animals and birds, including lions, monkeys, wild boars, peccaries, capybaras, caymans, otters, turtles, ducks, geese, pheasants, herons, parrots and vultures. Bus 109 comes here from Plaza Constitución via the east side of the bus terminal.

GUICHÓN AND THE RINCÓN DE PÉREZ
The main town in eastern Paysandú department is **Guichón**, 89km east of the capital on Ruta 90. Founded in 1907, it's a small agricultural centre of about 5,000 residents. Birdwatchers will be interested in the Rincón de Pérez, and the hot baths at Almirón round the day off very nicely.

The town lies to the north of a roundabout on Ruta 90, with the plaza two blocks to the east of the main road, Artigas. Restaurante Guayabos is on the plaza. On a hill directly off the roundabout at the southern end of town, the Alchimía spa (❦ *742 2206;* e *alchimiaspa@gmail.com*), opened in 2009, has accommodation for ten in four rooms, all feng-shuied and with air conditioning; TV and internet access are available in the dining area. An American breakfast includes juice from their own orange and lemon trees; there's a *parrilla* for *asados*, or a cook can come in. There are two pools (with a ramp and hoist), hydrotherapy (both medical and for relaxation), massage, reiki, treatments with mud or hot stones, as well as horseriding and boar-hunting. It's one of the few places in Uruguay that is genuinely wheelchair-accessible, and very pleasant anyway. Just west at km85.5, La Arisca (❦ *742 2144,* m *9972 7667*) has nice *cabañas* for up to nine (with kitchen, TV and fan) and farm-style rooms; meals can be arranged, as can boar-hunting.

The **Termas de Almirón** (*Ruta 90 km82.5;* ❦ *740 2203, 740 2891;* e *termas.almiron@paysandu.gub.uy*) are the only saltwater hot springs in the region, with good modern installations including open-air and indoor pools (④ *07.00–00.30 & 07.00–23.00 respectively, all year; US$1 entry to the complex*). Accommodation includes camping (*US$1.50 pp;* ④ *all year*) in the trees by the stream, where you might see otters, and one- and two-storey *cabañas* (*from US$30 for 4, US$40 for 6*).

Artigas continues north as a dirt road – nominally Ruta 4 – crossing the Arroyo Santana at km392, where there's a beach with free camping (toilets but no water except from the *arroyo*), and the Río Queguay Grande at km402 (Paso Andrés Pérez), where you can also camp (with dry-composting toilets). There's an interpretative nature trail on the south side just before the old bridge.

A kilometre to the north, a road turns left (west) to Colonia Juan Gutierrez. It's about 20 minutes' drive to the Rincón de Pérez, in the forested fork between the Río Queguay Grande and the Río Chico, where there's an unmarked path through a field to the right to the Cueva de Tigre, a cave inhabited by vampire bats. It's another 500m or so to the entrance to the **Reserva Ecológica Rincón de Pérez**, the largest area of native woodland left in Uruguay, where you'll find birdwatching hides and trails of about a kilometre in length. There's little infrastructure and no rangers here; to make the most of a visit you should contact Guichón's Junta Local (*Penza & 18 de Julio, a block east of Artigas;* ↘ *742 2225*) for one of the guides who have been trained as part of a sustainable-tourism project. Danny at the Junta Local can also put you in touch with the Club Queguay Canoas to organise a canoe trip down the Río Queguay. In January there's a mass descent of the river by hundreds of canoeists, from the Paso Andrés Pérez.

NORTH OF PAYSANDÚ Heading north from Paysandú, you'll pass a big interchange at km375, with a road west to the bridge to Colón (Argentina); 19km north of the interchange there's a toll and a bridge over the Río Queguay, and at km404 the start of Ruta 26 east to Tacuarembó. Ruta 3 crosses the Arroyo Guaviyú at km431, with the **Termas de Guaviyú** (↘ *754 2323;* e *guaviyu@paysandu.gub.uy;* ⊕ *all year; US$2*) to the left. This, like the Termas de Almirón, is run by the department, keeping prices moderate, although it's not the most modern of resorts. There are seven pools, with a covered complex at the north end and open pools to the south. In the centre are bungalows (*$$*) and to the south by the river a large campsite (↘ *750 4049; US$2.40 pp;* ⊕ *all year; $$*). Bikes and pedalos can be rented and there's a call centre and a butcher's shop to supply all those barbecues.

Across the main road is the Villaggio Hotel Termal (↘ *750 4041; www.complejovillaggio.com; dinner US$12; $$$$*).

From km453.2 a road leads west to the **Parque Histórico Meseta de Artigas**, where a 37m granite column bearing a bust of Artigas, 45m above the river, was raised in 1899 to mark the place where the first independent Uruguayan government was declared in 1815.

At km473.5 there's a turning to the left to the Hotel Termal Los Naranjos (↘ *73 69999; www.losnaranjos.com.uy; $$$$$*), the best in the Daymán area, with open pools amidst fields of orange trees. From km475 Camino Tierras Coloradas leads back southeast for 13km to the **Termas de San Nicanor** (↘ *73 02209*), where a former *estancia* is now the centre of one of the smaller and quieter hot-spring resorts, with two pools (slightly hotter than others, up to 40°C), four lakes (12–75ha), *cabañas* and camping. Horseriding is available at both places.

At km477 Ruta 3 crosses a long bridge over the Río Daymán (with good gallery forest for birding to the west) and into Salto department.

SALTO DEPARTMENT

SALTO Slightly smaller than Paysandú by most counts, Salto (at km487, two hours from Paysandú) is also a port shipping meat, leather and, more recently, citrus fruit down the Río Uruguay. It also trades with Argentina via the highway and railway across the Salto Grande dam, just to the north. For tourists it's a transport hub, and the centre of the thermal spas of the region.

It was founded here, in 1756, because of the *salto* (waterfall or rapid) blocking navigation just upstream. In 1811 Artigas led the Exodo del Pueblo Oriental

(Exodus of the Eastern People), crossing the Río Uruguay here with perhaps 10,000 soldiers and civilians into what is now Argentina. Development took off after 1830, and from 1860 considerable numbers of European immigrants arrived, as did the railway. The first Tannat grapes in Uruguay were planted here (see page 142), and by 1900 there were perhaps 100 vineyards around the city. Between 1880 and 1894 General Teófilo Córdoba ran the city, building the theatre, hospital, racecourse and other monuments.

Getting there

By car Arriving from the south on Ruta 3, the built-up area starts at the Rotonda La Gaviota (km483½), where there are some industrial buildings by Eladio Dieste to the right. Four blocks south of the bus terminal, in the northeastern part of the city, Calle Uruguay leads to the central Plaza Artigas, ten blocks west, continuing another seven blocks to Plaza Treinta y Tres and two more to the river.

By bus Buses arrive at the modern Terminal Salto about 1km east of the centre (*Avda Blandengues/Ruta 3 & Avenida Batlle*), which has a *depósito de equipaje* (*baggage store;* ⊕ *04.30–24.00*) and incorporates the Salto Shopping mall, with cinemas, restaurants, an exchange office and ATMs. Agencia Central (Chadre/Sabelin) has a booking office on Uruguay 711, just east of Sarandí (↘ *73 31717;* e *salto@ agenciacentral.com.uy;* ⊕ *09.00–20.30 Mon–Fri, 09.00–13.00 Sat*). Nuñez has a ticket office at Uruguay 930 (↘ *73 35581*).

From Montevideo Sabelin runs six buses a day (four direct on Ruta 3 and two via Durazno) and Cynsa/Nuñez runs three (via Trinidad); there's also El Norteño's overnight service to Salto and Bella Unión. Two of the Sabelin services run via Colonia, Mercedes, Fray Bentos and Paysandú, and continue to Bella Unión. From Paysandú Agencia Central (including Sabelin) runs seven buses a day, Alonso runs three (via Guichón), and Nuñez and Quebracho two each.

Heading north, Cotabu runs two services a day via Belén and Bella Unión to Artigas; Jote Ele (ie: JL) has two to Artigas via Rutas 31 and 4, and COA has three (two on Sundays) by this route. Agencia Central has a departure to Tacuarembó and Rivera at 03.00 on Mondays and Fridays only. Flecha Bus runs two buses a day to Concordia (Argentina), with connections to Buenos Aires and elsewhere, and COIT has two buses a week direct from Salto to Buenos Aires.

By ferry You can also go to and from Concordia in Argentina by *lancha (ferry; 08.35, 12.00, 14.30 & 18.30 daily, returning about 15mins later)*. Tickets (*US$2.20*) are sold from a basic shack at the entry to the port, at the west end of Brasil.

Getting around

By bus Bus 1, heading east on Brasil, is probably the best to take from the centre to the terminal. Note that north–south streets have different names on either side of Calle Uruguay.

By car Cars can be rented from Rentacar Daymán (*Amorim 368;* ↘ *73 40863, 34892,* m *9973 1188;* e *rentacar@adinet.com.uy; www.rentacardayman.com;* ⊕ *08.00–22.00 daily; also Brasil & Blandengues, 2 blocks from the terminal;* ↘ *73 41003,* m *9858 8715*) or Dollar (*Terminal Salto, Local 1;* ↘ *73 42347*).

By bike See page 291.

Tourist information There's a tourist information stand (⊕ *06.30–18.30 daily*) at the Terminal Salto. The main tourism office (*Uruguay 1052;* ↘ *73 25194, 34096;*

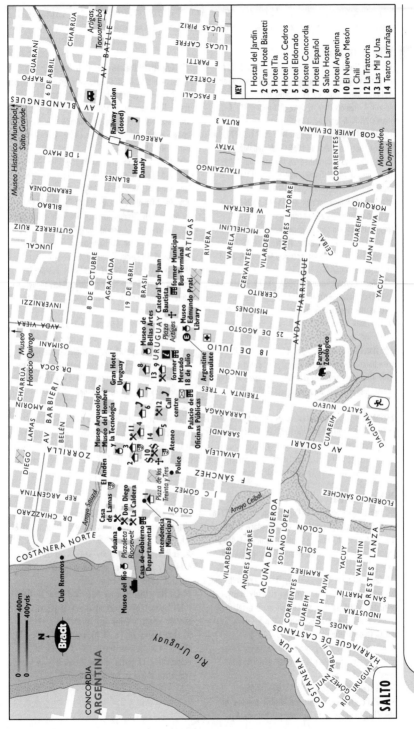

KEY
1 Hostal del Jardín
2 Gran Hotel Biasetti
3 Hotel Tía
4 Hotel Los Cedros
5 Hotel Eldorado
6 Hostal Concordia
7 Hotel Español
8 Salto Hostel
9 Hotel Argentina
10 El Nuevo Mesón
11 Chili
12 La Trattoria
13 Las Mil y Una
14 Teatro Larrañaga

SALTO

e turismo@salto.gub.uy; ⏲ 08.00–19.45 Mon–Fri, 08.00–12.45 Sat) is understaffed and usually busy taking bookings for the Arapey hot springs resort.

⌂ Where to stay

⌂ **Gran Hotel Uruguay** Brasil 891; ☏ 73 35197; **e** hoteluru@adinet.com.uy; www.hoteluruguay.com. A 1960s block with 40 AC rooms, this is very decent & friendly. Rooms have flat-screen TVs & there's Wi-Fi & parking. $$$

⌂ **Hostel Concordia** Uruguay 749; ☏ 73 32735. An historic place, opened in 1865, with delightful cool patios, this was refurbished at the start of 2009. The room in which Gardel stayed in 1912 is preserved as a museum. $$$

⌂ **Hotel Eldorado** Sarandí 20; ☏ 73 25042; **e** hotelleldorado@adinet.com.uy; www.eldoradosalto.com. A good business/tourist-class place. Rooms have AC, cable TV, Wi-Fi or ADSL. There's a PC for internet access, 24hr bar & good buffet b/fast. $$$

⌂ **Hotel Español** Brasil 822/826; ☏ 73 34048, 73 35400; **e** hespanol@adinet.com.uy. Not quite as nice as the adjacent Gran Hotel Uruguay, this has slightly dark rooms with AC & cable TV. Parking & b/fast inc, & there's internet access. $$$

⌂ **Hotel Los Cedros** Uruguay 657; ☏ 73 33984/5; www.hotelloscedros.com. A decent but dated place with 70 rooms, with AC & cable TV. There's internet access, buffet b/fast & a garage. $$$

⌂ **Gran Hotel Biasetti** Zorrilla & Brasil; ☏ 73 32141. Built in 1878 & once very grand, this is now run-down & eccentric, though not as bad as it seems from outside, & actually quite busy. Rooms are basic but come with bathroom & fan; there's TV in the lobby, with fine leather chairs & a circular bench. No b/fast. $$

⌂ **Hotel Argentina** Uruguay 892 & Soca; ☏ 73 29931. A discreet old-style place; some rooms have fans, some AC & cable TV. $$

⌂ **Hotel Danaly** Agraciada 2060; ☏ 73 35784; **e** hoteldanaly@adinet.com.uy. The only hotel near the bus terminal, a decent budget place with fan or AC as well as cable TV, barbecue & a garage. $$

⌂ **Hostal del Jardín** Colón 47 between Artigas & Uruguay; ☏ 73 24274, 73 32325; **e** hostalj@adinet.com.uy. A nice enough little place, though not quite the boutique it wants to be, with AC, cable TV & very soft mattresses. $$

⌂ **Hotel Tía** Brasil 566; ☏ 73 26574. Excellent value, this rambling place (definitely not disabled-friendly, with steps all over the place) has regular rooms with cable TV & private bathroom, & bigger ones in a 3rd-floor extension. There's a Wi-Fi signal only on the balcony (with swings). $$

Hostel The brand-new **Salto Hostel**, in an historic house at Uruguay 941 (☏ 73 37157; **e** info@saltohostel.com, saltohostel@hotmail.com; www.saltohostel.com; ⏲ all year; $$) has enthusiastic young staff, dorms with bunk-beds and lockers, family rooms, a kitchen, garden, barbecue, rooftop terrace and free PC and Wi-Fi. Rates include breakfast, and you can rent bikes.

✕ Where to eat

✕ **Don Diego** Chiazzaro & Purificación; ☏ 73 29376. Near the port, this simple & tasteful place is one of the best in town, although with a somewhat dated menu. Grilled fish, fondue & pasta are specialities. $$$$

✕ **Casa de Lamas** Chiazzaro 20; ☏ 73 29376. In an historic house near the port, this is fairly classy, with the usual meat & pasta options & a relatively good range of vegetarian dishes. $$$

✕ **La Caldera** Uruguay 235; ☏ 73 24648. A pleasant, rustic-styled place with a varied menu including parrillada, pasta & tasty desserts, & a good wine list. $$$

✕ **La Trattoria** Uruguay 754; ☏ 73 36660; ⏲ 09.00–01.00 daily. In the historic building of the Club Uruguay (with an internal balcony &

murals painted in 1945), this serves a good & very affordable range of chivitos, burgers, other meats & fish, pastas & pizzas. $$$

✕ **El Nuevo Mesón** Uruguay 564; ☏ 73 23726. A friendly parrilla that also serves pasta (but not pizza) & offers great value. $$

✕ **Las Mil y Una** Uruguay 906; ☏ 73 26331. Hardly 1,001 options, but a decent choice of pizzas, chivitos, salads & other fast foods. $$

✕ **Chili** Suárez 24; ☏ 73 23314; ⏲ 11.00–13.30, 19.30–24.00, Sun lunchtime only. A choice of 27 empanadas, 17 pizzas, quiche & salads – & yet the vegetarian choice is pretty standard. $

Shopping There's a big MultiAhorro supermarket in the Terminal Shopping, as well as Artè Salto (for leather) and other shops. There are three supermarkets on the three blocks of Uruguay between Larrañaga and Plaza Artigas. There's a big general market on Sunday mornings (food, clothes, jewellery and so on) on the Plaza Deportivo, on the way to the terminal. For genuine gaucho gear, go to the Talabartaria La Criolla (*Artigas 1005, just east of Rincón*).

Other practicalities

Banks There are plenty of ATMs on the 500 block of Uruguay (the first east of Plaza Treinta y Tres), and at the bus terminal, where there's also the Indumex exchange office (*Local 12;* ⊕ *10.00–21.00 daily*); there are also exchange offices on Uruguay.

Bike hire There's a big bike shop at Grito & Brasil, and they can be rented from the Salto Hostel (see opposite).

Communications The main post office is on Artigas just east of Larrañaga (⊕ *09.00–17.00 Mon–Fri, 08.00–13.00 Sat*), with postal services in various *farmacías* (including on the northeastern corner of Plaza Treinta y Tres) and in Salto Shopping at the terminal. Antel has four call centres (*Asencio 55;* ⊕ *09.00–20.00 Mon–Sat, 10.00–19.00 Sun; Artigas 1040;* ⊕ *09.00–19.00 Mon–Sat, 10.00–18.00 Sun; Artigas 1407;* ⊕ *08.00–24.00 daily; Blandengues 255, two blocks south of the terminal;* ⊕ *08.00–22.30 Mon–Fri, 09.00–13.00, 17.30–22.30 Sat–Sun*). There's public Wi-Fi on Plaza Artigas, and a weak signal on Plaza Treinta y Tres.

Consulate The Inspectoría de Migración is at Artigas 450 (✆ *73 32860;* e *i16salto@dnm.minterior.gub.uy*) and at the Salto Grande dam (✆ *73 26199*). The Argentine consulate is on the south side of Plaza Artigas (*Artigas 1162;* ✆ *73 32931;* e *consar_salto@yahoo.com.ar;* ⊕ *09.00–14.00 Mon–Fri*).

Emergency services The hospital (*18 de Julio 351 & Varela;* ✆ *73 32944*) is just south of Plaza Artigas. Police headquarters are at Artigas 450 (✆ *73 27031*) on the south side of Plaza Treinta y Tres, and there's a police station on 19 de Abril between Juncal and Gutierrez Ruiz.

What to see and do The central plazas Artigas and Treinta y Tres feel a bit strange – spacious, nicely laid out but a bit dead. Unusually for Uruguay, the focus of business life is along the main drag, Calle Uruguay, rather than on a plaza, making the city feel more European than many, with attractive streets with cafés and shops to explore.

Two blocks east of Plaza Artigas, on Córdoba between Uruguay and Artigas, is one of Eladio Dieste's best-known works, the former municipal bus terminal (1973–74), now the Agencia Central parcels depot, with its striking curved brick vaults, held by just a thin layer of concrete (see page 34). There are quite a few examples of Dieste's work in Salto, including another bus station, the Terminal Rural (*Latorre & Larrañaga*), a water tower and a boat shed at the Club Remeros (*Costanera Norte & Agraciada*).

On the east side of Plaza Artigas the **Catedral San Juan Bautista** (Cathedral of St John the Baptist), built in 1897, is large and impressive, with a Neoclassical façade, fine marble columns with classical capitals indoors, and a Neorenaissance ceiling. On the south side of the plaza, the library (⊕ *summer 07.30–12.30 Mon–Sat, winter 08.00–18.00 Mon–Fri*) houses the Museo Edmundo Prati, with works by the sculptor and others (the great equestrian statue of Artigas in the centre of the plaza is by Prati). Immediately behind the western side of the plaza the Mercado 18 de

Julio is a fairly standard cast-iron market hall, built in 1868, that now houses temporary art and photography exhibitions. On its south side is the Saltoko Euskaldunen Taldea (Salto Basque Group), which hosts social and cultural events for the local Basque community.

To the north of the former market is the tourism office and, across the road, the **Bellas Artes (Art Museum)**, properly the Museo María Irene Olarreaga Gallino (*Uruguay 1067;* ⊕ *15.00–20.00 Tue–Sun; free*). In this ornate Belle Epoque mansion is one of the largest and best art collections outside Montevideo, with a gaucho by Blanes, *Los Ombúes* by Carlos Roberto Rúfalo (1880–1975), a roomful of fine Cúneos (including two of the port of Salto), works by Rafael Barrada, Petrona Viera and Pedro Figari, and a maquette by José Belloni. Another room is given over to Carmelo de Arzadun (1888–1968), a pretty good painter from Salto. At the rear, the Sala Carmelo de Arzadun is actually a modern extension for temporary exhibitions, leading to the garden. On the stairs are more paintings by local artists and the Hungarian-born José Cziffery; upstairs, in addition to the original bathroom (with something like a stand-up jacuzzi) there's more contemporary work, by artists such as María Freira, Manuel Pailós, Bruno Widmann, Eduardo Sarlós (fine ink and gouache drawings) and Alfredo Ghierra. There's a room of work by Eriberto Prati, born in Paysandú and not very interesting.

Four blocks west along Uruguay and immediately north on Lavalleja is the Teatro Larrannaga, designed by British engineer Robert Wilkinson and opened in 1882, a grand Neoclassical theatre with 850 seats and superb acoustics. Currently being restored, it should reopen in 2010. Just across the road to the north, the former Mercado Central, built in 1909, now houses the **Museo del Hombre y la Tecnología** (*Museum of Man and Technology; Brasil 511;* ⊕ *14.00–19.00 Tue–Sun; free*). Apart from images of Gutenberg, Galileo and Leonardo, this is probably not what you'd expect, focusing on local history, from the development of the cattle industry and gaucho culture in the Jesuit missions, with an intact *pulpería* and a later Art Nouveau *confitería*, followed by citrus presses, typewriters, sewing machines and a battered 1980 model of the Salto Grande dam. There are some 10,000-year-old shaped stones from the Cultura Tangarupaense (Tangarupa culture), some later ceramics and the 2,000-year-old skeleton of a hunter from Salto Grande. The rather limited **Museo de Arqueología and Ciencias Naturales** (*Museum of Archaeology and Natural Sciences; same hours; free*) is downstairs, with a separate entry to the west. Here you'll see petroglyphs from north of the Río Negro and pictographs to the south, ceramics from 2,500 years ago, and bits of megafauna killed by hunters 9,500 years ago, such as sabre-toothed tiger (Smilodon), Mylodon, Hippidion, Pampatherium and the hippo-like Toxodon.

A block north and a block west, the Arroyo Sauzal leads to the Río Uruguay, past the former station of the Ferrocarril del Noroeste (Northwestern Railway) (1886, also by Robert Wilkinson) at Delgado & 19 de Abril, and opposite it the Sala Teatral El Andén (Platform Theatre), in a former goods shed. From here you can follow 19 de Abril parallel to the stream for three blocks to the *costanera* (waterfront road) and the Río Uruguay. To the left (south) is the *Aduana* (Customs), a fine pile built in 1829, and on its south side the shady little Plazoleta Roosevelt, laid out in 1946 around a fountain donated in 1930 by the Brazilian embassy. These look out on to the old port, with the Resguardo del Puerto (port offices) now housing the Museo del Río (Museum of the River), currently closed for refurbishment.

From south of the Plazoleta, Calle Uruguay leads east past the **Casa de Gobierno Departamental** (*Uruguay 1324*), an attractive single-storey mansion, and the Intendencia Municipal (*Uruguay & Gómez*), built in 1887. This looks over Plaza Treinta y Tres, a spacious square with palm trees and a fountain, remodelled in 1999, with the Salesians' church of Nuestra Señora del Carmen on its east side.

Built in 1855, this has an ornate façade and a simple cream-coloured Neoclassical interior housing a statue of the Virgin by a Guaraní woodcarver. Its bells (one dating from 1686) were brought from the Jesuit missions in 1832. On the south side of the plaza is the modern police headquarters, with the Neoclassical portico of the former *jefatura* (1862) still standing in front.

Immediately east of the plaza at Artigas 529 is the Ateneo (1895), with a 250-seat theatre, and a block further on, at Artigas 651, the Sociedad Italiana (1884). Another two blocks east, the Palacio de Oficinas Públicas (*Palace of Public Offices; Artigas & Treinta y Tres*) is a grand block designed in 1925 by Veltroni, with a tower that is one of the city's main landmarks.

From here it's six blocks south on Treinta y Tres to the rural bus terminal (see page 291) and, just east at the south end of Rincón, the **Parque Zoológico** (⊕ *10.00–19.00 daily; US$1*), one of Uruguay's best zoos. Between 2003 and 2005 it built new pens for lions, tigers and jaguars, and also has boars, foxes, peccaries, llamas, ñandues, emus, zebras, monkeys, deer, parrots, various raptors (including vultures which can fly in and out of open pens), caymans, snakes and turtles. One of Uruguay's four breeding herds of *venado de campo* (pampas deer) is here. There's also a summer theatre in the park.

Three blocks north of the new bus terminal is the Parque Solari (*Avda Blandengues*), an attractive and well-maintained place for a stroll; laid out in the late 19th century in Romantic style, it has a replica of the *Toilet of Venus* (the original Greek sculpture is in the Vatican Museum) on an islet. Immediately to the north across Avenida Amorin (opposite a 24-hour ANCAP station), the Chalet la Casona, formerly owned by the family of the novelist Enrique Amorim (1900–60), houses the **Museo Histórico Municipal** (*Municipal History Museum;* ⊕ *13.00–18.00 Tue–Sun; free*). Newly remodelled in 2009, it's a rural-style house with a large garden and carts in a shed; it has three rooms with historical relics, and a so-called Cultural Factory, for events and school groups. To the rear, Amorim's home, the Chalet Las Nubes (*Avda Amorim & Avda Artigas; not open to the public*), was built to plans by Le Corbusier.

Five blocks west is the **Museo Horacio Quiroga** (⊕ *14.00–19.00 Tue–Sun; free*), home of another local author (1879–1937), displaying first editions, personal objects and his bicycle; it also has lovely palm-shaded gardens. Quiroga's birthplace at Uruguay 860 is marked by a plaque.

The riverside *costaneras* are very popular for recreation. To the south the Costanera Sur passes fine villas, monuments to Quiroga and Lorca, two former *saladeros* (meat-salting plants), an altar where Pope John Paul II celebrated mass and, at Arenitas Blancas, 5km south, a fine hilltop viewpoint. The Costanera Norte passes the old railway jetty and the rowing club, founded in 1915, with its roof by Dieste (see page 34). The road is lined with beaches for 3km to the Parador Ayuí, a restaurant at the site where Artigas crossed the river in 1811.

AROUND SALTO

Termas de Daymán (*www.termasdayman.com;* ⊕ *07.00–23.00 daily; US$2*) It's 9km south to the Termas de Daymán, the largest and liveliest of all the hot baths in Uruguay, with families and busloads of youngsters pouring in on summer weekends. This has the hottest water of the Uruguayan springs (up to 44°C, from the Aquifer Guaraní, 2km down), and in most of the ten pools it's frankly too hot to swim much. There's cooler water at the Acuamanía water park (☏ *73 69222, 9322; www.acuamania.com;* ⊕ *mid-Sep–Easter 10.30–19.30 daily, except 23–25 Dec, 29–31 Dec; US$6.50, 3 days US$13*), with slides up to 70m long, pool basketball and other games, and mini-golf. The waters are meant to be good for rheumatic, neurological and musculoskeletal disorders, and for stress.

The baths are owned by Salto department and are surrounded by a great range of hotels (with 3,000 beds) and campsites; there's also access to the banks of the Río Daymán, immediately to the south. The 'Puerto-Termas' bus (*hourly 06.30–22.30, returning 07.00–23.00; US$0.60*) runs from the port and along Brasil to Ruta 3 (a couple of blocks south of the terminal).

Where to stay The hotels are immediately to the east of the entry to the baths.

Posada del Siglo XIX Barrio Jardines, just north of the resort (take Calle 10 just north of km478, then north on Los Sauces); 73 69955; e psxix01@adinet.com.uy; www.posadasigloxix.com.uy. There's nothing 19th-century about this place but it's classy enough, with nice gardens & swimming pools; internet access is available only in the reception area & the best rooms. $$$$–$$

Hostería Aguasol 73 69145/55; www.aguasol.com.uy. The nearest hotel to the river, at the south end of the resort, this is a good, fairly modern place with its own covered thermal pool & jacuzzi, gym, bikes, table tennis & a pool table, as well as Wi-Fi & parking. $$$

Hotel Aguas Calientes 73 69840; e aguascalientes@adinet.com.uy. A decent, modern place with no swimming pool but rooms with AC, cable TV, Wi-Fi & continental b/fast. $$$

Hotel Casablanca 73 69325. Friendly but slightly drab, this has rooms with AC, cable TV, & its own thermal pool. $$$

Hotel Géminis Calle Timbó s/n; 73 69108; www.geminishotel.com.ar. An apart-hotel at the south end of the resort, this has apts for 2–7, with kitchenette & microwave, cable TV & parking. B/fast is available. $$$

La Posta del Daymán 73 69901; www.lapostadeldayman.com. The only hotel west of the road, on a spacious site north of the baths, there's a 3-star hotel, hostal (simple rooms, though still with private bathrooms & Wi-Fi) & camping (US$4 pp), with an excellent restaurant (from

07.00 daily) with parrilla, pasta, fish & snacks, & choice of terrace or AC room. $$$–$$

Apart-Hotel del Pasaje 73 69932, 9661, m 9893 2932; e pasaje@adinet.com.uy; www.hoteldelpasaje.com. Facing the Acuamanía entrance, 18 new rooms have been added to the 19 apts & 4 cabañas, as well as a cafetería. Room rates include b/fast, those for apts & cabañas come with barbecue instead. All have AC, cable TV, Wi-Fi & access to a swimming pool. $$

Bungalows Archi 73 69959; e b.archi@adinet.com.uy; www.archi.com.uy. Motel-style suites each have dbl & sgl bed, kitchenette with microwave, AC, cable TV & parrilla. $$

Complejo Turístico San Francisco 73 69690; e aparthotel@starmedia.com. An apart-hotel opposite Acuamanía, very well set up & presented, with apts with cable TV, kitchenette & barbecue, & lots of PCs at reception, plus a bakery & other shops. $$

Hostal Canela 73 69121; e hcanela@adinet.com.uy; www.termasdayman.com/canela. HI-affiliated youth hostel a little way north of the resort (turn east at km478.6, then at once north on Los Sauces), a bungalow with 7 apts, swimming pool & kitchen. $$

Termal Daymán de Caute-Antel 73 69960, 73 69995; e termal@cauteantel.com.uy. A nice modern place (apart from the lack of internet access), with swimming pool & suites with AC & jacuzzi or 4/6-person cabañas with kitchenette & microwave. $$

Salto Grande At Salto Grande, 15km north of Salto and reached by a free bus service, are Uruguay's largest dam, hot baths, another water park and an isolated hotel.

The 4ha Parque Acuatico (*10.00–20.00 daily; US$5*) has three large pools, artificial waves and slides including the 73m-long Black Hole.

The **Represa Binacional de Salto Grande** (Salto Grande Binational Dam) was built in 1974–79 (with 14 Russian-supplied turbines of 135,000 kW each). When the 78km^2 lake is full, it can supply over half of Uruguay's consumption (with a similar amount generated on the Argentine side); even so, a 300kW solar plant is also being installed here, with Japanese government aid. You can take a guided visit (73 26131; e rrppmi@saltogrande.org; www.saltogrande.org; 08.00–16.00 daily except 1 Jan, 1 May & 25 Dec; free). These are also possible on the Argentine side, on a more limited schedule; take the signposted road to

Relaciones Publicas from just south of the Prefectura and the roundabout (at about km508) for the road over the dam.

On a headland just south of the water park and 2km from the road, the **Hotel Horacio Quiroga** (☎ *73 34411;* e *hhq@adinet.com.uy; www.hotelhoracioquiroga.com;* $$$$$) is an unassuming low, red-brick hotel that used to house army officers guarding the dam; it's adequate but still a bit institutional and not a destination in itself. It now has its own hot pool, sporting facilities, Wi-Fi, 80 air-conditioned rooms and a decent restaurant. With 218ha to explore, you can take a bike or a golf-cart, or arrange horseriding.

The green Trans 19 bus runs several times a day from Salto, picking up outside the bus terminal and opposite the Parque Solari, passing the turnings to the dam and the hotel, and after 15 minutes reaching the Parque Acuático. The hotel operates its own free transfers from a *sala VIP* in Salto (*Avda Blandengues, immediately south of the bus terminal*).

Termas de Arapey The most upmarket and exclusive of the thermal resorts is the Termas del Arapey (☎ *768 2005/6, 0800 8498 (TF); www.arapeythermal.com.uy*), reached by an asphalt road which leads 19km east from km548 of Ruta 3. A daily bus is operated by Argentur (*Uruguay 892 & Soca, Salto;* ☎ *73 29931; Termas del Arapey;* ☎ *768 2028; US$6, US$10 return*) from the Termas de Daymán (*10.00*) and Salto (*11.00, from south of the terminal on Avda Batlle; returning 19.00 daily*). Argentur can also arrange private *remise* transfers. A daily Chadre bus from Salto to Bella Unión also runs via Arapey.

There's accommodation in the Hotel Municipal Termas del Arapey (☎ *73 34096*), which offers *bungalows* ($$) and so-called *moteles* ($). This is the only resort in Uruguay that offers all-inclusive stays all year round, with rates including four buffet meals a day (including *merienda* or high tea). There are two restaurants, the better being the Restaurante Paradise (☎ *768 2441; www.restauranteparadise.com*), open every day of the year for buffet breakfast and à la carte lunch and dinner. There are six thermal pools and over 200 rooms, plus gyms, a business centre and an Ana Aslan anti-ageing clinic.

There's a large campsite (☎ *73 34096;* ⏲ *all year;* $), to the right of the entry, situated beside the Río Arapey.

7

The Interior

Away from the coast and the Río Uruguay, the interior of Uruguay – Artigas, Rivera, Tacuarembó, Durazno, Flores, Treinta y Tres and Cerro Largo departments, plus eastern parts of Río Negro, Paysandú and Salto (otherwise covered in *Chapter 6*) – is largely empty, aside from considerable numbers of cattle. This is gaucho country; passing through, perhaps on a bus towards the Brazilian frontier, you're likely to see a man in a beret, with baggy trousers tucked into leather boots, getting off at a gate in the middle of nowhere, usually with a walk of a couple of kilometres to his *estancia*. There are quite a few *estancias* that you can stay on here, offering perhaps less luxurious but more authentic accommodation than many of those to the south, with some real down-home farming experiences.

Although the soil is thin and unsuitable for growing crops, in recent years there has been increasing forestry, notably of eucalyptus for paper pulp. In addition, some vineyards have been established near Rivera, where there's also a limited amount of mining.

In the centre of the country (between Tacuarembó and Durazno departments) the artificial lake behind the Rincón del Bonete (or Gabriel Terra) dam can only be crossed in a few places, where resorts with watersports facilities have been established. At the dam, 22km east of Paso de los Toros, is the country's largest hydro-electric station, opened in 1949, with a capacity of 160 MW. Other attempts (especially by the military government) to boost the region's development have had little effect, and the departments along the northern border remain the hottest and slowest-moving part of the country, where the main activity sometimes seems to be selling bootleg Brazilian DVDs.

ARTIGAS DEPARTMENT

BELLA UNIÓN Tiny Bella Unión, in the northwestern corner of the country, seems like the town the government forgot, with its awful roads and sidewalks and an air of suspended animation. In truth, the town was victimised under the dictatorship, for this is the birthplace of the Tupamaros urban guerrilla movement.

Raúl Sendic (1926–89) was a labour movement lawyer who founded unions for rural workers such as those working in the sugarcane plantations in the late 1950s. Vicious repression led him to believe that armed struggle was the only solution, beginning in 1963 with a break-in at a gun shop in Colonia. Sendic was captured in 1970 and survived years of torture before being released in 1985 and dying in Paris in 1989. There's a monument to him at the junction of Artigas with Ruta 3. Sugarcane workers still live today in remarkable poverty, partly the result of price volatility which leads to frequent lay-offs. As cane waste can now be used to produce alcohol for fuel, it's possible that the industry will stabilise.

0 ━━━━━━ 50km
0 ━━━━━━ 50 miles

N

Bradt

BRASIL

Rivera

Cuchilla de Santa Ana

Tranqueras

R27

R5

Rivera

Minas de Corrales

Río Tacuarembó

Vichadero

Aceguá

Ansina

Cuchilla Grande

Isidoro Noblía

uarembó

R26

R6

Río Negro

R8

R7

Melo

Fraile Muerto

Cerro Largo

Río Branco

R18

Lago Merín

San Gregorio de Polanco

R7

Río Tacuarí

La Paloma

Tupambaé

Quebrada de los Cuervos

Blanquillo

Santa Clara de Olimar

Vergara

Laguna Merín

Treinta y Tres

Cerro Chato

R8

BRASIL

R6

Río Yí

Treinta Tres

R17

La Charqueada

Sarandí del Yí

R19

Cebollatí

Cuchilla Grande

José Pedro Varela

Río Olimar Grande

R14

San Luis Al Medio

José Batlle Y Ordóñez

18 De Julio

Cebollatí

Chuy

Alejandro Gallinal

R7

Lascano

Cuchilla de las Averías

R9

ATLANTIC OCEAN

Lavalleja

R8

Rocha

Bañados de San Miguel

Laguna Negra

Punta de la Coronilla

7

Founded in 1829 by Rivera and named after the meeting place of the Río Uruguay and the Río Cuareim, and of Uruguay, Brazil and Argentina, Bella Unión is home to the ALUR sugar mill and the Calvinor winery, but is of little interest except for the minor border crossings by boat to Monte Caseros in Argentina and by road (Ruta 3) to Barra do Quaraí and Uruguaiana in Brazil.

Getting there

By bus Buses heading north and east from Salto (see *Chapter 6*) join Ruta 3 near km481. Those to Tacuarembó continue eastwards, while those for Bella Unión head north on Ruta 3, passing the junction to the Salto Grande dam and the crossing to Argentina at km494. To the north is cattle country (with some sunflowers and sugarcane), broken by a few *arroyos* with gallery forest (km509, km541 and km613). It's 1 hour 40 minutes to Bella Unión, with a left turn just after km623 on to Artigas, leading to the central Plaza 25 de Mayo, 13 blocks west.

Bus offices are near the plaza: Chadre (*Agencia Central; Rivera;* ⎯ *77 92148;* e *bellaunion@agenciacentral.com.uy;* ⊕ *08.30–12.30, 16.00–22.00 Mon–Fri*) and Cotabu (*Artigas;* ⊕ *approx 06.00–08.00, 10.00–12.00, 14.00–15.00, 17.00–21.00 daily*). The main local bus company is El Norteño (*Rivera 480;* ⎯ *77 92676, 77 92385; 1–2 departures to Montevideo via Salto daily, 2 to Salto only*).

There are occasional buses from the plaza to Barra do Quaraí, but it's usually easier to take a *remise* (*US$2*) and then a local bus to Uruguaiana, from where there are bus connections across southern Brazil.

By ferry A small pedestrian ferry to Monte Caseros in Argentina (*09.00, 13.00 & 16.00 Mon–Fri; US$4*) leaves from the short pier at the west end of Attilio Ferrandis.

Entering Uruguay from Brazil, you must get your exit stamp from the Policía Federal in Uruguaiana.

Where to stay and eat

The only place to stay is the **Hotel Oriente** (*Rivera between Suárez & Asencio, 6 blocks east of the plaza; AC rooms with private bathrooms or rooms with fans & shared bathroom; b/fast extra; $$*). You can camp, with no facilities other than a bar, at the picnic area by the Río Uruguay, or 8km north at the Balneario Los Pinos, where there are better facilities, including electricity.

La Taberna, on the southeastern corner of the plaza (north of Artigas), and **Los Amigos**, a block east, offer pizza and grilled meats.

Other practicalities

Banks There's an ATM at the northwestern corner of the plaza.

Communications The post office is at Rivera 800 (⊕ *09.00–14.30 Mon–Fri, 09.00–12.00 Sat*). Antel's call centre is on Rivera a block east of the plaza (⊕ *09.00–20.00 Mon–Sat, 10.00–18.00 Sun*). There's public Wi-Fi on the main plaza and at the school on its west side.

Consulate For visa issues, the Inspectoría de Migración office is on the southeastern corner of the plaza (*opposite La Taberna, north of Artigas;* ⊕ *09.00–14.30 Mon–Fri*). Uruguayan Immigration border post is at the bridge to Brazil (⎯ *77 92080*) and in town at Romeo Bianchi & Artigas (⎯ *779 2835;* e *i05bellaunion@ dnm.minterior.gub.uy*).

Markets For food shopping, head for the Super San Jorge (*just off the plaza;* ⊕ *08.00–13.00, 15.00–23.00 Mon–Fri, 08.00–13.30, 15.00–23.00 Sat, 09.00–13.30 Sun*), or the small shop on the west side of the plaza.

What to see and do The grandest building in town is the Sociedad Fomento (1907–11) off the northeastern corner of the plaza. There's a small local museum and Sala de Exposiciones (*Exhibition Room; Rivera & Ferreira, diagonally opposite the post office;* ⊕ *from around 20.00*).

ARTIGAS Founded in 1852 (as Villa San Eugenio del Cuareim), the small city of Artigas (population over 40,000) is the remotest Uruguayan city from Montevideo, 612km away. It's known for heat – the summertime high temperature averages 33°C, with a recorded maximum of 42°C. In winter the average low is 7 °C, but temperatures as low as –4°C have been recorded. Artigas's average rainfall is 1,235mm per year.

Artigas department is known for its semi-precious stones, including agate and amethyst, from small mines just southeast of the city, especially near the Arroyo Catalán, also important for its archaeological finds.

Getting there
By car The most direct route from Salto is by Ruta 31 and Ruta 4. Travelling from Bella Unión, you'll head south towards Salto, then turn left at km619 on an asphalt road that bypasses the village of Tomás Gomensoro and continues as Ruta 30 across flatter grassland to the junction with Ruta 4. There you'll turn left and follow the main road (which becomes Avenida Artigas) in to Artigas (2½ hours from Bella Unión, 3 hours from Salto). From the bus terminal it's three blocks northwest to the main drag, Avenida Lecueder. Immediately to the left is the main Plaza Batlle, while the international bridge, the Puente de la Concordia, is ten blocks to the right.

By bus Turil has three services a day from Montevideo and Tacuarembó to Artigas (taking between seven and eight hours), and CUT (Corporación) has two a day. Jota Ele (JL) also has two buses a day from Salto to Artigas via Rutas 31 and 4, and COA has three (two on Sundays). Cotabu has two buses a day from Salto by this route and two via Bella Unión, and there's also a Sopel bus from Bella Unión at 17.00 (except Sundays). There are no buses from Rivera to Artigas – you can either take a bus through Brazil (from Santana do Livramento to Quaraí) and then a taxi across the border, or a local bus from Rivera as far as Tranqueras and wait there for a bus from the Tacuarembó direction to Artigas.

Traffic crosses freely between Artigas and Quaraí on the Brazilian side of the Río Cuareim (Rio Quaraí in Portuguese), but anyone going further must get their passport stamped on the Uruguayan side. Buses run along Lecueder and across the bridge, or you can take a taxi from the bus terminal or elsewhere. The Rodoviario (bus station) in Quaraí is just to the left (northwest), a block from the bridge. Entering from Brazil, you must get your exit stamp from the Policía Federal in Uruguaiana, then go to Uruguayan Immigration as you come off the bridge.

Tourist information The tourist information office (*18 de Julio 265;* ☎ *77 25202;* ⊕ *09.00–17.00 Mon–Fri*) is at the Uruguayan end of the bridge.

🏠 Where to stay

🏠 **Hotel del Norte** Lecueder 507; ☎ 77 22223; e hoteldelnorte@adinet.com.uy. Central & pretty nice, with patio, AC & a PC, but somewhat pricey. $$$

🏠 **Hotel Terminal** Herrera 438; ☎ 77 20599. This place looks far cheaper than it is. You'll find AC rooms with private bathroom & cable TV. $$$

🏠 **Hotel Concordia** Saravia 256; ☎ 77 22911. Large (over 50 rooms, with & without private bathrooms) & pretty comfortable for a 1-star hotel, but no b/fast. $$

🏠 **Hotel Ramón Correa** Lavalleja 466 & 495; ☎ 77 24666, 77 22736. A cheap place 100m east of the bus terminal, with 17 rooms, some with AC. $$

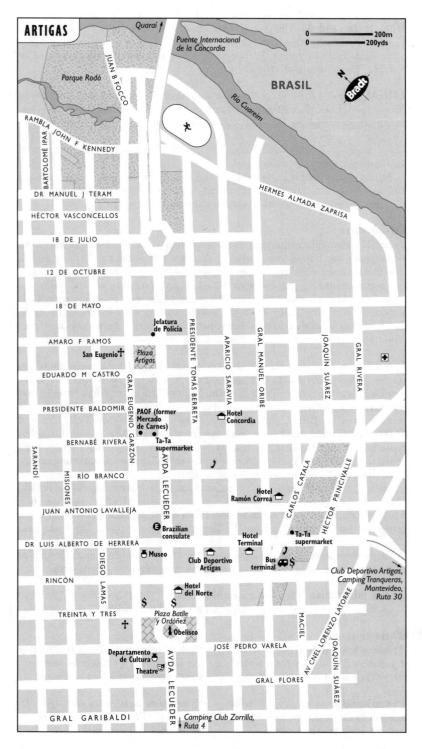

ARTIGAS

Quaraí

Puente Internacional
de la Concordia

Parque Rodó

BRASIL

Río Cuareim

0 ———— 200m
0 ———— 200yds

JUAN B FOCCO

RAMBLA JOHN F KENNEDY

HERMES ALMADA ZAPRISA

BARTOLOMÉ IPAR

DR MANUEL J TERAM

HÉCTOR VASCONCELLOS

18 DE JULIO

12 DE OCTUBRE

18 DE MAYO

Jefatura
de Policía

AMARO F RAMOS

San Eugenio †

Plaza
Artigas

PRESIDENTE TOMÁS BERRETA

APARICIO SARAVIA

GRAL MANUEL ORIBE

JOAQUIN SUÁREZ

GRAL RIVERA

EDUARDO M CASTRO

GRAL EUGENIO GARZÓN

PRESIDENTE BALDOMIR

PAOF (former
Mercado
de Carnes)

Hotel
Concordia

BERNABÉ RIVERA

Ta-Ta
supermarket

SARANDÍ

AVDA LECUEDER

RÍO BRANCO

MISIONES

CARLOS CATALÁ

HÉCTOR PRINCIVALLE

JUAN ANTONIO LAVALLEJA

Hotel
Ramón Correa

Brazilian
consulate

DR LUIS ALBERTO DE HERRERA

Museo

Hotel
Terminal

Ta-Ta
supermarket

DIEGO LAMAS

Club Deportivo
Artigas

Bus
terminal

Club Deportivo Artigas,
Camping Tranqueras,
Montevideo,
Ruta 30

RINCÓN

Hotel
del Norte

$

TREINTA Y TRES

$

Plaza Batle
y Ordóñez

Obelisco

MACIEL

AV CNEL LORENZO LATORRE

JOAQUIN SUÁREZ

Departamento
de Cultura

Theatre

JOSÉ PEDRO VARELA

AVDA LECUEDER

GRAL FLORES

GRAL GARIBALDI

Camping Club Zorrilla,
Ruta 4

302

Hostel There's hostel-style accommodation at the Club Deportivo Artigas in the centre of town at Berreta & Herrera (☎ 77 22532; $$).

Camping There are plenty of options for camping. One campsite is pretty central, at the **Camping Club Zorrilla** (*1km southwest on Avda Artigas/Ruta 4;* ☎ *77 24341;* $), which has a swimming pool and electricity. The others are to the south off Ruta 30, by the Río Cuareim: the **Club Deportivo Artigas** (☎ *77 23015;* $), about 2km east from km133 (you're supposed to check in at their hostel in town first, but you won't be turned away if you don't), and the Camping Parque Congreso de Abril (*Piedra Pintada;* ☎ *77 22261*), 4km southeast from km139½ by a dirt road (16km from the centre), where there's also a small menagerie. Both have swimming pools. The latter is reached by a bus (*07.30 & 17.00, returning 08.15 & 17.45, 30min later Sun*) from the roundabout by the international bridge and continuing past the terminal. Further south is the small, private Camping del Platano (*km140½;* ☎ *77 22000*), in trees to the west of Ruta 30.

Shopping For general shopping, there's a big Ta-Ta hypermarket across Herrera from the terminal, and a smaller Ta-Ta supermarket on Lecueder at Rivera. Lecueder is also lined with Free Shops, selling duty-free goods. Local specialities are amethyst and other semi-precious stones such as agate, available at shops such as Amatista (*Herrera 540;* ☎ *77 21053,* **m** *9977 2331;* **e** *sarnicola@hotmail.com*) and Carlos Ney Cigarán (*Sarandí 408;* ☎ *77 22030*); you can also visit some of the mines where these stones come from (see page 304).

Other practicalities

Banks There are ATMs at the terminal, on the northeastern corner of the plaza, and at Lecueder 299 and 533.

Car rental Cars can be rented from Rentacar Daymán (*Herrera & Oribe;* ☎ *77 32880,* **m** *9932 2805; www.rentacardayman.com*), opposite the bus terminal.

Communications The post office is at Beretta 385 (⏰ *09.00–17.00 Mon–Fri, 08.00–12.00 Sat*), and the Antel call centre is at Río Branco 379 (⏰ *09.00–20.00 Mon–Sat, 10.00–18.00 Sun*). There's public Wi-Fi on Plaza Batlle.

Consulate The Inspectoría de Migración is at 18 de Julio 29 (☎ *77 24041;* **e** *i04artigas@dnm.minterior.gub.uy*) and at the international bridge (☎ *77 24565*). The Brazilian vice-consulate is at Lecueder 432 (☎ *77 225414;* ⏰ *09.00–15.00 Mon–Fri*).

Emergency services The departmental hospital is at Castro & Rivera (☎ *77 23701*), and the police headquarters at Ramos & Lecueder (☎ *109, 77 23479*).

Events The city is famed for its *carnaval* celebrations, the longest in Uruguay (in terms of time period, not procession length), starting with the election of the *reina del carnaval* (Carnival Queen) in early February. It's more Brazilian than other Uruguayan *carnavals*, being the only one with samba 'schools' (up to a thousand strong) participating. Quaraí doesn't celebrate *carnaval*, so many of its population come to Artigas. Up to 20,000 spectators line Avenida Lecueder to watch the processions. Artigas itself has something of a Brazilian feel to it, with browner faces and rather Brazilian accents (and some Portuguese words, such as *churrasqueira* for a barbecue grill).

Carnaval is followed by Easter Week, marked with displays of horseriding and horse-breaking, and with traditional rural food and music. The 500 Millas del

Norte cycle race, a famous series of six 105km circuits around the city and nearby, has been held here every April since 1968.

What to see and do The modern bus terminal, opened in 2001, incorporates the former railway station, in use from 1891 to 1986; in a small plaza on its south side is a preserved steam locomotive, with level crossing signs and other pieces of railway gear. In front of the terminal is an *ibirapitá* tree brought from Paraguay in 1915, a descendant of one Artigas sat under in exile. There's also a clock donated by the town's Lebanese community in 1930.

Three blocks northwest is Avenida Lecueder, named after the department's first governor. Two blocks to the left is Plaza José Batlle y Ordoñez, covering two blocks on either side of the avenue. In the centre is a stumpy **obelisk**, raised in 1930 to the glory of the heroes of the independence struggle, made of 120 tonnes of granite from Pan de Azúcar. On the west side of the plaza is the **Departamento de Cultura** (*Varela 288;* ✆ 77 23094) with a theatre, municipal auditorium and library around the corner on Lecueder. Temporary exhibitions are held here, and this is the place to ask about events – and about whether the **Museo Departamental** (*Herrera & Garzón, two blocks northeast of the plaza*), with small collections of minerals, fossils, indigenous relics and stuffed animals, has reopened yet.

Three blocks northeast up Garzón, at Rivera 257, is the former **Mercado de Carnes (Meat Market)**, a Neoclassical structure by Juan Veltroni, inaugurated in 1919, refurbished in 2005 and now housing PAOF (Programa de Fortalecimiento de las Artes, Artesanías y Oficios), which trains young people in leatherworking, textiles and jewellery-making. There's a fine display of their work (including local amethysts) in the market hall, and a modern teaching wing.

Two blocks towards the bridge is **Plaza Artigas**, with a monument to the eponymous hero in the centre, raised in 1975 with 6,420 pieces of local agate on its base. On the northwestern side of the plaza is the church of **San Eugenio**, built in 1854, an unassuming little church which is only open a couple of times a week. On the northeastern side of the plaza is the castle-like **Jefatura de Policía** (police headquarters and jail), built in 1896 and the city's most emblematic building.

At the end of Avenida Lecueder is the 750m-long Puente de la Concordia, opened in 1968. By the river below are the Paseo 7 de Septiembre and Parque Rodó, with play and sports facilities, including a mountain-bike circuit, as well as a beach, recently closed by pollution. The campsite here is closed.

You can visit several of the **mines** from which the region's gemstones come. Some 60km south of Artigas, off Ruta 30 near the Arroyo Catalán, turn right at km178 towards La Bolsa and Meneses. It's 8km to the Mina las Amatistas, well set up for visits (*book at Lecueder 367;* ✆ 77 27833, 77 23627). La Limeña is an open-pit mine at km3 of the same road, and the Enzo Berardi y Andres Jacketti mine (✆ 77 25247) is further south at km16.

RIVERA DEPARTMENT

LUNAREJO AND LAURELES In the western corner of Rivera department, the 201km² **Parque Natural Regional Valle de Lunarejo** is one of Uruguay's newest protected areas, exciting those in the conservation and ecotourism businesses because of the rare ecosystems lurking in its steep-sided valleys. There are pockets of subtropical vegetation here (including tree ferns, orchids and epiphytic bromeliads), hidden from the wind and with plenty of water. Various neotropic mammals (at their southern limit here) include the last known populations in

Uruguay of the lesser anteater (*Tamandua tetradactyla*) and porcupine (*Coendu spinosus*), as well as one of the few Uruguayan populations of coati (*Nasua nasua*). Two new flower subspecies were found here in 2008.

Ruta 30 south of Artigas rises on to a parched altiplano-like (high-altitude plateau) grassland, crossing various streams including the Arroyo Catalán Chico at km167, with good gallery forest; there are also plenty of ñandues in this area. You'll pass the turning south to La Bolsa and the gem mines (see opposite), and another junction at La Charqueada, coming after 75 minutes to Masoller, where the departments of Artigas, Rivera and Salto meet. There's a memorial here to the Battle of Masoller, when the government defeated the rebel *caudillo* Aparicio Saravia in 1904.

Continuing into Rivera department, you'll soon see the Balcones de Lunarejo (↘ 65 06363) on the right at km230, offering camping, horseriding and an ecotourist guide. Then you plunge down the Bajada de Peña, the steepest hill in Uruguay, with hairpins restricted to 20km/h eastbound. The road quickly moves from windswept grassland to woodland, with eroded red hills on either side, and after 4km (km238, 90 minutes from Artigas) an unpaved road on the right leads to the Valle de Lunarejo.

The valley opens out here, with lines of hills all more or less the same height on either side. The Lunarejo road gradually swings away from the main road, coming in 1.5km to the tiny village of La Palma and, after a right-angle bend, the Posada Lunarejo (↘ 65 06400, m 9982 6348; *www.posadalunarejo.com;* ⊕ *all year;* $$), a fine base for ecotourism in this area. A single-storey colonial-style building in an attractive rustic style, it has just three double rooms and two family rooms, and offers horseriding (*US$3.50/hr*), mountain biking (*US$2/hr*) and nature tours in an open 4x4 truck (*US$2/km*), following the Arroyo Lunarejo to its source south of La Palma. Immediately south of the *posada* is a *bañado* (wetland) managed as a reserve, where you may see herons, egrets, ibis, vultures or teros.

Just south of Lunarejo, in the northern fringe of Tacuarembó department, the **Quebrada Laureles** (Laurels Gorge) is similar to Lunarejo and a little remoter, best approached from the south (with no public transport). There are some working *estancias* here preserving subtropical ecosystems in gorges which cattle can't reach, as well as about 20 waterfalls (of which perhaps five flow all year) and rock pools. The best place to stay is the Establecimiento Vichadero (↘ 63 02358, m 9522 5222; $$), run by Dario Fros, a great local guide, working with his neighbours to give access to gorges, waterfalls, swimming holes and even rope bridges. In some streambeds you may find quartz containing gems such as agate.

From the right-angle bend in the road in La Palma a track crosses a ford to reach Ruta 30 after about 2km (at km240.3). Here you can catch the occasional local bus (run by Boreal) from Masoller to Rivera via the village of Tranqueras, 11km east. The bus soon swings right on to a very slow dirt road (the former Ruta 30) to a bridge with the Camping Municipal (↘ 62 23803) alongside, then on a paved dual carriageway into Tranqueras, rejoining Ruta 30 at about km254. There's no hotel, but the campsite is adequate.

It's 10km east to km458 of Ruta 5 (from Montevideo and Tacuarembó to Rivera); turning left (north), it's 37km to the edge of Rivera, and about 5km more to the centre.

RIVERA Larger and livelier than Artigas, the city of Rivera (founded in 1867) is a more important crossing point, with the Brazilian town of Santana do Livramento immediately adjoining it (each with a population of about 100,000).

Getting there The Uruguayan and Brazilian *Aduana* (Customs) posts are 5km on either side of the actual border, and people can move freely in the area between them. There are no international buses crossing the border here; Uruguayan buses arrive at the terminal on Plaza 18 de Julio, and you must go eight blocks back down Agraciada to the Immigration complex on Viera between Agraciada and Sarandí (the two main streets leading to the border). On the Brazilian side it's ten blocks from the border to the Policía Federal at Silveira Martinez and Thomas Alboronoz for Immigration, then you'll have to come back eight blocks to the Rodoviária (bus terminal) at Filho and Alves. There are three buses a day (one overnight) to Porto Alegre, taking seven hours.

From Montevideo Turil operates five buses a day (including one *super cama*) via Durazno and Tacuarembó, Sabelin four a day, Agencia Central has four a day and Nuñez three, taking between six and seven hours. Nuñez has two buses a day from Melo (taking four hours. Posada has two services a day from Rivera to Melo and two to San Gregorio via Tacuarembó. Copay has two to Paysandú and Tacuarembó (the 16.00 departure only going as far as Tacuarembó on Sundays), and one to Tacuarembó via Tambores at 17.00 daily.

There are no buses from Artigas to Rivera – you can either take a bus through Brazil (from Quaraí to Santana do Livramento) and then a taxi across the border, or an Artigas-Tacuarembó as far as Tranqueras, waiting there for a bus from Tacuarembó to Rivera.

A CUT bus leaves Fray Bentos at midnight on Mondays and Thursdays, running via Mercedes, Trinidad, Durazno and Tacuarambó to Rivera; ETA has a similar service on Wednesday and Sunday nights. From Salto there's an Agencia Central bus very early on Monday and Friday mornings.

Tourist information There's a national tourist office (↘ *62 25899*), run by the Ministry of Tourism, at the Immigration complex. For city information there's a kiosk outside the Club Uruguay (*Sarandí 487; ⏱ 10.00–23.00 Mon–Sat, possibly closing for lunch*). Almost everything you'd want is on the main street, Sarandí, or Plaza 18 de Julio.

⌂ Where to stay

⌂ **Uruguay-Brasil** Sarandí 440; ↘ 62 23068; e urubras@netgate.com.uy; www.hoteluruguaybrasil.com.uy. The best in town, though still only an adequate 3-star. It's on the main drag with lots of pavement bars & restaurants nearby, but that also means it can be noisy at night. There's a lift, Free Shop & parking garage, internet access with 2 PCs & a Wi-Fi area, & rooms have AC & cable TV. There's a pretty formal restaurant & a reasonable buffet b/fast. $$$$

⌂ **Casablanca** Agraciada 479; ↘ 62 23221; e casablancahotel@adinet.com.uy, cablanca@adinet.com.uy; www.casablanca.com.uy. A slim 5-storey 1960s block, this is a very decent 3-star hotel, with lift, Wi-Fi, meeting room & Free Shop. Rooms have AC & cable TV, & superior ones (same size as standard, but more modern) have minibar. No credit cards. $$$

⌂ **Comercio** Artigas 1115. Very cheap & poorly run. If the Sarandí is still open that's definitely a better bet. $$

⌂ **Hostal** Viera 1181; ↘ 62 22900. A cheap place on a main road opposite the hospital & close to Immigration. $$

⌂ **Nuevo** Ituzaingó 411 & Paysandú; ↘ 62 23039. A cheap option very close to the border. $$

⌂ **Ferrocarril** Lavallejo 1008 & Uruguay; ↘ 62 23389. A very decent little 1-star place, with an AC comedor (dining room) & rooms with & without cable TV & private bathroom. No b/fast. $

⌂ **Sarandí** Sarandí 777; ↘ 62 35296, 66 23521. This is for sale & may close; in the meantime it's a slightly grubby but adequate 1-star place, with rooms with private or shared bathroom. $

Camping There's a decent campsite (↘ *62 523083*), 7km west on Paysandú in the Parque Gran Bretaña (a park donated in 1939 by the British ambassador, Sir Eugen Millington-Drake), where there's also a *parador* by a reservoir, a small zoo and

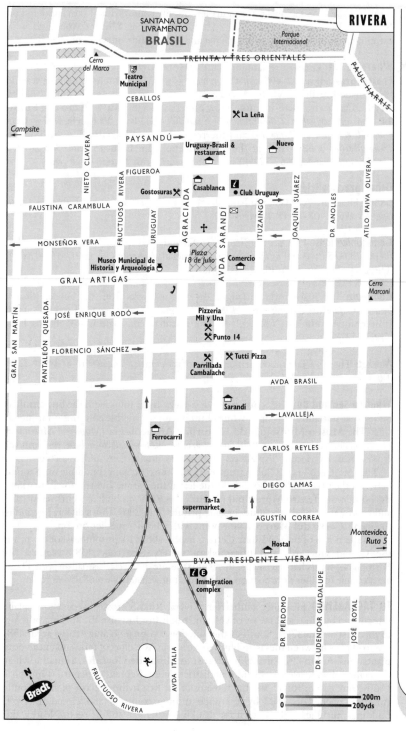

RIVERA

SANTANA DO
LIVRAMENTO
BRASIL

Parque
Internacional

PAUL HARRIS

Cerro
del Marco

Teatro
Municipal

TREINTA Y TRES ORIENTALES

CEBALLOS

✕ La Leña

Campsite

PAYSANDÚ →

Uruguay-Brasil &
restaurant

Nuevo

NIETO CLAVERA

FRUCTUOSO RIVERA

FIGUEROA

Gostosuras ✕

Casablanca

● Club Uruguay

JOAQUÍN SUÁREZ

DR ANOLLES

ATILO PAIVA OLIVERA

FAUSTINA CARAMBULA

URUGUAY

AGRACIADA

AVDA SARANDÍ

ITUZAINGÓ

MONSEÑOR VERA

†

Plaza
18 de Julio

Comercio

Museo Municipal de
Historia y Arqueología

GRAL ARTIGAS

Cerro
Marconi ▲

GRAL SAN MARTÍN

PANTALEÓN QUESADA

JOSÉ ENRIQUE RODÓ ←

Pizzeria
Mil y Una
✕
✕ Punto 14

FLORENCIO SÁNCHEZ →

✕ Tutti Pizza
✕
Parrillada
Cambalache

AVDA BRASIL

Sarandí

→ LAVALLEJA

Ferrocarril

CARLOS REYLES

DIEGO LAMAS

Ta-Ta
supermarket ●

AGUSTÍN CORREA

Montevideo,
Ruta 5

Hostal

BVAR PRESIDENTE VIERA

DR PERDOMO

DR LUDENDOR GUADALUPE

JOSÉ ROYAL

Immigration
complex

AVDA ITALIA

FRUCTUOSO RIVERA

N

Bradt

0   200m
0   200yds

The Interior RIVERA DEPARTMENT 7

The side text reads "The Interior RIVERA DEPARTMENT 7"

The Interior   RIVERA DEPARTMENT   7

motocross and car-racing circuits. Further into the countryside, 17km southeast on Ruta 27, the Balneario Paso Serpa (↘ *62 23803*) has 14ha of woodland with camping, electricity, barbecues, a *cantina* and soccer and volleyball pitches.

✕ Where to eat

The best restaurant is at the **Hotel Uruguay-Brazil** (↘ *62 23129*). **Gostosuras** (*Agraciada 490 near Carámbula*) is a small, homely restaurant serving homemade Brazilian-style food, salads, cakes, tea and coffee, and a buffet sold by weight. Otherwise there are quite a few pizzerias, notably **Tutti Pizza** and **Punto 14** (*opposite each other at the junction of Sarandí & Sánchez*), **Pizzeria Mil y Una** (*Sarandí 692 next to Punto 14*) and the relatively classy **Parrillada Cambalache** (*Sarandí 708;* ↘ *62 20767*) at the same junction. **La Leña** (*Sarandí 365 between Ceballos & Paysandú;* ↘ *62 32092*) is a café-pizzeria with a wood-fired oven.

Other practicalities

Banks There are ATMs along Sarandi. You can change money at Indumex (*Avda Sarandi 496;* ⊕ *08.00–18.00 Mon–Sat*).

Communications The post office is at Sarandí 501 (⊕ *08.00–18.00 Mon–Fri, 08.00–13.00 Sat*). Antel's call centre is at Agraciada & Artigas (⊕ *09.00–19.00 daily*). There's public Wi-Fi on Plaza 18 de Julio.

Consulate The Inspectoría de Migración is four blocks from the border (*Suárez between Carambula & Vera;* ↘ *62 24086;* **e** *i15rivera@dnm.minterior.gub.uy*) and at the Immigration complex (↘ *62 25254*). The Brazilian consulate is at Ceballos 1159 (↘ *62 23278*).

Markets There's a Ta-Ta supermarket south of the centre (*Sarandí 950;* ⊕ *08.00–22.00 daily*).

What to see and do

The centre of town is Plaza 18 de Julio, with the bus terminal on its west side and the simple, white church with red marble columns on its north side. The **Museo Municipal de Historia y Arqueología** (*Municipal Museum of History & Archaeology; Artigas 1090, just south of the bus terminal; closed between Christmas & New Year*) has decent displays on local history, archaeology and, as a rule, art.

The Art Deco-style Club Uruguay is the most striking building on Sarandí between the plaza and the border. To the left at the Parque Internacional, marking the border, the **Teatro Municipal** (*Treinta y Tres 970*) was built as a cinema in 1977 and run by the city, then controversially privatised in 2009. Immediately beyond is the basalt **Cerro del Marco**, a viewpoint with a border marker on top.

On the slopes of the sandstone Cerro Chapeu, about 10km southeast of town, are the Carrau vineyards and ultramodern winery (see page 138). Named (in Portuguese) for its hat-like shape, this is also the site of the city's small airport. There are a couple of other new bodegas in the hills immediately west of Rivera town.

TO TACUAREMBÓ Heading south from Rivera, Ruta 5 crosses a sandstone plain punctuated by plugs and mesas of volcanic basalt (for instance the striking outcrop to the west at km487½). South of the junction to Lunarejo and Artigas at km458, the road runs between mesas and limestone scarps, with lots of pine and eucalyptus plantations. At km426, Ruta 29 heads east to **Minas de Corrales**, a small town at the centre of an historic gold-mining district. At the Represa Cuñapirú (Cuñapirú Dam), 9km east of Ruta 5, are the remains of the first hydro-electric plant in South America, opened in 1882 by a French mining company and closed in 1959; buildings, turbines and a cistern for drinking water can still be seen. Nearby, the

San Gregorio gold mine reopened in 1997 under Canadian/Australian ownership, after being closed for over 80 years.

The main road crosses the Río Tacuarembó into the department of the same name, with a toll at km423½ and then rolling cattle and sheep country with pine plantations and some scrubby native *monte*.

TACUAREMBÓ DEPARTMENT

TACUAREMBÓ The eponymous capital of Uruguay's largest department, and the largest city in the interior of the country (with a population of around 50,000), Tacuarembó also boasts the only first-division soccer team outside the Montevideo area. Its biggest employer is Brazilian-owned Frigorífico Tacuarembó, which ships large quantities of beef jerky to the US. Sitting in a bowl without a river to cool it, Tacuarembó is known for its summer heat, with temperatures often rising into the 40s C.

A military post was established here in 1830 and the next year it was declared a town by General Rivera (as Villa de San Fructuoso, after his patron saint). In 1837 it became a departmental capital when Salto and Tacuarembó were split off from Paysandú. The area around the Arroyo Arerungá, west of Tacuarembó (now in Paysandú department), is known as the home of the last Charrúas, and the people of Tacuarembó have more Charrúa genes than other Uruguayans.

Getting there and around
By bus Ruta 5 bypasses the city to the east. From the north, at km393 the first turning to the city leads past the zoo and Parque Botánico, and after km390 (1hr 30min from Rivera) buses turn right (west), a couple of hundred metres west to the bus terminal. From the south, traffic turns left at km388 on to Avenida Pablo Ríos to the city centre, or continues to the turning to the bus terminal (*Avda Victorino Pereira 351*).

Turil has four Montevideo-Rivera buses per day calling at Tacuarembó (four hours 45 min) and Paso de los Toros, as well as a couple to Artigas; Nuñez has two buses daily from Montevideo to Rivera via Tacuarembó, and Sabelin/Chadre have four buses a day from Montevideo to Tacuarembó, continuing to Artigas or Rivera. Posada has four buses a day (two on Sundays) to Rivera, two a day (one on Sundays, at 07.00) to San Gregorio de Polanco, and two a day to Melo. Victor-Rony and Rocas also run a daily service each to San Gregorio.

Copay-Alonso has three buses a day (two on Sundays) to Rivera, two (one on Sundays) starting from Paysandú; they also send two (one on Sundays) north as far as Tambores. On Tuesdays and Fridays an ETA bus from Fray Bentos to Rivera passes through at 06.00, returning to Fray Bentos at 15.00. From Salto Agencia Central has a service to Tacuarembó on Mondays and Fridays, as does Toriani on Mondays, Wednesdays and Fridays.

The parallel streets 25 de Mayo and 18 de Julio run southwest–northeast, with three plazas between them. To the northwest, about six blocks from the terminal, is Plaza 19 de Abril.

By car Cars can rented from Dollar (*18 de Julio 351;* \ *63 22203*), Multicar (*Suárez 39;* \ *63 32446,* m *9588 5765; www.redmulticar.com;* ⊕ *09.00–19.00 Mon–Fri, 09.00–13.30 Sat*), Rentacar Daymán (*Catalogne 366;* \ *63 25367,* m *9937 5909*) and Turil (*25 de Mayo 256 & Sarandí;* \ *63 25350*).

Tourist information The departmental tourism office is at the west end of the bus terminal (\ *63 27144;* e *turismo@imtacuarembo.gub.uy*). There's also a bus information desk (⊕ *08.00–14.00 daily*).

⌂ Where to stay

⌂ **Hotel Carlos Gardel** Ruta 5 km387.5, on the southern outskirts; ☎ 63 30301/6; e infohcg@ netgate.com.uy. This is aimed at tourists in buses & cars, with a live tango show & *parrilla*, as well as swimming pool, disabled room & business centre. Bedrooms have internet access. $$$

⌂ **Hotel Tacuarembó** 18 de Julio 133, just east of the cathedral; ☎ 63 22104; e htacuarembo@ yahoo.com; www.tacuarembohotel.com.uy. The best in town, this is a professionally run 3-star with 62 AC rooms, Wi-Fi, parking & swimming pool. $$$

⌂ **Hospedaje El Progreso** 25 de Mayo 358; ☎ 63 20789. Opposite the El Progreso grocery, this friendly, simple place has rooms with private or shared bathroom. $$

⌂ **Hotel Central** Flores 300; ☎ 63 22341. Friendly, affordable & indeed central (rooms facing the street can be noisy at w/ends), this has spacious rooms with private bathroom & cable TV, & decent b/fast but no other meals. $$

⌂ **Hotel Plaza** 25 de Agosto 247, just off Plaza Colón; ☎ 63 27988; e hotelplazatbo@hotmail.com. A nice friendly place with AC rooms with cable TV, & internet access in the foyer. $$

Camping The Iporá campsite (*Avda Gutiérrez Ruiz, 7km north of the centre (no bus);* ☎ *63 22612;* ⊕ *early Dec–Easter;* $) has a *parador* restaurant and an open-air swimming pool. Camping is also possible at the Laguna de las Lavanderos, northeast of the centre, where there's an attractive lake, barbecues, a basic wash-block (and a better one at the northeast end that may be locked up).

✗ Where to eat
The Hotel Tacuarembó's Restaurant Don Juan is the best in town. Otherwise La Rueda (*Washington Beltrán 251 between Flores & Treinta y Tres;* ☎ *63 22453*) serves good traditional food (grilled meats, pasta, salads and snacks) at reasonable prices.

Other practicalities
Banks There are banks with ATMs at the junction of Sarandí and 18 de Julio, and on the south side of Plaza Colón. Money can be changed at M's Cambio (*18 de Julio 252*).

Communications The post office is at Izutaingó 262 (⊕ *09.00–17.00 Mon–Fri, 08.00–13.00 Sat*); Antel's call centre is at Sarandí 242 (⊕ *09.00–19.00 daily*). Plaza Colón is being remodelled and should have public Wi-Fi when finished, as will Plaza 19 de Abril; the school at 18 de Julio & Artigas also has a decent signal.

Emergency services There is an Emergency Centre on Plaza 19 de Abril (*18 de Julio & Herrera;* ☎ *63 24000*), and the police station is directly across the plaza. The hospital is southwest of the centre at Treinta y Tres 444 (☎ *63 22955*).

Market There's a Ta-Ta hypermarket at Suárez 259 (*Treinta y Tres;* ⊕ *08.00–22.00 daily*).

What to see and do On the southeastern side of Plaza 19 de Abril, next to the small **Cathedral of San Fructuoso** (1899–1917), the nicely restored Intendencia (1911) has an unusual Neoromanesque façade but a plain interior. The tower was added in 1930 and in 1960 it became a cathedral. Four blocks southwest is Plaza Colón, and six blocks further (out of the city centre) is Plaza Rivera. Another five blocks down 18 de Julio is the Cementerio Municipal, where the ornate Escayola and Escobar family tombs have been declared historic monuments.

The **Teatro Escayola** (*25 de Mayo 163*) was built in 1888–91 by Carlos Gardel's supposed father (see the box on page 312), with Carrara marble from Italy and a French grand piano; Gardel himself performed there in 1930. It closed in 1956, but in 2008 a campaign was started for the city to take over the building, now very run-down, and restore it to its former glory. There is a summer theatre at the

TACUAREMBÓ

Iporá Campsite

AV SECCO APARICIO

Laguna de las Lavanderas

Parque 25 de Agosto

Arroyo Tacuarembó Chico

CALLE 257

LÓPEZ AGUERRA

DR E FRUGONI

GRAL APARICIO SARAVIA

Swimming pool

Teatro de Verano

F SANCHEZ

LIB JUAN A LAVALLEJA

C C OLIVA

ZELMAR MICHELINI

FERREIRA ALDUNATE

LUIS BATLLE BERRES

JOAQUIN SUÁREZ

LUIS A DE HERRERA

Teatro Escayola

Hotel Tacuarembó & restaurant

WILSON FERREIRA

GRAL ARTIGAS

ITUZAINGO

Plaza de 19 Abril

Intendencia

MARÍA E CASTRILLÓN

PEDRO CHIESA

ANTONIO CHIESA

Rivera

Police

AGRACIADA

DR IVO FERREIRA

GRAL FRUCTUOSO RIVERA

Museo de Geociencias

San Fructuoso

Museo del Indio y del Gaucho

VICTORINO PEREIRA

R5

DR WASHINGTON

25 DE MAYO

18 DE JULIO

GRAL FLORES

Ta-Ta supermarket

Plaza Colón

TREINTA Y TRES

PEDRO VARELA

CARLOS QUIJANO

Hotel Plaza

Hotel Central

DR CATALINA

BELTRAN

JOSÉ SARANDÍ

25 DE AGOSTO

JUAN ORTIZ

DR BALTASAR BRUM

RAMBLA

DR CELEDONIO NIN

A FERREIRA

DR PUGNALINI

ORTIZ Y AYALA

Police

La Rueda

Hospedaje El Progreso

Hotel Carlos Gardel, Montevideo

N

0 — 200m
0 — 200yds

---

northeastern end of 18 de Julio, at the site where Artigas camped with his troops in 1813. Beyond this, 25 de Mayo crosses a bridge to the Parque de las Lavanderas (formally Parque 25 de Agosto), around the attractive Laguna de las Lavanderas (Laundrywomen's Lagoon), with waterbirds on floating islands, and teenagers hanging out drinking *maté*. It's about 6km further along Avenida Gutiérrez Ruiz to the Balneario Iporá ('clear water' in Guaraní), a leafy resort with an artificial lake, Olympic-sized swimming pool and campsite.

One notable feature of Tacuarembó is its *centros de barrios* on the outskirts of town, architecturally striking focal points for each quarter, which include health or sport centres.

There are two museums, neither of great interest. The **Museo del Indo y del Gaucho** (*Museum of the Indian & the Gaucho; Artigas & Flores; ⊕ 08.00–14.00 Tue–Fri, 08.00–12.00 Sat–Sun; free*) has large but dull collections of *bolas*, *rompacebezas*, ceramics, bows and lots of arrowheads, silver stirrups, gourds, bridles, carved cow-horns, lassos, pistols and swords, and one fine set of harness. The **Museo de Geociencias** (*Geoscience Museum; Artigas 191; ⊕ 08.00–14.00 Tue–Fri, 08.00–12.00 Sat–Sun, closed Christmas to New Year; free*) displays amethyst and other local rocks and minerals, as well as a dateline of the earth's geological history.

Events The **Fiesta de la Patria Gaucho** (Festival of the Gaucho Country), held at the Laguna de las Lavanderas in the first week of March, is one of the biggest of its kind in South America, with thousands of country folk coming from far and

When Carlos Gardel was asked about his place of birth, he used to reply, 'I was born in Buenos Aires, Argentina, at the age of two and a half years'.

One thing that is certain is that Gardel was not born in Argentina, despite being as solidly Argentine an icon as Maradona or Evita. Most written sources, including a birth certificate, indicate that he was born in Toulouse, France, in either 1887 or 1890, the illegitimate child of Berthe Gardès, who took him to Venezuela and then to Argentina. However, some Uruguayans, especially in Tacuarembó department, claim forcefully that he was born there, the illegitimate son of Tacuarembó landowner Carlos Escoyola with his wife's 13-year-old sister (who may in fact have been his daughter by his wife's mother!), and that he sent the child away with Berthe Gardès. In Argentina she worked as a washerwoman and brought Carlos up in the Abasto district of Buenos Aires. Gardel was certainly a regular visitor to Uruguay, including a trip to Tacuarembó in 1915 to convalesce after being shot in a bar, supposedly by Che Guevara's father.

Gardel may have encouraged the confusion about his origins in order to cover up the shadier aspects of his youth (there's speculation that he served time in prison), to avoid conscription into the French army during World War I, or to spare his mother the shame of an illegitimate child. In any case there is now a commission in Tacuarembó dedicated to proving Gardel's Uruguayan origins (in 2004 an Argentine court refused it permission to take a DNA sample from Gardel's remains). The museum in Valle Edén (see opposite) displays a copy of another birth certificate indicating that he was born in Tacuarembó, as do his application for Argentina citizenship in 1923 and the passport found on his body after his death in a plane crash in Colombia in 1935.

wide (including Brazil and Argentina), all in gaucho garb and many with their horses. There are parades, riding competitions, lasso, *boladera* and other contests, and huge *parrillas* producing a steady supply of grilled meats. In the evenings there's music and dancing, and traditional gaucho poetry recitals.

In December 2008 the first **Fiesta Gardeliana** was held at the Laguna de las Lavanderas, with lots of tango music as well as a Model T Ford rally.

VALLE EDÉN Leaving Tacuarembó to the southwest, Ruta 26 runs through fairly empty hill country with lots of native *monte*. Just beyond km208 (at the west end of the Arroyo Tambores bridge, 23km from Tacuarembó), an asphalt road lined with bamboo turns southwest to Valle Edén (pronounced 'bashay ayden'). Named Valley of Eden by the British engineers who built a railway here in 1890, this has similar flora to Laureles and Lunarejo to the north (see page 304), with subtropical characteristics, but is less well preserved.

Nowadays the area is best known as the supposed birthplace of tango legend Carlos Gardel, although this is naturally disputed by his legions of Argentine fans (see the box above). There's a good museum totally dedicated to proving that Gardel was born here.

Getting there From Tacuarembó's bus terminal, Calebus runs to Tambores, just beyond Valle Edén, three times daily; the 11.45 bus brings you right to the museum, returning at about 13.15, while the 06.30 and 18.00 buses leave you at the turning at km208. From where it's 500m to Camping El Mago (see opposite). A pedestrian exit leads to the road by a suspension footbridge (built in 1928), from where it's 500m to a police station. Here the road swings right and brings you in 300m to the museum, opposite the Posada Valle Edén at the end of the asphalt.

🏠 Where to stay

🏠 **Posada Valle Edén** Opposite the museum; ☎ 63 02345, 📱 9981 0567; e posadavalleeden@ gmail.com; www.posadavalleeden.com.uy; ⏱ all year. This makes a very pleasant stopover, in a house built of red stones in the late 19th century. There's a dbl & a trpl room, 2 cabañas with kitchen & barbecue (US$52 for 4), & 17 dorm beds (US$13). Meals are available, as well as preserves & liqueurs (from local fruits), mountain bikes, horses & a nature guide. $$

🏕 **Camping El Mago** (also known as Camping Valle Edén) ☎ 63 22275; ⏱ early Dec–Easter There's an open field with wash-blocks, then sites in native wood (with lots of epiphytic plants, as well as picnic tables & parrillas) along the Arroyo Jabonería (named after the arbol del jabón or soap tree, Quillaja brasiliensis). There are small fish in the river & various birds including chajá (southern screamer, Chauna torquata), whose squawk you'll easily identify. $

What to see and do

Museo Carlos Gardel (⏱ 09.30–18.30 daily; US$0.80) The museum is in a former *pulpería* (rural shop/bar) once frequented by Gardel, in a spacious, nicely laid out and maintained garden. It's delightfully cool inside, with a soundtrack of the man himself singing, interesting period photos and documents dedicated to proving his local origins. There's also a hall with a couple of horse carriages on display. Immediately below the museum is the former railway station (the line is still used by freight trains), where a couple of ancient and very decayed railcars await refurbishment.

Gardel was, according to many Uruguayans, born 12km further up the valley at the Estancia Santa Blanca; an unpaved road continues through native woodland (with plenty of birds) between low hills.

Estancia Panagea (m *9983 6149;* e *panagea@adinet.com.uy*) An hour north of Tacuarembó, Estancia Panagea is a working ranch offering hostel-style accommodation and a unique experience of rural Uruguayan life, very different to that of the traditional tourist *estancias*. Run by an Uruguayan veterinarian and his Swiss wife, globetrotters who settled here to farm as naturally and organically as possible, there's no TV, phone or internet access, limited hot water and no mains electricity, although a generator is cranked up most evenings to show one of their 1,900 films. Juan and Susanne run the farm with just one gaucho and his wife, the cook, saddling up at 07.00 to bring cattle and sheep in for pregnancy testing, vaccination, tick removal or a myriad of other reasons, returning for lunch and a siesta before riding out for another few hours. Guests are free to accompany them (you'll be kitted out in authentic gaucho garb) or to relax, play badminton or volleyball, walk, swim (in a creek 1km away), fish or birdwatch.

Accommodation is in the farmhouse (four double and two triple rooms), with simple and plentiful homestyle gaucho food, often barbecued meat or casseroles (vegetarians are well fed too, with advance notice); there's also plenty of wine (not included). For US$35 a night per person you get three meals plus snacks, fruit, tea and coffee, and plenty of horseriding (with ad-hoc lessons as required). They'll meet you at the Tacuarembó bus terminal on Tuesday, Thursday or Saturday at 11.00 or 18.00, with as much notice as possible, and return you there. Spring and autumn are the best times to come here.

PASO DE LOS TOROS Continuing south from Tacuarembó, Ruta 5 follows a remarkably un-straight line across flat grassland, where you'll see cows, sheep, *ñandúes* (see page 10) and cattle egrets. At km252, 138km (1½ hours by bus) from Tacuarembó (and exactly midway between Montevideo and Rivera), the town of

Paso de los Toros (Pass of the Bulls) stands at the north side of the bridge below the Rincón del Bonete dam. Founded in 1903 and rebuilt by the army after the construction of the dam and bridge, it's known as the birthplace of the writer Mario Benedetti (1920–2009), and of the Paso de los Toros brand of soft drinks (originally a tonic water concocted by Rómulo Mangini for British railway workers, later expanded to include soft drinks, and now produced by PepsiCo). The plant (Mangini 329, on the west side of the railway just south of 18 de Julio) now houses the Reserva Acuario, opened in 2008 with 37 species of local freshwater fish in tanks.

Getting there and away Ruta 5 bypasses the town to the east, meeting Bulevar Artigas at a statue of a bull at the north end of the bridge. Artigas leads a couple of hundred metres northwest to Plaza Artigas, with a Neogothic church on its north side. From here 18 de Julio leads west beyond the railway. The town centre (with shops and restaurants but no hotels) consists of the two blocks beyond the level crossing.

By bus Most buses from Rivera and Artigas to Montevideo bypass the town and will drop you off at the Esso station at the north end of the bridge. Otherwise buses stop at offices just southwest of Plaza Artigas: Nuñez and Cynsa (*Sarandí & Barreto*), opposite the former train station, Turil (*Hotel Sayonara*) at the same junction, CUT (*Sarandí, southwest of Bvar Artigas*) and CTTM (*18 de Julio 729*).

Where to stay and eat The Hotel Sayonara (*Sarandí 302 & Barreto;* ↘ *664 2535,* m *9986 4194;* \$\$) is a very decent one-star hotel with a restaurant/bar. At the dam, 22km upstream, is the more upmarket Hotel Rincón del Bonete (↘ *66 04875;* \$\$\$). By the northern approach to the bridge, the Camping El Sauce (↘ *664 3503;* ⊕ *Dec–Easter;* \$) is pretty good, with eight cabins, a *parador* (to the east of the bridge) and a small beach.

The restaurant Lo de Claudia (Club Social, Artigas 598) is pretty formal, serving *parrilla* and pizza. There's also the El Edén (*18 de Julio & Mangini*) and the Pinguï (*18 de Julio & Puyol*), both serving the same mix of food.

Other practicalities Antel has a call centre (*Mangini 357 just south of 18 de Julio;* ⊕ *09.00–21.00 daily*), and there's free public Wi-Fi on Plaza Artigas.

What to see and do South across the Río Negro is the village of Centenario, with a picnic area by the river to the east. Ruta 5 continues south through rolling cattle country, passing a military air base and crossing a high-ish bridge at km186 to enter Durazno, 66km from Paso de los Toros (50 minutes by bus).

Las Cañadas One of the most authentic working *estancias* that you can stay on is Las Cañadas (↘ *660 4048;* \$\$\$\$), 36km north of Paso de los Toros. Owned by descendants of the families that founded Fray Bentos and first shipped frozen beef to Europe, the historic *casco* (main house) has been lovingly preserved, with family portraits (including one president), leather chairs, wooden furniture and welcoming fires. It's a sprawling, low house with verandas on three sides, looking over rose and herb beds and across miles of rolling ranchland. There is a small swimming pool, and a wood-fired oven and grill where gauchos tend an *asado* fit to feed an army. Alternatively there's an open-plan room with low cupboards dividing a kitchen from the dining area, where huge meals of hearty traditional fare are served up four times a day, including *merienda* or high tea.

As a working farm (mainly raising Hereford cattle), the main activity is horseriding, either going with the gauchos to bring in cattle or just riding the placid *criollo* horses to the village or a swimming hole, with armadillos, hares, skunks and *ñandues* to see along the way.

There's no air conditioning or TV, but US$70 a day is great value for unlimited riding and the experience of living the traditional rural life.

SAN GREGORIO DE POLANCO At the eastern end of the Rincón del Bonete lake, where Ruta 43 crosses the Río Negro by a ferry, San Gregorio de Polanco is a peaceful little town known for fishing and for its 'living museum' of street-side murals, mainly north of the central Plaza Constitución. There's also a free Festival of Gospel Music on the first weekend of January.

Getting there and away By car, take Ruta 5 to km307, then Ruta 43 east for 59km. There's a surprisingly good bus service, with CTTM (*Artigas 159;* ✆ *369 4530*) running twice a day to Montevideo via Paso de los Toros and Durazno, Posada going twice a day to Tacuarembó and Rivera, and a couple of other services as far as Tacuarembó.

Where to stay and eat There's a campsite at the western end of the main street, Avenida Mollo. The only real hotel is Los Médanos (*Avda Mollo;* ✆ *369 4013/4074;* $$) by the river, which has a decent restaurant, and horses for rent. There's also the Apart-Hotel La Casona (✆ *63 31611/22019;* $$), Bungalows Artimir (✆ *369 4228,* m *9983 0649;* $), Cabañas Lo de Miguel (✆ *369 4220,* m *9964 7701;* $) and Cabañas de Carlín (✆ *63 22462/23292;* $).

DURAZNO DEPARTMENT

DURAZNO San Pedro de Durazno was founded at a ford across the River Yí in 1821 by the then Colonel Fructuoso Rivera, and it became his base, giving him fervent support. Many of its residents came from San Francisco de Borja del Yí (or San Borja del Yí), 10km east of Durazno on the border between the present departments of Durazno and Florida, the last mission settlement of the Guaraní people. In 1833 the 8,000 so-called Guaraní-*misioneros*, who had accompanied Rivera from the former Jesuit missions in what is now Brazil, were settled here. The settlement was disbanded in 1843 by the government of Manuel Oribe, and in 1862 the remaining inhabitants (the last pure indigenous Uruguayans) were forcibly moved to the towns of Florida and Durazno, where they became assimilated into the existing population. Many women and children became slaves on *estancias*, where their genes survive to this day.

Much livelier than the towns to the north of the Río Negro, Durazno now has over 33,000 inhabitants and is known for various festivals, notably the Pilsen Rock (see page 318).

Getting there and around
By bus Buses arrive at the terminal, southwest of the centre near Ruta 14 on the Avenida de Circunvalación (ring road). Tourist information is available here, and also at the zoo (by Ruta 5, arriving from the south). The local bus company is Nossar, operating both city buses and longer-distance services.

The Durazno-based Nossar operates at least eight services a day from Montevideo to Durazno (around 2½ hours), five continuing to Paso de los Toros, as well as four (two on Sundays) from Trinidad, three from Colonia (taking almost three hours), and five from Carmen and Sarandí del Yí. There are also services on Friday (17.00) and Sunday (19.00) to Cerro Chato, for connections towards Melo on Ruta 7.

Turil, Nuñez, Turismar and Agencia Central (Sabelin/Chadre) each operate four daily buses from Montevideo to Florida and Durazno, continuing to Paso de los Toros, Tacuarembó and Artigas or Rivera; the Nuñez buses and all but one Turil bus don't call at the terminal but leave you on Ruta 5 instead. In addition two of Agencia Central's Montevideo–Salto services run via Durazno each day. Bruno Hermanos and CTTM offer slightly less luxurious services via Durazno to Sarandí Grande, Florida, Carmen, Paso de los Toros and San Gregorio de Polanco. From Fray Bentos and Mercedes CUT/ETA run on Tuesdays to Fridays to Rivera via Trinidad, Durazno and Tacuarembó, returning the same afternoon.

From the terminal, Oribe leads northeast for nine blocks to Plaza Independencia. A block further on, you can turn left on to 18 de Julio, the main shopping street, known as the Microcentro. This leads in three blocks to Plaza Sarandí, from where 19 de Abril leads northeast towards the river and bridges.

By car Cars can be rented from Multicar (*Wilson Ferreira 481;* ℡ *36 24502,* m *9588 5764; www.redmulticar.com;* ⏰ *09.00–19.00 Mon–Fri, 09.00–13.30 Sat).*

🏠 Where to stay

🏠 **Central Hotel** Oribe 699; ℡ 36 20305; e hotelcentral@adinet.com.uy; www.hotelcentral.com.uy. A very nice modern place with wall hangings & arty photos in reception, as well as free Wi-Fi & 2 PCs, & AC rooms with cable TV. $$$

🏠 **Hotel Durazno** Herrera 937 & Brum; ℡ 36 22040/22371; www.hoteldurazno.com.uy. Rooms at this decent & affordable place range from *económico* (no window but fan & good bathroom) to standard, superior & suites; there's cable TV & Wi-Fi plus 2 PCs in the b/fast room (which offers a decent if limited buffet). $$

🛖 **33 Orientales campsite** Playa El Sauzal, by the river at the eastern end of Penza; ℡ 36 24500; e imdservices@adinet.com.uy; ⏰ Dec–Apr. A large, shady campsite, hectic on summer w/ends but much quieter at night. There's a *parador municipal* (restaurant), set on Corbusieresque columns, & decent wash-blocks. $

✗ Where to eat
Perhaps the nicest restaurant in the centre is **La Farola** (*18 de Julio, on west side of Plaza Sarandí*), with a good range of vegetarian and meat pizzas, *milanesas* and other standard dishes. North across the road from the bus terminal, **Don Armando** is a friendly *parrilla*. There's also the pleasant **Parrilla Don Pablini** (*Oribe & Zagnoli*), midway between the centre and the terminal.

Other practicalities

Communications The post office is at Rivera 428, north of Herrera (⏰ *09.00–17.00 Mon–Fri, 09.00–12.00 Sat*). Antel has *telecentros* at Rivera 564 (⏰ *09.00–19.00 daily*) and Penza & Artigas (⏰ *08.30–12.30, 14.30–19.00 Mon–Fri, 08.30–12.30 Sat*). There's public Wi-Fi on Plaza Independencia.

Markets Supermarkets include Ta-Ta (*18 de Julio 580 between Oribe & Zorrilla de San Martín;* ⏰ *08.00–21.00 Mon–Sat, 08.30–21.00 Sun*), La Familia (*Brum & 19 de Abril;* ⏰ *08.00–12.45, 15.00–21.00 Mon–Fri, 08.00–13.00, 15.30–21.00 Sat, 08.30–13.00 Sun*) and Supermercado 18 (*south side of Plaza Sarandí;* ⏰ *08.00–12.30, 14.30–22.00 Mon–Fri, 08.00–12.30, 15.00–22.00 Sat, 08.30–12.30 Sun*).

What to see and do In the centre of Plaza Independencia is the Monumento a Cristóbal Colón, raised in 1892 to mark the 400th anniversary of Columbus's 'discovery' of the Americas. Atop the column is a stone globe containing a time capsule, opened in 1992 and again, if all goes to plan, in 2092. On the southwestern side of the plaza, the **church of San Pedro** was built soon after the town was founded in 1821, and rebuilt in 1890–98, with a new façade added in the 1920s.

DURAZNO

Burnt out in 1967, it was rebuilt with a striking modern red-brick interior by Eladio Dieste, with a dramatic light-well at the east end. Inaugurated in 1971, it was declared a national monument in 1997. In 1975 Dieste also built a gymnasium six blocks northeast at the end of Zorrilla de San Martín.

On the northwestern side of the plaza, the **Casa de Rivera** was built in 1835 for Rivera (whose bust is across the road on the plaza) as the Comandancia General de Campaña, and he took the oath of office for his second presidency here in 1838. It became the effective seat of government until 1842 but had been split up by the end of the 19th century. The **Museo Casa de Rivera** (⊕ *08.00–20.00 Tue–Fri, 08.30–13.30, 16.00–21.00 Sat–Sun, 08.30–13.30 Sun; free*), opened in 1992, is very good, with lots of old photos and printed matter, though all in Spanish. Room 1 has a well laid-out display of indigenous stone tools, *bolas* and arrowheads (some at least 11,000 years old), as well as a dinosaur egg and a Lestodon bone. Antonio Taddei, born in Durazno, was the founder of Uruguayan archaeology, so the items displayed are not just from Durazno but include, for instance, ceramics from Isla Vizcaino. Room 2 is about Rivera (whose father owned land between the Río Yí and the Río Negro), with a few swords and bayonets, and (depending on the rotation of the displays) paintings by the English artist Francis Vincent. You can see Rivera's office at the eastern end of the building, and go down into the big, echoing *aljibe* (cistern) at the bottom of which various items, now displayed in the museum, were found in 2004–05.

The Casa de los Reyles, just east of the Casa de Rivera at Uribe 805, was bought by General Carlos Genaro Reyles, a pioneer of Uruguayan cattle ranching, who gave the building its present form. It has been a school since 1913.

Two blocks northwest of the Casa Rivera, the **Museo de Arte** (*Penza 719; west of Batlle y Ordóñez;* ⊕ *08.00–18.30 Tue–Sat; free*) is in the former home and office of Dr Emilio Penza Spinelli (a local doctor), a single-storey white building with a rooftop balustrade and a belvedere tower, built in the 1870s. It housed a school from 1921 to 1944 and a teacher-training college to 1981, and was restored in 2000 to house the town's art gallery. Two rooms display the rough-cut wooden sculptures of Claudio Silveira Silva (1935–2007), who moved to Durazno in the early 1960s and continued to visit after moving to Barcelona in 1978; there's also a room for temporary shows. There are some strikingly modern houses in Durazno, for instance three blocks further along Penza at Rubino. A little further, on the far side of the terminal and opposite the former train station, the new Museo de los Charrúas will preserve the memory of the area's indigenous inhabitants.

Following Ruta 5 (or the parallel cycle track) south for a couple of kilometres, you'll come to the **Zoológico Municipal** (*zoo; just south of km182;* ⊕ *daily; free*), modernised in 2008–09 with larger enclosures, a walk-in aviary and better visitor facilities. It houses 140 species of animals including lions, tigers, a dromedary, a hippo and a brown bear, as well as smaller mammals such as monkeys, deer, llamas, capybaras and anteaters, and birds such as toucans, storks, flamingos, ducks, egrets, southern screamers, black swans, ñandues and peacocks, mostly free to fly in and out. Well-tended gardens include palms and Brazilian araucaria trees. The most striking addition is a 120m-long wooden bridge south to the Parque de la Hispanidad, with a viewing platform overlooking lakes where many wild birds come to pass the night.

The Parque de la Hispanidad (*just south of km181;* ⊕ *07.00–21.00 daily; free*) is a spacious park planted with both Spanish and native trees and other flora. A large stage, built in 2000 in front of a lake, is used for festivals such as **Pilsen Rock**, the country's main rock festival (October) and the **Festival Nacional del Folclore** (early February), featuring guitar songs and vernacular poetry, as well as displays of gaucho skills. There's a new cafeteria building here, as well as the small Nueva Luna Parrilla at the zoo gates.

On the other side of town, Calle Penza (known for a short stretch as Avenida Morales) leads northeast to the Playa El Sauzal, the town's main beach, where half the town seems to set up camp on hot summer days. The **Movida Tropical Uruguaya** (Uruguayan Tropical Festival) is held here on the first weekend of January, with around 20 bands playing vaguely Caribbean music.

It is possible to continue on the beach and a path through the scrub to the left to the imposing long steel railway viaduct built by British engineers in 1879. Cotorras live in huge communal nests in the eucalyptus trees along Avenida Winston Churchill, which leads under the viaduct and on to the wooden Puente Sumersible (Submersible Bridge, also known as the Puente Viejo, although it was only built in 1903).

On the far side of the bridge is the **Campamento Artiguista**, a sandy area with trees and plaques reproducing the letters and proclamations that Artigas wrote here in January 1813, after crossing the river on his return from the Exodo del Pueblo Oriental (see page 15). There's plenty of native forest along the river, with good birdwatching, both here and in the other direction where Ruta 5 crosses the Yí; canoeing is also popular.

FLORES DEPARTMENT

TRINIDAD Trinidad, 192km from Montevideo on Ruta 3 to Paysandú (another 188km northwest), and 40km (25min) west of Durazno on Ruta 14, is not quite as nice as Durazno but it's quieter and makes a pleasant stopover, and has a fine zoo. Founded in 1804, it's the capital of Flores, one of the few departments not named after its main city. It's built on a tight grid pattern around the central Plaza Constitución, but through traffic on Ruta 3 skirts around its southern and western flanks.

Getting there and away
By bus There's no bus terminal. Bus offices include Nossar (*Ubeda, just east of the plaza;* ✆ *364 3786*), Agencia Central (*for Chadre and ETA; Berro 603 & Herrera, a block south of the plaza;* ✆ *364 2129/2460;* e *trinidad@agenciacentral.com.uy*) and Copay (*Ramírez, just south of Treinta y Tres;* ✆ *364 2653*). From Montevideo Agencia Central has seven services a day calling at Trinidad (five Sabelin services to Salto (two via Guichón), and two Chadre services via Ruta 5), and Nossar has three; Copay has four services a day to Paysandú via Trinidad and Young, and Nuñez has two to Paysandú and Salto by the same route. El Norteño's overnight service from Montevideo to Salto and Bella Unión also calls at Trinidad.

Nossar operates four (two on Sundays) from Durazno, three continuing to Colonia.

A CUT bus leaves Fray Bentos at midnight on Mondays and Thursdays, running via Mercedes, Trinidad, Durazno and Tacuarambó to Rivera; ETA has a similar service on Wednesday and Sunday nights.

By car Cars can be rented from Gol Rentacar (*Batlle y Ordóñez & Avda Brasil;* m *9987 4066*).

Tourist information Tourist information is at the southwest corner of the plaza (✆ *364 2210; www.imflores.gub.uy*).

🏠 Where to stay
🏠 **Gran Hotel Flores** Herrera 612 & Fray Ubeda; ✆ 364 2654/8; www.granhotelflores.com.uy. A

modern tower with free Wi-Fi & dataports in all rooms, AC, lift & outdoor swimming pool $$$

TRINIDAD

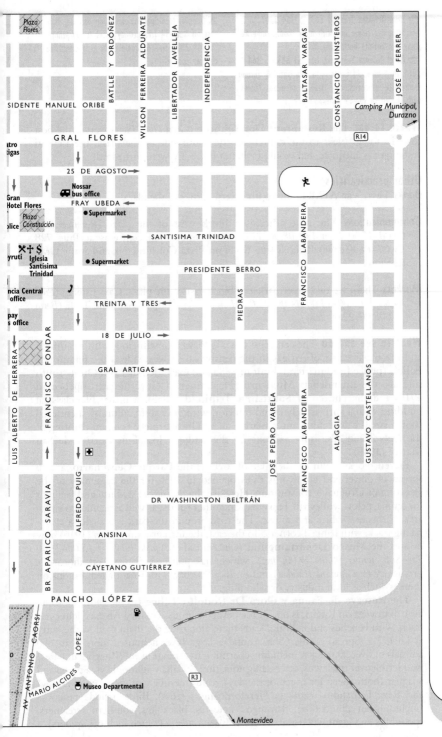

Plaza
Flores

BATLLE Y ORDÓÑEZ

WILSON FERREIRA ALDUNATE

LIBERTADOR LAVELLEJA

INDEPENDENCIA

BALTASAR VARGAS

CONSTANCIO QUINSTEROS

JOSÉ P FERRER

SIDENTE MANUEL ORIBE

Camping Municipal,
Durazno

GRAL FLORES

R14

tro
igas

25 DE AGOSTO →

Nossar
bus office

Gran
Hotel Flores

FRAY UBEDA ←

Plaza
olice Constitución

● Supermarket

SANTISIMA TRINIDAD

✗ ✝ $
yruti Iglesia
Santisima
Trinidad

● Supermarket

PRESIDENTE BERRO

FRANCISCO LABANDEIRA

ncia Central
office

♪

pay
s office

TREINTA Y TRES ←

PIEDRAS

18 DE JULIO →

GRAL ARTIGAS ←

LUIS ALBERTO DE HERRERA

FONDAR

FRANCISCO

JOSÉ PEDRO VARELA

FRANCISCO LABANDEIRA

ALAGGIA

GUSTAVO CASTELLANOS

✚

BR APARICO SARAVIA

ALFREDO PUIG

DR WASHINGTON BELTRÁN

ANSINA

CAYETANO GUTIÉRREZ

PANCHO LÓPEZ

LÓPEZ

AV ANTONIO CAORSI

MARIO ALCIDES

🗿 Museo Departamental

R3

↘ Montevideo

🏠 **Hotel Trinidad** Trinidad 663; 📞 364 2307. In a less attractive house but with nicer rooms, some AC; shared or private bathrooms. $$

🏠 **Hotel Potenza** Santísima Trinidad 643; 📞 364 2068. In a nice old house with cool patio & ancient leatherette armchairs, very clean & adequate. Rooms with shared or private bathrooms. $

🏕 **Camping Municipal** Balneario Don Ricardo, 8km east on Ruta 14 (reached by buses to Durazno); 📞 364 2009; free. A simple place at a creek-side bathing spot. $

✗ **Where to eat** The **Restaurant Don Quijote** (*Gran Hotel Flores*) serves the best food in town. Next to the church on the south side of the plaza, the Beyruti restaurant is adequate, but would be better if the TV were turned off.

Other practicalities

Banks There's an ATM on the southeastern corner of the plaza.

Communications The post office is a block west of the plaza (*Ramírez 620;* ⏱ *09.00–17.00 Mon–Fri, 08.00–12.00 Sat*). Antel's call centre is at Puig 728 (⏱ *09.00–19.00 daily*). There's free Wi-Fi on Plaza Constitución, and at the Gran Hotel Flores.

Markets There are two supermarkets a block east of the plaza: Casa Estefán (*Puig & Ubeda;* ⏱ *08.00–13.00, 14.00–22.00 Mon–Sat, 08.00–13.00 Sun*) and Ta-Ta (*Berro 474;* ⏱ *08.00–22.00 daily*).

What to see and do The centre of town is Plaza Constitución, with a fountain and the usual statue of Artigas in the centre; on its west side is the Jefatura de Policía (police headquarters), built in 1885 and expanded in 1911. On its south side are the Intendencia Municipal (Departmental Government), opened in 1916, and the church of **Santísima Trinidad** (1863), a heavy Neoclassical building with a surprisingly grand interior, with very solid columns, a coffered roof, a small baldacchino and a marble altar. The altarpiece is an oil painting of the *Holy Trinity*, the only painting by the sculptor José Luis Zorrilla de San Martín (1940).

Eleven blocks south on the edge of town is the **Parque Centenario**, a drab spread of gravel and eucalyptus trees opened in 1930 for the centenary of the swearing of Uruguay's constitution. Here are the municipal stadium and facilities for tennis, pelota, volleyball, basketball and other sports, as well as a children's play area, barbecues, tables and toilets. The road around the park is actually a cycle-racing track, with banked corners. To the east, the former train station (1916) now houses the **Museo Departamental** (*southern end of Alfredo Puig;* ⏱ *15.00–21.30 Tue–Sun, winter 09.00–19.00; free*), which has polished displays on the area's prehistory (see *Around Trinidad*) and on local history, with rotating exhibitions on themes such as local industry or schooling.

The **Reserva de Fauna y Flora Dr Rodolfo Tálice** (⏱ *till sunset Tue–Sun; free*), 3km west on Ruta 3, is one of the best zoos in the country. An excellent cycle track, with benches and lighting, leads there alongside the main road to the entry at km193½. Spread across 65ha around a large lake, it houses more than 600 animals of over 90 species, including charming free-range *maras* (Patagonian hares) wandering over the lawns, otters, alligators, tiny Brazilian titi monkeys, a puma and a jaguar (both asleep for much of the day), *coatis* (members of the raccoon family) and Raza Fernandina cattle (a Hereford/Angus cross). Birds include peacocks (including an albino one), flamingos, cotorras, black ibis, southern screamers, spoonbills and giant wood-rail. There's also a *reptilario* (which includes spiders), a sculpture park with a fair variety of pieces all jumbled together with no context, a children's play area, picnic tables, a cafeteria serving simple pizzas, *milanesas* and the like, and across the road the better Restaurant-*parrilla* El Portal.

It's also worth mentioning the **Zooilógico del Futuro** (*junction of Ruta 3 & Ruta 23, 5km south of Trinidad*), a collection of sculptures by local artist Martín Arregui. The iron cut-outs of native animals, weapons and symbols such as sun, moon and star allude to the threats to wildlife from hunting and other human activities.

AROUND TRINIDAD The Trinidad area has been inhabited for 13,000 years, and is known for its *pinturas rupestres* (rock art), pictographs carved around 2,000 years ago. The largest collection of these is at **Chamangá**, in the southeast of the department (between Ruta 57 and the Arroyo Maciel), usually found in triangular groups of three, mostly facing northwest. They consist of lines and zig-zags scored into the rock with a hard stone, and of outlined hands and other shapes in a reddish paint. Chamangá is part of SNAP, the new national system of protected areas, and can be visited by arrangement with the Comisión Departamental de Patrimonio (\ *364 3982 or 364 4863*). Trinidad's Casa de la Cultura (*Santísima Trinidad & Sarandí*) has a pictograph from Chamangá in its patio.

Almost 50km north of Trinidad Ruta 3 crosses into Río Negroon a long bridge over the artificial Lago Palmar, just north of the tiny village of **Andresito**. It's a very popular area for swimming and watersports, fishing, camping and picnicking. There's a *parador* with *cabañas* at the south end of the bridge, and a campsite in Andresito village. A casino and hotel are planned here. In January the Andresito Le Canta Al País (Andresito Sings to the Country) festival is held by the bridge, with folk singers from across the continent.

There are several excellent tourist *estancias* across the department. One of the most authentic gaucho experiences is at **San Martín del Yí** (*42km north of Trinidad; \ 360 4023; www.sanmartindelyi.com.uy*), east of Andresito. At the heart of the 1,830ha ranch is an L-shaped house built in 1850, with comfortably rustic rooms, and lashings of filling *criollo* food. You're welcome to work with the gauchos, looking after the thousand-plus sheep and 800 cattle, or you can relax by the Yí, paddle a canoe or watch the plentiful native wildlife, including parakeets, armadillos and ñandues. All-inclusive stays cost US$85 per person per day.

TREINTA Y TRES DEPARTMENT

TREINTA Y TRES Ruta 8 from Montevideo and Minas runs through rolling cattle country into the northeast of Uruguay, in some ways the most isolated area of the country. This region was in theory ceded to Portugal by the Treaty of Madrid in 1750, but continued to be administered from Buenos Aires. The city of Treinta y Tres (Thirty-three) was founded in 1853 at a ford over the Río Olimar and became capital of the new department of the same name in 1884. The railway arrived in 1911, since when the city has grown as an agricultural centre, with rice a major product (in the east of the department) along with cattle and sheep. Of the department's population of almost 50,000, more than half live in the city.

Getting there

By car Entering the department at km258, it's another 27km to the bridge over the Río Olimar (with an old road bridge and a rail bridge to the right – one of the city's iconic views). On the far bank is the Parque del Olimar, and immediately beyond you'll turn right after a 24-hour ANCAP station to enter the city, with streets named after each of the 33 heroes who crossed the Río Uruguay in 1825 to start the struggle for independence from Brazil.

By bus From Montevideo Nuñez runs at least six regular services (taking close to five hours) and two *directos* (taking four hours) via Minas to Treinta y Tres, two continuing to Río Branco (almost two hours further); Rutas del Plata runs three services a day to Treinta y Tres and Río Branco; and Tur-Este (Turil) runs four a day (two on Sundays) from Montevideo, and seven (four on Sundays) on to Río Branco. Expreso Minuano runs two a day (one on Sundays) from Montevideo to Treinta y Tres. From Melo there are five services a day with Nuñez.

EmTur has three services a day (taking three hours 20 minutes) from Maldonado, via San Carlos, Aiguá and Varela. Tur-Este has two services a day from Maldonado via Rocha, Aiguá and Varela; and two to Chuy. Turil and El Tala send two buses each to La Charqueada.

There's no bus terminal, the operators having offices just west of the central Plaza 19 de Abril: Nuñez (*Manuel Lavalleja & Freire*), EmTur (*Meléndez & Freire*) and Turil, Rutas del Plata and Minuano (*all on Zufriategui between Juan Antonio Lavalleja & Freire*).

Tourist information A block north of the plaza is the Centro de Información Turística (*Meléndez between Juan Antonio Lavalleja & Oribe;* ☎ *45 22911;* e *turismo33@imtt.gub.uy; www.imtt.gub.uy/turismo33;* ⊕ *07.00–19.00 Mon–Fri*).

🏠 Where to stay

🏠 **Hotel La Posada** Freire 1564; ☎ 45 21107, m 9512 6475; www.hotellaposada33.com. A fairly modern mid-range hotel with AC rooms, PC & parking, but no Wi-Fi. $$

🏠 **Treinta y Tres Hotel** Juan Antonio Lavalleja 1534; ☎ 45 22325/35; e treintaytreshotel@ starmedia.com. The best in town, with 3 stars but nothing very special; there's a garage, Wi-Fi, AC rooms & a restaurant (*closed for most of Jan*). $$

🏠 **Hotel Central** Juan Antonio Lavalleja 1241; ☎ 45 23095. Run-down, with simple rooms with cable TV & private bathroom, & parking. $

🏠 **Hotel Olimar** on the plaza at Juan Antonio Lavalleja 1414; ☎ 45 22115. The cheapest in town, an adequate 1-star place whose interior does not live up to its Art Deco façade. $

🏕 **Camping Río Olimar** Intendencia Municipal; ☎ 45 22108, 45 22456; ⊕ all year. On the southwestern edge of town by Ruta 8 & the river; simple but adequate facilities. $

✖ Where to eat

✖ **La Francisca** Juan Antonio Lavalleja & Meléndez. A decent *parrilla*-pizza restaurant.

✖ **Cervecería-Pizzería Don Rodrigo** Juan Antonio Lavalleja 549 & Zufriategui, west of the cathedral. A adequate beer & pizza joint.

Other practicalities

Banks There's an ATM on the west side of the plaza and others four and five blocks south on Juan Antonio Lavalleja.

Communications The post office is at Freire 1370 (⊕ *09.00–17.00 Mon–Fri, 09.00–12.00 Sat*). Antel's *telecentro* is at Gadea 1322 & Miranda (⊕ *09.00–19.00 daily*), and there's public Wi-Fi on Plaza 19 de Abril.

Emergency services The hospital is at Rodó 1831 & Zufriategui (☎ *45 22002*) and police headquarters are on the east side of the plaza (*Oribe 1439;* ☎ *45 22148*).

What to see and do The centre of town is characterised by wide, leafy two-way streets and single-storey houses. At its heart is **Plaza 19 de Abril** (the date of the landing of the 33 Orientales at Playa Agraciada), so well planted with trees that you can hardly see the surrounding buildings. In its centre is a monument to the 33 in

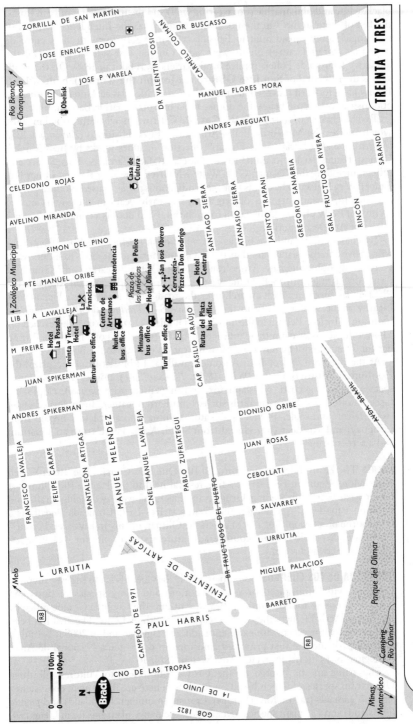

ZORRILLA DE SAN MARTÍN

JOSE ENRICHE RODÓ

DR BUSCASSO

Río Branco,
La Charqueada

JOSE P VARELA

R17 ♦ Obelisk

DR VALENTIN COSIO

CARMELO COLMAN

MANUEL FLORES MORA

ANDRES AREGUATI

CELEDONIO ROJAS

Casa de
Cultura

AVELINO MIRANDA

SANTIAGO SIERRA

ATANASIO SIERRA

JACINTO TRAPANI

GREGORIO SANABRIA

GRAL FRUCTUOSO RIVERA

RINCÓN

SARANDÍ

Zoológico Municipal

SIMON DEL PINO

PTE MANUEL ORIBE

Plaza de
los Américas ● Police

San José Obrero

LIB J A LAVALLEJA

La ✕
Francisca

Centro de
Artesanos ▦ Intendencia

Hotel Olímar

Cervecería-
Pizzería Don Rodrigo

M FREIRE

Hotel
La Posada

Treinta y Tres
Hotel

Emtur bus office

Núñez
bus office

Minuano
bus office

Turil bus office

Hotel
Central

JUAN SPIKERMAN

CAP BASILIO ARAÚJO
Rutas del Plata
bus office

ANDRES SPIKERMAN

DIONISIO ORIBE

FRANCISCO LAVALLEJA

FELIPE CARAPE

PANTALEÓN ARTIGAS

MANUEL MELENDEZ

CNEL MANUEL LAVALLEJA

PABLO ZUFRIATEGUI

JUAN ROSAS

CEBOLLATI

P SALVARREY

L URRUTIA

MIGUEL PALACIOS

BARRETO

AVDA BRASIL

Melo

L URRUTIA

TENIENTES DE ARTIGAS

BR FRUCTUOSO DEL PUERTO

R8

CAMPEÓN DE 1971

PAUL HARRIS

Parque del Olímar

Minas,
Montevideo

R8

Camping
Río Olímar

CNO DE LAS TROPAS

14 DE JUNIO

GOB 1825

0 ——— 100m
0 ——— 100yds

N

Bradt

black, white and pink marble (not wearing well) and the mausoleum of Juan Rosas, the last of them to die. On the north side of the plaza the Intendencia Municipal is a single-storey spread built in Eclectic style in the 1920s, with the Centro de Artesanos (Craft Centre) on its west side. On the east side of the plaza, the attractive Jefatura de Policía (police headquarters) was built in 1890. On the south side is the cathedral of **San José Obrero (St Joseph the Worker)**, built in 1871. It now has a modern red-brick façade and a simple Neoclassical interior with a flat end instead of an apse below the dome, and a big, pink-marble Baroque altar.

Two blocks east of the plaza is the **Casa de Cultura**, newly refurbished in 2009, which houses the Museo de Bellas Artes and Museo Histórico (*Zufriategui 1272 between Miranda & Rojas; free*). The art collection includes works by Juan Manuel Blanes, Blanes Viale, Joaquín Torres García, Rafael Barradas, Luis Solari and others, including the German Carla Witte who lived here near the end of her life. The History Museum has finds from the indigenous *cerritos* (raised mounds) of the department, documents and objects from the early years of the town, and an archive of B&W photos, many taken from the air. Next door is a cinema with a very attractive Art Deco interior.

Two blocks north and two blocks east, an **obelisk** (*Meléndez & Flores Mora*) rises 45m above a traffic island; raised in 1954, it's a memorial to the city's founders, with a bronze nymph at its base symbolising the Río Olimar. Nearby is the church of Cruz Alta, dating from 1868. At the western end of Meléndez, just off Ruta 8, is the Plaza de las Américas, with an arch over the road set up for Artigas's bicentenary. Nearby at the western entry to the city (*Ruta 8 & Fructuoso del Puerto*) there's a monument by José Belloni to the 'boy hero' Dionisio Díaz, who in 1929 rescued his 11-month-old sister from their murderous uncle (who had gone mad); he carried her for 7km to get help, but she died in the car on the way to the hospital.

At the northern end of Juan Antonio Lavalleja, 12 blocks from the plaza, the **Zoológico Municipal** (🕐 *08.00–18.00 Tue–Sun; free*) houses mainly native species, including coatí, grassland fox, hurón (similar to a weasel), carpincho, raccoon, otter, Geoffrey's cat, birds such as southern screamer, dusky-legged guan, stork, falcon and eagle, as well as alligator, a puma (more or less vanished from Uruguay) and axis deer (introduced from South Asia). There's also an aquarium and a serpentarium.

Events The Festival del Reencuentro 'El Río Que Más Canta' (The 'River Which Sings More' Reunion Festival) is a folk festival held in the Parque Río Olimar at Easter each year, with leading Uruguayan singers, as well as dancing, crafts and traditional foods. Also at Easter, the Treinta y Tres-La Charqueada Regatta is a waterborne procession (not a race) down the Olimar, mainly in kayaks and canoes. There are also various cross-country adventure sports events for 4x4 vehicles, mountain bikes and so on.

QUEBRADA DE LOS CUERVOS The Quebrada de los Cuervos is the largest canyon in Uruguay, with subtropical forest at its bottom and many species of birds and flowers otherwise found mainly in Brazil. Cut into the Cuchilla Grande range by the Arroyo Yerbal Chico, the canyon reaches a depth of 175m. The area has been well protected for years, with excellent paths and signage, and in 2008 it became a national park and the first protected landscape in the Sistema Nacional de Areas Protegidas or National Protected Area System (SNAP).

The name means 'Gorge of the Crows' but refers to vultures, all three Uruguayan species of which breed on its cliffs. There are three main ecosystems: *monte de quebrada* (ravine forest), *matorral serrano* (mountain heathland) and *pradera* (grassland) and 131 plant species (over 70% of the native plant species in Uruguay), with 87 trees and shrubs (including palms and cacti), 22 ferns, lianas, creepers, green and pink lichen, and 138 species of birds (with a toucan seen for the first time in 2008), about 20 amphibians, 30 reptiles and mammals such as Geoffrey's cat, margay cat, hurón, raccoon, foxes, *guazuvirá* (grey brocket deer) and armadillo.

Getting there and around The park is 45km north of Treinta y Tres, 24km west on a dirt road from km306.5 of Ruta 8. There's no public transport so you'll have to take a *remise* if you don't have your own wheels. From the north, a dirt road leads 33km from km328 of Ruta 8. From the visitor centre (⊕ *09.00–18.00 daily; US$0.50*) there's a 3km *sendero de interpretación* (interpretive path), with a viewpoint over the gorge after 800m (at the end of a wooden boardwalk), and other resting points.

⌂ **Where to stay and eat** There's a *parador* with barbecues 2km away, near the crystalline blue Laguna Redonda and a waterfall. The Camping Quebrada de los Cuervos (❧ *45 02394,* m *9985 3954;* ⊕ *all year; 6 cabins for 6;* $). At km14 of the road to the Quebrada de los Cuervos is the Cañada del Brujo, where an old school is now a simple but very friendly hostel (❧ *45 22837,* m *9929 7448;* e *vlatrilla33@gmail.com; also has cabañas;* $). Hiking and horseriding can be organised and bikes can be rented; meals are available and there's a kitchen to fix your own meals.

RÍO CEBOLLATÍ From Treinta y Tres, Meléndez continues east as Ruta 17 (there's also a northern bypass from Ruta 8), reaching the small river port of **La Charqueada** (also known as Pueblo General Enrique Martínez) after 61km. Tur-Este and El Tala run up to four buses daily on this route. Founded in the 18th century, it takes its name from *charque* (jerky), the dried beef once made here.

Swinging right at the plaza, Ruta 17 ends at a free car-ferry that crosses the Río Cebollatí to a beach in Rocha department, 7km from the village of Cebollatí. By the ferry slip is the *subprefectura*, where you can enquire about boats down the river, usually either a five-person launch or the 25-passenger *Dr Antiga*, which takes two hours for the 25km trip to Laguna Merín. Canoeing and kayaking are also popular, upstream and downstream from La Charqueada. There are massive oxbow bends, and impenetrable gallery forest (really an extension of Brazil's *mata Atlántica* or coastal rainforest), especially on the Rocha bank, with good birdwatching. Sport fishing is of far more interest to most visitors; possibilities include patí, boga, tararira, bagre, surubí and sábalo.

To the left of the ferry slip, the riverside Coronel Machado leads to the Cabañas Municipales (❧ *45 92256;* $), with 20 cabins with kitchenette and bathroom. There's also the free Camping Municipal (❧ *45 92204;* ⊕ *all year*), with hot showers, electric lighting and barbecues. Meals are available at the Parador Municipal.

From La Charqueada Ruta 91 runs north for 40km to **Vergara** (40km), 55km from Treinta y Tres on Ruta 18 to Río Branco. It's little more than a village, but is home to a modern Museo Antropológico (*Museum of Anthropology; Joaquín Suárez 1301 & Uturbey*). The eastern half of the department, now dominated by rice-farming, was home to a sizeable indigenous population, who left many *cerritos* (raised mounds) and village sites. The museum displays finds from these and also covers European colonisation and more recent history.

CERRO LARGO DEPARTMENT

From Treinta y Tres, Ruta 8 heads north, parallel to the Arroyo Yerbal, past the turnings to the Quebrada de los Cuervos (km306.5 and km328), and from km317 enters hillier country with rocky outcrops. the first settlement in the department of Cerro Largo (Long Hill), in the northeastern corner of the country, is Arbolito (km362), just south of which is a memorial to a civil-war battle in 1897. At km374½ the road crosses the Río Tacuarí, where there's a beach and wild camping. You'll start to see candelabra cacti, as well as groves of eucalyptus.

The border crossing with Brazil is at Aceguá, 60km north of Melo (the Uruguayan and Brazilian towns share the name). The Treaty of Aceguá in 1904 brought the last Uruguayan civil war to an end.

MELO Melo, capital of Cerro Largo department, was founded in three stages – first in 1791 as a military post known as the Guardía Vieja (Old Guardpost), near farms 5km south of the present city; then as the Guardía Nueva, on the site of the present cemetery, south of the centre; and finally in 1795 when Agustín de la Rosa laid out the present town on the orders of Viceroy Pedro Melo. Being close to the Brazilian border, it was captured by the Portuguese in 1801, 1811 and 1816, before becoming capital of Cerro Largo (one of the original six Uruguayan departments, cut down in 1837 and 1884).

This area has always been a stronghold of the Blancos (Partido Nacional), the main plaza being named as far back as 1845 after Manuel Oribe, Uruguay's second president and first Blanco president (it's now Plaza Constitución). General Aparico Saravia, the last of the great Blanco *caudillos*, lived at the Estancia El Cordobés (in the southwesternmost corner of the department), virtually the country's second seat of government from 1897 to 1903. Uruguay's first president, Fructuoso Rivera, died here in 1854. Juana Fernández Morales, later Juana de Ibarbourou, poet and novelist (see page 28), was born in Melo in 1892, and Wilson Ferreira Aldunate (1919–88), the Blanco leader who was the leading opponent of the dictatorship, grew up here.

Melo is now a city of close to 50,000 inhabitants, its prosperity based on trade with Brazil and on agriculture – largely cattle, for the PUL meat-packing plant and the Coleme dairy co-operative, but with rice increasingly important. It's still an old-fashioned, low-rise city, with a subtropical climate and a noticeably more Afro-Uruguayan population than most towns to the south. Pope John Paul II visited in 1988, the context of the 2007 film *El Baño del Papa* (The Pope's Toilet).

Getting there and around
By bus At about km392 Ruta 8 enters Melo (396km from Montevideo), buses continuing to the modern terminal nine blocks north of the central Plaza Constitución. The bus information office (✆ *64 22571*) is hidden away upstairs, and there's no specific tourist information office.

Direct traffic from Montevideo can also take Ruta 7, entering Melo from the west, although this bypasses intermediate towns such as Minas and Treinta y Tres. Ruta 7 and Ruta 8 cross in Melo, Ruta 7 going northeast to dead-end at Paso Centurión while Ruta 8 heads north to the Brazilian border.

From Montevideo Nuñez has five daily services to Melo by Ruta 8 (via Minas and Treinta y Tres, taking five to six hours), and two by Ruta 7 (via Cerro Chato, taking close to six hours); Turismar (Turil/Posada) has three a day by Ruta 7, and EGA has four (two on Sundays) by Ruta 8. From Rivera, Nuñez has a daily service (except Sundays) via Vichadero (taking four hours), and Posada has two a day via Tacuarembó and Ansina. From the Brazilian border at Aceguá Decatur has three daily buses (only at 08.00 on Sundays) and Nuñez has one daily.

From Río Branco, Nuñez has four buses a day, Turil has three, La Flota has two and Rutas del Plata has one (some of these starting at Lago Merín). Decatur/COTA

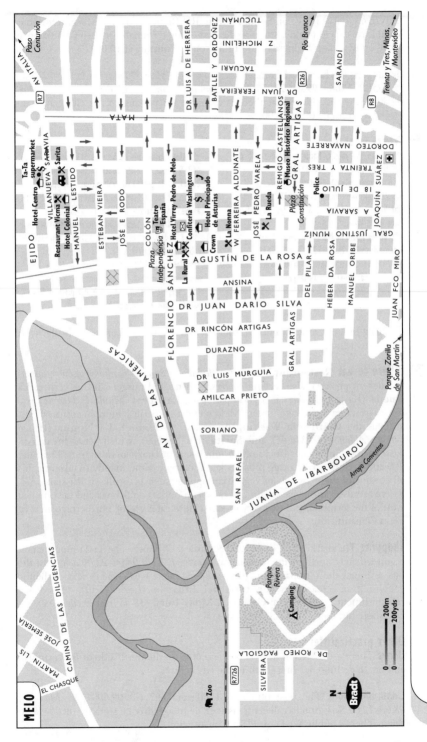

MELO

Paso Centurión

AV ITALIA

R7

EJIDO

VILLANUEVA SARAVIA

Ta-Ta supermarket
Hotel Centro
Restaurant Vicma
Hotel Colonial
MANUEL A LESTIDO
Sarita

ESTEBAN VIEIRA

JOSÉ E RODÓ

FLORENCIO SÁNCHEZ

Plaza COLÓN
Plaza Independencia
Teatro España
Hotel Virrey Pedro de Melo
Confitería Washington
La Rural
Hotel Principado de Asturias
Crown
La Nonna
La Rueda
W FERREIRA ALDUNATE
JOSÉ PEDRO VARELA
REMIGIO CASTELLANOS
Museo Histórico Regional
GRAL ARTIGAS
Plaza Constitución
Police
18 DE JULIO
A SARAVIA
JOAQUIN SUÁREZ
TREINTA Y TRES

AGUSTÍN DE LA ROSA

ANSINA

DR JUAN DARIO SILVA

DR RINCÓN ARTIGAS

DURAZNO

DR LUIS MURGUIA

AMILCAR PRIETO

SORIANO

SAN RAFAEL

JUANA DE IBARBOUROU

AV DE LAS AMERICAS

GRAL ARTIGAS
GRAL JUSTINO MUNIZ
DEL PILAR
HEBER DA ROSA
MANUEL ORIBE
JUAN FCO MIRO

DR LUIS A DE HERRERA
J BATLLE Y ORDOÑEZ
TACUARI
DR JUAN FERREIRA
Z MICHELINI
TUCUMÁN

F MATA

Río Branco

SARANDI

R26

R8

DOROTEO NAVARRETE

Treinta y Tres, Minas, Montevideo

Parque Zorilla de San Martín

Arroyo Conventos

Parque Rivera
Camping

DR ROMEO PAGGIOLA

R7/26

SILVEIRA

Zoo

CAMINO DE LAS DILIGENCIAS
JOSÉ SEMERIA
MARTIN LIS
EL CHASQUE

0   200m
0   200yds

N

Bradt

runs five services (three on Sundays) from Río Branco and Lago Merín. Ómnibus Vidal leaves Melo (on the street to the east of the terminal) for Paso Centurión at 08.00 on Monday, Wednesday and Friday only, returning at 10.00.

By car Cars can be rented from Multicar (*Francisco Mata 570 near Varela;* ↘ *64 24860,* m *9588 5766, 9980 0717; www.redmulticar.com;* ⊕ *09.00–19.00 Mon–Fri, 09.00–13.30 Sat*). Note that there is a charge for parking in the city centre on weekdays from 07.00 to 13.00.

⌂ Where to stay

⌂ **Crown** (54 rooms) Batlle y Ordóñez 609 & Agustín de la Rosa; ↘ 64 22261; e hotelcrownmelo@adinet.com.uy; http://hotelcrown.com.uy. Comfortable & friendly 3-star hotel with 54 rooms & 4 suites, all with AC, cable TV & Wi-Fi. $$$

⌂ **Virrey Pedro de Melo** (30 rooms) Plaza Independencia & Muniz 727; ↘ 64 22673, 6422411.Good 3-star hotel with AC rooms with cable TV, as well as Wi-Fi & a restaurant $$$

⌂ **Hotel Principado de Asturias** (15 rooms) Herrera 668 & Muniz, 5 blocks south of the terminal; ↘ 64 22064; e jorgeg1975@yahoo.com.ar. A spotless 2-star; all rooms have private bathroom & cable TV, as well as a garage & barbecue. $$

⌂ **Hotel Centro** Saravia 711, north of the terminal; ↘ 64 31469. Has rooms with private bathrooms & cable TV, & a cafeteria $

⌂ **Hotel Colonial** (6 rooms) Lestido & 18 de Julio, immediately west of the terminal; m 9481 7969 The cheapest (but also the noisiest) place in town has 6 rooms & 3 shared bathrooms. $

Camping In the Parque Rivera, on Ruta 7 across the Arroyo Conventos bridge west of the city centre.

✗ Where to eat

Where to eat **Restaurant Vicma** (*18 de Julio & Saravia, northwest of the terminal*) is a decent pizzeria, also serving *milanesas*, pastas and burgers. In the centre, **La Rueda** (*Varela & Muniz*) is a good *parrillada*; **La Rural** (*Muniz & Herrera*) is a *parrilla*-restaurant and café. In fact Melo seems to specialise more in coffee-shops, such as the **Confitería Washington** (*Muniz & Herrera*), **La Nonna** (*Wilson Ferreira Aldunate & Muniz*) and **Sarita** (*bus terminal*), which serve breakfasts, pastries and sandwiches (including *bauru*, a sort of Brazilian *chivito*). At Del Pilar 400 and Treinta y Tres a café sells cooked food by weight, mainly to take out; it's all cheap and there are lots of vegetarian options such as tortilla or Russian salad. There are also various ice cream and *empanada* outlets on Saravia and Lestido just west of the terminal, and two very modern kiosk cafés on the northern corners of Plaza Constitución.

Shopping The market is at 18 de Julio & Batlle y Ordóñez. The Ta-Ta supermarket is immediately north of the terminal at Saravia 777 (⊕ 08.00–22.00 daily). In the bus terminal the Criollas shop (*supposedly* ⊕ *24hr;* ↘ *64 21383*) sells authentic gaucho gear. Nearby is the Casa del Artesano (*Lestido 730*), closed for refurbishment in 2009. The Casa de la Mujer Rural (*18 de Julio & Aldunate*) is a café/shop, but there's not much for sale.

Other practicalities

Banks There are ATMs at Saravia 599 and 699, on the north side of the terminal, and on 18 de Julio, leading south to the city centre.

Communications The post office is at Herrera 667 (⊕ *09.00–17.00 Mon–Fri, 08.00–12.00 Sat*); Antel's call centre is at 18 de Julio 696 & Herrera (⊕ *09.00–19.00 daily*). There's public Wi-Fi on Plaza Constitución.

Consulate The Inspectoría de Migración is at Ruta 8 km460 (✆ *64 09027, 64 09156;* e *i03melo@dnm.minterior.gub.uy*).

Emergency services The police headquarters are immediately east of the cathedral at Del Pilar 718 (✆ *64 22421/2, 64 22018*). The hospital is at Doroteo Navarrete & Suárez (✆ *64 21002, 64 22480*).

What to see and do Plaza Constitución, nine blocks south of the terminal, is the city's central square, an attractive space with big trees and open space around the central monument to José Gervasio Artigas. On its south side stands the **cathedral**, clean and quiet, with light colours. It was built in 1857–76 in a simple Neoclassical style, the aisles added in the 20th century in exactly the same style. The apse seems to have been added in the 1970s, with an unusual arrangement of wooden slats and marble. Across Saravia immediately west of the cathedral is a tatty but very fine palace, south of the Club Unión – a less impressive Belle Epoque pile.

On the east side of Plaza Constitución, the **Museo Histórico Regional** (*Regional Historical Museum; Artigas;* ⊕ *07.00–13.00 Mon–Fri, 14.00–18.00 Sat–Sun; free*) displays mementos of the local *caudillo*, General Aparico Saravia (1856–1904), who led revolts against the government in 1894–97 and ran a virtual parallel government from his *estancia* of El Cordobés. He led uprisings again in 1903 and in 1904, and was mortally wounded at the battle of Masoller. There are lots of pistols and rifles, his carriage and safe, and even his branding iron. Upstairs are fossils, prehistoric arrowheads, *boleadoras* and grinding stones, and ceramics from the Jesuit missions in the west of the country, as well as some works by local amateur artists. You'll also see the rocking chair, hat, fan and prayer book of the poet Juana de Ibarbourou (see page 28), whose birthplace, a perfectly normal single-storey house two blocks south at Treinta y Tres 317, is not open to visitors.

The city's other main square is Plaza Independencia, southwest of the terminal. On the east side the single-storey, Belle Epoque Asociación Española de Socorros Mutuos (*Muñiz 770*), built in 1914, houses the **Teatro España**.

The Arroyo Conventos flows along the city's western side, with two riverside parks. There's a summer theatre in the Parque Zorrilla de San Martín, southwest of Plaza Constitución, while the Parque Rivera, on the far side of the Ruta 7 bridge, at the western end of Florencio Sánchez, includes a campsite, a *parador* and play areas. At its entrance is a replica of the house of Bartolomé Silva, where Fructuoso Rivera died on his way from Rio de Janeiro to join the ruling triumvirate. On the other side of Ruta 7 is a small zoo, with some native species plus tigers, lions, a black bear, llamas, monkeys and axis deer.

PASO CENTURIÓN From Melo, Ruta 7 continues northeast for about 50km to Paso Centurión, where it ends at the Río Yaguarón. A tiny portion of Brazil's *mata Atlántica* (coastal rainforest) has crossed the river into Uruguay here. There are butiá palms, creepers, ferns and bromeliads, animals such as anteaters, armadillos, porcupine, agoutí, margay cat, *guazubirá*, capybara and – a recent discovery in Uruguay – *cuica de agua* (water opossum; *Chironectes minimus*). The 120 species of birds include yellow-headed vulture, plush-crested jay, anhinga, saffron-cowled blackbird and rarities such as the reddish-bellied parakeet (or Azara's conure; *Pyrrhura frontalis chiripepe*), common or grey potoo (*urutaú; Nyctibius griseus*) and brushland tinamou (*perdiz montaráz; Nothoprocta cinerascens*).

First settled in 1778, this was a crossing point for cattle exports to Brazil, and the old Customs house and a military hospital can still be seen. Ómnibus Vidal leaves Melo at 08.00 on Monday, Wednesday and Friday only, returning at 10.00 – so unless you come by car or bike you'll have to bring a tent and stay at least two nights.

RÍO BRANCO Ruta 26 heads east from Melo towards the border town of Río Branco, after 13km passing the former **Posta del Chuy**, a stone coaching inn (*pulpería y posta de diligencias*) where two French Basques built a 85m-long toll bridge over the Arroyo Chuy del Tacuarí in 1855. Tolls were collected until 1917 and the *posta* is now open as the Museo del Gaucho, del Campo y de la Frontera (Museum of the Gaucho, the Countryside and the Frontier).

The Guardía Arredondo military post was built in 1792 near the present bridge, but in 1801 the Portuguese moved to the north side of the Río Yaguarón, leaving a settlement known as Pueblo Arredondo. By 1854 a new town known as Villa Artigas had appeared a couple of kilometres south, in 1912 renamed after the Barão (Baron) de Rio Branco (1845–1912), the Brazilian diplomat who guaranteed Brazil's frontiers and was responsible for the so-called 'free womb law' of 1871, which ensured that a slave's children would henceforth be born free. Today it's a quiet and unexciting town of around 13,000.

Getting there and around The road joins Ruta 18 from Treinta y Tres and Montevideo, and after just over an hour (km85) reaches the *paso frontera* (border post) at the western edge of Río Branco. Buses from Melo stop if required for Immigration purposes, continuing via Arredondo and Plaza Artigas in the town centre, turning around near the international bridge and returning to the centre. Empresa Moreira runs a local bus roughly hourly from the *paso frontera* to the plaza and the bridge. It's just over 3km to the plaza, if you should decide to walk.

The Barón de Mauá international bridge, opened in 1930, was at the time the longest bridge in South America (until the Paysandú–Colón bridge opened). It's 2,112m long, although the main span is only a couple of hundred metres; most of it is actually the approach ramp on the Uruguayan side, carrying both a road and a railway; there's a shorter ramp from Artigas in Pueblo Arredondo. There's no bus service across the border so you'll have to walk or take a taxi (*US$3 from Plaza Artigas to the Policía Federal*).

Nuñez operates two services daily from Montevideo, Minas and Treinta y Tres to Río Branco (at least six hours), and four from Melo (one continuing to Lago Merín except on Sundays); Rutas del Plata has three services a day from Montevideo. Turil has three buses a day from Melo and Rutas del Plata has one. Decatur/COTA runs five services (three on Sundays) from Melo to Río Branco and Lago Merín; and La Flotta runs two a day from Melo to Río Branco, one continuing to Lago Merín.

Where to stay and eat The only place to stay (other than the Excalibur 'love-hotel' on the Lago Merín road) is the **Hotel Status** (*Artigas, two blocks south of the bridge;* ✆ *675 2264; $$*), simple but decent enough. There are far more options in the attractive Brazilian town of Jaguarão, with cheap hotels near the bridge and better ones on the plaza, three blocks to the right.

There are *parrillas* on Artigas near the bridge and hotel. A block north of the plaza are the Restaurant-Pizzeria La Campana (*Arredondo & El Fanal*) and a Pizzeria-Churrasquería (*Arredondo & Ferreiro*). Six blocks south near the Nuñez bus office is the good Panadería-Confitería Esmeralda (*Arredondo & Arismendi*).

Other practicalities

Communications The post office is at Arredondo 963 (🕐 *10.00–16.00 Mon–Fri, 08.00–13.00 Sat*). Antel's call centre is at the southwestern corner of the plaza (*Gundin 881;* 🕐 *09.00–18.00 daily*). There's a Wi-Fi signal on the plaza but it's a bit weak. There are a few duty-free shops near the bridge and an ATM at the Banco República.

Consulate There are Inspectoría de Migración offices at the *paso frontera* (℡ *675 2638;* e *i014riobranco@dnm.minterior.gub.uy*) and at the bridge (℡ *675 2068*), and a Brazilian vice-consulate a block south of the plaza (*10 de Junio 379;* ℡ *675 2003*). On the Brazilian side, you'll have to get your entry stamp at the Policía Federal (*1572 Rua Júlio de Castilhos;* ⏰ *24hrs*), west from the lovely Rua X de Novembro. The *rodoviaria* (bus station) is on the plaza, with services to Porto Alegre (*3/day; 6hrs; US$35*) and Pelotas (*7/day, 5 Sun*).

LAGO MERÍN Laguna Merín is the second-largest lake in South America after Lake Titicaca, covering an area of about 3,800km². On its northern shore, 21km from Río Branco, is the beach resort of Lago Merín.

Founded in 1937, Lago Merín has always received many visitors from Brazil, and now sees around 15,000 on summer weekends. Some 60% of its houses are owned by Brazilians, many from the city of Pelotas. It's a simple resort, mainly attracting families, although it does have the usual hippies selling jewellery. The beach is sandy and slopes very gently, and the lake is not tidal, making it very safe for children. It has a maximum depth of 7m and often has a consistent breeze, making it popular with windsurfers and kite-surfers. There's also good fishing, notably for tararira.

The main festival is the Reina del Lago (*Queen of the Lake; www.reinadellago.com*), over a weekend in the middle of January.

Getting there and around

By bus Buses run five times daily (three on Sundays) from Melo via Río Branco, the last returning at 19.00. They run between huge rice fields (with lots of termite mounds) and enter on Calle 18, reaching the beach at km21 (where there are toilets and a *policlínica*) and turning right to terminate four blocks south.

By bike Bikes can be rented by the *policlínica* at the end of Calle 18.

Where to stay

Hostería Alcalá Four blocks south of Calle 18, on the rambla between Calles 2 & 4; ℡ 679 8893. A long-established hotel-*parador* with simple rooms & filling meals. Most visitors stay in rented *cabañas* $$

Hotel Laguna Merín Calles 18 & 11; ℡ 679 8033; e hotellagunamerin@hotmail.com; www.hotellagunamerin.net. The best place to stay, this nice 3-star place has a swimming pool indoors & one outdoors under a sunroof, plus Wi-Fi, gym & a good restaurant $$

Rincón del Lago Calles 18 & 13; ℡ 679 8804. Has nice apartments & *cabañas*, with AC & cable TV & a *parrilla*. $$

Camping Municipal Two blocks along from the Rincón del Lago; ⏰ all year. A simple, friendly campsite with hot showers. The Cabañas Municipales is on the other side of Calle 23. There is a police post nearby (*calles 18 & 23*). $

Where to eat There are shops and bars at the end of Calle 18, and a pizzería-cervecería with pool hall just to the north, as well as the Parador Municipal and casino, both closed (there's talk of a new hotel and casino in Río Branco). There are no fancy restaurants at all, except in the hotel.

It's worth mentioning the Laguna Lodge, run by Lake Merin Outfitters (*USA* ℡ *800 420 8707;* e *lakemerinoutfitters@yahoo.com, lakemerin@terra.com.br; www.lakemerin.com*), which aims to create an American-style duck-hunting atmosphere, complete with 05.00 starts and evenings with an open fire, satellite TV, Wi-Fi and hearty meals. They have various duck blinds 15–25 minutes away by 4x4 truck.

Appendix I

LANGUAGE

PRONOUNS

I	*yo*	they	*ellos*
you (singular informal)	*vos*	they (feminine only)	*ellas*
		me/myself	*me*
you (singular formal)	*usted*	you/yourself	*te*
you (plural)	*ustedes*	us/ourselves	*nos*
he/it	*él*	you (plural)/ youselves	*os*
she/it	*ella*		
it	*ello*	them/themselves	*les/se*
we	*nosotros*	them/themselves (feminine only)	*las/se*
we (feminine only)	*nosotras*		

NUMBERS

0	*cero*	19	*diez y nueve*
1	*uno/una* (m/f)	20	*veinte*
2	*dos*	21	*veinte y uno*
3	*tres*	22	*veinte dos*
4	*cuatro*	30	*treinta*
5	*cinco*	40	*cuarenta*
6	*seis*	50	*cincuenta*
7	*siete*	60	*sesenta*
8	*ocho*	70	*setenta*
9	*nueve*	80	*ochenta*
10	*diez*	90	*noventa*
11	*once*	100	*cien*
12	*doce*	101	*ciento y uno*
13	*trece*	200	*doscientos*
14	*catorce*	1,000	*mil*
15	*quince*	10,000	*diez mil*
16	*diez y seis*	100,000	*cien mil*
17	*diez y siete*	1,000,000	*un millón*
18	*diez y ocho*		

DATES

January	*Enero*	July	*Julio*
February	*Febrero*	August	*Agosto*
March	*Marzo*	September	*Septiembre*
April	*Abril*	October	*Octubre*
May	*Mayo*	November	*Noviembre*
June	*Junio*	December	*Diciembre*

DAYS

Sunday	*Domingo*	Thursday	*Jueves*
Monday	*Lunes*	Friday	*Viernes*
Tuesday	*Martes*	Saturday	*Sabado*
Wednesday	*Miercoles*		

TIME

today	*hoy*	week	*semana*
yesterday	*ayer*	month	*mes*
tomorrow	*mañana*	year	*año*
morning	*la mañana*	Good day/good	*Buenos días*
tomorrow morning	*mañana por la mañana*	morning	
afternoon	*la tarde*	Good afternoon	*Buenas tardes*
evening/night	*la noche*	Good night	*Buenas noches*
last night	*anoche*		

The 24-hour clock is used, so for '7pm' you can say either *son las diez y nueve* or *son las siete de la noche.*

What time is it?	*¿Qué hora es?*	12.00 (noon)	*mediodía*
01.00	*Es la una*	24.00 (midnight)	*medianoche*
02.00	*Son las dos*		

BASIC VOCABULARY

Hello	*hola*	You're welcome	*de nada*
Glad to meet you	*mucho gusto*	Sorry	*lo siento*
Goodbye	*adiós*	Excuse me	*disculpe*
Good/well/very well	*bueno/bien/muy bien*	Of course	*claro*
Yes/no	*sí/no*	Open/closed	*abierto/cerrado*
Please/thank you	*por favor/gracias*	Large/small	*grande/pequeño*

Directions and transport

here/there	*aquí/ahí*	unnumbered	*sin numero (s/n)*
left/right	*izquierda/derecha*	casi/esquina	*near/corner*
north/south	*norte/sur*	bus-stop	*parada*
east/west	*este/oeste*	bus station	*terminal*
northwest	*noroeste*	airport	*aeropuerto*
southeast	*sureste*	ferry	*barca*
straight ahead	*derecha/adelante*	jetty	*muele*
block	*cuadra*	return ticket	*pasaje ida-y-vuelta*
corner	*esquina*	I want to go to…	*Quiero ir a…*
street/avenue	*calle/avenida*	I want to get off at…	*Quiero bajar a…*
road/path	*camino/sendero*	Stop, please!	*¡Parada, por favor!*

Accommodation

Do you have a room?		*¿Hay un cuarto?*
What does it cost?		*¿Cuánto cuesta?*
Do you have anything cheaper?		*¿Hay algo más barato?*
with private bathroom		*con baño privado*
with shared bathroom		*con baño compartido*
too much	*demasiado*	single	*sencillo*
expensive	*caro*	twin	*doble*
cheap	*barato, económico*	double	*matrimonial*

air-conditioned	*aire acondicionado*		toilet paper	*papel higiénico*
shower	*ducha*			
towel	*toalla*			

Food and drink (*See pages 64–6 for some dishes*)

bread	*pan*		water	*agua*
butter	*manteca*		wine/beer	*vino/cerveza*
(without) meat	*(sin) carne*		juice/milk	*jugo/leche*
fish	*pescado*		tea/coffee	*té/cafe*
potatoes	*patatas*		knife/fork/spoon	*cuchillo/tenedor/cuchara*
vegetables	*legumbres*		Enjoy your meal	*Buen provecha*
fruit	*fruta*		the bill, please	*la cuenta, por favor*

Questions

Where?	*¿Dónde?*		When?	*¿Cuándo?*
Who?	*¿Quién?*		Why?	*¿Por qué?*
What?	*¿Cómo?*		How?	*¿Cómo?*

Typically Uruguayan words and phrases

a las ordenes	at your service	*bárbaro*	fantastic
¿Yo que se?	what do I know?	*rambla*	waterfront promenade
Que le pase bien	farewell	*balastro*	dirt road
¿Entonces, que pasa?	So, what's up?	*glorieta*	viewpoint
¿Que cosa?	What?		(not *mirador*)
¡Que calor!	It's so hot!		
Jaja	Yes yes		

Note that the word for government is often spelt *gubierno*, not *gobierno* as elsewhere – so the internet domain is .gub.uy not .gob.uy. The country to the north is spelt Brasil not Brazil (where Uruguay is spelt Uruguai, and its capital Montevidéu). The neighbour further to the north is called Estados Unidos (not Los Estados Unidos), and its people *americanos* (not *norteamericanos*).

Appendix 2

FURTHER INFORMATION

BOOKS
General

Delgardo, Mario *Boliches Montevideanos* Banda Oriental, Montevideo, 2006. A beautifully produced photographic guide to the most traditional, and significant pubs and bar-restaurants of Montevideo.

Jermyn, Leslie *Uruguay (Cultures of the World)* Marshall Cavendish, Tarrytown NY, 1999. Produced for school geography classes, this is a slim but well illustrated volume covering the country's geography, people, politics, economy and culture (including art, sports and food).

Lanza, Eduardo, Larrimbe, Miguel & Michelini, Margarita *Vinos y Bodegas de Uruguay* Montevideo, Fin de Siglo 2005. An attractive guide to the history of Uruguay's vineyards, focusing on their transformation from the late 1980s.

Morrison, Marion *Uruguay (Enchantment of the World series)* Scholastic, New York, 3rd ed 2005. Aimed at younger school-children, this is full of photos and entertaining boxes, as well as hints for further research.

Remedi, Gustavo (transl) Ferlazzo, Amy *Carnival Theater: Uruguay's Popular Performers and National Culture* University of Minnesota Press, Minneapolis, 2004. An academic investigation of the complex roots of Uruguay's popular culture.

Shields, Charles J *Uruguay (Discovering South America series)* Broomall PA, Mason Crest, 2nd ed 2009. A brief introduction for schoolchildren to the geography, history and culture of Uruguay, with extras such as recipes and project ideas.

Darwin

Aydon, Cyril *Charles Darwin* Constable & Robinson, 2002. A balanced account, placing Darwin in his social and economic context.

Browne, Janet *Charles Darwin: Voyaging* Princeton UP/Cape, 1996 and *The Power of Place* Princeton UP/Cape, 2003. This two-volume biography is the most detailed and up-to-date available.

Darwin, Charles *The Voyage of the Beagle* 1839; paperback editions by Penguin and Wordsworth Classics, UK, and NAL-Dutton, USA. Perhaps 'the greatest travel book ever'. Also: *The Autobiography of Charles Darwin* Oxford University Press/Dover, 1983; *The Origin of Species* 1859; paperback editions by Penguin, OUP World's Classics and Random House Modern Library; *The Descent of Man* Prometheus, US.

Keynes, Richard *Fossils, Finches and Fuegians: Charles Darwin's Adventures and Discoveries on the Beagle* HarperCollins, 2003. By Darwin's great-grandson.

Moorehead, Alan *Darwin and the Beagle* Hamish Hamilton, 1969/Penguin, 1971.

Ralling, Christopher (ed) *The Voyage of Charles Darwin* BBC, 1978.

Stott, Rebecca *Darwin and the Barnacle* Norton, 2003.

Thomson, Keith *HMS Beagle: the Story of Darwin's Ship* Norton, 1995. The remains of the Beagle have since been found.

Wertenbaker, Timberlake *After Darwin* Faber, 1999. Perhaps her best play.

History

Caviedes, César *The Southern Cone: Realities of the Authoritarian State* Rowman & Allanheld, Totowa NJ, 1984. A comparative study of the military dictatorships of Chile, Argentina, Uruguay, and Brazil of the 1970s and 1980s.

Gillespie, Charles *Negotiating Democracy: Politicians and Generals in Uruguay* Cambridge University Press 1991. An academic, but still fascinating, account of the negotiations behind the return to democracy in the late 1980s.

Labrousse, Alain *Les Tupamaros: des armes aux urnes* (1962-2009) Editions du Rocher, Paris, 2009. Only in French, but one of the best and most up-to-date accounts of the Uruguayan left's transition from a guerrilla campaign to forming the current legitimate government.

Parrado, Nando *Miracle in the Andes* Random House, 2006. The true story of the Uruguayan rugby club whose plane crashed in the Andes in 1972; after waiting for two months (and eating the flesh of their dead companions), Parrado and a companion made a ten-day journey to find help, and 16 of the 45 were rescued alive. Also told in:

Read, Piers Paul *Alive: The Story of the Andes Survivors* HarperCollins, 2002. Also a film.

Street, John *Artigas and the Emancipation of Uruguay* Cambridge University Press 1959, paperback 2008.

Vanger, Milton *Batlle y Ordóñez of Uruguay, The Creator of His Times, 1902–1907* Harvard UP, 1963; also *José Batlle y Ordóñez of Uruguay, The Model Country, 1907–1915*; and *José Batlle y Ordóñez of Uruguay, The Determined Visionary, 1915–1917*. An academic trilogy giving a detailed account of the creation of modern Uruguay as South America's first welfare state.

Weinstein, Martin *Uruguay: Democracy at the Crossroad* Westview Press, Boulder CO, 1988. An academic view of Uruguayan politics, at a time when its economy was stagnant and the restoration of democracy incomplete. Also *Uruguay: The Politics of Failure* (Greenwood Press, Westport, Conn. 1975), on the reasons why military dictatorship was able to supplant a democratic welfare state.

Literature

Boyd, William *Any Human Heart* Hamish Hamilton, London, 2002. The journals of the fictional writer Logan Gonzago Mountstewart, born in 1906 in Montevideo, whose mediocre life brought him into contact with many of the 20th century's most colourful characters; this is a substantial multi-layered novel (complete with footnotes and index) that soon moves beyond the confines of Uruguay.

Dumas, Alexandre père *Montevideo, ou une nouvelle Troie* Napoléon Chaix et Cie., Paris, 1850; Amis d'Alexandre Dumas, Le Port-Marly Yvelines, 2007. A very unusual book by the prolific novelist, a non-fiction account of the struggle for independence of the Banda Oriental between 1810 and 1848, this has not been translated from French; however parts were recycled in his *Mémoires de Garibaldi* (1861).

Fonseca, Isabel *Attachment* Random House/Chatto 2008, paperback Vintage 2009. About an American-British couple taking a sabbatical in the tropics, this novel is partly rooted in her life in Uruguay with Martin Amis.

Hudson, William Henry *The Purple Land* University of Wisconsin, 2002. First published in 1885, this was described by Borges as 'the best work of gaucho literature'; its English hero gradually casts off his Victorian stuffiness and comes to love the freedom and indeed chaos of the New World.

Travels

Green, Toby *Saddled with Darwin* Phoenix, London, 1999. Following Darwin's trail on horseback through Uruguay, Argentina and Chile, this is an entertaining but serious account by a talented young writer, combining accounts of Darwin's legacy and of contemporary rural life.

Wangford, Hank *Lost Cowboys* Indigo, London, 1996. In the country-singing gynaecologist's inimitable style, this is a funny and very informative pilgrimage through Latin America in search of the Hispanic origins of the cowboys; 40 of 300-plus pages are on Uruguay, where he found an unspoilt heartland of gaucho tradition.

Wildlife

Achaval, Federico & Olmos, Alejandro *Anfibios y Reptiles del Uruguay* Biophoto, Montevideo, 3rd ed 2007. A photographic guide to Uruguay's 66 reptile species and 48 amphibians.

Achaval, Mario Clara & Olmos, Alejandro *Mamíferos de la República Oriental del Uruguay* Facultad de Ciencias, Montevideo, 2nd ed 2007. A Spanish-language guide to Uruguay's mammals.

Arballo, Eduardo & Cravino, Jorge *Aves del Uruguay: Volume 1 Manual Ornitológico* Editorial Agropecuaria Hemisferio Sur SRL, Montevideo, 1999. With a second volume due, these weighty Spanish-language volumes will be the most detailed account of Uruguay's birds.

Azpiroz, Adrian *Aves del Uruguay – Lista e Introducción a su Biología y Conservación* 2nd ed 2003. Spanish-language list of Uruguay's birds, with information on conservation issues.

Brito, Ana Helena & Llano, Liliana *Bromelias del Uruguay* Librería Linardi y Risso, Montevideo, 2008. A Spanish-language guide to Uruguay's bromeliads (pineapple-like plants, many epiphytic).

Lahitte, B and Hurell, J A *Trees of the Río de la Plata* LOLA, Buenos Aires, 1999. In Spanish and English; fully illustrated.

Menafra, R, Rodríguez-Gallego, L, Scarabino, F, and Conde, D (eds.) *Bases para la Conservación y el Manejo de la Costa Uruguaya* Vida Silvestre, Montevideo, 2006. This large book on Uruguay's coastal biology costs less than US$20, due to funding by the US Fish and Wildlife Service; it consists of 63 academic papers by local scientists, covering not just the biology of the coastal zone but also geology, paleontology and archaeology.

Muñoz J, Ross P & Cracco P *Flora Indígena del Uruguay – Arboles y Arbustos Ornamentales* Editorial Agropecuaria Hemisferio Sur SRL, Montevideo, 1994. A Spanish-language guide to Uruguay's native trees and shrubs.

Narosky, Tito & Yzurieta, Dario *Birds of Argentina and Uruguay – a Field Guide* Vasquez Mazzini Editores. Buenos Aires, 15th ed 2003. The best field guide to Uruguay's birds, available through www.wildlifebooks.com in the UK.

Rocha, Gabriel *Aves del Uruguay – El País de los pájaros pintados* Ediciones de la Banda Oriental, Montevideo, 2004. In three volumes, this is a beautifully presented guide (in Spanish) to Uruguay's birds; the third volume includes information on ecotourism and birdwatching locales.

Wheatley, Nigel *Where to Watch Birds in South America* Princeton UP, 1995.

Health

Wilson-Howarth, Dr Jane, and Ellis, Dr Matthew *Your Child Abroad: A Travel Health Guide* Bradt Travel Guides, 2005.

Wilson-Howarth, Dr Jane, *Bugs, Bites & Bowels* Cadogan, 2006.

WEBSITES
Art
www.mnav.gub.uy/artistas.htm

Communications
www.correo.com.uy
www.antel.com.uy

Conservation and NGOs
www.retosalsur.org
www.karumbe.org

www.anong.org.uy
http://vidasilvestre.org.uy
www.avesuruguay.org.uy

Gay issues
www.alianzagayuruguay.com
www.outinuruguay.com
http://uruguaydiverso.blogspot.com

Health
www.fitfortravel.scot.nhs.uk
www.nathnac.org/ds/c_pages/country_page_uy.htm
www.cdc.gov/travel/destinations/uruguay.aspx
www.istm.org
www.netdoctor.co.uk/travel
www.uruguaywinetours.com

Horseriding and *estancias*
www.aru.com.uy
www.turismorural.com.uy

Immigration
www.dnm.mininterior.gub.uy

Maps
www.acu.com.uy/maparutero

Sport
www.auf.org.uy
www.uru.org.uy
www.wannasurf.com
www.olasyvientos,com
www.oceanmind.net
www.paipo.com.uy
www.aug.com.uy

Tourism
www.uruguaynatural.com
www.turismo.gub.uy

Travel
www.flypluna.com
www.buquebus.com
www.trescruces.com.uy
www.montevideo.gub.uy/stm
www.afe.com.uy

Wine tours
www.uruguaywinetours

Bradt Travel Guides

Africa

Africa Overland	£16.99
Algeria	£15.99
Angola	£18.99
Botswana	£16.99
Burkina Faso	£17.99
Cameroon	£15.99
Cape Verde	£15.99
Congo	£16.99
Eritrea	£15.99
Ethiopia	£17.99
Ethiopia Highlights	£15.99
Ghana	£15.99
Kenya Highlights	£15.99
Madagascar	£16.99
Madagascar Highlights	£15.99
Malawi	£15.99
Mali	£14.99
Mauritius, Rodrigues & Réunion	£16.99
Mozambique	£15.99
Namibia	£15.99
Nigeria	£17.99
North Africa: Roman Coast	£15.99
Rwanda	£16.99
São Tomé & Príncipe	£14.99
Seychelles	£16.99
Sierra Leone	£16.99
Somaliland	£15.99
South Africa Highlights	£15.99
Sudan	£16.99
Swaziland	£15.99
Tanzania Safari Guide	£17.99
Tanzania, Northern	£14.99
Uganda	£16.99
Zambia	£18.99
Zanzibar	£15.99
Zimbabwe	£15.99

The Americas and the Caribbean

Alaska	£15.99
Amazon Highlights	£15.99
Argentina	£16.99
Bahia	£14.99
Cayman Islands	£14.99
Chile Highlights	£15.99
Colombia	£17.99
Dominica	£15.99
Grenada, Carriacou & Petite Martinique	£15.99
Guyana	£15.99
Haiti	£16.99
Nova Scotia	£15.99
Panama	£14.99
Paraguay	£15.99
Peru Highlights	£15.99
Turks & Caicos Islands	£14.99
Uruguay	£15.99
USA by Rail	£15.99
Venezuela	£16.99
Yukon	£14.99

British Isles

Britain from the Rails	£14.99
Bus-Pass Britain	£15.99
Eccentric Britain	£16.99
Eccentric Cambridge	£9.99
Eccentric London	£14.99
Eccentric Oxford	£9.99
Sacred Britain	£16.99
Slow: Cornwall	£14.99
Slow: Cotswolds	£14.99
Slow: Devon & Exmoor	£14.99
Slow: Dorset	£14.99
Slow: New Forest	£9.99
Slow: Norfolk & Suffolk	£14.99
Slow: North Yorkshire	£14.99
Slow: Northumberland	£14.99
Slow: Sussex & South Downs National Park	£14.99

Europe

Abruzzo	£16.99
Albania	£16.99
Armenia	£15.99
Azores	£14.99
Belarus	£15.99
Bosnia & Herzegovina	£15.99
Bratislava	£9.99
Budapest	£9.99
Croatia	£15.99
Cross-Channel France: Nord-Pas de Calais	£13.99
Cyprus see North Cyprus	
Estonia	£14.99
Faroe Islands	£16.99
Flanders	£15.99
Georgia	£15.99
Greece: The Peloponnese	£14.99
Hungary	£15.99
Iceland	£15.99
Istria	£13.99
Kosovo	£15.99
Lapland	£15.99
Liguria	£15.99
Lille	£9.99
Lithuania	£14.99
Luxembourg	£14.99
Macedonia	£16.99
Malta & Gozo	£14.99
Montenegro	£14.99
North Cyprus	£13.99
Serbia	£15.99
Slovakia	£14.99
Slovenia	£13.99
Svalbard: Spitsbergen, Jan Mayen, Franz Jozef Land	£17.99
Switzerland Without a Car	£15.99
Transylvania	£15.99
Ukraine	£16.99

Middle East, Asia and Australasia

Bangladesh	£17.99
Borneo	£17.99
Eastern Turkey	£16.99
Iran	£15.99
Israel	£15.99
Jordan	£16.99
Kazakhstan	£16.99
Kyrgyzstan	£16.99
Lake Baikal	£15.99
Lebanon	£15.99
Maldives	£15.99
Mongolia	£16.99
North Korea	£14.99
Oman	£15.99
Palestine	£15.99
Shangri-La: A Travel Guide to the Himalayan Dream	£14.99
Sri Lanka	£15.99
Syria	£15.99
Taiwan	£16.99
Tajikistan	£15.99
Tibet	£17.99
Yemen	£14.99

Wildlife

Antarctica: A Guide to the Wildlife	£15.99
Arctic: A Guide to Coastal Wildlife	£16.99
Australian Wildlife	£14.99
East African Wildlife	£19.99
Galápagos Wildlife	£16.99
Madagascar Wildlife	£16.99
Pantanal Wildlife	£16.99
Southern African Wildlife	£19.99
Sri Lankan Wildlife	£15.99

Pictorials and other guides

100 Alien Invaders	£16.99
100 Animals to See Before They Die	£16.99
100 Bizarre Animals	£16.99
Eccentric Australia	£12.99
Northern Lights	£6.99
Swimming with Dolphins, Tracking Gorillas	£15.99
The Northwest Passage	£14.99
Tips on Tipping	£6.99
Total Solar Eclipse 2012 & 2013	£6.99
Wildlife & Conservation Volunteering: The Complete Guide	£13.99

Travel literature

A Glimpse of Eternal Snows	£11.99
A Tourist in the Arab Spring	£9.99
Connemara Mollie	£9.99
Fakirs, Feluccas and Femmes Fatales	£9.99
Madagascar: The Eighth Continent	£11.99
The Marsh Lions	£9.99
The Two-Year Mountain	£9.99
The Urban Circus	£9.99
Up the Creek	£9.99

Index